POGUE MAHONE **THE STORY OF** KISS MY ARSE

THE POGUES

POGUE MAHONE **THE STORY OF** KISS MY ARSE

THE POGUES

CAROL CLERK

OMNIBUS PRESS

LONDON / NEW YORK / PARIS / SYDNEY / COPENHAGEN / BERLIN / MADRID / TOKYO

Cover designed by Josh Labouve

ISBN: 1.84609.008.3
ISBN13: 978.1.84609.008.0
Order No: OP51073

The Author hereby asserts his/her right to be identified as the author of this work in accordance with Sections 77 to 78 of the Copyright, Designs and Patents Act 1988.

Exclusive Distributors
Music Sales Limited,
14/15 Berners Street,
London, W1T 3LJ.

Music Sales Corporation,
257 Park Avenue South,
New York, NY 10010, USA.

Macmillan Distribution Services,
53 Park West Drive,
Derrimut, Vic 3030,
Australia.

To the Music Trade only:
Music Sales Limited,
8/9 Frith Street,
London W1D 3JB, UK.

Every effort has been made to trace the copyright holders of the photographs in this book but one or two were unreachable. We would be grateful if the photographers concerned would contact us.

Typeset by Phoenix Photosetting, Chatham, Kent
Printed by MPG Books, Bodmin, Cornwall

A catalogue record for this book is available from the British Library.

Visit Omnibus Press on the web at www.omnibuspress.com

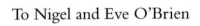

To Nigel and Eve O'Brien

Contents

Foreword   ix

Chapter 1 – The Importance of Being Irish   1

Chapter 2 - Going For A Burton   17

Chapter 3 – Nips And Rucks   28

Chapter 4 – The Rebel Yell   43

Chapter 5 – Pogue Mahone: Birth Pains And Beer Trays   57

Chapter 6 – The Advance Of The Young Old Men   71

Chapter 7 – Streets Of London   84

Chapter 8 – Stiff Records And Stiff Elvis   96

Chapter 9 – A Drunken Odyssey   109

Chapter 10 – Murray's Law   126

Chapter 11 – Rum, Sodomy & The Clashes   144

Chapter 12 – 'That's Poguetry For You'   159

Chapter 13 - The Raft Of The Medusa: Off With Their Heads!   170

Chapter 14 – Loose Porter In London   185

Chapter 15 – The One-Handed Drummer   199

Chapter 16 - You Promised Me Broadway Was Waiting For Me   210

Chapter 17 – Rain Dogs With Everything   226

Chapter 18 – Spain Killers   239

Chapter 19 – The Irish Rovers   252

Chapter 20 – The Terry Woods Solo Album   267

Chapter 21 – Falling From Grace   283

Chapter 22 – Strummer In The City   296

Chapter 23 – St John Of God's   311

Chapter 24 – Peace And Love: The Irony   329

Chapter 25 – The Bob Dylan Disaster   349

Chapter 26 – Gudbuy T'Shane   362

Chapter 27 – 'I Am Going, I Am Going…'   383

Chapter 28 – In The Death Of Afternoon   404
Epilogue   427

Pogues Discography   440
Acknowledgements   447

Foreword

"What fucking book?"

He looks up from the dinner he's been picking at, drops his knife with an enormous clang, and stares an unblinking, pale-blue stare that's accusing, terrifying.

Shane MacGowan has forgotten all about our appointment, the one we arranged in a phone call two days ago. He has forgotten everything he's been told by various other Pogues who for weeks, helpfully, have been suggesting to him that he might co-operate with this biography. Certainly, he has forgotten the trail of false starts and aborted interviews that have littered the way to our meeting here this evening.

The instructions had been vague enough to be worrying: "I'll be in The Boogaloo on Thursday night."

What time?

"Somewhere between nine o'clock and midnight."

The Boogaloo, described by *GQ* magazine as "the sweetest little juke-joint in all the world", is a pub and a venue for live music and literary celebration, high up in north London on the Archway Road. A hearty, bustling little hideaway from the mainstream, it has nevertheless become the focus of intense scrutiny by the tabloid press.

It was in The Boogaloo that star-crossed lovers Kate Moss and Pete Doherty were recently discovered on a date, Kate standing on her seat to jiggle along to the rumpus of Doherty's Babyshambles. And it was here, too, that the controversial couple were seen to clink a glass or two with Shane MacGowan.

Shane's an old customer and friend of Gerry O'Boyle, the proprietor of The Boogaloo. Previously, Gerry ran the esteemed Filthy McNasty's Whisky Café in Islington, and in both places, he has offered a home from home to the Pogue who likes to know that he's welcome to sleep wherever and whenever he needs to drop.

Not so long ago, Shane moved into a flat only minutes away from The Boogaloo. Sometimes he makes it home, sometimes he doesn't. It's comforting to live close to what you know; to have a safety net. But there was never any guarantee that the most unpredictable man in music would turn up in the bar tonight.

I'm lucky. It's only minutes after nine o'clock, and he's here already. It's just that he's not expecting me.

"What fucking book?"

He's at a table close to the bar, his back to the wall, surrounded by a coterie of friends including Gerry O'Boyle and one-time Pogues biographer Ann Scanlon. Shane sits upright, solid as anything, the charismatic centre of his company. He looks really, really well. He's dressed for whatever occasion it is in a jacket made of darkly red, shiny material. His hair is newly washed, fluffy, and there's a freshness about his face that belies the years of excess for which he's fabled. His complexion is that of someone who appears to have been eating his greens.

Tonight, Shane is periodically stabbing at a piece of fish and assorted vegetables. The suggestion that he might agree to an interview when he's finished his meal is met with an abrupt order: "Ask me a fucking interesting question."

For the next hour, Shane will continue to poke at his food while we duck and dive our way through an exchange that, at first, feels extremely uncomfortable. He refuses a drink, asking only for a glass of ice, and pours his own from bottles of wine that appear on the table as if by magic, courtesy of his bar tab.

We're face to face across the table, directly below a speaker which loudly cranks out selections from The Boogaloo's excellent jukebox. In these circumstances, MacGowan's tendency to mumble, his mangled, London-Irish slur and his absolute lack of teeth lead to the odd breakdown in communication.

Sorry, I didn't quite catch that. . .

When this happens, he drops his knife again, slowly and deliberately, and stares the unblinking, pale-blue stare, his body motionless, as he repeats what he has just said at the top of his voice. It's a bellow. It's a great impatience. It's a reprimand.

Friendly advice has it that Shane is fond of reminiscing about his days in Burton Street, the short-life-housing project and creative community near King's Cross, London, where the idea of The Pogues began to take root. What were the sights, the sounds, the smells, the atmospheres, of Burton

Street? Perhaps that might be a fucking interesting question, one which he might respond to. At the very least, it could be a starting point.

"It was a street with houses in it," snorts MacGowan. "Have you talked to the other members of the band?"

Yes, at length.

"Well, what do you need to talk to me for?"

Because you're the poet.

This doesn't go down well. Historically, Shane has not always been gracious with compliments, although I am trying to tell him that people are interested in his writing, in view of his considerable reputation, rather than attempting to curry favour or to insult the talents of the other band members and contributors.

He shoots back immediately with a list of Pogues favourites that are not of his making: "People have credited me with writing 'Dirty Old Town' and 'Misty Morning, Albert Bridge', which I didn't. People have credited me with writing 'Navigator' on *Rum Sodomy & The Lash*, which I didn't. That was written by Phil Gaston. 'Thousands Are Sailing' – I didn't write that. Phil Chevron wrote it. And, like, some people think that I wrote 'The Irish Rover'. Too much credit is given."

Notwithstanding the riches of the songs he mentions, it's obvious that this is a ridiculous statement, given the timelessness of the work that he has produced on his own and with co-writers, but it's a line with which he has tried and failed to derail interviewers in the past.

There may be a real modesty, maybe even an insecurity, at play here, or a desire to give others their due. None of these things would be out of character for MacGowan, according to some of his bandmates. At the same time, there can be no doubt that Shane is well aware of the weight of his achievement, and there have been troubled occasions when he has had to fight hard for his musical visions, or has vigorously defended his unique contribution to The Pogues.

Relenting slightly under The Boogaloo's blaring sound system, he admits: "I do feel I've contributed to Irish culture. Everybody in the group did."

The hostilities have subsided: Shane begins to react to questions with answers rather than arguments, and he becomes more thoughtful, more voluble, as the evening progresses, although he remains prickly. I'm always aware that when the guitars burst especially loudly through the speaker and when he is talking just that little bit more softly, more unintelligibly, I will have to ask him to say it again, whatever it is, and I will see the stare and I will hear the sound of the clattering knife.

I still hear it in my nightmares.

The other members of The Pogues, in hours of interviews, have been open about the many problems that they faced both personally and professionally as their pioneering, punk-fuelled, emerald-hearted romps and ballads pitched past pitch of success to a top three album, *If I Should Fall From Grace With God*, and beyond. Few would have predicted the spectacular popularity of their mission to pump some fresh new blood into traditional Irish folk music, a genre that was unfashionable and widely unloved, to revitalise it and to make it relevant and exciting even to people who had possibly never heard of a jig, a reel or an air, a cittern or a bodhrán.

It all caught on very quickly, at a time when Eighties audiences were tiring of the electronic precision of the new romantics. There was something irresistibly wild about The Pogues' reckless dash, something daring about their tales of drinking and brawling and sex, and something achingly romantic in their stories of love, loss, life and death. Importantly, though, the traditions that they rescued from the past, and the musical and literary influences of Ireland, the country across the sea, were counterbalanced by a realism set in the harsh streets of London. It wasn't always pretty, but the young especially understood it; they related.

For each of The Pogues, there was a price to pay for their seemingly effortless rise to fame. Jem Finer and Terry Woods have described the struggle to hold on to some semblance of family life in the years of enforced, relentless touring. Woods, Spider Stacy and Philip Chevron, all now teetotallers, have been frank about their experiences of alcoholism. Chevron and Andrew Ranken have revealed the strain of travelling the world while suffering from painful illnesses and also trying to cope with devastating events in their private lives.

Finer, Woods, Chevron, Ranken, Stacy, James Fearnley and Darryl Hunt have been honest, too, about the passing storms in their inter-personal relationships, from the difficulties of working with original bassist Cait O'Riordan after she fell in love with Elvis Costello to the confusion and hopelessness surrounding their gradual estrangement from Shane MacGowan.

In the years following his split from the band, MacGowan had some scathing and often deeply hurtful things to say in print and on videos and DVDs about The Pogues, their organisation, and the music they made with and without him.

Tonight, however, Shane has no intention of upsetting anybody. It's clear he has not changed his mind about Costello since an ancient run-in over 'A Rainy Night In Soho', and he makes his usual complaints about The Pogues' long-standing policy of democracy. But as far as the band members are concerned - "They're all my friends." He claims not to remember any details of the "fragmentation" that culminated in his departure, and he denies that other unhappy episodes recalled by his bandmates ever happened at all.

Once upon a time, MacGowan would describe the group's *Peace And Love* as a "really dodgy album" and its successor, *Hell's Ditch*, as "a real dog". At best, he might concede that "half of *Peace And Love* is all right". In The Boogaloo, he makes a dramatic U-turn: "I've always said *Peace And Love* would be recognised as the great album that it is one day." He adds: "I think all five Pogues albums [the ones he was involved in] are fine."

Clearly, there are reasons for Shane's conciliatory attitude this evening. The Pogues have, after all, reunited on an occasional basis for live shows and tours. There's every chance that at the time of his more poisonous comments, MacGowan had yet to work through his feelings about the split and why it happened and, anyway, he was usually always speaking from some altered state of consciousness.

Hopefully, there may be more than a grain of truth in Darryl Hunt's view of things: "When you see Shane today, he's so together. Now he really appreciates this group he's got behind him. *Then*, he started to lose that connection with the people he was working with. Not anything personal against us – it was caused a lot by the pressure he was under. Not many of us are that tough..."

Fast forward five weeks to December 21, 2005. The Pogues are playing the second of three sold-out, headline shows at London's Brixton Academy, and they're performing more vividly, more rumbustiously, than I have seen them do in 20 years. The utter mayhem in the audience bears testament to a fine and enduring repertoire, from 'Streams Of Whiskey' to 'Sayonara', 'Sally MacLennane' to 'The Sunnyside Of The Street', 'Thousands Are Sailing' to 'Tuesday Morning'.

There's a hugely emotional and passionate response: you can feel it swelling, all around the auditorium, and you can see it in the faces and the teary eyes of the fans, who come in all shapes, sizes - and ages. Sure, there are the faithful, those of the expanding waistlines and vanishing hairlines who saw it all in the old days. But there are younger people too, leaping madly and singing along with every word and pushing their way to the front in the T-shirts they've only just purchased from the merchandising stalls. They would've been learning to walk when The Pogues first did the rounds of London. Children of primary-school age bounce in their seats upstairs, thrilled, snapping pictures with the cameras on their parents' mobile phones.

The Pogues are delivering a song-and-dance act that links generations, that defies time. A jumble of men in motion, they are doing it with an athleticism that also seems to defy time, at least as far as accordion player James Fearnley and guitarist Philip Chevron are concerned, and with a finely-tuned sense of dynamics that simultaneously manages to sound abandoned in all of the grand rush and sweep.

And Shane MacGowan is on top of the game. He may blunder around the stage, kicking his microphone stand to hell, like the portly uncle of his previous, upstart self, but his offhand rasp hits home, gruffly, in all the right places more often than it ever did; he sounds almost exactly like you want him to.

It's the week that 'Fairytale Of New York' will once again ring bells all over Britain and Ireland, clinching the Number Three position in the prestigious UK Christmas chart and hitting the top spot in the Republic. The song begins to fill the room, unmistakeably, at Brixton, and its interwoven themes of tragedy, poignancy and humour are reflected in real life here tonight.

Kirsty MacColl's mother Jean leans forward in her front-row balcony seat, watching intently and with heartbreaking dignity as Ella Finer, daughter of Jem, walks on to sing the female part of the duet.

The snow machine sends showers of fake flakes fluttering down over the musicians, carpeting the stage, and there's a moment of comedic drama when Shane, conducting the traditional 'Fairytale' dance with Ella, keels over and brings her crashing down with him to the floor.

The whole hall feels for Ella, who recovers herself with grace. And as for MacGowan: he would have to be insane not to be enjoying and appreciating the power and the glory of The Pogues as they sound at this moment. No wonder he didn't want to rock the boat.

"Is that it?"

Shane looks at me with a mixture of hope and resolve. The scraps that remain on his dinner plate are too cold and limp to consider eating, and his night is still young. He is, of course, terminating the interview, although I am tolerated, just about; not dismissed from the company.

It's somewhere around midnight when Joey Cashman stalks into The Boogaloo. Cashman is Shane's personal manager, and more: he's a force of nature. In the next couple of hours, I learn more about Joey than I have discovered about my own friends over the course of years. He's a motormouth Irishman. He's witty, abrasive, confiding, cunning, ambitious, outrageous, critical, exhausting, unaccountably likeable, and quite unconcerned about what anyone else might think of him.

The clock shows 3am, and the other customers have long since left.

Shane and the companions with whom he started the evening have relocated to a table with sofas, and Gerry O'Boyle is making it plain that he would like to clear the premises.

"If you want to get anything more out of Shane," advises Joey, conspiratorially, "just follow him home."

I think about this, and the more I think about it, the less I want to shadow MacGowan and his entourage, paparazzo-like, to a private place where I've not been invited. Instead, I shake hands with Shane, bid my farewells and slip off into the night, to my hotel.

Cashman, the next day, is incredulous. He would be.

But the story already has an ending, a happy ending - or at least a positive one. Things have come pretty much full circle for The Pogues. Undeniably, the reunion of Shane MacGowan and the band must be financially beneficial to everyone involved, and they are certainly bigger at the box office together than they were apart, but it's gratifying to witness the healing of old wounds. In their younger days as tearaways on the up, roving wildly from one triumph to the next, there was at the heart of The Pogues a true sense of family. Like any family, they would rally round a stricken member, close ranks against the outside world, bicker, fight, fall out and make up. Years later, they have overcome their troubles on their own terms and for their own good, and ours.

"I think we'll stay together," says Shane. And I think he means it.

Carol Clerk
April 2006

CHAPTER 1

The Importance Of Being Irish

The year was 1977 and the place was The Cambridge, a large, traditional pub on the edge of Cambridge Circus in London WC2. It's still there, wrapping itself around the corner where Moor Street meets Charing Cross Road.

The Cambridge has never been recognised for its part in popular rock history. Day in, day out, tourists and pre-theatre tipplers mill around the two floors of an establishment that, 30 years ago, was serving drinks to a completely different clientele.

Shane MacGowan would sit there for hours, airing his thoughts about music and politics and current affairs with a gathering of friends who in their various ways were just as engaged and driven as he was himself. There were punks - early punks like Siouxsie Sioux - who were forming or championing bands and nipping off out to Neal Street to see what was happening in the legendary Roxy club. There were students from the nearby St Martin's School of Art. There were people who ran record shops and people who bought the records. Everybody was young. Everybody loved music. Everybody was eager to make a mark on the world, somehow, in a way that was individual and bold and creative.

Still, Shane MacGowan stood out from the crowd. Those who drank with him in The Cambridge remember someone who was forthright in his views and unassailably proud of his Irish background. They remember his keen intelligence, and the force of his ambition that he was going to make it in music, no matter what.

Phil Gaston was one of the regulars. Gaston was working at a vintage record stall called Rock On in the old Soho Market – later torn down by developers building the multi-storey car park at the Charing Cross Road end of Gerrard Street. A magnet for musicians, Rock On was also a hang-out with a social life all of its own.

"Shane must've been about 16 when he first came into the stall," muses Gaston. "He had matted hair down to his shoulders. You'd look at him and think, 'This guy isn't the full shilling.' He did look as if he'd been sleeping in doorways or whatever."

Over time, the people of Rock On became used to the strange, scruffy teenager who thumbed so avidly through the racks of vinyl records.

"But he quickly lost the hair when he saw which way the wind was blowing," adds Phil.

That wind blew an 18-year-old MacGowan into a Sex Pistols gig at the Nashville Rooms in West Kensington one evening in 1976. He had turned out to see the headliners, Joe Strummer's bristling pub-rock band The 101ers, but the Pistols changed his life instantly and forever. He was riveted by their amateurish, anarchic musical attack, by Johnny Rotten's sardonic vocal mannerisms and confrontational posturing and, particularly, by the fact that this group was brazenly flouting the accepted rules of rock etiquette. It was revolutionary. He was certain that he was witnessing the beginnings of something massive.

A familiar presence at their (sporadic) gigs from that moment on, he was captured in one famous film clip at the very front of the crowd, wide-eyed, probably legless and definitely in love. He would later frequently declare that the Pistols were "the best rock'n'roll band of all time". Shane admired the Irishness he came to see in Rotten as well his capacity for exaggeration and his superiority as a performer and a lyricist.

The Pistols, and early punk, provided MacGowan with an environment in which he felt alive and at home. Not long after a period of incarceration – and institutionalisation - in what he casually refers to as "the loony bin", he was delighted to connect with kindred spirits who shared his scorn for authority and conformity, people like himself who listened to good soul and dub reggae. He revelled in the nihilism and hedonism of punk in equal measure and he enjoyed its controversy and danger, but most of all he loved the fact that it championed the individual. There were no rules, no conditions and no exclusions on the grounds of gender, religion, class, colour, culture, looks or post code. For five minutes, back there, there was something that felt like equality.

Shane MacGowan became one of the innovators in the uprising, drawing on his imagination to create new fashion twists out of punk's array of staples. Among the drainpipe trousers, the leather and rubber and bondage gear, the mohair, fishnet and plastic, the ripped, home-made T-shirts, the winklepickers, brothel creepers and Doc Martens, the earrings and dog chains, the zips and studs and safety pins, the anarchy signs and swastikas, the riot of colour and the jumble of sartorial styles from years gone by, Shane cut a remarkable figure. He customised his clothes and wore unusual accessories, sometimes borrowing from the imagery of his Catholic background with crucifixes and rosary beads, teamed with a beret. He was, he claimed, ahead of the pack with that one.

The key thing was originality: Shane never bought into the "uniform". By the end of 1977, identipunk would have taken hold of the high street, where every other spiky-haired youngster wanted to be Sid Vicious, shoppers were shelling out ridiculous amounts of money to look that way and the level of gang violence against punks was escalating dramatically. MacGowan, who had appreciated the elitism and the purity of the original scene, would quickly become disenchanted, but he had learnt some vital lessons which he would take with him through his career.

Before all that, though, he made himself busy as 1976 flew past in a blur of amphetamine sulphate and chaotic activity, and his friends at Rock On observed his progress with interest.

"He was a *face*," says Phil Gaston. "He had his finger in so many pies. He was a catalyst for a lot of stuff. He was so central, without actually doing anything."

MacGowan was a godsend for journalists and photographers covering punk, and he was regularly featured in everything from *Sounds* to the *Evening Standard*. His most notorious appearance was in a lead review of The Clash at the London ICA, published in the issue of *NME* dated November 6, 1976 under the headline: "Cannibalism At Clash Gig".

Writer Miles described a fracas in the audience: "A young couple, somewhat out of it, had been nibbling and fondling each other amid the broken glass when she suddenly lunged forward and *bit his ear lobe off*. As the blood spurted she reached out to paw it with a hand tastefully clad in a rubber glove, and after smashing a Guinness bottle on the front of the stage she was about to add to the gore by slashing her wrists when security men finally reached her..."

The young lady was Jane Crockford, soon to come to prominence, briefly, as bassist of The Mo-Dettes, and the young man was Shane MacGowan. Still the proud owner of both earlobes, MacGowan later insisted that Jane was not his girlfriend but simply another crazy person in the crowd. They had been biting and cutting each other for "a kick" – one which he admitted to enjoying - and when blood started flowing copiously from a really rather minor wound, his legend was sealed: the whole affair raised Shane's profile enormously, not to mention his heroic standing in punk circles.

Meanwhile, Rock On was becoming something of a Mecca for the cognoscenti, with Phil Gaston and his colleague Stan Brennan receiving visits from such luminaries as The Damned, The Jam and various Sex Pistols. New York's Ramones arrived in search of records by Seventies British glam and bubblegum groups and, specifically, the tartan-clad Bay City Rollers whose 'Saturday Night' pop anthem had inspired their own mighty 'Blitzkrieg Bop'.

"Everybody who was in town just came down and hung around," remembers Gaston. "All the punky bands came. Mark Perry and the guys from [fanzine] *Sniffin' Glue* were down there. Everybody was doing fanzines. Shane started a little one."

MacGowan's fanzine was called *Bondage*. The first issue, which appeared in December 1976, had the Sex Pistols on the cover, with an inside editorial devoted to the furore that had blown up over the band's foul-mouthed TV confrontation with Bill Grundy earlier that month. "I hope that after this whole thing dies down, the Pistols carry on being more and more obnoxious," ranted MacGowan, before declaring 'Anarchy In The UK' the single of the decade.

Bondage also contained a review of recent Jam performances in Soho, one Upstairs At Ronnie Scott's and the other at The Marquee, with Shane proclaiming: "I think The Jam are fucking important. . . There's no way you can knock their youth, their energy, their skill and their songs, which are fucking great."

The fanzine had been handwritten – "Anybody who uses a typewriter is a GIRL!" – fixed together with safety pins, then photocopied. Shane took his project to various retailers - radical bookstores and record outlets including Rock On - and struck a deal: they would help towards the costs of having *Bondage* printed, and in return he would give them an agreed number of free copies to sell.

He did pretty well out of it, too, charging 50p per copy – more than three times the price of his many competitors' efforts. *Bondage* sold, it kept on selling, it made a small profit, and then it was over. He never did get around to the second issue. But then, he was busy. . .

Phil Gaston recalls his days in Soho Market with affection: "I loved doing music, opening up the shop and playing singles for the next eight hours, and the wheeling and dealing, and recordings coming in. . . You'd get some guy with four boxes of pristine bluebeat, or old blues collections from Chess.

"The pattern for us was that people would come into the stall at about half past five because everybody knew we'd be closing up at six. Then there'd be a whole gang go round to The Cambridge. We sat and drank and chatted about everything, not just about music.

"The Cambridge was the hub of a lot of stuff. There were people from Ray's Jazz Stall in Shaftesbury Avenue and from Dobell's music shop. There were lots of record shops in the small streets, in little nooks and crannies, the markets in Berwick Street... Then you had all the St Martin's students. Shane was there and he was great, a very, very funny man – really smart, really well-read.

"At some stage, we'd go out to have something to eat. There was the Barocca, a pasta place, and the Centrale. They were cheap and cheerful – we'd get lasagnes and platters – and everybody got stuck in with everybody else on long benches." The Centrale still exists and was recently voted one of England's top classic cafés.

"Then we came back to The Cambridge, drank more and figured out where we were going to go," continues Gaston. "There were gigs happening all over the place. There was the 100 Club, The Marquee and all the established ones. There were gigs in Camden Town. There was The Roxy in Covent Garden, not too far from where we all were. That was the sort of scrum that was developing."

The Roxy, a former gay club, had been opened as a punk venue in December 1976 by Andy Czezowski. The capacity was 250, but he regularly squeezed in up to 400 people. When it rather prematurely closed its doors in April 1977, Czezowski went on to launch the Vortex, a Soho punk venue, and later, the Brixton Fridge. As for The Roxy, it subsequently reopened under new management, but its first, bright burst of brilliance could not be recreated.

Another nightspot frequented in the early days by MacGowan and his cronies was Louise's, a lesbian haunt in Poland Street, where there was dancing to soul and disco music, and punks were made welcome. Here, the regulars were more than happy to buy expensive drinks from the cocktail bar for the colourful new customers.

It was only a matter of time before Shane joined a band. According to the 2001 memoir *A Drink With Shane MacGowan*, he'd already made one attempt, at the age of 17, when he formed an outfit called Hot Dogs With Everything. The name would soon surface again as the title of a Nips composition, the song itself later reappearing as one of The Pogues' contributions to Alex Cox's *Sid And Nancy* film soundtrack. Spider Stacy, who sang it, was never aware that any such group had existed.

It was a three-piece, said Shane, comprising himself and two equally long-haired friends called Berni and Charlie. They played dirty rock'n'roll music, loudly, and the sort of earthy, soulful R&B that distinguished Van Morrison's Sixties band, Them. Shane, Berni and Charlie had big plans for Hot Dogs With Everything. They intended that their live shows would be moody, mysterious and filled with feedback. It was a pioneering concept – they had effectively invented The Jesus And Mary Chain! – but for all of their ambition, the Hot Dogs never made it out of the rehearsal room, and such early MacGowan gems as 'Instrument Of Death', his first composition, have seemingly been lost forever.

A more solid venture, in 1977, was The Nipple Erectors, a group formed and named by bassist Shanne Bradley, another well-known character in the punk world.

Talking to an interviewer years later, Shanne confided, "I had a dream about a band – my dream band – who would look very futuristic wearing skintight, rubber body suits covered in nipples. I shall go no further... well, the name came from there."

"I was 15 or 16 when I had that dream, and I remember very vividly I had a purple bedroom," she adds today. "I used to like Bowie and I saw Jobraith and I suppose I was influenced by that."

She also memorably recalled her first meeting with Shane, across a crowded bar at a gig in the London Royal College Of Art: "I thought, 'Who's that mad bastard on a mission?' Those ears!"

Shanne and Shane had much in common, including the Sex Pistols. Bradley had happened across them early in their career, when they gate-crashed an event at St Albans School Of Art. Shanne, who was taking a foundation course there, decided they were bad enough to be brilliant. "I thought they were just taking the piss," she remembers.

She stayed in touch with the Pistols, travelled from her home in Hertford to attend their gigs, booked them back to St Albans and became friendly with many of the leading characters around the band, including Malcolm McLaren, Vivenne Westwood, Jordan, Sue Catwoman and Helen Of Troy, with whom she often stayed after late nights in London.

Bradley came into the city more often as events gathered momentum. She saw The Damned play their first gig, at London's 100 Club, on July 6, 1976. Impressed and acting on impulse, she offered them a second date, at St Albans School Of Art, replacing the Pistols who'd pulled out.

"They came along and they all came back to my house in Hertford and had a big party," she recalls. "They were trying to empty the booze cabinet. I don't think they succeeded..."

Shanne and Ray Burns [Captain Sensible] became firm friends.

"He turned up one day in Hertford," she laughs. "I came home from college and found him talking to my mum in the kitchen. He was a train enthusiast. He used to like catching trains and he caught one to Hertford. That was his story, anyway."

From then on, she made occasional visits to Croydon, where Sensible lived. There, she was introduced to a circle of like-minded souls including Johnny Moped's band. Captain had been in various incarnations of the group, and Chrissie Hynde sang with them for a short time. Shanne's first-ever recording session took place in Sensible's living room where Hynde was making a demo, Bradley singing along with Captain on the chorus of 'Precious' – an early version of The Pretenders' song. She adds, "Ray was playing drums on cardboard boxes."

Moving to London in the autumn of 1976, Shanne enrolled at St Martin's School Of Art to study fashion – "or *anti-fashion*, as far as I was concerned". On the day that she first visited the college to see around it, Chrissie Hynde was modelling for a class of students. Bradley walked out after the first term: her life now revolved around going to gigs, and learning to play the bass.

She received her first official lesson on the top deck of a Number 68 bus from Fred Berk, Johnny Moped's bassist, and Captain Sensible, who showed her how to play the entire Damned repertoire on the long journey from Croydon to Oxford Street. Stopping off at Rock On in Soho Market, they picked up flyers for a Jam gig that night, Upstairs at Ronnie Scott's Jazz Club. When they arrived at the venue, Shanne was still carrying the red toy bass that Berk had given to her that day: "It was electric and it did actually play," she confirms. Which was just as well: "Bruce Foxton broke his bass, so I lent him my new toy." She later sold that instrument for a fiver, but still keeps a photo taken of her that night with friends including Sensible and Shane MacGowan. It was one of the two Jam shows that MacGowan reviewed in *Bondage*.

Bradley, like Shane, strongly believed in the importance of appearance and personal style. She doesn't remember exactly how their friendship developed.

She says: "I had two friends I used to meet at the 100 Club – Claudio, aka Chaotic Bass, and Ray Pist. We had a group called The Launderettes. Shane wasn't around when we used to go to the 100 Club. He was always jealous cos he wasn't actually at the very first Pistols gigs."

Certainly, Shane and Shanne had become good buddies by the time they helped former Damned manager Andy Czezowski build the stage for the opening night of The Roxy, on December 18, with Generation X headlining.

Thereafter, Shanne would sometimes step up at The Roxy to sing backing vocals for Hynde and the Mopeds on 'Hard Lovin' Man', later saying of the fabled club: "It was wild, full of spontaneity. Most of the audience were in bands or wished they were. Stars were falling out of the ceiling. Yes, it was tatty with plenty of mirrors."

Shane MacGowan was perhaps an unlikely candidate for Bradley's "dream band", what with the ears and a mouthful of misshapen pegs where a pearly smile might once have been.

"I never always had bad teeth," Shane would protest in an interview with Adrian Thrills, published by *NME* on October 27, 1979. "But I got pissed down the Red Cow one night seeing The 101ers with a mate. We came out really drunk and he said that he'd give me a lift home on the back of his bike, but I tried to get off while he was still moving and I broke all my teeth on Hammersmith Road."

He added: "I suppose I was always made to feel like a bit of a wanker at school and I always found it hard to pick up girls at discos cos I was so ugly. I mean, the punk thing fuckin' changed my life. It didn't matter that I was ugly... nothing mattered. It was good."

Certainly, he was on Shanne Bradley's shortlist when, in the summer of 1977, she decided to disband The Launderettes and start another group: "Shane came round to my bedsit in Stavordale Road, Highbury, for an audition. I let him into my room and he went into this Iggy Pop impersonation, throwing himself around, rolling on the floor and just going mental. He made a horrible noise trying to sing, but it was his performance, his total attitude that grabbed me, the spirit of it. I thought, 'Well, that's the singer sorted out.'"

The Nipple Erectors began and ended with Bradley and MacGowan. In between, their revolving door ushered in and out something like 11 drummers and five guitarists, with Chrissie Hynde stealing Belfast man Gerry Mackleduff – 'one of the best drummers ever', according to Phil Garton – for the Pretenders. He played on 'Stop Your Sobbing'. The lifespan of the band also saw the start and finish of a tempestuous love affair between Shane and Shanne, and a search for musical identity that was brave but largely unfulfilled.

By the time The Nipple Erectors were getting down to their first rehearsals, both Shanne and Shane – *Sounds'* elected "Face Of '76" and its chosen cover star in April 1977 representing "Images Of the New Wave" - were dismayed by what they saw to be punk's absorption into the mainstream and by the dozens of emerging bands who were being signed to record deals, yet had clearly misunderstood the message. Instead of forging a proud and distinct path, they were copying. A lot of the music, sneered MacGowan, was "speeded-up heavy metal calling itself punk". Worse, the tabloid press had been covering punk frenziedly since the filth and the fury of the Sex Pistols' Bill Grundy interview. In so doing, the papers had given rise to an explosion of cartoon punks and had magnified what violence there was to the point that certain elements went right out looking for it.

Bradley: "It was a bit arty, I suppose, in the beginning. We just used to laugh all the time. It changed in 1977. It was all marketed. It was a bit *Daily-Mirror*-readers. People used to change after work and come to London to be a 'punk', whereas we'd never been punks as such. We didn't know what we were. It became more 'oi', there were lots of lads, and it got a lot more violent."

The threat of violence hung heavily in the air at the Camden Electric Ballroom, where Shane and Shanne regularly attended Teds' nights. Says Bradley: "We went to hear the music and it was quite interesting to be the only people who looked like we did, but it was scary. It was like dicing with death. My hair used to stand on end some of the time. You didn't know if you were going to get beaten up. I think Shane probably got beaten up in the toilets. He used to get beaten up all the time."

It was around this time that Stan Brennan first stumbled across Shane. Brennan had come to work with Phil Gaston at Rock On.

He says: "I knew about Shane a lot before we actually met. He was well-known around that scene. It was always the same 20 people at every gig. I actually met him first of all at The Roxy when they were recording *Live At The Roxy*." This was a compilation of live music from various bands playing at the club, and it's probable that Johnny Moped's group were on stage on the night in question.

Brennan carries on: "Shane and I met in the men's toilets and were very drunk and stole one of the recording microphones for a band he was forming at the time called The Nipple Erectors. At that time, me and my partner Phil were thinking of starting a record label. Out of that meeting with Shane, we decided to go and see his band."

The Nipple Erectors' first performance, complete with songs such as 'Abuse' and 'Stupid Cow', took place in the autumn of 1977 at The Roxy. It was reviewed by a punk 'zine called *Skum*, whose Mark Skum reported in the October issue that this was "one of the best punk gigs I have ever seen". He also published an interview with the band, conducted in The Cambridge, in which MacGowan insisted: "Basically all we want to do is earn as much money possible for doing *fuck all*."

Shanne Bradley describes her memories of the Roxy show: "Paul Weller and his dad John, who wanted to sign us - they were down there, and the guys from The Damned. Lots of people were there. It was great. We had a toy drumkit at that stage. The drummer used a kind of biscuit tin before that."

"The drummer was playing with bread knives rather than drumsticks," says Stan Brennan. "Shanne was good and Shane was a great showman, just putting everything into it. He was very young then, very visual – lots of dropping to his knees and all that kind of thing. He had what the

9

French call an 'ugly beauty'. He was very charismatic. He was very slim with high cheekbones, interesting features, punky hair. He attracted a lot of women, but it was never a classic pop-star look. We knew this was a band that would have to be sold on the music, and he was a really good songwriter. You could tell that from the melodies. That's what Phil and I were really blown away by – the quality of the songwriting. We signed them, we signed a publishing contract with Shane as well, and we started producing the records."

Stan Brennan and Phil Gaston also took on the management of The Nipple Erectors, and the drinking sessions in The Cambridge gained a new significance as the beer flowed into 1978. Someone who joined the company at this stage was Dee O'Mahony, a student at St Martin's School Of Art.

"The pub was very clearly divided between art students and punks," she remembers. "In the summer holidays, I was working in Ladbrokes, taking bets over the phone, and Shane started chatting to me in the pub with [Sex Pistols' roadie] Rodent. They were coming up with very creative scams as to how they could win money off Ladbrokes."

They never did, though.

"Shane was in The Nipple Erectors," says O'Mahony. "And the thing that I remember most clearly about those days was just his absolute ambition to get a Number One, to make it. He was really, really clear that that's what he wanted to do. He wanted to be a star. I can picture him in The Cambridge saying that. I can almost hear him.

"Shane was razor-sharp. He had a brain that worked so much faster than most, bar Spider's. And that's why it was always so amazing seeing himself and Spider together, cos the two of them were so funny and so sharp."

Peter "Spider" Stacy was a new friend of Shane's who had started accompanying him to pubs including The Cambridge in 1979 – and their easy, quick-fire banter would later become renowned and sometimes feared as they travelled the world together in The Pogues.

Dee carries on: "Something that I remember was the arguments Shane, Spider, Phil and Stan and myself and [another friend] Kathy MacMillan used to have. Just the sheer quality of the discussion and banter was amazing.

"I was Irish and that's one of the reasons I kind of stuck out. It was not hip to be Irish at that stage. Growing up in Ireland, there was a deep-rooted sense of shame at being not modern enough, that lingering insecurity. I was very conscious, in London, of keeping my head down due to the IRA's mainland bombing campaign in the seventies. I remember being very conscious of my accent, and I lost it fairly quickly. So here was this mad bunch ranting about Irish history and music, and it was the first time I'd met people who weren't afraid to talk about what it was to be Irish in London and to talk about Irish culture. That's one big thing I remember about Shane – his focused sense of what it was to be Irish.

"I really can't stress enough how *other* that was, this attitude about being Irish, about the Irish who'd gone to London. It was a completely different take. Shane was defiant in his pride, although it wasn't overtly nationalistic. That would've been there, but both Phil and Stan would've been too aware of the legacy of unionism and nationalism, so he didn't get away without a challenge if he launched into nationalist rhetoric."

That was the other thing. A huge and sometimes violent tide of anti-Irish feeling had been sweeping the country due to the IRA bombing.

"It was awful," recalls O'Mahony. "Shane would come into the pub with black eyes, covered in bruises." His experiences of "Paddy-bashing", as well as "punk-bashing", would result in some memorable injuries as the years went on.

Dee O'Mahony eventually married Phil Gaston and together they travelled the world and then moved back to Ireland. She hasn't seen much of Shane for a long time, but she has read and heard his interviews.

"When he talks now about being Irish, he seems quite sentimental," ventures Dee. "But he was never sentimental in those early days and he had this real respect for Irish culture and Irish music that wasn't necessarily hip Irish music. For example, he always talked about Luke Kelly and The Dubliners and that would've been at the time when the new wave of folk bands had come through, like Planxty and then The Bothy Band. Bands like The Dubliners would've been regarded as being very old-fashioned, but he was never ashamed of his passion for them."

For someone who'd been at the very cutting edge of punk, MacGowan would indeed stick up for the things he considered to be right, old-fashioned or not.

O'Mahony remembers, "The year I left college, 1979, my mum came over to surprise me. We were at the end-of-year party. I was somewhat horrified that she'd turned up – I was looking forward to a mad night out! I took her down to The Cambridge and Shane came in and he spent the whole evening chatting to her. For him, it was very important to meet people's families. The core values of family history and family stories and people's memories, and how much he and Spider between them could remember, meant a lot to them.

"Shane never judged people. He had an incredible generosity of spirit. He had an aggressive side, too – oh yes. And the thing that triggered it was mean-spiritedness, bigotry. He hated people being excluded because of somebody else's value system, and he would get very angry if fans were treated badly."

Dee O'Mahony has one other vivid memory of 1979, and it's of something that happened in the autumn: "Shane actually got caps on his stumps. He used to go up to the dental hospital and get them done for free. It was quite a long treatment."

"They filed his teeth down to put the caps on them," explains Spider Stacy.

Not that the caps lasted long. . .

"They got knocked out one way or the other," reasons Stacy. "I heard some rumours that he was in a fight. That means somebody took a swing at him. Shane's not a violent man. He's not the type of person that goes out and starts fights. I'll qualify that – his demeanour can possibly provoke people, fucking idiots who don't like the way he looks or talks. He's been the victim of people going for him, but he's not a brawler. On the other hand, he might have fallen off a bus and lost them that way."

Shane MacGowan was not born in Ireland, although there are many who think he was. He arrived on Christmas Day, 1957, in Tunbridge Wells, Kent, because his parents, Maurice and Therese, had taken a trip from their home country to celebrate the festive season with relatives.

The early years of Shane's childhood were idyllic. Growing up in the countryside near the provincial, north-Tipperary town of Nenagh, he belonged to an extended family crammed into a farmhouse that contained many more people than rooms.

It was a place where men were men, and they laboured hard, working the land with rudimentary machinery, mucking out sheds and killing poultry with their bare hands and a blade. They travelled the country roads on foot, on bicycles and by horse and cart. They smoked pipes and spat and swore and drank heartily. Shane adored the masculinity, the earthy character of his male elders, and he hero-worshipped his Uncle John.

At the same time, there was nothing slavish or self-pitying about the females who, primarily, ran the home, although they weren't afraid to get their hands dirty either. Some, including Therese, were avid readers, and they equally enjoyed the many evenings that found the farmhouse filled with friends, neighbours, laughter, music and alcohol.

Shane's mother, a notable beauty as a young woman, had been a prize-winning singer around the local music festivals, she'd won trophies for dancing and she became a sought-after model in Dublin where, in a pub, she met Maurice. He was a man of cutting wit who loved literature and poetry, whose musical tastes ran from jazz to country and blues to rock-'n'roll, and whose family line originated in Northern Ireland.

Therese described life at the farm to a film crew making a documentary called *If I Should Fall From Grace: The Shane MacGowan Story*: "My memory from the earliest days is a house of music and song and story-telling – it was also what I would call an open house, really."

Auntie Monica Cahalan revealed that Shane was a natural singer and actor from the moment he could walk and talk, and she fondly remembered his rendition of 'There's a Hole In My Bucket' at two and a half. "It was a scream to look at him," she enthused.

The sound of Irish music was woven into the very fabric of the society. Young and old joined together in the night-time singalongs, while various relatives played instruments such as the banjo, tin whistle, accordion and concertina and the age-old songs acquired a new lease of life as the children came to know and love them.

It was a lifestyle where, claimed MacGowan, he was allowed to drink, smoke, gamble and stay up until the early hours of the morning – all at the age of five. However, the Catholic obligations of the household were rigidly enforced. Shane was expected to attend mass and he didn't always manage to avoid the rosary meetings held round the kitchen table. He said his prayers. He was banned from blasphemous swearing, although the word "fuck" was deemed okay.

Here, death was treated with all the practicality of every other fact of life – there was, in the farmhouse, a "dying room" – and the history, myths and legends of Ireland were passed down eagerly and in colourful detail from one generation to the next. It was dramatic, sometimes scary stuff to young ears, gripping and unforgettable.

Shane was five when his sister Siobhan was born. And he was six, going on seven, when something happened that put an end to his days of herding geese and riding horses, his rambles along country lanes, his games of hurling and his fantasy wars in the overgrown fields around the farmhouse.

He moved to England. It was, said Shane, "a horrific fucking change of life".

Therese explained: "It was very, very difficult to get employment in Ireland in the Sixties. Many, many people had to go abroad to England or somewhere else to actually earn a living, and Maurice was one of those, so we had to go to London... We tried to leave Shane in Ireland as much as possible when he was young."

He remained at the farm, in the care of his mother's relatives, while Therese and Maurice set up home across the water. But the time came when he had to start his education, and his parents came back to collect him.

According to MacGowan, the family moved around quite a bit during their first couple of years in England, and he attended a series of different schools. In Ealing, west London, he went to a fee-paying convent, which he didn't mind, because the Catholicism and the nuns reminded him of Ireland. He was desperately homesick.

With Therese acknowledging that "his heart and soul always lay in Ireland, in Tipperary", Shane returned to the farmhouse every year in the summer holidays. In the half-term breaks, he went to stay with his Uncle Frank and Auntie Catherine whose Dagenham pub – the one immortalised in 'Sally MacLennane' – was frequented by workers from the Ford Motor Company.

Despite the disruptions in his schooling, Shane MacGowan was considered a gifted pupil with special abilities in English, particularly writing. His parents thought he might become an author, but he informed Therese that he saw his future in terms of writing songs, since "that's the way you communicate with people nowadays".

"He had a brilliant brain," confirmed Maurice MacGowan to the documentary-makers. "He still has - a few billion cells later."

Shortly after entering his teens, Shane won a scholarship to Westminster, a top public school with a history dating back to 1179. By now, however, he was being distracted by all manner of illicit pleasures. He'd become a "greaser", dressing all in black with a leather jacket and a quiff, and he was 13 when he smoked his first joint. He claimed that during his brief career at Westminster, he was an underage smoker and drinker, frequenting pubs, taking pills and acid, and going on shoplifting sprees.

Learning that he'd been busted for cannabis possession outside his house, the school authorities contacted his parents.

"We were invited around to the headmaster's study – a right wanker," recalled Maurice MacGowan. "And we went down there, the two of us, and he talked about the terrible 'crime' that Shane had committed. I listened to all this and I said, 'What do you want to do about it?' And he said, 'I'd prefer if Shane didn't come back.' I said, 'Fine. I don't want him to come back to this stupid fucking cunt of a place anyway.'"

It wasn't quite the end of the 14-year-old's formal education. After a string of dead-end jobs, including shelf-stacking, he agreed to go to college to study for some qualifications. He was 16 when he arrived for his first day at the Hammersmith College For Further Education, but he rarely attended classes and was soon asked to leave. He had, however, made some friends there, including Berni, with whom he reputedly formed Hot Dogs With Everything.

Shane now regarded himself as a "freak", having cultivated the collar-length hair that caught the eye of Phil Gaston at the Rock On record stall.

Freaks, said MacGowan, were harder than hippies. Freaks were into drugs and loud music. They listened to classic American garage bands such as MC5 and The Stooges, English mod bands including the Small Faces, and the hard rock and heavy metal albums released at the tail end of the Sixties and early Seventies by the likes of Black Sabbath and Led Zeppelin. They also liked Roxy Music.

MacGowan was beginning to enjoy life in London but, like his parents, he still missed Ireland and fully intended to return there in the future. Their lost life in Tipperary was the cause of much unhappiness within the family. A depressed Therese was the first to crack: she suffered a nervous break-down, and was treated at home with heavy doses of drugs including Valium. "I used to go up every morning and kick her and see if she was alive," remarked Shane, memorably, in *If I Should Fall From Grace: The Shane MacGowan Story*.

He himself was becoming "very emotionally disturbed," according to Maurice. Shane was experiencing depression, extreme anxiety and night-time hallucinations so frightening that he stopped going to bed altogether. He was also prescribed Valium – at 100mg a day, a lesser amount than his mother – but he supplemented it with speed, barbiturates and LSD, and washed it all down with alcohol. The eventual outcome was what appeared to be a complete mental collapse, resulting in Maurice admitting his son to the "loony bin" – the Bethlem Royal Hospital in the London borough of Bromley.

There, in one of two drug wards, both mixed, he was gradually weaned off the various substances he'd been abusing. For several months, he endured all sorts of programmes - individual therapy, group therapy, occupational therapy – and he was clearly a troublesome patient. He was still there on Christmas Day, 1975, his 18th birthday, unable to celebrate his coming of age with so much as a glass of shandy. By his own admission, he deliberately unsettled some of his fellow sufferers while making friends with others, he challenged the role of his psychiatrist and he formed an inappropriate bond with one of the nurses - an entirely sexual if unfulfilled relationship.

Finally, Shane MacGowan was declared sane and released from the loony bin. Disorientated, he struggled to cope with a life in which there was suddenly no supervision or timetable, later vowing that he would never again allow himself to become institutionalised, on tour, in rehab or anywhere else.

There followed a period of optimism. For the sake of her health, Therese had moved to the country, away from London, the place that had so oppressed her, and Shane returned to live with his father and sister in a flat in Wells Street, off Oxford Street. He took a job as a barman in the Griffin Tavern, a large Irish pub close to Charing Cross Station and renewed his friendship with Berni. Bored with the freak scene, they each had their hair razor-cut, quite short, into layers with a centre parting and a neat, springy top. They were soul boys, dressing up for nights spent dancing in discos in suits with wide lapels and collars and baggy trousers, upping the pose count with sunglasses and Italian shoes.

MacGowan, who had left Bethlem with a determination to avoid downers, said in *A Drink With Shane MacGowan*, a book of conversations compiled by his one-time girlfriend Victoria Clark: "I had a whole new attitude. I wasn't a wasted druggie zombie, and I wasn't constantly having rows with my parents... I felt sharp, alive. I had money in my pocket, y'know, I was into looking good... I wanted to just drink and take speed, and like... dance."

He was in exactly the right frame of mind for what was to happen next: the Sex Pistols.

CHAPTER 2

Going For A Burton

Spider Stacy was not too quick off the mark when punk started. As he puts it himself, "I woke up in 1976 and I got out of bed in 1977."

"I'd kind of gone to sleep," he explains. "In '73, '74, I was taking quite a lot of acid with a pal, and we used to listen to stuff like Genesis. Cos it's all trippy, I kind of got into that. I went to see Genesis a few times. I had a Nice album. But it wasn't really doing it for me. Not that I was looking for something to do it for me – I wasn't even consciously aware I was bored with the music I'd been going out and buying.

"Then I caught a glimpse of Eddie And The Hot Rods at ULU. I was really, really drunk, but it made a vague impression. And then a friend of mine had their 'Get Out Of Denver' EP, which I thought was really good."

In 1975 and 1976, adrenalin-fired pub-rock bands in venues around the country were setting the scene for what was to follow. They included Eddie And The Hot Rods, The 101ers and Dr Feelgood.

"I went to see Dr Feelgood and I was completely fucking blown away by them," remembers Spider. Still, when punk arrived in all its snotty glory, he was looking away. He'd stopped reading the music papers regularly, and although he was aware of certain names being bandied about, he only had a distant and strangely romantic idea of what they stood for.

"I picked up the notion that the Sex Pistols were French," he admits. "I'd heard of the Ramones, and I'd got this idea in my head that they were Puerto Ricans and they had pompadours and gold lamé jackets and stuff like that. I heard them on John Peel, but on a really dodgy radio. They were doing 'I Wanna Be Your Boyfriend'. It was an atypical Ramones song. I didn't know quite what to make of it."

The Ramones began to make sense at last to Stacy when he went to a dance at the Henrietta Barnett girls' grammar school in Hampstead Garden

Suburb, north-west London. "Someone put on 'Blitzkrieg Bop' and I was, 'What the fuck is *this*?'"

He made sure to be in the audience when The Ramones next came to town. Their first visit, to The Roundhouse in London's Chalk Farm in July 1976, had created huge excitement, encouraging the emerging English punk rockers to play harder and faster. The Ramones were seen as confirmation that the times they were a-changin', not just in small pockets of major British cities, but internationally.

For quite a while, though, the Ramones were appreciated more in the UK than in their native America, and so they returned with a European tour in the early summer of 1977. This time, they headlined two Roundhouse shows, supported by Talking Heads and The Saints, on June 5 and 6.

"Certainly, I've never seen a better band live than they were," says Spider – who has another reason for remembering his Ramones experience so affectionately. It was here, at The Roundhouse, that he first met Shane MacGowan.

"He was standing in the trough of the urinal chatting to a couple of guys about his fanzine," recalls Spider. "I'd started getting the music papers every week again, and I knew who he was because of the *Sounds* cover. He was a famous person. He looked quite menacing. He was tall. I was feeling a little bit conspicuous because I had long hair. A little while after that, I went out for a breath of fresh air and I saw him again. He said, 'Are you enjoying yourself?' That was like a little bit of acceptance. I thought it was nice of him. I said, 'Yeah.' He said, 'That's what it's all about then.' I went back inside."

After that, Shane and Spider would bump into each other at gigs from time to time, but it would be another couple of years before they got to know each other properly.

Once he'd discovered punk, Stacy was an instant convert. Working as a car salesman at a Renault garage a minute's walk from where he lived in the north-west London area of Temple Fortune, he spent his wages on records and gigs and dashed home at lunchtimes to listen to The Clash.

"Another thing," he adds. "I became aware that one of the things people were getting at here was going out and doing it yourself, not going out and watching other people doing it. That whole idea that anybody can be in a band, or write, or paint, or design clothes *et cetera*, although I saw it in specific relation to bands, really was a revelation. Anybody could do anything. The technical virtuosity or expertise was something that might come along later on. It was not by any means the be all and end all."

And so Spider formed a band, The New Bastards, with a bunch of friends from his schooldays. He himself had gone to Christ's College School For Boys in Finchley, but most of his friends were former pupils of Whitefields in Brent Cross.

"We would sit around and listen to all these punk records," says Stacy. "All sorts of things were coming out, and I'd say probably I liked all of it."

Spider took on the drummer's job in The New Bastards, even though he didn't own a drumkit and had never played one. The singer was John Golding, the guitarist was Matt Duguid and the bassist may have been Spider's best friend Matt Jacobson, although he's not sure. Together, they wrote a collection of rather rudimentary songs and rehearsed in bedrooms, Spider hitting a cushion with a rolled-up newspaper to create a drumbeat of sorts.

And then they played their one and only gig, a gloriously drunken spectacle, at Whitefields school: "We were supporting a band called Mister Meaner. We had to pull Johnny Golding out of the gents before we could go on, and it was fucking awful, a complete shambles - but it was great. Mister's drummer let me use half of his kit. I decided to ignore the pedals. I worked out that if I didn't use the pedals, I'd have a better chance of keeping time. The stuff we played was all self-penned except, I think, for a cover of 'Louie Louie' – the *Metallic KO* version of 'Louie Louie' [by Iggy & The Stooges]. It was a cover of a cover. There were a couple of *bona fide* punks in the audience, and they really enjoyed it."

Dizzy with the triumph of their Whitefields debut, The New Bastards did the only decent thing they could, and split. Matt Duguid formed a new group called The Russians, taking John Golding with him. Spider decided that drumming was not for him, and when he teamed up with friend and bassist Matt Jacobson to start his own new project, The Millwall Chainsaws, he became the singer. They recruited a drummer called Ollie Watts and called upon Matt Duguid to stand in on guitar when he was available.

1979 saw a dramatic exodus from Temple Fortune. Spider and The Millwall Chainsaws, together with other friends including Matt Duguid, had heard of a street in central London, near King's Cross, which was full of cheap housing, squats and a community of young people into music. Matt Jacobson's two brothers were already living in Burton Street, WC1, and everyone else followed en masse. That's when life got really interesting.

Things had been changing at Rock On Records. By 1979, Phil Gaston and Stan Brennan had bought the stall from owner Ted Carroll and changed the name to Rocks Off. When it was time for the bulldozers to roll into Soho Market, Gaston and Brennan moved Rocks Off to Hanway Street, tucked away behind today's Virgin Megastore in Oxford Street. It was here that they would later employ Shane MacGowan as a sales assistant. Carroll retained the other Rock On business he was running in Camden Town, beside the tube station.

The six-o'clock drinking sessions continued at more convenient watering holes. The gang had already abandoned The Cambridge for The Avenue, a pub at the top of Shaftesbury Avenue which has since been demolished, and now The Black Horse in Rathbone Place became a favourite.

The people involved in Rock On and the newly named Rocks Off were connected through a network of cross-border friendships in Ireland that would also grow to embrace The Pogues.

Phil Gaston and Roger Armstrong had been schoolmates in Belfast at the RBAI boys' grammar school, locally known as INST. Both went on to Queen's University where they met Stan Brennan and another student called Michael Clifford and, together, the four developed the Esoteric Music Society. "It originally was just a bunch of people going down into the cellar in the university building and playing Frank Zappa and Pink Floyd and all sorts of weird stuff," explains Gaston. In time, they graduated to promoting gigs, most successfully in conjunction with local record shop owner Dougie Knight. The Society, now known simply as EMS, continues to promote gigs in Belfast.

"Roger was determined to get into the music business," continues Gaston. "He worked for Jim Aiken [the leading promoter in Northern Ireland]. He went down south and he was working with bands down there. He managed The Chieftains, and a pop band called Chips."

In Dublin, Roger Armstrong met Ted Carroll, who co-managed Thin Lizzy, and Frank Murray, their tour manager. Many of the road, sound and lighting crew working for Lizzy, Horslips and other groups in their circles at this time would later be employed by Murray when he became The Pogues' manager.

Carroll sold his interest in Thin Lizzy early in the Seventies, soon after they had relocated to London. He used the money to set up the first Rock On, an arcade stall at 93, Golborne Road, off Portobello Road. Specialising in rare rock'n'roll imports, R&B, rockabilly, Northern soul and American garage music, the stall attracted customers who themselves were on the brink of memorable things. They included Malcolm McLaren, Joe Strummer and the American music writer Lenny Kaye, who assembled and annotated the influential *Nuggets* compilation of garage and psychedelic music, and went on to play guitar in the Patti Smith Group.

Phil Lynott celebrated his former manager's latest venture in the lyrics of Lizzy's 'The Rocker', released as a single in 1973: *"I get my records from the Rock On stall/Rock'n'roll/Teddy boy, he's got them all. . ."*

From Notting Hill, Carroll moved Rock On to the premises in Camden Town, having secured a partner called Barry Appleby. Both Dee O'Mahony and Philip Chevron, the future Pogues guitarist, would take jobs here further down the line, although by then, Appleby would have sold his share of the business to Ted and set up his own shop, Sea Of Tunes, round the corner.

Phil Gaston, meanwhile, had moved from Belfast to London after leaving Queen's University in 1972, using both brawn and brain to earn a living. "I was driving trucks, and teaching physics and chemistry in Holloway Boys' School," he reveals. "It was the kind of school where, if you gave out 10 bits of equipment, you had to count them and lock the door."

Before long, he moved into a squat in Carol Street, Camden, with Roger Armstrong, Stan Brennan and Michael Clifford.

"Then Ted Carroll decided to expand into the West End, and the record stall in Soho Market opened up," says Gaston. "Roger had been applying for jobs in studios and stuff like that – his interest was more in the recording end of things - but then he got into Rock On, and he was sent in as manager to start off the stall."

That's when Gaston got involved: "We spent a summer sawing planks and putting boxes together, making a counter and building the stall. Roger managed it for a good while, and I worked for him. Then he got more involved in setting up Chiswick Records and [its subsidiary label] Ace with Ted. I was left alone at Soho more and more. That's when Stan Brennan, who'd been working at the Camden Rock On for a little while, came to work with me."

Ted Carroll and Roger Armstrong launched Chiswick in 1975 with The Hammersmith Gorillas, Vince Taylor, The Count Bishops and The 101ers. And their future signings would include not only Shane MacGowan's Nipple Erectors but Philip Chevron's inventive Dublin band The Radiators From Space.

Michael Clifford, meanwhile, became the manager of the original Virgin Megastore in New Oxford Street. He spent some time working with Gaston and Brennan before returning to Northern Ireland to go into business with Good Vibrations hero Terri Hooley and subsequently to open up Heroes And Villains, his own record shop. Clifford now teaches English in Cambodia.

"It was like fate that one of the first bands I should see when I came out was a bunch of people who looked like they ought to be in a loony bin," observed Shane MacGowan in his memoir, *A Drink With. . .*, referring to his release from Bethlem and his subsequent first encounter with the Sex Pistols.

Shane was holding down his job at the Griffin Tavern in Charing Cross, even though he wasn't cut out to be a barman. The hours were long and tedious and, besides, he didn't always like the customers or want to talk to them. But he was still pulling pints there at the time of the Ramones' first, legendary UK gigs in July 1976, first at The Roundhouse and then at Dingwalls, the small but estimable club venue just a hop and a skip down the road.

Not too long after that, MacGowan made up his mind that he'd rather be unemployed, on the right side of the bar, than on the wrong side serving drinks to other people. He was still living with his father and sister in the Wells Street flat, which was perfectly located for his perambulations around Rock On, The Cambridge, Louise's, The Roxy and any number of pubs and gigs that demanded his attendance. He became a constant presence on the streets of the West End, and he was at the same address when he met Shanne Bradley and auditioned for The Nipple Erectors in 1977, according to her recollection.

The early days of the group were exciting, fun for everyone.

Phil Gaston: "Stan Brennan and myself were running the band out of an old red phone box at the end of Gerrard Street. Our management company was called Piss Artistes. People would be getting calls from Piss Artistes about The Nipple Erectors. The phrase used to be, 'If it's easy and it's cheap, go and do it.' We'd go up and down in buses, or we'd be trekking round the place on a bike with things in carrier bags. I went round the shops, printers, distributors and suppliers on a Honda 50, a red Vespa scooter and a Honda 250 until I got hit by a truck."

Gaston and Brennan were nothing if not enterprising, once helping The Jam make an unorthodox open-air appearance near the stall in October 1976: "We ran the electricity out of the market into the car park," says Phil.

Jam drummer Rick Buckler later confessed that the band had only attempted the performance because they hoped to be arrested, for publicity. In an internet interview, he said: "The Clash were there. They lived in a squat nearby and strolled past us as we were playing. . . The old bill did turn up, but they just watched the show. They didn't even ask us to turn the music down. We had to play one set twice, as we ran out of numbers to play. So we got fed up, packed up and went back to Woking."

Gaston and Brennan called their label Soho Records. It was "inspired by the neon signs of the strip clubs".

"Everybody was making records," remembers Gaston. "Singles were coming out in picture covers. Bands would go round all the record shops. They'd go in with their box of 25 and they'd say, 'Right, they're 50 pence each.' You'd give the guys £12.50 and you'd sell the records for a quid each.

Until the Pistols went and took it a level higher, it was all very do-it-your-self, and it was very easy to sell the records. We knew that if we made Nipple Erectors records, we could do the same kind of thing."

'King Of The Bop' c/w 'Nervous Wreck' was produced by Stan Brennan and issued in the early summer of 1978 by Soho Records. Although Shane is generally regarded as the band's primary songwriter, both songs were credited to MacGowan/Bradley/Towndrow. MacGowan later told *ZigZag* magazine: "When we recorded it we were all drunk and on drugs. Shanne was in a coma."

"I remember being passed out in the toilets at the back of the studio," confirms Bradley. "Then I remember being incapable of getting up. I could hear this horrible noise, and it was Shane doing his vocals. It was freezing in there as well. Other people seem to think the song is a classic, but I would-n't say I like it. It's the first thing we ever did. It was a learning experience."

By this time, the band had moved on a little. Now, they were firing the essential blast of their early, raw punk sound right up the skinny backside of rockabilly, with a quiffed-up MacGowan taking on the appearance of a typical Ted. *Sounds*, reviewing a show at the Moonlight Club in west Hampstead, christened them "rockapunky rebels", and ran an interview in the issue dated May13 in which Shane declared, "If I don't make any money, I'm gonna wanna know why." The next month, *NME* reviewed a Cambridge show and described The Nipple Erectors as "hard, fast, tight to the point of suffocation and instantly memorable". Alan Lewis, assessing 'King Of The Bop' for *Sounds*, noted that it was "perhaps the first record which will genuinely appeal to Teds and punks alike".

It didn't exactly sell in its millions. MacGowan later confided that, "It was meant to be a rock'n'roll number but we weren't that good at playing... it came out like a mixture of punk and rock'n'roll." The Nipple Erectors were suddenly saddled with the tag of "punkabilly", a reference to the contem-porary upsurge of rockabilly, even at a time that they were already march-ing towards a future that would find them bedding down with R&B, pop and mod.

Dee O'Mahony describes her impressions of the band: "I saw them several times. I was nonplussed the first time. I remember the whole energy of the band, and Shanne in her bedraggled ballgowns looking like some-thing from a zombie movie (I believe she wore a badge that said 'housewife, superstar'), and just the sheer energy of Shane onstage."

Gigs and radio play were pretty hard to come by for The Nipple Erectors, purely because of the name. They finally agreed to shorten it to The Nips, much to the annoyance of Shanne Bradley, who thought they were selling out, and the indifference of Shane MacGowan, who had tired of it anyway.

"I feel like all these guys took the whole thing over at that point," remarks Shanne, referring to Phil Gaston and Stan Brennan. "I think they were heavily patronising. In the studio, they started putting on all these Fifties things and handclaps, and it was like, 'We're producers and you know nothing.' It was a very sexist environment. Despite all that thing about punk changing the world, when we got involved with these people who wanted to make records, they treated me very badly as a woman. And they always said we owed them money."

The honeymoon period was clearly over.

"They were unhappy, especially Shanne," comments Phil Gaston. "They worked really very hard. They did all the gigs we asked them to. We were hiring vans and driving round in the back of a transit and we weren't making any money on that. Usually we were second on the bill, and you had to pay the first-on-the-bill's PA guys to turn the sound on for you, never mind mix it."

To charges of sexism, he replies: "I seem to have managed to work with and befriend quite a number of very strong, very feminist women in the music business without any problems at the time – Chrissie Hynde, [*Sounds* journalist] Jane Suck, Sophie Richmond [office boss at Malcolm McLaren's Glitterbest company] – and the women around Dee at St Martin's were all very upfront. I seem to recall enjoying their company and they mine, but then again, maybe they would tell you different. Maybe it wasn't sexism at all. Maybe I just didn't like the person that was Shanne Bradley? It happens."

He also rejects the suggestion that anyone hijacked The Nips' music: "The great thing about Shane was that he had ideas coming out his ears. Artistically, he called the shots and that's exactly what we wanted him to do. If we thought we could've done what he was doing, we would have tried. We couldn't and so we didn't. You can track Shane's image and influences. Into Iggy & The Stooges – scream and yell, rip off shirt and get bloody. Into rockabilly – wear suede brothel creepers and drapes and write 'King Of The Bop'. Going mod – buy expensive mohair suits and rip off Otis Redding.

"Shane was a zeitgeist-surfer, finger on the sweaty pulse better than anyone. So, yes, 'King Of The Bop' had handclaps – big deal. I don't think any band is ever happy with their production. The Nips were no different. But we didn't force them into Teddy Boy gear any more than we made Shane go out and buy a Union Jack jacket, and we didn't write a rockabilly-style song called 'King Of The Bop'. Shane did, and we thought it was great."

"Shanne was very negative about everything," states Stan Brennan. "She was a very undermining personality, very critical. She had ridiculously high expectations of what was possible. It was very, very hard to get this band away. We really were going to have to work them with gigs, and we couldn't get an agency for them. We couldn't get a settled band. Musicians kept coming and going. None of the recordings were ever done in decent studios. We'd do six tracks in a night. There was never enough time to really work at stuff.

"Shane was really trying to find some direction for his music, but he kept getting distracted. There was almost this conflict between his music and his social life that existed as far back as then. To be fair to him, he always came to rehearsals, gigs, recording sessions. He always worked hard. Another thing was, Shane is high maintenance. He needed a lot of love and attention. You needed to take care of him a bit, because he couldn't really take care of himself. And I don't think he's ever taken himself that seriously as an artist, which is a real shame, because given time and some kind of commitment to his art, he could've been really special."

Another Brennan production, 'All The Time In The World', backed with 'Private Eye' – both written by Shane alone - followed hard on the heels of the first single, this time under the truncated name of The Nips. Musically, it tipped its hat to MacGowan's fondness for traditional R&B and for the urgent pub-rock bands who'd paved the way for punk. It was even less of a success than 'King Of The Bop'.

It would be more than a year, approaching the end of 1979, before The Nips released another single, but with 'Gabrielle', they could really dare to hope. The buzz around the song was electrifying: the press, the group, their management, their audiences, their peers – everybody knew that this one could do it for them. Only it didn't. And everything turned sour very quickly.

Shanne Bradley can't really pinpoint a time when her friendship with Shane MacGowan blossomed into something more intimate, although at some point fairly early on, "He moved into my bedsit. Eventually I moved out cos I couldn't stand it. Shane could be such an irritating bloke at times. I moved to Euston and became the carer of a disabled guy called Keith, who had polio as a child. I was a live-in helper, 24/7. Shane kept coming over all the time and followed me there and, meanwhile, a friend of his called Pete Petal had come out of prison, so he put him up in the bedsit.

"I had my 21st birthday while I was at Keith's, in 1978. I stayed looking after him for 20 months, and then I just went mad. Keith was a very eccentric character, and I had to get away. Pete Petal had discovered a house in Burton Street and said we'd be able to break into it and we'd have a squat, so we squatted there."

It was 1979. Shane and Shanne were once again reunited, shakily.

Stan Brennan proposes: "They had this strange sexual relationship which was very sado-masochistic. She would sleep with other men and rub his nose in it."

"I would have said it was the other way round," raps Bradley, wryly.

"I think there was a masochistic tendency to Shane accepting it," continues Brennan. "She was the 'unattainable mother'. But I don't know if Shane's really capable of loving anyone. He has his own issues."

Shanne Bradley is widely regarded as one of the great loves of MacGowan's life. She comments: "We were great mates, that's the thing. We were always friends above everything, and still are. That thing of being 'a couple' – we were both born in the Year Of The Rooster [1957]. They say roosters peck at each other and I think that's what we did, and after a while one of them has to leave the coop.

"We made friends with some people nearby, at No 32 Burton Street. We were living in No 30. I moved into their house. I was trying to get away again. This was a bigger house, and I had a basement with no one else down there. It wasn't a squat, it was short-life housing, so suddenly I became an official short-life tenant." Before long, she would move away to Kentish Town, having met the man who would become The Pogues' first drummer.

According to those who know him, MacGowan carried a torch for Shanne for years. She was the muse for one of his most exquisite Pogues songs, 'A Rainy Night In Soho', which she describes as "very moving", and obviously for the instrumental 'Shanne Bradley' – "very sweet too".

"He's a bit of an old romantic in the truest sense," adds Bradley. "I did see that at the time. At one point I had the whole world coming up to me, saying, 'When are you going to get back together with Shane?' It was so annoying. It was as if I didn't exist as a person."

One of the residents of No 32 Burton Street, where Shanne had her basement, was Jem Finer – a relatively recent arrival in Burton Street.

"The first time I went there," says Finer, "Shane was standing on a doorstep and I thought, 'That's a very odd-looking character, an intriguing-looking young gentleman.'"

Finer, originally from Stoke-On-Trent, Staffs, had moved to London six months or so earlier, after spending a year travelling and "bumming around in England". With ambitions to break into photography, he embarked on a succession of jobs, some more interesting than others, and put his name down on every housing list he could find. In the meantime, he stayed with a cousin in Finsbury Park and then with various friends before moving into his own squat in Kentish Town.

Burton Street was his first offer of legitimate accommodation. Some of the houses in the street were derelict, quite a few were squats, some were owner-occupied, and others were temporary rentals run by Short-life Community Housing (SCH). Jem, who would later work, briefly, for the SCH, explains, "They had a licence from the council to use and rent these properties for a certain amount of time. So they were legal and short-term and very cheap to rent."

Shane MacGowan describes Burton Street as an "inspiring" place to live. Finer agrees: "It was very much a community, that's for sure. There was a real mixture of people – ne'er-do-wells, teachers, social workers, maybe even a lawyer or two. Art students, artists, musicians, people like me that were just doing this and that, although I was trying to be a photographer. Someone had a dark room across the street and I'd use it.

"There was all sorts of goings-on. It was an open enough community, although it became slightly incestuous at times. There was a lot of sub-groups. But it was a very thriving community, and all sorts of alliances were formed, and connections and networks, and for me it was very exciting because that's where I started to play music.

"There was this atmosphere there that people were very supportive and helpful and encouraging to each other. They were encouraging to me, both with the photography and the music."

Jem had never thought himself musicianly. He remembers: "I tried to have piano lessons once, but I was told I was tone deaf and there was no point. I was told that, musically, I was a no-hoper. Then I tried to teach myself guitar and got put off by these lads who were doing all this flash James Taylor-esque finger-picking. I kind of believed that for a bit - 'Don't even bother.'"

It wasn't until he met Spider Stacy's pals in and around The Millwall Chainsaws, who had descended chaotically upon Burton Street just before him, that Finer even considered picking up a guitar again. A short while later, Spider moved in too.

Shane MacGowan, Jem Finer and Spider Stacy – the three founder-members of The Pogues - were now living cheek-by-jowl in the centre of London. For the time being, though, they all had their own things to do.

CHAPTER 3

Nips And Rucks

Shortly after the release of The Nips' 'Gabrielle', towards the end of 1979, Paul Weller told *Smash Hits* that it was his favourite single of all time. The Nips and The Jam had been friends from the outset. They were still turning out for each other's gigs and the mutual admiration society between Weller and Shane MacGowan was as tight as ever.

Weller's enthusiasm for the band was infectious, with two of his writer friends catching the bug too. Gary Crowley, the soon-to-be broadcaster, reviewed The Nips at The Marquee for *NME*. Paolo Hewitt, now an author (who has reverted to the original spelling of his Christian name, Paolo), interviewed them for *Melody Maker*, describing 'Gabrielle' as "one of '79's finest singles". Other journalists agreed, referring to it as "a classic pop song", "a redoubtable classic" and "a miracle tonic", and primetime Capital Radio presenter Roger Scott raved about it as he spun the disc.

But who was Gabrielle? Shane MacGowan answered the question on everyone's lips in his interview with *NME*'s Adrian Thrills, published on October 27, 1979.

"Gabrielle was this girl who used to go down to that punk club Louise's. She used to have blonde hair and tight leather-look plastic trousers, and she used to model for Strawberry Studios. She was my first real love, but she wouldn't take me to bed with her. . . she had a bit of a hang-up about sex."

Shane's song about his reluctant lover had been recorded months before its eventual release, and a lot had been happening in the meantime. The Nips had engaged the managerial help of none other than Glitterbest's Sophie Richmond, although it would be a short-lived arrangement. Musically, they'd progressed from punk through punky rockabilly and on to a tougher R&B sound with MacGowan on harmonica. In May 1979, they advertised in *Melody Maker* for a rhythm guitarist into "rhythm'n'blues/rock'n'roll/soul".

The ink was no sooner dry on the ad than Shane, typically, was announcing changes. He told *Sounds* that he was interested in "pop songs with a good beat", and added: "There's lots of little bands doin' it, all the R&B bands. What I want is a healthy pop scene." It's what he'd hoped punk would become. "Instead," he complained, "it developed into all this new music. . . this *avant garde* shit," directing most of his vitriol towards acclaimed Leeds band Gang Of Four.

At around this same time, Shanne Bradley was starting openly to voice her concerns about The Nips' record production, with *ZigZag* reporting that she believed "Stan is over-producing them and would like a more rough-edged sound on their records".

Still, Shanne was pleased with 'Gabrielle' which, backed with 'Vengeance', was the last single Brennan would produce for the band. Both songs were credited to MacGowan/Bradley/Douglas. She says: "That was a great tune, my favourite tune that we did. I hoped it would make some sort of impact."

"We're loud, raw, leering pop!" proclaimed MacGowan, now calling himself Shane O'Hooligan, to Adrian Thrills on the eve of the single's release. Holding up The Undertones as an example of a band who'd got it right – "You play songs, and you play them loud and fast so that you can dance to them" – O'Hooligan also took the opportunity to lay into Gary Numan and, again, Gang Of Four.

Phil Gaston and Stan Brennan believed 'Gabrielle', with its 'Louie Louie' riff and its compelling *"Gab-Gab-Gab-Gabrielle"* hook, could be the breakthrough The Nips needed, and they were painfully aware that their own small operation at Soho Records didn't have the muscle to do the necessary. They struck a deal with their friends Ted Carroll and Roger Armstrong, licensing the band to Chiswick Records.

"We went to Ted and Roger because we trusted them," explains Gaston. "We didn't know our way around the big, huge companies. We knew that if we went to any of the major labels, Stan and myself, we wouldn't be able to stay in the picture; we didn't have the clout. Chiswick put out 'Gabrielle', but they weren't the kind of people who spent a lot of money on promotion and placement. They weren't a 'chart' record company. They were just the same as us, only bigger. If we'd been lucky and had a hit with that, everything in the garden would've been rosy, but the whole deal with Chiswick was then called into question."

Shanne Bradley felt "total disillusionment" when the single flopped. She contends: "They licensed us to Chiswick and it upped the bullshit. I think there was a big mess-up. Christmas came and Cliff Richard took up all the presses, and we couldn't press up enough copies. We were signed up to these people who didn't put any money in, and nothing was happening."

MacGowan – an "incredibly ambitious" person, according to Phil Gaston – was equally disappointed, his frustration quickly turning to anger as he savaged 'Gabrielle', his best Nips composition, as a "dumb, stupid love song" in his *Melody Maker* interview with Paulo Hewitt.

Three months later, in March 1980, he was still fuming when he spoke to the aptly named Alan Anger of *ZigZag* about 'Gabrielle': "It's a good tune, but Chiswick fucked it up and I am fucking ashamed to have been associated with a silly pop record."

Further trashing his previous achievements and passions while, characteristically, looking forward, he decided: "There'll be no more of that R&B shit once we work out some new numbers... In the future I want to play disturbing dance music – really strange stuff, but not fucking arty... Trash is what we're really all about... the Soho part of London, the side that's full of pimps, whores and junkies."

Punk, pop, loud, fast songs that you can dance to, seedy West End street scenes... it had been an erratic journey through The Nips, but MacGowan was exploring various avenues that would eventually come together in The Pogues. However, he had yet to recognise the potential of the music of his childhood: the riotous Irish singalongs and ballads that he played at deafening volume every night after closing time.

The residents of Burton Street tended to drift from house to house and more than a few ended up at No 32 – Jem Finer's place. Spider Stacy, the last of the Temple Fortune gang to move into town, started off across the road at No 5.

"There were various levels of organisation and competence in the squats," Spider explains. "Some people were real old hands, and it was difficult to tell their houses apart from a kosher place. Others were slightly more anarchic. Number 5 was sane for a couple of weeks. Two girls who lived there, Hayley and Bic, kept the place relatively sensible. Bic was in a band called The Regents, who were one-hit wonders."

The Regents enjoyed a Number 11 single with '7 Teen' in Christmas week, 1979.

Stacy continues: "A girlfriend of mine, Cath Best, was in The Regents too, and I moved into Burton Street initially with her, but she got sick of me, so that was that. Hayley and Bic moved across the road, and then it just degenerated. There were four guys living there, and we were all completely useless. One was Smut, the singer in my friend Matt Duguid's band. And there were these two skinheads called Nick and Norman.

"We lived next door to a derelict house. One night we decided we needed some money. Nick and Norman went and nicked the lead off our roof, and then it poured with rain that night. Why they didn't nick the lead off the adjoining roof. . ."

Before long, No 5 was almost uninhabitable. Stacy returned to his home comforts in Temple Fortune several times, but invariably made his way back to Burton Street.

"I would move around to different people's houses," he recalls. "I was terrible down there. I wasn't signing on or anything. I worked infrequently – I had jobs on building sites and I did washing up in burger joints and things. I never had any money. I'd just be sponging off people, getting food.

"Once I nearly set fire to the house that Jem was living in. It was one of the biggest houses, and one of the most organised, at least on some floors. On others, you might get people throwing armchairs through the window on a whim.

"One night I was sleeping upstairs on a mattress, with a lighted cigarette. It set fire to the mattress. Luckily I woke up, but it wouldn't go out. It just kept smouldering. Other people in the house woke up and they chucked it out of the window, and it fell down into the basement area. And at that point, I decided to leave."

Finer confirms: "It was actually quite close to catastrophe. Spider used to stay a lot and this friend of ours called Cathy Cinnamon [who also lived in No 32] used to look after him and give him money and feed him and give him dope. All I remember is waking one night and it was very smoky and I thought, 'This is a bit weird.' The mattress had set fire to the rubble at the back of the house. I think we dragged it through the house and put it in a skip. Yeah, and I remember Spider skulking off in the middle of the night."

"I didn't go back for about three weeks," confides Stacy. "When I did, it was with considerable trepidation, expecting the place to be burnt to the ground. Jem has never actually mentioned it to me. . ."

Finer was remarkably forgiving at times.

"I did something really bad to Jem once," says Spider, volunteering another confession. "I'd actually had a tax rebate and I'd bought an electric guitar with it. I never got to grips with learning it, and I sold it to Jem. But I also sold it to somebody else. It wasn't a very nice thing to do. I already had Jem's money, £20, nestling in my pocket.

"Jem's always been kind of quiet. He has a certain kind of self-assurance. He's usually quite a calm person, though he's capable of going off on one if you push the right buttons – or the wrong buttons, I should say. He's one of those people you feel is reliable and is generally going to have the right idea what to do in any situation. I always really liked him. I'm at a loss to explain why I ripped him off on the guitar, except that I couldn't refuse the lure of another £20, which was more money than I'd had in my life, probably."

"Spider was a bit tricky, really, at the time," says Finer. "He was a nice guy, but he was a bit of an 'opportunist'."

In time, the likeable if roguish Stacy would find his focus in The Pogues, and he would establish solid, lifelong friendships with his bandmates, including Jem Finer. Back in the days of Burton Street, however, Jem spent more time with Spider's friends, in particular the two Matts.

"I was pretty friendly with Matt Jacobson," says Finer. "He was playing bass in The Millwall Chainsaws with Spider and Ollie Watts, the drummer. We were just talking one day and I was saying how fed up I was that I'd never learnt to play an instrument, because I had all my life been told I couldn't. He said, 'It's not bloody hard. You should come and play with us just for a laugh.'"

At the same time, Matt Duguid, who'd split from Spider's first band, The New Bastards, to form The Russians, was on hand with practical help: "He wrote out a chart of the basic chord positions for the guitar and I practised this for a few hours for a day or two – simple progressions – and then I just went and played with Matt Jacobson and Ollie," says Finer. "That was great. I thought, 'Shit, I can do this!' And so I spent a lot of time just noodling round on guitar. I worked it out quite methodically, how the chords fitted together and how the keys worked, and I listened more closely to records, figuring out how different riffs went and how you did solos. And then I started playing with other people."

Things were very informally arranged in those days, and before long, Jem found himself playing bass in The Petals - a "psychotic, punky rhythm and blues group". They were named after their leader Pete Petal, a friend of Shane MacGowan's and a particularly colourful character. It was Petal – real name Peter Gates – who had moved into Shanne Bradley's former bedsit after being released from prison, and who had subsequently opened up the squat in which he, Shane and Shanne started out in Burton Street.

Most people who know Pete Petal attest that he was a victim of police harassment, and that his imprisonment was the end result of persistent hounding and goading. Shanne Bradley is not his biggest fan, although Jem Finer is among those who speak affectionately of him: "I think Pete would've liked to make records and stuff, but the situation conspired against him. He was a real radical socialist, always out picketing places. He did a lot for the miners' strike. At that time, people were a lot more militant than they seem to be now. He's very old-school Labour. There was a whole spread of people then who were actually very serious and felt things very deeply and it wasn't like a fashion. It appeared to be more widespread.

"He got set up by the cops on two occasions and ended up being put in prison for assaulting a policeman. I saw him quite recently, just out of the blue, in Hackney. He's a carpenter now. It was really lovely, and we played a couple of songs together."

For someone who'd only just learnt the basics of guitar playing, Finer's sudden move to bass reflected the spontaneity of the times. He remembers: "We did a few gigs. Being the bassist, I just had to play single notes but, actually, it was hard because the fretboard was quite long, so you had to stretch your fingers around a bit."

Cathy Cinnamon, the housemate of Jem's who had befriended Spider, was a schoolteacher but she played guitar and wrote songs in her spare time, and Finer played with her too, on guitar.

The Millwall Chainsaws, meanwhile, were continuing to make loud noises wherever and whenever they could. They had two floating guitarists who could be counted on to stand in if they were free. One was Matt Duguid and the other was The Nips' singer Shane MacGowan.

Spider says of the Chainsaws: "We were fucking rubbish, really shambolic. Shane liked the lack of any artifice, our sheer incompetence. Also, I think he liked the fact that we had this unshakeable belief we were a band because we had three or four songs and some instruments."

One of those songs was 'Skinhead Escapes', taken from the title of one of Richard Allen's novels about skinhead anti-hero Joe Hawkins.

Despite their limited repertoire, The Millwall Chainsaws managed two recordings. One was captured on a tape recorder in a Burton Street basement. The other was made in a small studio in Somers Town.

"Cath Cinnamon is quite important in the story," states Stacy. "She paid for us to do the second demo tape, but by this time, PiL's *Metal Box* had come out and we'd veered away from our one-chord roots to this dissonant noise ethic. We were even worse than we were before. I seem to remember us combining this with an ill-advised nod to the mod revival as well – Secret Affair, Purple Hearts, The Chords. . ."

The Chainsaws' career consisted of a "London tour" – a mere handful of gigs taking place over two years. One of the earliest was on New Year's Day 1979 (before Spider had followed his bandmates to Burton Street) at the London Film Makers Co-Op in Gloucester Avenue, Camden. Admission was 60p. The Nips were due to headline, but they pulled out. The Russians were also on the bill and so were the North London Invaders – who were about to change their name to Madness.

The official Madness website immortalises the occasion thus: "The

Millwall Chainsaws' set consists of gratuitous swearing and punky noise which causes many people already suffering from New Year's Eve hangovers to vacate the premises."

"We *were* shit," Stacy readily agrees. "But it was a good laugh. Madness - I really liked them in their very early days. My memory tells me that they were less ska-orientated and more in the vein of Kilburn And The High Roads. What I really remember about that gig is lugging the gear up a frozen fire escape. It was the first time I've ever had to do that, and the last time I ever chose to. When I saw that situation developing in the future, I made myself scarce."

The Invaders' manager John Hasler had started out playing drums and then singing in the band before bowing out of performing to make way for Suggs. Hasler would later become involved with The Nips' management, marry Shanne Bradley and join the original line-up of Pogue Mahone on drums.

As for the Chainsaws: "One of the gigs we did was at ULU, and our last gig was at a festival in the Hillview Estate [King's Cross]," reports Stacy. "It was actually very easy to get gigs like that - we were very, very cheap, if not free. We never built up that much of a head of steam. You have to pick up a momentum to keep going, and that never really happened with us. It was all stop-start, stop-start. I wouldn't say we had that much ambition. The thing to do was be in a band. We had a band and I think the name was great and that was enough, really. But we never actually split up. Technically we're still in existence and the tour of London is an ongoing thing. Any moment it could happen. . ."

The split, when it happened, was acrimonious — for a while. The Nips parted company with managers Phil Gaston and Stan Brennan almost immediately after the 'Gabrielle' disaster.

"It was very painful," recalls Brennan. "I think it was the first place I got a sign that Shane didn't really form relationships that meant as much to him as they meant to the people on the other side of them." At the same time, Stan concedes that, "I don't think any of us were brilliant managers."

Phil Gaston reflects: "I just think Shane deserved more than we could give him on the promotion. The Nips should've got much bigger."

By now, a character called Howard Cohen had arrived on the scene. "He just appeared out of the ether," says Shanne Bradley. "He was a balding, Jewish guy from the East End who was only 21 but looked about 50. He got us away from Stan and Phil. They didn't like him at all because he started to stand up for us against them, and he got things happening."

"Howard was a strange guy who was even more difficult to work with than Shanne," says Brennan. "He started managing the band. He knew someone who had an agency and he was into mod, and he was encouraging Shane to be a born-again mod. The Nips toured with Purple Hearts. Shane got this Cockney accent. I mean, Shane's this tremendous chameleon anyway.

"Howard had been recording The Nips live. I think I ended up with him up against a wall with my fist in his throat saying, 'If you don't bring me a tape I'm gonna come round your house.' The Nips had a recording contract with us. They couldn't record for anyone else. I got a tape off Howard and we put out a live album. Of course it's very poor quality, but it's something that was out there."

This would be The Nips' one and only contemporaneous album, the optimistically titled *Only The End Of The Beginning*, recorded at a gig in Wolverhampton and released by Soho in October 1980 in a limited edition of 1,000 copies. Described by Bradley as "a really rubbish bootleg album", it came in a black and white sleeve splashed with some of MacGowan's most memorable quotes.

"We'd broken up the formal management," explains Gaston. "We got a last record deal, which Howard was involved with, for *Only The End Of The Beginning*. We'd spent a lot of money on The Nips. We'd supported them and provided the vans and the trucks and the PA, paid for the studio time, paid for artwork and covers and distributed things. We were given the right to press 1,000 copies only of the album to sell and that was us getting our money back; that was the end."

For Gaston, it was also the end of his management career: "The Nips finished me with managing things. I wasn't cut out for it. I couldn't be tough or nasty enough. I'd rather be friends with people than be shouting at them to do things. I wanted music to be fun. We'd started with Johnny Moped and things like that, which I really enjoyed. Then we went into Skrewdriver, which was a bloody disaster, so I was getting cheesed off with the whole idea anyway. I didn't have the money or the spare time or the knowledge, really. I didn't have the heavy clout, the know-how and the know-who that you need."

There was no love lost between Shanne Bradley and her former managers. But after a short period of estrangement from MacGowan, Brennan and Gaston were once again lifting pints with him in the pub: he still regarded them as friends, and he continued his employment at the Rocks Off shop in Hanway Street. Shane had been working there occasionally, behind the counter, back in 1979 and had gradually increased his number of days.

"I'd go and meet Shane and Phil and Stan and we'd go into The Black Horse after they'd finished work at about six o'clock," remembers Spider Stacy. "It was a good time; we had a good laugh. People used to go to Bradley's Spanish Bar as well, in Hanway Street. Shane was working in Rocks Off at the time."

"Shane was a terrible employee," asserts Stan Brennan. "When he was *there*, he was great. He had an enormous knowledge of music. Everything we sold, he knew about. He could talk intelligently about any kind of music with our punters. But his drinking – and at that stage, it was still mostly drinking – was getting in the way of him working. Sometimes he would turn up at three in the afternoon stinking of booze, pretty rough looking, when he was meant to have been in at ten. I went a lot of extra yards to keep him working. It was like charity, really."

With Howard Cowen in tow, The Nips entered into their mod phase, going on tour with Purple Hearts.

"Shane was just exploring different things, and it seemed to influence the music we were doing," says Shanne Bradley. "We were learning. The fashions in the street seemed to change quite a lot. Mod came in. I think we were a bit directionless, really."

The band went into the studio to record some tracks with Paul Weller producing.

"Paul wanted to get us signed up to Polydor," says Shanne. "So they paid for us to do a demo. But they couldn't cope with the lyrics, so we didn't get signed by them."

Two of the tracks, 'Happy Song' and 'Nobody To Love', both MacGowan compositions, would be issued much later on Test Pressings Records. It would be the band's fourth and last single.

"We did a gig one night at Billy's club in Soho," says Bradley. "There was Gavin Douglas, aka Fritz, on guitar with Mark Harrison on drums. Gavin smashed his guitar up and said, 'I quit!' onstage at the end of the gig. So then Mark said, 'Oh, well, if he's quit, I might as well quit,' and then we all quit. It was just the tension of not doing a lot."

The Nips had already fallen apart several times before regrouping with different line-ups, but this time it looked serious.

In March 1980, the band issued a statement to announce that they were splitting but would honour gig commitments: "Basically this is a situation where the record company are a bunch of old tossers," they snarled, referring to Chiswick.

But there were other problems too. Shanne Bradley told *NME*'s Adrian Thrills: "We were just sick of each other and I hated the music The Nips were playing. Shane and I just weren't communicating. We were beating each other up all the time." It was reported elsewhere that cash problems also played their part in the general malaise.

The Nips performed a farewell gig at the Covent Garden Rock Garden on March 10, and Adam Sweeting captured the occasion for *NME*.

Likening Shane O'Hooligan to Plug from *The Beano*, he wrote: "Shane was angry and frustrated and mounted a fearsome assault which was sustained until the very last mauled and mangled semi-quaver. Spitting and snarling, he turned everything around him into the blandest of Co-Op wallpaper."

Sweeting continued: "Certainly it was a passionate set, though much of the energy was of the same genre as an exploding box of ammunition – potentially lethal fragments shooting everywhere."

James Fearnley, a former boy soprano from Lancashire, was buying *Melody Maker* every week, scouring the small ads for Musicians Wanted.

He'd arrived in London in 1974 for a three-year degree course at Ealing Technical College. A gifted pianist, he was nevertheless a guitar lover, brought up on the work of such blues-rock innovators as Alvin Lee, Carlos Santana, Peter Green, Rory Gallagher, Eric Clapton and Jimi Hendrix. Wherever James Fearnley went, his guitar went too and he would jam informally with fellow students and the people he met as he moved around west London mainly, living in rented flats and squats. Leaving college with an honours degree but no idea of what to do with it, he took a job at the London Chamber of Commerce - and also discovered punk and new wave music.

"I saw Elvis Costello at the Nashville Rooms when he had his residency down there," says Fearnley. "He was edgy and angry. I thought it was just fantastic." James liked The Damned too: "'New Rose' was on the pub jukebox where I used to live near Portobello Road. 'Neat Neat Neat' – I remember listening to all that. 'Pretty Vacant' by the Sex Pistols..."

He didn't last long at the Chamber of Commerce. "I was a research assistant," he reveals. "People would ring up – 'How much would it cost to move half a ton of smoked salmon from Norway to England?' I was good at looking things up. The guy that hired me thought that was very promising. I was on a probationary term for a month or two, after which instead of giving a week's notice to quit I'd have to give a month's notice. I didn't like the job enough to have even a month's notice hanging over me. While I was still able to give a week's notice to quit, I did so.

"Then I was moving out of the squat I was living in in Ealing. Every time I'd get up to go to the pub, I'd find five or six guys saying, 'That's a good idea,' and coming with me. You could never do anything on your own. It was a squat that I'd lived in a couple of years previously, and I was embarrassed to find myself back there, with all the same people. I decided I was going to fuck off to Germany and live there for the rest of my life. I'd done German at school and I was quite good at it."

Fearnley had shared a room in his first London flat with a German guy who played the flute and who subsequently went back to join a hippie commune in a farmhouse near Marburg, a small medieval town and student centre about an hour north of Frankfurt. In 1977, James rang his friend to say he'd be coming to stay.

"I didn't speak to him personally," explains Fearnley. "I spoke to one of his friends in this commune. There was a misunderstanding and by the time I got there, my friend had gone off to Spain."

Then there was another misunderstanding: "This girl woke me up in the middle of the night, mistaking me for someone else, and said, 'We're going to Berlin, do you want to come?' I went off with two girls to Berlin and I stayed there for three months."

James had little in common with the students he found himself living with in the city. He remembers: "They called themselves Apos, which is short for 'apolitical', but they were extremely, daftly and spontaneously activist. They'd get an idea to do something and then just disappear to, for instance, remove a wrecking ball from the machinery that operates it, paint the ball silver and deposit it on the front steps of Berlin town hall. How they did that I wouldn't know, but they did. I found it hard to understand what was going on. I didn't accompany them to many places."

Instead, he picked up his guitar. He was freewheeling, having fun, meeting other musicians and enjoying the fact that he could make a good fist of Hendrix's 'The Wind Cries Mary'.

And then: "I played with this black guy. He was African and I was accompanying him, playing guitar. I can't remember what kind of stuff it was, but I do remember he said: 'You're pretty good. You need to get yourself in a band when you get back to England.' It touched me quite a bit to have somebody actually say that. I hadn't known what I wanted to do until then. It was a real turning point."

James went home. He says, "The Fearnleys are builders in Manchester. I got a job on my dad's building site, earned money, bought an electric guitar and went back to London. I went from audition to audition, all over the place. I was up for anything."

One such audition, somewhere near the turn of the decade, was for Generation X, who had lost guitarist Bob "Derwood" Andrews.

"It was quite an official affair," says Fearnley. "It was a preliminary audition and the only thing they wanted to know was if I would dress in leathers. I said, 'Oh, course I will.' But I didn't end up going back to play in the end, cos next day I sprained my ankle and had to stay in bed.'' The position was snapped up by former Chelsea man James Stephenson.

By now, Fearnley was living in Teddington, in the London borough of Richmond on Thames. "I was in a bit of a relationship pickle which I had to bring to a close," he confides. "It was an extra-marital imbroglio – extra-not-*my*-marital, if you know what I mean." During this period, he auditioned for The Nips.

Following their belligerent announcement of a split and their "final" gig at the Rock Garden in March 1980, Shane MacGowan and Shanne Bradley had decided to give the band another go. By this time, Shanne was in a relationship with John Hasler, the former Madness manager, and he was working with Howard Cohen to reform and relaunch The Nips. They'd already recruited a drummer, Terry Smith, and now they had advertised for a guitarist.

"I was very nervous," says Fearnley of his audition. "I got the train up to London wanting the job very much, seeing as it might provide me with an escape from Teddington. The audition was at Halligan's rehearsal rooms in Holloway Road. Woody from Madness used to work there.

"I walk in and Shane is down the far end of the room, sitting on the floor with his knees up and his arms lolling on his knees. It was obvious that the core of the group was Shane and Shanne, and forbidding characters they were too. The only extrovertedly friendly one was Terry Smith. He had a bottle-green drum set, and he was the one you could relate to. But it was pretty clear that it was Shane and Shanne I would have to pay attention to.

"Shane said, 'Can you do disconnected shards of industrial noise?' I tried that – a guitar solo. Then we got into 'Sun Arise', the Rolf Harris song. We started it heavy, then on to a rollicking sort of beat – really, really good, very exciting. Then I was sent down to the pub on the corner to have a couple of pints and wait for the decision from the powers-that-be."

On the one hand, James felt that the musical side of things had gone well, especially 'Sun Arise'. On the other, the audition had been a discomfiting experience.

He recalls: "Shanne spent a long time looking at the bottom of my trousers. I thought I'd broken some kind of dress code straight away. I was wearing a linen suit-jacket and black trousers, blue sneakers or something like that, and a T-shirt. Probably not the coolest person – hair a bit long, perhaps. She made me feel a bit on the back foot. So did Shane, because he just looked a bit urchin-like."

Unbeknown to Fearnley, his appearance had been received with approval rather than derision. Shanne reveals: "We'd had all these guys with mohicans and leather jackets, gobbing everywhere, and James turned up in something very 'country gent' and he just looked so different we thought, 'He's the one.'" (James was once given a job in a band formed by Nick Wade, later of Alien Sex Fiend, simply because he turned up on a bicycle. He hadn't even brought a guitar. However, he didn't stay long with that group.)

Howard Cohen and John Hasler, The Nips' co-managers, arrived in the pub to break the good news to Fearnley, but before he accepted the offer, he insisted on one condition: "If you want me to be in the band, you have to get me somewhere to live."

He was directed to an SCH property above a gay bookshop in Marchmont Street, Bloomsbury, and was half-way up the stairs with his belongings when he was suddenly told there'd been a mistake: he was to go instead to No 32 Burton Street.

Jem Finer was away at the time, and so Fearnley slept in his room temporarily. He remembers his housemates: "Cath Cinnamon was upstairs and another girl called Jasmine. There was a group of people downstairs who were called The Beards. And Shane, of course."

Shane had moved into No 32 via No 30 and, then, No 34.

"Spider used to come round regularly and when he did, it got to be noisy," carries on James. "They had that sort of relationship, Shane and Spider. It was very full-on. I wasn't ready for the force of Spider at the time. Me being a reclusive northerner who had just come up from Teddington, I didn't want to get in the way of these lions that were roaring at one another.

"I remember one time trying to get to sleep. Shane and his girlfriend at the time, Mary Buxton, had a row and threw a table out the window. Cath Cinnamon was very upset about what had happened. She took up little pieces of broken glass and was throwing them on the corrugated plastic roof of this lean-to outside the house as she was sitting in the remains of the window.

"I was going to work every day – first in Soho at an electronics repair shop. Later, I moved to refurbishing a club on Charing Cross Road. There was quite a bit of mayhem going on in Burton Street and I tended to keep myself in my room, out of the way. I was shy. I didn't want to hang out with anybody. I had a typewriter, and I was just beginning to write stuff by myself. I've done that on and off ever since."

There were quite few musicians living and playing together in the street – members of The Nips, The Petals, The Millwall Chainsaws and a controversially right-wing band called Skrewdriver, whose drummer John "Grinny" Grinton had been in The Nips for a while.

"That added a strange nuance," admits Spider Stacy. "Those guys were completely hard core. Their politics were absolutely despicable, but when you're living in the same street as people like that, you're all in the same situation. You either completely ignore them, which can lead to unnecessary hostility or confrontation, or you try and rub along together. That's basically what I did. I tried not to discuss race or religion with them because it was pointless. There was this other band called Charge, who were a sub-Crass outfit, anarchist. Having them and Skrewdriver in the same street..."

Jem Finer notes that Charge's bass player, Dave Griffiths, also played drums for The Petals, who rehearsed in Charge's basement. Charge would later, briefly, be famous when their guitarist, the late, great Stu P Didiot, provoked a "Men In Frocks" controversy following his appearance on the cover of *Sounds*.

One of Finer's abiding memories of Burton Street is of hearing Irish music. Lots of it. "When Shane came to live in our house, we didn't really have much choice," he remarks. "He'd stick on The Fureys and The Dubliners very loud when he came home a bit pissed in the middle of the night. I'm sure on many occasions I wasn't even awake. I used to go to folk clubs when I was a kid and I knew quite a few of the songs, but I received a reminder and a re-education in the music during that period of time and enjoyed it a lot. I found it a lot more ballsy than English folk music."

The Nips made their comeback with a couple of pub gigs in venues such as Islington's Hope & Anchor, and they continued to play regular live shows. The biggest thrill for James Fearnley was the fans' familiarity with the set: "I had to do backing vocals. I'd step up to the microphone and suddenly everybody was singing what I was about to sing. I'd never experienced that before.

"I liked the energy of The Nips. Also, Shane's stagemanship was fantastic. I remember doing a gig somewhere south of the river once, where the audience hung around the walls of the club leaving the floor space entirely empty. Shane was wearing a quilted smoking jacket and he jumped out into the middle of the dancefloor and just rolled around on it. It was jaw-dropping."

As for MacGowan's potential as a songwriter, Fearnley confesses: "I couldn't see that at the time. I remember once saying to him, 'You've got a great talent for stringing swear words together.' He was a fucking livewire who was giving it out, and I found that exciting, but as far as songwriting talent goes, no, I missed that. The force of his personality, however, was something that you couldn't escape."

Fearnley remained respectfully wary of MacGowan and Bradley without realising the extent of their history together. He says: "There was a big bond between them. I remember sitting in a minivan at some point, a bit fearful of Shane and Shanne. They were talking about the merciless and cruel piss-taking they enjoyed foisting on their previous drummers and guitarists, and I can't say I didn't wonder when that was going to come my way, but I was laughing with them nonetheless, however cautiously.

"Shanne I found difficult to get through to, not that I tried particularly hard, because I was a bit in awe of her. Shanne and I have talked about this since. It seems so different now, and I don't know why it should be. I could see that Shane and Shanne were 'Nips' in a way that no one else could say they were, although I hadn't an inkling that they'd been an item. I hadn't much of an inkling that Shanne and John [Hasler] were an item."

Certainly, James detected no animosity between MacGowan and Hasler: "It wasn't until The Pogues had started up that I got a whiff or two that there was not a lot of love in the cottage, so to speak. I think Shane loved Shanne for a long time, and probably still does. I remember some sort of understated yearning about him that, at least in my presence, he would never express verbally."

Most of Fearnley's fondest memories of The Nips involve their social activities, usually arranged by Howard Cohen, the "head honcho" of the two managers.

"He would take us on outings – to Cambridge to see The Specials, to Aylesbury to see The Jam," says James. "I really enjoyed the outings, to go off with Shane and Howard and drink a lot and get backstage places and take adenoidfuls of speed, and stagger round Aylesbury on my own, trying to sleep in graveyards and allotments and eventually in a disused train on a siding somewhere.

"One high point – or low point – was to be invited to Paul Weller's birthday party at the Greyhound [in Fulham Palace Road] where Shane and I played 'Heatwave' with The Jam. Weller played piano. Shane sang. I played guitar, only I was so drunk that I couldn't get my head or hands around the chords. I appealed to Bruce Foxton to show me the chords throughout the song, but they remained beyond me, and he got understandably vexed. It was exceedingly embarrassing."

By the end of 1980, things had changed around The Nips. MacGowan and Fearnley, along with Jem Finer, the Chainsaw gang and all their friends and neighbours in Burton Street, had been unexpectedly evacuated from their homes. And the bubbly Terry Smith, with his bottle-green drumkit, had been replaced by Jon Moss – later to find fame with Culture Club. It was the group's last stand.

CHAPTER 4

The Rebel Yell

The bang on the door at No 32 Burton Street came early one morning, waking the inhabitants. Structural engineers from Camden Council had arrived to clear the building which, like most of the other houses in that part of the street, had been deemed unsafe. The fate of the residents was now in the hands of the SCH.

Jem Finer had been working for a while at the SCH offices and had taken the opportunity to add James Fearnley's name to the list of official tenants.

"He looked after me a lot, did Jem, as he has done throughout my friendship with him," remarks Fearnley.

At an emergency meeting with the SCH, James managed to blag himself a flat in Camden's Mornington Crescent.

"Shane was pissed off at me cos I was the one who got the nice flat out of it," says Fearnley. "He took a bit of umbrage, and why shouldn't he? I'm an upstart! I hadn't been living there long. That's going to rankle a bit. I think he felt he deserved better than he got. I felt bad for him. But I felt my need was greater than Shane's at the time. There was no way I could've gone back to Teddington, and I had nobody in central London to fall back on.

"I was driven up to Mornington Crescent that night by Les, who worked for the SCH. The flat had no electricity, or I couldn't find it. I had a mattress and a record player and a suitcase and some clothes. I woke up and found an extra room, so I had a living room, bedroom, bathroom and kitchen."

MacGowan remained ruffled for some time, says Fearnley. "This translated a bit later into – since I had a fairly sizeable flat, I should host the rehearsals. I think it was one of Shane's ways of making me pay for it. I remember arguing about that. Rightly or wrongly, I identified an agenda."

This marked the beginning of a creeping tension between James

Fearnley and the singer whom he nevertheless liked and admired in equal measure.

"One of my personal highlights of The Nips would be playing that Rolf Harris song, just wonderful to do," declares James. "I suppose that's the beginning of my relationship with Shane. Up and down as it's been over the years, I don't think I'm being fanciful in saying there's some bond formed there."

Jem Finer, meanwhile, moved into the Hillview Estate, King's Cross, where he lived in one of a number of tenement blocks built round a central courtyard. Finer's block edged on to Cromer Street, and where the two came together, there was a corner shop. Shane MacGowan moved into a flat above that shop, on Cromer Street.

And so the old community was scattered, but hardly to the ends of the earth. Indeed, in these new circumstances, MacGowan, Finer, Spider Stacy and Fearnley would soon come together to create a uniquely exciting music that would know no city limits.

First, though, The Nips would have to play out their final dramas.

Shanne Bradley was pregnant with John Hasler's baby. That was one thing. And then there was Jon Moss, an accomplished drummer but not the sort of character who would willingly take part in The Nips' more impulsive wheezes. This became clear at Christmas 1980 when they supported The Jam at one of London's most popular venues, the Music Machine in Mornington Crescent – right on James Fearnley's doorstep.

Shanne later recalled that it was one of her favourite Nips gigs: "I took some of my mum's old nylon nighties and dressed up the band," she laughed. "Shane had a pair of giant frilly knickers on, like a baby. Jon Moss was too embarrassed to come out for the encore."

James Fearnley elaborates: "Jon put up a big fight about this. I'm not sure if he actually put on a negligee. We might have made him. He struck me as a really, really good and careful drummer. He was a nice guy, funny, but he took his craft quite seriously. Those sort of people don't want to dress up." It transpired that those sort of people don't want to be playing ska versions of 'The Holly And The Ivy' either.

For Fearnley, it was a huge thrill to play with The Jam, this being one of a handful of gigs that the two bands did together at the time. "The only person who loved The Jam more than me was my brother Andrew," says James. "I remember standing in the VIP bit at the Music Machine and looking at my brother beside the PA stack and his trousers were just flapping against his legs because of the volume of air being pistoned out of the stack. He was in a zone. He loves Paul Weller still."

At The Nips' first Jam support in Leeds, Fearnley had been stunned by the normal routines of a major gig: "It was an eye-opener watching the fans spring to the front barriers. I was amazed at such lofty things as catering backstage, and in awe of Shanne who could play bass so pregnant."

When the opportunity arose to record some demos with Paul Weller, James – who had not been in the band at the time of the 'Happy Song' sessions – was elated. He relates what happened next: "For me, it was important because I'd never done anything under the aegis of someone so illustrious. Shanne was about to have her baby, so I said, 'If the recording needs to be done, I'm happy to play the bass.'

"Then I got a phone call from Shanne saying, 'You're not going to play the bass. You're out of the group.' But at that point, there was nothing happening and there was no group to be out of. I think it just discontinued. We just knew in the end that it was finished."

Shanne's first daughter, Sigrid, was born on March 1, 1981, but even then she had not given up on the idea of a career with MacGowan. She says: "When the baby was a few weeks old, I met up with Shane. John [Hasler] was trying to help us get the band back together in a managerial role. I'd had enough of this rock music. I wanted to do some sort of roots music. I really liked Cretan/Greek folk music – fiddle and bazouki and percussion. Shane was saying, 'Well, I like the Irish music and so on, so we'll try and do something that combines these things.'

"We found a Scottish fiddle player called Davy Rattray. John was playing drums standing up. He was also working as a talent-spotter, he'd seen a rockabilly band with a stand-up drummer and he was quite inspired by that. I was pretty busy breast-feeding at the time and I thought, 'I can't cope with this at the moment.' I met Shane in a pub in Finchley Road and said, 'We'd better work separately.' I was actually homeless. We were living in a hostel at the back of Finchley Road station, and we were waiting to get a council flat. It was all a bit too much."

Still, Bradley's musical career would last longer than her marriage to John Hasler. In 1984, she became a founding member of The Men They Couldn't Hang, a band that combined folk and punk, and she stayed with them until 1987. After that, she performed with Wreckless Eric and "a cast of millions", going on to have another daughter, Eucalypta. In more recent years, she returned to the Central St Martin's College Of Art And Design – so named after the original School Of Art merged with the Central School Of Art And Design in 1989 - and experimented with film editing. In 2001, she played live with Pogue Darryl Hunt's band, Bish, and she still maintains her friendship with Shane MacGowan.

Today, she looks back on The Nips with a mixture of affection and anger, stating: "Only The End Of The Beginning seems to be even now appearing on the internet in different guises. It makes my blood boil. There must be a few pennies somewhere. Where did they go? We must've paid for our rehearsal studio by now...

"A 'greatest hits' album came out through Ace Records [Bops Babes Booze And Bovver was originally released in 1987 on the Big Beat label]. They send me all the units we've sold and because of Shane's success in The Pogues and all the interest in punk, it steadily sells."

Additionally, unofficial releases such as The Lost EP and an album called The Tits Of Soho have appeared long after The Nips' demise.

Phil Gaston responds: "I found some Nips albums on the internet just recently. It was the first time I even knew they existed. They're bootlegs. Soho was given permission by the band to do a limited run of Only The End Of The Beginning to try to recoup some of the expenses paid out for the band. We stuck to that agreement and haven't pressed or marketed anything since."

Any subsequent reissues are therefore bootlegs, which Gaston has vowed to look into. He adds: "Shanne, same as Shane and the others, gets all publishing royalties paid directly to her from the PRS [Performing Rights Society] for all songs she has writing credits on. The Bops Babes Booze And Bovver album is discontinued and has been for a long time. As far as I know there hasn't been any (legal) Nips material available for several years."

At the time of writing, Bops Babes Booze And Bovver was being freely offered for sale online by such major outlets as Amazon and Pinnacle Entertainment, and it was also possible to drop Only The End Of The Beginning into the Amazon shopping basket.

Although Chiswick Records has long since bitten the dust, Ace director Ted Carroll and MD Roger Armstrong have built the label into one of the UK's leading reissue companies, specialising in everything from soul, blues, jazz and funk to garage, R&B and punk.

Spider Stacy enjoyed a nostalgic moment recently: "I was walking to the Festival Hall the other night, down Southampton Row, and I stuck my head into Burton Street. Walking round Russell Square, the smell in the air... it really, really took me back. Around that area was the whole stamping ground - King's Cross and the Hillview Estate between Euston Road and Cromer Street, stretching over to Rocks Off in Hanway Street and The Black Lion."

Shane MacGowan and Spider Stacy were almost inseparable drinking partners throughout 1981, with Spider travelling into King's Cross either from the address in Hornsey that he'd moved into with a girlfriend or from his parents' home: he stayed there often because "it was convenient and free".

"I was spending a lot of time with Shane," confirms Stacy. "We'd go out drinking, get bottles of cider, go back to his flat in Cromer Street after the pub and sit up talking about history, about politics, about sex, about music, about books, about violence, about *The Godfather*, about football. There was Shane trying to teach me how to play Gaelic football with a cider bottle, which ended up with me having to take him to casualty cos he'd gashed his foot...

"We'd listen to some of the old Irish records he had, or he'd be singing the songs and teaching me them. I learnt this whole litany of rebel songs."

Stacy and MacGowan would memorably attempt a selection of these rebel songs live with a one-off performance under the name of The New Republicans.

Prior to meeting MacGowan, Spider had not been entirely unfamiliar with traditional Irish music: "I'd been living at Temple Fortune, near Golders Green, close enough to places like Cricklewood, which are very Irish. We used to go up to The Castle in Child's Hill, at the top of Cricklewood Lane on Finchley Road, and occasionally to places like the Cricklewood Tavern where you'd feel like you were taking your life in your hands. Anywhere in London, if you spent any time going into pubs at all, you came across Irish music. With me, Shane had found someone who didn't know all of this stuff – 'So I'm going to play it.' He was evangelical in that sense. I was drawn to like rebel songs anyway. I'd heard a few things and I'd read Brendan Behan before I met Shane."

Behan stirred his imagination greatly, but this type of reading material also presented Stacy with what he now describes as a "slightly romanticised version of Republicanism". He continues: "You're talking about teenage boys here, without an understanding of what the reality of this stuff actually boils down to. I think it also was something that was going to cause deep offence to the representatives of law and order, of the British Government, of the establishment. You're going to be drawn to it if you're the kind of person who really does want to be going round sticking two fingers up to the establishment. It was more acceptable to walk down the middle of Oxford Street in full SS uniform than to wear the balaclava and a combat jacket.

"I remember sitting in the Harrison Arms in Harrison Street on Royal Wedding Day [July 29, 1981] and I started singing 'The Foggy Dew'. Shane was going, 'Shut the fuck up!' Our local was the Norfolk Arms in Leigh Street. I don't know why we went in there. The landlady was a real old battleaxe and I must've been barred about 20 times. I wasn't really doing very much either – kissing a girlfriend at the bar or something like that. Just general drunkenness."

It was at some point early that year that MacGowan and Stacy visited Cath Cinnamon, who had remained in the King's Cross locality after the exodus from Burton Street. "Shane picked up her acoustic guitar and started playing," recalls Spider. "He launched into 'Poor Paddy Works On The Railway' at 900 miles per hour, singing it very fast. It gave us the idea of playing acoustic instruments with that kind of punk energy."

MacGowan had introduced the same song to The Nips in their formative days, according to Shanne Bradley. He has also subsequently claimed that as early as 1975, on a visit to Tipperary, he and his friend Pete "Petal" Gates instigated a bar-room jam session in which they mixed Irish music with rock'n'roll. "So that really was the original Pogues," he decided in *A Drink With Shane MacGowan*, while admitting that he had not appreciated the potential of such a fusion then or for a long time afterwards.

Today, MacGowan vouches for Spider Stacy's recollection of a supercharged 'Poor Paddy Works On The Railway', although he contends that it happened earlier, in Burton Street, and not at the home of Cathy Cinnamon.

Stacy is adamant that his memory is true and is equally certain that for him, at least, "It was the genesis of The Pogues. That's where it all began, really. It's when we said to each other, 'We could do something with this.'"

Jem Finer could not have imagined the outcome of his decision to take a course in English-language teaching.

A university graduate, he'd been doing all sorts since arriving in London. He temped in warehouses, factories and an engineers' office where he fared so well that they wanted to keep him. He worked in bars and in an off-licence.

At the other end of the spectrum, Finer was employed as an outdoor clerk for a firm of solicitors, acting as a go-between in court for solicitors and barristers. "The barrister might ask you to do various things, or just take notes," he recalls. "It could be very intense. Sometimes I had to go to prisons and interview people, and that was fascinating."

Finer seemed to prosper in the community, where his talents were challenged: "I worked on adventure playgrounds quite a lot. My job was everything from helping build these big structures to looking after kids and taking them on trips and trying to stop them beating each other up and wrecking the place."

Eventually, enough was enough. Says Jem: "I'd run out of options. I decided I should go and live abroad cos nothing was really happening to me. And so I went on one of these courses – 'Teaching English as a foreign language'. That's where I met Marcia, who I fell in love with."

It was January 1981. Marcia Farquhar was an artist who had been working in Italy. She'd gone there after completing an art history and English degree at London's University College Slade School Of Art, and she intended to return to Italy to study film.

"Teaching English to foreign students was a means to an end for both of us," says Jem. "Marcia had been doing it before, but she needed the qualification to get a better job to pay for film school."

Finer gained his course certificate – and his life partner. He says: "Marcia was, and continues to be, an incredibly powerful force in my life. Without her, Lord knows what wouldn't have happened. She was the first person who ever really gave me the belief that I had the ability to do anything other than mooch around. It was like a light going on – 'Bing!' Pick up your guitar and walk. . ."

Jem and Marcia are still together with two grown-up daughters, Ella and Kitty.

It was during the teaching course that Jem applied for a job which, much to his surprise, he got: "It was at an intermediate treatment centre in Deptford. Instead of sending kids to borstal, the idea was to keep them in their communities and give them very special attention, which meant taking them horse-riding and doing all these activities, teaching them photography. I had experience of working with kids from the adventure playgrounds, and a very serious hobby of mine was photography. I enjoyed it for a while and I did get through to the kids. Then the guy who ran it left, and the one who took over was a bit ineffectual and it became more anarchic and nasty things started to happen. In the end I felt it was a waste of time, totally hopeless. While I was doing that, I was doing a lot of painting and decorating as well, with James Fearnley. We were very slow, very meticulous."

And at the same time: "I started the whole long process of working with Shane and, then, Pogue Mahone."

MacGowan and Finer would get together to play music at each other's flats. "Shane was someone I counted as a good friend," says Finer. "He was a very warm person. He had his eccentricities, but he's a loyal and very generous-spirited person too. He could be, if he got drunk and stuff, a bit of a pain, but no more than anyone else. Other people were far worse.

"In those days, I never really thought of him as Irish. I thought of him as London-Irish. He obviously identified with the Republic of Ireland, but I don't know if he even had an Irish passport at that point."

Shane and Jem also formed a band with Cathy Cinnamon who wrote songs, sang and played guitar. MacGowan was on bass, Finer on guitar and Ollie Watts on drums.

"We were quite into industrial northern funk, all these bands like Joy Division and A Certain Ratio," states Finer. "We were trying to play a bit like that. Cathy paid for us to do some recording. I don't know where the hell the demo tapes got to, but they bear no relation to anything Pogue Mahone-like." Cinnamon's teacher's salary also paid for the band's rehearsals, which continued through the spring of 1981.

One night in April, Shane MacGowan and Ollie Watts went out to one of their regular haunts, Richard Strange's new romantic club, Cabaret Futura, in Soho. There, they approached Strange with an impudent proposal: "We've got a band, we play Irish rebel songs and we'd like a gig here." Whether or not this was intended as a wind-up, Strange happily agreed, and the hastily assembled New Republicans found themselves with two weeks to get a set together.

Had Jem Finer been around, he might well have been the guitarist. In the event, he'd gone to Italy for a while and so the line-up comprised Shane MacGowan (guitar), Matt Jacobson and Ollie Watts from The Millwall Chainsaws (bass and drums) and John Golding from The New Bastards (guitar). It was agreed that Spider Stacy would be the lead singer.

"I was quite excited by it," says Spider. "It was just the kind of thing that happened – 'Oh, *course* we got a gig.' It was fantastic."

He remembers two weeks of rehearsals. One particular session had been booked for the Cathy Cinnamon band but was commandeered by The New Republicans. Shrugging off rumours of foul play, MacGowan says: "One day she didn't turn up, so we got a bit of free time to rehearse."

Stacy thinks Cinnamon – a loyal supporter of her friends – may even have paid for all of the rehearsals, which took place near Great Portland Street. One of these turned out to be a portent of things to come, at the gig itself, for Spider.

He says: "As well as working in Rocks Off, Shane was also working in the bar of the Royal Hospital For Nervous Diseases in Guilford Street. He got me a temporary job there. At one point, they told me they were thinking of giving me a permanent job, but then I realised they wanted a *proper* barman. At the end of my last shift, which was a lunchtime, I went round with one of those White's Lemonade bottles, filled it up with all the white spirits from the optics and poured in some orange juice. It was hideous. Then I went to a New Republicans rehearsal. I think I passed out in the middle of singing a song."

Spider didn't even get to sing one song at Cabaret Futura on the big night, and it wasn't just because of his hearty intoxication: "I'd lost my voice through a combination of nerves and smoking this really weird hash that I think had been soaked in gear-box oil or something. Shane had to take over the singing. I stood around the stage demanding to know where my pint had gone in my croaky half-voice. That was the one and only gig. I was there and I missed it."

He has no memory of the gang of British squaddies who were in the audience that night hurling handfuls of greasy chips at The New Republicans, resulting in the club owner – an Irishman - pulling the plug after six songs. "Great show, lads," he told them. "Never come here again."

Also watching the performance were Phil Gaston and Dee O'Mahony.

Says Dee: "There couldn't have been more than about 10 of us that actually knew the band, and the rest were the squaddies. Going to that gig was completely off the wall, completely different. Nobody was playing Irish music then."

Gaston adds: "They were a hoot, a shambles, and Shane up front spitting out the words... I always compared The New Republicans – and very early Pogues – to The Velvet Underground. That's what I saw up there, really raw, basic rock working on just two things: beat and melody. Everybody else was clanging around making noise in the middle.

"Previously, I had this piano accordion I'd bought in a second-hand shop with rhinestones all over it, a beautiful, beautiful thing. At the very start, when Shane was thinking of doing this, me, him and Jem would sit in Jem's place in the [Hillview] buildings and we'd do Irish songs and I plonked away on the piano accordion. We did it two or three times and then I dropped out.

"I hadn't much of a clue about Irish traditional music. I'd had my fill when I was a kid. I'd got all the Dubliners and Tommy Makem albums and I'd seen The Chieftains but I didn't have the sort of knowledge that Shane had from his background in Tipp of the really beautiful old stuff, not the rebel songs. His mother gave him a lot of really nice stuff. I was quite dismissive at the time. If he was going to do that, it wouldn't interest me. I missed my chance of fame there, or notoriety. When I saw The New Republicans – that's when I saw what the point was."

Spider Stacy reflects: "Anybody who enjoyed the gig was probably impressed by the idea behind it, not what they actually saw. Doing a set comprised entirely of Irish rebel songs wasn't really the way forward, but there was a germ of an idea there that was worth cultivating."

For the time being, Spider and Shane continued their pub crawls around King's Cross and the West End, and then Jem Finer came back from Italy. At this time, The New Republicans were being regarded as an ongoing concern.

"I was going to be the guitar player at the next gig," says Finer, "but that never happened. All the other people kind of disappeared. There wasn't a band. I don't know where Spider was; I didn't see him for bloody ages. So it just left me and Shane. He started teaching me more songs and we started fleshing out other songs he was writing."

It was a long but fulfilling process, taking place over many months, with MacGowan beginning to produce some sensational material including 'Streams Of Whiskey' and 'Dark Streets Of London' – believed to be his first compositions for the band that would become Pogue Mahone. By now, he was clear about his mission: he would recharge the batteries of Irish folk music and bring it to new, modern audiences via the spirit, the spontaneity, the attitude and the language of punk. Primarily, it would be music that stood for fun, to dance to and to drink to.

Says Finer: "Shane would show me these songs he'd written. I'd learn the instrumental bits and the chords and work out the parts to play with him. I was quite into country music and I liked bluegrass banjo music, and I'd be playing the guitar, trying to make it sound like a banjo. I'd show him odd things I'd written. I might go away and come up with something I thought fitted one of Shane's songs, and then it would either go in or not. Things usually worked.

"'Streams Of Whiskey' I thought was really brilliant. I loved the words, and it was really catchy. It was an amazing synthesis. It sounded like it had always existed, though infused with something that felt typically MacGowanesque. It had a beautiful simplicity and clarity and was really like nothing I'd heard before. Of course it had its resonances of tradition, but in a contemporary context. It was unique.

"I'd always really liked folk music, although I like the rougher stuff. I like the tunes a lot, often more than the performances. What I really liked about Shane's approach – I loved the tunes but I loved the fact that it was actually being performed more like punk than a folk song. I thought, 'There's these very simple things that people come up with sometimes that open up huge possibilities,' and the idea of taking traditional Irish folk music but playing it in this way was one such stroke of genius.

"I thought, 'It's really exciting. It's music I feel I'd really like to play. I've got something to contribute to.' Quite quickly I started making up bits that went into songs. I made up the instrumental bit to 'Dark Streets Of London', which is half based on the melody and half I made up. 'Boys From The County Hell' has a spaghetti western-esque introduction. It never occurred to me to write music or songs, but once I started doing that, I thought, 'Right, I'll try and write instrumentals.' So then I started trying to write whole tunes."

Finer switched from guitar to banjo, reasoning that he might as well play the real thing instead of trying to make his guitar sound like one. He was also inspired by a cousin, Carole Finer, who had played banjo with the Scratch Orchestra, an improvisational Sixties ensemble.

He explains: "She played it in a weird way and I'd always been really intrigued. I liked her approach, so I thought, 'I'll try playing the banjo.' The first one I got hold of was a six-string. I thought I wouldn't have to learn anything new cos I could just do the picking patterns I did on the guitar. I didn't understand how all these different banjos worked, but then I realised I had to have a five-string to be able to play some of these styles I wanted to play in."

Shane and Jem went busking together round the streets of London, and they talked about the band they intended to form: clearly, all of this original material they were creating was bursting for an outlet. And so Jem asked Marcia Farquhar if she would consider playing the bass.

"She expressed a bit of interest," says Finer. "She'd played guitar a bit when she was a kid, and I had this red bass guitar in my room and I remember saying to her, 'Have a go on this.' She sort of plonked around on it for a bit and then the whole thing got forgotten. She didn't really want to do it. She wanted to concentrate on her art." Marcia, however, would go on to contribute valuable creative ideas to the group.

The main thing now was to find an accordion player: "It seemed to be a priority for some reason," says Jem. "There was a mythical female accordion player in Hillview who we never found. Then Shane had this recollection that James Fearnley could play the piano so he said, 'Well, if James can play the piano, he can learn the accordion.'"

Finer and MacGowan borrowed an accordion from a friend called Jane Swann, one of the former inhabitants of Burton Street. And then Jem went looking for James in Mornington Crescent.

"In those days, there weren't any mobile phones or emails," he notes. "If somebody didn't have a home telephone, you had to go and find them. I knew the block James lived in but not the number. I walked round listening through the doors - I thought, 'I'll hear his typewriter.' That was the sound he'd make in Burton Street all the time because he was writing, and I assumed he was still making it. Eventually I heard a typewriter coming through a door. I knocked on it and James opened it. I said, 'Right, I've got this accordion, James. Me and Shane are looking for an accordion player. Are you up for it? We're having a rehearsal tomorrow or the day after.'"

★

When The Nips split up early in 1981, Fearnley had resumed his old weekly routine of buying *Melody Maker* and going for auditions, although one job opportunity turned up on his doorstep in the human form of Jon Moss.

"He had a demo tape with him," remembers James. "I didn't have a tape player in my flat, so we had to go down to his car to play it. We were sitting in the car with all the lights out, tapping our feet – and the car was rocking. Whether anybody saw it, I don't know. He asked what I thought, and would I consider joining Culture Club as the guitarist. He went away but no serious offer came and I'm kind of glad."

In the endless round of auditions, there was one which took Fearnley back to Halligan's rehearsal rooms, scene of his first meeting with The Nips. It was for Tenpole Tudor.

"It was very funny," smiles James. "They were in leathers and I was in a baggy suit. They wanted me to stand with my legs as far apart as possible and strut my stuff. It was really embarrassing but he was nice, Eddie Tudor-Pole, a daffy guy." Fearnley was not invited to join Tenpole Tudor, but he would later meet Tudor-Pole again when The Pogues worked with him on the set of Alex Cox's *Straight To Hell* film.

Fearnley had kept in touch with some of his Nips colleagues. He was friendly with Howard Cohen, now managing an all-girl band called Dolly Mixture - whose vocalist Debsey Wykes (later to sing with Saint Etienne) was James' girlfriend for several years, until 1985 or thereabouts.

It was through Cohen that Fearnley and Shane MacGowan next worked together. Says James: "We went off to do a demo with Pete Watts and Dale Griffin [the Mott The Hoople rhythm section] at their house in Acton one afternoon. Howard knew them. Dale Griffin was an in-house producer at the BBC, and he later produced one of The Pogues' sessions. Anyway, we did some music that day and I remember playing the piano a bit. What we did and whether we recorded it, I haven't a clue now."

One band James auditioned for was The Cannibals, a Sixties-style garage outfit led by American Mike Spenser. Another – which he joined - was a soul group, at one time called The Scene.

"I think they were called something else when I played with them," remarks James. "In fact, we did some recording with Dale Griffin and Pete Watts, funnily enough, a rather over-produced single that never saw the light of day. It was called 'All People Go Mad When They Fall In Love', a bright, up-beat sort of soul thing. The drummer, Nick, was with The Vibrators for a time. We used to do our own songs, with not a lot of success. Then we were joined by a trombone player and a saxophonist – I really liked the combination - and we changed our name to The Giants. It was, unfortunately, my idea."

The Giants gigged periodically, but never recorded anything. Shane MacGowan turned up at one of the shows and paid Fearnley a huge compliment by comparing his playing to that of American guitarist Steve Cropper.

"It was an open-air gig somewhere," says Fearnley. "I was showing off onstage. This was before Philip Chevron showed me how to do it properly. Shane, I think, always liked the way I played guitar as did Joe Strummer, I'm told."

One day, he set out for another of his auditions and, on his way, dropped in on MacGowan. "I told him where I was going and we both realised I was unwittingly going back to the Cannibals guys' house. He persuaded me not to go.

"I really, really liked Shane, and I was privileged to be close to him in the period between The Nips and The Pogues, where it was nice to go and drop in for afternoon tea at his grotty flat in Cromer Street if I was in the area. He'd got his accommodation sorted out after I'd taken Mornington Crescent from out of his hands.

"There was stuff everywhere, lots of tapes. He had a rather fetching bar. It was like the prow of a ship with gunwales and everything. There was a wooden table and chairs, nice to hang out around, and a mattress up against the wall. The tea came in the filthiest mugs imaginable. Horrible. I don't know how I managed to put my lips to them. And the bath was full of bin-bags."

MacGowan's "bachelor pads" have become legendary for their extreme messiness, bearing out Stan Brennan's contention that "he couldn't really take care of himself".

On one of Fearnley's afternoon tea stops, Shane talked at great length about his ambitions for another group. "He was reading books about the Roman Empire. The idea was he was going to dress up in togas and I should be a gladiator," says James. "He was really, really keen on this. It was a nod in the direction of the new romantics, who were cutting a dash in London at the time. His big thing was Cretan music [an interest possibly sparked by Shanne Bradley]. I don't think he had a name, and I've no idea who else was going to be in the band, but he had all the music sorted out in his head."

MacGowan and Fearnley would also go out for the odd pint: "We went drinking in the pubs round Cromer Street. I remember coming from a pub with him to sit on his mattress on the floor and play the tin whistle for him. I'd been listening to a record called *Tin Whistles* by the Chieftains guy, Paddy Maloney, and Sean Potts. I learned a couple of tunes – 'Jimmy Mo Mhile Stor' in particular, which was an air, nicely named after me! – and I was playing this tin whistle with Shane dancing in the room with a bottle in his hand in a shuffly, drunken kind of way. It was really adorable. That's when I experienced his vulnerability."

Eventually Fearnley grew tired of his life of auditions and short-lived bands. He sold his Telecaster, picked up an ex-office IBM electric type-writer and retreated to Mornington Crescent to become a writer. He was going out with Debsey Wykes, and he enjoyed a summer on the roof of his building reading James Joyce's *Ulysses*.

"It was a case of, 'Clear the decks!' Just, change."

He enjoyed the writing. "I rather liked the physical discipline of learning to touch-type," says James. "I used to listen to Chopin and I'd play the type-writer along to it. There I was one afternoon, typing away, when there was a knock at the door and Jem's there with this lovely-looking white painted Hohner accordion. . ."

Within days, James was rehearsing with Shane and Jem at MacGowan's flat in Cromer Street around the same wooden table where he'd sipped his tea from rancid mugs, trying to master the ins and outs of the accordion.

He recalls: "My first reaction was, 'This might be a nice distraction.' There's something about an accordion you can't run away from. It's an attractive instrument, and a daft instrument too. I just thought it would be fun to have a go and see if I could. And it's nice to be asked to do something. It made a change from always seeking something out and travelling to Carshalton, Harrow, Lewisham and Teddington to find it. I didn't find the accordion difficult at all."

Fearnley had already discovered a natural talent for playing music: "Give me an instrument and if I know what I want it to sound like, I'll get it to sound that way. I cut the cloth to fit the suit."

Shane MacGowan, Jem Finer and James Fearnley were now working seriously towards the establishment of The Pogues. But MacGowan had a secret, and he kept it for quite some time. He had already decided on a fourth member: Spider Stacy was going to be the singer.

CHAPTER 5

Pogue Mahone: Birth Pains And Beer Trays

It was decided that John Hasler would play drums. He may have won the heart of Shane's adored Shanne Bradley, but MacGowan set aside what grudges he may have been harbouring – if any – for the greater good.

The summer of 1982 was gradually turning into autumn. It had been about a year and a half since the New Republicans gig, and Shane was anxious to get the show on the road. Hasler would not have been Number One on the wish list but he was available and, for better or for worse, he was known to all of the band members through the old Camden and King's Cross network that connected Madness, The Millwall Chainsaws and The Nips.

Says Spider Stacy: "I always suspected that Shane got John in the band so he could fire him further along the line, although I'm probably wrong. I think that's some kind of interesting, minor conspiracy theory."

Hasler would indeed receive his marching orders, and within a very short space of time. In the beginning he, too, was a secret, at least from James Fearnley.

"When I first went to rehearse at Shane's place," says James, "I thought that it was just me, Jem and Shane. I didn't know that Spider or John Hasler were in the band. One of the jokes we had later was that we operated by means of cells. One cell didn't know that there were members of any other cell."

The rehearsals were frequent and productive, and for some time into the future the fledgling band rehearsed at the Hillview flat that Jem shared with a friend called Rick Trevan and at the homes of various friends, including Kathy MacMillan, a regular at the West End pub nights that so inspired Dee O'Mahony. Kathy had a place off Oxford Street, near Marble Arch.

"We used to rehearse there quite a lot," says Spider. "Her upstairs neighbour was this really beautiful African doctor, who might not have been the sort of person to appreciate this pretty raucous racket we were making, but I think she quite liked us. That was early evidence of the breadth of our appeal."

Jem Finer reveals that what he calls "Poguebeat" came into being in Kathy MacMillan's flat. He says: "I imagine it was before the first gig. James and Shane and I were certainly there, just using a snare drum and a floor tom. We boiled it down to a simple, fast tom-snare, tom-snare, boom-chick, boom-chick – a driving, minimal beat leaving no room for the drummer to piss about hitting cymbals and doing rolls all over the place." Impact, not technical skill, was the vital ingredient.

The visual style of the band was important too. They would dress to be different, and immediately recognisable, in suits. But the suits would not be smartly pressed: they had to look as though they'd seen a few hedges backwards, or at least some nights of uninhibited merry-making. It was a dishevelled and particularly Irish look, easily affordable from second-hand shops, that matched the joyous, Celtic abandon of the music.

The group's debut was set for October 4, 1982 at the Pindar Of Wakefield on Gray's Inn Road – a pub venue now called The Water Rats, only a couple of minutes' walk from MacGowan's Cromer Street residence. "Shane drafted me in three days before the gig," says Spider Stacy. "I was meant to be sharing vocal duties with him because he was still playing guitar at that time."

Jem Finer was surprised; he hadn't seen Spider since he went to Italy, and that was before The New Republicans. But when Stacy turned up out of the blue for a band meeting, there was something even more pressing to discuss. They still had no name.

Various suggestions were bandied about. One was The Noisy Boysies. Another was The Men They Couldn't Hang – an idea which they would later gift to Shanne Bradley for her next band. "In the run-up to this first gig, we were feverishly trying to think of something," says Spider. "One of the things I'd picked up from Shane was the expression 'pogue mahone'. I came up with The Pogue Mahones. And that was it." Well, almost.

The name Pogue Mahone, meaning 'kiss my arse' in Gaelic, was the last piece of the jigsaw, a dual expression of attitude and Irishness.

"I remember us walking down the street like The Wild Bunch," says James Fearnley, recalling his steps to the Pindar for Pogue Mahone's first-ever gig. "We seemed to be right across the road, from kerb to kerb, and we were really thrilled that we didn't have to use a van." They didn't have a lot of equipment: a couple of guitars, a banjo, an accordion and two drums.

'Streams Of Whiskey' was the first song they ever played on stage and the set went on to mix other original compositions such as 'Dark Streets Of London', 'Connemara Let's Go' [later retitled 'Down In The Ground Where The Dead Men Go'] and the instrumental 'The Clobberer' with new arrangements of traditional songs like Brendan Behan's 'The Auld Triangle', a sombre depiction of prison life, and Eric Bogle's 'And The Band Played Waltzing Matilda', with its graphic descriptions of bloodshed during the First World War's ANZAC invasion of Gallipoli.

Pogue Mahone's performance was shambolic but spirited and awash with alcohol, as was the audience. At least two members were still trying to find their place in the band, and would keep trying for the next few weeks.

"I felt really quiet, not knowing what to do," confesses James Fearnley. "I'd been pretty much a shoe-staring guitar player. I just stood where I was and played accordion. At this time, of course, I was also held in place by the location of the microphone." Later, Fearnley would become one of the liveliest members of the group onstage.

Spider Stacy had the opposite problem. He had entered the line-up without the benefit of any instrument and with little direction as to what his role should be. Bolstered by a certain amount of Dutch courage before taking the stage at the Pindar, he drew on all of his punk experience to produce a performance that consisted largely of spontaneous shouting and screeching, scowling and face-pulling.

He recollects: "We finished with 'And The Band Played Waltzing Matilda'. Shane had run through it with me up in his flat in Cromer Street. But he hadn't played the little coda at the end where he goes into 'Waltzing Matilda' itself. I nearly burst into tears on stage. I'd had a drink or three. It was obvious that night that he was the singer. I just didn't have a voice that was capable of doing what was necessary.

"I'm sure there were times when I was pretty obnoxious. I can only put that down to alcohol, over-enthusiasm and ego – it goes to your head, I guess. You get a bit carried away with yourself. After you've had a sufficient dose of, 'Fucking hell, what a dick I was last night,' hopefully, you tone it down. Hopefully there also comes a time when you realise that you're not the best thing since sliced bread cos you're up on stage in front of a bunch of people."

James Fearnley suggests: "Spider may have suffered from having the same position in the band as, say, Bez in Happy Mondays or Paul Rutherford in Frankie Goes To Hollywood. I was a bit puzzled. I couldn't see how his function was integral to what we were doing."

Jem Finer was particularly upset by Stacy's first night as a Pogue: "We'd developed a whole aesthetic, wearing second-hand suits - which we did anyway, onstage or off. Spider turned up with some sort of weird, red dyed streak in his hair and a leather jacket. He looked like someone from another band entirely, and he spent the whole gig just screaming at inappropriate moments, he was probably pissed as well, he just got in the way, and it was really annoying. *He* was really annoying.

"I remember saying to Shane afterwards that I was really pissed off. It was just bloody rubbish having someone so completely out of synch with the rest of the band. I think maybe Shane was a bit shy and he wanted Spider to be the singer. He obviously really wanted him to be in the band.

"So I think Shane said, 'Look, Spider, get your hair sorted out, get your-self a suit and learn to play something,' and he did pull it together rapidly. The second gig we did, he'd got a nice second-hand suit on and his hair was more in keeping. I think he might've still had a bit of red in it, but it fitted. He looked like one of the rest of us. He probably did a few annoying things, cos he was a bit like someone with Tourette Syndrome, given to involuntary outbursts, but you could see the point of it then and people really liked him. He added to the chemistry of a very interesting set of people."

Shane MacGowan remarks: "Maybe Jem couldn't understand what Spider was doing there, but Spider, like everybody, had massive potential. It was all friends, and friends of friends, all the way through."

Stacy immediately started learning to play the tin whistle, with highly successful results. In the meantime, he introduced a new instrument to his live performance, and it was one which perfectly suited his madcap person-ality: the beer tray.

It would still take some time, however, for Finer and Fearnley to get used to Spider's exuberance and the wise-cracking double-act he'd formed with his drinking buddy MacGowan.

"He could still be a bloody annoying person," says Finer. "Very nice but at times very annoying. The Spider we know now is a much more focused, conscientious person. He's always been a really charming and very funny and very likeable, cheeky character, but at that time he could drive one round the twist."

Spider Stacy was born on December 14, 1958 in Eastbourne, Sussex. By the time he was two, his mother had taken him and his elder siblings Hazel and John to British Guiana in South America to join their father, who worked there. Mother and children returned to Eastbourne after the best part of a year, while Spider's dad took a job in Libya working for the Bechtel corporation – a company whose future president and director, George Schultz, would later still become Ronald Reagan's Secretary Of State in the American Government.

"There are probably more ideologically sound companies in the world than Bechtel," admits Spider. "As I understand it, what they were doing then was constructing oil rigs in the desert."

Before long, Spider and Hazel and their mother went to live in Libya, while John – 12 years older than Spider – stayed behind. "I went to Tripoli College, an English-speaking school," says Stacy. "We had segregated classes. There were Libyans there and they always seemed to be in different classes, but I do remember the Crown Prince came to the school and he was in our class, along with a couple of either rich or royal Libyans. Maybe it was just that the English and American kids had to be taught in English.

"Most Libyans seemed to be really quite poor. We were hardly rolling in money by any stretch. We lived in a block of flats on the road to the airport, but round the back was what had been an Italian army barracks, all over-grown. There was an Arab shanty town next to it. It struck me as a bit odd that we were living in this nice little flat and there were these Libyans living in corrugated iron and cardboard. The early awakenings of a social con-science..."

Spider was seven-and-a-half when he, Hazel and their mum went back to Eastbourne yet again. Their dad returned to England too, although he went to London to work. "My mum got this job as the assistant matron at Bigshotte, a boarding school just outside Wokingham, near Broadmoor, in Berkshire. It was a minor prep school and I attended it, although only for a term, maybe two. Then we moved to Horley, Surrey, and then to Temple Fortune, London."

Spider went to Hampstead Garden Suburb Junior School, transferring to Christ's College For Boys, Finchley, at 11. At around this same time, Hazel, who was eight years older, left England with her husband Peter, and Spider inherited their 100-strong record collection. He specially loved the Stones, The Who, Jimi Hendrix and MC5, although he never quite worked his way through all of the albums. "Sometimes I could just be put off by the cover," he admits. "I feel really guilty and I have to confess that I've still got some of them knocking around that I haven't played." Spider also took on a paper round which financed albums that he wanted to buy for himself.

The first live band he ever saw, at the tender age of 11, was Uriah Heep: "Me and a friend of mine, Tony Ollman, went down to the Imperial College to see them, just the two of us. I don't think we even knew who they were. The people on the door weren't going to let us in. We said, 'We've come all the way from Ipswich,' thinking this would soften their student hearts, and it did. They finally agreed to let us in."

One would hope that the Heep were worth all of that determined effort. "They were fucking atrocious," declares Spider. "I hated them." Oddly, though, he persevered with the band, two years later picking up a copy of their *Very 'Eavy... Very 'Umble* in a local record store after learning that the Stones' *Exile On Main Street*, the album he had set out to buy, was not in stock.

"So I listened to the Uriah Heep record and I quite liked it," says Spider. "I did then go and see them again, and they were great, and I did buy other records such as *Demons And Wizards*."

Spider was in his early teens when he first took an interest in Andy Warhol, a controversial character at the time, having seen him on an arts programme on TV.

"Then I saw the Velvets' first album [*The Velvet Underground And Nico*], produced by Andy Warhol. I'd heard their name and I bought it. Without wishing to appear cool and remove the sting of the Uriah Heep confessions, I put it on and thought it was the best thing I'd ever heard. That's still probably my favourite album."

At school, Spider's teachers recognised in him a huge intelligence but despaired that he seemed intent upon wasting it. He agrees: "I wasn't disruptive, but my attendance record was abysmal, particularly in the last year and a half. If I went to school at all, I'd leave the building when the fancy took me. I'd be mooching around, bunking into London Zoo, going on shoplifting expeditions to the West End and Knightsbridge. I used to go there on my own and steal books out of Harrods.

"One day there was a chemistry lesson and a bunch of people had been mucking around and had to stay behind. Me and this other guy said, 'We weren't actually doing anything wrong, so we're going home.' I was suspended and told, 'Come back when you can behave yourself.' I took three weeks off and then went back. They suggested I might be happier in an out-of-school environment."

Spider took a job in a car wash, the first of a series of jobs that were all, importantly, within a couple of minutes' walk from his home in Temple Fortune. He can't remember them all, but he did spend some time on the dole, he worked in an electrical wholesalers and he enjoyed two years selling cars at the local Renault garage.

"I was actually quite a good car salesman," says Spider, "and I would have sold more cars if I'd been able to drive. I had to get somebody else to take customers out for a test drive. If it was one of the other guys in the sales team, they would usually muscle in and take over the whole deal. It was a choice between losing money or getting the cleaner, George, to take them out. George had a glass eye and was deaf in one ear as a result of the Normandy Landings. He smoked the foulest pipe. It smelt like ostrich guano. He reeked of it, and also he didn't like the customers driving the cars, so he used to screw up your deals.

"On occasions, some customers were just so fucking awful that I'd get him to take them out. I'd think, 'Right, I'm going to give you a dose of George. That'll take the wind out of your sails.'"

This is where Spider was working, terrorising the general public with his secret weapon, George, when he discovered punk in 1977 and saw Shane MacGowan for the first time in the Roundhouse toilets.

Unlike Stacy, Jem Finer and James Fearnley came from settled homes and did well in further education. Nevertheless, both went out into the world without a gameplan. In their different ways, they felt restless and unwilling to strap themselves into the tidy futures that their qualifications made possible.

Jem Finer was born on July 20, 1955 in Stoke on Trent, Staffordshire. He was just about 10 when his family moved to the historic town of Knutsford in Cheshire, only a short drive from Manchester. He attended Wilmslow Grammar School, where he worked his way through the system. "I hated it," says Finer. "I found it very boring. I had lots of friends and so socially it was all right, but in terms of learning, it was a pain in the arse. 'Drumming in' isn't education at all, but that's what happened a lot at my school. Maybe some teachers have got the ability to drum things in in an interesting way but, unfortunately for me, most of mine didn't. The only way you can actually learn something or teach someone something is by allowing that person to make discoveries for themselves. I did enjoy the odd thing from time to time, but generally it wasn't much fun. I was very glad to leave."

Jem left with nine 0-Levels and three A-Levels, and that was at a time when these exams were extremely challenging and difficult. "It was easier doing my university exams than doing A-Levels," confirms Finer.

Although he had every prospect of passing his exams and qualifying for university, Jem had received some extraordinary advice from his school careers officer: "I didn't take his advice to be a gas fitter. Careers officers are absolute idiots. It's like the Gas Board announce, 'We've got openings for 320 new fitters.' And the careers officer says, 'Oh, maybe you can do that.'

"I had no idea what I wanted to do and my father advised me. He said, 'Why don't you be an accountant?' cos I was quite good at maths. It was one of the few things I enjoyed at school. Physics I enjoyed too. He thought, 'Well, that's a way you can make a lot of money, juggling your figures, and you probably can manage it, you halfwit!'"

Consequently, Finer applied for a course in accountancy but went off the idea quickly when he started reading up about it. At this same time, he met a student from Keele University and discovered that it offered a more flexible approach to learning.

"The first year was like a foundation year," explains Jem. "You had a series

63

of lectures covering many subjects. Then you could choose what you wanted to do as your degree for the next three years. I thought, 'That sounds like a really good idea because I haven't a clue what I'm interested in, except for teenage pursuits.'"

Finer's teenage pursuits included music and football. A committed Manchester United fan, he was lucky enough to see George Best play during his golden years with the team. And he had enjoyed music since his early teens, his tastes ranging from The Velvet Underground, Lou Reed and Captain Beefheart through T Rex, David Bowie, Mott The Hoople and Led Zeppelin to Yes and Hawkwind.

"I loved The Faces," adds Jem. "I saw them a lot. I used to love going to see bands. I saw Genesis, Lindisfarne, Stackridge... I had a totally uncritical, voracious appetite for anything that was live music."

After managing to disentangle himself from his accountancy application, Finer was accepted by Keele University where he decided to specialise in law and sociology. "Sociology was very easy," he says, "because you just made up your own course and your own exam questions. I guess I had a bit of a slacker mentality although, actually, it was quite interesting. I did a documentary film course, a semiotics course. But the law thing – I lasted, like, one lecture. I was doing computer science as a subsidiary subject and I really loved it, so I asked them, 'Could I just change and do this as a proper course?'" The answer was yes.

He concludes that it was "brilliant going to university", and he remains grateful to Keele for two unconventional but abiding lessons.

"I realised while I was at university that I was quite a naïve individual who had blindly gone along with this middle-class educational career," he recalls. "And I decided I wasn't going to commit myself to anything, or to living anywhere. I was just going to see what happened."

And also, crucially: "I learnt how to learn things - that if I became interested in something, I could learn all about it by myself. My true education started as soon as I left there."

Finer went travelling almost immediately. In Knutsford, he'd done his share of school jobs for pocket money. He'd tramped the streets delivering newspapers, he'd served in a fish and chip shop and he'd separated lettuces for a farmer. As a student in Keele, he'd worked behind a bar. Now he was in France, earning money on a barge.

"I felt stupid that I couldn't speak another language, and I wanted to do so," explains Jem. "I thought, 'If I hitch-hike round France, I'll have to speak French to people.' During the course of that, I found a job on a barge for tourists going on five-day gastronomic cruises in beautiful countryside. I was called 'le matelot' – 'the sailor'.

"I'd get up in the morning and clean the deck, and I'd go on this bike called a Solex. The motor drives it along by friction, by rubbing on the front wheel. I'd go driving down these lovely lanes alongside the barge, jumping off just before the locks, or driving ahead in a van, getting the locks ready. I had the best job cos I was the only person that ever got off the barge. I did that for a while."

Finer hopped off to Morocco after that, returning to England after three months. Some nine months later he packed his bags for London, staying first with his cousin in Finsbury Park before arriving, via his Kentish Town squat, in Burton Street.

James Fearnley had a thoroughly musical upbringing. Born in Worsley, West Manchester, on October 9, 1954, he was surrounded by family members who enjoyed performing. His maternal grandmother sang in 'The Messiah' every year in the local church, and his parents knew their way round a piano: his father knocked out tunes like 'Little Old Lady Passing By', while his mother preferred hymns. The young James desperately wanted a piano in the family home, and he pestered his parents until they acquired one from a neighbour and gave it pride of place in the dining room.

"We all used to have a go on it," says Fearnley. "I was the one who was keenest. I took to it quite naturally."

At family gatherings, everyone would sing a party piece, and in 1965 his father captured James's performance of 'To Hear The Angels Sing' on a Grundig tape-to-tape machine. This, his first recording, still exists.

In his last couple of years at primary school, Fearnley was called upon to sing solos. Then he moved to Ackworth Friends' School, a Quaker co-ed boarding school in Pontefract: "It was quite progressive, I suppose. There was no corporal punishment at all."

According to one definition, "Quakers respect the creative power of God in every human being and in the world around us. We work through quiet processes for a world where peaceful means bring about just settlements."

In his first couple of years at Ackworth, Fearnley's soprano voice was highly prized, and he did plenty of singing. He was in the Worsley St Mark's Church choir, and in school, he sang one of the three leading parts in the Bertolt Brecht and Kurt Weill opera, *Der Jasager* [translated, it means *The Yes-Sayer*].

He also broadcast to the nation as part of a traditional Christmas programme: "There's a convention – a boy soprano would sing 'Once In Royal David's City', which is on Radio 4 every year. He gets a note and starts the carol and the orchestra comes in. I did that two years in a row."

James recalls: "My voice didn't break until I was 16, the lateness of which was beginning to mortify me by then."

The first signs of this were spotted by a teacher who was too polite to tell his pupil what was happening: "He just gave me a cough drop and said that I had begun to sing flat. So then I finished with the boy soprano stuff."

Fearnley had also taken piano lessons at the school, but had given them up after 18 months because he lacked the discipline for regular practice, and he wasn't comfortable with the instructress. He says: "She used to stand over me with her arms round mine and her breasts in my back, pointing out where 'G' was.

"I asked the head of the department if I could jack it in and he said no, because I was rather promising. The last lesson, I had bandages up and down my arm, pretending to be injured – but the guy before me had done exactly the same thing. I was banned from playing the piano for a while. The head of the department said, 'If you're not having lessons at school, then you're not allowed to use the facility.'

"So me and a guy called Jonathan Bedford had this sort of contract together – 'Fuck 'em!' – and we just played whatever piano we wanted to when we wanted to. We had an experimental music group. One of the people who was in that with me was Peter Christopherson, who went on to work for [rock artwork company] Hipgnosis and then on to Throbbing Gristle. We'd liberate cellos from the music room, and percussion instruments and trombones and clarinets. The head of the department had his own wonderful Bechstein grand rosewood piano in this huge room. He caught me and Jonathan playing it and told us to go away and not darken his keyboard again."

At around 14, Fearnley formed a band with friends Malcolm Rich (drums) and Steve Brown (guitar), after the fashion of blues-rock trios such as Cream and Taste. He was to play bass. Returning home for the summer holiday, James wanted to buy a £29 model from a catalogue, but his father refused the money on the grounds that he should learn to play regular guitar first. In October, James was presented with a classical guitar for his birthday.

He remembers: "It wasn't going to help with the band at all, and I went to school with my tail between my legs. They played by themselves and I sort of strummed along. I never did play bass with the band."

Within a couple of years, Fearnley had become more interested in electric guitar: "There was an American guy who had one we used to borrow. We'd play Allman Brothers things. We had a new English teacher who liked Roxy Music, and we did 'Jumping Jack Flash' with him. At the same time I was composing long, episodic things on the piano and performing them at school."

He was also hanging around the school radio station listening to everything from Syd Barrett to Amon Duul and Can, as well as the day's leading guitar heroes.

However, it wasn't music that distracted him from his studies. "I fell in love, big-time, and it was seriously intense for the last two years of my being at school," says James. "I threw away my A-Levels on account of that. She was in the year below me. Then she went off with somebody else. She stayed and I left, without sufficient qualifications to go to university. I had to spend a year at Eccles Sixth Form College retaking exams, and I did sufficient to get myself to Ealing Technical college in 1974."

Real life came as a shock to James Fearnley. He explains: "When you leave a boarding school, you go around under a cloud for a bit. It's happened to so many people that I've seen and know. I think I went very inner. You've lost that sort of social system. All the friends you've been with for seven years are flung around the country and it's harder to keep in touch. I think I just floated in all sorts of respects."

At Ealing, west London, James began a course in modern European studies. He says: "I felt like I needed to be plugged into the modern world. I should have known myself better than that. I'm a bit of an airy-fairy sort of person. It was all economics and history and statistics. I lasted six weeks. I wish it hadn't lasted that long."

Transferring to humanities, majoring in English, Fearnley settled into his coursework, studied the development of modern music, listened to esoteric music by the likes of John Cage and lived in a succession of squats. Leaving three years later, in 1977, he took up his brief employment with the Chamber Of Commerce, travelled to Germany and came back to London, to the Musicians Wanted ads that led him, eventually, to The Nips.

Pogue Mahone were already expanding – and their latest addition would bring an explosive element to the chemistry. The band had played their first gig as a five-piece: Shane MacGowan (vocals and guitar), Jem Finer (banjo), Spider Stacy (remarkable noises), James Fearnley (accordion) and John Hasler (drums). But they wanted a bass player and, as chance would have it, MacGowan bumped into the very person.

Originally, it was Cait O'Riordan who had sought out Shane the previous year. One of her first ports of call was the Rock On record shop in Camden. There, she had got to know Philip Chevron, a Dublin producer and musician whose last band, The Radiators, had been signed to Chiswick Records. Chevron would later join The Pogues. At this time, however, he was working for Ted Carroll at Rock On.

Says Chevron: "Cait had been asking about Shane, so I pointed her in the right direction." And that was towards Hanway Street, where MacGowan was still driving Stan Brennan mad with his timekeeping at Rocks Off.

"I remember when Cait first started hanging around the shops," states Dee O'Mahony. "She was only 16."

Legend has it that O'Riordan happened across Shane in Oxford Street the day after the Pindar gig, and they went for a drink. Settling down in a pub called Hog In The Pound in South Molton Street, Cait spent most of that week's dole money buying streams of whiskey for MacGowan. He told her all about the gig and she told him all about the black bass guitar that she kept at home under her bed. It was a cheap one and she didn't know how to play it, but she loved it all the same.

Later, she remembered: "Full of my whiskey and my giro, he said, 'You're in the band.'"

And so Cait turned up at a pub in Cromer Street prior to the next Pogue Mahone rehearsal, ready for a crash course in bass playing.

James Fearnley remembers: "I said, 'Oh, hi, you must be Cait the bass player.' She says, 'No, I'm just Cait.' So she set the tone straight from the get-go. I was a bit taken aback. I don't know what she was trying to tell me. She might not have been trying to tell me anything. I was probably understanding that she was confronted with somebody who thought that he was a musician, or it was me thinking that *she's* thinking that I thought I was a musician. The intimidating, overwhelming thing was that it might have sent a sharp point into my pretension to being a musician."

Spider Stacy was delighted by O'Riordan's sudden appointment to the bass: "I thought it was fucking brilliant. When I saw her I thought, 'She can only be an asset.' I wasn't in any position to consider her musical ability because, at that point, I didn't know if I was able to play the instrument I was trying to learn [the tin whistle]. But even if she'd only just started learning to play the bass, why should that disqualify her? That's what I understood the whole thing was about.

"Cait was ferociously intelligent and she had an instinctive, very clear understanding of what we were doing. I think girls in bands, like Maureen Tucker in the Velvets, Tina Weymouth in Talking Heads and Charlotte Hatherley in Ash, are a positive thing for all sorts of reasons. A band looks good when it's mixed and a strong female presence adds something very, very important to the dynamic – the other half of the human race for a kick-off. When The Pogues were all boys together, it was never too testosterone-fuelled, but that can happen, and having women around makes a difference."

Shane MacGowan considers what O'Riordan brought to Pogue Mahone: "Sex appeal and a youthful figure and a feminine presence. Without that, we descended into a bunch of little schoolboys, getting into arguments about rubbish." Which is not to say that they couldn't still behave like little school-boys, getting into arguments about rubbish, if they felt like it.

"We taught Cait to play the bass," declares Jem Finer. "We might have even written numbers on her fretboard. She picked the rudiments up fairly easily."

For now, that was enough.

Cait O'Riordan was born in Nigeria on January 4, 1965 to an Irish father, from Lahinch in County Clare, and a Scottish mother hailing from Musselburgh, a settlement seven miles east of Edinburgh which lays claim to being the country's oldest town. Cait's father Martin worked for an oil company in Lagos, but before she had reached the age of two, the family fled the onset of the Biafra War and set up home in Hounslow on the out-skirts of west London.

As she grew up, Cait identified most strongly with the Irish side of her heritage. The O'Riordans were living in a London-Irish community and their home was filled with the sound of country and western music, MOR songs played by Radio 2 and her dad's collection of records by Johnny Cash and The Dubliners. The family belonged to an Irish club in Teddington, and Cait would munch crisps and sip glasses of pop on Sunday afternoons while she absorbed the traditional songs on the jukebox.

By the time she was 14, O'Riordan had discovered John Peel's late-night BBC radio show and like generations of young people before her, tuned in as she snuggled under the bedclothes. One of the songs she heard, and loved, was The Nips' 'Gabrielle'. Later, in the early Eighties, she took to the music of groups such as Orange Juice, the ones who were signed to Scotland's Postcard label, and those were the first acts she went to see live.

Cait became acutely aware of the anti-Irish feeling that was gathering in pockets of England, subsequently telling an interviewer: "We were the 'weirdos' with the funny names and the dodgy accents. It was horrible. Our London-Irish identity was very strong. We knew we weren't these dogs or crazed animals that the Brits wanted us to think we were. But there was no focus for it apart from Irish dancing and the St Patrick's Day parade. Until Shane came along."

Cait played her inaugural gig with Pogue Mahone at the Clapham 101 Club on October 23. They were supporting King Kurt, one of the leading bands in the city's burgeoning psychobilly scene. King Kurt had a strong comedic value: they played songs about a real-life rat, Kurt, and their gigs were pure slapstick.

Says Jem Finer: "They were fun. They were mad, and really nice, but playing with them at the 101 Club was a bit messy because they made us go on second and the stage was just covered in goo and gunk. They'd throw around lots of flour and water and dead rabbits and offal. You'd keep treading on squidgy things and look down and find a bit of rabbit's liver."

It was Pogue Mahone's second gig, and Spider was happy with his reduced role as a backing vocalist. He was also brandishing a beer tray which he bashed wildly on his head. It made a wonderful, smashing sound, like a drummer hitting the big cymbal.

"It was another of Shane's ideas," says Stacy. "I said, 'You're fucking joking, of course... oh, all right then.' I'd really hit myself hard; I didn't fuck about. Shane also suggested I should do it on my knees as well as my head, which is really difficult to co-ordinate. I know there's an art to it, but the knees were just ridiculous. It was like I'd been playing football with Roy Keane in a bad mood. Shane will probably say it's a legitimate musical instrument and he'll reel off a list of exponents of the art, people he feels have been deprived of their place in the pantheon of musical greats. I felt it was a cheap laugh at my expense, but one which I didn't mind indulging in cos I thought it was quite funny and people seemed to like it. Which is why it's been reintroduced; I'm doing it again now."

MacGowan duly remarks: "The beer tray is a very old Irish thing. It's just an instrument, you know. It looks great and it sounds great live."

The six-piece Pogue Mahone, complete with beer tray, embarked on a string of gigs around pub venues in London. To an extent, they were growing up in public, learning their trade onstage.

"James had never played an accordion before," says Jem. "I'd never played a banjo and could barely play the guitar. Cait couldn't play the bass. Being able to play an instrument wasn't a necessary qualification." More important was the ability to learn.

Says MacGowan: "We were all naturally musical people, and what we got together to do in the first place was to get extremely old-fashioned and extremely powerful music and play it to an audience that had been waiting for something. We started off our repertoire mainly from the body of Irish popular music, which is a very wide one, from The Clancy Brothers, The Dubliners, The Fureys, to Planxty and De Danann, hundreds of people that you get on record. Some people thought Dexys [Midnight Runners] were doing it with 'Come On Eileen'..."

There was a world of difference between Dexys and Pogue Mahone. There was also a world of difference between Pogue Mahone and the great Irish folk musicians they listened to. As MacGowan once, succinctly, put it: "We played faster and took more speed."

For now, the band had only one more thing to do before they arrived at their first stable line-up, and that was to find another drummer.

CHAPTER 6

The Advance Of The Young Old Men

Spider was making good headway with the whistle. He'd been studying an instruction book called *Soodlum's Irish Tin Whistle Tutor*, which contained a selection of slow airs, ballads, dance music and popular tunes such as 'Silent Night' and 'Amazing Grace'.

He says: "When Shane first suggested the whistle, I said, 'Oh, that looks quite easy. How hard can it be?' I really didn't know what the fuck I was talking about. Luckily I found I could actually get a sound out of it. The book had diagrams of the whistle with the holes blacked out. As I could make the sound, I found it quite simple to figure out what you were supposed to do with your fingers. It was a couple of months before I played it onstage."

Certainly, Stacy was armed and dangerous with his instrument in the new year of 1983, when Pogue Mahone played a gig at Dingwalls in Camden Lock. He says: "I remember at the soundcheck, I was playing my whistle into the microphone and the engineer was saying, 'The noise actually comes out of the hole at the top, not the one at the bottom.'"

It was a disastrous performance for many reasons, not least because the band had parted company with John Hasler and had yet to find a full-time drummer.

"That gig was bloody awful," admits Jem Finer.

Spider Stacy adds: "The early gigs were certainly pretty drunken and quite chaotic, but rarely were they as much of a shambles as that Dingwalls one was. There has to be some kind of purpose underneath all the anarchy, a sense of something going on. We wanted to be able to get up and actually play the songs. They deserved to be played with a certain amount of cohesion. Although we *were* in the process of mastering instruments. . ."

Finer was especially industrious. James Fearnley remembers, "He was assiduous in trying to figure out the banjo, working so hard it would eventually become second nature to him to get all these complicated figures down for his left hand and, particularly, his right hand. He had metal picks on his fingers. He worked for hours doing that."

James, Spider and Cait had also been putting in their practice, and within two months of joining the band, O'Riordan felt sufficiently qualified to confront John Hasler. The bust-up happened just before Christmas 1982.

Stacy says: "John wasn't a very good drummer, which was a bit of a handicap. Cait said to him at a rehearsal something along the lines of, 'You ought to take a bit of time off to practise more.' I think his reply was, 'Maybe I should just take a bit of time off, full stop.'

"I don't think Shane was that keen on him in the first place, and there might have been some personal animosity between John and Cait. She was finding it a bit of a pain playing with a drummer that didn't have the knack. She was herself learning at the time, but she could do it. There was no doubt that she was a natural. It's not being unfair to John to say he wasn't a natural drummer."

"John was very badly treated," counters Jem. "Cait took a disliking to John. He probably wasn't the best drummer, but he didn't deserve to be treated so badly. I felt rather sorry for him. He got booted out without us having a good alternative. So then we didn't have a drummer."

Stacy continues: "We tried out various people. A friend of mine called Worth came down to audition. He was a good drummer but was maybe a bit too rock'n'roll in the flamboyant sense of playing for what we needed. And there was a guy called Pete who stood in for us at Dingwalls. He wasn't that great either. Peter Gates, who'd been the leader of Jem's band The Petals, got up onstage and started playing drums cos this other Pete wasn't doing a good enough job."

It wasn't until March 1983 that Pogue Mahone finally got their man. They'd already auditioned Andrew Ranken once. Ranken was living on the Hillview Estate, where he'd met Shane MacGowan.

"We were on nodding terms for quite a while in the local pubs," says Andrew. "Some of them had Irish songs on the jukebox. Eventually we got talking about Irish music."

He'd also got to know Jem, and it was probably he who made the phone call. At the time, Ranken was in the third and final year of a course in media studies and sociology at Goldsmiths College, part of the University Of London. He was also playing in a band called The Operation which had started out as a busking outfit. At any given time, they numbered anything up to 14 members.

"I got this call from one of them [Pogue Mahone]," says Andrew. "They were putting this band together to do Irish songs and would I be interested in auditioning to play the drums? I went along to this audition. I don't think it was particularly formal. It probably consisted of lots of cider drinking. And then I didn't really hear anything for quite a while. Eventually they got back to me and said, 'Would you come and audition again?'

"They'd done a few gigs with other people by then. They'd decided they didn't want a conventional drummer. And so I went along to this second audition and they said, 'Right, this is the deal: you've got to stand up and you're only allowed to have two drums, but you can have this little saucepan as well to bang on if you like.

"I thought this was quite a challenge and quite interesting, so I had a go at it and found I could do what they seemed to want and got the job. I was very keen to try something different. Everything was a bit up in the air anyway, because I was in my last year at college and I was seriously thinking about getting a proper job – 'Oh, God, I'm going to have to start going to interviews and I'll have to get a suit.' Well, I had to get a suit to play in The Pogues anyway, but it wasn't the sort I'd go to an interview in."

"He fitted us like a hand in a glove," says Spider. "It was obvious."

Jem adds: "He didn't fuck around trying to be flash. It was really exciting. It was like, 'Wow! This guy has really got it.' I remember then we went to the pub and we said, 'Do you want to join the band?' 'Oh, I don't know, really.' We said, 'We've got a gig. Do you want to do it?' 'Oh yeah, I'll do that.' It took a while to get him to be in the band properly because he was playing with The Operation as well for a while. There might have been one or two gigs we couldn't do cos Andrew couldn't do them, but generally he came along."

Andrew Ranken was born in London's Ladbroke Grove on November 13, 1953. His paternal grandfather Edmund, a builder, was Irish and his grand-mother Mabel, a nurse, was from Lancashire. They met and married while working on a mission in Africa, and Andrew's father, Michael, was born in Malawi. The family moved to Ireland, leaving for England when Michael was three. They settled in Lancashire.

Years later, Michael married Barbara French and they moved down to London, where Andrew was born.

"My father didn't play a great deal of Irish music," says Ranken. "I think he was a bit too anglicised, but he did used to sing odd songs and his father, who I was very fond of – I picked up some songs from him. There were various trips to Ireland. Also, where I grew up in Ladbroke Grove, it was full of Irish and West Indians, so it was a nice cultural mix."

The family relocated to Abbots Langley, near Watford, when Andrew was five, and moved again a year later to Heathfield, Sussex, where they remained for the next decade. Andrew passed the 11 plus exam at the local primary and went on to Lewes Boys' Grammar School, which became Priory Comprehensive while he was there.

"English and art were my best subjects," he recalls. He had also taken an early interest in music, having grown up listening to his parents' jazz records – "not a bad place to start". Then he had fallen hard for The Beatles and the Stones, citing the Fab Four's 'She Loves You' as the first record he bought.

He got into drumming by accident: "I had an older cousin who'd been trying to learn the guitar. He was so frustrated he gave the guitar to me, and I didn't realise for a long time that it was virtually unplayable. The action was so high it made your fingers bleed. I persevered for a few months and I found it impossible. Somebody gave me a pair of bongos and I thought, 'Oh, God, this is much easier.' Little did I realise. . . I gradually progressed to a full drumkit. I'm sure my parents found it intensely annoying at times, but we had a big house with an attic and they were able to isolate me fairly well."

Ranken was 14 when he joined a school band as the drummer. They went through various name changes but eventually settled on Joshua Bagmat. It was a blues-rock outfit, inspired by British blues-boom musicians including John Mayall and Peter Green.

"From then on," says Andrew, "I started getting into the original blues artists, Muddy Waters and Sonny Boy Williamson and everybody else."

Joshua Bagmat's leader was Stephen Warbeck, who has since become successful in film and theatre music, winning an Oscar for the music in *Shakespeare In Love*. (Ranken and Warbeck still play together, when they have time off, in a long-running band called The hKippers – with a silent "h" - also featuring *EastEnders* and *Holby City* actor Paul Bradley on vocals, guitar and Sellotape.)

Two other schoolboys in Andrew's year would also come to prominence musically: Pete Thomas, who went on to drum for Elvis Costello's Attractions, and Eric Goulden, later known as Wreckless Eric.

Joshua Bagmat played locally in Lewes and the surrounding areas but disbanded when the members left school. Ranken moved to London to attend the Central School Of Art And Design. There he answered an ad on the college notice board – "Drummer wanted" – and got the job.

"A couple of guys and a woman from the sculpture department were starting this funk band," he recalls. "I was into all that, particularly James Brown."

The female student was none other than Lene Lovich, who had yet to develop the unique, yelping vocal style with which she would become famous. "She was a great soul singer, very straight and very powerful," says Ranken. "She always seemed very nice to me. I think she had a reputation for being a bit highly strung. Her boyfriend, Les Chappell, was one of the guys in the band, and he was still with her when she got signed to Stiff. I don't think we did very many gigs. We mainly seemed to be rehearsing. They were in their last year when I joined the band, and it fizzled out because they were doing their finals."

Ranken dropped out of art school, disillusioned, after his foundation year: "I wanted to be a painter. I always did quite small, figurative stuff, and what they encouraged were these huge, abstract, expressionist canvases. They just said to me, 'You should be doing graphics.' I said, 'Well, I don't want to be a graphic designer.'" Andrew had also taken an interest in conceptual art, which was sniffed at by the college.

After selling his drumkit to raise some cash, Ranken and a friend, Richard, decided to go travelling in Europe with the intention of producing a book of writings and drawings, a sort of *Down And Out In...*

First they went to stay in a squat in Amsterdam – an ill-fated adventure: "We came home one day and our room had been broken into and all our stuff had been nicked. We managed to get jobs working in a peanut factory out in the suburbs. We had nowhere to live so we moved to a campsite and another friend, Stephen Skull, who'd been in the school band with me, came out and joined us. He had the luxury of a one-man tent, so the three of us lived in it for a month until we got paid. Then we rushed out and bought ourselves new tents."

By the end of another few weeks in the peanut factory – and, worse, the tents - Andrew, Richard and Stephen were starting to feel stir-crazy, so they split up and went their separate ways. Ranken went to France and then Italy where all the drawings and writings he'd produced for the book were stolen. Returning to France, his luck worsened when he developed a bad tooth abcess. By now, he'd been abroad for a year.

"I was in some little village where they didn't have a dentist," he remembers. "I went to a doctor and he said, 'You need some specialist treatment. You need to have some teeth out.' I figured it was going to be very expensive to do it in France. And it was winter. I was cold and I was bored of going to different places and not having anywhere to call my own. I didn't really know what I was doing any more. Eventually I crawled home not feeling very well, and I ended up living for about a year with my parents, who by then had moved to Epsom. It's a God-awful dump, but I was broke and a bit stuck.

"During this time I got a call from Stephen Skull. He said, 'Are you interested in getting a band together?' I said, 'Yeah, sure, but I haven't got any drums.' He said, 'All right, you can be lead singer then.'"

And so Ranken became the frontman for a band called The Stickers, playing "new-wave R&B" material which was nearly all original. He says: "It was less straight-down-the-line than Dr Feelgood; a bit more like The 101ers. We didn't know any of that existed. This was probably just at the beginning of the whole pub-rock thing."

Andrew remained with The Stickers for several years through a succession of line-up changes, gigging once a week or so, and he enjoyed singing. He and Stephen Skull moved into a tiny basement flat in Islington, north London, and Ranken took on "a series of horrible jobs".

He did painting and decorating and building work, and he toiled in a screw factory near King's Cross, which was "mindlessly boring". He had a few periods on the dole. He was casually employed by Barts Hospital as a porter on several occasions, dating back to his art school days, and he quite liked it there, so when Manpower, the temping agency, sent him to St Leonard's Hospital in Hackney, he had no inkling of the horrors that would confront him.

"I had to work the incinerator," he explains. "I had to fire it up every morning. Then this lorry would come with all these very ominous sacks that I would chuck in and destroy. There were amputated limbs, but there was also stuff that came from, I think, Barts Hospital where the students used to do dissections on dead animals.

"When I finished work, I'd have to close everything down and just hope everything had burnt properly. Anyway, I came in one morning and obviously the fire had gone out a bit too early. I opened the incinerator and there was this half-burnt Alsatian dog inside it. It smelt like bacon, funnily enough. It made me retch. I couldn't bear it any longer. I walked out."

That was when Ranken decided to go back to college and began his three-year course at Goldsmiths. It was 1980. He received a mature student's grant, which seemed like a fortune, and immersed himself in his studies.

By now, The Stickers had come unstuck. "Me and Stephen were in this flat in Islington," relates Andrew. "Then both our girlfriends arrived and moved into this two-bedroom flat with us and it became severely overcrowded. Then his girlfriend got pregnant, and so we decided it was time to find somewhere else to live. My girlfriend and I moved into a flat in Huntley Street, a whole street that was squatted, just off Tottenham Court Road.

"The Stickers never made any money, the line-up was always chopping and changing and it just got impossible to sustain. I always thought we should've turned it into a hardcore punk band, but there wasn't a lot of interest from the others in doing that. There were too many people pulling in different directions, and it fizzled out in a not-very-pleasant way. After that, I felt that if I was going to do anything musically, I just wanted it to be fun and without any pressure to try and achieve anything."

With the emphasis on fun, Andrew joined The Operation, a busking band playing blues and country, with two brothers of his girlfriend, a couple of other old friends and various people who came on board along the way. Again, he was singing.

"This was in the days before busking was regulated," says Ranken, "but it was after they'd redeveloped Covent Garden, and we used to go down there and play in the main square. Amazingly enough, for the first time in my life, I actually started making money out of playing music. We always tried to put on a good show and make it a proper event.

"We used to do the South Bank outside the National Film Theatre, and they liked us enough to invite us inside a couple of times. We used to get a lot of work out of it, people stopping to listen – 'Oh, would you come and play at my party?' We did some quite funny posh parties."

By the time Ranken was getting his teeth into his media studies and sociology at Goldsmiths College, there had been a "huge military-style eviction" from the Huntley Street squats.

"There was a big campaign to get everyone rehoused," he explains. "And we did get rehoused, on the Hillview Estate."

Living there, Andrew became acquainted with Shane and Jem, auditioned for Pogue Mahone, joined the band, and then: "Things started happening really fast."

Jem Finer and Marcia Farquhar were married on March 12, 1983. The wedding was a small family affair, and so the happy couple decided to hold a celebration party in May for their friends. It took place at a bar in King's Cross, and the band that played was Pogue Mahone. Well, all but one of them. Cait O'Riordan had had "a bit of a bust-up with Shane", according to Spider, and it was the first of several memorable occasions where she didn't turn up for a gig.

"I had to play the bass at that party," says Jem. "There might have been a couple of songs where I was able to play the banjo where we didn't need the bass."

"Everybody got very, very drunk," recalls Spider. "I remember myself,

Stan Brennan and Gavin Martin singing 'The Sash' [the Orangemen's most famous anthem] at about three o'clock in the morning."

Martin, a music journalist from Belfast, would later cover The Pogues comprehensively for *NME*.

The group spent much of 1983 playing around London's popular pub and club venues, notably the 100 Club in Oxford Street, the Bull & Gate in Kentish Town, the Hope & Anchor in Islington, the Sir George Robey in Finsbury Park and, regularly, the Pindar Of Wakefield, scene of their first-ever performance.

"In the very early days, there was a whole group of us and we went to all the gigs," says Dee O'Mahony. "There was a hard core of 40 or 50 people who used to go. I really enjoyed the band, but I thought they were too left-field to break through. I didn't think they were going to make it, initially."

Still, Dee urged everyone she knew to come and see this amazing bunch of characters playing Irish songs with such ebullience and daring. One person who took her advice at the earliest opportunity was Philip Chevron, who was working alongside Dee at Camden's Rock On shop.

Chevron had known Shane MacGowan for quite some time. "He'd seen The Radiators and I'd seen The Nips," says Philip. "But mainly I knew him from being a drinking buddy up in Camden. I knew Spider from his being a drinking buddy of Shane's. Most people who were half-way interesting gravitated to The Devonshire Arms in Kentish Town Road. That's where I would sit and have a drink with Shane. Once the conversation was going great guns, he'd fumble in his pocket – 'Do you want a drink?' 'Yeah, I'll have a pint of bitter.' 'Well, lend us a tenner...'" This was a routine later immortalised in The Pogues' 'Boys From The County Hell' – *"And it's lend me ten pounds, I'll buy you a drink."*

Chevron continues: "Dee always had her ear to the ground. She was the one who pointed me to all the good Sixties northern soul all-nighters, Gaz's Rockin' Blues, rockabilly clubs and all the places that weren't the Blitz and Billy's, all that new romantic bullshit. The psychobilly thing was happening at the same time with The Stingrays and The Meteors, and the garage/trash thing was going on as well. The undercurrents which followed punk were simmering under the surface and connecting with each other in many ways.

"Out of this, I saw one of The Pogues' early gigs. It might have been late 1982, early 1983. I said to Dee, 'If it's Shane, I want to go and see what it is.' I took to them straight away. I loved the idea, the simplicity of it, approaching Irish music with a punk attitude, and there was something about the people: they had wonderful charisma. They had the old Oxfam suits, and they looked great in them. Jem, I remember, was wearing a flat cap at the time. They reminded me of something out of *The Plough And The Stars* [Sean O'Casey's play], or an Irish novel."

The Pogue Mahone set of 1983 expanded to embrace MacGowan compositions 'Streams Of Whiskey', 'Dark Streets Of London', 'Boys From The County Hell', 'Down In The Ground Where The Dead Men Go', 'Transmetropolitan' and 'The Battle Of Brisbane', an instrumental; Spider Stacy's first composition, 'Repeal Of The Licensing Laws', another instrumental; and vivid arrangements of traditional fare such as 'Poor Paddy Works On The Railway', 'The Auld Triangle', 'Muirshin Durkin', 'And The Band Played Waltzing Matilda', 'Greenland Whale Fisheries', an old seafaring favourite, and 'Dingle Regatta', again an instrumental.

There were other covers, including 'King Of The Bop' [The Nips] and 'All Tomorrow's Parties' [The Velvet Underground]. Finer took the microphone for his "Country Jem" version of Kris Kristofferson's classic 'Me And Bobby McGee', sometimes forgetting the words and informing audiences that, *"Bobby put her finger up my bum"*, and Cait O'Riordan delivered a much-admired 'Don't It Make My Brown Eyes Blue'.

When Pogue Mahone were up-tempo, they whooped and shrieked and hollered as the music careered along at a furious pace and Spider battered his head insanely with the beer tray if he wasn't giving forth on the whistle. During opposite moments of balladry, they could be supremely emotional, due in no small part to MacGowan's delivery – a rusty, trailing deadpan, or a sneery contempt. The fact that he looked and sounded like someone both lamenting and cursing the woes of the world at chucking-out time simply added to the atmosphere, the authenticity, of the Pogue Mahone experience.

The six members of the band would be strung out across the front of the stage in a line, in keeping with MacGowan's position that there should be no obvious leader. He says: "I thought we had a brilliant line-up with no frontman, like the original six-piece. You had Cait, you had Spider, you had me, you had James, you had Jem and you had Andrew, and it was a united front."

It looked sensational, and as the weeks passed, Pogue Mahone began to match the visual impact and the attitude of their gigs with a more focused musical energy. There was to be no repeat of the Dingwalls fiasco.

Jem Finer comments: "It was a really great period. From the start, we had an audience that were really into it. The word got around pretty quick that there was this really weird band. We were quite in the face of fashion at the time. Even though there were a lot of trashy rockabilly bands and garage rock bands, they were all electric and loud whereas we were acoustic and loud, and bloody fast as well. When I look back at early photos of us, I can imagine people thinking, 'That's a band I'd really like to see because they just look so great. What are these people doing? They don't look like anything else. They look like young old men, and they look quite stylish, and they've got these weird instruments.' People didn't expect those instruments to be loud and abrasive.

"I always thought, 'This is just unique and wonderful, and it's got this great quality of timelessness.' If you want to make music that's going to last, it has to start from a premise of something that's already old or rooted in tradition. If you just latch on to what's current, it's going to sound rubbish in a year or two. That's one of the things that I thought was a stroke of genius – to tap into this tradition and other traditions as well. I always saw it as much more than just tapping into Irish folk music. I saw it as tapping into tradition full stop. And, obviously, Shane was writing these really great songs."

MacGowan adds: "We all knew why we were doing it. We didn't know what was going to happen, but we didn't care."

"When I joined, all the original stuff that's on the first album was already there pretty much," says Ranken. "We all knew right from the start that Shane was on to something. He was definitely coming up with the goods.

"The gigs went from being a complete shambles to being very exciting and different. We very quickly attracted a following and it went from strength to strength. It was very encouraging. It wasn't clear how far it was going to go, but for the first few years it just went up and up. I think it was a case of being in the right place at the right time and providing something people were really looking for. Obviously, we'd hit the nail on the head."

"Andrew joining was the final thing we needed to turn us from a great idea and a bit of a laugh into a serious proposition," says Spider Stacy. "With the quality of Shane's songwriting and the originality of what we were doing, we were always going to be a serious proposition, but we needed to find a drummer who could do the job. With Andrew, we got the perfect guy. Once you start playing with a proper drummer, it makes all the difference in the world. You could get four or five disparate people, all great musicians, but there might be no chemistry there. All the individual components of The Pogues, once Andrew had joined, were in place."

Ranken arrived as a living contradiction of the old joke: "How many drummers does it take to change a light bulb?"

"He certainly bucks the usual stereotype," says Spider. "I did and do like Andrew very much. He's quite a complex man, very intelligent. He's very well read and he has a highly developed social conscience. He's a Leftie. He was always the most political of the band. He would be the first to say that he wouldn't have any truck with releasing records in South Africa, not that any of us ever would have. He's also extremely funny and he has a brilliant, deep, bass singing voice."

People didn't get to know a lot about Andrew in the early days; he seemed quiet. "He was usually pretty quiet in interviews," agrees Spider. "He's placid in the sense that you could watch a bull elephant munching on a thorn tree and think, 'That bull elephant looks pretty placid.' You rub him up the wrong way and you can find yourself in a very messy situation indeed. But he's a lovely guy, Andrew. He really is."

Andrew Ranken was nicknamed The Clobberer after a MacGowan composition of the same name, and because he was a drummer. Finer was Country Jem, for obvious reasons. James Fearnley was The Maestro because he tuned the guitars and banjos before the gigs, and his understanding of music – "I knew about harmonic structure" – brought him into partnership with Jem Finer, working out chord sequences for each batch of new songs.

Cait O'Riordan, a towering stage presence and a formidable character to boot, was dubbed Rocky.

"That was pretty apt," remarks Spider. "It was a *nom de guerre*. She was the lone girl and so I think she sometimes felt the need to leave a bit of a mark, make herself noticed. And certainly, 'Don't fuck around with me.'"

"Cait was all right, actually," decides Finer. "She was a bit of a difficult person. The thing that was annoying about her was that she had an attitude that she was great and some other people were shit, and that was out of keeping with the rest of us. We were all very much like members of the audience who got up and played something. On the one hand I really liked her but on the other hand, I didn't like that side of her. Sometimes her bass playing left a lot to be desired, but sometimes all our playing, including my banjo, left a lot to be desired, so it's probably unfair to say that."

Fearnley adds: "She was tough because she was very young when she started, and I liked her spirit, and I did like her attitude. It was hard to deal with sometimes, but she was as sweet as anything with me. I remember arguing with her once about something where I just couldn't get her to see what was the best thing to do in a certain situation and getting so frustrated with her that I had to go and hit something inanimate. I might've thrown a drink or something."

O'Riordan and MacGowan were equally hot-headed and, especially when they'd been drinking, they were not the sort of people to temper their behaviour just because they happened to have an audience. They would sometimes get into brawls onstage, much to the surprise of the rapidly expanding Pogue Mahone audience.

"Cait and Shane were an item for a while," explains Stacy. "The fights in public sort of added fuel to the fire. Their relationship didn't last very long. Apart from the odd fight, it never really got in the way of the band. Cait could be a real loose cannon. She was quite unpredictable. But she was a very, very powerful force in the band."

"She was quite a volatile person," confirms MacGowan. "But we were all volatile people. We all had arguments with each other, but they were forgotten in no time at all."

Philip Chevron bears testament to the arguments. He says: "I only saw the Pistols once and I remember the overwhelming feeling of them being a dangerous band. Pogue Mahone as well - you didn't want to get too close in case you got hit by something, possibly Cait's bass. They even had rows onstage about what they were going to do next."

James Fearley says: "Some of the gigs did dissolve into bitterness half way through. We were all splattered with that mud. I remember one gig up at the Sir George Robey. We had such fighting onstage - not fisticuffs, but a snarly kind of thing with some kicking of beer glasses around, your plastic ones.

"We couldn't quite figure out how to get from one song to the next, which was quite messy. We didn't have the techniques to help ourselves get through a show from beginning to end without some argy-bargy. I'm a middle child and a Libran – not that there was turbulence in my family too much – and I tend to be. . . not a peacekeeper so much as somebody who tries to put fires out, and I did a lot of running around trying to put fires out rather than go for a lasting solution. I couldn't bear all that stuff. I used to get very upset. When blazes start onstage, I become the middle kid. Elsewhere in the set-up, I can be a little bit sententious. I think Shane always thought I was a bit on the sanctimonious side."

The occasional conflagration did no harm at all to Pogue Mahone. Indeed, Chevron observes that, "It was all part of the show, almost. It became part of the reason you went to see them." Their audiences multiplied and their reputation mushroomed to the point that *Music Week*, the record industry bible, voted them the band "most likely to succeed" at the end of 1983, before they'd even released a single.

Says Spider: "It was starting to dawn on me that this was taking shape. It was more than I'd expected. For a start, we weren't just playing around King's Cross. We became regulars on the London circuit, building up our own following, and there was this buzz that I was very, very aware of. I think Shane was on something of a creative roll.

"It was all fun and it was really exciting. It must have spurred him on. Then again, I guess he was also discovering in himself something that maybe he wasn't aware he actually possessed. We all knew he could write songs. Some of The Nips' songs are brilliant. But he was coming into something else here, and I think he was really enjoying flexing his muscles and stretching himself and discovering his own talent. I was constantly being knocked out by the quality of what he was writing, and this was to continue for the next few years. It was like when we were all going to see punk bands in the early days. Even though I came to it relatively late, there was still that sense of being part of something. It was something that was new and was yours and that not many knew about yet.

"Here I was actually being part of the thing that something was forming around, and that was a fantastic feeling – 'We're the dog's bollocks, aren't we!' I was developing a sense of our own greatness, not mine but the band's as a band. I thought The Pogues were fantastic."

CHAPTER 7

Streets Of London

Pogue Mahone had an office of their own, run by their management team of Shane MacGowan and Jem Finer. The Office was in fact an old shortbread tin, and when it wasn't on the road with the band, it stayed with Jem and Marcia, now living in a small one-bedroom flat in Wicklow Street, between King's Cross Road and Gray's Inn Road.

"I still have The Office," reveals Finer. "Bits of paper would go in it with things to remember, and receipts. Money would go in and then it would go out."

When Ella Finer, the couple's first daughter, was born on October 9, 1983, the mobility of The Office was especially useful if Jem was working: "To try and be quiet, I used to drag The Office and the phone into the little loo in our flat," says Jem.

He continues: "Shane and I ran the business in the band. I did all the donkey work, the organisational stuff, although I wouldn't make decisions on my own. We'd always confer about things. We were the team to whom the world made offers, and we plotted and planned. James was very good about helping get the gear from A to B and back again. I was, annoyingly, involved in both those things, the business and the gear. I don't think the others actually did very much on that score. I can remember one of my first dreams I wished to come true – to do gigs where I didn't have to carry bits of equipment round. We had to go to some gigs on buses, carrying things. I know one was in Hammersmith."

Certainly, Spider Stacy made a point of avoiding any movement of gear wherever possible, following his icy, mid-winter experiences with The Millwall Chainsaws on the night they played with the embryonic Madness. Still, nobody held it against him, least of all Shane MacGowan: "At one point he said I should be the manager," says Spider, incredulously. "I don't think for one minute anybody took that seriously – 'That's a great idea, Shane! Why don't you let him do the accounts as well?'"

From the outset, Pogue Mahone were intent upon democracy, and they held weekly band meetings to discuss every aspect of their career. They would congregate in various pubs around King's Cross, usually the Pindar Of Wakefield, the Norfolk Arms in Leigh Street and The Boot in Cromer Street.

Andrew Ranken, who has kept James Fearnley's typed-up minutes of the first-ever band meeting, says of these gatherings: "There was a lot of healthy arguing and probably a lot of unhealthy arguing as well. We used to divvy up tasks for everybody to do. Someone would have to get some flyers photocopied, and someone else would have to phone such and such a record company. We had general, all-purpose discussions about everything."

As managers and as musical collaborators, Shane MacGowan and Jem Finer made for a quietly effective partnership. Yet it was Shane's unholy alliance with his boisterous drinking buddy Spider that attracted all the attention: even today, writers are anxious to analyse the chemistry, the intuitive spark, between the two. They remain the best of friends, although MacGowan lives his life the way he always did while Stacy long ago renounced the drink and drugs that gave rise to some of his more outrageous behaviour at a time when he was viewed, albeit with great affection, as the resident, obnoxious brat-punk of Pogue Mahone.

"I don't think I was really like that," he considers. "In the beginning I was a little too extreme onstage, but I'm not talking GG Allin. I think it comes from the beer tray and stuff like that. Before I was playing the whistle, maybe I was doing a bit too much gurning and sneering into vacant microphones. People mistake high spirits for aggression. Especially when there's drink involved, you can get carried away in the heat of the moment. I hope it wasn't something I made a habit of. I guess there's no smoke without fire, but I would hope that any specific examples of that kind of behaviour can be put down to too much to drink and possibly an over-inflated sense of one's own importance in the heat of the moment.

"The Pogues were not ever an aggressive band. People could've been forgiven for maybe getting that impression, but the thing that gives the lie to that is the fact that there was rarely any trouble at Pogues gigs.

"I recall seeing only one pitched battle ever, which was in Carlow, and that was down to a flare-up with the Wicklow Barmy Army who'd come looking for their Carlow counterparts. There was this big set-to, but I guess that would've happened whoever had been playing that night. I've never seen any serious trouble. It's never been what the band was about."

Talking about his friendship with MacGowan, Stacy says: "If you hit it off with someone, the relationship develops as you spend time together. If you've got things in common where you think the same way, you can spark off each other and you do get that very quickfire banter. It's just a product of the chemistry you get with people sometimes. I think the other members of the band had a different type of chemistry with Shane. Jem's the one I'm thinking of. He has a very real chemistry with Shane, and it's something I've observed at close quarters over the years.

"My friendship with Shane, obviously, is very tied up with the band but at the same time, it's apart from the band. Its nature has had a different effect. The crucial relationship in The Pogues has been that between Shane and Jem."

Finer comments: "I don't like blowing my own trumpet. Everyone's friendships have different functions and in that sense, certainly from the point of view of getting the band together and keeping it going and musically, to an extent, I'd say I probably was crucial. On the other hand, Spider's friendship with Shane was crucial too in different ways. It gave him something that probably I couldn't give him.

"It was a very creative friendship that I had with Shane. There was just me and him for a year. We formed the band from the ashes of The New Republicans, we went through this experience of putting the band together and that must have established some sort of relationship that's just carried on. We'd spent so long together, from the first principles of learning the songs to starting to write songs together, with me contributing the odd little instrumental bit and so on. We were the dominant musical force, and there was an increasing collaboration in the music as time went by.

"We were certainly very close in the running of it. Shane was someone I'd always want to make sure something was all right with, before anyone else, really. We used to go to the same places and hang out with the same people. He's a pretty good friend.

"But there are other people in the band too. It's like an organism. Different bits form different functions, and you put it all together. The Pogues couldn't really exist without all of them. James was someone I liked a lot, and Andrew. And Spider, of course, but Spider would come and go, and he did sometimes tend to annoy me quite a lot. I'm sure I annoyed him too. I hope he'd understand me saying that, in the most affectionate way possible. But having said that, I liked everyone. It was generally a good laugh being together."

"I think I'm probably closest to Jem over the years in The Pogues," says James Fearnley. "I remember Shane laughing at the pair of us, how northern and sort of formal we were, although Jem's from Cheshire and I'm from

Lancashire. And Spider... he's quite a monumental force, a brilliantly clever guy with a photographic memory. He's extraordinary."

Stan Brennan and Phil Gaston may have been overthrown as The Nips' managers, but they didn't let that put them off Pogue Mahone. Together with Gaston's partner Dee O'Mahony, they turned out for all the early gigs, they became goodwill ambassadors, and they discussed the possibility of managing the band.

Gaston backed off from the idea almost straight away, having hated his experience of management with The Nips. He says: "I decided I wasn't going to get involved. There was tension between me and Stan as well. He was probably much happier managing Pogue Mahone by himself."

Still, Gaston wasn't averse to lending a hand, he would later take on driving duties from time to time and he genuinely enjoyed the band although, like Dee, he doubted that they had the potential for a serious commercial breakthrough: "It was very hard for people in the punky pop scene to see the difference between what Shane was doing and what these Irish bar bands were doing every Friday night in Hammersmith Broadway – ballads and rebel songs. The record-company view would've been, 'How are we going to make any money out of it?' There was all sorts of question marks over it. We brought people to see them and they couldn't play.

"But Shane was a huge fan of all types of music, and he could lift little bits from everything and put them all together. Then you had a Shane song. That's the bit of genius that he put into The Pogues that took them above the Hammersmith Broadway bar bands.

"The Pogues' attitude was, 'We don't want to sound like The Bothy Band, Christy Moore, Moving Hearts – we want to sound like we've just been ploughed up by a tractor and thrown onstage.' The idea was to keep it raw. They were inventive and creative and punky and Irish [sounding] at the same time, and that was fine."

As Spider says, "The whole thing was that punk attitude that The Pogues had which hadn't been done before. I think someone would've thought of it sooner or later. Well, I don't know... would they?"

Stan Brennan confirms that his friendship with Gaston was under strain at this time: "Phil and I were perceived by people we worked with as complementing each other. I think we frustrated each other quite a lot. He's an easy-going sort of chap, Phil. He takes things as they come much more than I do. I tend to want to make things happen, and I felt that our ideas didn't gel terrifically well. It was much easier for me to work with The Pogues by myself."

The band, however, were looking after their own affairs for the time being, and Brennan admits that in whatever managerial capacity he worked for them, it was as a volunteer because, "There wasn't any official title."

Anyway, he had bigger ambitions for his dealings with Pogue Mahone: "What I was really interested in was producing them." To this end, Stan offered to record and release their debut single.

The band had already recorded a couple of makeshift demos at the home of Justin and Vicki Ward, a couple who lived locally and who had booked their first gig at the Pindar Of Wakefield during a series of "alternative" nights at the venue. The group's first recording, towards the end of 1982, was a disappointing attempt to capture 'And The Band Played Waltzing Matilda', 'Poor Paddy Works On The Railway' and 'Streams Of Whiskey'. They tried again in the summer of 1983 with a hired eight-track, by which time Andrew Ranken had joined up. This was a more successful venture, with five tracks adequately completed, and they decided to film a video for 'Streams Of Whiskey' so that it could be used as the bait for a record deal.

They didn't have much of a budget, but the King's Cross network yet again turned up a saviour. "Video Rick" Elgood was the friend of a friend – Darryl Hunt – and Elgood agreed to make the promo for a fraction of the commercial cost.

Darryl was already a veteran of several bands and he was a Pindar regular, often playing or DJing at the venue. He greatly admired Pogue Mahone, who had in their early days supported his group Crazeology at the Bull & Gate, and throughout 1983, he helped out with their transport, being the owner of a VW Variant. He remembers: "Jem would call me up and say, 'Can you give us a lift to the gig?' I could get the gear in, and maybe Jem and Shane as well. Shane was very tall, and I thought he was quite dignified. Jem was very approachable."

As well as ferrying the gear around when the band were stuck, Hunt was borrowing their bass player, Cait O'Riordan, for an occasional group called Pride Of The Cross; she was the singer.

Hunt says: "Jem had the idea to do a video for 'Streams Of Whiskey'. We all lived in the same area, Jem and Shane and me and Andrew, and Jem knew Rick through me. Rick directed it, a little punk video, assisted by Dave Sketchley. They're both friends of mine from college days in Nottingham."

The video, much loved by Pogues fans although rarely if ever screened at the time, is memorable for the less-than-glamorous winter's scene in which MacGowan and Finer are seen relaxing in deckchairs beside an empty Regent's Canal, up by York Way - in nothing but their underpants.

"That was my idea," nods MacGowan. "It was a piss-take of [Wham!'s] 'Club Tropicana', that bit. It was freezing. Basically, I think the whole video is fun. It cost £60 to make. That was for film and expenses. A very enthusiastic friend and fan [Rick] who was a film student managed to get hold of Super 8 film and we did it in one afternoon."

Spider: "I've just got this image in my head of Shane and Jem in their Y-fronts and deckchairs, sitting in the mud and slime on the side of the canal. It was the antithesis of the sun, sea, suntan, cocktails sort of thing that you saw in videos around that time. I think they're both drinking cans of lager." Either that or cider.

Other parts of the video were shot in a courtyard at the Hillview Estate, with various band members springing up out of big council dustbins. This has since been interpreted as a reference to playwright Samuel Beckett's bin-bound characters Nagg and Nell in *Endgame*, but as Finer points out, it's more like The Flowerpot Men. Elsewhere, James Fearnley and Dave Sketchley gamely attempt a display of breakdancing, Spider bangs his head against a wall, Cait shows off some nifty footwork – as does MacGowan's sister, Siobhan – and Darryl Hunt throws stones into the canal. The live section, a thoroughly riotous affair, was filmed at the Pindar Of Wakefield.

Pogue Mahone were absolutely right to choose 'Streams Of Whiskey' as their best introduction to the music industry. If there is any merit in the idea that the hardest song to write is a simple one that will rise above all the other simple ones and outlive the era in which it was written, then Shane MacGowan had delivered something truly exceptional. It sounded like one of those classic Irish songs you'd known all your life.

"I am going, I am going/Any which way the wind may be blowing/I am going, I am going/Where streams of whiskey are flowing..." It may not have been the most thoughtful refrain MacGowan would ever pen, but there was something about the galloping *joie-de-vivre* of the music that caught his words and turned them, perfectly, into a feeling. For some, it was the heady feeling of a Friday night. For others, it may have evoked the fantasy of escape into a life of impulsiveness and pleasure. No matter what else the song did, it quickened the pulse and stirred the senses. It was wayward and uplifting, and it still is.

The verses established various other trademarks of MacGowan's writing. Relating the story of a dream about dramatist and novelist Brendan Behan, the lyrics acknowledge Shane's familiarity with Irish literature, they contrast the harsh realities of violence and imprisonment with the romantic freedom sought in the choruses, and they present the idea of alcohol as a refuge, an armour, a tonic and, importantly, a fuel for great creativity.

James Fearnley remarks: "I was a sort of Seventies rock listener and, of course, when you get fed as your staple diet Free and so on, I never listened to the lyrics because I knew they were crap. So I found my tendency in the band was not to listen to lyrics. There was a job of work to be done, which was to figure out how to play the songs. But 'Streams Of Whiskey' did stand out as, 'Wow! That's amazing.'"

Philip Chevron was shocked to discover that none of the six members of Pogue Mahone were in fact Irish. He wasn't the only one. So persuasive and *living* were their cover songs, so convincing their original compositions, that most people coming to the band for the first time were taken aback by James Fearnley's uncompromisingly northern speaking voice, for instance, or by the Cockney bias of MacGowan's original Tipperary accent. None of Pogue Mahone had been born in Ireland, and only Shane had lived there.

Accordingly, they were not too happy to be parcelled up as an "Irish band" – a convenient shorthand for writers and fans who were trying to describe them.

Jem Finer makes the point: "It's a London band whose influences are from living in London but who have got this element of an Irish experience, although not exclusively so. Shane's songs are the songs of a displaced person, not the songs of a native of a place. Shane, you could say, had the experience of feeling marginalised. To be Irish in those days was quite difficult in London, probably a bit like being a young Muslim now. A lot of people in the band had their own very separate experiences of being outside or marginalised slightly. That's probably quite an important component in the chemistry and energy in the group. We all empathised with the sentiment of the songs, the much more universal element rather than just the fact that many of them were Irish.

"I do think that everyone has not a total feeling of assimilation into the status quo. That all, I think, contributed to a very unique and interesting set of people. Cait – she probably had a hard time in many respects. She certainly seemed to have a chip on her shoulder. James had been at boarding school, and Spider had too for a short while. I think Spider may well have had a strange childhood.

"We all came from very different communities and backgrounds. I came from an odd sort of family. My father was a Jewish guy from a family from Chapel Market, and my mother was from a Christian family. I was brought up with a bit of both. I always identified more with the Jewish side. A lot of that was to do with the fact of when I was a kid, people would take the piss. They'd say, 'Yid,' and things like that, which wasn't very nice. It does forge a sort of identity. I always felt I was more Jewish than anything else."

Andrew Ranken adds: "The whole Irish side of things was very much to do with seeing Irish music through the eyes of the emigrants. It was more the Irish experience in London that we were talking about. I mean, it's no coincidence that the first single was called 'Dark Streets Of London'."

"I'd say The Pogues could never have happened in Ireland," remarks Chevron. "I think it needed that distancing of cultures, and the distancing of emigration."

Darryl Hunt adds: "Shane got a lot of his influence, obviously, from Ireland but also from the multi-culturalism of London. It's always been a hotbed of creative ideas. The world has always come to live here, usually as refugees or whatever. We were part of what was happening in London, but we were also observers. I think Shane's powers of observation, observing a cusp time in London life, are quite important."

The London slant of MacGowan's own lyrics, and the wider influences of everything from punk to pastiche that were present in the music were, ironically, the very things that enabled Pogue Mahone to set about helping to change British attitudes towards Irish music and culture. They became relevant, exciting, first to the young and later, as their success grew, to a wider cross-section of people.

Ranken: "Outside of the Irish communities themselves, I don't think there was any recognition of Irish culture or music. You could go to Irish pubs, but if people didn't have Irish connections, they tended to avoid them. There was never much of a thing about St Patrick's Day. It didn't seem to me that it was on the cultural map as much as it should've been, given how much of the place the Irish actually built. . .

"Traditional music and folk music get some of the worst snobbery. Bands like The Dubliners, who were really loved, had a bit of a hard time at certain points with people thinking they weren't purist enough or reverential enough. One of the big attractions for us was their lack of reverence. You find the same with the English folk tradition. Folk clubs in Sussex used to really piss me off – the finger-in-the-ear stuff, and being told to shut up.

"The subject matter of a lot of the music is usually down-to-earth - sex, drinking, violence. Nobody owns that stuff, or an awful lot of it. It's from a tradition, and people borrow bits from other songs and other tunes. It's all recycled in a way that I really like. It's the same with jazz and blues. They are always revisiting themes and sources, and new people come along and put a different slant on things. It refreshes it and revitalises it and at times makes it accessible to a whole new audience.

"So, yeah, I think we took something which could have been in danger of becoming very stuffy and preserved in aspic and shook it up a bit and tried to do it in a way that was more contemporary and fresh."

Philip Chevron made the connections straight away. He says: "What really interested me about Pogue Mahone, although there was scant evidence of it in the early days, was that they could connect with the whole London-Irish constituency in a big way, that they could somehow reflect the anger and the frustration that people felt growing up Irish in London.

"As an Irish person migrating to London, I was very aware of second-generation London-Irish – people whose Irish parents had come over in the Forties, Fifties and Sixties. These kids grew up learning Irish dancing and hearing Irish songs on pub jukeboxes. They needed the physical manifestations of Irishness. They valued the culture, in some ways indiscriminately I'd have to say, and they kept it going.

"The custodians of it were these London-Irish. I learnt that one of their great frustrations was that they were considered to be 'plastic Paddies'. When they went to Ireland, they weren't quite Irish because they were living in London, and they weren't quite English because they were Irish-born. They had double racism. Now that, to me, was an entirely new phenomenon. I went to London not knowing that.

"The Pogues could see that their audience was immigrant Irish or second-generation Irish. They arrived as an epiphany for me. They saw the merit of writing both within and against the tradition. I hadn't quite connected with the whole thing of being Irish without being born in Ireland.

"The band couldn't have happened anywhere except London or except with the combination of people it did happen with – that sense of everybody being in the right place at the right time, and all the stars lined up in the right sort of order."

This is an idea also expressed by James Fearnley, although in a more scientific manner: "It's like Brownian motion, where you enclose molecules and you can watch how atoms react with one another. There are all these swirling atoms everywhere and now and again they hit one another. With us in London, it was a complete accident of people who came together and we got a spark. I don't believe in fate. It's just one of those things that happens. I got a kick out of the spark that I had."

The right place and the right time for Pogue Mahone was Margaret Thatcher's Britain in the early Eighties. Thatcher had been elected Prime Minister in 1979, and her steely, headmistressy style of leadership and right-wing Conservative policies were giving rise to howls of protest, rallies, strikes and pickets up and down the country. The young were naturally united against a common foe, and in musicians' circles, many bands absorbed the general atmosphere of discontent and rebellion, and gave voice to it naturally in their music. Pogue Mahone was one such band. They would go on to appear at a whole string of benefits and awareness-raising concerts, for specific causes such as the miners' strike of 1984/85 and for blanket concepts including the almost impossibly vague Self Aid in 1986.

However, life wasn't too tough for the band members themselves when they were starting out. They may have been among Mrs Thatcher's "have-nots", and some of them may have been included in the millions of unemployed who were famously hectored by Norman Tebbitt - "Get on your bike!" - but as Darryl Hunt points out, they belonged to a community in which they didn't really have to have a ton of cash to survive.

"One of the key things was that we were able to live without needing money," he states. "You could live in legalised squats in a central London position, in King's Cross, in the days when you could still sign on. A couple of us had left college and you could walk round the clubs and pubs with hardly any money and develop something without the financial pressure to have to work. I think that had a lot to do with a lot of things that were going on at the time.

"The Mutoid Waste Company came out of Gray's Inn Buildings. They could hang out and experiment and they could be lazy idiots. They could do what they wanted. You go to that part of London now, you have to be a millionaire. That had a lot to do with it. It was the last great flowering of the inner city.

"We all used to go to the same clubs and it was very exciting – Cabaret Futura, Gaz's Rockin' Blues... Everybody used to rub shoulders with everybody else. It was a real mix. Shane used to go to a lot of those things. When I was working with The Mo-Dettes in the early Eighties, there was a whole scene going on there. Bands like Pigbag, The Slits, The Raincoats were all involved. Shane was into that scene too. Joe Strummer was very big in it with all his mates, always sleeping on different Mo-Dettes' floors. He had his space on the floor, and his little pile of records, at Kate's place [Kate Korus, Mo-Dettes guitarist] near Marylebone Station."

Philip Chevron agrees that London's squat culture was a fertile breeding ground for musicians. He comments: "There was always a variety of people around - Mike Spenser from The Cannibals, Nigel Lewis from The Meteors and Tall Boys, the girls from the Shillelagh Sisters. To me, it was really interesting. It was what I imagined the initial impulse of the punk scene was in London, that organic sense of people being attracted to each other's company and ideas. In a sense, The Pogues came out of that.

"Most of these people were living in squats in the same area, so they knew each other from being squat neighbours and the same thing happened as happened in Camden – interesting people gravitated towards each other and they connected with the London-Irish scene that was going on there. There were different scenes going on in parallel, but they also crossed over. You had Jon Moss in The Nips and in Culture Club. If you'd been in the wrong pub on the wrong night, any of us could have ended up in the wrong band. The whole Camden/King's Cross scene was like this. It [The

Pogues] was probably one of the few times that those things happen in your life where all the right elements are in place."

However, Chevron would not make his entry into the band for some time yet.

Stan Brennan wasn't actually sold on Pogue Mahone, but he wanted to work with them anyway. He recognised MacGowan's potential as a writer, citing later songs 'The Sickbed Of Cuchulainn' and 'A Rainy Night In Soho' as the proof of the pudding, but he confesses: "I always had this conflict. I wasn't really mad about the Irish stuff they did. I don't like it when they go all 'ceilidh band'. They kind of lose me there."

The group, in 1983, had started playing regularly at the Pindar Of Wakefield, sometimes at a weekly club night called Haywire. It was run by Darryl Hunt with two women friends – Fiona Murray and her pal Sharon. Justin Ward, who with his partner Vicki had organised the alternative nights at which The Pogues made their debut, took charge of the sound at Haywire events. Another friend of Hunt's, Dave Scott, was the compere. This was the gathering place for a circle of musicians who would later emerge as part of a "movement" in bands such as the Shillelagh Sisters, the Boothill Foot-Tappers, the Blubbery Hellbellies, the Skiff Skats and The Men They Couldn't Hang, Shanne Bradley's latest venture. Andrew Ranken and James Fearnley stood in with the Men on several occasions. The music of these groups, invariably informed by punk, took in rockabilly, country and Celtic tradition, and Pogue Mahone for a while would find themselves roped into the scene which was given several labels: punkabilly, countrybilly, countrypunkabilly, hokum hillbilly and cowpunk, the name that stuck.

Says Dee O'Mahony: "The fashion thing began to enter into it then. We adopted the Aran sweater. There were several women – myself and the Shillelagh Sisters – and we wore berets and old costume jewellery. There was a very conscious effort to dress up to match the boys' black suits.

"Funnily enough, Fiona Murray, who used to run the club with her friend Sharon – I work with her now, over here in Ireland. I'm an artist and I teach at art college in Galway, and so does she."

Brennan was also running live shows at the Pindar, on Mondays, and Pogue Mahone turned out for him too. Stan's nights were intended as a showcase for Media Burn, the label he'd set up after Soho Records, as a vehicle, mainly, for garage bands such as The Stingrays.

"The idea with The Pogues was that we'd do a single together. I would finance that and produce it and release it. I started a label called Pogue Mahone."

In January 1984, the band recorded 'Dark Streets Of London' at the cramped Elephant Studios in Wapping, with Stan Brennan at the controls.

They also recorded 'And The Band Played Waltzing Matilda' for the B-side. It was the first time in a studio for some of the members.

Says Finer: "Everything was very exciting in those days although record-ing the single was a bit fraught for me. I'd hired a really nice banjo cos I thought I'd get a better sound, but actually it had heavy strings on it, and it was much harder to play than my own banjo. It was quite an unpleasant experience. I'd have been better off with my old clunky one – which got stolen in Vienna, actually."

Spider Stacy had put in a lot of preparation. He remembers: "It's the only time I ever did this – I sat down and properly worked out a whistle part by playing along to a rough demo or a backing track and then playing the backing track and the whistle on to a machine with a blank tape in it. That was the limited technology that I had available to me. I became lazier after that.

"I'd moved back home and I almost certainly worked out my whistle part in the living room, babysitting my sister Hazel's kids while she was visiting her husband. He was in prison for smuggling hash. I wrote 'Repeal Of The Licensing Laws' under similar circumstances. My four-year-old niece was watching *Playaway* and I was just fucking around on the whistle and it came to me."

'Dark Streets Of London', a jaunty, light-handed recording, shows off a merry interplay between banjo, accordion and whistle that contrasts sharply with the tone of the story. Here, MacGowan tells of innocence lost forever in the city, the summer breezes and wintry days spent in warm pubs and bookies declining into hopeless poverty and despair. He makes apparently autobiographical references to *"the place where they gave ECT/And the drugged up psychos with death in their eyes"* – although MacGowan has declared that he never received Electro-Convulsive Therapy in the "loony bin" – and there is no happy ending, only a bleak and degrading survival of sorts for his character: *"And I'm buggered to damnation and I haven't got a penny/To wander the dark streets of London."* It's a theme to which he would return, memorably, with 'The Old Main Drag'.

Stan Brennan recalls: "The matrix number was PM1. I pressed up some-thing like 234 white labels and a friend of theirs, unbidden, knocked up about three or four hundred rectangular stickers with Pogue Mahone on them. We stuck the stickers on these white covers, and we sold them at a gig at the Irish Centre in Camden Town [March 16, 1984 – the eve of St Patrick's Day]. That was the first place Pogues records were ever sold. Then I think we pressed up about another 2,000."

The band had already started building quite a reputation for themselves. With the release of the single, their notoriety would skyrocket.

CHAPTER 8

Stiff Records And Stiff Elvis

Pogue Mahone had upset the BBC. In February 1984, they were invited to record a session for John Peel's legendary radio show. Interestingly, they chose not to promote the single they were about to release, opting instead to record 'Streams Of Whiskey', 'Boys From The County Hell', 'The Auld Triangle' and 'Greenland Whale Fisheries'.

Two things went wrong. One was that Cait O'Riordan started knocking back her drinks a little too rapidly when the band met up in the BBC bar across the road from the studios.

Spider says, diplomatically: "You have to hang around quite a lot. People get bored and their thoughts turn to drink. I do understand expensive equipment and everything, but they can be a little arsey, the BBC. Cait was just a bit pissed and they were worried she was going to break something. And I'm sure that if they asked her to stop doing whatever she was doing that annoyed them, she wasn't possibly as polite as they might have liked. I'm sure she didn't do anything that bad. It was eventually suggested that Cait go home, which she did, and James played her bass parts." Jem Finer also helped out, taking over the bass for one song. He believes it was 'Greenland Whale Fisheries'.

Fearnley recollects: "She got drunk very quickly and as the afternoon wore on and whispered meetings were had with ourselves and the producer – Dale Griffin, I think, from Mott The Hoople – who looked more and more likely to down tools and walk, and with the whole thing looking like going to shit because she just couldn't play, we started to encourage her towards conceding those facts.

"Eventually some of us had to wrestle her out of the building. There were sharp turns, narrow corridors, jogs in the passageways, lots of pipes and narrow doorways to jam her feet against, all the time her body snapping the way a freshly landed fish does. I sat with her on the steps outside and tried to understand her. She put a bit of her behaviour down to the sad state of her relationship at that time with Edwyn Collins [the then Orange Juice frontman], and something to do with smack.

"I ended up ringing Collins a couple of days later, to have him quit giving our bass player smack. I'm quite sure he hadn't the slightest idea what I was talking about. It could so well have been a matter of my being given the run-around by Cait. I was always on the gullible side. Cait seemed more likely to be on the factitious side. We were a perfect match in that way.

"Anyway, then she walked off down the road, and I went back in to play probably most of her bass parts. I do remember experiencing a deal of difficulty with some of the basslines, not that they were difficult in concept but that they were hard to play with that 19-year-old, fish-out-of-water, only-girl-in-the-band feel. This part of the afternoon is cloudier than the earlier part – though I have to say it was dark, and the streets were wet, when I sat on the steps outside with Cait, trying to understand what was up with her, amazed that anyone could be so bloody-mindedly contrary.

"Here's another recollection of that day that just came back to me: someone vomited in the corridor, which was deemed to be the height of egregiousness at the time."

Stacy continues: "I think we might've put Cait on a drinks ban as a result of what happened. Cait was put on several drinks bans. She was quite volatile when she was drunk, which translates roughly as everyone was scared of her."

The other misfortune, as far as the BBC was concerned, was the language in 'Boys From The County Hell'. Perhaps the powers-that-be objected to the line in which Shane's character – with, perhaps, a certain real-life axe to grind – describes a pub landlord he worked for as "a miserable bollocks and a bitch's bastard's whore". There again, they may simply have disliked the reference to breaking mine host's "fucking balls" and leaving the premises with "fuck all". The song was deemed unsuitable and omitted from Peel's broadcast.

Shortly after this, The Clash played three nights at London's Brixton Academy, from March 8 to 10. Ever the hustler, MacGowan persuaded Joe Strummer, an old friend, to allow Pogue Mahone to support on one of the dates. It was their biggest gig so far.

"This was The Clash Mark II," says Spider. "They were still doing their soundcheck as we walked in, and Joe called a halt to proceedings in order that we could get our soundcheck."

Now, that is rare behaviour indeed from a headline band, but it was typical of Strummer.

"I was quite impressed with that," says Stacy. "I don't recall actually meeting

Joe on that occasion. Shane knew him quite well, but I'd have been too nervous to go and say hello. If there was one person I was in awe of, it was him. Yet, as I later discovered, he was completely normal and approachable."

Jem Finer adds: "He seemed like a very considerate and warm person. They all did."

It was the beginning of a long association between The Pogues and Joe Strummer.

The band trooped on to the stage with Spider declaring, "Good evening, we're not The Clash!" and then appearing to take issue with the wag who retorted: "The Clash are better than you." From that rather unfortunate start, in which neither party intended any real hostility, Pogue Mahone went on to earn a generous reception from a capacity audience.

The venue has never looked so huge to Finer as it did on that night. The Pogues, of course, have since returned to play many sold-out shows of their own at the Academy, but Jem insists: "It's a bit like going back to places you've been as a kid. They look much smaller now."

Only days later, the band scored another first by inaugurating the tradition of a St Patrick's Day celebration – something which would become a staple in The Pogues' calendar. Hard on the heels of their appearance at the Camden Irish Centre, they whisked a coach full of London fans up to a gig in Wolverhampton on March 17, and took the opportunity to sell more white-label copies of 'Dark Streets Of London'. According to Spider, a fan called Mick, who was in charge of the singles, was picked on by a bunch of locals. There were also reports of a ticket mix-up, whereby not all of the party were able to get into the gig, and of a blocked toilet on the coach's homeward journey, but all things considered, the band look back on Wolverhampton as "a really good night".

Pogue Mahone dashed out of London, briefly, for a show in Oxford, returning for a weekend booking at the 100 Club. However, they would play it without their singer. The night before the gig, MacGowan was badly beaten up in the toilets of the Electric Ballroom.

"That's not the first time," says Shane, shrugging it off. "It wasn't the last time. There was a bit of shouting about the IRA, and there was a lot of them. I was lying in a pool of blood in the Electric Ballroom. I've been there before..."

This was an example of the sort of violence that Irish people, or those associated with the Irish, might have been unlucky enough to encounter in the early Eighties in London.

"Paddy bashing," asserts MacGowan. "You know what I mean – 'No blacks, no Irish, no dogs'. Paddy bashing obviously didn't work. Black bashing didn't work and Paki bashing didn't work once the younger generation, my generation of Asians, decided they weren't going to take any more shit from fucking whites. It's how much shit are you prepared to take? It was the same for all of the persecuted ethnic minorities. And if you were caught by the cops, then you were in a lot of fucking trouble."

As for Pogue Mahone: "We were part of a rising tide of pride in the Irish abroad."

Sometimes, MacGowan was attacked because of the way he looked. During the time he was living with Shanne Bradley in her bedsit in Stavordale Road, Highbury, he was regularly set upon by Teds.

Says Bradley: "Shane got his face smashed in so many times. I remember once I was up in Hertford visiting my mum and he called me up from a phone box near the Nashville Rooms. He said there were some Teds outside and, 'I think they're going to beat me up.' Anyway, he said goodbye after a while and later on he phoned me up and he said, 'I was right. They kicked the shit out of me and I'm in hospital.' He went back to the bedsit and his head was like the Elephant Man. He was unrecognisable. There's been so many. . ."

James Fearnley proposes that, at times, MacGowan has a knack of saying the wrong thing to the wrong stranger: "Not that long ago he got belted in a pub by somebody. Shane just says what's on his mind, and that's fantastic, that's really great, but it's going to get him in trouble because some people take umbrage and they kick him around like a rag doll."

After the Electric Ballroom incident, MacGowan went round to see Jem and Marcia. "His face was all bruised up," says Finer. "We were quite concerned."

The next day, Shane turned out for the gig at the 100 Club because, "I thought I could do it."

James Fearnley remembers: "I was outside his flat with Jem and probably others, and Shane's face was out to here and he couldn't talk. I rather insensitively laughed – 'Oh, what do you expect?' I didn't even think at the time, 'Is he going to be able to get through a gig?' That was one of the first gigs that Spider had to finish off for him."

Says Stacy: "He'd taken quite a pasting. He went up to start singing and Stan said, 'Get him off.' He should've been in hospital. I think he was a bit concussed. I took over some of the songs, although when I say I 'did the vocals', I did them in the loosest possible way. I didn't really know the words sufficiently, and I was probably just bellowing into the microphone. I know that Jem would've done 'Me And Bobby McGee' and Cait would've sung 'Don't It Make My Brown Eyes Blue'.

"Everybody felt angry that Shane been beaten up, so there was a certain, 'Well, we're not going to let this get in our way.' I probably was really nervous but also wound up with self-righteous indignation, which cut through the nerves. It was an absolutely shit gig. It was rubbish. The audience reacted with indifference, although I think everybody would have been aware of what had happened, and they saw that we were trying."

Also joining Pogue Mahone on stage that night was their busking friend and occasional roadie Stefan Cush, who strummed along on Shane's guitar. Cush would soon join forces with Shanne Bradley as vocalist and guitarist in The Men They Couldn't Hang.

Suddenly, cowpunk was flavour of the month, and Pogue Mahone were swept in under the umbrella. This didn't bother Shane MacGowan, who was always of the opinion that any press was good press if it brought the band to wider attention, and the other Pogues were philosophical.

Says Spider: "It looked like there was this scene developing and we all got lumped in cos we all knew each other and we were playing acoustic instruments. I have to say I never really liked the name cowpunk, but *Time Out* once described us as leprechaunabilly, and I think that's worse. I didn't actually have a problem with it, but I didn't see how we tied in. There was more to us than checked shirts and a vague nod to country and western. We were entirely different. Eventually, that scene either died away or we simply outgrew it."

For the time being, though, Pogue Mahone made the most of their opportunities.

The first, on Easter Monday 1984, was a concert at the Electric Ballroom billed as the Alternative Country Festival. There, they played with the Boothill Foot-Tappers, the Blubbery Hellbellies, the Skiff Skats and Hackney Five-O.

At the same time, London Weekend Television broadcast a *South Of Watford* show about the new phenomenon, focusing on Pogue Mahone, the Shillelagh Sisters, the Boothill Foot-Tappers and the Skiff Skats. As part of the programme, MacGowan was asked how the band's material differed from traditional Irish music, and he replied: "The stuff we play is more fucked up, cos you are more fucked up if you live in London than if you live in a nice little town in Tipperary."

In those days, the use of the F-word on TV was hugely controversial.

Stan Brennan recalls: "Ben Elton was presenting that. He did interviews with me and Roger Armstrong and Shane. They set up a gig at the Fridge in Brixton and we all played that, and The Pogues just blew everybody off-stage. The whole thing was kind of set up by the Shillelagh Sisters' management and it was going to be a showcase for them. The rest of us were there to provide local colour. The Pogues played brilliantly and Shane interviewed brilliantly – it was that 'fucked up' interview. Two-thirds of the show was really given over to The Pogues, and nearly all the live stuff shown was them."

Elton, undoubtedly reacting to the strength of MacGowan's language, made an ill-judged prediction, telling viewers: "I think it will be a while before Pogue Mahone – Gaelic for 'kiss my arse', by the way – are on *Top Of The Pops*. Some of the other bands may stand a better chance of breaking through to a wider audience. But in the long run, it's likely that countrybilly will stay where it's at its best – in the boozy, sweaty, raw atmosphere of live performance."

As a result of the sudden exposure arising from the Electric Ballroom gig and *South Of Watford*, 'Dark Streets Of London' attracted a fair amount of interest.

"It started selling quite well," remarks Brennan. "John Peel picked it up. He liked the fact that it was so 'minimally' designed. He'd got one of the white labels. He played it on the radio." So did David Jensen, Mike Read and Peter Powell.

But the airplay came to an abrupt halt towards the end of April when a Gaelic-speaking producer at BBC Radio Scotland took offence at the words Pogue Mahone and complained to Beeb headquarters. The single was not officially banned: Radio 1, a few months earlier, had seen Frankie Goes To Hollywood rush to Number One with 'Relax', a smash-hit success that was certainly helped by its being blacklisted. It was just decided, quietly, that Pogue Mahone should simply not be played during the day, and John Peel remained their only champion.

Still, it was the record companies who proved the toughest nuts to crack, according to Brennan, who was doing the rounds as an unpaid representative of the band. He knew that they needed the weight of a name company behind them to be able to progress any further.

He says: "You name it, I'd been there. We'd been voted by *Music Week* as one of the bands expected to succeed in 1984, so it looked hot for a deal. As far as the press went, people kept phoning us and saying, 'Can I interview so and so?' I didn't think there was going to be any problem, but I couldn't get a deal anywhere. Irish music – the labels didn't want to know. Nobody would touch them with a barge pole.

"At the same time, and I'm not bitter and twisted about it, I feel that the band didn't quite know what was going on. They were a bit like swans, sailing serenely across the water, and I was the feet paddling away. I don't think they realised what was involved in trying to get them a deal. Bands don't see that happening. They think it all works by magic.

"Shane was very well-known around the business as a songwriter.

Industry people really expected him to be the next Elvis Costello or Paul Weller figure, and it was a real shock to them that he came up with this Irish thing. They didn't see how they could get record sales. It was 'clearly a limited market'. That's what I kept hearing. The negativity was enormous, and we were also getting a lot of negativity from entrenched camps - old Nips fans and Irish music fans.

"We did a gig in Tottenham Court Road at a huge club which is now Spearmint Rhino. I had people saying, 'Stan, when are you going to get him to go back to Nips stuff and stop doing these Irish songs?' At another gig, at the Bull & Gate in Kentish Town, this woman came up to me and said, 'These people are prostituting Irish music.' I said, 'They have great respect for Irish music. You don't get it. You're not hearing it, are you?'"

At the same time, Brennan was watching the audiences broadening and growing. He states, "Something was clearly happening. When a band's breaking, you start to notice that at gigs, there are fewer and fewer people you know, and that's what was going on. The most open-minded people were the second-generation Irish, people who'd been born in England from Irish parents. They'd heard The Dubliners, they'd heard Willie Clancy and loved it, although they were too embarrassed to play this sort of music at parties with their mates. But they also loved punk, and they got the Pogue Mahone synthesis very quickly. There were a lot of those kind of people at the gigs."

Spider Stacy confirms this: "The number of people who've come up to me and said, 'I never even realised that I liked that but now I hear it in a completely different way.' The music that your mum and dad like might be deemed to be quaint and a bit of a relic that hasn't got much to do with what's going on, whereas it has and it can do. It's never actually irrelevant. Maybe in order to be relevant it has to be presented in a form you find easily digestible. Another thing: it shouldn't have to be something you need to spend time figuring out. The impact has to be immediate, otherwise it doesn't work."

"I think the folkies loved it too, people who knew about Eric Bogle and things like that," carries on Brennan. "Ian Anderson [a musician and editor of *Folk Roots* magazine] was a big champion of The Pogues in the early days. He was saying, 'Folk music needs a kick up the ass.' I don't think Shane himself had a sense of where the audience was going to be.

"But I was in despair. I was thinking, 'This is going to slip away. Nobody's interested in signing the band.' And then Dave Robinson got in touch with me."

Dave Robinson, a Dubliner, had started Stiff Records in 1976 with partner

Jake Riviera who subsequently left to manage Elvis Costello, one of the label's first and most successful signings. Stiff had been purchased by Island towards the end of 1983, with Robinson given special responsibility for reviving the fortunes of the new parent company. This he had decisively done, first with the launch of Frankie Goes To Hollywood and then with the release of the universally adored Bob Marley compilation, *Legend*, in May 1984. But he still had his eye on the ball, and that eye had been watching Shane MacGowan for a long time.

"I'd been keen to get The Nips," says Robinson, "but they didn't sign to me. They went to Chiswick."

Stan Brennan sighs, "I wish I'd gone to Dave at the time. He'd liked 'Gabrielle' very much, but we took it to Chiswick and they did nothing with it. I think we all over-rated Chiswick."

Robinson continues: "When Shane had a new band, I thought, 'I'll get them.' It was probably February 1984 I became aware that Pogue Mahone were around. Somebody just told me the name of the band and I thought, 'That's witty.' I went to the Pindar Of Wakefield to see them and it was packed out. They were very funny. In the third song or so, Cait went into the audience closely followed by Shane and, before long, by several other band members. They never came back. The drummer kept playing and when the crowd disappeared, I went to the bar and Shane was there. That was it. I thought, 'I'll definitely sign them.' Stan Brennan came to see me and then I met the band and we did the deal. We worked out a very cheap budget to make the first album and we, Stiff, put the money up."

The initial deal was for a single, with the option on an album and another single, and as Brennan admits, "We didn't get a penny for actually signing to Stiff. But they were great."

Spider remembers: "I was really excited that we were getting a deal. It made me think, 'We're a proper band with a proper record company', the coolest record company, we thought, in the world at the time."

"They said, 'Make an album,' and that was brilliant," adds Jem Finer. "Although it was slightly weird because we had to change our name."

Nobody made a big fuss about this condition of the record deal. Other bands might have screamed blue murder about censorship, but MacGowan had been through it all before, with The Nipple Erectors having to shorten their name to The Nips, and he was no more upset than his colleagues in Pogue Mahone about this latest development. If they had to tone it down in the interests of publicity and advancement, then so be it. Everybody called them The Pogues anyway. It was no big deal to make it official.

There were also reports that Stiff required the band to become a little less openly enthusiastic about drinking. If this was the case, then it wouldn't have been taken too seriously, and it certainly didn't last for long.

Finer comments: "Stiff had the famous T-shirt – 'If it ain't Stiff it ain't worth a fuck'. They had that sort of image, so I don't think they would've said we had to pretend to be clean-living people, although they were certainly prepared to say, 'Please, no drinks in this photo cos we want to get this in *Smash Hits* or *Woman's Own*,' or something like that. That's not an uncommon thing."

James Fearnley remembers The Pogues being photographed round a pool table in a pub and having all their drinks taken out of shot. However, this was later, and he attributes this to their future manager rather than anybody at Stiff.

The Pogues, as they were now known, set off on a string of dates around London including some with their old friends, the offal-flinging King Kurt. Philip Chevron, meanwhile, was continuing to spread the word to everyone he met, and he arranged a fateful outing with Elvis Costello to the Diorama Arts Centre at Regent's Park on June 22, where The Pogues were playing.

Says Chevron: "I was utterly sold on this band. I dragged Elvis to see them at the Diorama and he spent half the gig saying, 'The bass player. . . isn't she wonderful? Isn't she wonderful?' Me being innocent, I didn't realise he fancied the pants off her and was looking for an introduction. So anyway, he took it upon himself then to make his own connections with The Pogues."

Darryl Hunt adds: "The Diorama was where Elvis fell for Cait. I think it was quite an immediate thing, which is understandable. It's quite easy to fall for girls onstage. Their attractiveness is enhanced. It's like an amplifier. I wonder if it's the same the other way round?

"Elvis seemed quite a charming man. We hadn't met him before. He got very interested in the group and, obviously, one of his motivations was the bass player, but also he must have been impressed by the potential of The Pogues."

Costello would become a key character in the band's rise to fame. He would take them on a major tour, he would produce one of their finest albums and a highly regarded EP, he would travel with the band wherever they went and he would win the hand of Cait O'Riordan. Yet, Elvis didn't have an easy ride ahead of him. The Pogues were not starstruck by his extremely hip celebrity, and they would subject him to all kinds of schoolboyish abuse – most but not all of it good-natured – as they drove around together in their little van. Elvis would come into open conflict with Shane MacGowan over his production ideas. He would also be at the heart of O'Riordan's gradual estrangement from the band, and her most notorious walk-outs.

However, this was all a long way into the future as Costello gazed at the striking Cait onstage at the Diorama and enthused to Chevron, yet again: "Isn't she wonderful?"

Philip Chevron, for his part, was dreaming of producing the first Pogues LP. He confides: "That was obviously going to be *the* great album of the year. I was angling to be their producer. There was talk of them doing a one-off thing with Ace Records which, had it happened, I would have produced. But the whole thing went to Stiff and it ended up the way it did."

That was with Stan Brennan at the helm, although it had been by no means a certainty: Stan remembers Dave Robinson being keen to bring in a big-name producer, specifically Clive Langer who, with Alan Winstanley, had been responsible for all of Madness's recordings.

The band, however, were not about to ditch their loyalties to Brennan. He says: "The Pogues honoured every agreement that we made. I'd said the whole time that I wanted to produce the album and Jem actually pushed for that. He said, 'We want Stan to do it.'"

The sessions for the album, *Red Roses For Me*, began in Elephant Studios in August. Says Brennan: "Stiff paid for the album. It cost £5,000 to make. There wasn't any drink or drugs involved at all, including me. That was an agreement we made right at the start, because we had four weeks to record the album and a week to mix it.

"We set the band up live in the studio. We did the live track to get the drums, and I think I may have kept the bass from the live track as well, and then everything was overdubbed. The fact that the album sounds as tight as it does is quite a triumph, considering where the band were at. They hadn't been playing live a lot - they didn't have that tightness of a live band - and there was a very wide range of musicianship. Most of them were playing instruments that were quite new to them.

"James was a consummate musician and was very easy to record. He was a pianist, so he was quite comfortable with the accordion. He was very interested in what was going on, and he stayed around for the mixing of the album. He wanted to see how it was done. He was very involved."

Fearnley – "The Maestro" – also supplied the guitar parts for the album, despite the fact that this was MacGowan's role onstage and one he carried out with a ferocious strumming, a wild if sometimes erratic rhythm playing.

At the other end of Brennan's ability rating was Cait O'Riordan. "Her bass playing was incredibly limited," says Stan. "It's just two notes all the way through, but it's on the beat."

Spider Stacy, he remembers, was "incredibly nervous" but, "He did really well, I thought."

Brennan adds: "We had to do a lot of rearranging the parts to get what we got. Jem's banjo playing we had to tweak a bit. I think Andrew was solid enough, although I felt his drumming wasn't quite on the beat.

"When I did 'Gabrielle' with The Nips, we spent ages and ages on the vocal, doing drop-in lines and drop-in words. When we did the vocals for *Red Roses*, Shane came walking in and I think except for 'Sea Shanty', where we did a lot of call and response, he just sang the vocals live. I don't think we did more than two takes on anything."

This was the way MacGowan liked to do things. He had little patience for endless takes and he would in the future rebel against producers who expected him to work that way.

It may or may not be a coincidence that he says today of *Red Roses For Me*: "It's my favourite Pogues album."

After the initial excitement of being in the studio had worn off, some of the band members became bored during extended periods of inactivity, while others found the new environment challenging and interesting.

Spider spent hours sitting around waiting to be called: "Partly I think I engineered it that way," he admits. Possibly through nervousness, he wanted to put off the moment of playing. "I did the whistle parts as overdubs rather than as backing tracks and I was always the last to be called." As a result, his days became pretty tedious.

Jem Finer agrees: "Recording can be bloody boring when you're waiting around a lot, although I'd imagine when we were doing the basic tracks it was fun."

Offering an alternative view, Andrew Ranken states: "I really enjoyed the whole process of going into the studio every day and recording the album. It's a process I still really enjoy. I love it."

James Fearnley has many fond memories of the sessions: "It was my first prolonged studio experience and it was great for me personally because I got to play guitar on everything. I really, really enjoyed playing the guitar."

None of The Pogues are sure exactly why it was that James and not MacGowan should have done this. If Shane was upset about it at the time, then his objections have apparently gone unrecorded and unremembered. However, in months to come, with Philip Chevron joining the band as a full-time guitarist, both Fearnley and MacGowan would confess annoyance at losing their guitar jobs in the studio and on stage respectively.

Says James: "It fell to me to be the guitar player for most of the songs on the first couple of albums, and that might've hurt Shane a bit, although he always rated me as a guitar player from my days in The Nips with him. Nonetheless, it's not unreasonable to think now that that might have been hard for him, when he'd been playing the guitar live. There's room for disgruntlement around the place through the years."

One of Fearnley's most memorable *Red Roses* recordings was 'The Auld Triangle'. He explains: "I went out into the studio to play guitar and one of the engineers, Craig [Thompson], said to me, 'You can hear the pick too much. You can try this pick,' a felt pick. Then it was, 'We're just going to have to cover you over with a blanket and put the microphone on the other side.' They put this blanket over me and I played the track on the guitar. I didn't hear anything when I'd finished so I lifted up the blanket and I could see, through the window of the monitor room, everybody pissing themselves laughing. They hadn't recorded a damn thing. They just wanted to see the guitarist under a blanket."

James also enjoyed helping to create the colourful sound effects that festoon the album. He says: "For 'Down In The Ground Where The Dead Men Go', me and Shane were making all the clanky noises with bits of bells, and then there was all the screaming as well – Cait's got a great scream.

"When Stan was mixing, he had this machine that was new to the studio. It was some sort of effects box that he would put all the drums through. He was having a lot of fun with different sounds. There were sound effects we did that were separate from the box, like anvils and throwing cymbals around and stuff, which Andrew and Spider had good fun with. These were actually instruments, sound sources."

Fearnley's only problem in the studio was that the producer and the engineers faced the opposite way to the musicians: "I wasn't keen on just seeing the backs of people."

The Pogues went into Elephant with a surfeit of material.

"They were mostly songs we'd been playing," says Jem. "It wasn't really, 'Oh, shit, we've got to make a record.' It was more a case of, 'Which ones shall we not do?'"

MacGowan is credited alone for all of the album's original material and he, Finer and the other Pogues take a bow for the arrangements of the traditional songs, although Jem, for one, added extra elements to some of these.

"We'd play around with them and see how they worked best," says Finer. "It's hard to say who exactly did what. With 'Greenland Whale Fisheries', an old bluegrass tune was put on to that. It's one of the first tunes I learnt when I was starting to play the banjo. Various things like that happened. 'Dingle Regatta' is a traditional tune and the rest of it is a tune that I made up."

There were differing views about the finished product.

"I'm really, really proud of that album," says Stan Brennan. "It suffered very badly from the way it was mastered. It sounded nothing like it sounded in the studio. I wasn't invited to the mastering. Stiff just rush-released it because they were so skint. The great thing about it now that it's been remastered is that you can hear more of what it sounded like."

"I think it's a really good album for an unknown band," comments Andrew Ranken, echoing James Fearnley's opinion. "It was very kind of rough, but I didn't mind that. It sort of reflected how we were anyway. I'm sure things could've been done better, but we were doing it on a shoestring. I think it stands up really well."

"The production is possibly a bit thin," ventures Spider. "Although hearing it when it's been remastered and remixed, it sounds really, really good, really raw and really fresh. The essence of the band, the way we sound live – I don't know if it's ever been satisfactorily captured. I'm certainly not going to say that's any fault of Stan Brennan as a producer when people like, say, Steve Lillywhite may equally not be able to capture the essence of the band. I don't think anybody ever could, but I think *Red Roses* comes closest."

"I've thought for a long time that it wasn't a good idea for Stan to produce it," says the dissenting voice of Jem Finer. "I think Shane felt a responsibility towards Stan, which compromised things."

According to Brennan, it was Jem who had voiced the band's insistence that he should produce the album. If Finer had any personal doubts about this at the time, he kept them to himself, preferring to uphold the group's decision and any loyalties to Brennan as a matter of principle.

"No disrespect to Stan," continues Jem, "but I think we could have benefited from someone who had more experience. I just thought the whole sound of it could have been better, and listening to old Peel sessions and stuff, that's much more how I wanted to hear things, more live and bright and in your face.

"We were trying to make a record with instruments which weren't designed to be played the way we played them, and that needed a very particular approach, especially with the engineering. Nick Robbins didn't get the best sound out of them. But the producer has to say to the engineer, 'That sounds great,' or, 'It's not good enough.' The buck stops with the producer. But to actually have the album was great. It was really exciting."

Red Roses For Me was released in October 1984, and by that time The Pogues were on tour with Elvis Costello, eventfully.

CHAPTER 9

A Drunken Odyssey

The Shane and Cait show carried on in its normal, warfaring manner: The Pogues were banned from Soho's Wag Club, in Wardour Street, after an onstage altercation, although Spider believes the spat was used as an excuse to punish the band.

"The people at the Wag Club were wankers," he says. "Shane and Cait had a fight onstage, which looked a lot worse than it actually was. But something else happened that night. We had one of those broomsticks with beer-bottle lids on it that you shake as a percussion thing. That, very briefly, was another one of my duties. They accused us of banging holes in the ceiling with it, but it wasn't us, it was the Skiff Skats who had a similar device. We took the rap. The Wag Club took it out on us because of Shane and Cait's little brouhaha. There was a subsequent argument between Cait and the guy who ran the place."

It was also around this time, on August 8, that the band played the tempestuous gig at the Sir George Robey which had so distressed James Fearnley, the fire-stopper.

By the end of August, Elvis Costello had invited The Pogues to accompany him on his autumn tour of the UK and Ireland, which provoked a flurry of activity. The group now had to go into rehearsals, while attending to the many small tasks that accompany the imminent release of an album. For some, it was time to give up their regular employment.

"Up until then," says Jem, "we hadn't been working as a professional band. James and I were still doing our painting and decorating. Shane was probably still down the record shop*. When the Costello tour came along, that's when I stopped all other jobs. For the few months before that, I'd been

---

* Rocks Off

teaching computer skills to adults in the Mary Ward Centre in Queen Square, WC1. When the tour came along, I had to be away for a month so I packed in the teaching. It was the last proper job I had. After that, I just tried to make a living from the band."

The Pogues invited Darryl Hunt to join the tour as their driver, out-front soundman and road manager, although Hunt acknowledges: "Jem was as much a tour manager as anybody else. He used to look after the money. We used to have these meetings every week in the Pindar to pay everybody's wages."

As Spider succinctly puts it, Darryl was to be "the crew". The Costello tour effectively dealt the death blow to Pride Of The Cross, the band that Darryl had established with Cait O'Riordan on vocals. They'd been playing gigs about once a month, although things had been fizzling out due to The Pogues' record deal and their rapidly increasing workload.

Hunt had met Cait and Shane for the first time in a pub called the Pakenham Arms in Pakenham Street, just off Calthorpe Street in King's Cross, later bumping into them and other Pogues members in a variety of bars in the area including the Norfolk Arms in Leigh Street and The Boot in Cromer Street, where Kenneth Williams' father would play piano on Friday nights.

"We were all short-life housing people," says Darryl, who was living in Gray's Inn Buildings. "There was a tie-up between these areas of housing, the Hillview Estate and all those places. They were all ex-squats that had been legalised."

Hunt at the time was bassist in a part-time group called Baby Lotion with Dave Scott, a friend from his art school days who had gone on to play guitar with Spizz Energi and Athletico Spizz. Scott lived in the Hillview Estate, near Andrew Ranken.

"It was all coming together," reflects Darryl, before returning to the subject of Baby Lotion. "We were doing mostly weird, Spizz stuff Dave had written. It was quite good. There was one song called 'Questions In The House' about the sleaze in the House of Commons. Justin Ward put us on at the Pindar (where Scott also compered). We didn't really split up. We metamorphosed into Pride Of The Cross when Cait said she wanted to sing with us. I thought she was quite zany; likely to fly off the handle."

He wasn't wrong there.

"We had a trombonist called Paul Taylor," continues Hunt, "and we did versions of other people's songs. We used to go to places like the Hope & Anchor and we'd put tablecloths on tables, and candles, and create a terribly sleazy club vibe."

Pride Of The Cross were among the bands hanging out at the Pindar Of Wakefield during the cowpunk craze, although they were more of a lounge act than anything else, and they had as their champion Phil Gaston. "I thought Cait had a huge talent," says Gaston. "Her voice is great, and she was hilarious onstage. The Pindar gigs were just so funny. 'The Day Before You Came', the Abba thing, was just beautiful, and she did 'Is That All There Is?', a Peggy Lee song. She adapted to what was happening. The trombone player was wonderful. The Pindar set-up was like a cabaret. You had the Boothills coming up, then you had the Blubbery Hellbellies, and there was no big deal to it. You just got up and did your thing.

"Me and Darryl played a gig there. We formed a band called Pearl And Dean and we got up in the Pindar and did 'King Of The Road' and that. We made a tape called 'The Ballad Of Pogue Mahone'. Darryl had a girlfriend called Julie whose dad had been part of a Eurovision Song Contest–winning group*. He had a big house in the stockbroker belt with a studio in it, and me and Darryl did a couple of numbers there. 'The Ballad Of Pogue Mahone' was to the tune of 'Old Orange Flute'. We went through every member of the band, how bad they were and how they couldn't play their instruments."

During this same period, Hunt launched *Haywire*, a one-off music fanzine relating to the Pindar club nights. One memorable feature was a photo story, shot by Darryl, in which Julie and Cait were cast as two girls fighting over James Fearnley.

"There were drinks flying, and there were all these little speech bubbles," smiles Gaston.

Towards the end of their days together, Pride Of The Cross recorded a single, which was produced by Phil Gaston. He had written the A-side, 'Tommy's Blue Valentine', for O'Riordan, to acknowledge her admiration for Tom Waits. The B-side was a version of the old Peggy Lee hit 'Black Coffee'.

Says Gaston: "It was the best version of 'Black Coffee' ever. I really enjoyed making the single. Cait had started going out with Elvis by then. He came down to the studio, although he didn't actually do anything. He was hovering over the proceedings. He was a nice enough guy, and he was a really big Pogues fan. He was just part of the crowd at the time. It was quite egalitarian, although obviously he was leaps and bounds ahead of where we were."

The single was picked up by Roger Armstrong and Ted Carroll, who released it on Ace Records' Big Beat label in 1985, after Pride Of The Cross had split.

Phil Gaston had decided to try his hand seriously at songwriting. He'd written 'Navigator' specifically for The Pogues, which they accepted. They were already playing it live, and they would eventually record it for their second album, *Rum Sodomy & The Lash*.

---

* Brotherhood Of Man, who won Eurovision in 1976 with 'Save Your Kisses For Me'.

Gaston was still in partnership with Stan Brennan in Rocks Off in Hanway Street. By this time, they'd expanded their empire, having opened another shop, Vinyl Solution, in Hereford Road, off Westbourne Grove, W2, with a Frenchman called Yves Guillemot. They also started a third record outlet at Railway Approach, London Bridge. Brennan was running Rocks Off, Guillemot was in charge at Vinyl Solution, and Phil Gaston spent his days under the arches at London Bridge.

"That's when I wrote 'Navigator'," says Phil. "Shane just said, 'This is great. We'll do it.' They worked it up and they did it. It was great. I think it's a good song too."

Gaston continued writing songs in various styles, some of which were snapped up by such different performers as The Men They Couldn't Hang and German cabaret singer Agnes Bernelle.

But there was trouble in retail paradise. Says Stan Brennan: "We just couldn't get on with each other. We had terrible personality clashes. When the partnership with Yves ended, we let the London Bridge shop go, cos that never got off the ground, and Phil and I ran the West End one together." Before long, Gaston would opt out of the business entirely.

Darryl Hunt, meanwhile, accepted his offer of employment from The Pogues and even though he had said goodbye to Pride Of The Cross, he started another pet project.

"Me and Dave Scott had to do the Hillview Festival," remembers Hunt. "We did it every year. So we got a group together called The Troubleshooters. In that group was James's girlfriend Debsey [Wykes]. She was the singer and she was a wonderful writer too."

As time went by on the Costello tour and beyond it, whenever problems arose, Darryl would think about The Troubleshooters, eventually making up his mind to return to them. If fate hadn't intervened at the 11th hour, he would not be playing bass with The Pogues today.

Getting a record deal may have been the hard part, but the sleeve for *Red Roses For Me*, a seemingly simple matter, threw up a bunch of unforeseen problems for The Pogues – and history would repeat itself with their subsequent albums.

Stiff Records had furnished the band with matching, long, pale-blue, western-style duster coats, with black collars and cuffs, which they showed off in an outdoors location on the back of the sleeve. But MacGowan, whose sartorial style was a matter of great personal pride, turned out for the photo session with a walking stick and a plaster round his foot, having broken his ankle in a disagreement with several flights of stairs. There was a

The Pogues wrap up warm against the cold winter breezes blowing along the Thames at Chiswick during a photo session for 'A Pair Of Brown Eyes', released in March 1985. The dog, affectionately nicknamed Satan, arrived as a "prop". Says Spider: "We were a bit wary of him. He was an English bull terrier, very strong, and he nearly pulled my arm out of its socket." Clockwise, left to right: Spider Stacy, Andrew Ranken, Cait O'Riordan, James Fearnley, Jem Finer and Shane MacGowan. *(BARRY MARSDEN)*

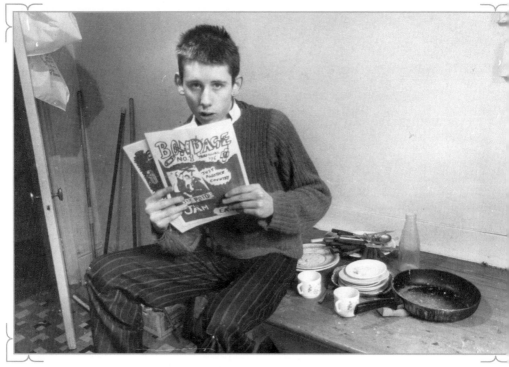

Shane, aged 19, shows off the one and only issue of his legendary fanzine, Bondage, in his family flat in Wells Street, London. The magazine, which appeared in December 1976, championed the Sex Pistols. "I hope... the Pistols carry on being more and more obnoxious," wrote the young editor. *(SYDNEY O'MEARA/GETTY IMAGES)*

Pictured up front at a Clash gig in the Harlesden Colosseum in March 1977, Shane was already a familiar figure on the punk scene, regularly making headlines, most notoriously after a previous Clash show at the London ICA when it was reported that he'd had his ear lobe bitten off. *(IAN DICKSON)*

Spider makes an early appearance with The Millwall
Chainsaws at the Tonbridge Club, King's Cross,
in 1980. "We were fucking rubbish, really shambolic,"
he recalls. *(SPIDER STACY ARCHIVE)*

Spider (left) and Shane share vocal duties at
the Hope & Anchor, Islington, in 1983.
MacGowan never wanted to hog the spotlight.
He says: "I thought we had a brilliant line-up with
no frontman, like the original six-piece… it was
a united front." *(DEIRDRE O'MAHONY)*

Cait and Darryl Hunt in Pride Of The Cross,
pictured at the Pindar Of Wakefield in 1984.
"The Pindar gigs were just so funny… the set-up
was like a cabaret," remembers Phil Gaston.
(DEIRDRE O'MAHONY)

Shane MacGowan takes a hands-on approach
to his beloved Shanne Bradley as The Nips
throw some shapes for their new record label,
Chiswick, having signed in 1979 for the release
of their 'Gabrielle' single. "We're loud, raw, leering
pop!" said Shane, reasonably. Drummer Rogers
Williams (left) and guitarist Gavin Douglas.
(CHRIS GABRIN)

Pictured on a rather spartan stage during a gig at London's Royal College Of Art in November 1983 are, left to right: James, Jem, Shane, Andrew and Spider. *(DEIRDRE O'MAHONY)*

Stefan Cush, a busking friend and occasional Pogues roadie, on stage with Jem and Andrew at the 100 Club in spring 1984 (above). Shane had pulled out after being beaten up by yobs. Cush later formed The Men They Couldn't Hang with Shanne Bradley. Spider (right) playfully grapples with Bal from The Stingrays as he manfully covers for Shane on the same night. *(BOTH PICTURES: DEIRDRE O'MAHONY)*

The Pogues – minus Andrew - at the Camden Irish Centre in 1984, posing with JFK for the cover of *Red Roses For Me*. Due to mistakes at the original session, this second shoot was arranged – but Andrew was on holiday: "So they pinched my picture off the back and stuck it on a stupid little doiley on the front." *(STEVE TYNAN/STIFF RECORDS)*

The love affair between Elvis Costello and Cait was a source of droll humour for The Pogues – before tensions and problems began to set in. Says Frank Murray, the band's manager at the time: "I knew it would lead to Cait leaving the group." *(RICHARD YOUNG/REX)*

Spider demonstrates the art of playing that ancient Irish instrument the beer tray at the Mean Fiddler in January 1985. "It looks great and it sounds great live," says Shane, while Spider explains: "I'd really hit myself hard; I didn't fuck about." Among the wildly enthusiastic audience that night was film director Alex Cox. *(PAUL SLATTERY)*

Cait takes issue with sieg-heiling neo-Nazis at The Loft in Berlin on April 20, 1985 – Adolf Hitler's birthday. "You need to tell the audiences in Germany who you are," says Philip Chevron. "If you don't they think they're entitled to turn up at a Pogues gig and honour The Fuhrer." *(ANDREW CATLIN)*

Relaxing at Ireland's Kenmare Festival in June 1985, left to right: Andrew, Philip Chevron, James, Debsey Wykes and Phil Gaston. It was here that Terry Woods first saw The Pogues: "The things that instantly got me were (a) their irreverence and (b) that MacGowan was writing songs from an emigrant's point of view." *(DEIRDRE O'MAHONY)*

The unstoppable double-act. Spider and Shane (top) share a joke in Germany in April 1985 and (below), go head to head at the Self Aid concert at Dublin RDS on May 17, 1986. Says Dee O'Mahony of the unholy alliance: "It was always so amazing seeing them together, because the two of them were so funny and so quick." *(BOTH PICTURES: ANDREW CATLIN)*

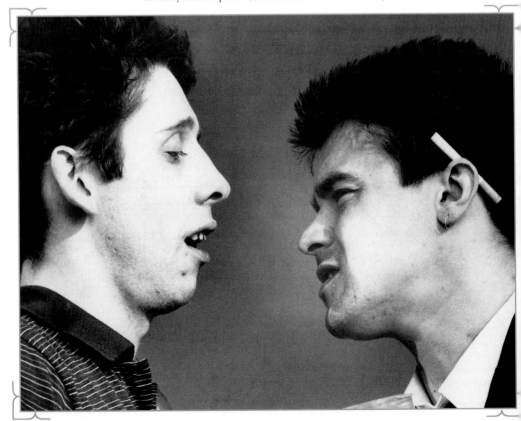

small possibility that alcohol was involved. On the same day, the photographer shot for the front-cover photo.

Then came bad news: there would have to be another session for the front of the sleeve. It duly took place at the Camden Irish Centre, with the group arranged around a portrait of John F Kennedy. The trouble was that Andrew Ranken wasn't with them: he'd gone away.

"It was really stupid," says Ranken. "Something as stupid as the photographer not having a film in his camera the first time. If you look at the back picture, then you'll notice on the front cover there are various different haircuts, cos the photograph was taken several weeks later when he realised he'd fucked up the first session, which I was in. I'd gone off on holiday somewhere and they couldn't find me. I wouldn't have come back anyway. So they pinched my picture off the back and stuck it on a stupid little doiley on the front."

It was a ridiculous solution, and other design features added to the group's dissatisfaction.

Dave Robinson admits: "I encouraged the art department to put on the lettering. . . and the band hated it."

Things were happening too quickly. The Pogues were next advised that they must film a promotional video for 'Waxie's Dargle', even though there were no plans to release it as a single. It was, however, a show-stopping album track and it remains Spider Stacy's most anarchic and exhilarating example of beer-tray-bashing. But Andrew was still on holiday and, by now, so was Jem Finer.

The answer this time was to replace not one but two Pogues. A shady lookalike wearing a hat was brought in to approximate Finer, and Darryl Hunt – an accomplished multi-instrumentalist when he wasn't being "the crew" - played drums in Andrew's place.

"I loved it," says Hunt.

The video was later unleashed upon the nation on *The Tube*, the coolest and most irreverent TV show in the country, broadcast weekly on early Friday evenings by Tyne Tees. Happily, this coincided with the release of *Red Roses For Me* and The Pogues' support tour with Elvis Costello & The Attractions.

"Elvis was taking a bit of a risk" says Philip Chevron with delicious understatement.

The Pogues were forging a formidable reputation: they were hailed as the wildest bunch in town, a boozing, brawling band of outlaws whose presence on any tour could only spell trouble.

It wasn't wholly their fault that, even then, they had been caricatured decisively by their supporters in the weekly music papers. Not all of the members were excessive drinkers, and they were by no means the only outfit in the hedonistic Eighties to fly the flag conspicuously for the right to party – and also, in MacGowan's case, the right to make a choice that was rooted in his own background and in the example of the great Irish writers and poets for whom alcohol was the key to inspiration and vision. It's possible to argue that The Pogues were singled out for special treatment due to the "Paddy factor". Yes, they drank, but so did lots of other bands, and it wasn't a problem – yet – for anyone.

At the same time, MacGowan, Cait O'Riordan and Spider Stacy were capable of sustained intoxication and riotous behaviour. They were unapologetic about it, with Shane typically insisting that it didn't matter what journalists wrote about the group as long as they were writing something. O'Riordan, quoted in Ann Scanlon's book *The Lost Decade*, said: "I just drank steadily for about two years. I never even thought about not drinking, so all I remember is getting horribly drunk."

For sure, Andrew Ranken and James Fearnley had chaotic moments too. And it's undeniable that a large part of The Pogues' appeal was the whiff of the bar-room wafting through their lyrics, the irrepressible gallop of their up-tempos and the teardrops in their ballads.

"Irish popular music is guts, balls and feet music," MacGowan once told an interviewer. "It's frenetic dance music or it's impossibly sad, slow music."

What finer accompaniment than a drop of the hard stuff? You would've had to be mad, back then, to think of experiencing The Pogues in a state of sobriety. This was all about fun and celebration. The people in the audiences were just as drunk, many of them drunker than the band.

Which wasn't the Costello vibe at all. Elvis had come to prominence in the late Seventies as a star of the new wave, an angry young man with a biting tongue. Although he didn't preach sobriety, he carried himself in a manner that suggested he had little time for frivolity and he deliberately distanced himself from the music press, creating an aloof, tetchy persona that was encouraged by his quick-tempered manager Jake Riviera. Inquiries into Costello's past were met with stony faced silence and the threat of a thumping. Now his career was temporarily in the doldrums with *Goodbye Cruel World*, an album that both the critics and Costello himself disliked when it was released in the summer of 1984, although it nevertheless made the Top 10. He was falling out with The Attractions[*], he was hanging with a new musical collaborator, T-Bone Burnett, and he had recently returned to his

---

[*] Keyboard player Steve Nieve (aka Steve Nason), bassist Bruce Thomas and drummer Pete Thomas, all experienced musicians well capable of performing Costello's demanding material.

interest in folk music, which tallied nicely with his meeting The Pogues. All the same, at least one member of the band privately believes that they would never have been invited to join the tour had it not been for Elvis's growing infatuation with Cait O'Riordan.

But it wasn't Elvis Costello who gave The Pogues a hard time when they took to the road together at the end of September 1984. It was his road crew.

Jem Finer: "We were all really naïve. When we turned up for the first concert in Belfast, Elvis's crew were saying, 'You're going to have to pay us £15 each to do your sound and move your gear offstage.' I thought, 'Oh my God, that's all the money gone already.' We sorted it out eventually."

"Everybody was very high on the idea of being on the road," recalls Darryl Hunt. "It was all a bit naughty. We used to invariably turn up late to soundchecks and get told off by Elvis's crew. It was like being back at school in a football team, getting hauled in by the master in charge of sports and told that if you don't turn up on time, you'll have to do extra revision. We didn't know rock'n'roll worked like that."

James Fearnley adds: "Elvis had a soundman called The Bishop. His crew were great, but this soundman seemed to wield quite a lot of authority. He just took a disliking to us. When it came time to do a soundcheck, it wasn't guaranteed we were going to get one. He'd down tools and say, 'Everybody has to go and have their dinner now.' Oftentimes we'd be left with Flakey, the roadie who took pity on us and helped us set up.

"For the longest time, doing gigs was problematic for many of us, not knowing the difference between onstage sound and front-of-house sound. That's how technically wet behind the ears we were. I think we were reasonable to assume we'd get some sort of help wiring all the stuff up and making it sound like something. This Bishop guy didn't want that so we ganged up on him backstage one evening. We were very angry. We pinned him up against a wall and said, 'We can't tolerate this any more.' It did get better after that."

Aside from the arguments over money and sound, Costello's road crew had other reasons to be infuriated by the support band.

"I think we caused quite a lot of trouble," remarks Andrew Ranken. "We were threatened with getting thrown off the tour on at least two occasions. In Portsmouth [October 7] there was a bit of a fracas in our dressing room and some bottles ended up being thrown out of the window and nearly landing on the heads of the crew who were loading Elvis's truck." This escapade has been attributed to Cait.

"Then there was another time in Bournemouth," carries on Andrew. "Jem was wearing his duster coat. He'd filled the pockets with sand off the beach and he'd made little holes in the pockets. Wherever he walked, he left this trail of sand which then got into all Elvis's effects pedals."

It probably didn't help the harmony of the operation, either, that The Pogues insisted on raiding the road crew's alcohol supplies from Costello's dressing room whenever possible.

"Elvis was a complete gentleman, which was just as well," says Ranken. "He managed to smooth things over and he kept us on the tour. At the end, he presented us with a supermarket trolley full of booze. Very magnanimous. It didn't go amiss."

Eventually, the Costello crew came to tolerate and then befriend their travelling companions. "Initially they thought we were a bunch of oiks but then they saw the point. We were there because Elvis had invited us. It settled down and they seemed to like us," remembers Finer.

Spider Stacy comments: "I got the distinct impression that the crew thought Elvis's band were up their own arses. They were very, very serious, The Attractions, whereas we didn't really care. I think they enjoyed having us around."

For The Pogues, the tour began in the manner in which it would continue. The first part of the journey involved a ferry trip from Holyhead in Wales to Dun Laoghaire, just outside Dublin. They would spend a night in the city and then travel north, across the border, to Belfast for the opening gig at the Ulster Hall. "We missed the ferry cos it took about an hour to get Shane out of his flat in Cromer Street," remembers Spider. The problems of moving MacGowan from A to B would become an important consideration in Pogues tour management from then on.

It was the first time that they'd been on the road properly and they were in high spirits, cooped up together for the best part of five weeks in a hired transit with Darryl Hunt at the wheel. Hunt had brought along some tapes, and all of the band remember with great affection the compilation of Irish music he'd made especially for the tour and the rowdy singalongs that it induced. Another favourite, particularly with Hunt and MacGowan, was a tape of Them, the Sixties R&B/soul/garage band led by Van Morrison. Also popular was Darryl's "serious" reggae selection, covering everything from ska to dub.

"There was a very particular feel to that tour, which was like no other," reveals Spider. "It was a kind of drunken odyssey. The seven of us just bouncing around in this little van listening to Brendan Shine and The Dubliners, all the Irish stuff on this cassette of Darryl's... Driving around Ireland was a real laugh. I'd never been there before. It was very exciting."

Stan Brennan, still carrying out voluntary managerial duties for The Pogues, was unable to join the tour full-time because of his commitment to the record shops, although he showed up for the gigs in Ireland. The band received a terrific response in Belfast and, the next day, piled into the van bound for Galway.

"That was a mad little journey," says Stacy. "We stopped off in Killashandra, County Cavan. All the others went to a pub to get soup and stuff, and James and I went to another pub to get away from everybody else, just to have a drink, and we got chatting with the landlord. He was asking us what instruments we played and he said his daughter played the tin whistle. She came downstairs and they got me to play something. I played the theme tune from *The Year Of The French*, a TV programme I'd seen about the '98 Uprising [which involved French military efforts to help the Irish Rebellion in 1798]. She then reeled off some incredible thing, and it turned out she'd been the under-18 all-Ireland champion whistle player. I thought that was a bit unfair. Meanwhile, the others were up the road drinking a lake of Irish coffee."

The Pogues arrived in Galway to find that their gear was missing, due to a loading error in Belfast. In its place was a flight case belonging to an orchestra from Northern Ireland. The show went on, however, with the band playing electric equipment borrowed from Elvis and The Attractions.

They were reunited with their own instruments in Dublin, where different problems arose. The National Stadium felt cold and damp, and the Costello fans took their time trickling into the auditorium. The Pogues were also worried about the prospect of bringing their anarchic brand of Irish music to Dublin.

"We didn't know whether people would think we were taking the piss or not," says Jem Finer. In the event, says Stan Brennan, "The people of Dublin were very welcoming, if a bit nonplussed by things like 'Waxie's Dargle' at a thousand miles an hour."

The Pogues then sailed back across the Irish Sea to begin the month of dates on the British mainland, with the itinerary including a weekly Monday-night residency at the London Hammersmith Palais. This particularly benefited Jem, who was anxious not to have to spend long periods away from Marcia and their young daughter Ella.

The first Hammersmith gig marked a turning point in the tour. "We'd decided unilaterally that we weren't going to shave for the whole time," explains James Fearnley. "But we all bottled out when we got to the Palais. We all shaved because it was an important gig."

One escapade followed another as the band drove the length and breadth of the country. "I can remember Spider having a piss on the carpet in the lobby of the hotel in Leeds and Elvis getting into trouble about it cos he was staying in the hotel and we weren't," grins Darryl. On that night, while Costello was being told off by staff at the plush Dragonara, The Pogues were slumming it in a gay temperance hotel. They themselves, via the Stiff press office, were responsible for untrue newspaper stories that as a result of an early-hours drinking session, they had been banned from every temperance hotel in the country.

Some of the tour anecdotes have passed into Pogues legend even if various members recall the events slightly differently and others don't remember them at all. The gig at Loughborough University was one such occasion, and it all began with James Fearnley taking inspiration from Shane MacGowan.

Says James: "He's so committed to meeting life in the face - go into the bar and drink 15 pints of beer. It made me want to do it. We'd all met in Yates's Wine Lodge. We were drinking port for breakfast and I remember driving to Loughborough with my head out the window, just drinking it all in, the air, the fields and everything. 'Streams Of Whiskey' has got that down. It's really, really nice to get that feeling."

"Then James and I kind of blew up the dressing room at the university," says Spider, taking up the story. "It was James's fault. We'd bought a lot of fireworks in Nottingham, and all these bottles of white port and madeira from Yates's Wine Lodge. We drove to Loughborough. James started letting off fireworks in the dressing room, and I had to get into the act. I think I threw one at Shane, and I think he responded by throwing the contents of a bottle of port at me, which missed. I found myself kneeling astride him with a tin whistle raised in my hand about to drive it through his eyeball into his brain. That's Yates's Wine Lodge for you."

After the gig, The Pogues tumbled into the van for the 17-mile drive back to their hotel in Nottingham. "Earlier that day, there'd been some argument about whether a tomato was a fruit or a vegetable, and they got very angry with each other," says Darryl Hunt, who may or may not be talking metaphorically.

James Fearnley remembers that shortly into the journey, there was "a lot of shouting – big shouting, this was". He believes the band members had been yelling at MacGowan about his drinking. Other sources say that Shane and Spider had become unbearably loud and obnoxious. Whatever happened, Jem Finer asked Darryl to stop the van.

Says Fearnley: "Jem said, 'I can't take this any more. I'm off,' and he just jumped ship. We went into a panic about it because there he was, not in the bus, walking in the middle of fucking nowhere in the middle of the night."

Minutes later, Spider also decided to get out of the van and take his chances walking to Nottingham. He ended up stumbling in the dark into a ditch full of nettles.

Oddly, Finer remembers Stacy's walk-out but not his own. "I'm not denying it," he says, evenly. "There were certainly lots of times I felt sick to the back teeth with the whole thing."

"We went up the road quite a way," recalls Hunt. "But we did go back and pick them up after about half an hour."

The Costello tour was vitally important to The Pogues. Not only did it offer the experience of playing in major venues, but also it built on the buzz already happening on the streets and in the press, and it introduced them to large crowds of people who hadn't necessarily heard their material. Touring insisted upon a certain discipline, a daily routine, and the music became tighter, more intuitive, as the weeks went by. Generally, they went down extremely well, which was a great encouragement.

"The Elvis tour was what really kicked things off," says Andrew Ranken.

"It was a very good experience to play so much," notes Jem. "It really got us round the country. I suppose if you're in a band and trying to make a go of it, it's a dream come true to get that sort of opportunity."

"It was crucial," says Darryl. "It transformed The Pogues from being a band that just played in London pubs for a few pints of beer into something that had more ambition. It seemed to focus everything."

Costello – already nicknamed "Uncle Brian" - was usually gracious towards his support band, and he turned out not to be quite the inveterate cynic of his reputation. "He tried hard to be the cool customer," remarks Hunt. "I think that was a persona he developed in the early days when he was with Stiff. People try to be something they think the audience want to see. But underneath it all, that wasn't Elvis's true personality. He was actually a softer, gentler person who liked to be involved in discussion and express himself a bit. He was fun. He had a little portable TV that we could watch the live football on, on a Sunday. He did hang about with us quite a bit as well, more so before the tour. Once we went on the road he became more 'professional'. He was just a bit of a pop star. But he was very decent. He offered to waive the lights and PA costs because we had no money."

"I suppose he had his ups and downs," says Jem of Costello, "but he was pretty accommodating and sociable on the whole."

"Elvis was fine," declares Spider. "He was busy ensnaring Cait or she was busy ensnaring him. They were very matey."

Costello and Cait had seemingly formed a relationship before the tour began, and it blossomed when they were on the road. Despite their early attempts to keep things "under cover", as Andrew puts it, the band weren't fooled. Before long, the couple became more openly affectionate. At this stage, no one could have foreseen the divisive implications of the partnership, and The Pogues' reactions varied from indifference to an amused acceptance and an occasional curiosity.

Jem Finer pulls no punches: "Cait made a beeline for Elvis, but then she did to anyone who was famous. He was the most famous person around. He seemed to enjoy her attentions."

James Fearnley: "Elvis seemed to be dead nice, although there was a lot of bizarre behaviour which could illustrate the relationship between him and Cait. The last show of that tour was in Norwich, and Cait and Elvis had to part for a time*. I don't know if any commitment had been made, one to the other. I think Cait wanted to send a message of some kind, so she shaved all her hair off, down to her skin, except for a crown of long, black hair on the top. It was like Ernie from *Sesame Street*. It was really, really strange. We couldn't let her onstage looking like that, so we insisted she wrap her head in some kind of turban. There was some sort of message in her being shorn. Something was going on, and it was definitely to do with Elvis."

This was also noted by The Attractions, who thought Cait an unusual girl and nicknamed her Beryl, after *The Topper*'s cartoon tearaway Beryl The Peril. They joked openly about O'Riordan, and how much younger she was than Elvis**. Outraged at this perceived disrespect towards himself and Cait, Costello's already frosty relations with his band became glacial, and he would drop them completely within a couple of years.

Attractions bass player Bruce Thomas told Costello biographer Graeme Thomson: "She [Cait] was very like Elvis. Intense, volatile, pretty cerebral. I went in the room and she was shaving her head, she had all these little razor nicks all over her scalp, and she carried a teddy bear all the time."

Despite the hilarity surrounding their fine romance, Uncle Brian and Beryl would go some distance together.

With The Pogues forced to live in each others' pockets throughout the weeks of the Costello tour, they were getting to know each other very quickly and very well. The atmosphere in the transit could be jovial one minute, argumentative the next and explosively bad-tempered in the blink of an eye. Yet, the prevailing mood was usually one of huge excitement. The album had been released, the gigs were going well, the press was unanimously enthusiastic, and all the signs were that the band was heading towards a good future indeed.

"It was either on the Costello tour or the trip to Germany not long after

* Costello was about to tour Europe with T-Bone Burnett.
** The situation was further complicated because at the time Costello was facing divorce proceedings from his wife Mary over his affair with Bebe Buell, an American model and serial rock-star girlfriend.

that, and I remember Cait and I sitting next to each other in the van," recalls Spider. "I said to her, 'You know what, Cait, we're the best band in the fucking world,' and she said, 'I know.' We really, really meant it. It wasn't said with any kind of ego. It was more like feeling lucky and being part of something really special. You always cringe when you hear people talk about how they're blessed, but I did feel that way about The Pogues. I didn't feel it was as a result of anything particularly that I'd done. It was more like it was something that had happened to me."

Stacy adds: "The Pogues' sense of community was a very important thing about the band. It contributed to our longevity and the atmosphere around us, because it was a really easy one. Egos possibly did raise their heads to a certain extent at some later point, but not in the way that they do and have done in other bands. That's never been the case with The Pogues."

It was an extremely protective and loyal community. Rows erupted and were quickly resolved, and no matter what the disagreements within the group, they presented a united front to the world at large. Various members reveal today how, in times of personal distress, the other Pogues could always be counted upon to rally round.

Darryl Hunt remembers: "There was so much talking and bantering. Now people live in their own worlds of headphones and laptops. We actually communicated a lot between us, sometimes in quite a fraught way, on the Elvis tour and subsequent tours. So much went on, so much was consumed. We lived such long, hard days with little sleep and lots of travelling. If we'd carried on like that, we'd have burnt out very quickly. It was all right for the first few tours, but you can't keep it up.

"I think everybody was pretty good with each other but sometimes things would get volatile mainly because of the amounts of drink being consumed. Cait seemed to hold up very well. There didn't seem to be any problem between her and everybody else other than the sexual tension you'd naturally get if there's a girl and five blokes, although in terms of sexual tension, I wasn't one of those blokes and neither was Jem. Cait used to go out with Shane, and there was still a bit of residue of all that. They seemed to trundle along okay. Shane would come out with the odd barbed remark about Costello. Cait would bite her lip and accept it. Sometimes she could get very tense. She was a very angry person. She seems to still have quite a bit of anger in her, I don't know where from. I was fine with her on the tour."

Andrew Ranken adds: "I think one of the reasons we managed to stay together was cos we did actually get on with each other quite well most of the time. You can't expect there not to be the odd tiff."

By now, the Shane and Spider double-act was in full swing. It was a thing of wonder and a force to be reckoned with, especially by the person on the receiving end. However, Andrew says: "Most of the time Shane was easy to get along with on the road. Most of the time Spider was as well."

At the same time, Andrew was beginning to experience problems with Cait, which made things slightly awkward since they were the rhythm section. For Ranken, she was more of a Rocky O'Riordan than a Beryl The Peril.

"I have to say I had a few run-ins with her," he reveals. "I did find her quite difficult to work with, I'd say from pretty early on. She was just quite famous for fighting and arguing generally. I can't really remember what the last straw was but, basically, she ended up not talking to me for about two years. Or it seemed like two years. I think we're friends again now, though. As a bass player, she was an apprentice. She was on the way, but she was a learner. I was quite prepared to hope for the best, that she'd get better quick, but then when we stopped communicating too. . . I mean, drummers and bass players have to communicate, they have to work together. It just wasn't working in the way that it needed to work."

Within any community, certain friendships are stronger – or more fragile – than others. Group roles are established and observed, and Darryl Hunt and James Fearnley had the misfortune on the Elvis tour to be cast as the victims of everyone else's jokes.

"The band were pretty horrible to Darryl," asserts Finer. "I think he was treated badly, people taking the piss and treating him like a dogsbody when he was doing a really difficult job, driving, lugging gear around, doing sound. Really, he's a very brilliant musician, and so I think it was good when he later became the bass player, because people started treating him like a normal human being. Groups of people seem to have this thing they can't help, which is that they like to gang up and pick on someone. When a lot of those humans are drunk people in the back of a van, and when you're a band or a team of some sort, I suppose some horrible kind of bonding experience makes you likely to hurl abuse at the person driving you around. It's rather like going on a school trip, hurling abuse at the coach driver. In general, I don't think I treated Darryl with the respect he fully deserved. I don't necessarily think I was as bad as some other people, but I don't think I'm an innocent party.

"Poor James – he used to get a bit of stick as well, probably because of his northern accent and his bluntness. We'd all tease each other. It's like being in the playground, being picked on a bit. I did get upset on James's account. Spider recently reminded me that I once called him and Shane 'malicious little shits' for being horrible to James."

Shane MacGowan denies point blank that any such behaviour took place, even though the other Pogues have confirmed that Hunt and Fearnley did tend to be picked on.

"No, they didn't tend to be picked on," he says. "I never had any fucking problems with James or any of the rest of them. That's rubbish if James said he was picked on. Darryl was never picked on by me once. No. They're all my friends."

Fearnley: "It was hard for Darryl because he's a canny musician in his own right. To find himself driving a band around who are his mates and things are going well for them… he was stalwart, although I think it might have been baffling for him. I think he got a bit of short shrift from Shane in those days. I'm not saying that Shane was a tyrant or anything, but Darryl's life was a bit difficult at Shane's hands. He had to suffer quite a bit. It wasn't mickey-taking… it was just some unpleasantness. It's horrible, but I was always relieved when Darryl got shit sooner than me – 'Oh, thank Christ for that.'

"Even in The Nips, Shane and Howard [Cohen] would laugh about people and say the most horrible things about them, and it was strange to me. It was part of some culture that I suppose I should've been more familiar with than I was. It's like joshing in pubs – I understand that, but I'm not sure if I understood something that didn't seem to be just joshing. It was malicious, I suppose. Yeah.

"For a while, and I suppose I'm still like this, I was a sanctimonious git sometimes, and most of The Pogues might know me for that. There's a certain moral rectitude with me that goes to shit sometimes, a level of behaviour beneath which I can't tolerate, but I didn't actually do anything proactive to stop it happening, except once. Later, we had a roadie called Roger who used to get shit from Shane and from Frank [Murray, manager] and Charlie [MacLennan, production manager]. I didn't understand what their gripe was with Roger and I shouted at Frank about it. I said, 'It's gotta stop. It's not right to treat people like that.' Maybe I should've shouted at Shane.

"To some degree, I probably wound Shane up. There was something about me that needled him the same way that things about him needled me. I used to get shit from Spider as well. Even in his cups, he was very bright and could run rings round me. I consider myself to be slow-witted and dim in comparison to both Shane and Spider, especially in the connections that they make verbally. Jem's a very clever guy, but I never had to suffer Jem running rings round me because he didn't really want to, but Shane and Spider used to. Jem used to josh me, but that's just joshing and everybody did it."

No one is suggesting that either Hunt or Fearnley were undervalued as contributors to the band. On the contrary, MacGowan states: "Darryl was a driver, road manager, medic – when people got ill, he looked after them. I don't think he felt put-upon. He was a genuine fan. He always had been."

James's musical contributions were extremely important. He was, after all, The Maestro, and it was James and Jem who would be the unsung heroes of some of MacGowan's best-loved compositions, helping to pull his musical ideas into shape. However, Fearnley's relationship with MacGowan was and remains a complex matter, with James liking and respecting Shane as much as he has been infuriated by him.

He admits: "The only person I dream of more than I dream of Shane is my dad. The Pogues are people I spent 12 years with, and with the reunion gigs, I'm spending time with them again now. One of the sources of conflict in the early days was that I allowed myself to be stopped in my tracks by the assumptions I was making about Shane, but with middle age coming on, it's a lot easier now for me to understand what I think I should've understood then, which is the extent to which he is like a Lost Boy, as in *Peter Pan*. I never really got that. I remember him asking me if I thought he drank too much. I said, 'Well, you know what, if you're finding that you have to drink in order to go to sleep at night, then you probably are.' He said, 'Yeah, well,' or something.

"When the first reunion thing came up [2001], I was very leery about that. I spoke to Jem or Spider about Shane. I seemed to be closest with them – I got really close with Spider after he gave up the alcohol, which is dead nice. They'd say, 'You know, he [Shane] loves you.' I said, 'Shit, I don't think so.' I remember reading in the biography of Oscar Wilde, 'You always hurt the one you love.' Maybe that's the thing, I don't know. I don't know if I can believe Spider and Jem when they say that he loves me. There's unmistakeably a connection there, and there always has been. Sometimes I don't really understand.

"I was talking to my brother about this. He said, 'You and Shane are like a couple of flints.' We've locked horns in an askance sort of way throughout the whole time I've known him, going way back to when I was living in Burton Street.

"I did have a lovely episode with Shane last year [2005] when we played in Spain. We'd come offstage and I ended up sitting next to him and gave him a slap on the thigh – next thing, we end up holding hands with fingers interlocked, which is kind of weird for two men to be doing, but not all that weird for two men from The Pogues. I wasn't going to break contact with him because it was just really valuable. And to have a chat with him on the bus about how great we felt about working together again was very nice. That's very rare for me [with Shane]."

Back on the Costello tour, despite the slings and arrows, Darryl Hunt was taking care of business. "I had too much to do to bother about getting on with people in the group," he declares. "You haven't got time for musicians' foibles. There's a job to be done. Certain people would be the centre of digs more than other members. Spider and Shane held court a lot of the time, but usually in a funny sort of way. I don't think the rest of us had the constitution of those two to go for it [drinking] all day, apart from maybe Andrew.

"It was actually a bit worse for James than for me, because he was on level terms with the group. He got quite a hard time from them, particularly Shane and Spider. Sometimes I used to get a bit of shit because of my job and where I was in the situation - I was the only 'outsider' on the road. I remember times when we didn't get on and there was shouting and ribbing going on. It wasn't so much Shane that did the picking: I think it was probably more Spider.

"A lot of it was water off a duck's back to me. I could walk out any time, and I had enough people in the group I had good relationships with. Andrew was a really fair guy. In a way, it's six of one and half a dozen of the other. I'm sure I irritated people. I'm sure James did. Some of the behaviour must have been incited. It happens with football teams - anywhere there are groups of men together. I didn't allow it to sink in very deeply. It's something that I think people now feel quite bad about. When I joined the group properly, on bass, everything changed. It was a different landscape. Suddenly I became respected."

Spider Stacy comments: "I guess if Darryl hadn't wanted to come on the road with us, then he wouldn't have done it. There wasn't very much for him in the way of money at that point. I never got the impression that he wanted to be off doing his own stuff. You always get someone who's going to be the butt of the jokes, and it was Darryl, and James as well. They filled that role, although I don't recall Darryl suffering particularly at Shane's hands.

"Everybody used to pick on Darryl and James. It wasn't just me and Shane. We're mouthy cunts. I will not stand idly by and have Shane deny that, but at the same time, it wasn't only us. It's not like Darryl and James were getting systematically bullied. Whenever there's bands or whatever going around, there's always people who are going to be the butts of jokes and people who are cracking the jokes. Maybe the people cracking them can dish it out and can't take it, whereas the ones that are the butts of the jokes are the ones who can dish it out and take it too."

Whatever the dynamics of this particular situation, change was in the wind and a new target of ridicule was about to emerge. Elvis Costello, their forthcoming record producer, was about to join the entourage, taking his seat in the bus beside Cait O'Riordan and gritting his teeth at the sniggering from the back row.

CHAPTER 10

Murray's Law

*R*ed Roses For Me scored a Number 89 chart placing, which wasn't bad at all. Despite the various complaints about the production and the mastering, the album did capture the unruly gusto of the band on tracks such as the opening 'Transmetropolitan', whose racing tempos and hearty chorusing whisk the listener through a veritable A–Z of The Pogues' London, from the comfort of "a fried egg in Valtaro's" to the sex shops of Soho and the "blood and glue and beer" of the back streets, from the "Camden Palace poofs" to the corridors of power in Whitehall, the BBC and the now defunct Greater London Council. At the other extreme is 'Kitty', a ballad that MacGowan learnt from his mother and the final song on the album. A portrayal of Irishmen saying goodbye to their families as they leave home to escape police scrutiny and detention, it's performed with perfect instrumental sensitivity and an unabashed emotion from Shane.

Certainly the most arresting track is MacGowan's 'Down In The Ground Where The Dead Men Go', a horribly vivid imagining of the fates of all those who died in the Irish Famine of the late 1840s. Carried along by a dark and frantic bounce, the song rises to a cacophonous climax filled with cries and screams and wails.

"We were on tour with Elvis when the album came out, and we were in Oxford," says Spider. "We went into a record shop and there it was. It was brilliant. I was really, really excited. When I got home with it, I went round to see my mate Terry, who lived on the other side of Hampstead Garden Suburb. He was the older brother of a guy I'd been to school with – the guy we used to go and buy dope off. He was actually really impressed, not by the fact my band had made a record, although that was quite something... but he *liked* it."

Stiff Records had re-released 'Dark Streets Of London' in the summer of 1984, just after inking their deal with The Pogues. Another single, 'Boys From The County Hell', immediately followed the album from which it was taken. Once again, by way of some lively musical cheer, MacGowan dwells on the seamier side of London, the greed of employers, the dream or reality of violence, and the prevalence of junkies, alcoholics, pimps and whores. He also effects a witty twist on the old counting song 'Ten Green Bottles' with the lines, "Five green bottles sitting on the floor/I wish to Christ, I wish to Christ/That I had fifteen more," leading up to the famous crowd-pleasing punchline: "And it's lend me ten pounds, I'll buy you a drink..."

Like its predecessor, 'Boys From The County Hell' failed to dent the singles chart, although it was a strong composition.

"We'd been playing it for a long time," says Finer. "I remember Shane showing it to me around the time of our first gig. We were sitting playing it and I came up with the spaghetti western intro. I suppose it was a good enough choice for a second single. Some of the lyrics were quite violent. I think Shane had to re-do the vocal for the single, changing the words to make it more radio friendly."

"I remember when I first heard it," says Stacy. "I thought, 'Shane's really coming up with the goods now.' It had so much attitude. It's really sort of punky. It just seemed that everything was happening as it should be. I along with other people always knew that Shane could write great songs and it was obvious he could go on to greater things. But it was just the sheer quality. Writing in that kind of idiom, writing the kind of songs that he suddenly started writing, it was fantastic."

It was especially gratifying for Spider that his own composition, the nimble 'Repeal Of The Licensing Laws', was the single's B-side, if not an album track.

He remembers presenting it to the group for the first time: "I was a bit nervous, but less nervous than I would be later on. It was a straightforward little tune. I took it into rehearsal and we all took part in arranging it. I wish it had gone on the album. If I'd known then what I know now, I might have fought a bit harder for it. I'd like to have known that you get a lot more money from songs on albums, unless you get a really big hit single. It's on the remastered version of the album now as a bonus track – 20 years too late!"

Stan Brennan recalls a certain opposition to 'Boys From The County Hell' being the follow-up single to 'Dark Streets Of London'. This was because the album also contained 'Streams Of Whiskey' with its infectious rush of blood to the head, its headlong fling into hedonism and its whole-hearted suggestion of liberation. Incredibly, it was never released as a single.

Says Brennan, who was continuing to deal with managerial matters, voluntarily, on behalf of the band: "Jem wanted to release 'Streams Of Whiskey'. I thought it was too similar to 'Dark Streets', but I think now he was right and it should've been released as a single. It's the most complete production on the album. It's why it always appears on all the best-ofs. It works really well - although I remember when we were doing it in the studio I kept singing, 'I am sailing' along to it. I probably let my need to be in control get in the way of a good decision there."

By now, Brennan believes, a certain conflict had arisen between himself and Finer.

"I think there was probably some acrimony. I think Jem was upset that I didn't let 'Me And Bobby McGee' go on the first album. We did it in the studio and I didn't feel it fitted. But Jem did do a lot of work for The Pogues, and I don't have an axe to grind. I think probably the fact that I couldn't come out on the Elvis Costello tour didn't help matters. Shane certainly was not managing the band, but I daresay Jem was doing a lot of work that wouldn't be normal for the banjo player to be doing."

Jem certainly was. With The Pogues' profile and popularity increasing enormously, The Office was getting busy: the trusty shortbread tin was far too small these days to accommodate the huge volume of in-coming material that demanded attention. It was time to hand over the reins.

Says Finer: "During the Costello tour, I thought, 'If we're carrying on like this, I just can't keep on doing all this stuff with Shane. We need someone to do it for us.' I talked to Shane about it and we talked about Frank."

The Pogues had met Frank Murray at one of their Monday-night gigs with Elvis at the Hammersmith Palais when they hopped out for a pint in the pub next door, the Laurie Arms. A Dubliner, Murray had been a tour manager, taking care of everyone from golden-era Thin Lizzy to the 2-Tone package – The Specials, The Selecter and Madness, who were replaced mid-tour by Dexys Midnight Runners. Now Murray was managing Kirsty MacColl and Philip Chevron.

He remembers: "I'd seen Shane with The Nipple Erectors, and I saw The Pogues for the first time at the Hope & Anchor. Ted Carroll was a friend of mine and he told me they were a bit of fun. Another friend, Dave Jordan [The Specials' engineer and co-producer, and The Pogues' future monitor man], had just come back from living in Kendal. He'd left London and gone back up north to get healthy the year beforehand. He gave me a call and I said, 'Come on, we'll go and see The Pogues.' I thought they were great. I'd never heard a band like them before. I liked the mixture of musics they were playing, Irish folk and American country and everything with that Pogues punk sensibility. They were laughing, having a good time. They weren't too serious about anything. I saw them a few other times, including the gig in the 100 Club that Shane couldn't do, and I became a casual fan of theirs.

"There were a few bands coming out of the Camden area – The Men They Couldn't Hang, The Boothill Foot-Tappers and the Shillelagh Sisters. I was in discussions with The Men They Couldn't Hang about managing them.

"The Pogues played several nights at the Hammersmith Palais on that Elvis Costello tour and on one of those nights, The Men They Couldn't Hang were opening. After, I went into the pub next door with Cush, from The Men, and various members of The Pogues came in. I was talking to Jem, and he was asking me what they should do to take the next step. I told him they should go back to all the places they'd just played and play them again so people still remembered them. I told them they should get themselves an agent and concentrate on playing live, just giving that kind of general help and advice."

It was after this that Jem and Shane had the conversation about Murray. "I'd never met Frank before that," says Finer, although MacGowan had. "We decided it would be a good idea for the band to meet Frank and talk about it. I think Frank had been quite clever and put the idea in my head without actually saying it that he could manage us."

Murray takes up the tale: "About a week after, I started getting messages at home saying Jem, the banjo player from The Pogues, wanted to talk to me. I arranged to have a meeting with them at a pub in Parkway, Camden. Everybody turned up.

"Earlier that week, I'd had a meeting with The Men They Couldn't Hang. It was like the inquisition. They were saying that they didn't want to be associated with The Pogues, that they were different bands. They saw The Pogues as too out-of-control, not too focused. I met The Pogues about two or three days later, I gave them my ideas on things, they were cool with that and it was all done in half an hour. So then I became their manager."

Finer says: "Frank was a very charming man. He still is. He can be very funny and engaging and warm."

"I didn't know anything about him," admits James Fearnley. "We all went to this meeting in the pub and in comes Frank, characteristically sucking on his teeth, which somehow gave him an air of importance. There was something a bit restless about him, as if he had some other place to go, and I liked that energy at the time. He seemed to be pretty straightforward – 'I'll do what I can.' And he did do what he could."

Spider adds: "He seemed like the right kind of guy to do the job. He had a very confident air about him. He had a real swagger, Frank, and he said all the right things. I don't mean that he was being duplicitous in any way, but he looked and sounded the part. I think he was the right person for the first number of years."

Shane MacGowan was the only person to sound a note of caution from the outset. He says: "In the first place, I was the only person who didn't vote for Frank to be the manager. We were on varying terms of friendship with him, but I knew him better than anyone else and at the meeting where we decided to offer him to look after us, he did warn us we'd probably all hate him within a few months. But I never hated him."

Looking back now, MacGowan concedes: "I think Frank did a great job. He didn't make any promises. I think he was the right man for The Pogues at the time."

Murray immediately signed The Pogues to an agent – Derek Kemp at The Agency – so that they could embark on a touring blitz. Already, Jem Finer was beginning to regret the haste with which The Pogues had committed to their new manager.

He remarks: "It wasn't very well thought through. And, you know, I certainly hadn't bargained for what having a manager in the mould of Frank meant. He's a very old-school rock'n'roll manager. He loved being on tour. He loved that kind of life. His *modus operandi* for the band was we'd just tour the whole bloody time and, through that, you built up a following so that when you're eventually allowed a couple of weeks to go and record a record, someone just might buy it. This wasn't great news for me at all.

"Managing The Pogues was a bit of a no-brainer. Here was a band with a huge amount of potential. We'd made an album and there was a lot of interest in us. Obviously, there was great songwriting potential and a very charismatic singer with an amazing voice, and the whole band was very charismatic as a bunch of people.

"We said to Frank, 'Look, we need someone to manage us. Are you interested and what's the deal?' He said, 'Yeah, I'll manage you. It's 20 per cent of your earnings gross.' We thought, 'All right.' We were just fucking stupid. When you go on tour, you might get paid £100, so that's £20 to the manager and £80 to you. Well, for a start, that's crap because there were six of us. Already we were getting less than the manager. We should've thought, 'No one should get more than anyone else.' Even worse, when you're talking about gross – if £100 was going in our biscuit tin, he'd get his £20 and then all the expenses would come out of the £80 and then we'd split what was left between us.

"It wasn't really a living, but it wasn't like breadline either. You get a bit more popular and you might make a living wage out of it. We just sold ourselves down the river instantly. Without realising it, we agreed to that and consigned ourselves to this life of constant touring. Very quickly we were in debt. Initially, Frank would only take a bit here and there because we couldn't afford to pay him. Then we were in debt to him. Once you're in debt, the only way to earn more money to pay it back is to go on tour. But when you're earning more money, you're making more of a debt."

Later, when The Pogues were "presented with a contract", they negotiated with Murray a different rate for live shows, being either 15% of the gross or 10% of gross, according to a formula.

"Obviously, a certain amount of touring is a sensible thing to do," reasons Finer. "It was necessary for us to build up a following. Touring was *a* way to make the band big, but there's a compromise too. A lot of people in the band weren't that worried about it, because it was a good laugh and a novelty and they were enjoying that lifestyle. For me, it was a bit of a nightmare scenario.

"I feel we were all incredibly naïve. Frank wasn't being unpleasant. We said yes to something we should never have said yes to. That's not his fault. I wasn't happy with it, but we'd invited this guy in, and he was doing things the way he wanted to do them. He wasn't doing it to be horrible to me. I'd somehow sanctioned a situation which was really not very good for me.

"And we went around touring and we got more and more popular and that was great, but for me it came at a price. I was torn between wanting to be with my family and wanting to see the band get better. There was also a financial price to pay, though we didn't realise at the time quite what we'd let ourselves in for on that front either."

The touring problem was something that Finer was never able to resolve successfully during Murray's management. As time went on, Andrew Ranken, and then other members, would support his protests.

Meanwhile, only one thing remained to be done at the end of the Costello tour – and Darryl Hunt caused something of a sensation when he returned the van: "The guy at the hire company called all the workers out to look at it, just to show everybody how disgusting it was. And that was after I'd cleaned it out. . ."

It was a stimulating and productive period. The Pogues had a big surprise in store for anyone who assumed they'd have trouble with the time-honoured "difficult second album", which Stiff was now inviting them to record. Far from using up all of their best material on *Red Roses For Me*, they had some great ideas left over from that period, and they were coming up with new songs too.

James Fearnley remembers working on 'The Old Main Drag' with Shane and Jem round the wooden table in Cromer Street, early on in their career.

131

Gradually the song would take on the simple but affecting character that has so engaged generations of Pogues fans. A slow waltz with the merest click of percussion and the gentlest touch of banjo and accordion, it gives MacGowan the space and the spotlight for a vocal that's almost stately in its melody and affectingly straightforward in its delivery. Ignoring the obvious opportunities for melodrama, Shane once again tells it like it is (or was) in London, focusing on the violence and the cops, the drugs, the drunks, the dossers and the rent boys sloping in and out of back alleys for a fiver a favour. He has often declared his fascination with the seedy underbelly of the city and his inclination to illuminate and sometimes celebrate it, but 'The Old Main Drag' memorably raises the prospect of a lonely death on the street.

'A Pair Of Brown Eyes' – regarded by some as MacGowan's finest composition – began life even earlier. Finer says: "It's a brilliant song. I think it's one of Shane's real classics. It had another name originally. He wrote it about the time of the Falklands War [1982], and it was called 'Me And Hanley' or something like that. It had totally different lyrics. I liked it then. I played it with him in Cromer Street or in my flat. We may well have busked it. Then he rewrote it. It's still got elements of war in, but it's much more than a linear song – all kinds of different elements came into it which weren't originally there. I found it a very exciting song, both lyrically and musically."

Possessed of a haunting and beautiful melody, 'A Pair Of Brown Eyes' tells of a pub encounter between an old man who cannot forget the horrors he has seen in wartime service and a pissed-up youth who doesn't want to hear his reminiscences but nevertheless can't forget them.

The Pogues, of course, were already playing Phil Gaston's 'Navigator', and it would figure largely in their future plans. Then there was 'Sally MacLennane', a new song of MacGowan's which was rooted in the bar-room culture he absorbed as a youngster, staying at his Uncle Frank's pub in Dagenham. It should be pointed out that Sally MacLennane is neither a buxom barmaid nor a long-term love interest: it, not "she", is a type of stout. This was another in the vein of 'Streams Of Whiskey': recklessly tuneful with a rousing chorus, effortlessly Irish to the point where you could hardly believe it had not been sung loudly in snugs and lounges across the Republic for decades.

This was all phenomenal song-writing, quite extraordinary from someone who was then so young.

"I thought for the longest time that 'Sally MacLennane' was a traditional song," agrees Fearnley. "Lots of them come across like that because they're so perfect. I was watching the Bob Dylan documentary [Martin Scorsese's

No Direction Home]. The way that he explains his position in folk music and how he writes his songs - you could take Bob Dylan out of that equation and put Shane in. It's part of an idiom, it's part of a culture, it's part of history. Shane's songwriting was just so informed by the force of all his experience, and that experience includes as much Irish music or as much folk music as he ever heard. There's something timeless about it.

"'Sally MacLennane' sounds like it had already been written. And I love the abandon too, which is something that I get a big kick out of with The Pogues, and the sound of the instruments, the banjo and the accordion and the whistle doing stuff together particularly. It was unhinged. And I really like the way it melds with the way that Shane writes songs."

MacGowan is credited with some of the most evocative lyrics in popular music. Still he bridles at any mention of the word "poet" as though it were some sort of poisonous accusation, and he has stated that although he would never want to churn out words that were lame enough to insult the Irish tradition, his priority has always been the music. That, however, was something that required help from his fellow Pogues. In the early days, when Shane was very focused, their assistance ranged from instrumental suggestions to harmonic advice although as time went on they played an increasingly important role.

"Rehearsal was fun," says James. "I really enjoyed trying to wrest out of Shane what it was that he was trying to do with the chords to a song. Although he mightn't have known what they were, he knew what they weren't.

"It was difficult to hear him thrash away at a song in front of you and then forget where he was in the words, and then the timing would go wrong, and the metre would be all over the place. It was really, really hard but great fun to do. It was me and Jem mostly. Jem's a little less judgemental than me, less reactive than I was in those circumstances, and he was able to calm everything down. He would display a gentleman's befuddlement about what it was, so Shane would go through it for him in a more measured manner. It worked because Jem is pretty diplomatic.

"In listening to Shane's discourse sometimes, I found it extraordinarily difficult to follow the connections that he makes. That's throughout the time I've known him. You've got to go with him. Sometimes that's hard. You don't want to appear foolish because you don't understand. So it's a bit of a ride and sometimes it's like tying yourself to a stake and not moving further than the ropes are going to let you go, otherwise you're lost."

The other Pogues also had input. Andrew Ranken remembers endless hours of endeavour, stating: "Working out songs with Shane could be a very long, drawn-out process. We'd go all round the houses trying to understand what he was getting at and we'd go through all these permutations only to end up where we started. Then he'd say, 'Oh, yeah, that's what I meant all along.' I think anyone who's written a song has a vision of how they want it to go. It's very hard to get anything to come out exactly the way that you hear it in your head, and it can take an awful lot of thrashing around trying to get somewhere near it. Sometimes you just have to accept that you're not going to get exactly what you want and sometimes it's this nebulous sort of thing that you can't fully explain. Two people can play something the same technically, but they'll always play it with a slightly different feel. An awful lot of what makes The Pogues' music good to me is the feel. Cover bands never sound quite like the band that they're covering."

Spider adds: "Everybody had a hand in a lot of the songs here and there. A couple of lines I contributed to Shane's songs. In 'The Old Main Drag', "I've been spat on and shat on and raped and abused" – that's mine. Shane will probably fucking say that it isn't, but actually it is. There are little bits and pieces like in 'Transmetropolitan' where it's got the tune from 'The Boxer' and 'The Rare Old Times', and that was my idea as well. So really I'm the secret genius at the heart of The Pogues!"

In December 1984, the band were back on the road for a tour titled Lock Up Your Drinks Cabinet.

Says Frank Murray: "The Pogues were darlings of the underground scene in London. Journalists asked about them. There was a 'movement' coming out of Camden, but the rest of the country wasn't picking up on it. The best thing, I thought, was to get them back out there playing. We started to go the length and breadth of England and Scotland, and we went to Wales and Ireland. Through that, I got to know the band, the music, the fans and how people were reacting to them. I got a really great sense of what the band were and what they could become.

"I was interested in the next album, of course, and in seeing what the development would be from the first one to the second one, and what direction the songwriting was going in and what the standard of the songwriting was.

"The band were easy to deal with at that early stage. There was chaos, but I enjoyed the chaos. There were things that would irritate you. You'd always have to wait an hour for Shane in the van outside his house; dumb shit like that would piss you off, but everything was fairly good."

Despite Cait's incapable behaviour at The Pogues' first BBC recording, the band were invited back for another John Peel session, which was broadcast, helpfully, at the beginning of the tour. They performed two traditional songs, 'Whiskey You're The Devil' and 'Danny Boy', a closing-time favourite, plus Gaston's 'Navigator' and MacGowan's sparkling 'Sally MacLennane'. This time the recording passed without incident or censorship, and Peel pronounced the band to be "the finest soul act" of the year. Accolades were coming thick and fast, with *NME* readers voting The Pogues among the best new acts of 1984 and the journalists placing *Red Roses For Me* at Number 11 in their list of the year's finest albums.

And so to New Year's Eve, which found the band headlining at the London ICA as part of Harp Lager's Rock Week. For most of the band, as for most of the country, it was a night of celebration, but not for Jem Finer.

He recalls: "Frank would say, 'I'm going to do this, I'm going to do that,' like he was the band. Fucking annoying. And I remember being in the dressing room and he was saying he was going to do this and that. I felt my heart sinking and I thought, 'Jesus, I can't do this.' It was one of the most depressing New Year's Eves I've had. I walked home, towards the house, being thoroughly miserable and thinking, 'Shit, I've been through all this to help create this wonderful thing and now it's become a nightmare to me.' I'm not saying that it was for anybody else. And so I started thinking, 'I don't know if I can actually carry on like this.' Marcia said, 'You've got to carry on.'"

By now, Marcia was pregnant with the couple's second child.

"Our arrangement in life had always been, when we first had a kid, that we would take equal responsibility and we'd both do our own stuff as well," continues Finer. "So Marcia was going to carry on with her art and studying and I was going to do whatever. This whole development meant she was suddenly left looking after Ella [with another baby on the way]. It was a lonely thing for her – not much money, and the frustration, and not being able to get on with other stuff that's important too. But somehow it all carried on. It wasn't all bad. I still had a good time as much as I could, but it was a bit of a horrible thing too. And it got worse."

For Frank Murray, who had only just started working with The Pogues, this was a sudden and disturbing crisis: "I had to talk Jem into staying in the band." James Fearnley also remembers trying to persuade Finer not to leave. Like Jem, he took a long walk after the ICA gig.

He says: "I walked up to Islington to deliver a Happy New Year card to my poor beleaguered girlfriend Debsey who had had a pretty shit year, in the hope that my card, home-made, would propel her into a good one. I remember Jem ringing me up within the next few days to tell me he was going to quit. I remember being very alarmed that he was going to leave and, regrettably, not so sympathetic to his circumstances but more scared of what would happen to me if he left, and rather flattered that he should ring me to talk about it. I rather think I might have persuaded him to stay on with The Pogues at that time. I can't remember what arguments I used, but I do remember his coming round to my way of thinking about it."

While Finer may well have taken on board the advice of others, it was through his conversations with his wife that he made his final decision to stick it out.

The rest of the band made the most of the traditional boozefest. Says Spider: "I remember very little about the ICA gig except for a shambolic rendition of 'Auld Lang Syne'."

On January 11, the band appeared on *The Tube* and it was there that they experienced for the first time the aggressive side of their manager. "We could have stuck in at least one extra song," says Spider. "But we didn't, and Frank really blew up because we hadn't taken advantage of the opportunity."

Frank Murray made a lifelong friend during his days at the Drimnagh Castle Christian Brothers School in the south of Dublin. Paul Scully, a fellow pupil, became Murray's partner in crime and together they bunked off to have adventures in the city and surrounding countryside, often going riding on horses "borrowed" from a local gypsy encampment. At 15, both took up business studies at Rathmines College Of Commerce, an establishment also at one time attended by Irish Prime Minister and EU President Bertie Ahern.

The pair were more interested in rock'n'roll, blues and soul than they were in business studies, and in 1967, when the rest of the world was turning on to psychedelia, flowers, peace and love, Murray and Scully came across a teenage Phil Lynott leading a band called The Black Eagles. They became fans, then friends, and when Lynott joined the Irish group Skid Row as their singer, he invited them to jump on board as roadies.

Murray and Scully eventually quit the band to move to London, where they took up regular employment and lived with an aunt of Frank's in Maida Vale. In 1970, they heard again from Skid Row, who by now had signed a deal with CBS and lost Lynott along the way.

"He got sacked because they became one of those sort of Cream trios," explains Murray. He and Scully returned to the band as roadies, along with Ted Carroll. All three – and Skid Row – moved into a house in East Ham and embarked on a life of international touring - one which Murray enjoyed thoroughly.

After the band's first American tour, Murray and his friends took over a house in Belsize Avenue, Hampstead, vacated by the Irish band Granny's Intentions, who had split. Paul Scully had worked for a while with Granny's

– and it had been with them that Gary Moore made his recording debut at the age of 17.

During 1971 and 1972, travelling between the UK and Ireland, Murray took up some additional opportunities, tour managing Reverend Gary Davis at the Cambridge Folk Festival and looking after the sound for B. B. King in Dublin.

Leaving Skid Row for the second time, in 1972, Frank began working with two of the Irish musicians who were living in the house in Hampstead. Terry Woods, a player of great repute, and his wife Gay had previously been in Steeleye Span and Doctor Strangely Strange, with whom Murray had "done a few stints". Now they were forming The Woods Band. Scully, meanwhile, returned to Dublin to devote more time to his interest in the Divine Light Mission and its guru, Maharaj Ji.

Murray became sound engineer for The Woods Band, and accompanied them on various tours until they split, although Woods and Murray remained friends. Frank went back to Dublin where he bumped into an old pal. Phil Lynott was now fronting Thin Lizzy and had enjoyed a hit single with 'Whiskey In The Jar'. Murray returned to London to become Lizzy's tour manager, and the arrangement continued until they lost their guitarist, Eric Bell, and then his replacement, Gary Moore. The band took six or eight months off the road to sort themselves out.

Yet again relocating to Dublin, Frank was employed by The Dubliners' manager and theatrical producer Noel Pearson as a production manager, overseeing first a revue called *Jacques Brel Is Alive And Well And Living In Paris* and then other musicals including *Jesus Christ Superstar, West Side Story* and *Joseph And His Amazing Technicolour Dreamcoat* as well as Jason Miller's drama, *That Championship Season*. Murray had a particular interest in acting, and would later appear in several films: Alex Cox's *Straight To Hell*, Elizabeth Gill's *Gold In The Streets*, Nicola Pagett's *I Could Read The Sky* and Peter Richardson's *Comic Strip* Movie, *Eat The Rich*. He would also, notably, win a small role in *Father Ted*: 'The Mainland', episode four in the third series of the classic comedy sitcom, also features actor Richard "Victor Meldrew" Wilson appearing as himself. Murray is seen calling the police when an excitable Mrs Doyle comes to blows with her friend in a tea shop.

In 1976, Thin Lizzy were hot to trot with the recruitment of dual lead guitarists Brian Robertson and Scott Gorham, and Murray resumed his former tour managing role for the next two years, during which the band released their most important albums - *Jailbreak, Johnny The Fox, Bad Reputation* and the double *Live And Dangerous*, widely considered one of the finest live albums of all time.

Murray ventured into promoting in the summer of 1978, launching

Camden's Electric Ballroom as a rock gig. His opening act was a "super-group" – The Greedy Bastards - comprising Steve Jones and Paul Cook of The Sex Pistols and Thin Lizzy. Continuing on a similar theme, he booked The Vicious White Kids, bringing together Damned drummer Rat Scabies, the Pistols' original bassist Glen Matlock, Sid Vicious as lead singer and his girlfriend Nancy Spungen making even more appalling vocal sounds. It was Vicious' last gig in his home country: titled Sid Sods Off, it was also a fund-raiser for his and Nancy's trip to America, where both died.

The venue was shortly forced to close due to inadequate soundproofing, and Murray returned to tour managing. His experience with Elton John was eventually less than happy, although Elton's manager John Reid did pass on one piece of advice which stuck, that Murray should go into manage-ment. This he duly did after the 2-Tone tour, taking on an all-girl band called The Bodysnatchers who had two minor hits for 2-Tone in 1980: 'Let's Do Rock Steady' (Number 22) and 'Easy Life' (50).

"I'd built up a lot of road experience, and I learnt a lot from Chris Morrison and Chris O'Donnell, who managed Thin Lizzy," says Murray. "Then I took over Kirsty MacColl. I was with her when she had her hit singles, 'There's A Guy Works Down The Chip Shop Swears He's Elvis' on Polydor and 'A New England' on Stiff. We mutually agreed to part company in 1986/87 when she started becoming a mother. I also tour managed artists including Ian Dury, Blue Oyster Cult and The Commodores. I did a tour with Squeeze. I worked also as a production manager with [promoter] John Curd, doing Sunday-afternoon shows at The Roundhouse when he started the punk thing going there."

Finally, Murray added to his management books Philip Chevron, the former Radiator. Chevron, still working in Rock On in Camden, had been involved in production work, most recently for The Men They Couldn't Hang.

In time, Murray would bring many of his friends into The Pogues' family: Philip Chevron and Terry Woods would join as musicians, Paul Scully as a sound engineer, Dave Jordan on monitors, "Big" Charlie MacLennon as production manager, Paul Verner for lights and John Sharp as a backline and general roadie.

"The word was that Elvis Costello was crazed about Cait," remembers Dave Robinson. "Love is a great thing. It was very useful."

Stiff Records had got wind of a rumour that Elvis wanted to produce a couple of tracks for The Pogues. Frank Murray had heard the same report.

"I kept hearing all these stories about the band on the Elvis tour," he says. "Some of them were horror stories about their behaviour. I kept trying to figure out which stories were true and which weren't. They were all talking about how Elvis had been courting Cait. I didn't know whether Elvis wanted anything more to do with The Pogues or not.

"Jake Riviera was a friend of mine. I called him up. I said, 'There are all these weird rumours going round that Elvis would produce The Pogues.' I think Jake was horrified by the notion just, I guess, because of their experiences of the band on the tour. He said, 'I haven't heard anything about that, Frank, but I'll tell you what, I'll ask Elvis.' He rang me back two days later and said, 'Surprise, surprise. He really is interested in doing it.' I thought, '*Yes!*'

"I didn't think the band needed a producer to come in with a sound. They had their own sound, and it had to develop. When Elvis said he was a fan of the songs, I knew he'd treat the songs with respect."

"You couldn't just *get* Elvis Costello," asserts Robinson. "Getting him to do a Stiff band other than this one wouldn't have happened. The whole thing was remarkable. I thought, 'What a great thing.'"

The Pogues and Costello repaired to Elephant Studios to record 'A Pair Of Brown Eyes' and 'Sally MacLennane'. Both were potential singles, although the band's choice was the former. Stiff Records begged to differ.

Says Murray: "The relationship with Stiff was good. Almost anything we asked of them they gave us. They wanted 'Sally MacLennane' out first as a single. We said, no, we wanted 'A Pair Of Brown Eyes', and they gave us that."

"I think Costello did a great job producing it," opines Jem Finer. "I'm sure he taught Cait the bassline – it's very simple, but it's got a sophistication. It's more melodic than most of the formulaic Cait-type basslines - we'd just tell her to go 'boom boom boom'. Cait doing a backing vocal as well was really great. Elvis introduced a couple of elements into the arrangement – a tambourine and a mandolin part, which is beautiful. They were just very simple things which really enhanced it. He was very good at that. It's a really brilliant song. It was very exciting recording it. It was the first recording I thought, 'Jesus, this sounds so great' – what I'd imagined the band could sound like."

The sessions went so well that Elvis decided he wanted to produce the album, and that's when Stan Brennan came to the end of his work with the band and also with Phil Gaston, his partner in the record shops.

The arrival of Frank Murray had been the first blow. Brennan now saw no place for his endeavours in The Pogues' organisational structure, and coincidentally, he was coming to the conclusion that it was time to step back to attend to the complications in his own life.

He says: "I had to make a choice. I had a child, we were going to have another child, and it was all about putting bread on the table. At that stage, The Pogues weren't earning any money. Stiff didn't pay any production royalties for at least five years. I had a family to support and a mortgage to pay and I didn't feel I could put that at risk. I had my own issues with drink and drugs, and I had to think, 'Is working with The Pogues going to help me with this?' I had to make a big decision – 'Do I want to be with my children as they grow up?' More importantly, I had to deal with my own demons.

"The other thing was this terrible resistance. There was a Belfast guy called Paul Charles who was running the Costello tour. He was really positive about The Pogues but when I talked to him about signing them to his agency, Asgard, there was this resistance. It really was like pushing a rock uphill. One of the things with Frank was that he had an agency he was connected with and later the band would start getting lots of gigs, which is really what broke them. At the time I thought, 'This is where I need to exit.' I spoke to Alan Cowderoy [Stiff general manager] and said, 'It's a decision I've made myself,' and he said, 'If you feel all right about it. . .'

"I had a meeting with Shane and told him I was going to drop out. I might have been about to be sacked, I don't know. Really, I sacked myself. He didn't say an awful lot. He was very low-key about it. There was a part of me that wanted him to say, 'I want you to stay.'

"I don't know what kind of relationship you ever really make with Shane. For me, having had the first experience of Howard Cohen and The Nips, I didn't want to get hurt again. I thought the best thing I could do to protect myself was to pull out, and I believe it was the right decision. I never heard what the other members of the band felt. But I was still interested in producing the band."

That hope died when Costello offered his services.

"I really regret that I didn't get to do the second album," admits Brennan. "I'd love to have produced 'A Pair Of Brown Eyes' and 'The Sickbed Of Cuchulainn'. I met Frank Murray one night and he said, 'Elvis is doing the next album.' From Frank's point of view, it was a good move. It gets me out of the picture, and that's good for Frank, and getting Elvis Costello to produce the album as a career move helped The Pogues. It gave them a higher profile. But I think I understood The Pogues' music probably better than anyone else. I'd love to have done *Rum Sodomy & The Lash* with them.

"After that, I'd go to occasional Pogues gigs. I still do. But I got very busy with my own label, Media Burn; it was starting to do very well. I was signing up a whole group of bands that were playing in London. I worked out my relationship with Phil and I bought him out of the shop."

The pair had already given up the shops in London Bridge and Hereford Road, leaving only their Hanway Street outlet: "I was running that myself and running Media Burn and another label Absolutely Free, and running live gigs," says Brennan.

"In the middle of all that work, I was in therapy for about five or six years, dealing with my own issues around drink and drugs, and the emotional issues. I was starting to feel like I didn't want to be in retail all the time. From doing my own therapy, I thought, 'I could do this.' Out of all the early work, I'd always been very interested in dealing with people.

"Groups are so needy. I'd spent so many years being an unpaid psychotherapist, working with about 15 groups as a label owner. In 1991, I would've completely finished with the shop and that's when I retrained as a psychotherapist. I now have a private practice in Highgate, London, working with individuals and groups of people."

Phil Gaston had been happy to dissolve his business partnerships with Brennan because he intended to go travelling with Dee. He says: "I was doing a bit of PR here and there. It just took me away from the whole thing. The kids came along, and then you get caught up in stuff and you don't have the same kind of attitude."

Gaston and Dee eventually went back to Ireland, settling in County Clare, where they still live.

"We got our little cottage out here," says Phil. "It's just lovely. Dee got herself a post lecturing in the art college and I ended up as the director of a music school called Maoin Cheoi An Chlair – 'The Gift Of Music In Clare'. I have several hundred kids learning to play the piano and do their scales. Clare is the heart of the musical tradition. The musicians round here are unbelievable. Now I've gotta get back to writing songs again."

Phil and Dee continued to turn out for Pogues gigs before they set off on their travels, with Gaston remarking: "People still haven't assimilated what The Pogues did. There's no equivalent. The Saw Doctors, Black 47 – they all think all they have to do is play it really fast, really loud and put electric instruments in it. There's an artistry that Shane had. You can't just do it by formula. The Pogues are still unique."

Brennan comments: "I look back on the Pogues era with a mixture of excitement and lost opportunity. It almost feels like sometimes these situations are presented to you at a time you're not ready to take advantage of them. If I'd been as solid a person as I feel myself to be now, I probably could've done a better job, maybe been more open about what was going on for me and asked more about what was going on for them instead of making so many assumptions. I thought there had been such an interesting synthesis going on in the early days that got lost the longer the band went on.

"My partner Sophie was and is still very friendly with Marcia and Jem, and I meet Shane at the Brixton gigs occasionally, but we don't have much time together. I find it quite painful being with Shane. My memory is this really bright, articulate, knowledgeable, interesting guy. It was so exciting being around him. He really brought out all these great parts of you. While he's still intelligent and interesting, I find it very painful to see the effects of these years of abuse. I have no idea how he's survived all that. The number of people I know who've died... he must have an extraordinary constitution. But there's surviving and surviving, and the Shane I knew hasn't survived.

"To me, the band is a bit like [Oscar Wilde's] *The Picture Of Dorian Gray*, and Shane's the picture in the attic. If you want to see the cost to The Pogues, you just have to look at Shane."

By 1985, the band were being asked in every interview they did about their drinking habits. There was rarely any tone of disapproval: most people who experienced The Pogues enjoyed and shared in their dishevelled revelry. Still, there was rarely any acknowledgement that various members of the group might actually be more likely to roll a spliff than to crack open a bottle of something strong.

Sometimes they would deflect journalists' enquiries with a deft one-liner, or a lightning burst of repartee. MacGowan, however, was more likely to rise to the defence. For months, he had been explaining that the music was rooted in an age-old tradition that also involved alcohol.

In a typical example, in August 1984, he told *NME*'s David Quantick: "Look, the point is the sort of stuff we do – which is a mixture of Irish and Scottish folk, country, a bit of rockabilly – obviously, all those types of music are played in bars, y'know. It doesn't mean that everybody has to get drunk, but it's played in places where the idea is the band are whooping it up and the people are whooping it up with them... I mean, alcohol is a social drug..."

MacGowan, Stacy and O'Riordan – the three most obvious consumers of the social drug – were not about to apologise for it either, which resulted in a certain chicken-or-egg controversy. Quantick voiced it: "Is there any danger of encouraging the 'drunken Paddy' stereotype?" to which Jem sharply retorted, "Rubbish. Complete crap."

The Pogues believed that at a time when excess within bands was commonplace, the stereotype had been unfairly foisted upon them. James Fearnley: "It became really wearisome that journalists' and the public's perception of The Pogues should centre so firmly on drink. Yeah, we did drink a lot, but I don't think any more than anybody else did. It was always the first question out of a journalist's mouth."

"You'd think, 'The best way to actually scotch that – ha ha! – is not to go onstage with a full bottle of wine,' but we weren't going to stop that because that's Shane's life. We sort of became the ambassadors of alcohol: 'You want to find out about drink? Ask The Pogues.' This happened to the exclusion of lots of other considerations. We got pissed off with it. We were hoisted by our own petard. You wondered if there was something racist about it – 'Irish music, and they're all drinkers, and they're all stupid.' That bugged us a lot."

A more dangerous line of questioning was emerging in relation to MacGowan's lyrics, his literary heroes (many of whom, for instance Brendan Behan, had IRA involvement) and the traditional Irish songs that the band chose to cover. Were they a subversive political band? Were they Republicans? The unspoken part of the question was: did they secretly support the IRA?

MacGowan would later, in *A Drink With Shane MacGowan*, assert his sympathies with the historic activities of that organisation, while qualifying his support: "I wouldn't join the IRA now under any circumstances. I don't agree with killing civilians. I don't think I'd be any good in the IRA, is another reason."

Back in the Eighties - with the bombing campaign still striking fear into the heart of the mainland, inciting suspicion and hatred of Irish people and anybody thought to support Republicanism - it was an association that The Pogues could do without. Half of the band had no connection to Ireland at all, and not one member, including MacGowan, could claim to understand the intricacies of the civil war in the North, much less take sides in it. Behan's 'The Auld Triangle', sometimes offered as "evidence" of a Pogues party-political allegiance, was, they explained, a song that described the life of a prisoner almost anywhere in the world.

Finer: "I dealt with it all by saying, 'No, I'm not a Republican and I'm not a loyalist.' If pushed, I'd have said that while not supporting violent protest through bombing and stuff, I had a lot of sympathy with the Republican cause, but that doesn't make one a Republican. I still think that's the case, and I still think going round blowing people up is a really shitty thing. I wouldn't want to associate with it. That's the way all of us felt about it. In that climate then, it was probably a big problem. Things are very different now. I'm sure things haven't been solved at all, really, but we're now in an age where the IRA have finally decommissioned their weapons. We live in a very different world from one where there's an active bombing campaign going on.

"To be perceived as an IRA propaganda tool, self-appointed or otherwise, would have been a terrible thing. I mean, it would have been complete rubbish but it would have been quite a liability to life and limb. I think we were all at pains to point that out."

CHAPTER 11

Rum, Sodomy & The Clashes

In 1985, they toured and toured and toured. A string of dates in January and February brought a couple of important visitors to their shows.

One was Alex Cox, the maverick film director and writer who had come to prominence the year before with his debut, *Repo Man*. In the course of his promotional interviews for the movie – now a cult classic - he was quoted as being a fan of The Pogues.

Frank Murray wasted no time in extending the hand of friendship, and sent Cox a copy of *Red Roses For Me*. With Cox being hailed as a revolutionary talent and *Repo Man*, an intense and savage film, acclaimed as a fitting product of the Eighties punk era, Murray proposed that he might like to direct the video for 'A Pair Of Brown Eyes'.

Cox had no interest in making videos, but he found the album so uniquely exciting that he agreed to see the band playing live at the Polytechnic in his hometown of Liverpool.

"Shane and I were walking down Lime Street," says Spider, "and we saw this guy in a light-green trenchcoat with this orange spiky hair coming towards us. I said, 'That's got to be Alex Cox,' and indeed it was. He said, 'Ah, Pogues!' Later that evening Cait slammed the dressing room door in his face cos she didn't know who he was."

"It was a great show," remembers Cox. "They all stayed at the Adelphi Hotel. I stayed there too, and it was great. So I agreed to do this promo called 'A Pair Of Brown Eyes'."

Cox caught The Pogues again, at the end of January at the Mean Fiddler in Harlesden, London, and was amazed by the wild scenes they generated. The Fiddler was a real hotspot for the band and, some months earlier, the scene of a gig that made a lifelong impression on Frank Murray.

He says: "The place was really, really packed to the walls, and the crowd were singing songs off the first album. They knew the lyrics. Something clicked in my head when I saw that. People had listened to this band a lot more than I thought they had, and it was a criss-cross sort of selection of people watching it. Also, there was an intense excitement which I'd only ever witnessed before on the 2-Tone tour. Because of the skinhead thing, with that tour there was a danger. There was no danger with The Pogues. It was an exceptional excitement. The audience were really part of the show and the band gave out that vibe naturally. They were very connected to the audience."

February took the group to Scotland for the first time and back to Ireland where Murray's old pal Paul Scully ventured out to a club in Dublin – later named McGonagles - to see The Pogues. Like Cox, he was astonished by the reactions they triggered, and he was also intrigued by their audacious musical hybrid. Murray was undoubtedly pleased to catch up with Scully, but he had another reason for encouraging his interest in the band. Frank had decided it was time to relieve Darryl Hunt of his duties at the mixing desk and to take on a professional sound engineer. Since Scully had throughout his roadie days specialised in sound, he was Murray's first choice for The Pogues, and he was invited over to the UK in March for their first major headlining tour, promoting the release of 'A Pair Of Brown Eyes'.

Says Murray: "We needed someone who had some kind of affinity with Irish music to be able to sit there each night and figure out what these guys were doing. Everything at that stage was shambolic. I gave Paul a shout and asked if he was interested in giving it a try. I knew also he'd have the patience to work with the band. I reckoned Paul would be the guy for the job. As it turned out, he was."

After parting company with Skid Row in 1972, Scully had worked briefly with Murray and The Woods Band before relocating to Ireland to make more room in his life for the Divine Light Mission. In County Kildare, Paul hooked up with Donovan and then retired from the music business for a while. In 1981, he took a job with a PA company in Dublin, and had moved on to painting and decorating by the time he was invited to join The Pogues.

Scully reported for duty at Nottingham Rock City on March 6. He would become their longest-serving lieutenant, remaining with the band to this day. "He's a real diamond geezer; a complete one-off," enthuses Spider.

The tour continued through March 1985, with St Patrick's Day an undoubted highlight. Celebrating the great event at the Hammersmith Clarendon, The Pogues were supported by Elvis Costello who was announced as "The King Of Pop" and who sang, 'A Man Can Be A Drunk (But A Drunk Can't Be A Man)'.

Phil Lynott, Frank Murray's hometown buddy, had turned up at the soundcheck with a bottle of whiskey and vague promises to make a guest appearance at the gig, where he would sing, appropriately, 'Whiskey In The Jar'. In the event, he didn't show, and when the gig was over, Murray decided to take the celebrations over to Lynott's house in Richmond with various companions including Shane, Spider, Cait and Elvis.

By now Philip Chevron, who also knew Lynott, was very much a part of The Pogues' entourage, having produced the two B-sides for 'A Pair Of Brown Eyes', but he opted not to join the party that night.

Chevron admits: "I didn't feel like getting a taxi all that distance. Also, I was with friends. I didn't realise I wouldn't see Phil again. I never actually 'hung out' much with him, but saw him at gigs and, frequently, in studios, notably at Good Earth in Soho, owned by Tony Visconti. Phil was always ducking in to record something when ourselves [The Radiators] or David Bowie weren't using the place; it would not get designated a Phil Lynott track or a Thin Lizzy track until later. We viewed each other with the mixture of respect and hostility common in such circumstances, he the master, me the young pretender.

"By the time of the Clarendon gig, Phil was very much a stay-at-home, waiting to have the drugs brought in. He was already on the slide. He'd put on a fair amount of weight. He was going into that Burger Elvis kind of mode. Spider got him a St Patrick's Day tie with shamrocks on it."

"He seemed fine, actually," says Spider of Lynott. "I don't really remember very much about it. We went to the pub the next lunchtime and he poured snakebite into me and we had a gig that evening in Aldershot. He gave me his GI helmet that I insisted on wearing onstage, which was too heavy for my neck. I was banging the front of the helmet against the microphone."

Darryl Hunt looks back on this particular tour as "the start of the real thing for the group", adding: "We'd got an agent, we were headlining tours, and we got an accountant, Anthony Addis, who is now our manager. He's very fond of us and he still refers to us as 'the boys'. Frank got us involved with him, and a lot of people who proved to be very helpful to us in the future."

"I liked Frank a lot, although I didn't like his bursts of anger from time to time," remarks James Fearnley. "He was a very concerned and caring guy a lot of the time, too, with a lot to think about."

Chevron attests to the changes that took place once Murray had taken charge: "He was the only person in the London music business to take The Pogues as seriously as The Pogues took The Pogues. He was so excited at where it was going that he thought it could go as far as anybody has ever gone. That's a good start. Not even Stiff took the band seriously – 'We'll sign them up as a novelty act. They'll probably get pissed and split up after one album anyway.' And they were the only record company that would take the band on at all. But Frank made everyone sit up and take notice, including Stiff Records, and he was the only one who could do that. He banged heads together when he had to."

Frank Murray says of his relationship with Stiff: "We dealt mainly with Philip Hall [head of press]. Philip played a huge part in getting The Pogues going. He was brilliant, genius. The other person we dealt with was Simon Ryan in the art department, John Whyton in legal affairs and Alan Cowderoy. Dave Robinson was busy most of the time with Island affairs – although he was always aware of what was going on with The Pogues."

Murray and Robinson had known each other of old. Says Murray: "He managed Graham Parker & The Rumour. I gave them a gig with Thin Lizzy on the *Jailbreak* tour. He also managed a band called Clover, and I gave them an opening stint with Lizzy as well on the tour. At the time he signed Madness, I was tour managing the 2-Tone tour. Obviously we were both from Dublin, and I'd known him from that pub rock scene."

Still, this was one fellow-Dubliner with whom Frank did not get along too happily. He says: "I made sure that the band always had 100 per cent creative control of what they were doing, and I think that's a huge part of the manager's job. The actual business and the other periphery stuff I dealt with."

Murray did not encourage direct contact between the band and the record company, and this annoyed Robinson, who says he enjoyed interacting with the musicians in the way that Stiff, an informal company, had been used to.

"I encouraged Frank to be The Pogues' manager, which was a fatal mistake from some points of view," says Robinson. "Frank's idea was to (a) get between the record company and the band so he could be more powerful and (b) take Shane down the pub. Shane didn't need anybody taking him down to the pub. I resented that, at the end of the day. I got Frank the gig cos he was on his uppers. He didn't have any money or anything. He brought me Kirsty MacColl [who had a 1985 hit for Stiff with 'A New England']. He's a charming, bright bloke, but he distanced the band from the record company. I wasn't allowed to speak to Shane in those days. I had to go through Frank."

Murray retorts: "Dave called members of The Pogues at home, but they always referred him back to me. I said, 'Call the band if you wish. If you want to put anything to them, put it to them,' but there was no real reason. The only time he might have wanted to get through and talk business with

The Pogues would've been if it was to suit himself. Dave could not help getting involved with everything, and I mean this in the best possible way. He had management experience and he saw managers as a hassle. He liked bands that had weak managers so he could manipulate the acts. We didn't need any influence from Dave Robinson."

As individuals, The Pogues were perfectly friendly with Dave, although as was par for the course in those days, they also liked the colour of his money. Spider: "I always got on fine with him. A couple of times I'd borrow a tenner off him and Shane would always say, 'Why didn't you tap him for £100?' Asking him to lend you only £10 was an insult, really. Although, even then, he didn't get the tenners back directly."

The inter-band dynamics continued as they had started. Everyone was thrilled by the up-turn in The Pogues' fortunes and they, for the most part, were having a wonderful time, although MacGowan and Stacy remained a fearsome combination, Shane and Cait would row from time to time, Finer was increasingly unhappy about being constantly on the road while the arrival of his second child was getting closer, Darryl Hunt and James Fearnley were still bearing the brunt of the teasing, and Fearnley was concerned about the growing tension between himself and Shane.

"It was a struggle with Spider," remarks Fearnley. "On a lot of the early tours, we got awfully angry with Shane and Spider when they would get into this banter on stage and nobody, least of all us, could understand what they were saying. It seemed to be self-referential. Once we got going a bit, we'd review ourselves after gigs. They weren't planned reviews. They just happened because somebody was disgruntled about something, right after we'd finished, where there'd be some sort of smouldering anger about behaviour, or something that might have been building for a bit, or something had happened on stage that was just not okay behaviour-wise. And it seemed to centre at that time on Shane and Spider going at one another – which oftentimes can be entertaining but which, on stage, pretty much excluded both the audience and the rest of the band.

"It became too enclosed – 'This is our party and we don't care who else is in the room with us.' Not that we wanted to be involved. We'd rather that if it was going to happen, talking on stage, it should be directed outwards. It was so quickfire as well. I just waited for it to finish before we could play another song. I couldn't contribute to it. I didn't have the rapidity of thought that Shane and Spider had."

Fearnley also believed that he had blotted his copybook with MacGowan yet again. Having first deprived the singer of his desired flat in Mornington Crescent after the Burton Street clear-out and then replaced him as The

Pogues' guitarist in the studio, James had innocently committed another *faux pas* during an interview.

He recalls: "We were at The Cricketers at The Oval, doing a gig, and there was a round of interviews. They were shared around the dressing room, and my job was to talk to the people from *In Dublin* magazine, which is like a *Time Out*. Shane had finished his interview with whoever it was and he came in and saw me talking to a couple of Irish guys and he asked, 'What's he saying?' I got all defensive and reactive: 'I've just told these people that I think Ireland stinks.' It was a joke, but it was a joke that backfired and which lasted for quite a long time. I don't know how Shane could have believed I would say and actually mean anything like that.

"I was identified as the 'Brit' in the group for a long time, from the accent and the attitudes and a bit of the sententious outspokenness that I have. That rankled with Shane a little bit too, with a lot of cause."

Fearnley and other members of the band, including Andrew Ranken, were careful in their dealings with MacGowan. It must have felt a little like walking on eggshells.

"I know James does feel like that," agrees Spider. "You have to watch what you say, with Shane if you want to maintain a vague level of sanity. It depends very much on the mood and the circumstances. Certain things you can say to him sometimes, he's going to get the wrong end of the stick – go down some very long but blind alley.

"Sometimes Shane can be really quite obtuse, and also he'll get an idea in his head which is completely wrong and you can't shift it, no matter what evidence you may present to him. And then maybe six months later you'll hear something that indicates he knew this all along and that you're sup-posed to be the one holding the opinion he had previously held."

Of his own antics, Stacy jokes: "I was a horrible piece of work, a nasty little piece of work. Everyone else was really nice." In fact, Spider had bags of charm, which was usually enough to get him off the hook in all but his most drunken and/or annoying rampages.

'A Pair Of Brown Eyes' reached its highest chart position of Number 72 at the beginning of April 1985. It was backed with two traditional songs pro-duced by Philip Chevron – 'Whiskey You're The Devil' and, on the 12-inch format, 'Muirshin Durkin'.

Chevron had been rushed in for the sessions because Costello had gone on tour. They were done hurriedly, early in the year, on a day when most of The Pogues were reportedly hungover.

Finer comments: "I don't think they are particularly brilliant recordings. I think we just knocked them off, really. The ones I like that we did with

Philip are 'The Parting Glass' and 'A Pistol For Paddy Garcia'."The latter, an original Jem Finer instrumental, would later appear as the B-side of 'Dirty Old Town', with 'The Parting Glass', an all-band arrangement of an old song, added to the 12-inch.

Chevron, for his part, had been extremely impressed by 'A Pair Of Brown Eyes' and 'Sally MacLennane', the MacGowan songs that Costello had recorded. He says: "Those two tracks made very clear that Shane was going to be a force to be reckoned with, 'A Pair Of Brown Eyes' in particular."

It was only after the single had been released that The Pogues shot the video with Alex Cox and co-director Martin Turner.

"The Pogues were marvellous," says Cox. "They had such character faces. I'd think, 'Jem can play such and such a guy and Fearnley can look like this...' Everybody had a character they could play. Shane was the hardest one. He could only ever be himself. Everybody else had a bit of the actor in them."

"I thought Alex was an interesting and engaging character, quite eccentric, a bit nutty," says Finer. "I'd seen *Repo Man* and thought it was a really good film. When people whose work you admire want to work with you, it's a really nice thing. He was quite a laugh. Obviously, he had a very surreal take on things, and he had a weird way of talking American when he obviously wasn't. I have some reservations about things we did with him later on. Maybe I should've been a bit more suspicious about people to start with..."

In the video, says Jem, "I was an old man on the tube, and in a paper bag I had these brown eyes, which I show to a young girl." One of Cox's themes is the appearance of the eyes in unlikely places – on the end of a pool cue, on the tube train's hand grips – before they disappear into a bulldog's stomach. The passengers on the tube are blindfolded and wearing headphones, surrounded by images of Margaret Thatcher where the adverts would normally be, and the cast includes various Pogues playing police officers and border guards, Elvis Costello with a pair of chest expanders and a pantomime horse cavorting around Hampstead Heath with the band.

Cox's treatment of the song had little to do with its lyrics. Indeed, he was quoted as announcing, grandly, on set: "Neither The Pogues nor Alex Cox is interested in literal interpretation."

Rather, this was a comparison of Thatcher's Britain to a police state. It was a place of perilous military complicity with the US, aided by a population who were too plugged into Walkmans, ghetto blasters and television to notice or worry about the dangers and iniquities of the regime. In one sequence, The Pogues were seen spitting at a poster of La Thatcher, although an alternative scene was shot at the insistence of Stiff Records.

Few would have imagined that 20 years later, under a "New" Labour Government, Cox's protest would have become even more bitingly relevant.

"I did very much enjoy spitting at Mrs Thatcher," says Spider. "I think it should've been done more often. I liked that video. We were all willing to go with Alex's ideas. I was quite excited because he was a real-life film director."

The video shoot was covered by *NME*'s Don Watson, who at the same time reported several facts that would become more important in hindsight. One was that Cox was working towards a film about Sid Vicious and Nancy Spungen – although it wasn't known then that The Pogues would be contributing to the soundtrack. Another was Shane MacGowan's obsession with Sergio Leone's complex and masterful 1984 gangster movie, *Once Upon A Time In America*. This would become required viewing for The Pogues, and it would bring influence to bear upon them both professionally and personally. It's said that Spider could at one time recite the entire script. Perhaps he still can.

Watson's final revelation was that Shane MacGowan was on medication for alcohol abuse. He hadn't stopped drinking, although he had cut out spirits.

"Of course my state of health worries me," he confessed to Watson. "I realise now that I just can't go on drinking and drinking and never eating. I know my body isn't going to take it. It worries me, but I'm taking all the measures that I possibly can."

MacGowan also insisted: "I'm not knocking drugs at all – drugs heighten your awareness of things."

The pursuit of heightened awareness was seemingly at the heart of MacGowan's gargantuan appetite for drink and drugs, and he was quite correct: these things do hold a key to the magic kingdom, a place of sweeping emotional connection and creativity, although equally they can slam shut the gate at the point of over-indulgence. Writers, poets, musicians, artists – many of the world's most revered talents have fed their muse in one way or another over hundreds and thousands of years. It wasn't until later that Shane's excesses began to obscure rather than illuminate his way forward with The Pogues.

Not everyone was thrilled by Cox's video. Darryl Hunt remembers: "The band got quite a bit of criticism cos they'd gone out of that London cowpunk thing. After the 'Brown Eyes' video, some kid walked past us and said, 'So you've sold out, have you?' The Pogues doing a 'proper video' meant they'd 'left the roots'.

"But things progress or move you away. Anything that does that well is going to go out of your control and you have to let it go. When you think you can control everything, you're not in touch with reality. The slings and arrows of outrageous fortune cannot harm you as much as when you think you're in control of your life. It's got to be a little bit of a, 'What's around the corner I don't know.'"

The Pogues had no sooner finished the March tour than they were packing their bags again, for their first trip to Europe in mid-April.

It was at this point that Jem Finer would finally take some paternity leave, to be temporarily replaced on banjo by Philip Chevron. Finer's objections to back-to-back touring on family grounds were already well known, but he had also become dismayed by the way in which it disrupted the band's established routines of writing, rehearsing and recording. Suddenly, The Pogues were having to work up new songs on the road – not that that was always a bad thing – or in the studio, on the spot. And the sessions for their second album, *Rum Sodomy & The Lash*, had to be fitted in piecemeal around their live commitments through the first half of 1985. In fits and starts, the band recorded the album in Elephant Studios with Nick Robbins and Paul Scully engineering.

"This bloody on-the-road thing," sighs Jem. "It changed the whole creative process. Once you're stuck on this wheel where you go on tour before you make your new record, it changes the opportunities for rehearsing. We'd been used to meeting up once or twice a week and knocking things around."

By now, The Pogues were so used to Elvis Costello being around that they regarded him simply as one of the gang and not some sort of superstar producer.

Spider sums up the general attitude: "I wasn't that impressed, like it was a really huge, big deal."

"I think it was helpful that he was a musician and he was able to suggest things that the first producer [Stan Brennan], who wasn't a musician, wasn't capable of," ventures Andrew Ranken. "I like the sounds Elvis got on things."

Philip Chevron adds, "At this stage, Elvis and Cait were inseparable. Certainly none of the band were particularly enamoured of Elvis, because he'd become too familiar for that. He was 'Uncle Brian'. Cait had started calling him Brian, after Brian [the snail] in *The Magic Roundabout*. Then it became slightly scornful. The Pogues could be a cruel bunch if they thought there was fun to be had. So Elvis was besotted with Cait. What was going to happen? How was this going to affect them? All they saw was this lovesick puppy who was now asking to produce their record. It was far from, 'The great Elvis Costello comes down from Mount Olympus to produce The Pogues.'"

And another thing, says Chevron: "Elvis's view of the band wasn't always Shane's view."

"*Rum Sodomy & The Lash* is a great album," declares MacGowan, "but I was unhappy about what he [Elvis] was doing in the studio. We decided we couldn't work together." Shane complained bitterly about Costello's protracted efforts to nail the vocals, with the many takes that this entailed; he much preferred the rough-and-ready approach.

"Shane's got different views about it than I have," says Andrew. "Having to sing in the studio is quite different to playing an instrument where it's normal to do things over and over again. I've ended up doing hundreds of takes of things and, yeah, it does get really irritating sometimes cos you end up not being able to tell whether one's any better than another. But I don't remember it being a problem for me personally."

Chevron: "It's a complaint Shane would have to have levelled at every other producer, but somehow didn't. He just decided to be awkward about it, I think.

"Elvis wanted to capture the spirit of the band, to keep it as raw as he could. Shane was deeply suspicious of all producers and of Elvis's methods. It was easier for me to understand; I knew what it was like to be a producer. Shane tended to interpret it as, 'Elvis doesn't see how big a vision we have here. He thinks we're just this pub band.' Now that was deeply unfair to Elvis, because he would not have been wasting his time with the band if he thought that was what they were. Shane's head was full of orchestras and Frank Sinatra ballads. Elvis hadn't made that leap of faith. It tended to pull against all Shane's instincts.

"Partly, that was Shane's misunderstanding of what record producing was or could be. Once he's made up his mind about you, that's his mind made up for life. It's maddening. He decides what he thinks of a person right from the outset and sticks with it. I know a lot of people who have been very unfairly judged by him."

"Elvis made many suggestions for the arrangements," adds Darryl Hunt. "It was his idea to change the key in 'Dirty Old Town' in the middle break, where it was positive. He had quite a lot of musical input."

It was Costello's musical input that sometimes needled James Fearnley, who had been hoping to collaborate fully on the overdubs.

"I was a big fan of Elvis from way back in the Nashville Rooms when he had his residency there," explains Fearnley. "There was this nerdy guy in a suit with glasses and attitude, with this vein bulging on his forehead. Then to get him in the studio with us was really exciting. The best memories were

Elvis's pixie-ish presence on the other side of the mixing desk with his face turned towards us. He used to bring in a pomelo – a fruit that rhymes with his last name – which is a grapefruit with a very thick skin. But as for the recording – there were some difficulties.

"Elvis was a musician and if he had something in his head, a country-style guitar or a lap steel, he would just go and do it. I'd think, 'Jesus Christ, you're not in the band – I am.' He said, 'All right, if you have the idea, you go and do it. I've had the idea and I'm going to go and do it.' This was hard to take. It happened often enough for me to get all ornery about it, wishing I'd thought of that [whatever it was]. I used to so enjoy doing overdubs. There was probably some consulting, but often enough, Elvis just got up and did it.

"Then, on the other hand, when we recorded 'Brown Eyes', me and Elvis played mandolin in Greek style, in harmony and stuff, and that was such a thrill to me to play trilling mandolin, and looking at one another. Oh God, that was brilliant. 'Wild Cats Of Kilkenny' was fun to do. 'The Gentleman Soldier' was great, because I didn't have much idea what to play on accordion for that and Elvis said, 'Go home and think about what you're going to do.' So I came in with the Russian national anthem the next day and he said, 'That's all right.' It was nice to be given homework, singling you out and saying, 'You can make this happen.'

"'Jesse James' was, I think, the only time I've ever done backing vocals on a Pogues song. I volunteered. I knew what to do – strained, high-pitched harmony – but Elvis came with me and drowned me out. I was so pissed off. I knew how to make it sound right, but so did he, and his voice was so much more identifiable and louder than mine. That was a moment that was snatched away from me.

"Then, when Dick [Cuthell, horn player] came in to play on 'And The Band Played Waltzing Matilda', that pissed me off because it was always an accordion solo. It was always very plaintive and simple and direct. To have the horn on it never sat right with me. That was Elvis's idea. I'm sure Dick Cuthell's a nice guy, but I can't bear to hear him play it on the album even now."

The Pogues were lucky that they had some great songs already in the bank, both originals and covers. 'The Old Main Drag' pre-dated even the first album. 'And The Band Played Waltzing Matilda' was another early favourite. 'Navigator', 'Jesse James' [sung by Spider] and 'Billy's Bones' had all been around for a while.

"Some things evolved as we were touring," says Finer, giving as an example The Pogues' definitive reading of 'Dirty Old Town' – written in 1956 by Kirsty's father Ewan MacColl. "We'd always played it for a laugh. I can remember James playing it in Sheffield in a dressing room with the mandolin, and I was playing along on the banjo, and it seemed like a lovely way to do it.

"There were other songs that Shane had written but never had a chance to show us, so we just learnt them in the studio. 'The Gentleman Soldier' [a traditional song] we might have just done for a laugh there and then."

Finer had also started collaborating more fully with MacGowan. He says: "By then I'd thought, 'Well, if I'm going to write these little instrumental bits to fit into Shane's songs, I might as well write instrumentals.' I wrote one that fitted with something Shane had, that started with a Pink Floyd-ish bassline." The result was 'Wild Cats Of Kilkenny'.

"There are some really good songs on *Rum Sodomy & The Lash*," comments Spider. "'The Sickbed Of Cuchulainn' – I remember the first time I heard that. I hadn't been at the session the day they laid down the rough version of it. I heard it in Sweden in the back of a van. I thought, 'Fuck! This sounds really, really good.'

"Shane was getting into gear as a songwriter. Everything seemed to be accelerating. One of the reasons I thought we were such a good band and was pleased to be in The Pogues was the strength of his songwriting. If he was here, he'd immediately start saying, 'I didn't write "Misty Morning, Albert Bridge"...', full steam ahead and 'everybody else did everything', which is a complete sea change from what he said in Victoria's book [*A Drink With Shane MacGowan*]. But he definitely was writing really, really good stuff."

'The Sickbed Of Cuchulainn' is a gripping opener for the album, its darkly troubling, slow passages all the more forbidding for their proximity to the bounding accordion, whistle and banjo ringing out their madly addictive tunes and dances. Taking its name from that of an Irish mythological superhero, this is the song of a man on his deathbed flashing back through a life lived to the max, one in which his Catholicism never stood a chance against the demon alcohol, its joys and its rather more unfortunate consequences: *"They took you up to midnight mass and left you in the lurch/So you dropped a button in the plate and spewed up in the church..."*

The 'Sickbed' still reminds Philip Chevron of an old feud with Philip Lynott: "When I expressed reservations about his all-things-Irish-are-brilliant-and-lend-themselves-to-lame-puns song 'Black Rose', on the grounds that it failed to convey any of the complexity or paradoxes of being Irish, Phil might have argued, with some merit, that as he was himself the living embodiment of a complex, paradoxical Irishman, he had no need to elaborate further, but instead he chose to lay into 'writers like you who always want to slag off Ireland and expect me to be slagging off Ireland too'.

"I write about Ireland more in sorrow than in anger, and Shane's love for the oppressor, England, expressed in so many of his songs, comes from a similar place. And while Shane tends to err in favour of the Irish – Boyzone and Westlife are the 'best' boybands, Foster & Allen are 'brilliant' etc – he is not above a little troublemaking. Frank Murray, enthusing to me about a new song of Shane's he had just heard in 1985, described it to me as 'Shane's "Faithful Departed" [Chevron's Radiators classic]'. The song was 'The Sickbed Of Cuchulainn'."

Also outstanding is the traditional arrangement of 'I'm A Man You Don't Meet Every Day', a ballad whose ownership is claimed by both the Irish and the Scots. The story of a wealthy, philanthropic land-owner, it's believed to have originated in Ireland before being edited and re-written for adoption by Scotland. Whatever its beginnings, The Pogues' superb twist was to have Cait O'Riordan supply a breathy lead vocal, so plaintive that it queries the apparent generosity and bonhomie of the central character, Jock Stewart. Perhaps his shooting of his own dog was not a mercy killing...

"I think it's a really brilliant album," says Jem Finer. "And it's pretty good after all these years to still think so. I could lose 'Jesse James', for example, but that's just being pernickety. Elvis captured the vitality of the band. He did a good job."

"I found Elvis's production just a little flat although it wasn't terrible," counters Dave Robinson. "Anyway, the songs were so good. 'A Pair Of Brown Eyes', 'Sickbed'... I enjoyed all these."

Rum Sodomy & The Lash would crash into the Top 20 when it was released at the end of the summer.

Jem's second daughter, Kitty, was due any day, and so he opted out of the European tour that started in April 1985. Finer was temporarily replaced on banjo by Philip Chevron, who then decided that he didn't want to leave the band. Luck was on Philip's side: before long he was able to join The Pogues by switching full-time to guitar.

Chevron recalls the fateful conversation with his and their manager, Frank Murray: "We were talking about The Pogues and Frank said, 'We've got some dates coming up in Germany and Scandinavia, but we're going to need a banjo player cos Jem has to take some time off.' I just heard myself saying, 'I'll do it.' I convinced myself that I could, although I'd never picked up a banjo in my life." Murray took the idea to The Pogues, who were agreeable.

"By this stage I was getting cold feet," confesses Philip. "I was thinking, 'How does a banjo go?' I've always been able to get a noise out of an instrument, so I had a try and I thought, 'Okay, I can do that,' not with the technique of Jem, and I couldn't do all that finger-picking stuff, but I knew where the notes and chords were and how to get an approximation that would do in his stead. I did one day's rehearsal with them. Then we went to Germany."

Jem flew out for the first show in Munich, at the Alabamahalle, because it was being filmed for German television and the band didn't want to take any risks with an inexperienced banjo player. The gig was a wild success, but its memory would be overshadowed by the other things that happened in Munich.

There was a convivial afternoon in a café or restaurant somewhere in the town, with Murray and The Pogues ordering rounds of drinks and chatting animatedly about their most recent recordings. And it was during this conversation that Andrew Ranken uttered the phrase that gave them their album title: *Rum Sodomy & The Lash*.

He explains: "It was a quote from Winston Churchill. I think it was his description of the British Navy. I'm pretty sure that we'd been talking about a nautical theme before I came up with the idea. I must've been reading George Melly's book at the time – *Rum, Bum And Concertina* - which is a variation of the same quote. I didn't expect anyone to agree to it."

"It cracked me up," says Murray. However, an extraordinary suggestion made by Frank around the same table would be met with rather less hilarity. He advised The Pogues that they should expand their line-up. The new member would be someone they'd never met, and he would be Murray's old friend, the accomplished Irish musician Terry Woods.

"I was afraid that the band were going to get stuck in a rut," explains Frank. "They'd become known for speeding through their songs, amphetamine-laced, and there comes a time when you have to play, really. And I needed a player in the band that could anchor it. I knew one day the critics were going to say, 'Oh, that's great, but can they play?' I thought Terry would be a good anchor. I knew his style of playing and his attitude towards music. He wouldn't be put out by the treatment that the music was getting, really being ripped apart and thrown up in the air, and it needed to be."

The Pogues were puzzled if not outraged.

Says Finer: "I wondered where Frank was coming from. We weren't a traditional Irish band. We were from London and, to a large extent, we had reinvented a way of playing Irish folk songs, but we also had a very distinctive style that was going in different directions too, absorbing all manner of influences. Terry was a kind of rebel in the context of Irish folk music, and brilliant. I loved his Sweeney's Men album that I had, but I didn't see why we needed to have someone else in our band.

"Frank seemed to think, 'It will give you this sophistication and he'll bring all this experience of how to play this music.' Maybe he thought it would give us some credibility in Ireland, I don't know. I thought, 'That's a fucking dumb idea. We don't fucking need that. We've invented our own way of playing. We don't need anyone coming in to show us how to play it.' So this idea was mooted, and then it disappeared, and I can remember thinking, 'I'm glad everyone's stopped talking about this Terry Woods guy.' I feel a bit bad talking like this about Terry. He's someone I count as a very dear friend, but at the time I'd never met him. Anyway, it wasn't talked about for a while. And eventually it was again."

Much later that night, Jem and Andrew were rather the worse for wear. It had been a long day.

"It was the first time we'd been to Germany," says Finer, "and I think it was the first time we'd played abroad, so it would've been doubly exciting. More than anything, I was excited about my imminent new child. I used to share a room with Andrew at that point. I can only really remember that at some stage of the evening we were in a restaurant trying to order a cab to take us back to the hotel, which mystified all the waiters. We were actually in the hotel we were trying to order a taxi to."

The next day, Finer went home, no doubt hungover, leaving Philip Chevron to his tour of duty with The Pogues. Everything was changing, and things would seem worse before they got better.

CHAPTER 12

'That's Poguetry For You'

Chevron's first shows with the band were nothing if not eventful. He made his debut in Stuttgart on the second night of the tour: "It was a great gig, but I wasn't sure about my own performance. I thought it was terrible - 'I've let them down! I'll have to go home!' I discovered afterwards they thought it was great. I suppose I was being over-critical, but I was disappointed that it wasn't what I'd hoped to do. Nobody was in the mood for being sympathetic, so I thought, 'Okay, fine, now I can enjoy this.' One thing I did playing Jem's banjo was to move around with it. The Pogues had always been very stationary. I brought a sense of edginess and theatricality. Much to my surprise, other people started to pick up on it, James in particular – he now does all that. It adds to the showbiz sense of it. It picks it up another gear."

James Fearnley confirms, "The showing off that I do onstage is all to do with Philip. He inspired me. It was nicely competitive." Certainly, an accordion is a much weightier instrument to brandish than a banjo or a guitar. "It kept me fit," explains Fearnley. "When I was a kid I had a book about judo and, in judo, you use your opponent's weight to vanquish them. I did that with the accordion. You send it on a path and then you just get out of the way. That's where my fitness – and also my curvature of the spine – comes from. I also wore off all the hair on the outside of my thigh, and there was a time after playing shows when I did not have the strength in my fingers to hold anything, even a tin of beer, in my left hand. A doctor gave me hormonal cream that you get from a pig's gland to rub into the muscle and he recommended swimming. The instrument I had at the time was huge, easily 40 pounds of accordion. I play a lighter one now." And he still swings it madly as he jumps around, dashes out to the front of the stage and crashes to his knees. He's ruined dozens of good suits.

The band were travelling round Germany in a minibus driven by Darryl Hunt, arriving in Berlin for their gig at The Loft on April 20 – Adolf Hitler's birthday. No surprises, then, that their audience included a minority of neo-Nazi skinheads who were out to celebrate their hero's memory by disrupting The Pogues' performance with chants and slogans.

"Myself and Cait took it upon ourselves to deal with it," says Chevron. "She lashed out at a couple of them with her bass. I actually stopped the gig and changed the running order – 'In honour of The Fuhrer's birthday, we'd like to play this anti-war song, "And The Band Played Waltzing Matilda"'. It took everybody by surprise, including me, having only been in the band for a week. But you need to tell the audiences in Germany who you are. If you don't, they think they're entitled to turn up at a Pogues gig and honour The Fuhrer."

"That was a nice gig to get away from," remembers Andrew Ranken. "I was so pleased to get back to the hotel I just ran into my room, took a running jump on to the bed and the bed collapsed. I landed on the floor in a heap of matchwood."

The presence of racist skinheads at their concerts was something the band most often ran into in Germany and France, but occasionally closer to home. Ranken says: "We got tear-gassed by the National Front in Swansea once. The gig was packed, and I think we'd heard there were some skinheads in the place, which wasn't anything new. We did occasionally hear a bit of 'sieg heiling'. But this time, they let this stuff off and suddenly everybody started crying, including us. They got chucked out, although nobody else had to be evacuated. We just ploughed on in tears."

The Pogues returned from Germany to play a "Jobs For Youth" benefit concert for the GLC at the Dominion Theatre with folk guitarist Richard Thompson, headlining, and the Boothill Foot-Tappers.

"They blew Richard Thompson offstage," says Dee O'Mahony, recalling a performance that resulted in a stage invasion and was described by the *Daily Mirror* as a "total riot".

Meanwhile, Kitty Finer's unwillingness to observe her estimated time of arrival meant that Jem and Marcia were still parents-in-waiting, and Philip Chevron again stood in as a hired hand when The Pogues set off for their next foreign trip, to Scandinavia. The journey involved two nights on a Finnjet ferry sailing from a port near Lubeck in Germany to Finland.

"The ferry made the Holyhead boat [to Ireland] look like a floating convent," declares Spider, who took advantage of the bar immediately after boarding.

"I got really, really drunk," he says. "I was nearly put in the brig, and it was only Cait's intervention that saved me. I remember coming round, giving her a whole mouthful and her looking really upset, saying, 'I just kept you out of jail.' I don't know why I did that. I'm not particularly proud of it."

The next night's victim was Philip Chevron who, in true Scandinavian fashion, embarked on a schnapps binge with James Fearnley. It started out as a friendly drink, a bonding, getting-to-know-you session, and ended in a Helsinki hospital.

Says Fearnley: "Philip and I sat up with a bottle of schnapps that I had, in this viewing observatory. Philip talked about his childhood and his interest in musicals and about Agnes Bernelle, everything about his life, and I did the same. We were drinking and looking out at the dark of the sea and the little lights of Latvia and Estonia. It was quite a cementing experience."

"I was entering into the spirit of being a drinking Pogue more than was good for me," concedes Chevron. "And it had a bad effect on the ulcer I'd had since I was 11. I had a very painful stomach for my teenage years and much of my adulthood. It was a nightmare at times. It renders you incapable of concentrating on anything else. They used to think you had to whip ulcers out. My dad had his taken out and it had a bad effect on his general health. When they announced they were taking his boy's out, he said, 'No.' I'm so grateful for that, because as recently as 12 years ago, they found out by accident that an ulcer can be cured with antibiotics, as mine eventually was. At one stage, they invented this very chalky substance and pills that sort of helped. The most effective anti-ulcer pill was later re-marketed as an indigestion tablet, and it's widely available over the counter.

"On this ferry, my ulcer got in such a bad state that I was panicking. Only once before had I felt as bad as that. I didn't know how far or near to shore I was. 'I could die! They'll have to fuck me overboard!' I probably did think I was dying and Spider probably did believe me."

Spider: "Philip got really, really ill. James was sharing a cabin with him. He went and got Andrew, who came and got me and Shane. Philip was just lying in bed looking awful, whiter than white, whimpering faintly. Me and James stayed with him, and Shane and Andrew went off to find help. They ended up walking on to the bridge and completely freaking out the captain."

"Philip made it through the night," continues James. "He looked the next day like someone had attached a hose to him and sucked everything out of his body. His skin was so tight to his skull, and his eyes were closed, and he was as pale as anything. We drove the minibus off the ship when we docked, and every bump we went over, you heard Philip go 'Uuuuuhhhh!' He was in such pain. I felt a little bit conflicted about staying up with him all night pouring schnapps down his throat. It was as if I'd tried to kill him off before the tour had really started."

Chevron concludes the tale: "I was taken to hospital in Helsinki. They kept me on a trolley for a couple of days giving me fluids and milky substances. I had a couple of days' rest and I was okay. I only missed one gig. I still had a remnant of the pain through all that tour, but it was manageable. All the same, it went down as 'Chevron's tour from hell', but that's Poguetry for you. Everybody has a different version of what happened.

"Shane had had a pretty hairy experience in Berlin on the German tour. He ended up in hospital being patched up for something or other. [MacGowan claimed, rather unconvincingly, to have fallen over.] These things just become battle scars. All you know is they inconvenienced you slightly at the time. My problems only really began much later on in that they were constantly debilitating rather than something which just put me off the map for a couple of days."

Two things occurred simultaneously. Despite his dramatic illness on the Finnjet ferry, Chevron developed a burning desire to stay in The Pogues, even though Jem would soon be returning. And MacGowan and Stacy, in one of their drinking sessions, decided they wanted to keep him.

Says Spider: "It seemed to work really well with Philip, so Shane and I went to Frank and demanded that he should join the band permanently as the guitarist. A lot of it was down to the fact that Shane didn't want to keep playing guitar, and that *was* actually his idea no matter what he may have said since."

MacGowan, while subsequently admitting that he found it difficult to sing and play rhythm guitar onstage at the same time, has certainly groused about being "sacked" as the guitarist. Today, he says simply of Philip's appointment: "It wasn't a big problem."

Frank Murray adds: "You've got to be on the button if you're playing rhythm guitar. Shane was in various stages of sobriety and unsobriety and I suggested to him that he should give up the guitar and he said yes at that time, cos it suited him. But he would often feel later on, 'I should be playing guitar again.' I don't think anybody ever stopped him playing guitar again, although I didn't encourage him."

When the band returned from Finland, Sweden and Norway (where the subject of Terry Woods had arisen again), Chevron found himself at a crossroads, losing both his home and his job at Rock On. He moved from the Camden Town flat he'd rented for two years into temporary accommodation with Roger Armstrong. From there he found a home in Kennington with Phil Gaston and Dee, staying with them for a couple of years until they'd finally saved up enough cash to go travelling.

Marcia gave birth to Kitty on May 14, 1985 and Jem was determined to spend as much time as possible with his wife and newly expanded family. The Pogues meanwhile invited Chevron to join them for a number of summer festivals.

He says: "I went back to Rock On and I'd worked out a schedule. I presented Ted Carroll with a diary saying when I was going to be available to work in the shop and when I wasn't. The arrangement we'd always had was that I could take time off to work in music, but this was taking the piss. Ted read through it, tore it up and said, 'You're fired.' He said it in such a way we both knew he was making the right decision. He cut me loose from my safety blanket. I had still been earning a wage at Rock On, but it certainly wasn't guaranteed in The Pogues. They were paying me as a session man at that stage."

This coincided with the band's decision to recruit Chevron as a full-time member: the very thing he most desired.

"What happened, in a way, was that Philip had found his family," observes Murray.

"To an extent Frank is right," responds Chevron. "It's a slightly glib way of putting it. I had found a group of people to whom I felt instinctively I belonged for the first time in my life. All gay men seek their family because they don't automatically marry into one. As a general rule, the gay people I know have adopted a group of people who essentially function in the same way as a family. In my case it almost inevitably happened to be in a band. To find a bunch of people who I was sharing music with and sharing my life with, who I really liked for all their foibles *et cetera*, did seem to be a happy place to be. What I had to do over a period of time was to learn that it wasn't the healthiest place. I needed to strike out and be independent of them as well, which I did eventually do."

Chevron's first months as The Pogues' guitarist were in many ways confusing. No one had explained the permanence of the post to him – he was simply offered a series of gigs - and the continuing debate about Terry Woods' possible entry into the group filled him with uncertainty: "I wasn't sure whether Terry being drafted in was going to knock me out of the band – that I was going to fulfil my obligations and then have to leave. It just never got discussed.

"Frank didn't want me to be in The Pogues. He felt I should have continued with being a producer, and I had all these ideas for a solo album. There may also be the fact that Frank, in a business sense, felt that he'd lost a client. But I had ended up in a situation that suited me very well."

At the same time, Chevron had to work his way through the "new boy" period. He says: "It was like being in *Big Brother*, where they bring in somebody new in the third week. It's not nice being that person. It positions you differently in the chemistry. I had issues with that for a while, getting to know people from scratch, how you connect with them, what your contribution is, and it's a more difficult thing to do when at the same time you're on the up and you've got chart albums for the first time in your life and you're touring and you're under all this additional pressure and surrounded by all these stimulating people. It took me a long time to find and assert my position in the band.

"In any band, nobody will invite you to assert yourself. Because I had problems with alcoholism bound to self-esteem problems, I was not naturally inclined to give myself the position I necessarily deserved. It's a long, elaborate growing-up process. One of the beautiful things is that now we're all grown up, we know our shortcomings and foibles and can laugh at how we were with each other in the past."

The rest of The Pogues were delighted to have Chevron aboard. While they had enjoyed the rough, wild energy of MacGowan's acoustic guitar strokes, Chevron brought a certain precision that Andrew Ranken, for one, appreciated.

"Musically, it freed up Shane in terms of singing, and as much as I like Shane's playing, Philip was a bit more sophisticated – although he was still also capable of playing quite simply and powerfully," states Andrew. "It started to feel that there was proper fusion happening with the basic drums and rhythm guitar, whereas before it had always been a bit haphazard and messy.

"There was a feeling at the time that The Pogues was becoming quite a family, and we were all getting on with each other extremely well. We were having an enormous amount of fun together – and the bigger the family, the more fun it was."

Darryl Hunt adds: "The group was very strong before, but when Philip joined, it did make the rhythm sit better. It was tighter, more solid. He brought a more focused front line vocally, and he brought a few songs like 'Thousands Are Sailing'."

Shane MacGowan received Chevron in an equally friendly manner. Says Philip: "Shane loved the idea that I was in the band. He welcomed that hugely. He was actively giving up playing the guitar. Shane accepted the fact that, by accident, he'd become the frontman when it was always going to be Spider, originally. But when all the attention focused on him, especially around the time of *Rum Sodomy & The Lash*, he had to stand in front and be the lead singer and focal point. His act of rebellion was, 'I'm not going to play the guitar, then.' That only became an issue in retrospect when he thought, 'I should've been playing the guitar.' Under the influence of 20 tabs of acid, some cunt could've said to him in an airport somewhere, 'Isn't it a shame you gave up the guitar?'

"Occasionally a guitar will appear with Shane, and it only signifies that he's doing some writing when he's on the road. It's something that he's picked up in a junk shop, in a plastic bag. He never says, 'I think I'll play

164

guitar on this song.' It never happens. It's not something he's discussed in 15 years. He knows damn well the contribution I've made to the band, but once he establishes something in his head, it stays that way. In his mind he'll always be the right person to play guitar with The Pogues."

Unexpectedly, the one band member who experienced some problems with the new guitarist was Chevron's schnapps-buddy and room-mate James Fearnley.

"I really liked Philip although there was a certain amount of competition with him as well," says Fearnley. "For all that time I'd been The Maestro and then in comes Philip. I remember doing a rehearsal at Nomis studios and there was a blackboard on the wall. And here's Philip figuring out the chords. I thought, 'What the fuck do *I* do?' When it came to recording, sometimes I wanted to be in there doing the overdubs before Philip. I was shouldering my way into some position and shouldering him out of the way. I did feel my position was being usurped. It all sounds really petty now, and I should've known better. There's a lack of self-awareness about it that's kind of alarming. I think probably I was aware of what I was doing but did it anyway. Philip might have put it together. But nothing was ever said as far as I remember.

"Then Philip plays the guitar on all the records, and a good guitar player he is. I think one of the things that bugged me about Philip at the start was that he didn't play the guitar like me. It annoyed me that he didn't hold the pick the way I did, which is really stupid. I think things got sorted out just by getting on with it, moving on, I suppose. Something else happens for you to worry about."

There were further twists in Chevron's friendship with Fearnley.

"I took an instant shine to James," declares Philip. "I just loved James. I actually fell in love with James, which was awkward. That complicated matters for a while. The Pogues are wonderful, fascinating, lovely people. It's hard not to fall in love with them, which is complicated if you're male and homosexual in a heterosexual band. It's the sort of thing you might have to look out for if you were the only girl in the band. It caused me pain from time to time because, obviously, nothing was going to come of it.

"James dealt with it in the most gentlemanly and human and sophisticated way possible. He was a sweetheart. There must have been times when I was placing emotional demands on him which he was far from capable of. All men love being adored. There isn't a man on earth who isn't flattered by the notion that somebody's in love with them. But all you can do is be very good at dealing with it, or not very good.

"In a situation like that, you're open to emotional outbursts and traumas, at your most vulnerable. The other person has to be rather good to deal with that and not throw a complete wobbler and tell you to fuck off. And they wouldn't, because they're human beings. I think people understood that alcohol increased the likelihood of an emotional outburst."

Fearnley was surprised to discover that Philip was in love with him, and he decided that this should remain their own business and nobody else's.

Says James: "It only concerned me and Philip and how I dealt with somebody who's a homosexual being in love with me, not wanting to lead him on or give him any hope where there was none. I was trying to be very, very decent with him. We were sharing rooms, and I'd comfort him when he got into the extremes of pain, because he was in a lot of pain about it, and I'd chivvy him along a little bit – 'It's time to go to sleep now and forget about all this.'

"There would be like lovers' tiffs between me and Philip. He seemed to be so dogged with me, like my shadow for a lot of the time, and it came to a head when we were in New York. I was at my wits' end what to do. I didn't want to hurt Philip, but it had to stop because it was doing neither of us any good. So I told Frank Murray about it in a club one night."

Murray comments: "James was not going to turn. I tried to talk to Philip and I had to say the cruellest thing to him – 'You can't share a room with James any more because it's not going to work.' I think everybody handled it in a very sensitive way."

"It seemed to dissipate after that," concludes Fearnley. "It's really weird how things happen without you realising that they've happened, and then they're all over without you realising they're all over."

None of the other Pogues knew about any of this until it was history.

Spider: "I have a photo image of the particular part of Paris we were staying in when I was told about it. I wasn't altogether surprised. If you're going to fall in love with someone, you could do a lot worse than James Fearnley."

"Yeah, it's true we took the piss out of Elvis Costello," admits Shane MacGowan.

By now, Costello had become a regular member of the touring party, and his status in the outside world cut no ice with The Pogues. He was subjected to the same merciless ribbing as everybody else in the entourage and sometimes to the "special" treatment previously doled out to Darryl and James.

"He took the piss out of himself," explains MacGowan, adding that, "At the time, he was the kind of guy you'd just take the piss out of. We all used to take the piss out of each other and everything else. He came on tour with us. This is after we'd supported him and, like, I never had anything against him being there. It wasn't any problem – I like taking my girlfriend on the road with me. I didn't realise it would lead to Cait leaving the band. If we'd stopped him coming round with her, she would have left the band quicker."

Jem Finer: "When you've got a bunch of people living together in such close proximity in a little van and in shared rooms in hotels, there's no way you could ever get your own space. It seems to be a cruel trait of human beings that they find things to have a laugh at and I guess it probably became Cait and Elvis instead of Darryl and James.

"There were things about Cait and Elvis that made one want to take the piss. They wore the same sort of clothes and they were always reading hard-back books, and the rest of us couldn't afford hardback books. There was probably other things. Some couples get very symbiotic. Well, they certainly did. If you've got a group of people travelling round together and someone is always off with their partner enjoying a symbiotic relationship, they wouldn't be spending so much time with the other people. That was her choice."

Frank Murray could sense trouble brewing, although it wouldn't come to a head for some time yet. "The romance between Elvis and Cait blossomed, and I knew it would lead to Cait leaving the group," he declares. "Elvis and Cait would sit sometimes in the back of the bus reading their books. And if we finished a tour somewhere in northern Germany, we would have a long trip back home. Elvis would go, 'Fuck that, I'm getting on a plane,' and him and Cait would fly back. I'd do the same myself.

"Shane now and again would feel needled by Elvis for some reason, I don't know why, and Shane and Spider were quite a dynamic duo at the time. They would often make fun of Elvis, but they did it in front of him. Shane used to do imitations of Elvis singing songs. I always thought it was just good fun. I can't see any reason why anyone would be upset."

But Costello was starting to feel the heat, although he tried to shrug it off and explain it as a by-product of the band's particular genius.

Graeme Thomson, in his Costello biography *Complicated Shadows*, notes that The Pogues' sense of humour "became increasingly cruel and crude as Elvis's relationship with Cait developed and deepened". Elvis himself would tell *NME*, in March 1986, that, "Groups like The Pogues, groups that are in a class of their own, can be very cruel. When I'm about, the cruelty just transfers to me."

Thompson ventures, further, that the ridicule only succeeded in bringing Elvis and Cait closer together. Their touchy-feely behaviour, their constant smooching, may at times have been embarrassing for the other members of the band, particularly when they were trying to work in the studio. But there can be no doubt that Costello found in O'Riordan a partner who refreshed and inspired him, personally and musically.

"It was a bit like John and Yoko for a while," says Andrew Ranken. "They were like a law on to themselves. And then she just started drifting away and wanting to be with him all the time and not with us. I thought we had a lot of laughs with Elvis. We used to take the piss out of everybody, including ourselves, and I think most people realised that was the way we were and that, on the whole, it was pretty superficial. I'm sorry that Elvis felt uncomfortable about it."

Spider adds: "Quite honestly, I always got the impression Elvis could take it. We were only joking. Probably. Some of us might have been joking a little bit less than others, ie Shane, but that would've been softened or diluted by those of us who were, in fact, only joking. It didn't seem to deter Elvis from turning up. The way they were did get a bit annoying sometimes, because it was taking her away from the rest of us, but until she went away permanently, I didn't know what the problem was.

"I remember once we were in Austria and we went to Salzburg and Elvis and Cait went over the border to Switzerland for lunch or something like that, and that got up people's noses. I'm one of the people whose noses it got up. I don't know why. It was a really petty sort of thing. Maybe it was because they could. Maybe because he had money. Maybe it was because there was a sub-conscious realisation that this could lead to a permanent split. But again, it was part of the piss-taking as well."

Philip Chevron reasons that the introduction of any strong personality into an existing group of equally strong individuals can't help but affect the chemistry.

He explains: "The fact that it was Elvis Costello lends an extra dimension to it because it's somebody who's also a colleague or collaborator. When someone's sitting there being all lovey-dovey, it impinges on your gang mentality or your solidarity. It makes people uneasy, despite their intellectual reasoning on it.

"You're never allowed to get above your station if you're around The Pogues. It was, 'Don't lose the run of yourself,' as my granny used to say. We were all aware that Elvis sniffed this rarefied atmosphere in tour buses and airports and The Pogues weren't interested in accommodating that. If you were going to be hanging round with The Pogues, you got in the van. Elvis needed no instruction in how to be at ease with The Pogues any more than I did. Essentially, he became part of the furniture.

"Elvis turned up everywhere, and he got in the van at the same time as the rest of the band every day. Everybody's little nooks and crannies got discovered on those tours: there was always somebody who would reveal something of themselves that they hadn't previously talked about. It wasn't even a question of letting your guard down. You had to be part of the fun or else feel alienated from it. Elvis was just another of the people travelling around on this mad adventure. Along the way, there'd be little bits of needling from Shane. He would say things in a slightly jocular way, but Shane says nothing entirely as a joke. It was just a reminder of who's the boss here. There was a sense of that between Shane and Elvis. In fairness, Elvis never tried to be the boss and never would've done."

Costello was on hand at many of the festivals and events that The Pogues played over the summer, beginning with the Kenmare Festival, an important folk-rock gathering in County Kerry, at the beginning of June. Frank Murray had invited Terry Woods to come along and meet the band and see them play, having already suggested to his old friend that there might be a place for him in the line-up.

Terry had by now opted out of the music business. He was working by day in a factory and playing by night for fun and drinks in a "mad little band" called The Gartloney Rats.

Woods remembers: "I didn't quite know what The Pogues were doing. But I knew who they were and every now and again Frank would tell me stuff about them. He said, 'You'd fit into this. It would be really good. You'd give them some of the stuff that they need, and they'd give you some stuff that you need.' I went to see them at Kenmare. The things that instantly got me were (a) their irreverence and (b) that MacGowan was writing songs from an emigrant's point of view. That was one of the aspects of Irish music that I'd never experienced."

Jem Finer had remained in London with Marcia, Ella and the newborn Kitty, so he missed the chance to meet Terry on that occasion. Spider Stacy also missed the chance to meet – or to remember meeting - Terry, explaining: "It was a great event, Kenmare – but, as you might imagine, a festival in County Kerry wasn't exactly a temperance weekend."

Philip Chevron says, "We were there for about a week living in these cottages. I remember Elvis coming over with a tape recorder and rough mixes of *Rum Sodomy & The Lash* in his pocket. The album was very much an ongoing process. He was having to do it whenever we could and he could. Frank also made a point of inviting Terry down, and it was the first time we'd met him. We hung out with him a bit."

Woods' entry into The Pogues was never going to be a stroll in the park. Despite great misgivings, the band would eventually come to accept that this was a Frank Murray *fait accompli*, and they were prepared to give it a chance, however reluctantly. But the stakes were higher for Terry Woods who was being encouraged to give up his job security and to disrupt his idyllic family life in the Irish countryside to get into a transit with seven people he didn't know.

With remarkable understatement, he admits: "I was a little uneasy about it."

CHAPTER 13

The Raft Of The Medusa:
Off With Their Heads!

'Sally MacLennane' fared slightly better as a single than 'A Pair Of Brown Eyes', charting at Number 51 in June. Backed by traditional pub favourites 'The Wild Rover' and 'The Leaving Of Liverpool', the latter additional on the 12-inch, it was overlooked by daytime radio programmers in spite of its vivacious melody and an arrangement, complete with rat-a-tat-tats, that animates the song perfectly.

The Pogues promoted the single with live appearances around England and Scotland, but the character of the summer was defined more by their one-offs. There was a jubilant performance at a boggy Glastonbury, where Frank Murray bumped into one of his Dublin friends, a lighting engineer called Paul Verner. A veteran of Thin Lizzy, Horslips, Bow Wow Wow and The Undertones, Verner was now working with The Boomtown Rats.

Murray: "When The Pogues were playing bigger venues and selling them out, you needed to up the production. So the next thing we needed was a lighting guy. Naturally enough, I talked to a friend of mine. Paul Verner, as he was fond of pointing out, did the finale at the first Live Aid." Soon he would join The Pogues' crew.

The band performed in front of 80,000 people at the GLC's "Jobs For A Change" event in London's Battersea Park and electrified the masses at WOMAD. On July 13, 1985, while the world was glued to the global jukebox that was Bob Geldof's Live Aid and Paul Verner was tending to the lights at Wembley Stadium, The Pogues were playing a miners' benefit at The Fridge in Brixton.

Dee O'Mahony was there: "It was just us, 40-odd diehard fans, and the miners and their wives. I remember doing waltzes in this huge cavern in

Brixton. It was an absolutely incredible gig, brilliant. Subsequently The Pogues did another really amazing one somewhere in north London and they really gelled. The rawness of it was startling. They were so tight, so visceral almost from the beginning, with Spider's head-slapping and Shane's voice tearing through the song. There was no letting up there. That's when suddenly I realised they were definitely going to fly."

Philip Chevron adds: "Elvis came to the miners' benefit with the words of 'All You Need Is Love' [which he'd performed, with irony, that afternoon at Live Aid] written on his hand."

Also held at the Fridge was Alex Cox's benefit concert for the Sandanistas in Nicaragua, starring Joe Strummer, The Pogues and Elvis Costello.

Says Cox: "There were 2,000 people in the Fridge and another 2,000 people outside who couldn't get in. The Pogues and Strummer together were this amazing draw." The concert gave Cox the idea of taking the same acts on a package tour of Nicaragua in August 1986: "I thought we could get it funded by a video company and we could support the revolution." That idea would eventually collapse, but since the musicians had already set aside the time for the project, they were invited instead to appear in Cox's next movie, the hurriedly conceived *Straight To Hell*.

With "Jobs For A Change", the miners' benefit and the Nicaraguan fundraiser, The Pogues were among those bands who were happy to try to make a difference in Thatcher's Britain and to help to raise awareness of global problems.

"We'd always done things for causes we felt some empathy with," comments Finer. "We did a couple of miners' benefits in 1984. The unemployment one was an obvious one to do. We weren't one of those overtly political bands who were around at that time like The Redskins, but if we were asked to do something and we could, then we would. Unemployment is something a lot of people in the band had experienced. If your job's playing music, you're pretty fortunate, really, so it was good to be able to use our position to try and help in some way."

Spider says: "We'd all come out of that quite politicised squatting thing, so it was the normal thing to do. There was all that Rock Against Racism stuff as well. The Pogues came out of punk, and there were so many elements of the Sixties counterculture in it, just the alternative kind of thing. Take The Clash and somebody like Joe Strummer – they were very much a part of that squat scene. The 101ers were a definitive 1975/76 squat band, and that scene was thick with those real late-Sixties counterculture politics. It wasn't even a hangover from the Sixties - it was very much alive.

"There were a lot of benefits and causes flying around through the Eighties. That whole kind of thing died out after a while. Not that there's not a lot of things to protest about now, but people seemed more prepared to get up and do stuff then. You had the miners' strike. You had Thatcher galvanising a large percentage of the population to fight against her. It's not like we haven't got an enemy now, but when you've got an enemy you can really get your teeth into. . .

"I suppose I'm almost nostalgic for Margaret Thatcher when you look at what we've got at the moment [the Blair administration]. I'd never say anything in her favour, but at least we knew what we were getting. We knew what she stood for, and there was quite a radical scene going on. Today's Government – they've betrayed their party and the causes they were supposed to stand for."

By now, The Pogues had substantial pulling power as a live band, and it says a lot for their principles that they decided to play a small venue in Scotland purely as a favour to a pal. Nick Stewart, a fan of the band, had originally befriended them in Manchester on their first headline tour. When they subsequently played in Hull, Stewart and his friends plied them with drinks and more drinks, before, during and after their set.

The Pogues repaid this generosity by driving up to Shotts, just outside Glasgow, to perform two gigs at The Mucky Duck, a small pub venue run by Stewart, whose hospitality again was boundless.

"You know those situations where everybody wants to buy you a drink and the last thing you should do is accept anyone's offer?" asks Spider, ruefully. Of course, he accepted every offer going, and was incapacitated for the whole of the first night. Taking refuge in the van for his own comfort and safety, he emerged, briefly, from his stupor only after the band had finished playing.

"Somebody woke him in the van," recalls Chevron. "His first remark was, 'Have we played yet?' Whoever it was said, 'Yeah, yeah.' And he asked, 'How were we?' 'Well, the Pogues were very good but, incidentally, you weren't there.'"

Spider continues: "Nicky Stewart put me up on the sofa and his wife made me breakfast next morning. I had a visit from Jem and Andrew informing me that I was on a drinks ban. I was the only person apart from Cait to be put on a drinks ban."

There was never any attempt to discipline Shane MacGowan in such a fashion. "That would have been pointless," laughs Spider.

"We did some incredibly mad things which were huge fun and also sowed the seeds of some later downfalls among us," reflects Chevron. "I suppose you see how far you can go. You test limits. It's always that weird mix of the sacred and the profane. You know in your heart that you're on the side of the angels, but the devil will always come and get you when he wants you. We did stuff you only do when you're in your mid-twenties."

Spider made it onstage for the second of the two Mucky Duck gigs, and The Pogues still see Nick Stewart when they play in Glasgow.

An even more memorable weekend was on the cards next, with the band booked to play at the Vienna Folk Festival. There they would meet their great inspirational heroes The Dubliners, who were also on the bill.

"We flew out to do the festival," says Spider. "We were just making our descent and I think it was Andrew said to me, 'I think there's a couple of Dubliners on the plane.' Then somebody went, 'Shane, there's one of The Dubliners over there.' And he says, 'Which one?' and James goes, 'The one with the beard.' They were indeed The Dubliners and Shane was really over the moon. They were *the ones*. Of all the Irish bands, they were the closest to us. It's my understanding as well that like us, they attracted problems from the purists, cos they were just about having a laugh and being a bit raucous. The Dubliners have always been very open. They understand that music is a living, breathing thing and you don't put it up on a plinth."

"Oh, fantastic!" enthuses Fearnley. "The Dubliners were nice guys. So were Muzsikas [a Hungarian folk band]. It was our first meeting with them too. The only thing I remember about the gig was Jem smashing his mandolin up because it was old and decrepit and he just thought he would. He said he was going to. It was amazing. It was so rockist, but then not. It was really exciting.

"Me and Spider were the last people to leave the place where the festival was. We'd been hanging out with [The Dubliners'] Barney McKenna and John Sheahan in the bar, trying to play the bagpipes that one of the guys from Muzsikas had. We couldn't get any sensible noise out of this damn thing at all, but we tried and tried. It was a great night with the bagpipes and just general raucousness and shouting and drinking, and The Dubliners and the Hungarians."

This marked the start of a personal friendship between The Dubliners and The Pogues, and it was one which would pay dividends professionally too.

At the end of the summer, the band went to France to promote their next single, 'Dirty Old Town', and the album, *Rum Sodomy & The Lash*. The Pogues were very popular in a country where their reputation as drinkers was a huge advantage,

Stiff's Dave Robinson explains: "The French have a genuine love of people who lash the booze in. If The Pogues were coming over, the record company people we were dealing with in France would give up a day, and as soon as the band got off the boat or the train or the plane, they'd shoe them into a bar and they would have a whole big alcoholic day."

The Pogues had made their first appearance as a seven-piece - with both Jem and Philip in the line-up - on the *Old Grey Whistle Test*, BBC2's ultra-serious alternative music programme, shortly after the Kenmare Festival. Television in France was a completely different proposition, as The Pogues would discover at least once on the trip.

Robinson: "On this occasion, they were taken into the bar and then they went for rehearsals, which were shambolic. French TV shows in those days were variety shows. You might be the rock band, but there would be a juggler and a comedian... it was like the old *Sunday Night At The London Palladium*. Usually you did it live, but they decided to have them mime. The Pogues were given bottles of champagne as they went onstage to do the song. They were so hysterical at this point that half way through the song, Shane stopped 'singing' and started pouring champagne over the head of Spider, who was playing the whistle at the time. They all started pouring champagne over each other and spraying it. Everybody fell on the floor in hysterical laughter.

"I remember hearing about it by telephone from one of the French companies. Frank, the public – they all thought this was hilarious." The result was that thousands of French TV viewers rushed out to buy both 'Dirty Old Town' and *Rum Sodomy & The Lash*.

Philip Chevron remarks: "We had no reason to stay sober for the television recording. The French took it very seriously, as though, somehow, if you're a complete drunk, what you have to say must be twice as much worth hearing."

Philip Ryan – later known as Philip Chevron - isn't sure of his date of birth. It could have been June 16 or 17, although it was definitely in 1957. His passport states June 17, although nobody made a note of the time of his arrival in the middle of the night in Dublin's Rotunda Hospital, also home to the Gate Theatre.

"I was never far from the theatre," he observes.

Chevron was, however, born on Bloomsday – an annual commemoration of Irish writer James Joyce and his famed novel *Ulysses*. The celebration takes place every year on June 16, but carries on until 6am the next morning.

His father and grandfather were also called Philip Ryan: "My father, it turned out, wasn't Philip on his birth certificate, but he was on his christening certificate. All his life he was called Brendan – his middle name – to avoid confusion with his father. 'What are we going to put on his tombstone?' I come from a family of confused identities."

It was through his dad that Philip developed his lifelong love of the theatre and its various traditions, including variety and vaudeville. Brendan had always pursued twin interests in food and entertainment. As a teenager, he attended catering college while privately writing sketches for Dublin comedians, producing and performing his own revues and establishing a company called The Irish Theatre And Cinema Players.

Brendan moved up the catering ladder, working for Rank cinemas, theatres and restaurants, and began to make his name in management. Marrying Philip's mother Christine LaGrue and starting a family, he went on to spend "a fairly unhappy time" as a catering manager in Dublin's Mater Hospital.

"He was saved in later years by his own bad health," says Chevron. "He developed a disease of the lungs that forced him to take early retirement. He focused on what he'd been doing for a few years – writing books on theatre." One of his biographical subjects was Jimmy O'Dea, the great Irish comic and star of movies including the 1959 children's favourite, *Darby O'Gill And The Little People.* He followed on with the life story of stage, film and TV actor Noel Purcell.

When Brendan died at 69 in May 1997, he'd nearly completed a book titled *The Lost Theatres Of Dublin.*

Says Philip: "It was a love letter to the city as well as the theatres and history of the people that played in the theatres that are no more. His deathbed promise from me was I would finish the book for him, which I did, and it was published the year after he died. It helped me get through the grieving process. I felt so incredibly close to him, just out of sheer necessity."

Chevron's mother was descended from original Dublin settlers the Huguenots. Tradesmen specialising in weaving and book-binding, they gradually moved towards the middle classes. Philip's maternal grandparents settled in the newly affluent area of Terenure in the south of the city, where his grandfather supplied potatoes to crisp manufacturers and became the proud owner of a Dodge car, the first in Dublin.

By contrast, Philip's father's family had a background in printing and trades unionism, and they had connections to James Connolly – the leading trades unionist and socialist who commanded Republicans at the GPO during the 1916 Easter Uprising, for which he was executed by firing squad.

"My grandmother was in Cumann Na mBan," says Chevron. "They were like the female wing of the original IRA, and apart from providing safe houses and nourishment, they actually were militants. My grandmother would hide guns in the babies' prams cos it was one place the Black and Tans [paramilitaries employed by the police force to suppress Irish rebellion] would never think of looking, until they wised up. The women never came under suspicion then. There was no precedent."

Brendan's family had lived in Ballybough, the first poor inner-city residential area. "Some of the characters from Sean O'Casey's plays were based on real-life people who my father and his family would've known," reveals Chevron. "Fluther Good in *The Plough And The Stars* was a genuine Ballybough character. He took them to court for using his name. He was awarded ten shillings, which lasted all of one evening."

The young Philip attended the local Sisters Of Mercy convent school in Larkhill, a Dublin suburb which aspired to the middle class. His parents spent almost every penny they had on the mortgage repayments, with the result that the house was usually unheated and the children wore home-made clothes. However, Brendan and Christine were creative in protecting the youngsters from the harsh financial realities: Philip never had an inkling of his family's relative poverty. Rather, he remembers: "I was deeply loved and nurtured by both my parents."

After three years he transferred to the O'Connell Christian Brothers School in North Richmond Street, where James Joyce had studied for a while.

Says Chevron: "I went there for the rest of my school career. I hated most of it. All the things I did in my school years that made me happy were on the periphery of my school experience. I ran the school magazine for a while, like a punk fanzine. It was an excuse to go and talk to Horslips and Christy Moore. I had an issue banned for using the word 'funk'. I'd seen it in my sister's *Jackie* magazine. I couldn't adequately explain to the school what it meant and it was assumed to be some subversive if not seditious word.

"I saw I was being fed a tissue of lies and, not only that, the lies were coming through a regime of violence and abuse of one form or another. Corporal punishment had grown so much part of the system that no one ever questioned it. I started to equate Catholicism with punishment from the word go, and it always had to do with negativity and violence, the opposite of what it was proclaiming itself to be to do with. The indoctrination was pretty severe. You really are carrying in your unfortunate young head all this stuff about hellfire as well. On one side, you have a sense of reason and freedom of thought to think, 'This must be bullshit,' but there's a strong enough residue of, 'What if it isn't? I'll burn for eternity.'

"The church and the state were so intertwined. Physical abuse beyond classroom punishment, sexual abuse − all of that was known to the Irish Government and they were complicit in it by doing nothing about it. The English were 'bad guys' and protestants were all going to hell. That sort of thinking led us to 35 years of the troubles in the north, and it all stemmed from this co-existence of church and state. They were prepared to overlook and encourage the downsides of the other.

"The whole thing about Ireland was the secrecy. I remember hearing a great phrase in rehab when, eventually, I got there: 'Secrets keep you sick.' There was always this great elephant in the room in Ireland and it was this secret that was Pain. No one ever talked about it."

Philip saw music as an escape. The Sixties revolution that had happened overseas was still making waves in the Republic in 1973/74, and the 15-year-old Chevron joined the rock'n'roll search for enlightenment with his conversion to the Divine Light Mission and its chubby, teenage guru Maharaj Ji. During this period, he met fellow converts Paul Scully and Terry O'Neill, who had managed Horslips and Thin Lizzy and would later become The Pogues' press officer in Ireland.

Chevron quickly realised the hypocrisy of the guru and had disassociated himself with the organisation within 18 months. Meanwhile, things had not been going well with the Christian Brothers. For four years, he'd been playing truant.

"I felt a desperate need for education that I wasn't getting in school," he explains. "I felt I could get it best by exploring my fascination for this great city I was born in and that they weren't prepared to tell me about, other than the dogma. I spent days walking round it, connecting with it, which is where *Ghostown* [Chevron's Radiators' masterpiece] began."

At the same time, Philip was having a "traumatic" time at home, with his father, an alcoholic, suffering a relapse – and he was also mulling over the gradual realisation of his homosexuality: "I found it interesting, without ever being shocked and frightened by it – 'I wonder what repercussions that will have?' I was quite pleased I was attracted to men. I certainly fancied a lot of blokes. But I was very much aware of the social problems it was going to incur, not least the fact it was still illegal in Ireland and would remain so until the Nineties. My parents didn't find out until much later. I was deeply closeted. This was Ireland in the Seventies. If you *were* out, you had to be circumspect. There was an enduring fear among homosexuals in Dublin that the police were going to burst in at any time."

By the age of 17, Chevron knew he was going to be a songwriter. He'd been writing songs since the age of 11 and forming bands for almost as long. First, there was The Jangles, a pop group he started at 12 with his lifelong friend Kieran Tyrrell and their two sisters. A couple of years later came Aisling, a "Horslipsian" outfit which incorporated traditional Irish instruments. Aisling covered several pieces that would later become familiar in The Pogues' repertoire, including 'Dingle Regatta' and 'The Rocky Road To Dublin'.

Philip was driven by the influences of his heroes: Horslips, David Bowie, James Dean – and Agnes Bernelle, the Berlin-born director and cabaret actress. While still at school, he became her apprentice.

He recalls: "I heard her on the radio on a biographical series and I was completely mesmerised by it. When I discovered she was living in Dublin, I just had to find her, introduce myself to her, ingratiate myself with her, cultivate her. I sought her out at the original Project Arts Centre."

This was, and still is, a vibrant, hard-working theatre, cinema and gallery complex.

Says Chevron: "I said to Agnes, 'Hello, my name is Johnny Juke – I'm a pop star and a journalist and I want to make records for you cos I understand you haven't made any.' She looked at that unpromising 14- or 15-year-old dressed in his father's clothes, which were intended to be Ferry-esque or Bowie-esque..."

The unlikely pair became fast friends and collaborators: "I did everything from stage managing to recording to sound jobs to posters and appearing in her shows, eventually."

The Project Arts Centre was an inspirational place for Chevron, peopled by some of the great directors, actors, choreographers, playwrights, screenwriters and film-makers of the future, the likes of Gabriel Byrne rubbing shoulders with Neil Jordan, Jim Sheridan and Peter Sheridan, with whom Philip wrote a musical. "The people working there were much more interesting collaborators than the rock people I knew," he says, "and were closer to the ideal of what I was trying to do, to dramatise my own life and experiences as a young Dubliner. If there was a unifying force in teenage artists in Dublin, it was the need to break from the shackles of the Catholic church-state conspiracy and to find a voice for Irish literature, film and music." Virgin Prunes and Gavin Friday were among the centre's more musically inclined *habitués*.

Chevron: "The place started to do weekend rock gigs, at which point it attracted The Boomtown Rats, and I remember seeing U2 play to 15 people. It became an all-encompassing sort of place."

In 1975 at a free, open-air concert in Blackrock Park, Chevron played his one and only gig under the name of Philip Taylor, complete with a *pierrot* mask that hoped to salute the spirit of Bowie rather than Leo Sayer. He was leading a band, including the current Saw Doctors drummer Fran Breen, who performed rough versions of some of the songs from *Ghostown* for the first time in public.

These were portraits of Dublin, a city where the characters who had lived and died there, the good, the bad, the misjudged and the unspeakable, continued to haunt the streets that Philip had wandered endlessly on his illicit holidays from school. Here were the joys, the secrets and the hypocrisies of a place still darkened by the shadow of its own history, a place where indoctrination and bigotry remained at odds with the famous Irish welcome.

The songs would not be complete until Philip realised what they lacked: "That's exile. They needed to be written from a distance." And so he left them simmering on the back burner when in 1976 he formed the band that would, after some name changes, become The Radiators From Space with Jimmy Crashe, Mark Megaray, Pete Holidai and Stephen Rapid. He had by now decided to adopt the more street-credible surname of Chevron.

He says: "The band wasn't ready to address the scale of ambition required for the *Ghostown* songs. We were still figuring out how to do what we did. Other aspects of being young in Ireland we could write about. It was much better getting up people's noses. We played songs written by the band. It was collaborative at that stage."

Philip had already secured a record deal for Agnes Bernelle with a label called Midnite which was run as a hobby by Jackie Hayden, one of the chiefs at CBS Ireland, and Horslips drummer Eamon Carr. Agnes's album, *Bernelle On Brecht And...*, was released in the autumn, with Chevron credited as production co-ordinator. He also appeared in two Dublin shows involving Bernelle, one of which he scored, and he would continue to work with her into the Eighties.

The Radiators went into the studio to record a demo for Midnite. Carr, on a trip to London, took the tape to his friend Roger Armstrong, hoping to sell the band to Chiswick in return for a percentage, while keeping the Irish rights. The Radiators had signed to Chiswick by the end of 1976, and CBS via Midnite would release their records in Ireland.

Their first album, *TV Tube Heart*, which explores the idea of TV as a trigger for change in Ireland, was released to much acclaim. Following a period of sustained gigging in and around Dublin, the band went to London in 1977 to promote the album and ended up staying there after a Thin Lizzy support tour, where they met Frank Murray. They racked up a phenomenal number of gigs and then took six months off to record *Ghostown* with producer Tony Visconti.

They showcased some of the new songs in October 1978 at the Electric Ballroom, supported by Stiff Little Fingers, where they discovered to their horror that the new generation was unwilling to accept their music. The band had moved way, way beyond punk, but the audiences had not, and they made that very clear.

"It was just shattering," says Chevron. "It had never occurred to us to question whether we would be received well or not. We knew what we'd done was really good. To be dismissed so summarily was a shock." It was the last British gig they played – until they reunited in 2005.

Because of cash-flow problems at Chiswick, the band, now simply called The Radiators, had to sit around for a year, until 1979, waiting for *Ghostown* to be released. Even then, Chiswick could find little spare change to promote it and many of the reviewers liked it without ever looking past its wondrous melodies and harmonies: the word 'pop' cropped up quite often. Chevron and the band could only watch, heartbroken, as their album slipped into obscurity, and they returned to Ireland.

"It was crushing," says Philip. "Our momentum had been so startling and so strong and so purposeful that the comedown was always going to be horrendous. I love *Ghostown*. It stands up very well, and I think it's still got hidden depths. It yearns for a changed society, so it's always going to resound."

Lovingly, ingeniously crafted and arranged, the album draws on a wide range of musical influence, from the vaudevillian 'Kitty Ricketts' to the Spectoresque dramas of 'They're Looting In The Town', along the way taking in 'Song Of The Faithful Departed', since covered by the likes of Christy Moore - a poetic but pointed summation of the things that had so disturbed Chevron about the motherland. *Ghostown* has since been widely recognised as one of the all-time great Irish albums.

But back in the early Eighties, after a couple of blatant attempts at hit-single-making, the cupboard was bare and The Radiators, gutted, disbanded in 1981. Ted Carroll gave Chevron a job in the Camden Rock On shop. At the same time, Philip maintained his links with the theatre, took on part-time A&R commissions and developed a sideline producing bands including The Atrix, Lash Lariat & The Long Riders, The Prisoners, Tall Boys and, successfully, The Men They Couldn't Hang, also recruiting Frank Murray as his manager.

In the shop, Philip received "a crash course in music, exposing me to country and jazz and R&B and soul at a level I hadn't previously experienced", adding: "Sooner or later, everything comes back to Ted Carroll. I learnt a lot from him and all the other people who passed through the shop. Elvis Costello had famously been a Rock On customer when he came in and bought a whole bunch of soul records one day, and went away and made the *Get Happy* album."

By now, Costello had set up his own label, Imp, as an outlet for a single called 'Pills And Soap' which he released as The Imposter. Chevron, having recently put out a mini-EP of Brecht & Weill songs and performed them to an ill-mannered Moving Hearts audience in Dublin, was ready to get back in the saddle. He wanted to record a version of 'The Captains And The Kings', from Brendan Behan's play *The Hostage*, and he quickly persuaded Costello to produce it, along with a new version of 'Faithful Departed' on which Elvis played all the instruments. It was released on Imp.

"One of the things Elvis wanted me to do was to reconnect him to the

London gig scene," says Chevron. And that's when he suggested that they should go and see The Pogues.

Jem Finer and Philip Chevron did the unthinkable: they went to see Dave Robinson at Stiff, without Frank Murray. Murray was on holiday at the time. And The Pogues were worried about the video for 'Dirty Old Town'. Alex Cox had been in the frame to direct it, but now he was being vetoed.

"Dave Robinson gave us his talk on how he saw The Pogues, how he wanted to market us, how he thought our ugliness was beautiful, and how if he had his way he would be directing all our videos," says Chevron. "He said, 'I knew how Madness should look, and I was right about Madness.' He said he wanted the video to be soft-focus, showing people 'how beautiful you are but in unconventional ways'. Jem and I looked at each other and said, 'Whatever.' The bottom line was that Alex wasn't getting to do it. In Robbo's case, whatever bullshit he spouts, it's always about money. He could do the video cheaper than anyone else.

"It's the first and last video Dave Robinson supervised. Frank tore a strip off him when he came back from holiday – 'You're the record company. You sell the records the way I tell you.' And it was the last time any of us were ever allowed into a record company until after Frank. His whole position was, 'That's my side of things. Just let me take care of that.' There were a lot of instances where he had to go out and bat for the band. If he hadn't been as tough as he was, a lot of things wouldn't have got done." The video was filmed onstage at Brixton Fridge, but without any audience scenes, it was distinctly lacking in atmosphere.

Spider: "'Dirty Old Town' did relatively well. Stan [Brennan] never wanted us to do that song. We started playing it quite early on, but he hated it so much that he managed to convince us not to do it, for a short while anyway."

"I think it's a brilliant rendition," says Finer. "I like the arrangement, which Costello had a lot to do with. I don't think Ewan MacColl liked it, though..."

MacColl, its composer, damned it with faint praise: "I didn't care for 'Dirty Old Town' much at first, but I find it sounds better with each hearing. I like the other tracks a lot..."

The other tracks were Chevron productions: Finer's 'A Pistol For Paddy Garcia' and, on the 12-inch, 'The Parting Glass'. Finer used the character of Paddy Garcia as a symbol for his spaghetti western-styled compositions, later penning 'A Needle For Paddy Garcia' for the *Sid And Nancy* soundtrack.

"I wrote a third one, a something else for Paddy Garcia, but I never even showed it to the band. Then I suppose I grew out of my spaghetti-westernesque phase and got into something else, be-bop or something. Who is Paddy Garcia? He's no one. I'd written 'A Pistol For Paddy Garcia'. I remember tapping out the melody on a crocodile-shaped xylophone, one of Ella's instruments, on the night Kitty was born. The kids' toy instruments were always quite good for composing. I wanted to give it a spaghetti-westernesque title. I think Frank phoned up and said, 'We need a title,' and I said, 'Oh, I don't know, "A Pistol For. . ."' He said, 'In Mexico you get these Irish-Americans with names like Paddy Garcia.' I said, 'All right, I'll call it "A Pistol For Paddy Garcia".'"

The single received some daytime airplay, which was a step in the right direction. It reached Number 62 in the UK in September 1985, and it was a major hit in France. But the big excitement was *Rum Sodomy & The Lash* which had scored a Number 13 chart placing the month before.

"August was a 'Stiff month'," explains Dave Robinson. "We always used to release something new in August because [with the lack of competition from other record companies] it would be more likely to get a chart position."

The LP was launched on July 30 with one of the greatest parties in rock legend, aboard *HMS Belfast* on the Thames. This was the brainchild of press officer Philip Hall who later won a prestigious *Music Week* award for his *Rum Sodomy. . .* campaign. The Pogues dressed up in Napoleonic costumes to play a selection from the album, and there were copious supplies of free rum for some 400 guests from the media. The *Melody Maker* contingent made the most of the hospitality, with sub editor Richard Fenn finally flinging himself overboard. He was dragged out of the murky waters, heroically, by rock'n'roll guitarist and singer Rene Berg. Fenn survived although Rene, alas, died many years later.

Dave Robinson: "I went and hid. I thought the band might be thinking, 'Let's throw the record company in next.'"

"I thought the whole thing was magnificent," says Andrew Ranken. "It was hilarious."

"It's a bit of a two-way thing," ventures Finer. "British warships are a bit dodgy. . . But it's always fun dressing up. The costumes were rather becoming."

Rum Sodomy & The Lash was broadly welcomed as one of the most exciting album releases of the year, and its lasting popularity proves the true worth of the songs. The cover image – a striking adaptation of Gericault's painting *Le Radeau De La Medusa*, with The Pogues' heads transposed on to the original characters – still immediately identifies the album at a glance, although the ill-feeling it aroused between Jem Finer and Frank Murray has also endured to this day.

"It's a brilliant, brilliant image," begins Finer. "If you look inside, it says, 'Sleeve concept Frank Murray'. It's actually a bit generous of Frank to give himself such a prestigious position in its conception.

"There'd been a lot of talk about having some kind of nautical theme. At some stage, Frank came along and said, 'We've got to get this cover together.' I was talking to Marcia about it and she, being an art historian, has an encyclopaedic knowledge of paintings through the ages. She says, 'There's this amazing painting in The Louvre called The Raft Of The Medusa [*Le Radeau De La Medusa*], and it's also a very Pogues-like subject.'

"It was painted as a political protest cos there was this ship, *The Medusa*, off the African coast and it was too heavily laden. The captain was compromised by either a politician or the owner or something into sailing too close to the coast or in bad waters, and the ship was wrecked. Because it was overladen and there weren't enough lifeboats for the people on it, those from the higher stations saved their skins while a lot of people were left to perish. Some of them built this raft and were set adrift. They were floating around with no food or water and in the end they had to start eating each other. It's a typical story of the under-classes being shat on by those from above. Lots of Pogues songs deal with that. 'And the Band Played Waltzing Matilda' – all these poor bastards are sent out of the trenches by some idiot and blown to pieces.

"It was a double-whammy. There was this great image and a great story behind it. It worked with the whole idea of the band and the material, so I took a book with the painting in it down to where we were playing. I said, 'Here's a suggestion.' Everyone's going, 'Oh, fucking brilliant!'

"Now Frank claims it was his idea to stick everyone's heads on. I don't think it was entirely his idea. One thing Marcia did from time to time was make collages, and she did a really early one for Jack Brennan, Stan and Sophie's son, who was born while we were on the Costello tour. She made him a card that had The Pogues' heads stuck on babies. And so this notion was already in circulation. I'm not saying Frank didn't think it was a good thing to do, but for him to take full credit for the sleeve is a bit rich. It would've been nice if he'd had the generosity to share the credit with Marcia. I remember being quite upset about that.

"I actually really liked Frank. I found him a very entertaining character and I could have a real laugh with him. There were a lot of things I liked about him. I'd have liked him a lot more if he wasn't our manager. As time went on, I started thinking more and more that he took far too much credit for things. I was upset by the workload and also by the financial commitment we'd made. That was our own fault. But this was a new sort of incident for me where I felt he was appropriating something, taking some credit, which I felt was very unfair. Very nicely, Spider, on the reissue, made sure Marcia's name was put in. Spider went some way to redressing the balance."

As a final complaint, Finer asserts his dislike of the lettering on the sleeve every bit as much as that on *Red Roses For Me*.

Frank Murray insists that he came up with the idea for The Pogues' heads on the afternoon that he enjoyed drinking with the band in a Munich café during their first German tour – at the same time as Andrew's *Rum Sodomy & The Lash* brainwave.

Murray says: "I was suggesting that they should have an album sleeve like a Bruegel painting and there'd be a little face of each of The Pogues on a Bruegel character. So then Andrew got me thinking. It went from a Bruegel painting to a naval one. I gave as an example to the band when they came back the famous death scene of Nelson on the *HMS Victory*. I said, 'I need a sea-going painting.' One day Jem came up to me with an Oxford University book of various paintings and he said to me, 'What about this one?' It was The Raft Of The Medusa. I said, 'That'll do.' I then went into Stiff Records and I had the book with me. I said to Simon Ryan in the art department, 'This is the painting we're going to put the faces on.' Dave Robinson put him on a plane the next day. He went to The Louvre and bought a slide of the painting. We went about photographing the band members and having their faces put on the heads of the survivors."

"I think to Frank it was just a painting with ships and sea in it," complains Jem. "I don't think he really understood the subtext – why it was so much more than just some nautical painting with the necessary quota of violence and abject misery."

Philip Chevron was not photographed for the cover image, since he hadn't officially joined the band at this point, although he is pictured in other parts of the album artwork. Despite his absence from the painting, he opines: "It portrays the band in an interesting and funny way. It also served notice that we weren't prepared to be parcelled up in shamrock."

James Fearnley notes that Crash Test Dummies later used The Raft Of The Medusa as their artwork for a single, although they made no amendments to it.

"It festered with Jem for a while and with Marcia as well," says Murray of the disagreement over the sleeve credits. "Later on, I think Jem took a dislike to me, towards the end somewhere. To reinforce it, stuff like that came up."

Generally, though, The Pogues were happy and increasingly busy. They had a Top 20 album, and their career was taking on a new momentum.

CHAPTER 14

Loose Porter In London

Journalists were still asking about the drinking, of course. And if they weren't, they were patting themselves on the back for not asking about it. But with the release of *Rum Sodomy & The Lash*, they found a new line of questioning. Why, they wondered, were The Pogues so preoccupied with death? Danny Kelly, reporting for *NME*, pointed out that in addition to the cover painting, which speaks hugely of catastrophe, some nine of the 12 album tracks were about death.

"Ten actually," corrected Spider. "The instrumental's about death too. The 'Wild Cats Of Kilkenny' claw themselves to pieces 'til there's nothing left."

Shane MacGowan replied, as he would on many other occasions, that, "The songs we do, and this includes the traditional ones, confront, or rather just mention, death casually. There's no big fuckin' deal about it." This, after all, is a man who had lived in a community where people regarded the inevitability of death as just another part of life and matter of factly arranged their homes to include a "dying room".

He also explained that 'The Sickbed Of Cuchulainn', for instance, with its final twist, is about coming back from the dead: *Then they'll take you to Cloughprior and shove you in the ground/But you'll stick your head back out and shout, 'We'll have another round!'"*

Finally, he insisted that his songs were not built around grand themes but were "just stories", albeit stories that were often filled with characters and situations he had personally observed, such as those in the Piccadilly streets of 'The Old Main Drag'.

Certainly, no one could come out of *Rum Sodomy & The Lash* feeling morbid or miserable, such is the hurtling vitality of 'Billy's Bones' with its contagious tin-whistle riff, the bawdy hilarity of 'The Gentleman Soldier', complete with MacGowan's excitable role-playing, the irrepressible 'Sally

MacLennane' and the vigorous surges of 'The Sickbed Of Cuchulainn' -
although there's certainly space for some quiet reflection with 'A Pair Of
Brown Eyes' and 'And The Band Played Waltzing Matilda'.

The weekly music papers were all still very much in love with The
Pogues, which was rare.

"The press we got was so approving that the odd bit that wasn't could be
dismissed and thought of as the work of some crank," says Spider. "We were
very lucky in that respect. We got a very, very easy ride from the press right
up until *Peace And Love* in 1989. It used to be if one paper liked a band,
especially a new band, there was a good chance that one of the other papers
might say, 'Well, hang on a second...' But it wasn't like that with The
Pogues. The press was universally very approving. You could sit back and
complain about the misconceptions and stereotyping – 'All they ever do is
ask about why we drink so much' – but at the same time people were asking
questions couched in the most glowing terms."

Andrew Ranken says of the constant references to alcohol: "It did piss us
off. I can't say that it wasn't founded on fact, because it was, but it was
annoying. I mean, we did have this quite rowdy audience right from the
start who were interested in having a few jars, and we never discouraged
them. But I remember seeing The Faces and they were all obviously completely plastered and it didn't seem to bother anybody. It might have had
something to do with people's perceptions of us as an Irish band. Every time
anybody did a piece of artwork for us, it always seemed to have a shamrock
slapped on it somewhere. It did seem like sometimes we were just part of an
advertising agency for the Irish Tourist Board and Guinness."

"You can't have too much publicity," counters Shane MacGowan.
"There's not much point in nobody knowing who you are. If you're in a
band of entertainers, what's the problem with having your face on the cover
of fucking magazines every fucking week, or two or three of the group, or
even the whole group sometimes? We were labelled as hell-raising, rabble-
rousing, anything to take people's minds off the lyrics and the tunes and the
music. I wouldn't say I was a hell-raiser or a rabble-rouser, not any more
than anybody else that I've met in groups and a lot less than most of them.
Now I don't read it [the press].

"Most people could make up their minds – either they like the music or
they don't – and the best thing of all, of course, is that older people love it
and kids love it, and neither of them are interested in bullshit or any of that.
They tell you straight out whether they like it or not. If they're smiling and
dancing around then they're having a great time. Our audiences don't come
to our gigs to have a bad time and we don't do it to have a bad time. The
most important thing was having a good time."

The Pogues were about to start a 20-date September tour of the UK and Ireland when Terry Woods received the call from Frank Murray.

"I'd been trying to get the band to make a decision about Terry," says Murray. "They had a meeting, a very half-hearted one, and James got on the phone to me. He was saying, 'I'm not sure about your mate, Frank.' And I said, 'Why, what's wrong?' He said, 'He might be too good for us.' I said, 'James, for fuck's sake!' That was the end of that. We had some rehearsals, so I told Terry just to get on a plane and come on over. Terry was bemused. He didn't know what was happening. I don't think he knew whether the band wanted him or didn't want him. The band were neutral."

Terry Woods had a semi-legendary reputation in Ireland, where he was also seen as something of a renegade. Shane MacGowan, Philip Chevron and Jem Finer certainly knew who he was. MacGowan claims to have seen nothing strange in Murray's proposal that Terry should join, but the other Pogues, who knew little or nothing of his achievements, were perplexed.

"I was a bit bemused," admits Spider. "It seemed to be presented as a done deal, so I thought, 'All right, let's see how this works out.' I really like Terry, but it was a strange thing for Frank to do. I suppose I can see what he was trying to do, but it makes me feel that in some ways Frank didn't necessarily understand what the band was all about. It's not the first thing I would've thought we needed. How it worked out is a different story, but it was just a rather odd thing to do, definitely, at the time. But there's serendipity – he might've been some God-awful old wanker."

Andrew says: "I was a bit cautious. I could see that it might be a good idea in terms of broadening the scope of things, but I don't think I went for it in terms of getting in a well-respected Irish musician who had some sort of authenticity or whatever. I didn't see any need for that. I thought, 'There's no harm in giving it a try.'"

"The line we were given was that Terry would make us more sophisticated or provide a link with modern-day Irish folk music, which I have to say now is a bit puzzling," says James Fearnley. "We seemed to be doing quite well without anybody's help. Maybe Frank just wanted to get Terry a job. Another thing that was weird was that Terry seemed so much older than us."

Woods had a lot of things to think about. He confesses: "It took me a while to figure out what to bring to the party. They already had an established set-up. They didn't need somebody to come in and upset the apple cart. It was a question of fitting into The Pogues, to gel with that without causing it to fracture. . ."

What Terry did believe he could bring to the party was, "my experience in coming from folk music - my background that would've been helpful to them. My immediate thing was not to be one of the writers. It was to get involved in the music and help Shane in the music and help settle it. That was where I needed to fit.

"When I met Shane first, he was a tall, thin, young fellow who dressed very smartly and took great big steps like a big Irish country guy. He was a real character. He still is. People misread Shane. He's a very well-read, well-educated man. An awful lot of that education he's done himself. He knew me from my band Sweeney's Men. He knew various things I did, some of which he would've liked and some of which he wouldn't."

Woods, a multi-instrumentalist, also had to decide what instrument he would play: "They didn't need a guitar player, they didn't need a banjo player and they had an accordion player, so I had to find a niche that didn't get in everybody else's way but that would add power to the band. I needed something between the guitar and the accordion, so I settled on a cittern, which is mid-range, and it helps the banjo and gels a lot of stuff together."

It was a daunting prospect. He says: "Frank, fair play to him, said, 'Give it a chance. It'll work.' Up until then in most situations, I was one of the leaders. To suddenly get into something where you weren't a leader... one thing they wouldn't have accepted is if I'd gone in and started a takeover situation. So for me, it was a bit unnerving.

"But I couldn't see myself carrying on working in the factory. And at that point in time, there were very little opportunities. I'd been making my living as a musician for, let's say, 20 years, since the early Sixties. I wouldn't have been incredibly employable in Irish eyes unless it was in the music business somewhere. With The Pogues, there was a chance to invigorate myself musically and earn a living at the same time or work in the factory. No contest."

The Pogues were rehearsing in a room at the Boston Arms, a music pub in Tufnell Park, north London, when Terry Woods walked in with Murray. "I thought, 'Fucking hell, this is really annoying,' says Jem. "I didn't like his manner. He seemed very uptight. He didn't seem to acknowledge anyone. He said, 'What's the loose porter like in here, Frenchie?'"

Roughly translated, that means, "How's the Guinness here, Frank?"

"So Frank and him started drinking a couple of pints of Guinness," continues Finer. "We all met up and I thought, 'Well, maybe he's shy and it's all a bit weird for him too. It must be intimidating coming over here, and the poor guy doesn't know what he's letting himself in for.'"

Frank Murray admits: "I've never asked Terry how he felt that day. He probably felt a little uneasy. Spider started to talk. He struck up a conversation with Terry, and that took a lot of the tension out of the air."

James Fearnley – The Maestro – took on the responsibility for musical liaison. He remembers: "I sort of assumed rather arrogantly it would befall me to be the one to tell Terry how everything went. So I did. I think it went fairly well."

Suddenly, Terry Woods had become the eighth member of The Pogues, and it was time to go on tour.

"The first gig I did was in the Barrowlands in Glasgow," says Woods. "It was a bit of a nightmare, it was nerve-wracking, but it was very enjoyable at the same time and I learnt a lot from it. There was a great atmosphere around the band at that time. It was a roll, electric. When you're in a band, you *know* when something is beginning to happen. You can feel it. Nobody can put their finger on one specific thing that's making it all go, 'Boomph!' It's an electrical charge or something. When things are happening outside of one's control and they appear to be good things and this charge is going on, you think, 'This feels wonderful,' and The Pogues was a bit like that. The reactions we were getting at gigs was astounding. The build was beginning."

Terry Woods was born on December 4, 1947, in the Dublin area of Kilmainham, famous for its jail and, now, for the Irish Museum Of Modern Art. He was a primary and secondary pupil at the James Street Christian Brothers School.

"I hated every minute of it," he states. "I had, frankly, a hard time at school. The Christian Brothers in the Fifties weren't exactly renowned for their gentility: it was all based on violence. I couldn't wait to get out. I left at fourteen-and-a-half, and I regret it because I didn't get an education. I educated myself after I left school."

It was not through any encouragement of the Christian Brothers that Terry discovered his natural talent for soccer. His first ambition was to become a professional football player. But then he discovered music.

"My mother and father, William and Sarah, weren't musical," he says. "But my grandfather was a snare drummer in the Barrack Street Band in Dublin, a fife and drum band, at the turn of the 20th Century. Funnily enough, he was the champion snare drummer of the British Isles. I can only presume that whatever music I have I got from him."

In the early Sixties, Irish radio programmers fed their listeners a narrow diet of showband-type music, so there was little excitement to be had on the airwaves. It wasn't until Terry started going to live events with his sister May, six years his senior, that he started to take a real interest in music.

"I was a bit of a lost soul at that period," he admits. "May had been going to anything of interest that was happening in Ireland. Flamenco troupes used to come in. She would go to Radio Eireann Symphony Orchestra concerts. She'd say, 'Why don't you come along and have a look at this?' The folk revival was in its infancy, I went to a couple of sessions, and then I was hooked. I'm afraid football went out the window and music came in the door."

Before long, Terry decided to learn an instrument and acquired his first guitar. He also took up a boring, civil service job with the Post & Telegraph. He then became an apprentice draper at a wholesale drapery warehouse owned by Ferrier, Pollock & Co, the company where his father worked, but eventually left to concentrate on music.

He formed a band called The Apprentice Folk, later shortened to The Prentice Folk, with his girlfriend Gay and various others who came and went. For the next four years, they played music which Woods now likens to The Carter Family. Terry and Gay got married in 1968.

"Folk music did things to me that pop music couldn't," says Woods. "But the narrow Irish point of view of that time put me off Irish music. You had the Christian Brothers beating it into you one way and the restrictive radio beating it into you in another way. It took me until Sweeney's Men to get into it again."

Terry turned his attentions to American old-timey music, developing a fondness for banjo players Clarence Ashley and Buell Kazee, and for Scottish artists including The Galliards and Josh McCrae, who became a mentor to the Woodses when they travelled to Scotland.

Through McCrae, Terry and Gay met Appalachian folk singer and dulcimer player Jean Ritchie from The Ritchie Family in Kentucky. "Having met her," says Terry, "she asked, 'What part of America are you from?' We said, 'We're not.' She was gobsmacked by what we were playing. She asked, 'Would you not fancy coming to live in Kentucky?' and to this day, from a musical point of view, I regret not actually going. That type of singing and playing from the Appalachians and the Ozark Mountains – that really is what attracted me, that way of delivering songs."

Woods accepted an invitation to join Sweeney's Men – "to be able to look at Irish music again" – with Andy Irvine and Johnny Moynihan, early in 1967. The three had been friends for some time in the scene later described as Ireland's new folk underground. They recorded two singles, 'Waxie's Dargle' and 'Sullivan's John' as well as an album, 1968's *Sweeney's Men*, on Transatlantic.

"These men were nearly ten years older than I was," says Woods. "I learnt a lot from both of them. Moynihan and Irvine introduced the bouzouki into Irish music. Andy used to play the mandolin. I was playing a 12-string guitar, so we had the double-stringed sound going on. It became *our sound*. People still do talk about Sweeney's Men."

Irvine left the band in 1968, later becoming a founder member of

Planxty, and was replaced by guitarist Henry McCullough, who had toured with Hendrix and would go on to play with Joe Cocker and Wings. "Henry is a lovely man, and I still regard him as a good friend," says Terry.

Sweeney's Men started to develop an interest in electric music, in line with the records Woods was listening to by The Byrds, Bob Dylan and The Band. Unsurprisingly, they had their "Dylan moment" at the Cambridge Folk Festival when the crowd loudly disapproved of the electric instrumentation. Nevertheless, the McCullough line-up of Sweeney's Men has been credited with kickstarting the British folk-rock movement.

Henry McCullough quit Sweeney's Men when he was offered a guitar job with Joe Cocker's Grease Band, and Woods and Moynihan struggled along for a while as a duo, completing a second album called *The Tracks Of Sweeney*. However, they weren't getting along.

"We were so disenchanted with each other that an awful lot of the album was done separately," says Terry. "And it shows. We'd gradually fallen away from each other, musically and personally. It's never been repaired. We haven't seen each other for 20 years, maybe. I wouldn't seek out his company and I doubt he'd seek out mine."

By this time, Woods and Moynihan were ready to part company, with Johnny later to join his old friend Andy Irvine in Planxty. They had been spending a lot of time in London in a bid to really make something of Sweeney's Men.

During this time, Terry was meeting kindred spirits at the Prince Of Wales pub in Highgate - the highlight of the week being the Sunday football games that kicked off after the pub had closed for the afternoon. One of his fellow-drinkers was Fairport Convention bass player Ashley Hutchings.

Woods and Hutchings agreed to form a new group – "an Irish/UK band that would be something like The Byrds". They were joined by Terry's wife Gay and various combinations of musicians who didn't work out.

"Tim Hart and Maddy Prior came into the situation, unfortunately for Gay and me," says Woods. "I found Tim Hart an impossible person to deal with. He was a very manipulative type of person, and he wanted to be the top dog in the band – which was Steeleye Span. The agreement was that the name belonged to the five of us, but Tim went off very swiftly and copyrighted it for himself. That only came out years afterwards.

"It was engineered in such a way that the band broke up after the first album [*Hark! The Village Wait*]. Gay and I went to her sister's in Nottingham to recover from it all and while we were up there, we heard Martin Carthy had 'joined Steeleye Span' and we'd 'left'."

Woods had all the while been travelling back and forth to Dublin where he was a familiar face in musicians' circles.

"We all knew each other," he says. "It was a very small place and there was a number of us who had similar interests. I used to hang around with the guys in Skid Row. When Philip Lynott was turfed out of the band, he used to come down to my flat and we'd look at songs. We played in a school for the disabled on Island Bridge, just below Kilmainham Jail, the night that America landed on the moon [July 20, 1969]. I saw the remainder of that when I got home."

Woods and Lynott became good friends: "We understood that each of us had ambitions. My ambitions weren't as extreme as his. When he'd made it big in Thin Lizzy, he was always on at me – 'Get in, get really into the music business!' I was into alternative living. It wasn't the normal working-class family life, especially in a country like Ireland which was still very backward and repressive in lots of ways. I would have been an odd one in Philip's mind cos I tended to live down the country. I was very much a hippy, although I didn't see myself like that. We lived in a cottage and we split our time between playing and growing vegetables and living a fairly quiet exist-ence. Philip was the opposite. He loved the rock'n'roll lifestyle and lived it to the Nth, which killed him. I couldn't live it 24 hours a day in that way. But I would've regarded Philip as a close friend up until his death."

After the Steeleye Span disaster, Terry and Gay played a European tour with Doctor Strangely Strange and in the early Seventies, they put together The Woods Band with a variety of musicians, living and rehearsing in Benson, Oxfordshire. The group went out on tours of the UK, Europe and Ireland and were highly regarded, pre-dating the emergence of the Celtic-rock movement spearheaded by Horslips. Indeed, it was Horslips' future manager, Michael Deeny, who organized one of The Woods Band's Irish tours. At one point, they were supported by Planxty at Dublin's National Stadium.

The band fell apart after signing to a new record label, Greenwich Gramophone Company. Although they had been courted by other compa-nies, they decided to go with the smaller label which looked as though it might put good time and energy into its acts. With Terry's friend, Colosseum bassist Tony Reeves, as the company's A&R man, things went well in the beginning, but six or seven months later management problems became apparent and the company went into decline. Terry and Gay, fed up with the "twisted business" of the music industry, returned to Ireland to play as a duo, picking up musicians wherever and whenever they needed to.

Author Colin Harper once memorably remarked: "Before the Osbournes, there were the Woodses."

Terry laughs, "That's quite funny. We were naturally volatile at that point, the two of us. We probably did some really good gigs, but they were always fairly edgy and it could erupt into the Third World War without anybody really doing anything. I was a fairly volatile young chap."

Harper also observed that Woods had "a somewhat exaggerated reputation for belligerence". "Maybe my reputation at that time was a bit like Shane's is now," agrees Woods. "You get a reputation for anything, it tends to travel ahead of you. I've never suffered fools gladly, and I hate being taken advantage of. But that's the music business."

Terry and Gay toured extensively around Europe with session musicians and released four albums before their marriage broke down irretrievably in 1980. He says: "My personal life and my musical life were in ruins. An awful lot of my music was intertwined with hers. I was at a loss."

He carried on gigging under his own name throughout 1981 and 1982. During this time he got together with his future wife Marian and her daughter Alex, from her marriage to Keith Donald, a sax player noted for his work in Moving Hearts. Marian and Alex moved into the lake lodge home – rented from Johnny Moynihan – where Terry had lived with Gay near Oldcastle, County Meath.

"It was a sad place for me," reflects Woods. "It was closely associated with yer woman. I think Marian was incredibly brave to take it on. But once she did, we made it our own – very much so."

Terry and Marian had two children together, Sarah and Hazel, and Terry then quit music.

He explains: "I needed to earn a living, and I had two babies at that point. Marian and I wanted to buy a house. I'd become very dissatisfied with my life musically. I would've had to leave Ireland to re-establish a musical career. I took a job at a plastics factory in Oldcastle, an appalling job pulling things in and out of machines. It was absolutely hateful, but it had to be done. We had this mad little band called The Gartloney Rats up the country. We didn't play for money – we played for drinks. And it was a really, really good time, apart from the job. It kept me on the straight and narrow and it paid the bills. Marian and I were developing a life together and it was a good life, living in this little lake lodge in the country. We were never going to be millionaires, we were never going to be thousand-aires, but we were happy."

In 1984, they bought a country farmhouse three or four miles from Oldcastle, near Virginia, County Cavan. And then, a year later: "I got this phone call from Frank Murray . . .

"Frank had been part of my life since the Skid Row days in London. We were fairly tight friends. He worked with me with The Woods Band and Steeleye Span. Frank, Ashley Hutchings and myself put a Steeleye Span football team together and we played Fairport Convention in Bishop's Stortford, where they were living. We destroyed them! There was always a bond between Frank and me. We mightn't see each other for months and years, and we mightn't even speak, but the bond is still there."

Terry and Marian finally got married just a few years ago, with their children grown up.

"We had a very long engagement," jokes Terry. "We wanted to be sure we were doing the right thing."

When Woods was invited to join The Pogues, he discussed it at length with Marian. "We decided, 'We'll take the chance.' Of course, in the midst of all that, it wasn't planned that I would go bananas. I became as bad as the rest of them. We lost the plot for a little bit of the time. I'm teetotal now. Absolutely. I retired defeated."

The September 1985 tour was also notable for a new and important character joining the crew. Paul Verner had left The Boomtown Rats at the beginning of the month and was now The Pogues' lighting engineer.

"Frank brought in a lot of people he knew and they were all really great," says Jem Finer. "We'd already got Paul Scully, and Paul Verner was a lovely guy. Lights wasn't something I'd thought that much about. It was good to have someone doing that for us."

Little by little, The Pogues were becoming more professional – although there was always room for the unexpected. And the most unexpected event of the tour took place in Dublin when the band was invited on to a panel of traditional musicians, journalists and fans to discuss Irish music. The debate was to be broadcast by RTE, and it was chaired by presenter BP Fallon – a larger-than-life rock personality and an incorrigible Irishman who in 1970 somehow talked his way into playing tambourine for John Lennon's Plastic Ono Band on *Top Of The Pops*. From there he went on to become a PR and general Mr Fixit, firstly for Marc Bolan in the T. Rextasy era and later for Led Zeppelin.

The Pogues soon found themselves under attack, with Planxty's concertina player Noel Hill suddenly denouncing their music as "a terrible abortion". Compounding the insult, he also condemned the band along with their heroes The Dubliners and The Clancy Brothers for playing "rowdy ballad music".

In the course of the ensuing argument, Andrew Ranken – normally the least truculent member of the band – hit back at Hill: "I think it just comes down to sex. I mean, are you a better fucker than me?"

"I think it was a bit of a set-up," decides Andrew. "They wanted to get us into a confrontation, but we were quite up for it ourselves. Ever since the Sex Pistols on the Bill Grundy show, we'd thought it would be a good laugh to go on the television or radio and swear at someone, so we did. Noel Hill started the whole thing off. Basically he said that we couldn't play Irish music and we were a bunch of upstarts and we shouldn't be allowed to get away with it. We were murdering traditional Irish music, or something along those lines. And, well, we rose to the bait, so we just called him lots of names. We might have upset a few more purists, but they would've been upset anyway.

"What I was trying to get at with what I said was the fact that we weren't really talking about music at all and we might as well have been talking about sex, and it was all quite irrelevant. I was trying to point out the stupidity of the whole thing. I was trying to say, 'Well, who's got the authority to say who's better at something than somebody else, and what makes you think you've got the authority?' I thought I'd illustrate the point by putting it into another context."

Jem: "There were certain people in Ireland saying we were shit and a travesty and we were destroying a great tradition, and there were other people like The Dubliners and Christy Moore saying, 'Thank God – here's a band that's actually revitalising and reinventing a great tradition. That's how a tradition survives, by growing and mutating. If Noel Hill and people like him think they're playing music exactly the same way it was 400 years ago, they're talking bollocks. We don't live 400 years ago. Folk music is an expression of how people feel, and it's got a long history. It's the way people passed stories around before books and newspapers. To make something contemporary, you need to play it with some kind of contemporary energy. That's all we were doing. We were doing them all a favour and they didn't realise it.

"We had a very great respect for that music. Basically a song is some words and a tune. You can't say it has to be played on this instrument or that instrument and the instrument has to be 300 years old and have a bit of woodworm along the bridge. It's a living thing. They wanted to preserve it as some kind of monument. We are keeping it alive and passing it on. One day people will listen to Pogues versions of things and go off and do it their own way."

Referring to the purists, Philip Chevron observes: "It drove those fuckers mad when me and Terry joined, because they couldn't even call the band 'plastic Paddies' any more. In fairness, a lot of people who were entrenched at the time just decided to take against The Pogues on principle. Half the people who slagged us off had never heard us. We were assaulting all their sacred cows. We just gave them a nasty reminder of the true nature of Irishness – more free-thinking and more pagan, perhaps, than they wanted to believe or cherish or aspire to. It hurt everything they held sacred. I'd already been in England long enough to see all that stuff I'd grown up with was complete bullshit. But most of the people who were agin us have in subsequent years told us or said on the record that they were wrong. They weren't so entrenched that they weren't prepared to learn."

"I do believe we opened up a lot of people to Irish music," adds Terry Woods. "It's music by the people for the people. It shouldn't be owned by any one set of people. It's there for everybody."

At some point in the argument, Cait was reportedly called a "pig", to which she responded with "an outburst of grunting and snorting", according to Andrew.

As a postscript to the whole affair, Finer titled one of his instrumental compositions 'Planxty Noel Hill', and it later appeared on the 'Poguetry In Motion' EP. "It just seemed to be a good way of taking the piss," explains Jem. "It was obvious he'd hate it." Although he doesn't know for certain. "I'm not personally in touch with Noel Hill."

The news that Terry Woods had joined The Pogues provoked varying reactions. Dave Robinson at Stiff thought it was a very good thing, whereas Stan Brennan was astounded. "I would never have done that," he admits. "It struck me as utterly bizarre. It felt to me then that the band became entirely different."

"It shocked and surprised a lot of people in Ireland," contends Chevron. "They couldn't understand. This was *the great Terry Woods*."

With typical nonchalance, Shane MacGowan comments, "Terry brought a stabilising, anchoring influence. He was, like, a bloke with former experience."

The stabilising, anchoring influence didn't extend to Philip, who had still received no reassurances about his own place in The Pogues. He says: "By osmosis, it all eventually fell into place, but there was an unhappy period where Terry and I seemed to be rivals, and I think Frank liked to encourage that feeling. He liked to use 'divide and rule' whenever it suited him. Terry had an unhappy beginning in the band. I suppose he never knew whether he was welcome or not, because he knew he was Frank's boy. I don't know if anybody made him feel enormously welcome."

Woods claims to have experienced few problems with his new bandmates, stating: "The Pogues were always like a family, a dysfunctional family a lot of the time, but nevertheless a family and if you hit one, everybody cried. Outsiders or people at the edge of the band who were trying to do something with or for them were always made to feel very welcome."

He had the familiar friendships of Frank Murray and Paul Scully, he grew close to James Fearnley over time and tours where they roomed together, and he enjoyed his musical relationship with MacGowan: "I loved working with him. Some of his ideas are nuts, but I love it. He comes up with really quirky things, things that I might think about but throw away. Shane would make them work. Often you'd say things to him and he'd have them in a song in no time. I'd say, 'Why can't I think like that?' But I don't. He does. And that's what makes him unique."

Andrew Ranken felt that Woods enabled the band to reproduce more of their studio capabilities on stage, adding: "One of the things I liked about Terry was that he wasn't an Irish purist at all. He was into American stuff, Appalachian stuff."

Darryl Hunt considers that, "Terry brought his sort of melodic awareness into the group, and his real understanding of Irish airs and all these incredible things in his head that he could apply. He brought in another dimension which I don't know was ever properly utilized in the way it could have been because he subjugated himself to the group thing. I suppose he also brought an element of authenticity - suddenly this semi-legend of Irish music had joined The Pogues, this ramshackle bunch of Londoners. And Terry brought 'Young Ned Of The Hill', which is a great tune, and 'Battle March Medley', which ended up on the B-side of 'Fairytale Of New York'."

"I was never happy about why we needed Terry in the band," says Jem. "As time went by, I grew to really like having him round both as a person and a musician, although we did have our ups and downs. I know I upset him on occasion, and I'm sorry about that, but I always had strong feelings about the band and the music. Anything I felt was screwing it up, I'd try and change. There were things I found very difficult musically and they never really worked, but there was other things I thought really did. I'm not sure whether he really changed the direction that much.

"For him, things were very difficult too. Sometimes he found our punky approach to things pretty obnoxious. And for him, too, it was pretty difficult being away from home a lot. Very quickly as a person I grew to really like him, but musically it was a bit more of a struggle to come to terms with. He's a very brilliant musician but coming from the position of being a band leader maybe not the best team player. It was finding a meeting between what he was doing and what I was doing and what I was interested in seeing the band grow into. I'm still not clear whether it was a brilliant idea or not. Regardless, I love Terry. He's a brilliant guy and a beautiful musician."

James was struck by "an air of otherworldliness about him", and Philip declares that, "Terry brought some ancient wisdom to the whole thing." He elaborates: "Terry seems to have been around for centuries, and we kid him about that. There was that sense that he brought the whole burden of Irish history with him in a very authentic way and also incorporated into that the entire history of the journey of Irish music. Appalachian music – he reintroduced that sensibility to Irish music. He had foundation and substance, and he endowed The Pogues with a sense of confidence that we were on the right path."

However, it took some time for Philip to feel secure with Woods also in the line-up. He recalls, "The Dubliners tell stories about how people didn't actually join the band. They just looked round 25 years later and they were all there. It probably never occurred to anybody to consider whether Terry or I should be asked officially to join. By the time of the third album, we were very much in the band. It happened without anybody taking incremental steps to formalise it.

"Ultimately Terry and I got on extremely well together and are still very close friends. He found it tough feeling his way into the band. He would have been aware of all this mind game stuff going on with Frank. After a while, I said, 'This is fucking bullshit.' We got close when Phil Lynott died*. Terry was just devastated, and I was there to comfort him and our friendship just went from there. It was bigger than any disruption that anybody could put in front of it.

"We figured it out quietly without any of us ever mentioning the topic. The Pogues is a great, self-adjusting organism. If there's a fly in the ointment, it will push the fly out of the way. No one will ever say, 'Let's have a meeting about this.' It just ran on group dynamics. We all implicitly understood how we needed to be in The Pogues. I don't think Cait ever clicked into Poguetry. Elvis distracted her from that, inevitably, through no fault of his own."

Cait O'Riordan was becoming increasingly isolated from the group: there were troubled times ahead for the bassist.

---

* January 4, 1986

CHAPTER 15

The One-Handed Drummer

The Pogues had decided to record a Christmas single. In the second half of 1985, in between bouts of touring, they'd been rehearsing and recording a number of new songs with Elvis Costello, some of which would materialise on the 'Poguetry In Motion' EP.

Frank Murray had given each group member a tape of a song by The Band, 'Christmas Must Be Tonight', suggesting that it might be an ideal cover. Shane MacGowan and Jem Finer had other thoughts, setting their minds to an original composition. MacGowan was dreaming of something sumptuous, with strings, while Finer chewed over ideas for lyrics and melodies. It may have been a deliberate attempt to write a seasonal hit record, but whatever they came up with, it had to have quality too.

Finer had only just mastered the art of writing full-length instrumentals. Now he intended to venture into whole, structured songs.

"I thought the idea of a cover was a bloody stupid one," he says. "We thought, 'If we're going to do a Christmas song, let's write one. Come on – we're songwriters! Why do someone else's song that isn't even very good?'

"The idea had been knocking around for a while of Shane and Cait doing a duet. I wrote one song, a duet. It's embarrassing to think about, cos it wasn't very good. At that time, I'd started to write songs without words – a melody and chords and instrumental bits – or songs with words which I'd always expect Shane to rewrite because his lyrics were going to be better than mine. So I'd written this duet with crap words. Often, I'd try out my new material at home on Marcia. On this occasion, I played her this song. It was very banal, a miserable song about a sailor being away from home. He was singing his bit and his wife or lover back home was singing her bit. I think at the end he committed suicide or something. Rubbish. Marcia said the sailor romance thing was naff, that it didn't ring true and how Christmas was always a battle with the true events or circumstances of anyone's life – the way the call to have fun, go shopping, kiss under the mistletoe and all that crap appears like some evil spotlight and only shows up how miserable, poor or furious you might be in your circumstances.

"I said, 'Okay, well, you tell me a better story.' I remember her saying that I should think of something that was more like the sort of song I'd want to hear. She suggested a couple having a row at the time of peace and good-will, trying to crank up some Christmas spirit but failing and fighting, lost in recriminations about money and other disillusions. The guy takes what they have got, and he's meant to be out buying stuff for Christmas. He goes out to the bookies and the pub and he drinks and gambles it away, which causes an altercation. But she warned that the song shouldn't end on a bleak note and there should definitely be some kind of redemption for the end of the story, that it should end in a weird romantic truce that just couldn't be helped, a little glimmer of uncanny hope amidst the torture of packaged party time. I thought, 'Okay, I take the point.'

"I wrote a second song which had that plot to it. It was based on the people who lived across the street from us. We went into the studio and we rehearsed 'Body Of An American' and, I think, 'London Girl'. I took these two songs of mine along. Shane took them away and he wrote 'Fairytale Of New York' using the melody of the first song I'd written and the storyline of the second one, which he then transposed to New York, and he made it into what it is now.

"So then we had this embryonic 'Fairytale' which we tried to record, with Cait singing, and it just didn't really work. The arrangement was all wrong. It was far too complex. It was a very ambitious song for us. It really was aspiring to new levels of sophistication. We just couldn't play it well enough and the lyrics needed more juggling around."

Philip Chevron adds: "I think Shane and Jem always knew it was going to be a big song if they could get it right. The Elvis recording is very obvi-ously an early draft of the lyric. Some quite significant bits aren't yet in the song. It just talked to me. It started out with this grand scheme to include quotes from other songs, although the only ones left are 'Galway Bay' and 'Once Upon A Time In America', the theme from the film.

"Shane had this vision of a huge, Sinatra-esque ballad. Elvis was the wrong person to get it. His work on 'Fairytale' isn't great. He doesn't attempt to put any shape in it. We needed to recruit somebody who was not a musician but a producer to come at it from a different angle."

The Pogues abandoned the song for the time being, and it would not see a release that Christmas. But they kept returning to it in rehearsals and in recording sessions, experimenting with the arrangement while MacGowan worked away at the lyrics, refining and redefining them. It would take a long time to get the song the way they wanted it, and another age to get it into the studio for recording with a different producer – Steve Lillywhite.

The tour dates had continued into October 1985, but no sooner had The Pogues come off the road than they were back on it again, this time bound for Europe in their first-ever tour bus for four weeks of dates in Holland, France, Germany, Switzerland and Scandinavia. Revelling in the novelty of a video machine, they watched endless re-runs of *Once Upon A Time In America*.

"Ennio Morricone's music is just extraordinary," says Chevron. "It's one of the best scores in film history. It stayed with us. The first few notes of the main theme are the first few notes of 'Fairytale'. It's based on that, and it's a cue to why we approached 'Fairytale' in the way we did. We wanted it to be epic and poetic and telling a cinematic story. It wouldn't have come about if we hadn't seen Sergio Leone and heard the soundtrack. It fed into 'Fairytale' in an enormous way."

At other times, the band listened to hours of Tom Waits music on the stereo, especially his newly released album *Rain Dogs*, and worked on new ideas of their own.

"We would while away six-hour coach journeys by playing music and experimenting with sounds and stuff," remembers Chevron. "It was a very fertile time. Everybody was exploring what these Pogues might be capable of, whether there were any boundaries that we needed to observe at all. We seemed to be able to pick up on things like jazz and Spanish music."

So far, so good. They were about a week into the itinerary when Andrew Ranken cut his finger slightly, which didn't cause any undue concern. He recalls: "We were in Germany and I'd gone onstage a bit pissed and whacked my finger on the side of the snare drum by accident. I might have done the same thing if I was sober, but it was less likely. I didn't really hurt it. The next night [in Munich], I did exactly the same thing in the same place and then it started getting really painful and turning black.

"I went to see a doctor and he said, 'You've got blood poisoning. We'll have to put the finger in plaster, and you'll have to have your arm in a sling. Come back later and we'll see what sort of a state it's in. If it's not any better, we'll have to chop the finger off.' I was so ill with this blood poisoning that I missed two gigs."

Darryl Hunt stood in on drums on the first night, to be replaced by Elvis Costello on the second.

Says Darryl: "It was great fun being a drummer in The Pogues. It's the best job of the lot. The rhythms are really good fun, not like rock rhythms.

They're something else. I think I did a better job than Elvis. He wants to be on stage all the time – although we're all a bit like that – and as he was the bigger nob, he got the job on the second night."

Hunt had become used to Costello being treated as a bit of a buffoon, taking some of the pressure off himself and James. But Elvis's takeover on the drums signalled in some small way to Darryl that Costello might be swinging back into favour – a needless worry, as it turned out.

Andrew, who watched both shows as a member of the audience, offers his verdict: "Elvis was better at hitting the drums hard, but Darryl was much better at actually playing them."

"Elvis was like Joe Strummer would be later," says Chevron. "He got to do lots of different jobs in The Pogues. He stood in for Shane, he stood in for Andrew and he stood in for our roadie, changing a guitar string."

Returning to the doctor's, Ranken was relieved to find that he could keep his finger and was back on stage for the rest of the tour, albeit in a one-handed capacity. As a direct result of the scare, he stopped drinking before gigs: "Sometimes we were just too pissed to play properly. I don't think there's anything wrong with having a couple of drinks to calm you down, but sometimes it would go a bit beyond that. I'd make up for it afterwards."

Andrew was something of a "sporadic" drinker anyway because of his susceptibility to a condition called cluster headache. "They used to think it was some sort of migraine, but it isn't," he says. "It's something I've had all my life, but it's only fairly recently that it's been identified. It's an absolutely agonising headache which builds up over a period and fades away again. When I get it, I tend to have three or four attacks in the night, and each attack can go on for up to 40 minutes. It's not an allergic response to any-thing, but odd things can trigger it off, and one of the commonest is alcohol. When I'm suffering from cluster headache, I can be off the booze for a good six months. I don't feel in the slightest like having a drink."

On other occasions, Ranken would be more than happy to join in the post-gig celebrations although his bandmates did not follow his example of abstinence before showtime.

Terry Woods comments: "We'd go to places and fans would turn up and out of their generous hearts, they'd hand you a bottle of whiskey, and they'd like you to drink it with them. But then you had to go on stage… Eventually it was one of the things that was doing Shane in, because he couldn't find peace no matter where he went. Jem was always a very, very steady, upright man, something I still admire about him. He doesn't get knocked off his path easily. But I, unfortunately, for a while – I lost the plot. Things like this become insidious because you're constantly touring. You're passing yourself by at night on airplanes and spending an inordinate amount of time away from the wife and kids. But never is there any need to be there. You're there at the behest of the music business."

At the same time, Philip Chevron was dealing with – or, rather, not dealing with – a burgeoning drinking habit.

He says: "It's a fact that for better or for worse, the Irish soul is the most receptive to ideas and creativity very often when it's under the influence of alcohol. There's a huge link between Irish art and alcohol. There's no getting round it and no reason for getting round it. You might even go so far as to say there were some scientific alcohol experiments, like the time where Jem drank the worm at the bottom of the mezcal to see how he would play that night. It was like a piece of conceptual art. That's precisely the sort of thing that Jem does.

"Alcohol was very much for the good – until it became a problem for you, at which point you had to take a different view of it. The Pogues always had a relationship that understood that. I remember Andrew saying to me quite early on, 'You know, Phil, you shouldn't drink so much.' He spotted that I was a problem drinker. We were that clued into each other. Nobody would judge you, but they wouldn't be afraid to say something to you. I certainly wasn't going to admit it until I absolutely had to. Alcohol made me feel like the person I thought I wanted to be. It took me away from the person I was that I thought I didn't want to be. That's all about self-esteem and stuff like that. It took me a long time to figure out that it was okay, I didn't need to drink any more."

The immediate problem in Germany was how to accommodate a one-handed drummer – and the solution was one that changed the look and the sound of The Pogues forever. Rather than standing up and playing two drums with his hands, Andrew was permitted to sit and presented with a hi-hat and a bass drum he could operate by foot and a snare drum he could play with his good hand.

"I did the rest of the tour like that," says Ranken. "Then they decided they liked the bass drum so much that they wanted to keep it, so I got to sit down from then on. It was a great relief. It was always quite uncomfortable playing the drums standing up. It was also very limiting. I wanted to be able to do other things."

Jem: "It was great that Andrew did the standing-up for so long. It was part of the whole madness of the appearance of the group. Drummers can play far too complicated. That's one of the reasons when we invented the Poguebeat, we invented it for the two drums. By the time Andrew started to play the minimal kit with the kick drum and the snare, I suppose we felt it was giving it an extra bit of energy that was worth pursuing. It was part of the progression."

By the time The Pogues came to record their third album, *If I Should Fall From Grace With God*, Andrew's kit would be bigger still. Says Darryl: "I don't think a lot of the songs on that album would've been possible with just two drums."

With the band, their one-handed drummer and Elvis Costello carrying on into Scandinavia, Shane MacGowan became the next tour casualty when he was diagnosed with pneumonia.

"That was really awful," shudders Spider. "I was sharing a room with him. We were in Malmo, in Sweden. He was in his bed in the hotel and he was kind of asleep but groaning. He was in real pain from his back. I told Frank and we got a doctor and Shane had to go to hospital. We all went home, but before that, we did go ahead with that night's gig." It was possibly one of the most drunken Pogues performances of all time, with Costello, Spider, Philip and Terry sharing the vocal duties.

"It was a shambles," says Spider. "I said, 'I've got a bit of a sore throat, so if you want me to sing you'll have to get me some whiskey.' People in the club brought all this whiskey and everybody got really, really drunk, Frank, Costello, all the band, all the crew – and the audience were really drunk anyway because it was Sweden."

"The image I have is this very dark stage with a pillar in the middle of the place and this bottle of whiskey going round," says James Fearnley. "Things were falling apart."

"The spirit of the gig was just get drunk and get through it that way," adds Philip. "I had no recollection of it at the time. That's why you stop drinking, so you can feel the moment and remember it. It becomes unbearable to not know what your life is like. Somebody has to tell you whether it was any good or not. I remember going back to the dressing room, saying, 'Hey, we rocked!' and conking out in the corner."

Those who had not conked out remember outrageous scenes.

Spider: "We trashed the dressing room. It was the only time with The Pogues there was any kind of rock'n'roll vandalism, and it was started by the management [Murray] and the guest international singing star [Costello]. They started to throw crockery around and everybody else joined in cos we thought it was the right thing to do. We were following the example of our elders and betters. It was a fitting end to the evening cos the gig had been really shocking."

Apparently, Spider is exempting the fireworks escapade in the dressing room in Loughborough from the charge of "rock'n'roll vandalism".

"Okay, that's twice it happened," he concedes. "That was different, though, because it was James who started that, and James is not the kind of person you would associate with that kind of mindless, arrogant destruction."

James remembers Malmo as "a fairly savage evening". He explains: "There were rows and ructions between Cait and Elvis. I was like the middle kid again, trying to separate people and appeal to reason, but they were too far gone. There was fisticuffs and weeping and irreconcilability. I think Elvis might have connected somewhere [with his fist]. I think they were both at it, not just Elvis. It was quite a public spat. I know about Cait's temperament: she's a very fiery woman.

"But the end of the evening was very nice. When we've had trouble before, I've ended up with Jem talking about stuff in a room, without judgement. On this occasion, after all the ructions and the gig and Shane going into hospital, me and Jem ended up in the linen closet in this hotel, talking. It was a quiet place and comfortable with linen everywhere and these shelves to sit on. It was a really, really pleasant experience. It was a little eddy in the maelstrom that was going on."

Elvis Costello was not usually so aggressive in The Pogues' company.

"He really quite enjoyed coming out on the road with us," continues Fearnley. "We'd talk and listen to new music, and it must have been really cool for him to sort of muck in with us. To illustrate that was a gig we did in Toulouse with the Nyah Fearties, a Scottish band. There was just two of them. They'd go out and scavenge for things for their gig, shopping trolleys and bits of metal to hit. They were folky, punky, loopy people with a bass and guitar and they'd hit things for percussion. They're great friends of Andrew. So we were out on the road in France, and it was a very hot gig. Outside the gig, there was a swimming pool. We'd stripped off and gone in. I'm swimming in the water when this enormous black shape goes over the top of me, and it's Elvis Costello in his coat, straight in, fully clothed. He probably had his shoes on too."

The band cancelled the rest of their dates and headed home for MacGowan to make his recovery.

"Shane's health was always fragile in the early days," says Philip. "He had various things wrong with his stomach. He kept bottles of Pepto-Bismol in his bag. He also had an unhappy knack of breaking limbs. The trouble about that – most people will be patient enough to sit there and wait for the cast to come off after six weeks. He'd discharge himself from hospital after three days and limp down the road with the cast dragging behind him. He never gave his body a chance to properly heal. Staying up late, drinking, touring, all those things combined just put him out of action."

MacGowan was later reported as saying, "When the hospital started treating me, they shoved paracetamol up my bum. That felt a bit strange, but some of the nurses were nice..."

Surprisingly enough, the story of Malmo has a happy ending, because

Chevron recently heard a bootleg of the gig and, despite his worst fears: "It was fine!"

December brought yet another tour of England, Scotland and Ireland, and Frank Murray called on another of his cronies to join the crew as a monitor man. Dave Jordan had been with Murray when both saw The Pogues for the first time at the Hope & Anchor in 1984.

Jordan, from Cumbria, had gained some solid experience since his early days in London when he worked for Island Records as a van driver. He soon notched up some impressive qualifications in sound: he was a recording engineer for The Rolling Stones, and he worked on The Specials' debut album with Elvis Costello and was consequently offered a full-time position with the band. It was during this period that he struck up a lasting friendship with Frank Murray, who'd been tour managing the 2-Tone package.

When The Specials split, Jordan became the producer for Fun Boy Three, a splinter band formed by Terry Hall, Neville Staples and Lynval Golding. He was responsible for their hit single, 'The Lunatics (Have Taken Over The Asylum)' and their debut album, *Fun Boy Three*. A year later he was sacked, reportedly for bad timekeeping, although his lateness may well have been related to a somewhat excessive lifestyle. After working with a variety of little-known acts from overseas, he went home to Kendal to recover his health and returned to London a year later, in 1984.

The resumption of his friendship with Frank Murray resulted in Jordan producing for Kirsty MacColl, among other artists, and the offer of a job looking after the monitor desk for The Pogues. Here, he was reunited with another old pal in the entourage: he had once recorded some tracks for one of Darryl Hunt's old bands, The Lemons, in the 2-Tone town of Coventry.

Dave Jordan took up his new employment at the start of The Pogues' Christmas tour, in Sheffield, on December 3.

It was the tour that saw The Pogues reaping the rewards of their exhaustive gigging, their exhilarating live shows and a pair of albums that combine an expert grasp of songwriting, a colourful lyrical balance of the romantic and the realistic, a people's choice of cover material and an impulsive cheek that jumps out of the speakers, effing and blinding.

The spacious bus in which they had travelled the motorways of Europe, watching *Once Upon A Time In America* and rasping along with Tom Waits, had gone back to the hire company, and the band were once again huddled together in a modest van. But this time they were headlining serious venues, the biggest you could get before you hit the arena circuit, with an experienced and creative crew. They were selling out everywhere, and the crowds were going mental.

There was no such thing as a "typical" Pogues fan. They came in all shapes and sizes, ages and persuasions, and there was no dress code. A Pogues gig was all-inclusive.

Says Jem: "The music itself has this great timeless appeal. In a way, it's hard to dislike. If you've got a great tune and fantastic words and a simple but very powerful beat, and a lot of energy, you can't go far wrong. And then what we sang about I think struck a chord with people. It wasn't just nonsense. If there were songs about love, they had a real edge and realism to them. We had songs about life, and stories, and things that appeal to people – the timeless appeal of story-telling translated into something you can dance to, presented with great verve and energy and an anarchic strand by a charismatic band with a singer with a great voice. To see a bunch of people with these acoustic instruments playing at such speed and volume was a complete novelty at the time. Then, I think, when people met us they could have a laugh. We were an approachable bunch and largely intelligent people as well, and not sort of starry, stand-offish types. People enjoyed hanging round with us."

Philip adds: "There was never a hardcore Pogues constituency that could be identified by its demeanour or nationality or ethnicity or street style. It was a mixture of age groups and people. Rockabillies, punks, old folkies – it was always mixed. That cross-section just got bigger, amplified and magnified over and over again. And it's pretty much stayed like that.

"Rock'n'roll depended for many years on the existence of the generation gap. One of the reasons there isn't one now is that bands like The Pogues came along. We weren't interested in not playing to kids or older people. Old women might want to take care of Shane, but they understand who he is; that he's a great Irish talent."

The London gig took place at the prestigious, 4,500-capacity Hammersmith Odeon (now the Apollo) – the proof, if any were needed, that the band had arrived, big-time. They were joined by various guest artists including Elvis Costello, who came on for 'The Wild Rover'. And uileann piper Tommy Keane and fiddler Henry Benagh, both of whom had contributed to *Rum Sodomy & The Lash*, were welcomed onstage for 'Dirty Old Town'.

James remarks: "I remember that little bar at the back of the venue, backstage. I remember how puffed-up Frank was because I think, to a degree, it was more important for him to do that gig than it might have been for us. It's a hugely important gig to play, but for Frank, it was a matter of sticking it in the face of people who said we couldn't do it. I don't think we ever had that agenda, but Frank did, and he wanted to show the nay-sayers. It was a feather in his cap. I remember being slightly aware that it was a feather in his rather than one in ours. That's Frank's character: he's a pugnacious fighting guy. I don't think it was part of our agenda, somehow, to fuck the begrudgers."

Jem's foremost memory of the evening is a bitter one: "We'd been given some silver or gold discs, and someone stole my disc from the dressing room." He adds: "The other thing – it was really weird playing there cos we couldn't really hear what the audience was like. It was one of these gigs we weren't used to, slightly removed from the audience. But I think it went quite well. I remember listening to a live recording and being surprised."

The Pogues concluded this leg of the tour in kilts at Glasgow Barrowlands where, as usual, the crowd was wildly enthusiastic.

The level of touring that The Pogues were now undertaking was the very thing that Finer had dreaded all along. Frank Murray remembers having a conversation with him, one which probably took place on this December tour although it could well have been even earlier, in September.

"After we'd done *Rum Sodomy...* we were up in Scotland and Jem came up to my hotel room one afternoon," says Murray. "He was warning me that he was going to quit the band for family reasons. His wife had recently given birth to their second daughter, Kitty, and both Jem and Marcia were concerned about him being away for long periods at a time. I spoke to him for about an hour and I guess I convinced him to stay.

"This band were worth being in. They'd just released *Rum Sodomy...* to great critical acclaim and they could only get better. I also told Jem, 'Even just stay in the band until you make your next record.' Then you could have replaced him to go on the road afterwards. I encouraged him to write songs and get his work put on the next album. He said he'd go away and talk to Marcia and think about it, which he did do, and he told me he was going to stay for a while, and that was it. I never told anybody in the band about that conversation. I thought it was better to leave things the way they were and just let him think about things without any pressure."

Jem was caught in the dilemma which he would never really escape during Murray's tenure as manager, although his desire to see The Pogues fulfil their true potential carried him through the worst of times.

He states: "I didn't want to spend all my time away from home. It's difficult when kids are really small. It would've been different if they'd been older. Ella and Kitty were at that age where kids get ill a lot. One time we arrived in France for a three-week tour and I phoned home to find they'd both got whooping cough. It's just terribly worrying and stressful.

"I was very rooted in having to keep at least one foot on the ground by having a very young family. It was always in the back of my mind. I don't mean that in the sense that I couldn't have a laugh, I wasn't walking around

New York, New York. The Pogues arrive in the States in March 1986 for "the most Babylonian tour ever" and bite chunks out of The Big Apple. Says Philip, "It was total insanity: 'Welcome to New York – we've been waiting for you guys all our lives.' We decided to plunge in." Left to right: Cait, Andrew, Philip, James, Shane, Jem, Terry Woods and Spider. *(GEORGE DUBOSE/LFI)*

Jem, Philip, Andrew and Shane resplendent in uniform at the launch of *Rum, Sodomy & The Lash*. One of the most famous parties in rock history, it took place on HMS Belfast on July 30, 1985. "It's always fun dressing up," says Jem. "The costumes were rather becoming." *(ANDREW CATLIN)*

"Baby Pogues" – the collage Marcia Farquhar made for Stan Brennan's baby son Jack. It was an idea later taken up for the cover image of *Rum, Sodomy & The Lash*. *(MARCIA FARQUHAR)*

Jem and Marcia at the Empire State Building, NYC, in November 1982 – four months before their spring wedding. "Marcia was, and continues to be, an incredibly powerful force in my life," says Jem.

(JEM FINER)

Darryl, in his capacity as roadie, attends to Philip's guitar. "I didn't want to continue doing this job," admits Darryl, who was later rewarded with a new role – as The Pogues' bassist – when Cait walked out of the band. Left to right: Shane, Jem, Cait, Philip, Darryl, Andrew. *(ANDREW CATLIN)*

Getting into character during the filming for *Straight To Hell* in the desert near Almeria, Spain, in the late summer of 1986. "Great!" says Shane. "Going to Spain and getting paid for it, and there was a fiesta on as well." Left to right: James, Cait, Shane, actor Xander Berkeley and Spider. *(ADRIAN BOOT/URBANIMAGE.TV)*

James has lift-off at Sheffield in June 1986, and he doesn't let a little thing like an accordion get in his way. "The showing off that I do onstage is all to do with Philip," James explains. "He inspired me. It was nicely competitive." *(ANDREW CATLIN)*

The Pogues in the Soho streets from which Shane has taken so much inspiration.
Left to right: Darryl, Philip, Andrew, Terry, Jem, James, Spider and Shane. *(ANDREW CATLIN/LFI)*

Kindred spirits. The Pogues and The Dubliners formed a mutual admiration society which gave
rise to all kinds of high jinks and a hit single, 'The Irish Rover', in March 1987. "It was brilliant,"
says Shane MacGowan of the collaboration. "It was a big thrill." *(ANDREW CATLIN)*

Producer Steve Lillywhite was at the helm for
The Pogues' best-selling album, *If I Should Fall
From Grace With God,* and he helped them perfect
a Christmas song they had been working on
for ages – 'Fairytale Of New York'. "We gave it
some tempo and some joyfulness," says Steve.
(EBET ROBERTS/REDFERNS)

Shane and Matt Dillon at the video shoot for
'Fairytale Of New York', set in a real-life NYC
drunk tank, in December 1987. Dillon, a huge
Pogues fan appearing as a cop, was too respectful
of Shane to push him around as roughly as his
part called for. *(MARTIN SHEERIN/RETNA)*

Celebrating St Patrick's Day at Brixton Academy on March 17, 1987 with their most spectacular show to date,
The Pogues dressed as New York cops performing in front of a backdrop of the Manhattan skyline, designed
by Andrew. The Pogues with crew members Dave Jordan, Charlie MacLennon, Joey Cashman and Paul Sculley
in the back row, with manager Frank Murray in the centre. *(ANDREW CATLIN)*

Terry and Joe Strummer at the Boston Metro in December 1987. Strummer was deputising during a three-week American tour for Philip Chevron, who was hospitalised with crippling stomach pains from an ulcer. "Joe brought a real, sussed professionalism to being on the road," reflects Darryl. "Everyone got on with him. He did a lot of good work for us." *(BC KAGAN/RETNA)*

Kirsty MacColl, pictured onstage in March 1988, had become an honorary band member with her much-loved performance on 'Fairytale Of New York'. Her presence on this UK Pogues tour was her first, important step in a personal bid to overcome stage fright. Says Andrew: "Coming on the road with us was meant to be a way of trying to gently ease her back into it without the spotlight being on her too much." *(ANDREW CATLIN)*

Filming the video for 'Fiesta' on the roof of Gaudí's Casa Mila building in Barcelona, May 1988, The Pogues were joined by Joey Cashman (third left) on sax. Most of the band had fun with the shoot, directed by comedian Ade Edmondson, although James, for various reasons, reveals that, "I didn't enjoy that particular day." *(ANDREW CATLIN)*

By 1988, The Pogues had become one of the most popular live bands in the country, marking St Patrick's Day with six sold-out nights at the Kentish Town & Country Club and another at Brixton Academy. Left to right: James, Philip, Jem and Shane enjoy the luxury of monogrammed bathrobes backstage in London. *(ANDREW CATLIN)*

in a permanent cloud of misery, and it didn't stop me having some fun. I think having a laugh is one of the more important things in life and without a sense of humour we'd never have got to the point we're at now. We've had a lot of laughs. A band, for some people, can be a perfect place to extend an adolescence. But if you've a partner and two young kids that you feel a responsibility to, obviously it puts a different complexion on things. The flip side is that it's a very creative thing having young kids. It stimulates the imagination in ways that not being round young children can't."

Christmas brought another slew of media awards for The Pogues. They were honoured with four entries in John Peel's annual Festive 50. *Melody Maker* voted *Rum Sodomy & The Lash* Number Two in its albums of 1985, and Shane MacGowan was its runaway winner of Chap Of The Year – a privilege bestowed for outstanding merry-making and quotability. 'A Pair Of Brown Eyes' was the year's ninth best single for *NME*, with *Rum Sodomy...* voted into 18th place in the album listings. Philip Hall was hailed Press Officer Of The Year by *Music Week* for his inspired promotion of *Rum Sodomy...*

The Pogues had barely time to digest their Christmas dinner before they were called up yet again for active service, leaving on Boxing Day for a major tour of Ireland. Cait O'Riordan was the only band member not to turn up for the flight, claiming to have mistaken the day of departure. "Cait and Elvis didn't get out of bed," says a blunt Darryl Hunt, who stood in for the errant bassist in Waterford.

"I had to stand with my back to the audience reading these charts on top of the amp," continues Darryl. "Even though I knew the music very well, you don't necessarily know the chord structures."

O'Riordan arrived in Ireland in time for the next gig, in Tralee. It was the first sighting of her new piece of jewellery – a glittering diamond and emerald ring.

CHAPTER 16

You Promised Me Broadway
Was Waiting For Me

Irish winters can be bitterly cold, and this one was no exception. James Fearnley remembers shivering his way through the whole tour.

"None of the heating worked in any of the hotels," he declares. "Before one gig, I was so cold – numb - that I had to lie in the bath in hot water before going onstage. It was miserable, as I remember."

One vivid memory, however, was the band's visit to County Clare, where they sought out the Cliffs of Moher, one of the country's great scenic attractions with spectacular views over the Atlantic Ocean. "That was fantastic, to stand on the cliffs in blasting winds," says James. "Shane gets all sort of *inner* when he sees magnificent Irish things like that. I've seen him do that in Norway as well."

It was during this tourist trip that the band stopped off at Lahinch, the hometown of Martin O'Riordan, Cait's father. "Shane and Terry, with the rest of us backing them up, told James that it was a tradition in Lahinch, when you arrived there, to stand with your back to a house and throw a banana backwards over it," relates Spider. "It was very juvenile, but James did that. He was pretty daft to fall for it."

After Waterford and Tralee, the tour carried on through Dublin and Belfast, reaching Dundalk on New Year's Day 1986. Then came Claremorris and Galway where the band appeared at Leisureland on January 4. It was Cait's 21st birthday, but her celebrations were naturally subdued by the news that Phil Lynott had died. Frank Murray had already rushed off to his bedside in London after hearing that his old friend was dying from multiple organ failure.

"I remember sitting round the back of the stage in a corridor somewhere when somebody told us that Phil Lynott was dead," says Fearnley. "Terry was done in, because he was a friend. All of them were. Cait seemed to be very upset as well. All I can remember is birthday cake being thrown around because people were in extremis. I can't say I was all that miserable myself about it. To me, he was a bass player, and I really enjoyed his phrasing, his playing and all his singles from the second coming of Thin Lizzy. But as an emotional issue, I wasn't there, really."

There were better times ahead: the tour wound up on home turf for Shane MacGowan with a gig in Tipperary. Many of his old friends and family turned up for the show in Kennedy's Bar, Puckaun, and got into the spirit of The Pogues with a vengeance.

Says James: "We were on this stage where the only source of heat was some sort of range at the side that we were gravitating towards. We did the gig, we finished, and then for some reason the family got up on stage to be introduced to everybody that they knew anyway. An uncle and a younger relative just stayed there, and we played a couple of encores with these people standing in the middle of the stage. There was still some charm about us that we could go and play in Shane's hometown in the local bar."

The tour support was a duo comprising Elvis Costello and Ron Kavana, an Irish R&B artist who was well regarded on the London pub circuit.

"There were some terrible shenanigans going on with Ron Kavana," remembers Fearnley. "He's from County Cork and the majority of the other people, of course, were from County Tipperary. He accused somebody from County Tipperary of borrowing his radio, if that's what it was. It was some sort of electronic thing that he had. You don't accuse County Tipperary people of theft, especially if you're from County Cork. There was a distinct serious edge to it, and Ron was very upset."

Their first visit to America was coming up in February, but The Pogues had things to attend to first in London. Antoine De Caunes arrived to produce a half-hour documentary about the band for French TV, mixing live footage from a January 16 Mean Fiddler gig with video clips and film shot in the studio and The Devonshire Arms.

The next major project was the 'Poguetry In Motion' EP, which was intended to keep the band's profile up between albums and to show off several different aspects of their music. For Terry Woods, it would be "one of the gems in The Pogues' catalogue – a real pointer as to what the band could do". They'd been working on some strong new material before Christmas, and one track in particular, 'A Rainy Night In Soho', was destined to become an all-time classic. Ironically, it was this song which would lead to an enormous bust-up between MacGowan and Costello and to the end of Elvis's working relationship with the band.

They and Costello went into Elephant Studios to complete the recordings. "It was a really nice thing to do," says Andrew Ranken. "I always liked the format of the EP, which is something that's been lost. It's just a nice, easily digestible chunk of music."

MacGowan's opening track, 'London Girl', a hop, a skip and a jump with a simple but memorable call-and-response refrain, arrives as a showcase for James Fearnley's accordion playing, and he remembers the overdubs in particularly bizarre detail.

"I played my heart out in my little accordion room that I had," he recalls. "It was really, really hard to do, but fun like anything. I'd never played anything so tiring, but it was that sort of delicious tiredness afterwards that made it so nice to stretch out. I fell asleep on the couch. The next person up for overdubs was Terry. The way that his playing was coming in and out of my dreams, it sounded for all the world like the acoustic version of somebody's testicles hanging out through a pair of boxer shorts. It was as if somebody was struggling to keep their testicles inside their underpants but one testicle kept dropping out. That's the way it came into my head – although I wouldn't want one of Terry Woods' testicles in my dreams. It's just the way it connected up with me when I was half-awake and half-asleep."

Another Shane song, 'The Body Of An American', works in a few of The Pogues' favourite tricks, its sedate opening waltz suddenly shooting off at speed, at the point where the wake described in the lyrics moves from sadness to celebration, towards a hearty, singalong chorus. Deft, stop-start punctuation and Spider's whistle, fluttering around on high, add extra zest to the main event.

'Planxty Noel Hill', Jem's lively instrumental response to the BP Fallon radio debate, is included as the EP's closing track. While Finer would like to think that it annoyed Hill, who had shown so little humour on the day of the argument, other members of The Pogues are not so sure.

"I'd hope he was pissed off," says Spider, "but I think he probably wasn't, because he's been immortalised. It's not like we did some insulting rap. At this point in time, I'm having a debate with myself about the effectiveness of having an instrumental as an expression of disregard. The Pogues were strictly spiteful, although our stance has softened with the years... possibly."

Philip Chevron proposes: "A lot of Jem's things are almost like installations, and 'Planxty Noel Hill' is one of them. This 'tribute' to Noel Hill is about as contrived and clichéd a piece of music as you can ever invent. It's like that sort of tune that everyone thinks of when they think about Irish dancing. Irish music needs to have enough space that the fiddle player can take off with a version of the theme. There's not an awful lot of that you can do on 'Planxty Noel Hill'.

"Elvis never understood why 'Planxty Noel Hill' had its own merits. He never saw it as an art installation, a piece with a point to it. He thought it was 'that crappy instrumental'. I think Noel Hill got the joke. He knows we were smart enough that if we'd wanted to write something in praise of him, we would really have tried harder.

"We'd done quite a nice cover of The Lovin' Spoonful's 'Do You Believe In Magic' with Cait and Shane – in Elvis's view, a very attractive inclusion for the EP. But for it to be on the EP required another song to disappear, and it would've had to be 'Planxty Noel Hill'. Jem stood behind that, cos he'd written it. If there's going to be a royalty on the record, better The Pogues should get it than John Sebastian. It was a pointless argument and Elvis was never going to win it. I thought he was right, but I knew that the chemistry and politics of the band were that we were going to have 'Planxty Noel Hill' on the EP. I was surprised that Elvis couldn't see that."

Still, any strife surrounding 'Planxty Noel Hill' was as a molehill compared to the mountain of trouble that came with 'A Rainy Night In Soho', which presented a very simple problem. Shane MacGowan wanted a cornet on the track, and Costello didn't. He substituted the cornet with a cor anglais – an oboe-like woodwind instrument sometimes referred to as an 'alto oboe'.

MacGowan snorts: "I think he didn't understand the difference between a cornet and an oboe. It was obviously a jazz ballad – and he wanted an oboe on it. I wanted a cornet. I wrote the bloody song and that was the arrangement, and he knew that."

Philip Chevron is the only band member to support Costello's preference. He says: "I thought Elvis did a great job. Shane's instruction was he wanted a Sinatra-type big ballad. I was there the day the strings were done. Myself and Elvis and [engineer] Nick Robbins mixed it. The oboe sounded exquisite. I felt really moved – 'That's just a great mix.' We all gave Elvis the high five. Shane heard the mix and immediately despised and loathed the oboe. I don't know if he despised the oboe or he despised Elvis Costello's oboe. There was a bit of brinkmanship going on between him and Elvis. He needed to express his distaste that we were being produced by the bass player's boyfriend. He demanded that we do that track again, strip it down and put a smoochy Chet Baker-type cornet or trumpet on it.

"It was an unnecessary row - people go in and remix tracks all the time. It was just that Elvis decided he was going to stand by his work. Not only that but the guitarist in the band loved his work. I suggested Dick Cuthell. He came in and did this smoochy cornet and it lent a completely different sound to the thing, more jazzy, more nightclubby, more cool. No doubt about it, it worked. And that's the version that went out – although the 'oboe' version did get released in various places including America. There are something like 13 versions of 'A Rainy Night In Soho' with different edits of the two recordings."

In the meantime, says Philip, "Elvis phoned me up – 'What is this shit about the oboe?' I said, 'I'm only one of the band.' He said, 'What can we do?' I said, 'They're probably going to put trumpet on it,' one of those trumpety-type things anyway. He said, 'I just want you to know I've washed my hands of it now.' I said, 'Don't take it personally from me.' He signed off the record in a bad mood – and we'd done so much work together."

Frank Murray recalls: "None of us liked the cor anglais, so I had to call Elvis and tell him we wanted it off, and Elvis refused. I said, 'Elvis, you have to give the band what they want. We'd prefer a trumpet or a cornet.' Elvis said no. Then he was saying, 'If that happens, I want my name taken off the record.' And I said, 'Okay, whatever you want.' I called out Dave Jordon - and he produced it. Dick Cuthell put down that trumpet and cornet at the end of the song, and it suited it a hell of a lot better."

Chevron: "Elvis never had quite enough sense to realise the chemistry of the band is different from the chemistry of Elvis Costello & The Attractions. It shifts and alters very subtly, usually for the right reasons. I don't think he was ever on top of The Pogues' chemistry. I find it very hard to blame Elvis for this. He understood and knew us as people, but he would push for things beyond their natural limit. All he was doing was standing by his work and the inevitable consequence was, 'If you don't like my work, let's not work together again.' Obviously we'd come to the point where we'd done all we could together. We'd spent a lot of time together, so much that his office seriously thought he'd lost his marbles. It became acutely embarrassing for Jake [Riviera] – 'Who are these people Elvis spends all his time with?'

"It was kind of coming to a natural end. In the end, 'Poguetry In Motion' stands up as a great piece of work. I think Shane has probably forgotten how far he pushed against Elvis. There's always compromises to be made – even now, when we're old men, we still have huge disagreements. This just happened to be something Shane felt strongly about, and 'Planxty Noel Hill' was something Jem felt strongly about, and Elvis made the unfortunate mistake of taking it personally. Elvis played a part in leading us to where we went. I certainly don't think anyone else could've done it that well. But there was a point where we had to move on from each other."

'A Rainy Night In Soho' is a triumph of mood and atmosphere, the richness of its melody and the clarity of Shane's vocal perfectly carried by the smoky, late-night ambience of the instrumentation, the stateliness, the intimacy, the rise and fall of the piano, the strings and Dick Cuthell's horns. Usually interpreted as a love song to Shanne Bradley, there's nothing maudlin or unrealistically hopeful about the words: this is a genuinely moving tribute, delivered with a dignified acceptance that something has passed yet still matters: *"You're the measure of my dreams."*

"Shane was still getting over Shanne when he wrote it," says Philip. "He's got the softest heart in the business. I think 'A Rainy Night In Soho' was part of the process of coping with his torch for Shanne."

By the time 'Poguetry In Motion' was released, MacGowan was beginning a new relationship with Irish-born Victoria Clarke, the on-off, live-in, live-out friend and lover who continues to share his life. Victoria had met Spider first, in her local pub in Golders Green, and it was through him that she came to know MacGowan.

"I met Shane in London in 1982 when I was 16 and he was 24," Victoria told the *Daily Mail* some 14 years later. "I was working for Sock Shop, he was working in a record shop. Nothing happened for four years but in 1986 our friendship developed into something more."

That began on the night of her birthday, when she received a kiss from MacGowan.

"Shane isn't an obvious sex symbol," continued Clarke, "but he is a lovely, talented person with nice eyes and a good physique. We shared many of the same interests – we both love 18th Century literature and 17th Century poetry. We once spent 13 hours in a restaurant, just chatting."

In the documentary *If I Should Fall From Grace: The Shane MacGowan Story*, Victoria declares: "One day I just looked at him and saw beauty where before I'd seen hideous arrogance." She came to admire his capacity for doing things that she herself wouldn't dare to do, his "sheer nerve and imagination".

MacGowan, meanwhile, still bristles at the mention of Elvis Costello, and James Fearnley offers a final twist in the tale of 'A Rainy Night In Soho': "Elvis gave Shane his Ovation Jubilee guitar. This wasn't a peace offering, I don't think. Shane never let it out of his sight for a very long time after that. He wanted that guitar there because it was like having power over his feelings about Elvis, like there was some sort of weird curse on it – a curse on Shane. Maybe there was just a general bad vibe about the guitar because it was Elvis' guitar. Shane wanted to be in control of it. That's my guess. He was so concerned about where the guitar was all the time. I do remember him going on about a curse but, of course, Shane is a very creative, fanciful, mythological sort of person."

It certainly wouldn't be creative or fanciful to suggest that Costello's next dealings with The Pogues would bring a heap of misfortune to the band.

The Pogues were in the States when 'Poguetry In Motion' reached its highest UK chart position of 29, early in March 1986. It was the first time in America for most of the band, and a long time in the plane for those, like Shane MacGowan, who were not good fliers.

Says Spider: "I remember once going up to Newcastle – the first time I'd been in an airplane since I'd come back from Libya when I was seven and a half – and neither Shane nor Cait had been in an airplane before."

Presumably, Cait had been in a plane when her family returned from Nigeria to settle in London but as little more than a toddler, she was unlikely to remember anything about it.

"They were both really terrified," continues Spider. "Cait just crossed herself all the way. Shane felt it necessary to take lots of tranquillisers. It's cruel to make fun of people cos they're scared of flying, but sitting there crossing yourself constantly – it was quite amusing. I was taking the piss."

The Pogues, travelling for once without Costello, decided that rather than cross themselves all the way across the Atlantic to New York, they would drink. James Fearnley describes the mixture of fear and wonder with which he flew into one of the world's most exciting cities.

"I was scared shitless," he reveals. "I suppose my assumptions I mostly got from American television programmes. I assumed it was an inherently dangerous place, a society gone mad. Drinking all the way, on Air India, was lunatic. I know how to travel now: I don't drink on airplanes, and I get some sleep. But then I was so excited and nervous together – we must have made the other people's travel a misery. There was clambering over the seats and bottles of whiskey and we had all the window blinds up, looking down at the ice floes and Greenland when you're supposed to close the blinds and let everybody get some rest, and all the sights we could see and all the shenanigans we could get up to... I'd say I was one of the worst offenders.

"It was miserable lining up for customs, which I hadn't expected at all, and it was really, really difficult to shuffle forward with a hangover and lack of sleep and a time difference. The condition I was in and the queue snaking round – 'Welcome to the United States', and there's the picture of President Reagan.

"We were picked up by limousines, which we've never had since [except, I have to say, the first time we went to Los Angeles], and it was fabulous. I sat next to the guy that drove it, in the front, and there was Philip and Dave Jordan in the back and maybe Terry. I couldn't get enough of the guy that was driving because of his accent, his gritty face and this mauve, plush seat in the front... there was some vibe about it. I wanted to hear him talk. I kept asking him questions and drinking him in and drinking it all in outside – the water towers and bridges, the water, and those grotty little houses you go past on the expressway, the type of stone they make the bridges out of."

Jem Finer, not a newcomer to America, was less impressed by the travel arrangements: "I never used to like going in limousines. I thought it was shit. Horrible vehicles. I'd rather just get a cab or something."

The Pogues, not at all sober, checked into the Iroquois in West 44th Street, at that time one of the favoured hotels among rock bands visiting New York, and immediately headed for the bar.

"We've gotta get out of here," said Philip to James. "I've just found out we're quite close to Broadway."

James replied: "I want to go and find a proper bar instead of this hotel bar shit."

"Whenever we do 'Thousands Are Sailing'," says James today, "I always think of the night we got there. I went out drinking with Philip, and I'm not sure if he's talking about me in the song – *"And in Brendan Behan's footsteps / I danced up and down the street"* – but I've chosen to think it's about me because that's what I did."

Chevron, who started writing the great Pogues anthem during this first trip, confirms that James "looms quite large" in the song, although not in those particular lines. "Dancing up and down the street was what Brendan Behan was supposed to have done when he first came to New York," says Philip. "Although Shane always said Behan was a terrible dancer...

"What happened was that James and I walked down towards Broadway and when we got there, I held him back. I said, 'Stop. We've gotta do this properly.' I took his hand and said, 'Now, come with me,' and we walked on down to Broadway." This is immortalised in the lines, *"We stepped hand in hand on Broadway / Like the first man on the moon"*.

Chevron and Fearnley soaked up the atmosphere of New York's legendary theatre district and then carried on drinking. "We went into bars and I had a camera with me," says James. "I took photographs of people. I got straight into it."

"When you go to America for the first time, you realise it's just like the movies, only more so, as Quentin Crisp said," adds Philip. "I was as mad as everybody else with the whole New York experience. It was the most Babylonian tour ever. Everyone experimented with drugs. We were all doing bits of everything and people were giving them up the same day – 'I don't like this one.' It was total insanity: 'Welcome to New York – we've been waiting for you guys all our lives.' We decided to plunge in."

What the band plunged into first was a couple of days of press and promotion. The tour was focused on New York and the surrounding area, and Frank Murray had hired an independent press officer to drum up as much interest as possible. The Pogues' American company, MCA, was also taking its responsibilities seriously, especially since college radio had picked up on 'A Pair Of Brown Eyes' and the 'Poguetry' EP. While

MCA's efforts were well-meaning, they showed a fundamental misunderstanding of the band.

Says Chevron: "They sent a photo out to the press. It's the one on the back of 'Poguetry In Motion' except that they'd airbrushed and filled in Shane's teeth, and put shamrocks all around. There was a hell of a lot of 'Kiss me quick, I'm Irish,' sort of thing that had nothing to do with what we were doing, and it was in danger of consigning us to next week's bargain bin. Being Elvis's pet group didn't help at a certain point. It became yet another obstacle to negotiate.

"It was getting irritating to be asked by every American journalist, 'What's it like to work with Elvis Costello?' The question came with baggage that The Pogues didn't like and didn't need. There's the danger of being thought of as 'this little band that Elvis picked up and they're all Irish and they all drink'. It was on the edge of doing us harm, and that wasn't Elvis's fault but nevertheless he got blamed for it, I would say mainly by Shane. This is all tied up with the whole thing of 'drunken paddies' and 'plastic paddies'. Shane understood more than anybody where this could go pear-shaped. He wanted people to take the band seriously, and his need to be taken seriously went beyond being on Dave Robinson's jokey little record label and having Elvis Costello come in and do stuff for us."

The tour proper began on February 28 at a recently opened New York club called The World. The Pogues sold it out easily, and they played an all-conquering show to a crowd who surprised them by mouthing along with all the words. Hollywood actor Matt Dillon was there that night, he became an instant convert, and he subsequently turned out for other gigs on the tour. An enthusiastic and friendly character, his conversations were nevertheless a little limited. He talked about The Clancy Brothers, and he complimented The Pogues in variations of one sentence only: "Hey man, I dig your shit."

NME writer Mat Snow and photographer Bleddyn Butcher were covering the tour and, early the next morning, leaving the Iroquois in search of breakfast, the pair bumped into a woozy-looking Cait O'Riordan in the lift. She introduced her companion, a bearded fellow, as a rock journalist, before vanishing into the city streets.

Later, the band were milling around the lobby, ready to depart for the next gig in Washington, DC, when it became apparent that Cait had not only left the building, she had left the tour and was about to leave America.

Frank Murray recalls: "We'd been doing our usual Pogues drinking till five or six in the morning, taking advantage of the licensing laws in New York. And we got up in the morning and we started to look for Cait. We couldn't find her anywhere. And then we got really worried.

"Somehow, after three or four hours, I tracked down a guy called Bill Flanagan, a writer who knew Elvis. He'd been part of the conspiracy to get Cait out of town. I think Elvis called him and he arranged for her to get on a plane. You'd think that Elvis, being a musician, would have called and left a message with us rather than leave a band stranded with the bass player gone, and rather than being behind the scenes masterminding it."

"There was a right bloody brouhaha," says Jem: "The implication was that Elvis had to get her out of the clutches of the 'evil Pogues'."

"I got angry at Bill Flanagan," continues Murray, "because no one had called us and because he'd facilitated this whole thing one way or another. In the end, we all got in our bus and we drove out to JFK to stop her getting on a plane. We got to the airport, and there was no way: Cait had gone."

The Pogues were furious at O'Riordan's secret escape and at Costello's part in arranging it. "I seem to remember spluttering over my morning coffee when I heard the news," says Terry Woods. MacGowan and Stacy did more than splutter over their coffee. Sitting in the bus on the futile dash to JFK, ignoring the fact that a journalist was present, MacGowan and Stacy poured out their anger in a stream of abuse. Snow, finding himself in the middle of a major scoop, did only what his editor would have expected. He reported the whole incident, including the insults dealt out by Shane and Spider to the absent Cait and Elvis.

"We let rip," admits Stacy today. "It would've been the same no matter who'd gone walkabout. They would've come in for the same treatment. What we said was absolutely vile. We're all quite articulate, and that can sometimes stoop down to the gutter as well as reach up to the stars. It was just fucking banter, really. Cait had left us in the fucking lurch and I think we knew what the end of this story was going to be. She was going to go, and that was a shame. She could definitely be a real pain at times. By nature, she's quite stroppy and she says what she thinks and she can be a bit of a nutter sometimes. She was only 21 and she was the only girl with a bunch of guys. I think that makes a difference.

"But her disappearance came out of nowhere. She'd been acting a bit moody and then she'd skipped off and we were without a bass player. We were probably also quite over-excited and hungover and it's a potent brew, a volatile mix. So we were venting. Really, it should've been seen as venting and it shouldn't have been printed. I suppose if you've got a journalist with you, you should watch what you're venting. He deemed it appropriate to put down a conversation between two members of the band that wasn't even off-the-record never mind on-the-record. He was in our fucking bus. He should've shown some tact."

At the time, though, none of The Pogues had any inkling that this was going to happen.

Frank Murray put in a call to Cait and left a message: "No one's angry with you, all is forgiven, come on back – we need to finish the tour." Eventually O'Riordan did fly back, but not for a few days. In the meantime, Darryl Hunt was quickly appointed to bass duties, and as the band drove on to Washington, DC he frantically ran through the set with James, Jem and Philip.

The gig, at the 930 Club, was a grand success for the band and for Darryl. Paul Scully had now taken over the sound and the band had an American driver for the tour, which meant that Hunt had seen his responsibilities greatly reduced. Now he was a roadie, and he was tour managing too, and he was delighted at the chance to play with The Pogues instead of running around after them.

He says: "I was actually going nowhere fast. Being a roadie wasn't something I wanted to develop as a career. All of our crew were incredible, dedicated, amazing people. I don't think I'd have had the strength to do their jobs at all."

Darryl stood in for O'Riordan at subsequent gigs in Baltimore, Boston and New York's extremely hip Limelight Club before she eventually reappeared. "I think I was disappointed she came back," confesses Darryl. "By that time, we'd all got used to me playing bass and I was enjoying what I was doing – 'Oh, this is quite nice. I could do this job.' I didn't understand why the group put up with her behaviour. If I'd been in charge, I'd have given her her cards there and then for quitting on a tour. She wasn't exactly the most important member of the band, and there was quite a bit of anger that she'd gone off."

The showcase that they performed at the Limelight Club was a turning point for The Pogues. It proved that they could win over any audience, even one full of the New York elite: press and posers and celebrities including David Johansen, the one-time New York Doll, Brat Pack actress Molly Ringwald and their besotted new fan Matt Dillon.

"It was a big fucking deal," says Stacy.

It was such a big deal, accomplished so impressively, that the Limelight management gave the band gold membership cards for the VIP lounge.

"They put you in this roped-off area and look at you," explains Philip. "You don't even have to pay for your drinks. When you tell The Pogues *that*... We discovered Long Island Iced Tea very quickly and ordered it by the bucketload. There was a point where you just forgot where you were."

"We were flavour of the month," says Terry Woods. "All sorts of doors were open to us. They made a terrible mistake in giving us those gold cards.

They didn't realise the type of animal they were dealing with. Every night we were in the bar and we drank them dry. They were horrified. One night I fell asleep and fell over a couch and Spider did the same thing on the same night. They mustn't have found us. They put the lights out and left. We woke up there in the morning with the cleaners, started again, and made our way back to the hotel. I still have the gold card, funny enough."

Not everyone took full advantage of the Limelight's hospitality.

"By the end of it, I hated the place and its elitism," reports Jem. "I think there was a lot of us around one night and there was probably some altercation because they wouldn't let someone in who was a friend. I put my gold card down the drain as a protest – 'Bloody dump anyway!' Not that anyone was paying the slightest attention."

The other noteworthy happening in the Limelight – but don't mention the war! - was that Spider met a disco singer whom he married seven months later. This is something that the usually talkative Stacy refuses to discuss to this day, on the grounds that he made a serious mistake he would rather not think about.

The entourage travelled on to Hoboken in New Jersey, and Northampton and Boston in Massachusetts. John F Kennedy Jr and Joseph Kennedy – sons of American President JFK and his brother Bobby – dropped into the Spit/DV8 club in Boston where they watched The Pogues deliver an incendiary set and met Frank Murray. And then, via Providence in Rhode Island, the group returned to New York for the final gig of the tour, at the Danceteria, on March 8. Here, they effortlessly attracted yet another full house with a new sprinkling of celebrities including the endlessly cool punk prototype, Richard Hell.

It was an especially interesting night for Andrew Ranken who, despite having given up drinking before going onstage, had not ruled out the ingestion of other substances.

He reveals: "That was my first experience of ecstasy, which I don't think I've ever repeated, at least not to that degree. The whole tour, we'd been hearing all this stuff about this new drug, and I remember reading something about Grace Jones saying it was fantastic and it made you feel wonderful and loving. We were all thinking, 'God, we must try and get hold of some of this stuff.' We went through all the dates unable to get any and finally ended up in New York at the end of the tour. By this time, there was a big buzz about the band. Lots of people turned up, and it was quite an important gig.

"Of course, this was the night somebody said, 'Does anybody want any ecstasy?' So of course we got some and of course, me being a drummer in the proper sort of Keith Moon tradition [laughs], I took mine before we went on and it started taking effect just about the minute we walked onstage.

"And we started the first number and I found it really difficult to play, not physically but mentally. It just seemed such an aggressive thing to be doing, and it got worse and worse and I was standing there thinking, 'God! *I can't do this to my drums!*' I actually stopped playing for a bit and everyone was giving me strange looks and saying, 'Get on with it.' I tried again and it just wasn't happening. Eventually I got to the point where I just couldn't bear it any longer so I jumped off the stage and into the audience.

"I thought the band sounded wonderful, so good they didn't need drums. They cajoled me back on to the stage. I don't know if any of them realised or not that I'd taken some ecstasy. From my point of view, it was a wonderful gig, but drumming-wise it was a complete shambles. I think we got away with it somehow. Years later, I saw Michael Blair, who was Tom Waits's drummer at the time. He'd been at the gig and he said, 'Do you know, everybody really loved that. They didn't know what to think. It was so *avant garde*.'

"But it was a real downer for me because by the end of the gig, the effects had worn off and I was just feeling terribly guilty that I'd let everybody down and made a complete fool of myself. But then, you see, everybody else took their ecstasy and they were all having a great time while I was feeling completely mortified and miserable."

The Pogues' first foray into America had been a victory beyond their wildest dreams, and all of the members flew home with great memories, especially of New York City.

"It was fantastic," states Andrew. "God, what a place. I really loved it. It's like nowhere else on the planet. Some people did get our music, definitely. I think we were viewed as underground and alternative and cultish."

Jem: "We played in very Pogues-friendly places, where there was a liberal attitude towards music and/or an American-Irish population. If we'd gone to Texas or Utah it might have been a very different thing. I've got a feeling that Shane never got over the jetlag to this day. He always kept weird hours, but they got a lot weirder after we went to America."

Terry Woods says, "I was amazed by America. What The Pogues did for me – they opened up the avenue of emigrants' music and it gave me an understanding of how it felt for the Irish in particular being elsewhere. Previous to that, I would've been fairly dismissive of American attitudes to 'the Oirish'. I then understood that an awful lot of this stuff has been handed down in families and it surfaces in whatever way it surfaces for them, and it's as valid as me being born and reared in Ireland. New York opened my eyes to a lot of things like that."

Shane MacGowan later told an interviewer: "We've got a black sense of humour which is perfectly suited to New York. I think that's why we're understood in New York much better than we are anywhere else in America."

James Fearnley, now living in LA, quite recently met a bartender who once worked in the Limelight: "He's a parent of one of the kids in the school my daughter was at. He remembered Spider and Terry and myself getting drinks at the Limelight. He thought we were great."

Nobody asked Cait O'Riordan why she'd run away from New York in the first place. James and Spider were convinced it was because she'd missed Elvis so much she felt compelled to rush home to him. The *NME*'s Mat Snow suggested that Cait was experiencing the ill effects of "forty-eight hours of sleepless partying". Costello biographer Graeme Thomson concurs, alleging that she suffered some sort of breakdown due to the combined effects of cocaine, alcohol, sleep deprivation, isolation within the male environment of The Pogues and an inability to cope with the sudden flurry of attention in America. Thomson further contends that Costello became so worried about Cait's safety that he asked his friend Bill Flanagan to get her on the first plane out of there.

O'Riordan says in *The Lost Decade*: "I was just full of vodka and consequently went extremely psychotic for a few days, but I sobered up. Once I was away from the free drink and the fawning, I was fine."

Philip Chevron: "I don't think she was particularly well-suited to the level of attention we started getting when we first went to America. It was so terrifying for her that she phoned up Elvis and asked him to come and get her. Bill Flanagan intervened to get her out of the hotel on Elvis's behalf. To this day, I don't know if Elvis was using that as an opportunity to get her out of this band. . .

"Because she's Cait, we never did get to find out what was on her mind. If Jem or James asked, 'What went on there?' she'd say, 'What do you mean what went on there? I'm here now.' She never felt close enough to confide in anybody.

"The first American tour for any group is a bit of a culture shock. If you're hot, you're hot. We were in a goldfish bowl where we were the toast of New York and every celeb and rock star in town was coming to see us. The record company were buzzing around us like flies, promising we were going to make megabucks. 'Megabucks' became a catchphrase on the tour. Cait was unexpectedly vulnerable to this sudden fame and fortune. Perhaps she would've responded better had Elvis been there. I think he may have estimated that The Pogues didn't need Elvis Costello hanging around with them on their first tour of New York. He was actually being generous in not accompanying her. He found he had some work to do. That was my read on it anyway."

There was no rest for the wicked. Back in England, The Pogues played a couple of gigs up north before travelling down for the annual celebration that they were popularly reviving in London: St Patrick's Day. This time they played two shows, on Monday and Tuesday, March 17 and 18, at the Hammersmith Palais, accompanied by a new roadie. Joey Cashman, a friend of Philip Chevron's, had been invited along to help Darryl, and then: "They gave me every show that came afterwards."

The first gig, a wild and wonderful homecoming, saw some serious mayhem in the crowd, although the Tuesday night show was slightly less uproarious – maybe because of what was going on behind the scenes.

Mat Snow's *NME* feature had been published that day, and The Pogues' attacks on Cait and Elvis, uttered in the heat of the moment in their van in New York, were now laid bare for public consumption. Somehow they looked worse in the cold light of day, printed out neatly in black and white.

"Her bra looks like the business end of a Roman catapult" – Spider on Cait.

"If Frank just wears a couple of melons down his jumper. . ." – Shane on a possible replacement.

"We should post her Elvis's head with his cock in his mouth" – MacGowan.

"We should all dress up as Michelin Men and gangbang her" – Stacy, referring to Costello as Michelin Man.

"Elvis always used to get a bit outraged, a bit pissed off, to say the least, by The Pogues' wicked sense of humour," says Terry Woods, backtracking to the days before America. "Unfortunately for him, he was trucking with The Pogues, and The Pogues were not going to stop for anybody, including Elvis Costello."

But then came Cait's great escape: "The unfortunate thing that occurred was that two guys were sitting in the back of the bus writing stuff down and some of it ended up in print. Hence, Elvis got very upset. The written word is master. You can say, 'Look, I didn't mean it that way,' but in print, it looks what it looks, and it just didn't look good. It didn't have the humour that it had in the live situation on the bus. MacGowan can say anything to you and you have to be there when he's saying it to get it. I think that's what really set the cat among the pigeons."

Frank Murray: "I arrived down for the show at the Hammersmith Palais and the place was crazy. Elvis is in a room with Cait, and he'd read the *NME*, and the band were in another room. That caused embarrassment all round. Cait seemed quite calm about it. I said to Elvis, 'Listen, man, you know Shane and Spider and their *Once Upon A Time In America* stuff.' Everybody had a right to be angry over Cait leaving at that time."

MacGowan and Stacy now had to face O'Riordan.

"We were both quite nervous, understandably," remembers Spider. "We were very apologetic and she was cool about it, or at least seemed to be, but it possibly might have upset her a bit."

Philip says: "Elvis knew that everybody found him a figure of fun and would talk about him quite openly. Sometimes that would go into entertaining little riffs between Shane and Spider, but when it happened in front of a journalist, that would hurt like hell for Cait. Elvis Costello was smart enough to know that anything that altered his public image was a good thing anyway. He accepted the position he'd put himself in, but I don't think Cait ever did. She didn't like reading what people appeared to think about the man she really loved. Shane and Spider are great comedians, but in print, it doesn't look that funny."

A typically contrary MacGowan later insisted that it was "a fucking brilliant article" because it added to The Pogues' legend.

However, there's no doubting the truth of Terry Woods' conclusion: "It didn't help Cait's relationship with the band."

CHAPTER 17

Rain Dogs With Everything

It was supposed to be a low-key evening, a pleasant chat with Alex Cox around the dinner table in Khans, an Indian restaurant in Westbourne Grove.

MacGowan and Stacy had a few things to discuss with the director. The Pogues were finishing off the recordings they'd been making for the soundtrack of Cox's *Sid And Nancy* movie, and they were looking forward to another collaboration in August. This was when they would film *Straight To Hell*, the spaghetti western parody that was made instead of Cox's original plan for a rock'n'roll package tour of Nicaragua.

All went well until Shane, Spider and Cox left the restaurant.

"We were just walking across the road," says Spider. "There was a taxi on the other side of the road. Shane was slightly behind me, and suddenly I heard this bang. I looked round and Shane wasn't there. There was a taxi very near to where he should have been and then there he was, further on down the road, on his back. The very first thought was, 'He's dead', but then I saw that he wasn't almost immediately.

"It was that slow-motion thing – it really did happen like that. I think the taxi driver came round the corner too fast. The road is quite brightly lit and it's a busy street. I think I might have been shouting at the taxi driver at one point, which probably wasn't very helpful. An ambulance came. I know I went to the hospital and I know I phoned Frank, and I don't actually remember doing it."

Alex Cox remembers the incident quite unusually: "It was very dramatic and very emotional and strangely prosaic because we're so used to people being mown down by cars. Shane and Spider always used to do the thing, 'Lend me £10 and I'll buy you a drink.' They were just so funny. Anyway, Shane says this thing to me, 'Lend us £10.' I said, 'Fuck you.' He turns away, turns into the street and gets hit by a taxi and knocked into the air. We thought he'd been killed. He was lying in the road and Spider was next to him. It was the weirdest thing, this being Shane and being this musical poet genius and so incredibly vulnerable – and it's just another road accident. You get kind of inured to accidents. Everybody has got a family member who's been killed by a car."

MacGowan was pretty badly hurt. He had a fractured arm, injuries to his face and major damage to ligaments in his leg. He had the cuts on his face stitched up, he underwent surgery and he had his arm and his leg put in casts which he had to keep on for the next month. As a result, The Pogues had to cancel upcoming tours of France and Germany.

"I think Shane did us all a big favour," remarks Andrew Ranken.

During the lay-off, the band members were able to take a rest and to pursue some individual activities. MacGowan and Stacy, reunited after Shane's near-death encounter, spent more than a few nights in the pub, usually the Devonshire, where they dreamed up a new, humorous project – a band called Shit – with a bunch of friends. In their short career, Shit played a gig at the Town & Country Club in Kentish Town where they knocked out a selection of old songs by the likes of The Nips. Spider only vaguely remembers Shit, and has no recollection of the Town & Country show, which is hardly surprising. By all accounts, his contribution was to yell loudly into any available microphone, much in the way he had done at the first Pogue Mahone gig.

At the other end of the scale, Jem Finer and James Fearnley played for an audience of pre-school children at Thomas Coram's Nursery School, near Bloomsbury, which Jem's daughter Ella attended. This, according to James, was "one of the most harrowing experiences you could have". He adds: "They'd love you if you just stood there with your instrument and didn't do anything and just smiled at them. There's no judgement. It's such a purgative experience, although it was really, really good at the same time."

MacGowan was also writing songs during this period using a Casio keyboard, among them 'The Broad Majestic Shannon', a pacey ballad intended for Liam Clancy and Tommy Makem who, disappointingly, never recorded it. A song about Shane's childhood in Tipperary, it relives old times with great fondness while acknowledging that they can never be recaptured and there's no point crying about it: *"For it's stupid to laugh and it's useless to bawl / About a rusty tin can and an old hurley ball."* In part of its melodic progress, 'The Broad Majestic Shannon' bears a certain resemblance to 'Fairytale Of New York', a song which already existed in some shape or form. It's thought that at this time Shane also completed the lyrics for the giddy 'Turkish Song Of The Damned' – the title inspired by a German fan's muddled attempts to converse with him about 'The Turkey Song' by The Damned. Both songs would later appear on The Pogues' third album, *If I Should Fall From Grace With God*.

Finer and Fearnley had created the Middle-Eastern flavours of 'Turkish Song Of The Damned'. Says Jem: "At that time we were listening to Tom Waits's *Rain Dogs* a lot. He's got jazz in there, and East European and Brechtian music and all sorts of stuff. It's quite nice to think you can really mix up styles and make a cohesive record. I was always getting obsessed by discovering new musical styles.

"Middle-Eastern music was something I was quite into – those weird scales. One of the tracks on *Rain Dogs* starts with Middle-Eastern accordion. James started playing around with that. I asked him what the scale was."

James: "Jem and I have been conducting a musical dialogue for years, including things like Doric modes and so on, and I came across eastern scales that contained intervals that might jar a westerner's ears. So we went over the scales I'd found, and had been working on at home on a mandolin, on a tour bus in Germany, around the time we were listening to *Rain Dogs*."

"I wrote this instrumental with this scale that I'd learnt," continues Jem. "Shane and I would get together from time to time and show each other songs and bits and pieces. On one of these occasions, I said, 'Check this out for "Turkish Song Of the Damned".' He turned up some weeks later and said, 'I've written some lyrics for it.' We played it through and said, 'Yeah, that sounds brilliant.' The first time we did it was on a Radio 1 session."

'Turkish Song Of The Damned' contrasts the Middle-Eastern qualities with more typically Poguish melodic passages. A spooky tale about the sailor who left his 83 shipmates to perish when the vessel went down, the song is bathed in the cries and sighs of the lost souls: *"The dead have come to / Claim a debt from thee."* The song ends with a fleet-footed dance to the finish, presumably signifying the freedom that the repaid debt will make possible.

Finally, The Pogues took advantage of their enforced break to finish the soundtrack recordings for *Sid And Nancy*. It was their first attempt at film music, and probably not an orthodox introduction, judging by Cox's methods.

"It's not real, technical soundtrack music," advises James. "I've actually done a soundtrack since, where you have to synchronise it to the film. We just played songs, basically, and whatever Alex could do with the material we came up with, he did."

Cox explains: "The Sex Pistols' music and other punk music was in there. The principal people who wrote music specifically for the film were The Pogues, Joe Strummer and a band in San Francisco called Pray For Rain. It's more like casting. I didn't really give them a brief. You can't give much in the way of notes to the composer. You just hope they'll figure it. I was extremely pleased. There was an undercurrent of the film that was trying to be romantic. The instrumentation that The Pogues used was quite old-fashioned. They were going for something as sentimental and as sincere as they could, and I think they did a really good job."

The band began work on the recordings before their trip to America, and fitted subsequent sessions in as and when they could, with some members more involved than others.

Terry Woods, for instance, had more important priorities to consider. He says: "There are occasions that things came up for The Pogues that I wouldn't have been particularly involved in. Everybody else was living in and around London, but I was still living in Ireland, so I would've come home. My involvement with the band took a big toll on my relationship with my wife. I don't know how she stuck it, but she did stick it. At that point we were living out in the country and my two girls were very young. Sarah was born in 1981 and Hazel in 1982."

Nor was Spider one of the driving forces. He admits: "I had very little involvement. I had no problem with the idea of doing soundtrack music. I must've played on some of it but I think it probably just didn't fire me up particularly at the time for whatever reason – laziness, really. Lack of motivation and kind of swanning around."

The rest of The Pogues were much more enthusiastic.

"I thoroughly enjoyed doing that," says Andrew. "It was a chance to do something a bit different and not have to go out and play gigs, and I've always really enjoyed studio work anyway. I thought Alex was a good laugh. I really enjoyed the *Straight To Hell* stuff as well. I thought we were pretty good at doing film music. I'm surprised we didn't get more jobs."

The lack of direction from Alex Cox was only a problem until the band decided to seize the chance to venture outside their more usual territories and, as Fearnley puts it, "have a dig around in influences that we've always enjoyed".

He explains: "The Velvet Underground, for one, was a big influence and they came from the location of maybe half the movie as well, with it being New York. We were excited to get into stuff like that. I got to play violin on one of the tracks, 'Junk Theme'. It was the aural equivalent of sticking your fingers down your throat. I was really chuffed that it came out like that."

Jem Finer says: "By then, I'd been writing all sorts of bits and pieces, some of which weren't Pogues-like at all. I thought, 'This is really exciting – it's an outlet. We can really expand things here, do stuff we wouldn't normally do.' I wrote quite a few bits and pieces for it. Shane wrote a couple of songs.

229

We went into Elephant Studios and we recorded lots of stuff very quickly. Dave Jordan was helping with the production."

Finer's contributions include 'Junk Theme', which accompanies a scene in which Vicious is shooting up, a romantic waltz called 'Love Kills In Paris', and 'A Needle For Paddy Garcia', which picked up Jem's fascination for spaghetti-western music.

The band also revived The Millwall Chainsaws' 'Glued Up And Speeding' and an old Nips song, the extremely rude 'Hot Dogs With Everything'. This, of course, was the name that MacGowan has claimed to have given his first-ever band.

James remembers: "We tried to play 'Hot Dogs With Everything' in all sorts of ways, the point being not to play it the way The Nips used to. I think we were being too careful about that. I lost my way with the recording and couldn't see where it was supposed to go. Nothing seemed to work and I was turning into a musical wanker, basically. It wasn't until Frank Murray told us to quit fucking about that we cranked everything up and tore into it the way it's supposed to be played.

"I think that song had me playing bass for a bit in the mixing studios or something I have a recollection was in Wardour Street. This might have been the time that Jem tipped a bottle of wine, by accident, into a very expensive mixing desk."

"One of the experiments was to see if we could be a straight-ahead punk band," adds Philip Chevron. "You wouldn't know it's The Pogues. We were using the studio as a creative place to be, trying weird instrumentations and stuff. There were bits of French restaurant-type music. Most of our stuff is in the film, albeit fleetingly, coming in unusual places like the car radio."

"Alex Cox's reaction was very positive," says Jem. "Some of the stuff we gave him got used in the film more than once. It was really exciting to see *Sid And Nancy* and to hear the music. That was a whole new experience. It made the film, I reckon. It wasn't the best film, but it had some good performances in it. I think our stuff works great on the soundtrack album. I don't think that much of the other stuff on it. I think they should've used more of ours."

The final track recorded for Cox was Shane MacGowan's love ballad, 'Haunted'. Cait O'Riordan sang the lead vocal, while Craig Leon produced it.

"There was competition between me and Philip even with the recording of 'Haunted'," remembers James. "Maybe sneakily, I did the guitar solo overdub when Philip had gone off to a doctor's appointment. It's just me hitting an electric guitar with some teaspoons. By the time he came back, I'd already done it, and other overdubs as well."

Released as a single by MCA in August, backed with 'Junk Theme' and with 'Hot Dogs With Everything' extra on the 12-inch, it would reach Number 42 in the UK singles chart. However, 'Hot Dogs With Everything' would be removed from the film soundtrack album by MCA who deemed its lyrics too obscene for record-buyers in America.

After what had proved to be quite a productive lay-off, The Pogues played alongside many of Ireland's greatest musicians at the 14-hour Self Aid marathon held at Dublin's RDS arena on May 17. The concert, broadcast over the RTE TV network and by Radio 2 in Ireland, aimed to highlight the country's rising unemployment problem, and to secure donations and job pledges. The slogan for the day was 'Make It Work'.

The whole idea was criticised at the time for being a rather woolly concept which failed to address the underlying causes of unemployment. However, the assembled musicians saw it as a show of strength and unity, a world-class display of Irish talent, and many bands, including The Pogues, simply enjoyed a great day out.

Giving their services for free, the big attractions included U2, Van Morrison, Rory Gallagher, The Boomtown Rats (playing their last-ever gig), The Chieftains, De Danann, Christy Moore, Moving Hearts, Paul Brady, Chris De Burgh, Chris Rea and Elvis Costello, who was permitted to be "Irish" for one day only.

"I still don't know what that was in aid of," remarks Chevron. "It was spurious at best. Everyone involved regretted it almost immediately. If the organisers had paid for all that talent, they'd have had to charge £300 or £400 for a ticket. I do remember some people took a conscientious objection to it, but everyone was won over ultimately by the bill. It was irresistible. Purely in terms of the talent involved it was worth doing. The charitable aspect of it can be more or less forgotten."

"I'd love to know where the money went," adds Woods. "I never ever saw any figures after that. It's probably like everything else in this country – well and truly buried."

Woods is inherently suspicious of the glittering, fund-raising tradition inaugurated by Live Aid in 1985 and most recently continued with Live 8. He says: "The people on these stages are incredibly wealthy pop stars and they're playing to this audience who have already paid their income tax. But most of these pop stars, the wealthy ones, they've all got tax dodges, like most corporations. These people are up onstage saying to the G8 people, 'You've got to do this and you've got to do that.' U2 had just played in Dublin three times in a week, and they earned something like eight grand for every two minutes they were onstage. You've got the likes of Madonna,

Coldplay… and I don't know where the ego ends and the altruism begins. There's something that seems rather strange in all of this.

"The populus go along with it because they're now fed this culture of bullshit from the media in terms of celebrity and stardom, which is very little to do with music or anything else. They all buy into it. I don't understand how the world is becoming dumbed down to such an extent. It's all instant. Sometimes I think, 'Hold on, it's your age.' But for me, music is ruined. Whatever feeling was there, it's just ruined. I wouldn't even know how to begin to repair it now. Everything is a sell."

Back at the RDS, several members of The Pogues made such an early start on the business of getting merry that they managed to miss great chunks of the day, or could not remember it afterwards.

Andrew Ranken says: "What I remember about that gig was seeing Rory Gallagher for the first time. He's a guy that I used to like a lot. He was the first act I saw where I thought, 'Yeah, this is what it's meant to be like.' I remember meeting my current partner Jane's brother afterwards. I didn't really know him at all at the time, and we fell asleep on a table together, backstage at the gig. There was a lot of Guinness consumed."

James got into a similar condition. He says: "I don't remember the gig all that much. I mean, I drank and drank and drank, and when it came to the customary grand finale with everybody together onstage [for 'Whiskey In The Jar', a tribute to Phil Lynott], I was one of the first people to march out to do it. I was so gung-ho. I don't think I had an instrument with me. I was so drunk I tripped over this monitor wedge and fell on the stage on my face. I got up and ended up at the centre microphone with Bob Geldof's arms draped over my shoulders and likewise. So that's quite an embarrassing thing for me."

"Nobody knew the first verse of 'Whiskey In The Jar'," recalls Spider. "Everybody was like playing round it. Bono stepped up to the microphone in typical fashion and took over, and he remembered the words. I guess it was good that somebody did it. I think I was fighting for microphone space with [The Chieftains'] Paddy Maloney and didn't quite realise who it was. Shane was sort of tugging my arm."

Philip Chevron was the only Pogue to opt out of the festivities. "I had one of my sporadic bad stomachs that week," he explains. "I wasn't feeling so hot. Once we'd done our bit, I went to the hotel and watched it on television. I was thinking, 'I bet I know what they're all doing now.' Next thing I see them all on the TV, obviously having had several drinks, Andrew and James on stage singing 'Whiskey In The Jar' with Bob Geldof and Bono, the whole company, all rat-arsed. They'd been enjoying the day. It could only ever end that way."

Costello, during his performance, dedicated a song called 'Leave My Kitten Alone' to Cait – "my kitten from Clare". However, the couple did not publicly announce their happy news.

"Cait and Elvis supposedly got married that day," says Philip. "What they did was exchange rings in a church, privately, with no preacher man and no legal documents."

It was also at Self Aid that Shane MacGowan first chatted at length to Big Charlie MacLennan, a friend of Frank Murray's and a former member of the Thin Lizzy entourage. Charlie and Shane were among several people who enjoyed a laugh and a joke with Bob Geldof in his backstage caravan. Before long, Big Charlie would become The Pogues' production manager.

During this particular visit to Dublin, The Pogues were persuaded to film a "Just Say No" anti-drugs message for television. "We couldn't really say no without appearing really churlish or like drug addicts," laughs Spider. "We had our fingers crossed behind our backs."

Andrew: "I think Frank Murray agreed to it – 'It'll get you seen on television, lads.' I don't think anyone took it seriously for a minute. We all just stood in a line and looked stupid, not very convincing."

Later in May, The Pogues set out on a short tour of France and Finnish festivals with the Nyah Fearties, before returning for another TV appearance on the *Whistle Test* and a string of UK dates which saw them travelling by coach rather than by van. They were accompanied again by the Fearties and also by Joey Cashman who was this time acting as the tour manager.

"The atmosphere in The Pogues was brilliant in those days," remembers Cashman. "I was such a smartass, making jokes about people, and everyone was laughing. I also started this whole scenario of drawing everyone in the band – not very nice – and I made each person a *Viz* character. I made laminates with the drawings inside. Spider was Spoilt Bastard and Shane was Brown Bottle. I was Postie, a nasty bastard who used to rob children's Christmas presents, and I was also named by Spider and other people Doctor Sex, 'the man who knows everything about sex'. Spider insisted on giving this name to me. Terry Woods was Terry Fuckwit The Unintelligible Idiot. He laughed his head off and wore it with pride. Jem was Mr Logic. He was livid. I once drew him without even realising the significance of the double meaning. The slang for 'Jew' is 'four-be-two'. I drew him as a plank of wood. So he took it both ways, a four-be-two and a plank of wood, and he threw it in the bin. Then he saw other people wearing them and laughing, and he sneaked it back out."

Joey was hoping to be invited to join the band on their forthcoming three-week American trip, a more far-reaching tour than the first one, which began towards the end of June in Washington, DC. Joey wanted to take a holiday with a friend who had a yacht, but The Pogues did not have provision in the budget for an extra return flight. Cashman made his way to America under his own steam and caught up with the band two or three gigs into the tour, in New York.

"I thought, 'Great!'" says Cashman. "They can give me a lift up to Newport, Rhode Island. I can do a few shows roadying just for expenses and *per diems.*' We got to LA where Frank gave me wages for the whole tour and paid my fare back to Boston so that I could meet up with my friend."

Within hours of arriving in the United States, Spider Stacy had split his forehead after, allegedly, falling out of bed. He received four stitches but nevertheless continued to smash himself over the skull repeatedly with the beer tray as the tour moved through Philadelphia to New York. There, The Pogues built on the success of their first visit by blowing 1,500 minds in the sold-out Ritz.

"I rather think we went to a première of *Sid And Nancy* in New York," says James. "Joanne Woodward and Paul Newman were sitting in the seats in front of me. He was wearing exactly the same suit that I was, I think in a Prince Of Wales check."

The Pogues, supported by an anarchic duo called Mojo Nixon and Skid Roper, carried on to Trenton, New Jersey; New Haven, Connecticut; Boston; and north into Canada for two shows at the Quebec City Summer Festival. Returning to the States, the band headed for Columbus, Ohio – the scene of Jem Finer's notorious mezcal experiment, which ended with The Pogues completely legless – followed by Detroit, Chicago and, finally, Los Angeles.

It was on this tour that Frank Murray and Terry Woods earned the nicknames of The Lone Ranger and Tonto respectively, due to their habit of going out on the town together for all-night drinking sessions.

"To my undying shame, we probably did," nods Woods. "Our relationship goes back a long, long way. It was inevitable that when we'd go anywhere, we would gravitate towards each other. We'd a lot in common. Frank, myself and Paul Scully came from the same Irish background. We did a gig one time in Finland, a festival. It was during the summer and I think I went to bed about six times. It never got dark. I kept getting up and going back to the bar. Night didn't happen. We just kept going."

Murray says of The Lone Ranger and Tonto: "We were called lots of things, actually. We had this kind of dream, I guess, from the time we were younger which centred on American traditional folk music and a lot of things about America, and this was the first time we really got to be together there. We were in Detroit and we got to see Doc Watson play. We would never have thought 30 years before that the two of us would walk into a club and sit down and watch Doc Watson. That's why we'd go on drinking sprees together. You see certain things. Each one knows what to point out to the other when you're walking along. I was close to Terry. I was close to Paul Scully, but I hung out a hell of a lot more with Terry and Paul Verner."

Asked if his position as manager compromised his friendship with Woods, Murray replies: "Not then, no. Later on it did."

The highlight of the tour for most of The Pogues was the opportunity in Chicago to meet another of their big heroes, the man whose music they'd been playing in their bus for months, weeks, days and hours on end. Tom Waits was starring in a show called *Frank's Wild Years* in the Briar Street Theatre. It was presented by the Steppenwolf Theatre Company who were testing the production in Chicago for a possible move to Broadway that, in the end, didn't happen.

The Pogues were playing their own gig that night at the Vic Theatre, but they were able to attend a matinée performance of *Frank's Wild Years* where they met Waits, his mother, and his wife and co-writer Kathleen Brennan. James Fearnley enjoyed the performance perhaps a little too loudly.

He says: "Paul Scully went in with a cassette tape recorder to record the show, which was against the law. I was sitting right behind him and the only thing he could hear on the tape afterwards was me – 'Yeah, Tom, haw, haw, haw!' I'm a good audience. I got such a kick out of seeing the show."

Later, Kathleen Brennan went along to see The Pogues' gig and Waits was subsequently quoted as saying, "She flipped. You have to give them awards for standing up, first of all, and anything that follows… afterwards we all went out to a bar and got up and sang and played all night. Yeah, The Pogues are something else."

Two members of the band did not accept Waits's invitation to drinks in a nightclub after their show was over. Philip Chevron was still suffering from stomach pain. He says: "That whole summer must've been a pretty bad one for my stomach. I was avoiding the after-show craziness and veering towards early nights throughout most of that period, and that was one of the nights I cried off."

Still nobody can explain why Shane MacGowan, possibly the most fervent Waits fan in the group, avoided the party. "As far as I can remember, I couldn't make the whole evening on that first time," he says, rather lamely. "I've been out drinking with Tom Waits over the years since, two or three times. He's got a great sense of humour. He isn't really a growling zombie, but he isn't far off… but then neither am I."

Says Chevron of Shane's refusal to go to the club: "I don't know what the foundation of that is. It may be something like shyness. When a shy person encounters another shy person, intuitively they just avoid each other."

"I think Shane was a bit overwhelmed," suggests Stacy. "I think he was genuinely star-struck. It was all a bit much for him. He threw a sickie – although he wasn't displaying any signs of illness."

The Pogues were met at the Vic Theatre by actor Aidan Quinn, whose mission was to guide them out of their own gig, shake off the hangers-on and whisk them off to the club where Waits and his band and his fellow-cast members were in residence.

"I didn't have much to do with Tom Waits that night," recalls Fearnley. "He seemed awkward. He's a deferential sort of person – nice, but Dickensian. I hope he enjoyed the night."

Andrew Ranken remembers that experience of Waits quite differently: "He was absolutely fine, a very charming man. He had his mother with him, so I guess he was on his best behaviour. He was great. We drank jugs of beer for hours and played the piano and sang songs. I think he was quite chuffed that we knew all the songs off *Rain Dogs*."

James takes up the tale: "Tom Waits got up and played a song or two. Then it was, 'All right, anybody else want to do anything?' So Elvis got up and sang that song, 'Leave My Kitty Alone', which was manifestly about Cait. I think Cait might've sung a song. Somebody said, 'Anybody else?'

"I got up and I walked to the front and I played 'Exodus' on piano, because I knew the chords on the left hand and one finger on the right hand. I decided the best thing to do would be to play it as a tango. I don't know if the applause was thunderous. When I got back to the table where I was sitting with Terry, there were tears rolling down his cheeks."

"Funnily enough," adds Andrew, "I was talking to this guy Wilson Milan, who was the producer of *Frank's Wild Years* in Chicago. He's still a theatre producer and I did a bit of work for him a couple of years ago. It was a play by Martin McDonagh called *The Lieutenant Of Inishmore*. Wilson directed it for the RSC in London and he also knows Stephen Warbeck, who's my friend in The hKippers. He approached Stephen about music for the play and Wilson said, 'What I really want is The Pogues.' Stephen said, 'The drummer's an old friend of mine. I'll put you in touch.' I went and met this guy and ended up getting the job, and I brought in Philip, Jem and Darryl. Anyway, the first thing he said was, 'Do you remember that night in Chicago?' He was at that drinking session, although I don't know if I actually met him on that occasion. He told me that James Fearnley had ended up on the piano playing the theme tune for the film *Exodus* seemingly for hours on end and that for the rest of the run of *Frank's Wild Years*, whenever he turned up in the theatre, the cast were always whistling 'Exodus'."

A big surprise was in store for James Fearnley when he woke up the next day in his hotel room: "I lifted myself up – and then this head appeared at the other end of the bed. It was Mojo Nixon. Mojo and Skid Roper had invited themselves into the room I shared with Terry."

Chicago marked the start of a lasting friendship between The Pogues and Tom Waits.

Back in Blighty, the Pogues and Elvis Costello set off for Birmingham where, on August 2, they appeared at the NEC's YIVA! Festival – a benefit organised by Oxfam and Artists Against Apartheid for oppressed people in South Africa and Namibia. Elvis and Cait had become a celebrity couple, and it was here that Costello memorably told journalists: "We're the Sonny And Cher of the Eighties – and I'm Cher."

Cait also talked about her situation in The Pogues: "The biggest drawback is putting up with these drunken bastards, when they are drunken bastards. Sometimes they're absolutely loveable... It was fine when I was as pissed as they were – or even more drunk – but now that I'm a refined, mature young lady, I find it all a bit wearing... I love them. I wouldn't be without them."

That last sentence wasn't quite true.

The band squeezed in a 10-date festival tour of France before their trip to Spain for the filming of *Straight To Hell*. They appeared at some unusual locations, from bullrings to Roman amphitheatres, and James Fearnley – no longer going out with Debsey Wykes – found a new girlfriend.

"I fell in love hook, line and sinker with a 16-year-old French student," he reveals. "She came to the show in Nîmes. You know how you meet people who are really, really hard to impress? She was falling asleep through The Pogues' gig until we played 'Turkish Song Of The Damned' and then she decided to listen. That set the tone for our relationship. We got talking, as you do, about French philosophers and things, because she was still at school.

"When you meet somebody and you're footloose and fancy-free, as I was, sometimes something just flashes up. You tend to meet people like that when you're in the throes of being with people you're so damn familiar with. It's really fun to duck out and get into something that cuts quite deep. I found myself yearning for experiences like that, just to duck out, whether or not it was with a person. I used to go for walks after the gigs, through towns and stuff, and take it all in. I think it's all part of the same desire. You kind of ache for the place to throw something up, and mostly it doesn't, but when it does, it can get a bit biblical."

James met his young love again when she came to a Pogues gig in Paris three months later, in November, and he visited her after Christmas.

He says: "It continued for a year, or something. It was one of those things that gets fanned by absence and language difficulties and age as well, because I was old enough to be her dad, basically. I was 32 at the time. It fizzled out in the end. It was a matter of trying to understand letters in French and trying to write them in French, and it just got more and more difficult."

As The Pogues set off for Almeria in Spain to meet up with Alex Cox and his motley collection of rock stars, storm clouds were gathering on the horizon. Cait O'Riordan and Elvis Costello were becoming increasingly remote from the band. And there were rumours of serious financial problems at Stiff Records.

"There's a famous story about Dave Robinson," says Stan Brennan. "What Stiff did with their bills was put them in a hat. Every week they'd draw three or four out of the hat and they'd pay those. Somebody once phoned up who was furious about not being paid, and Dave said, 'If you don't fucking stop bothering me, you're not even going in the hat this week.'"

Stories such as this were reaching the ears of Frank Murray. He decided that he must, at all costs, prevent The Pogues' next recordings from getting into the hands of their record label. It would cause long delays in the release of their biggest-selling and, in some eyes, their finest album, *If I Should Fall From Grace With God*.

CHAPTER 18

Spain Killers

Originally, the movie was going to be called *The Legend Of Paddy Garcia*, which would undoubtedly have necessitated another spaghetti-western instrumental from Jem Finer. Then there was a title change.

Straight To Hell sounded harder, more punky, in line with the spread of musicians that Cox had assembled as actors: The Pogues, Joe Strummer, Edward Tudor-Pole, Elvis Costello, Courtney Love, Zander Schloss, Grace Jones and Amazulu. They were flanked by professional actors including Sy Richardson, Dennis Hopper and Dick Rude, who had co-written the script with Cox. Jim Jarmusch, the accomplished director, writer and actor, also had a part, as did Kathy Burke, who was just at the beginning of her career in films. The ubiquitous Joey Cashman was present as a sound assistant.

One person was missing from The Pogues' entourage. Darryl Hunt felt like a break, and so after the French festival tour, he drove the gear back to England and stayed there.

"I was just the roadie and the odd-job man," he explains. "I knew that if I went with them, I'd be running round after people in the hot Spanish sun just doing errands. Paul Scully ended up doing what I would have done. He didn't have any role in the film."

The province of Almeria, part of the greater region of Andalucia, lies in the south of Spain, and its capital city, also named Almeria, is located on the coast. In the Sixties, the province built up a strong partnership with the American movie industry because of its Tabernas Desert, which became a much sought-after location. Three major film sets were established there, and Mini-Hollywood — now a theme park - was the first. It provided the scenery for many famous movies of the Sixties and following decades, but its legendary connection was with the spaghetti western. Here, in the Wild

West set that had been built at the heart of Mini-Hollywood, was the setting for Sergio Leone's "Dollars" trilogy.

However, Alex Cox was intent on filming his Island-funded million-dollar production in Blanco Town, one of Mini-Hollywood's less famous sets. And he had decided that *Straight To Hell*, a comedic spaghetti-western spoof, would be based not on any of the huge box-office hits but mainly on Giulio Questi's *Django, Kill!*

These were the only things that Cox seemed sure about. As shooting began, it became clear that *Straight To Hell* was a work in progress, one in which things could change or happen of their own volition with little regard to the script, such as it was. Cox is open about the fact that he and Rude dashed it off in three days.

The Pogues were based in the Grand Hotel in Almeria, an historic city populated by an even mix of Spanish and Africans. Jem Finer and Terry Woods brought their families out to enjoy a holiday while they played at being cowboys, although no one had envisaged that their stay would coincide with a week-long fiesta – a barrage of music and noise and lights that carried on all night, every night. This was either a good thing or a bad thing, depending on which member of The Pogues you were. Alex Cox hated it.

He says: "We'd shoot out in the desert and it was hot and then we'd go back to town, to the hotel, seeking peace and instead there would be this ghastly noise, and this hellish music playing all through the night. The hotel was built like a big boomerang. It would catch the echo on the two sides of this building and it would ricochet about. 'All Night Long' by Lionel Richie did play all night long. People were hanging out in the streets, drinking brandy, and throwing balls and trying to win hideous dolls called chochona dolls. They played this damn tune when anybody threw the ball – 'La, la, la, la, la, la, la...' So you had this cacophony of traffic noise, horns honking, you had Lionel Richie reverberating off the front of the building and you had the chochona thing, 'La, la, la, la, la, la, la...', all night long."

Jem Finer: "For a week you couldn't get any bloody sleep, if you'd wanted to get some sleep, which I did. Sleep's kind of nice sometimes. The hotel was right next to the fiesta. It was bloody disturbing, cos it was so loud and there were these mad tunes that played through it."

The sounds of the fiesta are captured in all their jangling inanity and insanity in the subsequent Pogues song, 'Fiesta', from the whooping of the brandy-swigging revellers to the chochona theme at the end of the track.

"As a cathartic experience as much as anything I wrote this song without words," says Finer. "The instrumental bits were quoted from these tunes and jingles that were playing at the fiesta. I showed it to Shane one day round at his place. He just wrote the words to go with the tune and added a chorus, I think."

MacGowan's lyrics are amusing and directly related to the Almeria experience, particularly the fiesta which he personally enjoyed: *"We have the song of the chochona/We have brandy and half corona..."*

"We then got sued for one of the tunes," continues Jem. "Now we have to share the publishing with this German bloke who reckons he owns the rights to this tune from the fairground, the 'Lichtenstein Polka'. This had been playing non-stop at the bloody fiesta."

Cox comments: "Even though the song is very funny and entertaining and high-spirited, it was actually a nightmare to be stuck in that fiesta."

James Fearnley suffered even more of a nightmare, rooming next door to actors Tim Robbins, John Cusack and Fisher Stevens. Robbins and Cusack had already been sacked from *Straight To Hell*.

James recalls: "Alex had them come out to play jarheads[*], but they showed up not realising what being a jarhead meant as far as the haircut went. They were unable to consent to having a haircut because of other contracts when they got back. So Alex said, 'You're no use to me, then.' They just hung out in Spain. They were partying and going out to the fiesta until three o'clock in the morning. I'd been having difficulty with the fiesta outside and I'd had enough of being woken up, and so this one night, I got out of bed and put my pyjama bottoms on and went out and their door was open. I just walked in and they're all shouting and drinking. I stood in the room until somebody noticed me. I said, 'Can you not shut the fuck up?' I left and slammed the door behind me.

"Later that morning. I heard a knock on my door and there was Tim Robbins, and he gave me a piece of yellow Plasticine as a peace offering. Then they departed back to the United States. I kept the Plasticine for a long time, until it went off and turned into a brick."

Andrew Ranken was one of those who made the most of the fiesta. He says: "It just became one of those things that you couldn't escape, so you just had to give in to it and enjoy it, which was fine. You'd get to bed to this din and you'd wake up to another din. The hotel is right next to this major traffic junction. There were always policemen out there from seven o'clock in the morning blowing their whistles all the time and directing the traffic, and the drivers were all blaring their horns and shouting and yelling at each other. And all day long you're out in the desert shouting and firing guns and charging around. . . "

---

[*] A reference to the 2005 film of the same name featuring crop-haired US Marines.

As for Philip Chevron, he slept through everything. "I'm completely deaf in the right ear," he explains. "I sleep on the good ear. The best guess is that the deafness was caused by an infection I got when I was six months old. It's really awkward. Engineers, once they get to know me, know to put everything in mono in my headphones.

"It doesn't mean you hear nothing in that ear. If I'm in a loud disco and you come over and talk to me in my good ear, I probably won't hear what you're trying to say to me. Because I'm not hearing with both ears, my brain isn't able to unscramble what you're saying to me. Whereas if you were to go and talk to me in my deaf ear, my good ear would compensate and I'd hear what you're saying.

"I can only ever be on the phone on one side. And if something comes on in the distance – if we're in a shopping mall or something and my mother hears 'Fairytale' playing – I won't hear it. I hear noise, but I won't be able to hear 'Fairytale' until I come to a different relationship with the source of the thing. But it doesn't affect my life at all, except in ways I've learnt to adjust to, and it does have its plus points, like I could blot out the fiesta.

"I actually only embraced the fiesta one night where I didn't have to get up the next day. I bought candyfloss and sticky toffee and went round looking at the craft stalls and then I went to the harbour and lay down in the rising sun and woke up there about three hours later. It was a great night. I was just glad I hadn't slipped over into the harbour."

The band were cast as members of the blood-thirsty MacMahon family, a group of gun-slinging, coffee-swigging townsfolk living in a settlement where violence is the norm and strangers are anything but welcome. Jem Finer, having already played an old man in Cox's video for 'A Pair Of Brown Eyes', was again allocated a senior role: this time he was Granpa.

"I think that was a bit unfair," concedes Cox. "But Jem looks so good, and he plays the part so well. He's a very good actor. I think he would rather have played the younger gunfighter."

On this occasion, Finer was happy enough with his part since, as Granpa, he made fewer appearances than the rest of the MacMahons and was therefore not required to be on set so often.

"I didn't particularly enjoy working on *Straight To Hell*," he admits. "I somewhat distanced myself. I thought it was a dumb script, a missed opportunity. It could've been really good. I've read interviews where they [Cox and Rude] proudly say, 'It only took us three days to write the script.' Some joker once retorted, 'Hey, what took you so long?' If they'd taken a week, it might've been better. It turned into a big star-fuck for Alex Cox, basically. It was all just a bit pathetic and annoying.

"Alex liked his power as a director and used it as a way to humiliate people, to an extent. This 'old man' thing was the particular humiliation he chose for me. But it actually suited me in *Straight To Hell*. I was very glad that I was Granpa, because it gave me some time off. The rest of the band had to be around the whole time the shooting was going on. I could hang out with Marcia and the kids. There was so little time then at home. This was the only chance we had to be together somewhere that wasn't London. It was nice being in Spain, and I really loved Almeria. We've been back there as a family virtually ever year since. We stay at Cabo De Gata, which is next to Almeria. But it was frustrating and boring doing the actual film."

Andrew comments: "When we got there, people were very excited. They were saying, 'I'm not quite sure what Alex is doing, but he's making a great film here.' As it went on, they started saying, 'I'm *really* not sure what he's doing, and I'm not even sure if he's making a good film.' It ended up, 'I still don't know what he's doing and I think he's making a crap film.' Alex was trying to do more than he could possibly achieve in it. I think he was trying to get at several pretty major themes, and I don't know that it was the right vehicle for any of them. There were all these loose ends. I started off thinking, 'It'll all get tied up,' but it didn't. It just became looser.

"I thought there were lots of interesting things about it, and the looseness is part of it, but I still ended up thinking, 'Well, what was all that about?' He's getting at all sorts of different issues but not resolving them. Maybe he just wanted to point them out."

While Jem believes that Cox enjoyed humiliating his actors, Ranken is sure that the director set out to make divisions among them.

"I think Alex, in his devious, mischievous way, thought that one way of achieving tension in the film was to actually create tension within the cast," ventures Andrew. "So we had this situation where The Pogues were all in the same gang, and Joe Strummer and Courtney Love and all the other guys were in this rival gang, and we actually led quite separate existences because we stayed in the hotel in Almeria. I don't know about Courtney, but the others all lived out on the set, so they were in the desert the whole time. They did turn up at the hotel occasionally, and they'd sort of swagger around making out that they were the real tough guys cos they lived in the desert. We were all wimps cos we came back to sleep in the hotel, although we weren't sleeping. We were out playing on the dodgems all night. The whole thing was pretty childish - but in general it was good vibes."

Philip Chevron takes up one of Andrew's points: "It was like Alex was picking up on the psychology of the people he'd employed and mixing that up with the characters he was asking them to play – the dynamic between Cait and Elvis, say. He'd staged this thing where Cait is torturing Elvis – I think that scene made it to the DVD as an extra. There's a lot of very direct mind-fuck sort of things. He knew that if you put a bunch of people who'd never acted before into a movie, especially a western, they will conform to childhood type. He wanted to create an atmosphere of mayhem and sexual tension on the set."

Alex Cox declares that he found The Pogues "very agreeable, quite pissed, very sweet, very loveable". He adds: "There was a loving, warm vibe about them, I think Shane enjoyed himself enormously on *Straight To Hell* because it was so much fun, but I don't think he took it seriously. He's not interested in being an actor, or even a conventional pop star. He looked good, and he was himself. Spider was a very good actor. Frank Murray is a very good actor. Elvis Costello didn't like climbing hills, but apart from that, he was a star actor."

MacGowan comments: "*Straight To Hell* – great. Going to Spain and getting paid for it, and there was a fiesta on as well."

Some of The Pogues took their roles, and their acting, very seriously. Unlike Jem, Spider "really did enjoy the filming, the whole process, very much".

"We were getting up very early every morning, which in itself was quite unusual," adds Spider. "I just really had fun. It was very, very hot, very dusty, and we were all wearing these Mariachi costumes which were very difficult to get out of if you needed to go to the toilet. I think it was me and James that Alex seemed to be taken with."

James comments: "There are some aspects of Alex that were just not for me. Generally speaking, he's one of those English eccentric types. He's a very protean sort of person, and quite fiery, which you have to be if you're a director. You have to make things happen. He was awfully funny to watch with his red bandana round his head and his shorts and his long legs and his desert boots and his not-quite-Wirral accent. He had a lot to contend with. We all got a speech. I practised and practised mine in front of the mirror to get it right, and I was happy with what I did."

Terry Woods was another who got into the spirit of the occasion. He says, "I had a whale of a time. I liked Alex. But because it was after a tour, it was straight from the frying pan into the fire. We were all still in the tour mode, so there was a hell of a lot of drinking involved.

"At some point during the movie, a gun went missing and because of The Pogues having an Irish connection, there was mayhem. Apparently, if you've got guns, you have to have security people. It isn't just as simple as having guns in the picture. All that stuff has to be accounted for. This was during the IRA era of Northern Ireland, so they got very nervous about us and we were being blamed for the gun going missing. It had fallen off a table and gone down behind something. We didn't get an apology as far as I remember, but we laughed about it cos it was typical.

"The acting experience was very enjoyable. It was something I was always interested in, and I was prepared to immerse myself in it and learn. I've actually done several movies. I was in [the Comic Strip film] *Eat The Rich*. There was a Ken Loach movie about the shoot-to-kill policy in Northern Ireland. Then I was in *Michael Collins*. That was the last thing I did. I was being asked to speak lines, and my voice is very bad these days. I can never depend on it. My larynx is a bit knackered, and it would take an operation to maybe help it, but they couldn't guarantee that it would be any better. It may end up even worse than it is."

Like Fearnley, Philip Chevron had practised his speech night after night in front of the mirror. But when it came to the filming, he was disappointed first that there seemed to be little loyalty to the script and, second, that far from being expected to endow his character with some personality, he was actively discouraged from doing so.

"The film was being made up as we went along, to all intents and purposes," he explains. "The first day I arrived at the location, there were camels walking around. Alex had ordered them. They were shipped in from Morocco, across the sea. But then he decided he didn't like them and they went back on the same boat they came on after having had a walk round the Almeria desert. There was serious madness going on and, frankly, a lot of red wine. It was midday, desert sun, mad dogs and Englishmen.

"I had been taking the script as The Bible. I said at one point, 'It says here that I say this.' Alex said, 'Oh, does it? You'd better do it then.' So I did it and because I was prepared and got it right the first time, it stayed in the movie. That's the bit where I can't kill the bad robber.

"I'd decided that my character would be the gay one in the MacMahons, twirling my gun unsuccessfully. I incessantly practised twirling my gun badly. Every time I did it, Alex is going, 'Leave the gun out, Phil.' I decided I was going to make the most of it, even if it was only in my own head. I created the character although I wasn't being asked to, and to me, he really lives there on the screen. The reason he can't kill this man, Willy, who comes into their midst is because he fancies him. Suddenly, he finds it's either him or the guy, face to face with guns, and he can't do it, so Willy shoots him instead. It's the most unrequited love affair in cinematic history."

The Pogues are more or less unanimous in their views of their co-stars. Everybody loved Joe Strummer, nobody liked Courtney Love, Dennis Hopper was a charismatic and charming gentleman – "not a drug-taking, psychotic nutter from the dark side," according to Jem - and Kathy Burke was adopted as a dear personal friend by all except an unfriendly Shane MacGowan, who had formed one of his stubborn first impressions.

"It took Kathy years to stick up for herself," says Chevron. "She said to Shane, 'I'm not the kind of cunt you think I am.'"

Strummer took a method-acting approach to *Straight To Hell*. "Joe stayed out at the location, living in an old beaten-up car," says Philip. "He never changed his clothes or washed. There's a scene in the movie where he's flicking back his hair with oil from an oil can, and he did, he started every day by putting oil in his hair and was just completely living out the character. He never came into town except once, for his birthday."

Finer comments: "Marcia and Gabby [Strummer's partner] became very good friends, and it was afterwards, through them, that I really got to know Joe. We both had two young daughters, about the same age, so we all used to hang out quite a lot. I didn't really have anything to do with him on *Straight To Hell* because I wasn't in the method-acting camp."

Alex Cox recalls that Strummer was eventually unhappy with the film: "He wanted to restructure it. He thought that it should be re-edited, and new sequences shot. He decided that the hardware store-owner should become the hero and it should be his story, set in a bunker underground in the year 2050. I thought it was fine the way it was."

Cox also believed that Courtney Love socialised well with the rest of the cast.

Shane MacGowan says simply: "I didn't get on with her."

But Jem Finer echoes the wider feelings of the whole band when he declares: "I found her one of the most obnoxious people I've ever met in my life. She was a brash, loud, ignorant, boorish, unattractive, talent-free jerk. She had no idea how to conduct herself. She pissed so many people off.

"I can remember in the hotel having breakfast one morning and she was so awful the way she treated the staff. I have a feeling that maybe I said, 'Why don't you just fuck off?' For some reason, she left, and the waiters were going, 'Oh, thank goodness, this woman is a nightmare,' in Spanish, which I understood. After that we met her in New York a few times and she actually seemed really nice, like a completely different personality. She seems to have reverted to type spectacularly since then."

Chevron: "I didn't like her at all. Everything that she was in the movie – whiny and bitchy – she was like in real life as well. She was a pathetic sort of creature, still expecting that the world somehow revolved around her. Checking out of the hotel, she couldn't pay her extras bill. She'd run up a ferocious tab. Her whole logic was, 'I tried to pay them but they wouldn't take my money.' It's left to somebody else to pay. That was her take on life in general. All these people were just extras in her life. On the other hand, I instantly took to Joe Strummer. Even when he was in his mad methoding-out, he was still Joe, as heart-warming and soulful as he ever was."

James Fearnley decides: "One of the best bits about Spain for me was meeting Kathy Burke. I've been firm friends with her ever since. Sy Richardson I had fun with, and [actress] Jennifer Balgobin – I had an enormous crush on her. She's quite, quite beautiful and she's dead nice. I did go to stay with her in Los Angeles once, but it was clear enough nothing was going to develop."

The Pogues, in common and in competition with most of the musicians in the film, were writing voluminously for the soundtrack, although they had started work on this before arriving in Spain and would continue afterwards. It was an inspiring place to be.

Andrew says: "It was generally a very creative time, and the whole band were involved. Some of it actually happened on the set, because there was an awful lot of sitting around doing nothing in between takes. So we had a few instruments out there, and back at the hotel, and people came up with ideas and when we got back to England, we took a lot of the stuff into the studio that we'd already pretty much worked out in Spain. There was a lot that didn't get used on the original soundtrack, and Philip pretty recently put it together on another album."

Ranken, Fearnley, Finer and MacGowan all receive composers' credits for the film, with Shane contributing 'Rake At The Gates Of Hell', his imagining of the vengeful, brutal fantasies of a dying gunslinger. 'If I Should Fall From Grace With God' – the title track of The Pogues' next album – was also composed for *Straight To Hell*, another "cowboy death song" with a jaunty pace, distinctive country flavours and a chorus imploring *"Let me go boys, let me go boys..."*

Two other songs destined for the band's own album were conceived in Spain. Obviously, 'Fiesta' was one. The other was 'Lullaby Of London', a MacGowan composition that he wrote in Almeria with a Spanish guitar. A delightful ballad delivered tenderly by Shane, it tells of a father trying to reassure his child at bedtime that the ghosts and demons of his fearful imagination are not there, while sending out a hopeful message of his own: *"May they all sleep tight/Down in hell tonight/Or wherever they may be."*

Straight To Hell was slagged to hell when it was released the next year, and that's if it got reviewed at all.

Alex Cox confesses: "I hadn't really planned it for a long time and hadn't invested a huge amount of time or emotion in it other than the time spent doing it. I was into something else anyway then. I was making a film called *Walker* [which Spider appeared in]. It was Joe more than anybody who had to carry the can for *Straight To Hell*, cos he was in London. It was very honorable of him to do that."

Philip proposes: "I think Alex's vision of the film was much bigger than what eventually was given out to the cinemas. It seemed to me it needed to be a three-hour epic. Most people go along with the line that it's just an extended in-joke. [Spider refers to it as a "glorified home movie".] It comes out as that because of the sacrifices Alex had to make as a director in the cutting room. He must've said, 'Oh, fuck this, they're not going to let me make the film I want to make. I'll just make a popcorn movie.' I saw some of the rushes and they were just extraordinary. The cinematography was gorgeous. Some of the characterisation was very interesting. Those were some of the things that had to be sacrificed that broke Alex's heart."

Nevertheless, *Straight To Hell* has quite recently been reassessed in some quarters as a cult classic, with its British Film Institute reissue on DVD, packaged with Cox's *Death And The Compass*.

"What happened was when the BFI did this new edition, that was the magic ingredient that made the whole focus change and yes, it started to get serious reviews," says Philip. "Also, the second soundtrack album of music which didn't make it on to the original, a beautiful album which I supervised, came out recently. All of that helped to build up the credibility of the film. What does it take? It takes the BFI to acknowledge you before you get a good review in the broadsheets – academia says *Straight To Hell* is cool!"

Darryl Hunt was feeling disillusioned with his role in The Pogues. He didn't want to be a roadie forever: he wanted to be a musician.

"I'd started off as driver and tour manager and I did the sound," says Darryl. "Now there wasn't even any driving needed. I was reduced to changing strings on guitars. I was pondering leaving the outfit, cos I didn't want to continue doing this job. I got it [the teasing] particularly rough after Frank joined, when I didn't have so much responsibility any more. Maybe that's one of the reasons why I wanted to do something else. I didn't want to be involved in something with negative vibrations."

Hunt was thinking of returning to his old band, The Troubleshooters, which included his old friend Dave Scott and James Fearnley's ex-girlfriend, Debsey Wykes. He had told Frank Murray of his intention to quit The Pogues and in preparation for this, he was training Joey Cashman to take over his job. Darryl was one of the few people not to suspect that the band might have a vacancy for a bass guitarist coming up in the near future.

"I didn't really see Cait leaving," he admits. "We'd just had a very successful album. She sang 'Danny Boy' in *Straight To Hell*. Everything had settled down quite a bit. If she had any sense, she wouldn't leave something that was going places. Why take your bets off a winning horse?"

When the group returned from Almeria several members, including MacGowan, Philip, Spider, Terry and James, contributed to a charity album, *Irish Ways – For the Children*, for the London Irish Live Trust (LILT). The organisation was set up by Ron Kavana as a peace initiative, opposed to sectarianism in Ireland, and its beneficiary was the Belfast Charitable Trust For Integrated Education.

"I just sat down for an afternoon and played some guitar," says James. "Any peace initiative, I'm going to support. I was brought up as a Quaker, and that's as pacifist as you can get."

The Pogues regrouped at the end of September 1986 for rehearsals. They had a John Peel session coming up, they were writing for the *Straight To Hell* soundtrack and they were planning to record the material soon. In addition, a European tour had been booked for November.

It had become clear to most if not all of the band that O'Riordan's mind was not on the job. "Things were pretty shaky with Cait," confirms Andrew. "I think we all realised it was on the cards that she'd leave, and I don't know if anyone was that keen to persuade her to stay. It seemed that she was much more interested in being with Elvis Costello and she was losing interest in the band, and it just didn't seem to be working, really. I was probably not on speaking terms with her. I don't know which particular row it was that led to us not speaking. I think I had quite a few with her.

"Really, I wanted her to be much more committed and to work with me much more closely, and it wasn't happening. It got worse instead of better. Nobody could tell her anything – certainly not me, cos we weren't speaking. She did go off into her own world a lot of the time, and that became more and more pronounced. I think it must've been obvious, even though it wasn't said for quite a long time, that she was sidelining herself and eventually would go.

"This was at a time when things were really starting to snowball, and we probably chose not to think about it too much. It was more a case of trying to keep going and doing what we had to do. We weren't ever that great at planning for the future. We never knew what was round the corner anyway."

Jem Finer ventures: "Probably one got the feeling that things were coming to an end, but at the time I'm not sure if I even cared. I think it was the case that Cait didn't talk to any of us. I think she got quite stand-offish. She was the only one that would blank people, and she had a starry attitude. And she could be quite unpleasant. Well, I suppose we all could. But there's a certain humility that's attractive in human beings and a certain arrogance, which is definitely not. Musically, she didn't deserve to be arrogant. She was a great singer with a lovely voice, but her bass playing wasn't that fantastic. Obviously, she had a certain charisma but she wasn't always the most pleasant person. So, in that sense, I wasn't her greatest fan."

Philip: "I felt an estrangement between her and the rest of us in Almeria as she got ever closer to Elvis and simultaneously ever more torturing him. She was drifting away from us further and further."

"I knew she'd leave the band," adds Frank Murray. "I was quite resigned to it. I'd been around musicians all my life and to me it was very, very obvious. Elvis was doing a lot of travelling and going to LA a lot, and Cait was going with him. Hanging with Elvis in LA with his friends was a different life than going round Europe with seven or eight guys in a cramped bus. I didn't think the relationship would be able to withstand him going in one direction round the world and us going in the other direction."

At the same time, The Pogues became aware of Darryl's plans to leave. "I don't think anyone was particularly surprised," comments Andrew, "because we used to tease him mercilessly all the time, and he put up with it, but probably enough was enough. And also he had other fish to fry. I think the feeling was probably, 'Oh, fuck! Where do we find another Darryl?'

"It was around that time that Joey Cashman came in. I got on all right with him most of the time. I didn't always like his way of doing things. I think he was quite often in cahoots with Frank, and he had this old-school rock'n'roll attitude which, a lot of the time, I find pretty arrogant and insulting and unnecessary. It always seemed to me to be symptomatic of the way that they were trying to get us to work, on the road all the time. I did feel that there was too much touring, and certainly Jem did, and most of the others as well."

Darryl was in rehearsals with the band one day, showing Joey the ropes, when Cait went absent without leave, and failed to phone in.

"I said, 'See if her bass is around,'" recalls Murray. "Elvis had given her a really cool Fender bass. Someone said, 'It seems to be gone.' I said, 'Well, she's not coming back.'"

This is where The Pogues have conflicting memories. Some say that her bass was still there, and that she later came to collect it. Others insist that it had vanished, and that she had claimed the night before that she was taking it home to practise. Whatever the case, Cait had walked out on the band just as suddenly as she had done in New York, only this time she had no intention of returning. Both Jem and James made phone calls to try and track down O'Riordan so as to get to the bottom of her latest disappearance.

"Next thing, she was on the west coast of America with Elvis," says James. "He was staying in his hotel under the name of Napoleon Dynamite. I had to speak to one or the other of them, and I spoke to Cait. My reaction was, 'Where the fuck are you and what's going on?' It annoyed me that she should bugger off without telling anybody what was happening. I don't remember the conversation all that well, but I got the gist of it, that she had actually left."

"I remember phoning her and asking if she was coming to rehearsals," says Jem. "She said, 'No,' and I said, 'Oh well, are you likely to be coming at any point?' and she said, 'No.'"

Shane MacGowan claims to have been surprised at Cait's departure, adding: "I was pissed off."

"It was a very shocking moment for all of us," adds Philip Chevron, "because somebody had left, for the first time, in the middle of a very exciting period. I felt a mixture of relief and disappointment. There was no doubt that she was a great Pogue and a great asset to The Pogues."

"I was really, really sad when she left," recalls Spider. "I thought she was going to be a difficult person to replace. She was such a strong character, such a powerful figure, both within the dynamic of the band and the way they looked and worked onstage. She was turning into a very good bassist as well."

Cait received little sympathy from the other band members or from Frank Murray who states: "I didn't care, because I knew it was coming. I didn't really have any run-ins with Cait but after she left the band and went off with Elvis, she never spoke to me again. She had a lot of the band thrown out of an Elvis Costello gig in Paris, within about six months of her leaving. They'd arranged to go down and see Elvis. I could smell trouble. They went backstage and someone said, 'Come on, Pogues, you've gotta give back your passes.' According to the guys from Elvis's road crew, she insisted they weren't allowed back there."

Stiff's Dave Robinson remarks: "Frank was happy to get rid of Cait, cos she wouldn't play the ballgame. Frank had now got rid of an anti-vote. He had [most of] the lads behind him and he could tell them any old story he wanted."

"I thought it was the best thing for everybody when she left," says Finer.

And Andrew Ranken comments: "I wouldn't call it a disaster, but it was problematic cos we needed someone to play the bass. I think the other side of it was that everyone realised it was an opportunity to get some fresh blood into the band – and then drink it."

CHAPTER 19

The Irish Rovers

Cait O'Riordan took no further interest in The Pogues. She ignored their albums, and had no further contact with any of her former band-mates for another 17 years.

In an interview with Irish TV listings magazine *RTE Guide* in January 2005, she said: "I only just heard *If I Should Fall From Grace* and it's a great album. So it was my loss. I should have checked in with the band and enjoyed the music. Sometimes when you leave, though, you just can't look back. It's too much of a head wreck."

While O'Riordan was starting her new, Pogue-free life with Elvis Costello, touring the world and notching up writing credits on his albums, Darryl Hunt was stepping into the job she had vacated. He'd been invited, first of all, to stand in on bass at the John Peel session and the *Straight To Hell* recordings.

Hunt had covered for Cait before, he knew the band and their material inside out, and so he was ideally placed to become her full-time replace-ment. Astonishingly, The Pogues did not consider this, instead drawing up a list of possible candidates for the post. They included Ron Kavana, Nigel Lewis from Tall Boys and, according to Frank Murray, Shane's old flame Shanne Bradley.

"Shane was anxious for her to join," says Murray. "He carried a torch for her for a long time. A few other names were mentioned, but we didn't have time to rehearse people and get the European tour done so I suggested, 'Why don't we let Darryl play the tour? Then when we've got time off, we can hold auditions and do whatever you want.' Darryl was the roadie for the band. He was part of the family."

Andrew Ranken and Philip Chevron realised straight away that Darryl was the man for the job, and they were aghast at the idea of auditions.

"It was very problematic getting Darryl into the band," reveals Philip. "Myself and Andrew had to work on this at some length. Darryl had been the guy who deputised in times of emergency. Apart from me and Andrew and Darryl himself, nobody thought of him as the logical replacement.

"Ron Kavana must've thought he'd been given the job. One time I was sitting with him in the Devonshire. He said, 'I know you can't say much at the moment, but mum's the word. Nudge, nudge, wink, wink, I'll be seeing you next month and we'll be doing some playing together.' I was extremely embarrassed because I didn't know what he was talking about. There were obviously people who thought he was right. Any combination of Frank, Shane and Terry [a good friend of Kavana's] is a fairly formidable bunch of people to have in your corner if you're looking for a job as the bass player in The Pogues.

"For Andrew and me, it was just so fucking obvious – why not Darryl? Paul Scully got involved in that too. Eventually we just had to grab the bull by the horns. We said, 'We think as the rhythm section that we've got a bigger say in this than most people, and we want to consider Darryl as the bass player.' This genuinely came as a surprise to some people. He wasn't a serious contender in many people's eyes. I thought, 'Surely they've just over-looked it because it's so fucking obvious, or is it that they don't want him in the band because he was a roadie?' Andrew and I could see that it was poss-ible for the first time to have a proper rhythm section."

"I pushed for Darryl to be the replacement," confirms Andrew. "I didn't see the point in looking any further. I was a bit dubious about Ron Kavana joining the band cos I didn't think it would last. We got on with him well enough, but I always thought he was too much of a performer in his own right to just stand at the back and play bass. He'd want to be out the front doing his own material. It was asking for trouble, really. Anyway, we did give Darryl some sort of a trial and, personally, I was perfectly happy with him."

James Fearnley looks back with some puzzlement at the band's original attitude. He says: "I remember us agonising about who was going to play bass, and the answer to that question was right there. For some reason we couldn't go that way. I don't know why. Maybe it was that Darryl's function was so solidly cemented in being a roadie and driver and all-round solid, trustworthy guy that we couldn't see him as The Pogues' bass player. It's ridiculous thinking about it now that we didn't do the obvious thing there and then."

Jem Finer notes that the band were still dithering about the decision at Christmas, by which time they'd completed the European tour and the tra-ditional slew of UK and Irish gigs, titled Back From Hell. On the other hand, Spider Stacy has no recollection of Darryl's lengthy apprenticeship.

He remarks, "I think once he'd been installed, temporarily or otherwise, he was in fact The Pogues' bass player. He'd been there from day one in one capacity or the other. He'd already done the job on a few occasions, and he'd stood in for Andrew on drums. It was really important we had somebody who was already part of the team. I personally felt it would be crazy to bring in someone from outside who would disturb the chemistry. To have brought in an outsider, we would almost certainly have brought in some arsehole."

"It was good that he'd been working with us for years and that he could play bass," nods Shane MacGowan. "He was playing the same basslines, and the dynamic didn't change."

It wasn't until way into the next year, 1987 – when the band had completed an American tour, with Joe Strummer standing in for Philip Chevron – that Darryl was invited to stay on permanently. By this time, he'd long since given up on the idea of returning to The Troubleshooters, and The Pogues had come to value greatly his musical quality. This also marked a turning point in Hunt's personal relationships with the other band members, who stopped teasing him more or less immediately.

"The band became a much more formidable force when Darryl started playing the bass," states Finer. "He's a lovely guy. I feel very bad about my part in taking the piss out of him. It's not something I'm proud of. I hope I didn't upset him."

Chevron remarks: "There's a funny thing that happens when a rhythm section really pulls together. It becomes almost this unified noise. It's hard to distinguish who's who in it. You understand each other's thoughts and you're predicting things almost telepathically. That simply hadn't happened with Andrew and Cait, although at the time, it wasn't something that I felt the lack of. You accept the conditions you're given.

"What Darryl did was he galvanised both me and Andrew into thinking and playing like a rhythm section. We began to find the foundation. We became the engine room, holding the thing together, and in turn that liberated everybody else in the band, the soloists and the lead-line players, to do what they do best. It gave them a solid bedrock. Whatever flights of fancy they went on, it was never going to get lost. To me, that was the defining point: when it became *The Pogues* was when Darryl did that. It turned the band into a different league as a musical entity. He was the final element that made the whole thing just fly. The previous line-up could not have pulled off the things that the later Pogues could pull off. Also, it galvanised me into becoming a much better guitarist.

"All the things that were irritating about Darryl are still irritating, but they are also endearing now. Just leaving the top off the toothpaste type things, the sort of things you have to put up with in all relationships. Something fundamental shifted in him when he joined the band. I had already realised that he has this great substance, but he just became a funnier person, more entertaining, almost as though he'd been liberated from this skin he was wearing as the roadie or the driver and there was this butterfly just waiting to emerge.

"It was startling. When people do in life what they're meant to be doing, they become comfortable in their own skin. To see that blossom was in itself quite a wonderful thing. All this time there was this great human being there who'd been half hidden away in this roadie shell. Darryl in becoming The Pogues' bass player became the man he was meant to be, and that was incredibly entertaining and beautiful to watch. It had a beneficial effect on all of us."

Darryl comments: "I think I made things work more easily when I joined the band. It seemed to be more positive. There was a little less tension. We all fitted into something that was already quite certain in its purpose. The main writer and singer at that time was Shane, and our job was to make his songs come to life, to make them Pogues songs, make them great songs. We were really attempting to get a definitive version of them. I've not heard many better versions of Shane's songs than the ones we did."

The dramas of Cait's departure were happening around the time that Spider, on October 9 [the birthday of both James Fearnley and Ella Finer], married the singer he'd met in New York's Limelight Club. It was an ill-fated and tempestuous union, which Philip likens to that of Richard Burton and Elizabeth Taylor. He adds: "They were always, always, always arguing, constantly. It was a really unhealthy relationship, two people not suited to each other."

The marriage would end acrimoniously, and Spider would become embroiled in other disastrous relationships – also taboo subjects – before falling in love with his soulmate and fiancée, Louise Nevill, to whom he dedicates 'Repeal Of The Licensing Laws' at every Pogues gig.

With Darryl on board, The Pogues could start rehearsing purposefully. They'd been playing the same old set for too long. Now it was time to work up some of their new songs to play live. Some, like 'Rake At The Gates Of Hell' and 'If I Should Fall From Grace With God', had been written for *Straight To Hell*, while MacGowan had been thinking of Tommy Makem and Liam Clancy when he penned 'The Broad Majestic Shannon'. Other tunes which became set staples at this time included 'Turkish Song Of The Damned' and 'Lullaby Of London'. All of these, apart from 'Rake At The Gates Of Hell', would later appear on The Pogues' Top Three album, *If I Should Fall From Grace With God*.

During this period, MacGowan was still apparently feeling the loss of his original guitarist's role. He wanted something to do that involved a little more than standing out front and singing, and so he took up the bouzouki. It was one of a number of "substitute" instruments that he would bring into the band, others being the bodhrán, the banjo [playing rhythm] and a Casio – although that came along much later, as he admits in *A Drink With Shane MacGowan* – "when I really didn't give a fuck any more".

The boys were also writing more new material while they were on the road and fitting in recordings for *Straight To Hell*, with Dave Jordan and Paul Scully producing, between bouts of touring.

"It was such a great period to go into the studio without any record company interference and muck about on things that weren't as Pogues-related as everything else we'd done," remembers James. "To do instrumental music is just so different from writing songs. They are bits of music in their own right, and we all had a go. We had all sorts of daft ideas.

"A lot of them came from what was going on out in the desert. There was one occasion where I was standing in the shade at a distance and I could see some San Miguel beer bottles that had landed bottom down in the sand, and the wind would pass over them and make a sort of droning noise. I thought, 'I'm going to have that.' So there was a piece of incidental music just called 'Bottle Drone', which I got by just blowing through a bottle, trying to get that sound of the wind in the desert. I put some pan pipes on it because that's the sort of music we enjoyed from *Once Upon A Time In America*. It had an Andalusian theme to it, with flamenco guitar. We used that guitar all over the place. It gives it a flavour."

Fearnley, who admits to borrowing bits and pieces from Anton Bruckner and Mussourgsky as well as taking inspiration from the everyday sounds of Spain, is only regretful that the band did not have the facility to synchronise their music accurately to the film. He cites the example of Jem's 'Tango' track, written to accompany a scene between Joe Strummer and actress Sue Kiel.

"We tried to synchronise events in the music to fit in with certain things that happened, like a look they give to each other at precisely the moment where you know they're going to have sex. We tried to get this event in the music, a crack from an orchestral whip to happen just as they looked at one another. Of course, it's not digitally synchronised, so the crack's somewhere else entirely when it comes to the finished product."

MacGowan's two songs were later described by Alex Cox as "marvellous", although James remembers Shane's concern about 'Rake At The Gates Of Hell', asking people both inside and outside the band if they thought he could get away with such extreme anger. 'If I Should Fall From

Grace With God', included in the *Straight To Hell* soundtrack, was later re-recorded to become the title track of the band's third album.

"I'd have loved it if The Pogues had been able to do *all* the music for *Straight To Hell*," admits James. "I'm not awfully keen on the music that Pray For Rain did, and I'm not even sure if I enjoyed Joe's contribution too much. It would've been great if The Pogues had done their own soundtrack. It's as selfish as that!"

Jem Finer tends to agree with Fearnley, stating: "Recording the stuff is exciting. Like with *Sid And Nancy*, you get the chance to write and record stuff you wouldn't normally do. But then it's frustrating, cos you've recorded whole tracks but the directors come along and they chop them up and change them and neuter them. A lot of directors don't have much of a clue about music or sound. There's a lot of other people's stuff on the sound-track. That's frustrating too. You've recorded this stuff and it's not repre-sented properly in the film and it's not represented in its entirety on the record. It's now been released with the tracks as we recorded them on this Big Beat CD called *Straight To Hell Returns* - full versions rather than messed-around movie versions."

Darryl Hunt was born on May 4, 1950 in the medieval town of Christchurch, situated on the Dorset coast near Bournemouth and the New Forest. The county boundaries have changed since Darryl was born, when Christchurch was officially part of Hampshire rather than Dorset.

Freely admitting to having been "a little bit of a middle-class lad", he went to a local prep school, Sopley Park, until he was 13 and from there transferred to a public school, a rambling old place called All Hallows, near Lyme Regis. "On the whole it was okay. I had a reasonable time and I had some good friends there," he says.

By the time he left school, his family had moved a couple of times – to Bournemouth and then to Devon, where his father ran trawlers from Brixham, fishing for Dover sole. "It was very good fish," says Darryl. "Top-class restaurant fish. He got good money for it."

Hunt's father introduced him at an early age to rock'n'roll and to the music of jazz drummers such as Gene Krupa and Buddy Rich, while his mother listened to classical music, especially Mozart. He began to make his own musical discoveries in the Sixties with the advent of the Stones, The Yardbirds, The Animals, The Kinks and The Who, and he started exploring classic soul music on the Stax and Atlantic labels.

When his eldest brother Ian joined a rock'n'roll band, he taught Darryl the important chords: "My training came from picking up his guitars and learning all my favourite pop songs." Before long, Darryl was playing in a school band. "I was on rhythm guitar, just doing the barre chords I'd learnt from my brother. There was a guy who was three years older than us who played guitar in the group. He was just like Jeff Beck... really good."

Leaving school, Hunt enrolled at Newton Abbot Art College to take a two-year foundation course and, at 20, moved north to study for a diploma in fine art at Nottingham Art College – now part of Nottingham Trent University. During his three years at the college, Darryl became involved in experimental film and music, and through these connections became a member of two different groups.

Moonlight Drive was an innovative electro-jazz outfit with a line-up that included Jan Kopinski, then one of the technicians at the college and now saxophonist with his own contemporary jazz band, Pinski Zoo. It was with Moonlight Drive that Darryl had his first experience of recording, and they played some gigs in the local area. He was also playing bass with a band originally called The Brothel Creepers.

"Us fine artists, we were making and using films a lot, getting more and more into these odd things," says Darryl. "One time we were making a film and we had to do a soundtrack for it. That's how me and Harry got together to do some music. We also had to form a group for a scene in the film. It went down quite well, and that's how The Brothel Creepers started."

Harry Stevenson was a fellow student, one or two years older than Hunt. He became the lead vocalist and guitarist. They were joined in the band by drummer Simon Bladon and two other guitarists, Duncan Kerr, from Trent Polytechnic, and Richard Booth, from Exeter Art College. The group became known as Glider. Later, Bladon was replaced by drummer Keith Gotheridge and, because a band called Glyder were threatening legal action, they changed their name to Plummet Airlines. Eventually, they would catch the eye of Stiff Records.

Meanwhile, Darryl was among the students creating light shows for visiting groups including Roxy Music, and he joined fine art lecturer Dave Measures in avant-garde jams at Leeds Art College.

Plummet Airlines gradually became a priority for Darryl. Leaving Nottingham Art College with a BA rather than the diploma he'd signed up for, he set aside any ambitions he may have had to work in the art world. The band was beginning to make a name for itself in London. Occasional gigs gave way to more regular appearances in the capital, and in time came packed residencies at venues such as The Marquee. They broke the existing attendance record at the Hope & Anchor.

"Harry used to write most of the songs," says Hunt. "They were rocky and quite guitary, but they could be ballady and gentle too. We were very good live, apparently."

There was a substantial interest in Plummet Airlines around 1975, but the advent of punk the next year queered their pitch somewhat. They supported some of the rising punk bands, including The Damned and The Stranglers, and Stiff Records released a single, 'Silver Shirt', backed with the more representative 'This Is The World', but the tide had already turned: "It was all a bit late. We had been quite popular, but the interest just sort of faded away."

When Richard Booth left the group, they carried on for another year during which time they released another single, 'It's Hard', on State Records. "That was another flop," says Darryl, "and then the group folded." They were commemorated with the release of a posthumous album, *On Stony Ground*.

Darryl, Duncan and Keith formed another band, a power-pop outfit called The Favourites. Their first single, a version of Abba's 'SOS', was an Annie Nightingale Single Of The Week on Radio 1. Released by 4 Play, it was followed by 'Anjelica'. By now, Hunt was writing songs, and he had taken over the lead singer's role, but he missed playing bass.

In 1979, when the band split, he moved to London where his ex-girlfriend Marnie (Harry Stevenson's sister), was living with friends in a squat in Hastings Street, King's Cross. Darryl, still on good terms with Marnie, moved into another squat not far away, in Judd Street, with his then girlfriend Karen Gwyther, a fashion designer. "We stayed there for a few months until they started taking the pipes out and turning the gas off," he recalls. "We got legalised and put into a short-life place in Gray's Inn Buildings.

"I was working for Manpower and doing all sorts of odd jobs for them, any sort of driving jobs. I was delivering letters to Number 10 and stuff. I once took a letter from Norman St John Stevas* to Margaret Thatcher. I had to give it to her. The whole cabinet was in there waiting to be seen by her, sitting in a vast hall with policemen with guns on their shoulders. The letter was asking for money for the Arts Council.

"At that time, an old friend of mine, Jos – he's working in The Pogues' crew now – said he needed a tour manager for The Mo-Dettes. I knew a lot of the Spizz/Mo-Dettes people through Gina Birch from The Raincoats. She was at Nottingham Art College, and she'd moved down to Westbourne Park Road where this whole Notting Hill scene was going on. So I did the tour managing for The Mo-Dettes. Soon after coming back from that, I went back to bass and I joined The Lemons."

The Lemons dressed in lemon-coloured suits, in the style of The

---

* At that time Tory Minister for the Arts

Coasters, and played an individual blend of ska and R&B. They released a single, 'English Summer', for The Specials' label, Race Records, and persisted for a couple of years until, in 1982, they threw in the towel.

Darryl put together a new band, Crazeology, named as a tribute to Charlie Parker, with David Quinn, The Lemons' sax player, and a keyboard-playing friend of his called Paul Holub. They were a jazzy, funky outfit who never released any records but played a few gigs, including one at which they were supported by Pogue Mahone.

At around the same time, Darryl hooked up with Spizz-man Dave Scott, another old pal from Nottingham Art College, to form Baby Lotion, a band who frequented the Pindar Of Wakefield and sometimes played there. Drinking in the pubs around his King's Cross neighbourhood, Darryl became friendly with the members of Pogue Mahone, and willingly helped out when they needed transport to gigs.

It was an honour, a privilege and a joy of joys. The Dubliners were making a double album – *25 Years Celebration* – to mark their silver anniversary, and they invited The Pogues to be among the guest artists. Both bands assembled at Elephant Studios on October 29 and 30 to record two tracks: 'Mountain Dew' and 'The Irish Rover', a tumultuous romp that delighted everybody involved.

Producer Eamonn Campbell, a Dubliners veteran of 20 years' standing, had dreamed of producing The Pogues since he first heard *Rum Sodomy & The Lash*, and he declared afterwards that the Elephant sessions were "the best thing I've ever produced", while declaring The Pogues "a great bunch of lads, the finest you could ever meet". It was a mutual admiration society of the highest order, and a collective friendship born from music and steeped in the barley and the grape.

"It was brilliant," says Shane MacGowan of the collaboration. "It was a big thrill. Us and The Dubliners – great. I mean, we can all arrange ourselves. It's simple, it's minimalistic. That's what it's meant to be all about. I worked with The Dubliners afterwards. I still work with The Dubliners every now and then."

Jem Finer suggests: "Maybe they saw us as some kind of kindred spirits, and it was something we were very happy to do. I could remember hearing Dubliners records in the middle of the night when I lived with Shane, so they'd always been part of the soup of things that were there before the band ever were. It seemed like a nice completion of a circle."

And a vindication in the face of the doubters?

"Yeah. But those same doubters would probably not have been the greatest Dubliners fans either. There are probably a lot of Irish musicians who think The Dubliners were a bunch of chancers too. They'd got quite a rebellious attitude. They do things the way they want to. They learnt within the tradition. But anyway, they were fine. It was very professional and amicable. It's not just a vindication: it's more than that. It's like becoming a new node in the timeless march of tradition."

James Fearnley took a particular shine to Eamonn Campbell: "He's a really cheery, instantly likeable guy who's always been great to me. Later on, in the fall-out of the relationship with the French schoolgirl, he took me under his wing. He took me out to dinner somewhere in Dublin and I cried on his shoulder all night. He just listened to me blethering on about this thing. Nice man. And John Sheahan was an awfully nice man too who, as a musician, I had a bond with."

"It was great craic, but it was also surreal," says Philip Chevron. "There was just so many people involved for a start, half of them with beards."

He remembers an initiative from MacGowan which had already been tried, unsuccessfully, on the Costello tour: "At one point, Shane ordered us to grow beards and after about two weeks, most people accepted defeat and shaved. We all just looked dirty. Nobody looked like they were going to have a promising growth at the end of it. The [would-be] beards got itchy and annoying and bristly."

Chevron found The Dubliners charming, amusing and full of stories. He adds: "I think they probably recognised something in us that reminded them of themselves when they were our age - the same spirit, the same sense that we were wiser beyond our chops. We meant what we were doing and we didn't need to justify it to anybody. It was Luke Kelly and Barney McKenna who put the banjo in Irish music.

"In a funny sort of way we were mirror images. Ciaran Bourke had had a stroke and was barely able to communicate with people, and Luke was dead, of course. It was a mirror image and a warning at the same time. They were way too smart to say, 'Don't do what we did, lads.' Everyone has their life to lead and their own path to take. But there was a sense in which The Dubliners were there to support and nurture us at some level without saying anything as corny as that.

"And they helped us confirm that we were as good as we thought we were. We knew when we played with The Dubliners that we were bloody good. We held our end up. The fact that it worked out so well musically was beyond our wildest dreams. It was so spontaneous and instantaneous. We had forged something completely new."

Chevron, with his background in theatre, was especially pleased to be involved with 'The Irish Rover', describing it as "an Irish music hall song". "It was written by a guy within living memory. It was still in copyright. We were doing something from the recent Irish theatrical past. The Dubliners had, in a sense, started out at the Gate Theatre. They were the Royal Court Theatre house band. They were highly thought of in theatre circles, as were people like Ewan MacColl. Ronnie [Drew] and I hit it off purely on that level, talking about theatre."

Finally, Chevron maintains that the union of The Pogues and The Dubliners has been more influential than is widely recognised: "We almost created a blueprint by which other bands throughout the world have made dozens of good and not-so-good albums. The Dropkick Murphys, The Tossers, Flogging Molly – there's dozens of them. Some are tribute bands and some are bands who've been influenced by us. It came out of this magic that got made when The Dubliners and The Pogues played together."

It was a magic that would give The Pogues their first Top 10 single, and they would keep on recreating it. The two bands bumped into each other regularly after that, most often in Europe and Ireland, and The Dubliners were always welcomed on to The Pogues' stage for encores when they were staying in the same town.

This happened almost immediately after the Elephant sessions, when The Pogues were playing Munich on their November European tour and The Dubliners stepped up, to a rousing reception, for 'The Irish Rover', 'The Wild Rover' and 'Mountain Dew'. There was a repeat performance in December when The Pogues, in Ireland on the Back From Hell tour, arrived for the final date at an old ballroom called The Top Hat in Dun Laoghaire. It was an uproarious occasion anyway, but the audience became even more frenzied when The Dubliners walked on for the same three songs.

In March 1987, The Pogues joined U2, Christy Moore and other notable Irish musicians, as well as The Dubliners themselves, for a special edition of the popular Irish TV programme *The Late Late Show*, celebrating the Irishmen's 25th anniversary. The Pogues, The Dubliners and Christy Moore gave forth with a spirited version of 'The Irish Rover', which was about to come out as a single. Remixed by Dave Jordan, 'The Irish Rover' was released by Stiff appropriately enough on March 17 – St Patrick's Day – backed with 'Mountain Dew' and, on the 12-inch, 'The Dubliners Fancy', without The Pogues. It rushed into the Top 40 in its first week of release.

Alex Cox had called on Spider's services. He was making his movie, *Walker*, with various actors from *Straight To Hell*, including Joe Strummer, Eddie Tudor-Pole and Dick Rude. *Walker* tells the story of an American soldier leading a mercenary corps into Nicaragua in the mid-19th Century to set up a new government, with himself as president, in a *coup d'état*. The invasion was bankrolled by an American multi-millionaire with an interest in the country.

Says Cox: "Spider was invited because I thought he was a good actor, and the casting director liked him a lot. He was one of the mercenaries."

The movie focused very strongly on the lead character of Walker, played by Ed Harris, and the other actors had less chance to shine than in *Straight To Hell*.

Cox: "Walker made himself the first American president of a free country. Parallels are very evident. All the actors got a bit short-changed, but it was for the greater good. And that's the end of my story with The Pogues, I think. I've seen them play a couple of times since. I saw Spider and Chevron a couple of times, and Andy 'The Clobberer' Ranken. And I've run into them recently because I was working with Chevron on the reissue of the *Straight To Hell* CD.

"My most profound memories of The Pogues are of seeing Shane getting hit by a taxi and of seeing Shane sober one day, somewhere around the time of *Sid And Nancy* – very lucid, not drunk, a sunny day and I had a nice drink with him down by the Thames somewhere."

While Spider went off to boil in the south American heat and struggle with an unmanageable costume for the sake of *Walker*, the other Pogues were travelling to Derry in Northern Ireland to appear with The Dubliners on the *Tom O'Connor Roadshow* – a trip that would end with three of the party banged up in prison.

"I've known The Dubliners for years and years," begins Terry Woods. "I would regard myself as a good friend of Ronnie's, and I was a good friend of Luke's. There was this television show in Derry City, and we were doing 'The Irish Rover' as part of the promo for the single. It was being held in the Guildhall, a very nice, big, red-brick building. We flew over the night before, had a few drinks and went back to the hotel.

"The Dubliners were coming from Dublin. Ronnie, at the time, didn't like staying in the north of Ireland, and he stayed on the Republic side of Derry that night."

According to James Fearnley, "Ronnie Drew fell off the wagon, which was quite a serious event for him."

"We all met up at the Guildhall the next morning," continues Terry. "Ronnie came in and he looked terrible. Whatever had occurred, they'd all gone on the batter. I said, 'Will we go and see if we can get a drink to calm the old nerves?'

"It was before opening time, but we were told about a pub. We were told, 'Knock on the door, the woman will let you in and she'll sort you out.' There was just me, Frank and Ronnie, and we went in. The cleaning ladies were there. They said, 'Look, help yourself and leave the money.' We did help ourselves and we did leave the money. I had a shandy, Frank had a pint of lager and Ronnie had a couple of pints and a couple of shorts. Then Ronnie was all right.

"We went back to do the show at the Guildhall, and it became quite a social gathering. John Hume [then SDLP leader] was there – he's a friend of some of The Dubliners. The Mayor of Derry thought, 'What a wonderful idea. We'll get all these people into the Mayor's chambers and we'll have some press photographs.'"

The polite gathering in the Mayor's chambers rapidly descended into chaos with the offer of hospitality. Says Woods: "I seem to remember him going behind the desk and pressing a button. The walls parted and out came a bar. He didn't know what he was dealing with. The locusts descended on the bar and in no time it was cleaned out."

"They were plying us with drinks," confirms Andrew. "Then they pretend to be surprised that you're drunk. What else do they expect? The thing I do remember is that at some point we all started singing 'The Auld Triangle'."

Terry takes up the tale: "The Mayor got a bit panicky – 'What kind of animal have I unleashed?' When the bar finished, he disappeared. It was then suggested that we go back round to that little bar we'd been in earlier, which would now be open, and we all did.

"I lived at the time outside Virginia, County Cavan, and I'd asked Ronnie, because we had three days off after this television thing – 'Will you be going back home? Would you drop me at Virginia? I'll go home for three days and I'll get my wife to pick me up.'

"Anyway, we ended up in the bar. Ronnie got sozzled fairly quickly and fell asleep, and I was thinking, 'Ah, Jesus, how am I going to go home?' The Pogues had been taken off to the airport in the afternoon, and I was the only one going to the country. I said, 'Ronnie, will you be all right to drive?' He said, 'Oh, no, we'll have to get Barney.' It came around to nine o'clock and I said, 'We'll have to go.' This is before mobile phones and all of that, and there was no real way of keeping in contact with my wife to let her know what was going on."

It was decided that Barney McKenna would drive, and so they loaded the instruments into Ronnie's car and set off. "Ronnie got into the front and instantly fell asleep," remembers Terry. "I was dozing off in the back. What I didn't know was that Barney had never driven an automatic car before. We must've gone down the road in stop-start fashion through two or three sets of traffic lights. All of a sudden, we were surrounded by the RUC [then the Northern Ireland police force] and the army. They looked at Ronnie and said, 'Look at the state of him.' They looked at me – 'Look at the state of him.' And they looked at Barney – 'Look at the state of him.'

"We were each given a Land Rover with police and army and taken to an enormous barracks. It was fairly forbidding – steel doors, big high walls. In we were marched to the area where they charge you. I was carrying Ronnie at this point, cos he was well gone. They charged us with whatever they were charging us with and we were taken downstairs to the cells.

"Barney got the first cell, I took the second cell and we put Ronnie in the third cell. I covered him up with a blanket. The cells were pretty dirty. I was sobering up at this point very, very quickly. I was thinking, 'Jesus Christ, how am I ever going to explain this to my wife?'"

Later, Terry heard Ronnie waking up in his cell. "He got up and he obviously wanted to go to the loo," explains Terry. "He came out of the cell and he bumped into Barney, who was coming back from giving blood and urine samples, in the corridor. He said, 'Jesus Christ, Barney, what kind of a hotel have you booked us into?' Barney said, 'You're not in a hotel.' 'Where am I?' 'You're in fucking jail. *Now* sing "The Auld Triangle"!'"

Later still, Terry became aware of more noises: "The RUC came down – 'We've got a few instruments and a few drinks – do you want to come up for a bit of a session?' I said, 'You must be fucking joking. You've just arrested us.'"

The trio were released early the next morning after legal intervention and heard nothing more about the incident, except from their nearest and dearest.

"My wife nearly killed me," sighs Terry. "I got a sound thrashing!"

The two bands met up again, less eventfully, a week later for another TV appearance playing 'The Irish Rover', this time on *Saturday Live*. It was hosted by Ben Elton, now championing the young band he had underestimated three years earlier on the *South Of Watford* show.

'The Irish Rover' entered the Top 20, and The Pogues and The Dubliners were booked for *Top Of The Pops*. "Nobody on the floor or in the control box quite knew what to do with us," laughs Philip. "They'd never had a band so big since St Winifred's School Choir. It was ridiculous. When the two bands were together onstage, it looked somehow that there were 50 people. It didn't look like just 15 – in fact, even less, because Spider wasn't there. He was off making the *Walker* movie.

"The Dubliners had been on *Top Of The Pops* before, with 'Seven Drunken Nights'. We hadn't. They immediately saw the funny side of it being their first appearance in 20 years."

Andrew comments: "The woman who was presenting it [Janice Long] I think had heard of The Pogues, but she obviously hadn't a clue about Irish music or The Dubliners. She introduced us as The Pogues and 'The Dub-Liners'. I think she thought they were some kind of reggae band or something."

"Working with The Dubliners," muses James, "is almost as if they're the grandparents, we're the parents and the kids are..? It feels that we have occupied a ledge in the rock face of folk-rock somewhere below The Dubliners, but I can't see who's underneath us. No one has established a relationship with us the way we did with The Dubliners. They were all fantastic."

Chevron recalls one sour note from *Top Of The Pops*: "There was potentially a situation where the Musicians' Union said they weren't going to let us continue because we didn't have a whistle player. We'd done that old tape-swap thing and we were miming to the record. 'Where is this tin whistle coming from?' Some smart Alec from the MU realised he couldn't see a whistle player. It was a dangerous situation that could've got us bumped from the show. Frank saw that and was not going to let it occur.

"Sean Cannon from The Dubliners was to all intents and purposes the only spare pair of hands. It wasn't as if they were going to miss another guitar. Frank got Sean and said, 'You're going to play the whistle.' Sean got all righteous on him. Frank said, 'I don't think I'm making myself clear, dickhead.' Next thing he had Cannon pinned up against the wall – 'When I tell you you're playing the whistle, you're playing the whistle.' And I think he played a couple of minutes of whistle.

"Frank always raised his voice. It was the first sign that things would be going badly for the other person. Underneath his charm is a most ferocious temper although, generally speaking, it was on behalf of the band rather than on behalf of Frank. Anyone who stood in the band's way for some reason that he considered fatuous or spurious would get the up-against-the-wall treatment."

The next week, 'The Irish Rover' hit its highest chart position of Number Eight. And it would be The Pogues' very last release for Stiff Records.

CHAPTER 20

The Terry Woods Solo Album

They'd been on the road almost constantly since the release of *Rum Sodomy & The Lash*, and the first months of 1987 gave The Pogues an opportunity to step off the bus, at least for a while.

The year had started with various projects they all really enjoyed: their promotional activities with The Dubliners, and their recordings for *Straight To Hell*, which had been challenging, absorbing and fulfilling, with only one false step along the way.

It had seemed like a good idea to revive Ennio Morricone's 'The Good The Bad And The Ugly', but after attempting a straight cover, they decided to go for something rather more unconventional. With Andrew's absence from the studio during one of the sessions, James Fearnley, Dave Jordan and [engineer] Nick Robbins enthusiastically took up Jem's idea of a hip-hop version, complete with Morricone samples and clips from The Pogues' own cover. To this, they added layers of heavy rock guitar and a lot of screaming vocals.

"I remember working all night with Nick Robbins putting it together and doing the drum loop and sampling Shane's voice," says Fearnley. "I got to play lead guitar stuff, so that was great fun for me. But then I have a feeling the tape was given to Rick Rubin to have a listen to, and I think he dismissed it out of hand, because he said if you're going to do that kind of track, you have to do it with live drums and not a drum machine."

Brian Downey, formerly of Thin Lizzy, subsequently laid down some drums, and Jordan mixed the track. He said, in *The Lost Decade*, "By doing exactly what Rick Rubin told us to do, I think we completely missed the point. What we had in the first place was a great track – it was completely mental but it was definitely The Pogues."

James comments: "I remember it being played in The Devonshire Arms and I desperately wanted to be so proud of it, but it just didn't hack it."

In another interesting side-project, several members of the band were invited to take part in The Comic Strip's satirical movie, *Eat The Rich*, which wags a disapproving finger at tabloid journalists, political activists and civil servants. Joey Cashman was a member of the sound crew. Shane, Spider, Terry and Frank Murray joined a host of other celebrities making cameo appearances, including Paul and Linda McCartney.

Philip Chevron complains: "Frank stole my part in *Eat The Rich*. They asked for four Pogues. The point is that if the budget allowed for some rather than all The Pogues, one of us was *always* going to be Frank Murray. The over-riding vanity that made him see himself as more than just a manager is one of the things that led to his downfall with The Pogues. He always aspired to be one of these personality managers, a character, rather than just somebody who is doing the band's business on earth.

"That's very fruitful in many ways, but there does come a point when you have to realise that when your intentions are going in a different direction from the band's, it's the band's you have to follow, not yours. His response to that would always be, 'They're not doing it right. They're not doing it my way.' We weren't there to do it his way, and he never quite came to terms with that."

The traditional St Patrick's Day celebrations were bigger than ever, with The Pogues selling out a major London gig at the Brixton Academy as the centrepiece of a handful of UK dates. It was decided that it would be their most spectacular production to date, and in line with this, the band dressed up as New York cops, with a backdrop depicting the Manhattan skyline - designed by Andrew Ranken.

Andrew recalls: "I think probably Jem had this idea of 'collapsing' skyscrapers, and I came up with this drawing. The skyscrapers weren't falling to bits - they were just at odd angles and leaning over. Some of the buildings were taken from real ones in Manhattan and some were just made up. Everybody seemed to like it, so we had it blown up to enormous proportions and it became a backdrop which we used for quite some time. It expanded after a while. We got some more skyscrapers added on to it."

It was at this time that Frank Murray invited yet another of his old cronies, Charlie MacLennan, to join the crew as a backline roadie. Eventually, "Big Charlie" would work his way up the ranks to become production manager, and he would be one of the band's "big four", an honorary Pogue alongside Paul Scully, Paul Verner and Dave Jordan.

"Charlie MacLennan was like a force of nature," says James Fearnley. "He was an inveterate rock'n'roll person, and the toiletries that he had in his hotel bathrooms were astonishing, like an Aladdin's Cave of hairsprays and body stuff. His quiff was perfect, near as dammit, all the time. He used to wear the tightest jeans you could ever come across. He was a barrel-chested guy with a sort of monotone Scottish accent which still people will impersonate – *'Don't even think about it!'* He had a very big presence in the group.

"There was a story somebody told me. Charlie was on a tour bus somewhere – I don't know if it was our bus – and he'd mistaken the exit door for a toilet door. He opened it and he walked straight out over the motorway, but he managed to hold on to the door and an alarm went off in the driver's place. He slammed on the anchors and brought the bus to a halt. Next thing, Charlie's standing at his window outside the bus saying, 'I was just looking for the toilet.'

"These stories build Charlie into this mythological, godly figure who was indestructible and would never die, and it was a profound shock to me when he did die. He was fantastic.

"Whenever we came offstage, he would make fists with both hands, and in between each finger there'd be a cigarette, and he'd have towels draped over his shoulders, so that when you left the stage, you'd pick up a cigarette and you'd take a towel."

Andrew confirms: "He was larger than life and, well, he was absolutely wonderful. He was a very big guy physically, he was certainly somebody that you wouldn't attempt to mess around with, but he had a very big heart."

Big Charlie had set out on his career in 1968 with fellow Scot Alex Harvey, after which he joined the Thin Lizzy team as Phil Lynott's guitar tech. At the time Murray invited him into The Pogues, he'd been working for singer-songwriter Joan Armatrading for several years.

Shane became particularly close to MacLennan, having bonded with him for the first time in Bob Geldof's caravan at Self Aid, and they would remain tight friends, colleagues and drug buddies after both had left The Pogues.

None of the band members report having any particular problems with Charlie. Frank Murray, however, would struggle with MacLennan's bouts of insubordination. "Charlie was a great friend of mine but he could be the most conniving bastard you ever met as well as the nicest and most gentle person," he says. "I gave a eulogy at Charlie's funeral and I meant every word I said, but Charlie could also be bad. In fact, at one stage I wanted to sack him, but it was during my last period with the band, they weren't really listening to me at all and they said no. Every so often, Charlie could get too arrogant and try to wield a bit of power, and that can cause problems with the chemistry. He could try to undermine stuff in a very sly way."

The leather-jacketed Joey Cashman had by now taken up the reins as The Pogues' full-time tour manager. He was "a motherlode of resourcefulness", according to James. He was also ambitious and eager to learn proper management skills.

"I like Frank Murray," Cashman proclaims. "He did me phenomenal good. When I became tour manager, he took me to meetings with the record company. Now, a manager does not take his tour manager to meetings, from fear more than anything else, but he taught me everything he knew. He wasn't mean in his attitude or sharing his knowledge. We managed other bands together as 50/50 partners."

Back in the early months of 1987, when everything was on the up and the team around The Pogues was united and working all-out for the greater good of the band, Frank Murray could not have known that he was training his apprentice to take over his own job. And Joey Cashman could not have anticipated the extent to which he would later grow to despise Big Charlie MacLennan.

"Charlie was an asshole, no matter what anyone says," spits Cashman. "He wasn't a wonderful guy. He was a sick fucker."

No members of The Pogues would endorse that opinion.

Most of The Pogues had come to the end of their tether with touring. Jem Finer had been vocal about it since the earliest days of Frank Murray's management, and other members of the band had started to agree with him.

Philip Chevron: "It was problematic from the outset. It was always being discussed and talked about in people's hotel rooms at three in the morning."

The Pogues devised a compromise which they all say they put to Murray, but which he claims not to remember: every three weeks on the road would be followed by two weeks off. (Some band members remember this as an equal three weeks on, three weeks off.)

"Every time a tour came up, there was always an encroachment on that," says Andrew. "And it was, 'Well, it's only another couple of dates.' But then, it wasn't, because the next batch of touring would start a couple of days early, so at both ends, it ate into your time off and this always seemed to happen no matter how often we put our foot down about it.

"Sometimes Frank would force or cajole us into doing extra bits of work. He'd say, 'It's really going to be good for you in the long run, it's a great opportunity,' blah, blah, blah, and he could be very persuasive. But at the same time, it was like he never really accepted that we'd decided on how we wanted to work and we wanted to stick to that. He should've been supporting us, not trying to undermine us."

Philip continues: "When we came off the road, it was still relentless. It wasn't really two weeks to unwind because there was still something else that needed to be done. After a while, it just stopped being observed anyway. People's families were beginning to fall apart, in two or three cases very seriously indeed.

"You have the syndrome that after three-and-a-half weeks on the road, you're partly insane. Tour madness takes over after two weeks. The normal day-to-day courtesies of life don't actually exist on the road. You come back and you've got tour madness and you've had a few drinks on the plane and you're like a monster, a roaring fucking beast coming through the door. There's this sort of debriefing period. Even at this late stage in the game, Bono's honest enough to say Ali [his wife] won't have him home for a week after a tour. He has to go and stay in a hotel. Ronnie Drew does it as well. You're a different animal from the one that left and, as the gaps grow shorter, increasingly you're just an animal all the time and it's something it's unfair to ask anybody to put up with.

"It becomes spousal abuse and it was something Frank never got to grips with. His family were always a rock'n'roll family. He could never quite accept that when we were telling him we were having trouble domestically, we meant it – 'This is seriously undermining my marriage, my family, my relationship with my children,' or whatever, and it was doing untold damage. Ultimately it wasn't Frank that was having to take the flak when members of The Pogues came back off tour."

James voices one particular memory cited by various Pogues, in which Murray would stress the potential rewards arising from short-term personal sacrifices: "He'd say, 'Just give me a year of your life. . .' The next year he'd say, 'Give me another.' And, 'Give me another.' And it went on like that. Jem had a really, really hard time, more than I ever knew until I had children."

Stiff's Dave Robinson takes a less emotional view of the subject: "Bands traditionally do object to being on the road at a certain point. Madness did. But the managers and the record companies want them to keep on because (a) it promotes the records and (b) if they're out live, doing things, they're earning income. Bands always think that once they get a flow of money, it's coming in forever. But like a footballer - you're only as good as your knees hold up. I didn't push The Pogues out on the road all the time. That was Frank's business. They were probably spending vast quantities on various substances."

There are certain members of the band who would take exception to that supposition.

Murray explains: "The thing was, they were an eight-piece band. So in order to survive any way economically, touring has got to be involved. The band didn't like to tour America for more than three weeks. You couldn't really do three weeks, come home for two weeks and start flying everybody out again - not for an eight-piece band, and then you've got crew and everything with you. Supposing you average five gigs a week – that means you do 15 gigs in a country that's got 50 states. It's a really hard task. We weren't getting played on mainstream radio. We weren't like U2. We could draw a lot of crowds live, but it wasn't always reflected in record sales.

"If you go to France and tour, there's no point coming home for two weeks and then going back to Germany, and coming back all the time. You can't do that. Touring is costly.

"We needed to replicate the success we had in Britain elsewhere. The Pogues did well in Germany, France and Scandinavia. Most of Europe we'd done very well in. That was mostly coming through live shows and not from album sales. If you're showing up in the national charts or in the *Billboard* charts, you can organise things differently then."

"Frank was very old-school in his approach," answers Andrew. "He used to talk about doing six-month tours of America and just playing absolutely everywhere. I don't know if that really works for everybody. As far as The Pogues are concerned, there are huge tracts of America where you might as well not go, cos it's just flogging a dead horse as far as I can see."

The rigours of touring also led to stresses and strains between the group members who were cooped up together in hotel rooms and buses for weeks on end, getting on each other's nerves. Sometimes there was a playful outlet for the tension and sometimes there wasn't.

James Fearnley: "I was sharing a room with Terry after I'd stopped sharing with Philip. We were like brothers-in-arms a lot of the time, me and Terry. We stood next to each other onstage and have done ever since, except on one occasion at Croke Park. Our relationship was problematic for me for a good long run, which was harder because we were sharing a room. There were arguments about the volume at which Terry played on stage. I would ask him to turn it down. He said, 'It's really hard to play single notation music if you can't hear what you're doing.' It was like my ears were being lashed with barbed wire a lot of the time.

"I got so wound up after one gig that I threw a glass of champagne at the wall and stormed out of the room. I would never throw anything at anybody – although I did throw an orange at Shane once and hit him full in the face, up in Scotland somewhere. He hadn't done anything to deserve it – I was just mischievous. He was livid. But it's really funny with Shane to incur his wrath like that, and then to hide from him is the easiest thing in the world: he has no idea where to look. He was hell-bent on revenge and chasing me round the dressing room, which wasn't very big. There was a pillar in the middle and some furniture and stuff, and I just hid and he hadn't a clue where I was. I escaped down the corridor. On another occasion, I remember hiding in an airing cupboard somewhere in a hotel to get away from him.

"I remember once being under a table, hiding, and I saw Shane's legs come past. I grabbed hold of the bottom of his pants and I ripped them all the way from his turn-up to his groin – the seam just came apart in my hands, all the way up. I was remorseful after that because Shane tended not to go on tour with much clothing, so I had to go to the dry cleaners and get them mended for him."

Fearnley admits that he was not so happy to be on the receiving end of MacGowan's pranks: "Shane was and still is quite a good teaser, and I'm not very good at taking it. If he recognised that and exploited it, I don't know. There was a period when I got into dressing nicely. I'd wear a suit all the time. I still like suits. You can live in them, work in them. So I lived in my suit and because I was so proud and happy about it, I hated to have anything done to it and I think Shane knew that. I remember sitting opposite Shane and Victoria at a table where we'd just had our band dinner, my head resting on my forearms. I heard laughter but was too tired to wonder what was causing it until I felt liquid in my hair. Shane had egged on Victoria to pour... I don't know what... over my head because he knew it would get to me, which it did. On such occasions, unfailingly I would provide him with the response that he wanted."

James concedes that a lot of the high spirits were fuelled by alcohol, and sometimes erupted in food fights. He states: "They occurred from time to time when there was a dressing room full of fripperies and things that we didn't really need. It's a bit of a temptation. They were something that Jem abominated, food fights, and I so understand that. It's so wasteful and horrible and childish."

To tour was to live in a bubble, and occasionally the bubble could burst. "Being on the road has got a mass about it that attracts a lot of gravity," says Fearnley, making another comparison. "I'm not saying it's a black hole, but it affects your other life very badly. Peer pressure, commitment, contracts, career, travel, personal politics, personal power and all sorts get mixed up into one sometimes horrible thing that binds everybody together so it's really difficult to make judgements.

"I jumped ship a few times. Once we were travelling from up north down to London and we got to Knutsford services and I couldn't take any more and I got off. I decided to hitch home to Manchester. But it was only when I knew I didn't have to be anywhere that night. It was never serious. I think I'm the only person who's never missed a gig, although I missed a video shoot once."

The enforced proximity also meant that the band members became privy to each other's private problems and sadnesses: "Say you're rooming with somebody," suggests Philip. "You know they've gotta phone home so you leave them in the room and go down to the bar for a couple of hours. By the time you go back upstairs, you'll have to contend with the grief that he's been given by the wife, and that will feed into a conversation that will go on for hours about, 'What's the matter with this band? The way we're doing things?' It's a system of destruction that is very corrosive. It starts to kill the goose that lays the golden egg. That started to happen to us very quickly, although we had a few periods, like the joy of making an album, sufficiently long periods of release that we could start looking forward to going back on the road."

April 1987, like the three months before it, saw The Pogues making only selected appearances, one of which was at France's annual music festival, *Le Printemps de Bourges*. Memorably for Fearnley in particular, it was here that they met the controversial but estimable French singer and songwriter Serge Gainsbourg.

"The show was quite warm," says James. "Serge, Shane, myself and Andrew sat up against the wall backstage in this rather Sixty-ish modern building, like a municipal building. There were metal staircases, yellow painted. We just hung out with Serge for a bit. He seemed to be interested in the fact I was so warm after the gig, covered with so much sweat, that I had to take my shirt off. He seemed to get excited by that. Shane used to get excited by that too. He used to poke fun at me when I walked around with just a towel round my waist. Serge was raddled. He didn't strike me as being awfully well, and he seemed a bit worse for wear. Maybe that's why we all sat down instead of being stood up."

The band were delighted to have jumped off the hamster wheel of solid touring for a while, but they didn't want to sit back idly doing nothing. It had been nearly two years since *Rum Sodomy & The Lash*, and they were desperate to get into the studio because they knew the strength of their new songs.

"We were just going nuts wanting to get our ideas down on tape," says Chevron. "We didn't want to lose the moment of greatest creativity, where people were going to be able to hear us at our best. We'd been playing ourselves into the ground writing all this stuff on the tour bus on the way to gigs, learning how to play new instruments. It was hugely creative and always in danger of just floating away."

Frank Murray had been thinking about the third album too. He was equally convinced that The Pogues were going to turn in a superb collection of songs, but he couldn't risk booking them into a studio for fear of alerting Stiff Records. The soundtrack albums and the Dubliners collaboration had succeeded in keeping the band in the public eye, but now they really needed to get to work in their own right.

"It was annoying and frustrating not to be able to go into the studio," declares Jem. "When you write songs, you want to record them."

Indeed, the band received a visit from Dave Robinson, who was also growing anxious about the lack of new recordings. Says James: "He came to see us at a rehearsal room somewhere wearing a car coat, and he looked so much the worse for wear – miserable, gaunt, unshaven. I think he tried to make some sort of case, but we weren't interested any more. I suppose we just knew that our time with Stiff Records should come to an end now. I remember feeling a little bit of sympathy for the guy because he looked so much like he had his back up against the wall – or else he just hadn't bothered to shave. We were adamant. We said, 'I'm sorry, this is over now.'"

Frank Murray explains: "I didn't know what was going on with Stiff at that period. There was lots of rumours going round and I think The Pogues were the biggest act on the label at the time. I knew that Stiff had royalty commitments to acts that had been on the label before. That money's got to come from somewhere. I was afraid that money being generated by The Pogues would be used to start paying other people and to maybe keep the record company afloat. And if that was the case, how were we going to be paid *our* royalties? At the time Stiff had lost the backing and the protection of Island Records and they didn't have any kind of set-up around the world for American releases and stuff like that."

Murray was reading the situation correctly. Stiff had been bought by ZTT, the company belonging to husband-and-wife team Trevor Horn and Jill Sinclair.

Jill became the victim of a horrific accident in June 2006 when she was hit by a pellet from an air rifle believed to have been fired by her 22-year-old son Aaron during target practice in the grounds of the family estate. At the time of writing, it was not known to what extent Jill – who suffered a severed neck artery – would recover. She remained critical but stable in intensive care.

In an interview for this book before the accident, Sinclair said that she'd had a good relationship with Dave Robinson while he was MD at Island – parent company of both Stiff and ZTT, which had enjoyed a massive sales boost with Frankie Goes To Hollywood. Stiff subsequently parted company with Island and was put up for sale.

"I bought Stiff to stop Dave going into liquidation," said Jill. "I knew he was going to lose his house in 21 days, maybe 28 days. I did it to save a friend of mine from going bankrupt. Purely, there wasn't another option for Dave. He'd spent several million pounds on Stiff. We thought, 'Why not? It could be good for him and it could be good for us.'

"Then we tried to work really hard on Stiff. But Dave's accounting policy was that he owed everybody money all the time. He worked on the basis that you were only as rich as the credit you could get. Robbo just borrowed from Peter to pay Paul. He was a wild character. He flew by the seat of his pants through his entire life. I was so browbeaten and so battered by him that I didn't know what to do. I was close to having a nervous breakdown. I thought the whole thing was going to tumble down around my ears. We used to have what we called a 'church barometer' on the wall. It showed the fortune that had been poured into Stiff. Would we ever, ever climb up to the top of the barometer? It was a horribly expensive time. Frank Murray's fears were not unfounded."

Dave Robinson contends that despite his hugely successful mission to save the ailing Island with Frankie Goes To Hollywood, Bob Marley's *Legend* and U2's *Under A Blood Red Sky*, he personally lost money in the process. The relationship between Robinson and Island supremo Chris Blackwell broke down irretrievably in September 1985, and Robinson took Stiff away to new premises in Coronet Street, Hoxton, where he tried to resuscitate the label. But by then, he says, "Stiff had been run down by Island's accounts department not paying Stiff's bills," leaving Stiff "not in a great state with its major suppliers". More cash was swallowed up by the court hearings that ensued when Dave sued his former friend Blackwell.

"There were a few rumours around about financial difficulties, which were true," says Robinson. "But we were trading our way through." And, he adds, he was pinning all of his hopes for Stiff's survival on the forthcoming albums from Furniture and The Pogues. However, those were not forthcoming.

"It was getting very, very difficult," says Robinson. "It was decided to try and find a partner to sell to, and so eventually we sold Stiff to ZTT. It was running in their offices and with their involvement, and I worked with Stiff for another year."

Frank Murray had already lined up a producer. He'd bumped into Steve Lillywhite in Dublin, in the office of U2 manager Paul McGuinness, just above Windmill Lane studios.

"Steve was producing a U2 session," remembers Frank. "Larry Mullen came into the office and he said to me, 'Steve Lillywhite is downstairs.' I said, 'Tell him I said hello.' Larry went back down to the studio. After about 10 minutes, Steve came up just to start chatting. I was telling him about The Pogues and how we were getting ready to do another album. He wanted to know who was producing it. I said, 'There's nobody producing it at the moment. Would you give it a shot?' He said, 'Yeah, maybe.' I had most of the album on tape from the live shows, cos we were doing most of the songs live, and I called Paul Scully and asked him to get a tape from the mixing board over to Steve at Windmill Lane. After a couple of days, I got the call from Steve saying, 'We should do it.'

"We decided to cut a few songs first to make sure we could all work together, so Steve booked Abbey Road. But for legal reasons we could not be in there as The Pogues. Until I was shown differently [about Stiff's finances], nobody was getting the tapes to the album."

The Pogues went into Abbey Road under the guise of making what became known as "the Terry Woods solo album". Terry was the only member of the band not signed to Stiff Records.

"The whole thing was to safeguard the band," continues Murray. "We had toured for two years so we had some money in the pot. Steve Lillywhite deferred his advances as a gesture of friendship and we only had to then pay the studio. So we paid for the recordings ourselves."

The Pogues spent a few days in Abbey Road studios making demos for songs that would appear on *If I Should Fall From Grace With God*. Terry Woods remembers: "It was very much cloak and dagger, and I think I used to have to take some of the tapes back with me to Ireland."

One of their guests at Abbey Road was country-rock icon Steve Earle, who described his visit as "very hush-hush and deliciously clandestine" – that is, until he actually walked into the building, where every man and his dog knew perfectly well that the band in residence was actually The Pogues and not The Terry Woods Quartet.

Time passed, and at the beginning of May 1987, the band finally went into Mickey Most's RAK studios with Steve Lillywhite to record the album proper – the greatest Terry Woods solo album that never was.

According to Murray, they once again paid for their own studio time: "Normally if a record company paid, if Dave Robinson was picking up the bill at RAK, he would've had rights to the tapes, but we were paying the studio ourselves. I believe some people came over to RAK and tried to get the tapes and they were told no, we had paid for them and they were our property."

Robinson tells a different story: "The recording cost and advance had been paid by Stiff."

While Frank Murray was keeping the band one step ahead of Stiff Records in his determination to outwit the label, The Pogues were dwelling on problems of their own. Various members felt that their contributions to the band's recordings were going unacknowledged and unrewarded. Shane MacGowan, the chief songwriter, was raking in the lion's share of the publishing money and royalties, but it was his colleagues who could dependably help to translate his ideas into real music, and to create the uniquely magical sound of The Pogues.

While feelings of dissatisfaction were starting to take root around now, it didn't become an issue for quite some time – but when it did, it would lead to Andrew Ranken threatening to leave the band.

It was around this time that The Pogues negotiated their first official management contract with Murray.

Andrew comments: "Frank is a charmer. I think gradually as we became more aware of his way of doing business we all began to feel kind of estranged, really. There was an initial honeymoon period where everything was on the up and he was almost like an extra member of the group for a while. But as things went on and we became more jaundiced with the amount of touring we were doing, we started asking questions. The initial period was all fairly happy-go-lucky."

Murray states: "I managed them for the first three years without a contract. I never asked them to sign one. They always knew what the deal was. So then we formalised it. I took a standard managerial contract negotiated with them and my lawyer. Jem was there, Philip was there and Darryl was there, representing the band, with their accountant and their lawyer."

The usually helpful Murray declines to specify the terms of the contract.

The Pogues emerged from RAK studios every now and again, usually at weekends, to play a series of summer events and festivals at home and abroad, starting with a short Irish tour at the end of May. In Dublin, they hosted a TV special for RTE, and their invited guests were The Dubliners and Joe Strummer, with whom they performed 'I Fought The Law' and 'London Calling'.

On July 18, they headlined what they'd hoped would be a sunshine party in London's Finsbury Park for 8,000 people. Instead, the Picnic In The Park was awash with rain and mud. "I remember it bucketing," says James. "And I remember a kid sitting cross-legged in the rain, just outside the tent. He was so drunk that he didn't know he wasn't under the canvas. Such a funny, funny image."

The Pogues returned to the Kenmare Festival where they'd first been introduced to Terry Woods. They played in Germany, Italy and Finland, where Fearnley was "flabbergasted" that the sun didn't go down all night. They were supported by Chuck Berry at a show in Geneva, they appeared with Christy Moore, Status Quo and The Wolftones at the Cork Festival, and they went back to Ireland on August 23 to headline the Tralee festival, which was attended by the winner of that year's Rose Of Tralee competition, a traditional, world-famous beauty contest.

"Paul Verner, our lighting guy – it made this day, his life!" says James. "To talk to the Rose Of Tralee herself! He was absolutely gobsmacked."

It wasn't grinding touring, and The Pogues enjoyed the chance to see the outside world again. But their most interesting venture, and an unaccustomed one, was into the world of stadiums, supporting U2 at selected dates on their Joshua Tree world tour during July and August. The first of these shows was at Wembley Stadium where the band played to an audience of more than 70,000.

"The great thing about that," says James, "is that me and Jem went down on to the pitch before the gates opened, and with an imaginary football, we ran all the way from the box at one end, passing the ball between us, to get to the goal mouth at the other end, and we each took a shot and we put the ball in the back of the net."

The support dates continued at Dublin's Croke Park, the enormous Paris Hippodrome and a windswept Murrayfield Stadium in Edinburgh.

The two bands got on reasonably well together, although Bono could sometimes appear a little distant and enigmatic. Even then, in some small way, he had taken up the humanitarian stance with which he now harangues world leaders.

Spider hilariously said at the time: "I met Bono in Cork when U2 had just played. I went up and said, 'How are you? What was the gig like?' He said, 'They've suffered in the city. They have a great spirit, they have great hearts, great souls.' I said, 'Bono, I just wanted to know what the gig was like.' I think he was on mushrooms. Either that or he'd had a very heavy prayer session. But they're all really nice blokes. Diamond geezers."

"They were very normal, very approachable and nice," says Jem Finer. "Adam [Clayton] was the more fun-loving one. I'm not saying the others weren't, but he seemed to be the one who was up for hanging out a bit. They're very friendly, not at all stuck up. We were their personal guests, and it was much appreciated."

Terry Woods adds: "The band were fine, but you wouldn't see very much of U2 anyway on the tour. In general, the gigs were good. We were doing very well at that point, and we didn't feel as if we were supporting U2. There was a large, Pogues-like audience there for us so it was really enjoyable."

"U2 were very respectful of us and our material, and Shane as a singer," says Darryl Hunt, who also describes the confusing aspects of backstage etiquette in such huge venues. "There were so many green rooms and red rooms. You didn't know what ones you were allowed to go into and what ones you weren't. There were other rooms you couldn't get into. But U2 were extremely good on that tour."

"I think we took it in our stride," comments Andrew. "I don't think we were fazed by the size of the places or anything. The U2 guys were okay. They were pretty down-to-earth. They were really going for this stadium-rock thing which Shane in particular was not keen on at all. I think Shane didn't really think we ought to be doing stuff like that, that it compromised us in a way. And I'm guessing, really, but I think he might've felt that it was destroying the intimacy and immediacy of our music. That's something that happens with that stadium stuff.

"I wanted to do the gigs partly for the experience. I wanted to see what it was like. But, actually, unless you're headlining, you don't get the whole picture anyway because you never have as much of the PA as the headlining band."

According to Darryl, The Pogues were granted a quarter of the PA's power. "The headline band don't want to be blown offstage," continues Andrew, "so they've got to come on with more power than anything that's gone before. Also, you don't get as much time to sort out your own sound on stage or anything. With that amount of equipment, you've really gotta work quite hard to get it sounding good. I think we did all right.

"It's a completely different sort of experience when you've got this sea of people in front of you and you're attempting to communicate something that works really well in a small room in a pub."

Says James: "I know that Jem was interested in The Edge's gear. I think they found time to talk about the kind of things that The Edge put his guitar through."

"I did want to try my banjo through his 1,001 effects," nods Jem.

Both bands wound up at the Cork Festival, although they were playing a day apart, and they got together in the city's Jury's Hotel to celebrate The Edge's birthday on August 8.

"I made him a birthday card from all of us," remembers James. "On the front I wrote, 'The Unquenchable Thirst'. We went to his birthday party. There's a story that has done the rounds over the years, and still surfaces from time to time, which features me dancing through the bar in Jury's Hotel on the night of Edge's birthday, though there was no danceable music playing at the time. 'I'm dancing to a tune that's going on in my head,' I say to The Edge and the people he's with. I was on a different plane that night, thrilled to be in such company. Bono and Spider and Shane were in a huddle somewhere in the corner, talking."

When U2 set out on the American leg of the tour in September, they invited The Pogues to support on two dates towards the end of the month. One was at Sullivan Stadium, Foxboro, near Boston, and the other at the prestigious Madison Square Garden in New York.

"It's a bit shit doing gigs like that," asserts Jem. "Madison Square Garden was virtually empty when we were playing. You're just the soundtrack to people finding their seats. Of course, there are a few people that want to hear you, but in a massive place like that it was a bit weird. When we played with them in Wembley, for example, the place was pretty full, so it was more like doing a gig to a bunch of people. Madison Square Garden is different to a stadium. It's a different kind of space and it's indoors. It was kind of impersonal because it was so big. I don't think it's hard to get the same enthusiasm onstage, but the connection is maybe a bit dissipated."

Terry Woods relates a terrifying experience at the Garden: "We were going to start off the set with one of my pieces, 'The Battle March'. It started with Paul Scully playing a very slow piece of music and the stage in darkness. We were doing this in our own gigs as well. I would walk out on to the stage, pick up the cittern, and when the fast bit started, the band would gradually come on stage and join me.

"The stage at Madison Square Garden was enormous. I walked out, the slow music was on, and there were all the candles. It was fairly moving, to say the least. To my horror, the cittern was knocked down on to the stage, but I was too far away for any of the road crew to see me and the stage was in darkness. I was like, 'Christ in the Garden of Gethsemane!' I was sweating blood. Two or three of the pegs were bent out of shape. All I could do was physically bend the pegs back and hope they didn't break, and then try and hear the instrument without making a noise.

"It got to the part where the slow piece stops that Paul Scully was playing and I had to pick up the tune. I really didn't know what was going to come out. It was one of the most frightening things that could ever happen. If the ground could've opened up. . . I was a puddle of jelly. By some strange quirk of fate, I was virtually in tune. After that, I had the most wonderful gig. I couldn't be fazed no matter what happened."

"The stage was just a metal grille, and it had nothing on it at all," recalls James. "The equipment and technicians were under the stage. To come out before 20,000 people on a stage made of a metal grille with angles and gradients around it, it was scary – scary on account of the multitudes of U2 fans and on account of the leather-soled shoes I was wearing that I didn't trust at all on the metal stage. But it was really, really great fun."

It was also at the Garden that the band were astonished to see Hollywood legend Faye Dunaway walking into their midst. "She'd gone into the wrong dressing room," explains Fearnley. "She was trying to go to U2's, but Charlie had shown her into ours because she needed to use the bathroom. It was so funny, Charlie MacLennan getting Faye Dunaway through our dressing room to the toilet."

Shane MacGowan says of the U2 tour dates: "We did what we usually do - worked hard to have a good time and make sure the audience is having a good time." And despite his previously reported disapproval of stadium gigs, he insists: "I didn't feel unhappy about doing them."

Frank Murray, meanwhile, was still working on the problems surrounding the release of The Pogues' third album. Very soon, he would be able to announce a breakthrough.

CHAPTER 21

Falling From Grace

Steve Lillywhite was exactly the right producer for The Pogues. A warm and patient person, he had the utmost respect for the group's abilities and their songs. "They're absolutely spectacular musicians," he says. "They're up with the best session players in the world."

Lillywhite paid careful attention to the rhythm of their working days, and he sought out the strengths and interests of each individual member. He saw that he had the makings of a fine album, one which would celebrate the essential sound and spirit of The Pogues while taking influence from a broadening spectrum of music – a consequence of their recent travels around the world.

"Oh God, the musicianship, the camaraderie... the atmosphere was all good," enthuses Steve. "They were very friendly. It was pretty crazy at times and it didn't come together really easily. I remember at the end of it, Spider coming up to me and saying, 'I don't know how you did it, but you did it.'

"Each member of the band I would work with individually to get the best out of them. It was all pieced together, one thing at a time. It wasn't really lots of performances, but I'm sure that it was very well weaved together. I'm quite anal. I know the sort of standards I expect and so you take a little bit of time, sometimes, to get the right performances out of them.

"There are two things about the music – things that need to be really precise and things that have the spirit. Sometimes you had to get the band early in the day. You wouldn't want to do some of that really intricate stuff at midnight. By then, you'd want to be recording backing vocals or raucous stuff. Part of my job was deciding what to do at what time of the day without breaking the flow. Artists need to feel that things are getting done and that every day something new is happening. My job is to start building that."

Shane MacGowan was more comfortable with Lillywhite than he had been with Elvis Costello, and there were no nasty arguments. Still, Shane liaised less closely with the producer than the other members of the band. He was, says Steve, "a sort of pussycat. He was shy as well as being arrogant."

The group, without exception, were delighted to be in the studio at last. They'd been touring the songs for quite some time, so had already worked out the fundamental dynamics of the material.

"It was like bursting a boil of frustration – 'Thank God, at last we can get this stuff out,'" says Jem. "They were really brilliant songs and everyone knew what they were doing and wanted to be doing it. We were used to being in studios and we finally had a real record producer. Steve had grown from being a tea boy to an engineer to a producer, and he'd worked with all sorts of different bands. Everyone respected him and had confidence in him. He was a very friendly, funny guy, very straight, no messing around. He wasn't bothered by any reputation we had, although that reputation was rather exaggerated anyway."

Andrew Ranken: "It was a huge step up for us in all sorts of ways – going into a big studio, this lovely area which had rooms with windows. We'd been stuck down in this basement at Elephant Studios which was all right at the time, but it did get pretty claustrophobic. RAK was a nicer atmosphere to work in, and the recording equipment was much better. We were able to experiment a lot and get sounds we hadn't been able to get very well before because of not having the equipment to do it on."

Ranken, by now the owner of a full-size drumkit, adds: "Steve was a very experienced producer, and he knew how to get a really big, fat sort of sound, which isn't the easiest thing to do with lots of plinky-plonky instruments like we had. I think he brought a sense of scale to it that had been lacking to some extent. He had lots of tricks up his sleeve.

"I found the whole thing really enjoyable. Every day I looked forward to going in and working there, and very quickly it became apparent to me that we were making a really good album. And we came up with this way of working which I really enjoyed as well. Me and Darryl would start off by getting the bass and drums down until we got that really solid and then we'd build everything around it. In the past, we'd done endless takes of everyone playing together and often it happened that things would start to gel for the rest of the band but at that point I'd be knackered and I'd be going off the boil."

"Steve Lillywhite was really good for The Pogues," agrees Terry Woods. "He has patience and knowledge, and he works very hard. He was and is a very, very good man."

The band also enjoyed the services of brass and string sections. Joey Cashman played tenor sax with the other brass men: Eli Thompson (trumpet), Brian Clarke (alto sax), Paul Taylor (trombone) and Chris Lee (trumpet). Ron Kavana guested on tenor banjo, spoons and mandolin, Siobhan Sheahan on harp and Fran Byrne on bodhrán.

Darryl Hunt remembers "incredibly inventive sessions". He says: "There were a lot of ideas from Steve. I thought he could hardly be bettered. He liked to work with people who wanted to get on with the job. He was very conscientious. And his tape ops as well were very hard-working. It seemed a very positive time."

Unlike Costello, who had sometimes lorded it over James Fearnley when the overdubs were being done, Lillywhite welcomed the accordion player's fascination and help. "I was the overdub king with Steve Lillywhite," says James, proudly. "I got on with him really, really well. He would sometimes swivel round in his chair and say, 'Well, what's Mr Fearnley got?' I think he was waiting for me to come up with things here and there. Steve was up for anything and everything, and it was a matter of great pride for me to get a phone call, while he was mixing, summoning me to the studio to supply some element, he didn't know what, to lift something – the 'Recruiting Sergeant' medley – and had me tattooing on a cymbal pressed to the floor under my foot, that sort of thing."

Fearnley loved the studio and prospered in an atmosphere of encouragement. Says Spider: "People would always listen to James in the studio, and still will, because if he says something it's worth listening to. His arranging abilities – not enough attention is paid when people talk about The Pogues musically. He plays a hell of a lot of different instruments, and he always has a hand in the arrangements. He's a really crucial member of the band. He's a lynchpin."

Fearnley always had a great ear for music, although he can't explain why: "My only experience was a year and a half of piano and being a choirboy. I did have an uncle who did solo, classical piano gigs, my mum's cousin David. He was a hermaphrodite, I found out later. He kept it very private. My dad used to have fun with that, in a very kind sort of way. My dad was a man of two parts. He was full of guff and sententiousness and, on the other hand, he was quite sensitive. Like me, basically."

James's duties often began with the presentation of any new idea by Shane MacGowan. Together with Jem Finer, he would "wrest the stuff out of Shane", going right back to the days of *Red Roses For Me*.

"Shane wanted me to play the piano on 'The Auld Triangle'," explains Fearnley, by way of an example. "I wanted to play the melody that Brendan Behan had based his tune on to begin with, but that was hard to do because

I didn't know the original, traditional melody. For Shane to explain how it went was quite difficult, but we got it in the end.

"I think all the way through I was an interpreter more than anything. Both me and Jem were lightning conduits to ground Shane. That was our chief work, and it *was* work. It was hard and dogged a lot of the time, because Shane was so cack-handed at playing the guitar and in his desperation to get this stuff out, things became really confusing. He'd play a snatch of something, he knew what he was doing, but then he'd stop and then he'd start off in the middle of a line with his guitar-playing and singing, and you wouldn't know where you were. The vase was smashed and we were trying to put it back together the way that he originally had it in his head. A lot of the time we might have put the handle in a different place from where he expected it to go."

Sometimes Fearnley tried to do the impossible. He cites the case of 'Streams Of Whiskey' where he faced the task of devising backing vocals. He admits: "Harmonies – we could never get into that with The Pogues. I remember trying to figure out what harmony vocals would go with 'Streams Of Whiskey' and nothing sounded right. I felt so bad. I just realised it wasn't going to happen and it would have to be unison singing, all of us."

Like MacGowan, James was not ashamed to borrow ideas from other sources. In 'Greenland Whale Fisheries', he'd sneaked in the "diddly-dit, diddly-dit" part of the *Captain Pugwash* theme tune; in the Lillywhite sessions at RAK, he called upon Paul Simon, endowing 'Birmingham Six' with the "township kind of accordion" suggested by the *Graceland* album. On the title track of *If I Should Fall From Grace With God*, he stole a Keith Richards lick and played it on an acoustic guitar.

Both Fearnley and Finer enjoyed the challenge of a new skill. "I remember when Terry Woods actually showed us a reel," says James. "Me and Jem learnt it - in the end. It was so difficult to get this Irish music down a lot of the time. You start playing the tune somewhere in the middle of it, as if it's been playing all the time. You pick it up and take it in a big 360 degree circle. The metaphor I had for it at the time – you play the tune and, 'There's that telegraph pole again.' It's like a never-ending thing. 'Down In The Ground Where The Dead Men Go' [recorded before Terry's time] is a tune with no beginning and no end: it's just eternal. Me and Shane playing the bells on the front of that song was a nice, engaging, intimate moment. Somebody brought some goat bells in and we recorded it together."

Fearnley was fond of sound effects, from the earliest days of 'Waxie's Dargle' to the latest carousing gaiety of 'Fiesta': "When we did a demo of 'Fiesta' at Abbey Road, when it was 'the Terry Woods solo album', I got metal ashtrays and did wolf whistles with my fingers to try and get the fairground noises," says James. "In the actual recording, we all of us did the noises. Someone got hold of a popgun, but that wasn't powerful enough, so it had to be augmented with me making gun noises with my mouth. I think the wolf whistles came in again. Both me and Jem worked hard with the brass section, the trumpeter particularly, because we didn't want it to sound like a soul brass section. It had to sound south of the Rio Grande, for me."

By now James had found a sweeping new confidence, accompanied by an irrepressible excitement about the material being recorded in RAK.

He confesses: "Apart from struggling, oftentimes with Jem, getting the blood out of the stone of Shane's curious inability to communicate, it wasn't until we got to *If I Should Fall From Grace With God* that I really started to get meddlesome. I wonder if a lot of that meddlesomeness might have found its wellspring in 'A Pistol For Paddy Garcia', which we recorded without Shane and with Philip producing? I got to play the electric guitar and the tubular bells and even to whistle and discover countermelodies that actually became part of the fabric of the song. That was a bit of a harbinger, that one."

James followed his instincts with vigour and, sometimes, a headmasterly severity: "With 'Sit Down By The Fire', I designed the marching-band bass drumbeat at the beginning, that rhythm that might hark back a little bit to 'Sun Arise', the Rolf Harris song we did at my audition for The Nips. And I remember getting very excited about the long crescendo before the final outroduction. I think the song's quite scary and might say a lot about Shane's life as a child and what a hard time he had of it. It's darkly funny. And really good playing by everybody. I've been listening to it in the car lately, and I think it's probably one of the best songs we've ever done. It just rattles along."

The lyrics offer spine-chilling tales of phantom creatures who will "rip out your liver and dance on your neck" – not quite the bedtime reassurances of 'Lullaby Of London'.

James continues: "'The Broad Majestic Shannon' is a towering song. I remember when Shane brought that in and the structure seemed all wrong to me. You think you're going to go into a chorus and you don't. It always felt unusual, and it still does. It's one of those songs that I think define folk music, or help to. It's extraordinary. I diligently tutored Terry in something that was just too simple for him to play, a descending line on the concertina of just three or four notes that I was convinced should go in. Oh, Terry's puzzlement and frustration, maybe, at being told what to do and then being restricted to playing it the same way each time."

The most amusing collaboration on the album happened between James and Andrew Ranken when they taped 'Worms', a gruesome glimpse into the grave.

Says Andrew: "It was a song that my father's father used to sing when I was a kid. He had quite a collection of comic songs, but that was one I really loved because it was so macabre. In late-night sessions in hotel bars every now and then I'd sing it, and I think Steve Lillywhite must have heard it at some time and thought, 'We must stick that on the album somewhere.' It wasn't my idea. We deliberately left that long gap at the end before it came in. It's not meant to be a serious part of the album. It's a little extra."

Andrew, who sang the lead vocal, adds: "We wanted to get this sort of creepy quality. Steve got us to walk around the room in a big circle on this wooden floor, treading quite heavily, with me singing and James playing the accordion, so we got the footsteps in as well."

"Tom Waits had a lot to answer for," comments James.

Jem Finer had been a major contributor to the songwriting, collaborating with MacGowan on 'Fiesta' and 'Turkish Song Of The Damned', Darryl Hunt's personal favourite. It was the first Pogues track Darryl had actually worked on himself, rather than having to trot out someone else's basslines. He adds: "I thought it was very powerful."

'Bottle Of Smoke' – the ribald story of a racehorse of the same name coming in at "twenty-fucking-five to one" – is the Pogues song that Philip Chevron would take to a desert island. "It's the ultimate good-luck song," he says. "The ultimate great overcoming the negativity of the world, overcoming all the bad shit, against all the odds. The Pogues and The Pogues' audience are the Bottle Of Smoke. That's what people identify with very strongly."

Jem: "That's another song where Shane had the words and the chords and I had an instrumental. They fitted together naturally though neither had been designed to go with the other."

'Metropolis' is entirely Finer's baby. He explains: "I had this simple title, 'Metropolis', and I was thinking of big American cities in the night-time, driving round them, and I wanted to write a jazz instrumental. I'd got really into jazz and especially be-bop and hard bop, listening to a lot of Charles Mingus, Art Blakey and all sorts of stuff. But I thought, 'No one's going to record it if I just write a jazz instrumental.' It wouldn't fit in. I tried to work out a way of having enough of a typical Pogues Irish-sounding instrumental and somehow mated it with brass playing some kind of mad, urban, night-time, blaring, traffic-jam jazz. There's this bass line that I worked out just by playing with patterns of numbers, applying them to music and seeing what they sounded like. At some stage, it occurred to me that that fitted with parts of an Irish-sounding tune I had, and it would also fit with these horn lines I'd started thinking about. It all started to coalesce around that. I was always trying to push things a bit, but it didn't always work."

★

Philip Chevron and Terry Woods – recording their first album with The Pogues – also received writers' credits. Chevron's song, 'Thousands Are Sailing', remains an essential part of the band's live set, and although he now sings it himself, it was MacGowan who recorded the vocal for the album.

For Philip, presenting a song for consideration by the group was a nerve-wracking experience. He says: "It seemed like an appropriate song because I could see that to some extent, part of the album was going to be about the greater Irish Diaspora, the place of the Irish in the world. By virtue of seeing more of the world ourselves, we widened our brief, I suppose."

'Thousands Are Sailing', a melancholy anthem, refers to the mass emigration from Ireland at the beginning of the Eighties, when the country was suffering a major economic slump.

Says Chevron: "Obviously I was aware that New York was full of Irish people because a lot of them were coming to see us when we played there. I've always made a connection between the past and the present. You start off in the past and connect to the present and blur the edges so you're not sure where you are time-wise. The song wrote itself because it became an obvious parallel [with the exodus in the mid-1800s due to the potato famine]. The heart-sickness in 'Thousands Are Sailing' is not so much about missing home as about the alienation of being somewhere else, that sense of not belonging anywhere.

"But it was daunting presenting songs to The Pogues. You're aware not only that Shane was considered the best writer in the band but also it's desirable to have as many Shane MacGowan songs on an album as possible. He would always arrive with as few songs as he thought he could get away with, and a few ideas that would never get tried out. You're up against the expectation that he's the main man and the thought that everyone in the band would rather hear a new Shane MacGowan song.

"I didn't introduce 'Thousands Are Sailing' until well into the album because I couldn't find the right moment. There was a huge self-esteem thing going on because of my alcoholism. You're aware of how other people present their work with a degree of confidence, an assumption that you'd want to hear this, that the person with low self-esteem doesn't necessarily have. So you're always looking for negative signals.

"I presented the song and Steve Lillywhite nodded approvingly, but I wasn't getting any feedback from the band. They were used to Shane coming in and not being able to explain himself terribly well, but they weren't used to somebody coming in and almost apologising for their song. Frank Murray was in the studio and all I saw in the control room was Frank laughing his head off – obviously at some kind of joke, nothing to do with 'Thousands Are Sailing', but I interpreted it as a snub. I'd gone from quivering wreck to jelly at this point. Frank and Terry went to the pub and when Terry came back, he said, 'Let me get into this song of yours.'"

Woods suggested a couple of chord changes. "And suddenly the thing kicked into a different gear," continues Philip. "Having initially accused Terry of being unsupportive, I realised he was the one that helped make it the great performance it is. He kicked off the magic. He was basically blurring the edges where they needed to be blurred.

"Then I realised I was in safe hands. I was thrilled and delighted. The song was working, the track was working and Shane was saying, 'This sounds great.' After that it got a lot easier presenting songs."

There were further problems with 'Thousands Are Sailling' when MacGowan refused to sing a couple of the lines. He didn't agree that Brendan Behan would have danced up and down the street in New York, so he changed the words on a nightly basis. "It used to irritate me," says Chevron, "because I realised he was doing it to argue with the song. I thought this was an argument we could have somewhere else."

And despite the blasphemous scenes MacGowan himself had written into, say, 'The Sickbed of Cuchulainn', he took umbrage at Chevron's line about "guilt and weeping effigies".

"He took me to task for that," remembers Philip. "He challenged me about it in the dressing room. I tried to see it from his perspective but I thought, 'There's no argument to be won because the song is the song and it can't be argued with.' He just agreed to repeat the words of the previous chorus." Chevron later reclaimed the song in live performance.

Terry Woods was also bringing new influences and insights to The Pogues, not only through his musical experience and the new material he was writing but in the potential covers he suggested to the band. 'Medley' combines three traditional songs: 'The Recruiting Sergeant', 'The Rocky Road To Dublin' [included in The Pogues' early sets and then dropped] and 'The Galway Races'.

"The fund of material that came along with Terry was really good to have," says James. "Terry knows a lot of tunes and so does Shane. I think the marriage of those two in the band was actually quite good for us."

However, it was a new Woods and MacGowan co-write, 'Streets of Sorrow/Birmingham Six' – a combination of two contrasting songs – that would make a big impression. 'Streets Of Sorrow' is a Woods composition about Michael Collins, the Irish patriot and revolutionary. Orginally a longer piece, it was trimmed to act as a prelude to Shane's 'Birmingham Six', the noisier half of the equation, which was eventually banned. Written specifically about the Birmingham Six and the Guildford Four, Irishmen who turned out to be innocent of the terrorist crimes for which they were imprisoned, the song can be interpreted more broadly as a comment on the perceived victimisation and oppression of Irish people by the British – or indeed, the experience of any minority group in the world that is suffering persecution.

"Terry has quite a fearsome connection with Ireland," remarks Fearnley. "I remember me and him and Dave Jordan got left behind at Frankfurt airport once. We missed a plane. We were drinking, and Terry brought himself down to this irreducible level of pain about what the British had done to Ireland. I never saw anybody talk about Ireland like that. It was astonishing to me to witness how deep it goes."

Of the album track, James says: "'Streets Of Sorrow' is very plaintive and well-meant, but I think that song could only work by taking it into 'Birmingham Six', which is a bit more gutsy and vengeful. They work together particularly well."

The Pogues were elated with the results of the sessions in RAK. Jem Finer believes that *If I Should Fall From Grace With God* is the band's most successful album artistically: "It had an expansion of influences into different styles, but it was cohesive and it was very identifiably The Pogues in the same way as 'Rain Dogs' was a very cohesive album that drew on a lot of styles. Everything came together, and it was very focused. That's really the creative peak for me, in terms of the whole band being on a wavelength. Everything had developed, and everyone was going in the same direction. That's not to say we became less creative after that but, for the most part, it felt to me like a less focused creativity."

Asked for his highlights of the album sessions, Steve Lillywhite replies: "Working in this wonderful studio in London - and recording a Christmas song in the summer."

They'd finally nailed it. 'Fairytale Of New York' had come together after months and months of trying and failing, working and reworking, tweaking and twiddling, and it was Lillywhite and his wife Kirsty MacColl who had finally brought the song bursting into life. It was dazzling.

Steve says of the original Elvis Costello version: "It was a little slower, a little bit darker in a strange way, whereas we gave it some tempo and some joyfulness. It's that wonderful thing of being a sad and a happy song. Maybe what I helped put into it was the happy part."

Most of The Pogues think it was Lillywhite who suggested Kirsty sing the female part. Steve remembers rather that the suggestion came from MacGowan: "I don't think he knew that Kirsty and I were married. He lived in Shaneworld."

Whatever, the two vocals were not recorded together.

Lillywhite explains: "I took the tapes home, cos I had a recording studio at home. I think Kirsty loved 'Fairytale'. We spent a whole day working on her vocals. I wanted to make sure they were really, really good, and her voice is perfect on the song. When Shane heard it, he went, 'Oh my God, I've got to re-do my voice.' So he re-did his part after hearing that, except for the very intro. That was done as a piano-voice part live. All the other stuff was done later. James Fearnley had a great input in 'Fairytale'. He came up with the cello line. And it was fantastic." James is credited with being the co-arranger of the strings, with Fiachra Trench.

Although there are no cheesy festive devices on the track, 'Fairytale Of New York' instantly means *Christmas* to everyone who hears it, like 'Merry Xmas Everybody' or 'Mistletoe And Wine'. It just happens to be better. Everything is beautifully delivered: the strings, muted behind the piano during Shane's bittersweet introduction, the zinging, stinging exchanges between the singers, the sound of their voices rising and falling together with Kirsty's crystal purity somehow ideally matched to MacGowan's crusty drawl, and the way that Shane snarls the word 'Christmas', with contempt.

Unlike Chevron's Irish emigrants in New York, struggling to find an identity in a new city and half-heartedly going about the seasonal celebrations with Christmas trees but no fairy lights in 'Thousands Are Sailing', the elderly characters in 'Fairytale', a drunken gambler and his junkie wife, have no hopes or illusions about their life in the city, only the memory of what they'd dreamed it would be and a lifelong bond forged from habit, resignation, endurance and a love expressed only by the hopeless husband, who'd broken all his promises.

MacGowan: "My part in the duet is the man who's got kicked out of the drunk tank on Christmas Eve night. His wife's in hospital, she's ill and he's just out of his skull. Then they're having a row and he keeps on bringing it on back to the good times and she keeps handing out all the shit... The guy is whining and saying, 'Forgive me', and she's saying, 'Fuck it, you're a waste of space.' She's right and so's he. They're both right and they're both wrong. But in the end they start getting sentimental and thinking about this and that, like old people do."

While the song is specifically about these two characters, Chevron believes that it takes its place as one of the great "universal songs of disappointment and loss".

"That song did have a long gestation, but Steve was really enthusiastic about it," says Andrew. "He encouraged us to persist with it. And eventually, it somehow all came together. It's done what it was supposed to do. There was a conscious decision to write a Christmas hit and it succeeded. It was always destined to be a big one, and I think that's why we took so long trying to get it right. There was no point just bunging it out half-baked. If ever I hear it now, I just think, 'Well, that's another couple of bob.'"

Over at ZTT, there was great anxiety about The Pogues' album. 'The Irish Rover' had been a Top 10 success and had widened the band's crossover appeal, especially into Irish audiences, considerably. Sales of *Rum Sodomy & The Lash* had been climbing again, and the group were now a huge live attraction. And so if anything was likely to help improve the look of Jill Sinclair's "church barometer", it was a new Pogues LP.

"The third album was obviously going to be the important one for The Pogues and Stiff Records," says Dave Robinson.

Frank Murray knew that he had an amazing album and a surefire Christmas hit single on his hands, and he was not about to give the tapes to anyone, especially Dave Robinson. Stiff may have been taken over by ZTT, but that fact did nothing to inspire Murray's confidence. He had heard that Dave Robinson was not prospering within the new company and, anyway, "I didn't think that ZTT was a label for The Pogues.

"Legally we were with ZTT and they started to hustle me for the tapes," continues Murray. "I still wasn't sold on them. Somewhere along the line, I think ZTT got pissed off with us and they decided they would move us on. They would sell us. So they called Chris Blackwell at Island. I [The Pogues] was on tour in America doing some shows with U2 on the Joshua Tree tour and I started getting phone calls from Chris Blackwell expressing an interest in the band."

Unfortunately for The Pogues, that interest went cold before the band had returned to England. Murray then arranged a meeting with ZTT.

"Steve Lillywhite had gone off to New York to work on a David Byrne album, so I let it be known that Steve had the tapes somewhere, I didn't know where, and that I had no access to them," says Frank.

"Jill Sinclair took me to dinner and she was coming on schoolmarmish. She told me that The Belle Stars were the biggest act on the label. I said, 'If ever I heard a reason for not going on your label, that's it.' So there was nothing going on then for a while."

"Frank's not the most rational person to speak to," remarked Sinclair. "I've gone through conversations where I've been making logical points and he'd turn round and say, 'Don't play fucking games with me.'"

Robinson says: "We'd put all our efforts into the new Pogues and Furniture albums. Both of these records had very decent orders, so financially Stiff would have survived. We'd been putting money into The Pogues' tours *et cetera*. Furniture's publisher withheld a licence for us to put their album out after we'd paid for that. We pulled everything together for these two records. But it took about a month or five weeks to get the licence required for the Furniture album. And just when The Pogues' album was ready to be delivered, Frank ran off with the recordings. We couldn't find him or the tapes.

"At the end of the day, Frank Murray was one of the reasons that Stiff came to financial ruin because he ran off with the tapes and we had to go through the courts to get them."

Murray: "I think it's very unfair of Dave Robinson to blame The Pogues for him going bankrupt. I'm a great admirer of an awful lot of things Dave's done. Like everybody else, sometimes you make a good move and sometimes you make a bad move. Dave had a lot of things going for him, but you don't want to be up against him when his back's against the wall. My principal interest was The Pogues and The Pogues only. They were my responsibility and they were the only people I had an obligation to protect.

"What happened was that Dave's 'key man' clause in our contract expired. The clause meant that he had to be part of Stiff and if he ever left Stiff Records, we could leave as well. The relationship between Dave and Trevor Horn and Jill Sinclair had reached a really low ebb. So when they found out that the clause expired, they saw no reason to have Dave around."

In one way, Jill felt bad about getting rid of Robinson. Stiff was his label, his passion, and he had built it up through blood, sweat and tears, inspired ideas, creative accounting and enormous debts.

"Dave hasn't kissed the Blarney Stone," she commented. "He's made love to the Blarney Stone. We did everything we could – I didn't want to take Dave away from Stiff. But in the end, we just had to ask him to leave. We had a meeting, my father came too, and we sat and listened. My father looked at him and said, 'You don't understand. It's over. It's finished.' There was absolutely no way we could spend another penny."

Sinclair also said that on a personal level, she was finding it hard to work with Robinson, despite his capacity for charm and persuasiveness: "Dave is very mercurial and very alpha male. It was new to me. I'd never met anyone like him before. People like him, they're bullies and they'll be shouting at you. You only want to have a little bit of intelligent dialogue to be able to come to a logical solution."

Neither Sinclair nor Murray have any memory of court proceedings involving Dave Robinson.

Says Murray: "I'm still waiting on the court order. I definitely haven't seen it."

Sinclair added: "My memory is that Chris O'Donnell, who'd left ZTT, came back. He's a very nice boy. He'd sorted all the ins and outs of getting

Dave out of Island. I don't think we ever went to court. It's conceivable that Robbo said, 'We've gotta do this,' and I said, 'Do it.' But my understanding was that we dealt with Chris O'Donnell. He brought those tapes in. He got the album from Frank Murray."

Murray explains: "Chris O'Donnell was a friend of mine. And Jill Sinclair started doing a deal for ZTT to go through Warner Brothers. So I had some meetings with Chris O'Donnell and things were turning our way then, having a very strong ally in the company. I had a meeting with Rob Dickens of Warners and that proved to be very positive."

"It was very tough to actually get the tapes," admits Sinclair. "And they refused for it to be on the Stiff label. So we set up a new identity which was Pogue Mahone Records. It came through ZTT but it gave them a label identity and made them feel emotionally better. They felt more comfortable because we at ZTT then took over the accounting policy."

"We got quite a large cheque – just an advance and stuff like that – for the album," concludes Frank Murray. "We got our own imprint. And that's the story of the Terry Woods solo album."

Dave Robinson looks back over the whole, sorry saga: "Having signed them and put a lot of effort into two years of The Pogues, it was a shame that things ended the way they did. The Pogues I really liked and admired because the music was fantastic. It was my own kind of stuff. When I finally got to hear *If I Should Fall From Grace With God*, having recovered it, I thought it was very good, but Stiff went down before this record came out.

"I have found that in the record business, you do live and learn but it's slow. I did have what I would have termed ten good and close friends. I probably have one of them now that I talk to. At the time Stiff ran into its difficulties, these people ran like pheasants from a gun.

"Realistically, I never had a friendship with Frank. He had his agenda, always. We got on to a degree. Also, Frank really was in the way of the band doing slightly better. Shane had been a drinker since The Nips. With a little policing and a little bit of effort, he would pitch up for the gig. Frank isolated him so Shane became his main buddy. He was in a completely terrible state forever. After Frank, he started taking some really hairy drugs, a lot of coke – 'Get as drunk as you like, take a bit of coke and it'll get you on stage.' Well, it only does for so long.

"I look back on The Pogues with great affection. I like to see them doing well. It's amazing Shane is still alive, and I'd like to see him making something of the rest of his life. He's done a great deal. Maybe he could've done more."

CHAPTER 22

Strummer In The City

The Pogues had become world-renowned for liking a jar, and then some. Shane MacGowan, of course, was a law on to himself. Spider Stacy, Philip Chevron and Terry Woods were developing serious alcohol problems which all three would eventually resolve. James Fearnley and Andrew Ranken enjoyed a glass or two, and although they were capable of pissing it up with the best of them, neither was on a mission all the time. Darryl Hunt and Jem Finer were never heavy drinkers.

Darryl quickly realised the reputation that had been foisted upon him simply because he had joined The Pogues.

He says: "Journalists kept asking us, 'How do you play when you're so drunk?' and all that sort of stuff. Some people in the band did like a drink, and some were as straight as dies when we did the gigs. We were all tarred with this sort of brush, which was slightly irritating. It was something that we'd have a little moan about.

"Of course Shane liked his drink. There *was* drinking, you know. But the press seemed to elevate that. We had to work bloody hard and, really, before the gig, the bulk of the group was on the case. Even Shane and Spider were pretty cool when they hit the stage. They did their thing; some of us held back. At the time I joined the band, a more professional attitude was going on.

"Most people really didn't have a drink till after the show, even the more serious drinkers among us. Then, certain people might go completely out to lunch. I'd like a drink after the gig, but I couldn't call myself a serious drinker. I'd be sick. We did like smoking a bit of pot, as everybody does. I was more likely to skin up a large spliff than have a drink. We weren't just this drinking group."

"Smoking spliffs – Jesus Christ, that was pretty constant, I think for

296

most of the band's existence," agrees Andrew. "Not everybody, but the majority. That always seemed pretty innocuous to me. It gets you cancer, of course."

Hunt: "I don't think our lifestyle was any different to your average stock-broker in the City of London on a Saturday night. It's just that people thought that."

However, a little further down the line: "There's no doubt that eventually drinking damaged people quite a bit and they had to stop."

The one person who had no intention of stopping anything was MacGowan.

"At the beginning, everything was fine," recalls Frank Murray. "It was the music business and we'd drink and everybody was guilty of the excessive drinking. We loved it. We could sit in our hotel rooms with ourselves as company and entertain ourselves for days on end.

"The first signal that Shane was possibly going too far was when we were doing a photo shoot for 'A Pair Of Brown Eyes'. We went back to the Island offices and Shane had been complaining about getting sick and having pains in his stomach. I think he'd coughed up blood, or something like that. He said he'd given up drinking and then I saw him with a beer. I think he said to me, 'That's not drink.' He'd define drink as whiskey and spirits. So there's a problem.

"Gradually, as Shane started to earn more money, I guess he started to enjoy himself. He had no restraint. Maybe because he'd been hard-up for a long time, he got this appetite for everything, and he loved to know that he had a wad of bills in his pocket. You could sit down with Shane in a bar and he'd order a gin and tonic, maybe a glass of white wine and a glass of milk and a cup of coffee, and he'd start drinking them."

Soon, Murray would have grounds to become seriously worried about MacGowan's relationship with alcohol and drugs.

"Sometimes one of the problems was you were looking at him and you were talking to him but he was under the influence of so many things it was hard to know whether you were getting through to him or not," says Murray. "I kept making excuses for him – 'This is not the real Shane.'"

However, it wasn't MacGowan but Terry Woods who came in for a telling-off when the band played a sprinkling of Irish dates in the autumn of 1987 after finishing their album recordings in RAK. The tour – and those following - was promoted under the banner of The Brother Wouldn't Look At An Egg, a literary reference to Irish novelist Flann O'Brien. It was the beginning of a long, live campaign supporting the band's soon-to-be-released new album, *If I should Fall From Grace With God*. The itinerary included two nights in Virginia, County Cavan, the home ground of Terry

Woods, and it was here that the loyal brothers-in-arms, Woods and James Fearnley, ended up in a fierce dispute over Terry's state of inebriation.

Says James: "I think Terry was very nervous about playing in his home-town. He got *very* drunk and I remember saying to him, 'It's your home-town, just lay off it a bit.' He was so angry with me. He rounded on me – 'Mind your own business.' He was very cross."

The Pogues followed on with a one-off concert at the London Electric Ballroom in mid-November.

It was my first introduction to Shane. Early afternoon and he was lying unconscious along the seating in the venue while the other Pogues waited quietly to begin the soundcheck. Rumours abounded at the time that the road crew held keys to MacGowan's flat so that they could march in at any time, pick him up and stretcher him out to whatever appointment he would otherwise miss. It certainly looked like that's what had happened.

Shane was a man who enjoyed staying up all night. Like John Lennon before him, he liked to be surrounded by all manner of information and entertainment, with open books, tapes and albums scattered round the room, a guitar and a pen and paper never far from reach, and the TV on at all times, blaring out regular broadcasting or videos. Smoking, drinking, reading, singing, listening, learning and viewing, he would spend the hours of darkness in a world of his own making, usually accompanied by friends and whatever drugs he happened to fancy at the time. Speed was still a favourite, by all accounts, and he had already started a period of experi-mentation with acid.

Andrew, Darryl and Philip repaired to the nearest pub and each ordered a St Clements - orange juice and bitter lemon. Spider, arriving later, had something a little stronger. And then it was time for somebody to wake MacGowan. He opened his eyes, picked up a bottle of port and drank it. Then he was ready to face the day. And first things first – a drink. Heading directly to a French restaurant just a couple of steps along the road, Shane announced more than once that you could "drink all day" there. This was important because, back then, the pubs closed at 3pm for a break before the evening session.

They seemed to know Shane in the restaurant, where he ordered a bottle of wine and a couple of starters: tomatoes with basil and a bowl of snails. It seemed to be the best part of his day: he was relaxed, expansive, welcoming towards the visiting *Melody Maker* reporter. It was a warmly enjoyable after-noon, punctuated by the sound of his famous, hissing laugh. But after the soundcheck, back in the restaurant for the formal interview, his mood changed dramatically. Having sobered up with unnatural rapidity, he became tense, snappy and suspicious, quite unlike the affable character who'd held court in this same place just a couple of hours earlier. It was a great relief to be joined at the table by Joe Strummer, a dependably courteous and gregarious companion.

Strummer was about to make his first live appearance in three years as a special guest of The Pogues. He said: "I would never have accepted an invitation from anybody else, you know. The Pogues are from the same tradition as The Clash. I don't wish to draw any divisions within the scene, but The Pogues are definitely from my side of the tracks. They're definitely something I can understand. I was really impressed when I heard their instrumental music in *Sid And Nancy*. I'd been thinking of one-dimensional Pogues and when I heard that, I realised that they had depth to them, this fabulous depth.

"They called me and said, 'Come up to Camden Ballroom.' It's a room that I've decorated with my own sweat on more than one occasion. I must confess to being a bit nervous. I'm frightened as hell. . ."

"It scares the shit out of me too," agreed MacGowan. "All that mania going on out there – it's been getting more and more manic in the last year or so."

MacGowan was now openly admitting the strain of touring. He revealed: "A lot of the time on the road, I feel like a nervous wreck. There's a lot of pressure. People are shouting and screaming at you all the way. You get hassled by people grabbing you, wanting to talk to you, asking you why they can't get in free, telling you why they didn't like your last record."

It was all getting to him: fans demanding autographs, photographs and keepsakes, yelling questions up to the band on stage while they were trying to play, and wanting to know the same things every night in every city.

The audience at the Electric Ballroom was, of course, as hot and as packed and as manic as Shane expected. The throng sang loudly along like a football crowd, dancing and cheering frenziedly, and things became even more tumultuous in the auditorium when Strummer walked on for encores of 'London Calling' and 'I Fought The Law'. The Pogues were more than capable of topping that, though, piling on the excitement with a final leap through 'Maggie May'.

"I sweated so much into my accordion that the wood expanded and the keys wouldn't work," says James Fearnley. "I had to unplug it and cavort around and pretend I was actually playing it."

It was a triumphant night for The Pogues and a "wonderful" occasion for Joe Strummer – who would find himself back on stage with the band a lot sooner than he expected.

★

Philip Chevron was in agony. His ulcer had flared up again, really badly, and he could barely stand. It became clear that he would not be able to join The Pogues for their three-week tour of Canada and the States in December.

Philip remembers: "I suppose the lifestyle and everything had contributed. I was exhausted from the sheer constant pain of it. We were on the verge of great things. The album was in the can, 'Fairytale' was about to be released as a single, and there was a tour of the USA in for December, which seemed to me unnecessary."

More immediately, there was a photo session for the album sleeve. Yet again, The Pogues' album artwork would become a problem for at least one member of the band.

"I woke up one morning and I could hardly get out of bed," says Chevron. "I phoned up Frank and said, 'I can't make it to the photo session today.' He said, 'If you don't get to the photo session you're not on the fucking album sleeve.' He said, 'Do whatever it takes, get yourself here and then you can sit down.' In fact, it's one of those things that worked in our favour. As soon as they knew I needed to sit down for most of the session, the photographer brought in this luggage."

The luggage was a big, old-fashioned trunk which Philip sat on for the photo shoot, surrounded by the rest of the group, all in black suits, holding their instruments. This would become one of the most famous – and appropriate – images of The Pogues.

"It looked perfect," says Chevron. "It spoke of emigrants, although the luggage was there mainly for me to sit on. That's why it arrived in the first place. Again, The Pogues turn disaster into triumph.

"I went home and sank back into my bed. When I had spells of pain from the ulcer, it made it very difficult to eat, and that made me even weaker. It was a self-perpetuating problem. I said to Frank, 'I've gone to the doctor. They want to take me into hospital this week.' They took me in two days later."

Frank Murray now had to find a temporary guitarist for the American tour. He says: "Philip was looking really, really bad. He was so weak a gust of wind would've blown him over. I was sitting at home one night and I thought to myself, 'If he comes on this American tour, he could easily die.'

"I called up Joe Strummer and I said to Joe, 'Look, are you busy over the next couple of weeks?' He said, 'Why?' I said, 'I can't take Philip to the States with us. I think it would kill him. He really needs the rest, but I can't cancel the tour.' I said, 'Will you come and play guitar with us?' Joe was thinking about it and he said, 'Philip's not been sacked, has he?' I said, 'No, I swear he's not. I think he's really ill.' He said, 'Well, if the band agree, I'll come on the tour.' So then I rang each individual member of the band. They all said,

'Okay.' I rang Phil and said I'd spoken to everyone, and then I called Joe back and said, 'Everybody agrees.'"

Philip: "Frank said, 'I've made arrangements for Joe Strummer to play guitar, but you need to go over to Joe's and teach him the songs. We'll send the car. Sit down, play guitar for two hours, show Joe how the songs go, don't worry about things and I'll see you in January.' So I have to do one final thing before I get permission to collapse in a heap. I did have that session with Joe, round his house in Ladbroke Grove. He understood he was dealing with somebody who was very fragile, and it was good. We just played guitars all afternoon.

"I showed him the songs and in the end, he reduced the entire Pogues guitar score down to this tiny little crib sheet which he Sellotaped on top of the guitar. It went with him through the American tour. I've got it. It's one of my great treasures – Joe's actual guitar sheet music. It's the one thing of his I'm really delighted to have because it's so personal to me as well. It's ours. And how gracious he was."

The rest of The Pogues still talk with awe of Strummer's little piece of paper, crammed with a whole set's worth of guitar chords in his miniscule handwriting. Everyone got on famously with the former Clash man, and this was a probability which had not escaped Chevron.

"I suppose I was a bit nervous that he might get on too well with them," concedes Philip. "That was just my insecurity. I was inclined to say, 'I'll meet you at some point on the tour. I'll come over next week.' Frank said, 'You can't. You have to be realistic. We need to do this tour. We don't want you falling sick in the middle of it with no insurance, so let's make a decision. Let's let Joe do it all.'"

Strummer had two or three days' rehearsal with the band before they flew off to New York, and The Pogues admired him on many counts, especially for his professionalism and sensitivity.

Jem: "Joe wasn't really like an outsider trying to find his place. I can remember being really impressed by the effort he put into learning stuff. He was a very meticulous guy. It was great to see that kind of dedication and commitment. He really wanted to get it right and do a good job. And he was a lovely person to have around.

"I think it created a little bit of excitement in America too. It was kind of nice to hardwire that connection, the spirit between The Pogues and The Clash. Joe was very reserved on stage. He was at the back playing his guitar, really working at it, and then he'd come to the front and do his numbers. He was a very charismatic frontman, but he played it pretty low-key. He didn't want to steal anybody's thunder. He fitted in as one of the band and then he took his turn in the spotlight."

Darryl adds: "Strummer had his own fans at the gigs. They knew which side of the stage he was standing – next to me, playing rhythm guitar – so I had the Strummer contingent in front of me. He brought a real, sussed professionalism to being on the road. He talked a lot of sense, simply through his experience of what actually mattered when you're performing. He had a great regard for the venues we were performing in. He also taught me to support your comrades, to be sure that people in the group were supporting the other members. You respect your comrades, you support them and you consult people. These things Strummer did without thinking. He had the respect of everyone from other musicians to the T-shirt sellers or whatever else. I learnt a lot from him. He had this side that was very, very sussed about the priorities in life – respect for others and their work and their art and their abilities.

"He was very good at standing by the person who was the least important or the least effective of the group. One time, later on, when Philip was having drinking problems and was not in a good way, Joe was very aware of that. He was producing *Hell's Ditch* for us, and he made sure Philip did the tracklisting. He'd designate something. He'd do the same for me. Playing on the team and being respected – that's how he liked to see things. Everyone got on with him. He did a lot of good work for us. He was a diplomat's son. With Shane he had no problem at all."

There may not have been any particular problem and MacGowan states today that he enjoyed having Joe on board, but Gavin Martin, covering part of the tour for *NME*, reported an "unspoken tension" between Shane and Strummer.

Strummer told Martin: "You're not the first person to mention it and I think you're right. I want to clear things with Shane; if I come aboard, I don't want to elbow in on anything. I just want to do justice to his songs."

Joe went on to describe MacGowan as a "genius" ranking alongside Lou Reed and Brendan Behan, before confirming that he was really enjoying his chance to play Pogues music: "It's ten times faster than punk," he said. "I've got callouses on my fingers I've never had before. They feel like blocks of wood."

In New York, at the beginning of the tour, The Pogues took time out to film a video for 'Fairytale', with MTV director Peter Dougherty. In a strange instance of life almost imitating art, several members of the band and crew were less than sober as they arrived to film in a real-life drunk tank, attracting some comment from the NYPD – who, incidentally, don't have a choir and are therefore unlikely to spend much time singing 'Galway Bay'.

Shot in black and white, the video follows the storyline of the song, with gum-chewing cop Matt Dillon bundling MacGowan through the station and up a staircase to spend Christmas Eve in the cells, while a wobbly Charlie MacLennan leans for stability on a desk, dressed as Santa. Such a Pogues fan was Dillon that he refused to rough up MacGowan, despite the singer's encouragement and insistence that it would add to the authenticity. Sleeping it off in custody with Terry Woods, MacGowan is reunited the next day with his young sweetheart, Kirsty MacColl. We see them walking through the city in the Fifties, a carefree couple whose happiness soon deteriorates into an unseemly display of pushing, shoving and haranguing. The video ends with the famous Shane and Kirsty waltz, dimly lit and romantic.

Interspersed through the film are shots of New York, a bagpipe band replacing the "NYPD choir" and a Pogues performance set in a smoky nightclub at probably two in the morning. Darryl plays double bass while James Fearnley, wearing Shane's jacket and rings, acts as his stunt double for close-ups of the piano keyboard.

"A lot about the video was influenced by our collective obsessions," explains Jem Finer. "This jazz video we had – a lot of Billie Holiday was in it, and it was shot in black and white in this beautiful way. There was a completely black background with just her lit. We said to Peter, the director, 'We want it like this Billie Holiday video.' The drummer had this huge kick drum and in the 'Fairytale' video, that's what Andrew's got. So that's where all that came from."

The tour finished with three nights in California, two of those supporting Los Lobos, who had personally invited The Pogues to play. The third show, in San Juan Capistrano, was a headline and a great success. Gavin Martin told *NME* readers that the band had acquired "a new fluency of playing which complements rather than smoothes over their essential rawness". He added that the live show "mixes a cornucopia of international musics with an emotional range stretching from gangland/party exuberance to heart-rending poignancy".

Somewhere, Bob Dylan's son Jesse, the latest convert to the band, has a video tape of the whole gig.

California was also significant to female fans of The Pogues who may have been devastated to learn that the band's very own Cary Grant – accordion player James Fearnley – had just met the woman who would take him off the market.

James remembers: "I first met Danielle when we were in Santa Barbara opening for Los Lobos. We agreed that we'd write letters to one another. We wrote letters a lot." The letters would whizz back and forth across the Atlantic for the next six months until James and Danielle could meet again in Los Angeles.

Gavin Martin, despite his great regard for the band and the ways in which they were progressing, sounded a note of warning about MacGowan, writing: "As Shane approaches his moment of greatest fame, he seems to be becoming increasingly bedraggled, sinking ever further into the mire. He looks more and more like one of the underclass victims described in a song like 'The Old Main Drag' and sometimes sad and kind of ghostly."

The Pogues returned for three nights of gigs at one of their favourite venues – Glasgow Barrowlands – from December 17 to 19. Here, they played their last shows with Joe Strummer (for the time being) and also proved the live potential of their bigger, broader, more ambitious sound with the help of trumpeter Eli Thompson and saxman Brian Clarke, both borrowed from support band After Tonite. Thompson and Clarke had been part of the brass section used on the forthcoming album. They were making their live debut in Glasgow, as was Kirsty MacColl, who was greeted with deafening cheers as she strolled on to sing her part in 'Fairytale Of New York'.

Glasgow, predictably, went apeshit for the band. Myrna Minkoff, reviewing for *NME*, described the fervour and diversity of the scrum: "By 'Sally MacLennane', most of the lads had their shirts off and were enthusiastically throwing themselves into a number of male-bonding rituals. Just in front of us, a housewife in her early thirties removed her top and spent the rest of the gig in bra and skirt, one arm wrapped round her husband."

Minkoff commented on the scope of the material, noting that MacGowan sounded like "a Middle-Eastern Tom Waits" on 'Turkish Song Of The Damned' and complimenting the "startling effects" of the brass section on 'Metropolis' – "with their simple, jarring intrusions". Moreover, Woods and Fearnley "elevated most of the pieces into a complex world of folk-jazz".

The Pogues, with a fully recovered Philip Chevron and Kirsty MacColl, made time to perform 'Fairytale Of New York' on *Top Of The Pops*. It had all the makings of a great Christmas Number One and all the quality of a great Pogues song.

Nick Cave, a long-time fan of the band, marvelled at the originality of this most unusual festive offering, stating: "You don't normally get Christmas songs so utterly hopeless." He later commented: "I think Shane is a kind of master of the opening lines of songs, unbelievably good – *'It was Christmas Eve, babe / In the drunk tank…'*"

'Fairytale' – backed with Terry Woods' 'The Battle March Medley' and with the MacGowan instrumental 'Shanne Bradley' additional on the 12-inch – was the band's debut release on Pogue Mahone Records. Frustratingly, it only reached Number Two in the Christmas chart: few would have foreseen its ascendancy blocked by Pet Shop Boys' cover of 'Always On My Mind'.

Smiles all round belie the fact that trouble is brewing. A certain "fragmentation" was beginning to take place in the group, escalating during the sessions for their ironically titled *Peace And Love* album in 1989. Shane was beginning to distance himself from his bandmates, and other members of The Pogues were becoming disillusioned. *(ANDREW CATLIN/LFI)*

Shane in Elephant Studios in April 1990, prior to the band's relocation to Rockfield to record
Hell's Ditch with producer Joe Strummer. Despite the growing estrangement between MacGowan and
the rest of The Pogues, Shane had been working on a batch of new and impressive songs for the album.
"Hell's Ditch had a sunnier outlook," says Philip. "It's a happier album, and one that was turning the
corner for us." *(ANDREW CATLIN)*

Joe Strummer was the unanimous choice to join the band when Shane was invited to leave in Japan. Joe, pictured with The Pogues in 1992, undertook several tours as Shane's replacement. "He was very easy-going," says Spider. "He was incredibly enthusiastic. It was just really good for the morale. Joe gave us the legs to continue." *(PAUL SLATTERY)*

When Strummer left to return to his solo career, Spider took over the lead vocalist's role. Pictured with the band in November 1992, he says, "I was really nervous about it but also I was drinking a lot, so a drunk arrogance swaggered into town." *(ANDREW CATLIN)*

Long-time friends Shane and Johnny Depp joined forces to promote The Popes' single, 'That Woman's Got Me Drinking', in October 1994. Depp, who played guitar on the track, directed and appeared in the video and made a string of appearances with Shane. *(TIM ROOKE/REX FEATURES)*

Shane and his friend Sinead O'Connor in 1995, when they scored a Top 30 hit with a new recording of 'Haunted'. They would fall out several years later when Sinead shopped him to the police for possessing heroin. Later still, he credited her with giving him a "wake-up call". *(DES WILLIE/REDFERNS)*

Shane meets up with old pals Nick Cave and Kate Moss in March 2005 at a party launching the release of *Hoping For Palestine*, a DVD of the benefit concert for Palestinian children held at Brixton Academy in October 2004. *(DAVE BENETT/GETTY IMAGES)*

The Pogues onstage at Brixton Academy in December 2001 – the year of their first reunion. Terry Woods sums up the feelings of the group: "The Pogues were too big a band to go out with a whimper. I was quite delighted about the reunion. It appeared if nothing else that we could put a proper full-stop after The Pogues." *(TABITHA FIREMAN/REDFERNS)*

Shane MacGowan waltzes with his leading ladies in 'Fairytale Of New York':
Kirsty MacColl, above left *(PATRICK FORD/REDFERNS)*; Cait O'Riordan, above right *(DANNY CLIFFORD/FILMMAGIC)*;
Cerys Matthews, below left *(HUW JOHN/REX FEATURES)*; and Ella Finer, below right *(MICK HUTSON)*.

In December 2004, reuniting after a year off, The Pogues line up with their original bass player Cait O'Riordan backstage at Brixton Adademy. Left to right: Spider, Darryl, Jem, Andrew, Shane, James, Cait, Philip and Terry. *(DANNY CLIFFORD/FILMMAGIC)*

Back to the classic *Fall From Grace* line-up. Together at the Fuji Rock Festival in Japan in July 2005 are, left to right: Terry, Philip, Andrew, James, Jem, Spider, Darryl and Shane. *(DANNY CLIFFORD/FILMMAGIC)*

The dynamic duo reunited! Shane and Spider joined the rest of The Pogues to be presented with a lifetime achievement honour at the Meteor Ireland Music Awards in Dublin on February 2, 2006. The audience was rewarded with a Pogues and Dubliners rendition of 'The Irish Rover'. *(BRIAN MCEVOY/WENN)*

Celebrating St Patrick's Day 2006 with a short, sell-out American tour.
Says Shane: "I think we'll stay together." *(ROBERT E. KLEIN/RETNA)*

"I was disappointed rather than pissed off," admits Jem Finer. "But most people seemed to think of 'Fairytale Of New York' as being Number One. It was the people's choice." In Ireland, it was even more of a smash hit, racing to its rightful place at the very top of the chart.

Andrew: "I think we were all pretty confident it would get into the charts and do quite well, but you don't know what the competition's going to be, especially at Christmas."

"We thought it would be very disappointing if it wasn't a massive, big hit," agrees Darryl. "We had a feeling it was something special."

Terry Woods had not anticipated the perennial popularity of the single. He comments: "We didn't give it a second thought that it would become a Christmas classic. I'd get pissed off – every supermarket I'd go into coming up to Christmas, it would be on. It used to irritate me, I got that pissed off listening to it. Now I have a nostalgic liking for it."

There had never been much time to relax after Christmas, and January 1988 was no exception. The Pogues jetted off to conquer new territories with a month of dates in Australia and New Zealand. While they were there, good news arrived from home: only two weeks after its release, *If I Should Fall From Grace With God* had zipped up the UK albums chart to Number Three.

"Retrospectively," says Darryl Hunt, "it's a very important body of work and very finely played. It's almost like a pinnacle. Obviously now it's considered a classic along with *Rum Sodomy & The Lash*."

The Pogues were widely judged to have fulfilled their potential and justified the hopes placed in them by their supporters over the years: they had moved forward, bravely, without any loss of their popular strength and individuality. And although this was more of an all-band effort than had been the case in the past, much was made of MacGowan's continuing genius as a songwriter. He was no flash in the pan: he was the real thing.

Talking in the DVD *If I Should Fall From Grace: The Shane MacGowan Story*, Nick Cave says: "I thought he was an incredible lyric writer, a great singer, and the songs were really beautiful. And then the next album came out *[If I Should Fall...]* and I just thought some of the lyric writing on that was unbelievable, kind of head and shoulders above what anyone else was doing. It had a simplicity and beauty about it that was just extraordinary, I thought.

"There was energy in the way that he wrote. From my point of view, I was writing very different sorts of lyrics. . . and from as early on as I remember, I was trying to make an effort in some way to show that I could write. And that's the difference between me and Shane, and what made Shane such a great writer - his complete effortlessness. It just looked like it dropped out of him. And there wasn't a bad line amongst it. It was just beautiful stuff."

However, the British tabloid newspapers were outraged by one of the songs on the album, and as a result of their shock-horror reporting, 'Birmingham Six' was quite some time later banned from broadcast. Campaigners had been protesting the innocence of alleged IRA terrorists the Birmingham Six and the Guildford Four, who were then serving long sentences for bombing pubs. Both groups of men would go on to be released after having their convictions quashed by the Court Of Appeal, the Guildford Four in 1989 after 15 years' imprisonment, and the Birmingham Six in 1991 after 16 years.

This was controversial stuff, so much so that James Fearnley's father took exception to his son's involvement. "He was very upset that I should be part of a group that would play a song like that," recalls Fearnley. "He said, 'James, you're in the entertainment business, and you've no business making political statements.' I tried to tell him it wasn't so much a political statement as the artistic expression of a political statement, and even if it was, so what? He couldn't accept that."

Even more inflammatory was the final verse, which contained this couplet: *"While over in Ireland eight more men lie dead / Kicked down and shot in the back of the head."* This refers to eight IRA men who'd been shot by British forces in Armagh, and it was this passage which was hurriedly faded out of a live performance of the song on a TV show hosted by Ben Elton before the ban was in place.

In interviews given to support the album release, at a time when fresh evidence was emerging about the Birmingham and Guildford pub bombings, MacGowan expressed his rage at a system which could set up and then incarcerate so many innocent men. "It's just so offensive and disgusting," he told me. "The song does also mention the things that go on in Ireland, the guys that got shot in the back of the neck by the SAS in Armagh, but the main thing is the Birmingham Six and the Guildford Four."

At the same time, MacGowan was unhappy to be asked about such recent atrocities as the Enniskillen bombing of 1987. Eventually, he replied that it was "a revolting thing to do". Jem Finer agreed, "It was horrible and it was self-defeating."

Shane carried on: "I don't believe in killing anybody, but some people are legitimate targets."

"If you see yourself as fighting a war," Finer interjected.

"Armed people are legitimate targets," said Shane. "If you're carrying a gun, if you're prepared to shoot somebody, you've got to be prepared to die yourself."

Frank Murray wasn't too concerned about the negative press. He says, "I didn't see it in those terms. It probably increased the band's notoriety. It was a great song. It was up there with 'Hurricane' by Bob Dylan. It was me who suggested it. People were asking us right, left and centre to do all kinds of benefits for the Birmingham Six and the Guildford Four. I asked Shane, 'If you agree with the whole thing, will you write a song about it?' He said, 'Yeah, I'll try.'"

James: "We met the wives of those people. We did some collecting for them, for the families, which they were awfully appreciative of. I remember after the album came out, we were playing in Belfast. Frank came up to us and said there had been a bomb scare in the venue and we all had to get out while the place was swept. I think Frank might've suggested it would be a good idea if we didn't play 'Birmingham Six' that night and we said, 'We're going to, because it's on the setlist.' That's what we did, and nothing happened."

Gerry Conlan of the Guildford Four subsequently came along to a number of Pogues gigs, and he became especially friendly with Joey Cashman.

The Antipodean trip marked the beginning of another period of intense touring, but The Pogues were happy enough for the time being, enjoying the chance to see Australia and New Zealand.

"I'd always wanted to go there," says Jem. "It's a bit shit having to be away so much, but if you're going somewhere interesting... Say you go to Europe, you're working the whole time and you just drive from one city to the next. Because of the distances involved in Australia and New Zealand, we'd play a night or two and have a couple of days off. We actually got time to hang out there and explore a bit, go on little day trips and so on. It was brilliant.

"Arriving in Australia, I immediately had this feeling of it as this really old, old place. The land feels very old and, in a sense, the cities and towns can feel very alien, like they've just been landed on this wild place. There's this place called Surfer's Paradise, this horrible resort-y place in Queensland. I was looking at the sea thinking, 'It's amazing. It could be millions of years ago.' And I turned round and these grey, high-rise things behind looked like they'd just landed. They literally looked like tombstones."

This observation formed the basis for Finer's composition, 'Tombstone', which would appear on the next Pogues album. He adds: "The lines *'The night is dark, the moon is full/Across the blood-red plain'* – that was my interpretation of the Aboriginal flag - that's the black and the yellow and the red. I was just trying to write a song very simply about what happened when the people of this land, who considered themselves to be part of this land, were colonised. It's a sort of ethnic cleansing situation. The white man comes along and wipes out the natives and covers everything with tarmac and concrete. I felt that quite strongly there.

"My favourite place was Byron Bay, a small surfer town in the eastern-most part of Australia, north of New South Wales. That was quite in the countryside. There was a beach and rain forest and a nice atmosphere, lots of people hanging out surfing. It was a lovely place. I'd have loved to be able to spend some time just driving to the outback and getting lost in the middle of nowhere. Obviously that wasn't possible."

At the same time, Finer had his own down moments, and it was as a result of one of those that he wrote probably his most celebrated Pogues song, 'Misty Morning, Albert Bridge'. "The first draft of it I wrote in some dump in New Zealand when I was feeling particularly lonely, like I was at the end of the earth," he explains. "I woke up and I wrote a poem which became the basis for the lyrics to the song. It's just this poem rewritten so you can sing the words.

"I can't remember what the town was called. It was a peculiar place. It reminded me of a book I had as a child – *The Ladybird Book Of A Town*. The weird thing about New Zealand is that a lot of it looks like another planet, where someone has recreated 1950s England. A lot of the planning is exactly like English planning but in a slightly alien landscape. There's a lot of melancholia about it. It reminded me of when I was a kid, probably sub-consciously, and it made me feel further away, not just in terms of distance but in terms of time as well. It was a very weird experience.

"So that's where that came from, and this idea of 'Misty Morning, Albert Bridge' – Marcia grew up living next to that bridge. I can remember one of our early dates, walking very early in the morning past it. I guess that's something that stuck in my mind."

Asked for Marcia's opinion of the song when she heard it, Finer replies: "I know she didn't give me a hard time like she did with my first draft of 'Fairytale'!"

But if Jem was having weird experiences in New Zealand, Shane MacGowan's were weirder still. Frank Murray revisits the scene: "We'd just toured Australia. I think we had to do about four gigs in New Zealand and then we were going home. This was probably our second-last gig, maybe in Wellington or Christchurch. For the previous gig, Shane had been a mess. Besides drink, he was doing speed. Anyway, he came off the stage this night and he'd done a really bad show. Everybody was getting on to him. We'd all been having a pop at Shane for about 20 minutes, and he kept giving us weird answers to everything. I think at one stage I said, 'What did you do that for?' and he looked at me and said, 'I done it for Ireland.' I remember Paul Scully came in and started ripping into Shane and asked him what the hell did he think he was doing out there on the stage."

Philip Chevron remembers: "There were times when Shane just didn't perform. He'd be incapable. He was there physically, but mentally he would not be in the same place. There were times when we were very concerned, very worried, and this was at a time when we had some very tense situations ourselves. The funny thing was, with awful gigs, it never mattered to the audience. They judged the success of a gig on how out-of-it Shane was. They're not the people who come and see us any more, but there was certainly an element of the audience who'd say it was brilliant when it was rubbish from start to finish – 'We're sorry we took your money.'

"There was this one situation in New Zealand when Paul Scully came backstage shouting, 'Is this how it's going to be? You're just going to watch the guy die in front of your eyes?' It was the tensest it's ever been. That's how it was increasingly coming across, as being that on the edge.

"We all froze. It was very strange because nobody had ever seen Paul lose his temper before. When somebody who doesn't *does*, you pay attention. We thought, 'There isn't really any answer to that.' Paul went into a corner and wept and then he went and started talking to Shane. Everybody was taking off in a different direction to cry on each other's shoulders and at 4am have that conversation in the hotel room yet again – 'What's the matter with this band?' We were in ever-decreasing circles of hell. You don't know how it's going to be from one day to the next."

Frank Murray: "The next morning, I discovered that Shane had painted his hotel room. He'd written all kinds of graffiti all over the walls. He'd painted his face blue and his chest blue, and he was refusing to leave the room. I asked him, where was all of his dignity gone to? What had happened to him? Why was he in such a state? Had he had a look at himself? I tried to reach some part of him. I remember telling him to wash himself because we had to get to a plane. Yeah, he washed himself and all that, and he came down and got with us."

In *A Drink With Shane MacGowan*, the singer claims that the hotel was built on a Maori graveyard, and that he painted himself blue because the Maoris told him to: "This particular night I started getting a very strong, totally real feeling that the Maoris were talking to me. You see, you talk to yourself in your head when you're speeding and you get turned into two people, who talk to each other in your head."

He added that he used to carry paints around on tour, and that he was instructed to use the colour blue because "it showed that I was a warrior brother". He was, he later reasoned, in some state of "depressed paranoid madness".

Andrew Ranken: "I never saw the result of the room redecoration, but I did notice that Shane was a rather strange colour one day. I thought it was more grey than blue. I wasn't sure if it was just lack of personal hygiene. I think it's fair to say that Shane's always been quite a messy person. I never saw him with a paintbrush, but I can sort of imagine him with one. He quite frequently used to do drawings, usually with felt tips, and he'd end up covered in ink."

It wasn't MacGowan's last alarming escapade: Frank Murray would have a lot more clearing up to do in the coming months.

CHAPTER 23

St John Of God's

"Frank was genuinely scared at times," reveals Philip Chevron. "He felt he was the only one who could take some sort of responsibility for Shane and get him from A to B. He took an awful lot of shit."

Chevron has come to believe that there may have been a theatrical aspect to MacGowan's nevertheless worrying behaviour. He reached this conclusion while flipping through *A Drink With Shane MacGowan* (not, he hastens to add, because he wished to read the book for his own pleasure but because he was curious to see the passages which had so upset some of his fellow Pogues).

Says Philip: "Shane does, it's very clear, have a much better recollection of the entire period than he ever indicated he was going to have at the time. He has a 100 per cent recall of things where he was apparently out of his tree, scaring people to death. There's stuff there that was clearly done to wind Frank up, that he remembers with such recall that he can't possibly have been quite as out-of-it as he appeared to be at the time.

"People had started saying, 'If The Pogues loved Shane they wouldn't let him go on tour.' Shane was the same when he was in The Devonshire Arms. If anything, he was probably safer with The Pogues than he was with his hangers-on in London, because we genuinely did care about him. It was a circular argument, put forward by some people who really should have known better. It also presumes a knowledge of Shane that I don't think they were in any position to claim – not that anybody has a legitimacy to a claim like that, including us in The Pogues. We never laid a counter-claim that we knew better.

"You try to help, but ultimately everybody's life is in their own hands. You can't go round being responsible for other people, especially when 20 years later you realise that Shane was more sentient than he ever appeared to be. He was perfectly aware of the dismay he was causing in certain circles."

"Shane often behaved badly," Victoria Clarke, his girlfriend, told the *Daily Mail* years later. "He was very much a part of the drink and drugs culture, and when he was drunk he did the most incredible things, such as painting himself with magic markers or lying down in the middle of London's Euston Road, screaming that the world was about to end. I didn't drink much, took no drugs and liked to go to bed early, so I always felt left out. I was convinced that the rest of the band and all the hangers-on hated me. It was pretty miserable at times."

Before the year was out, MacGowan would find himself in St John Of God's in Dublin – "a kind of loony bin for alcoholic nutters". In the meantime, there was work to be done: The Pogues were on the crest of a wave, and they pushed the simmering tensions to one side as they set about promoting their fine new album.

You can't keep a good fan down, and Joe Strummer was hot to strap his guitar back on when The Pogues hit London in March 1988. Due to their American trip in December, they hadn't been able to play the usual run of festive dates in the UK, and so instead they played the three in Glasgow and set up a major tour, Nobody Tells Me Anything, for February and March. This would also take in the usual St Patrick's Day rave-up.

The band were joined on all dates by Kirsty MacColl. Without her, they couldn't – or, rather, wouldn't – attempt 'Fairytale Of New York'. But for Kirsty, the tour had a far greater significance. Prior to her collaboration with The Pogues, she'd been stricken by such a severe case of stage fright that she'd more or less stopped performing. By coming on the band's UK tour, she hoped to face and overcome her fears.

"I didn't know Kirsty before 'Fairytale'," says Andrew. "I think Terry did. I remember Steve Lillywhite telling us about what a state she got into about live performances. Everyone gets nervous at times, but with her it got worse and worse. I think it got to the point where she could hardly bear to go onstage, and she'd be throwing up beforehand and really finding it very difficult.

"Coming on the road with us was meant to be a way of trying to gently ease her back into it without the spotlight being on her too much. If she didn't feel like coming on and singing a bit, that was okay. The pressure was not on her. She was a really wonderful person, great fun and great company and great voice, of course, and she was joining right in with the spirit of things, and it was a pleasure."

"She didn't have to take any responsibility," adds Jem "She could do as much or as little as she wanted. And I think she grew in confidence as the tour went on."

The Pogues – never a "blokey" band by any means – were pleased to have a female presence in their company again.

The dates opened at Norwich UEA on February 21. By the time the entourage had reached London, Kirsty was enjoying things so much she would stay on stage after 'Fairytale' to sing on 'Lullaby Of London', 'Dirty Old Town' and 'Turkish Song Of The Damned' as well as the encores.

Steve Lillywhite: "This was perfect for her. It wasn't her tour, but when people saw her walk on, they knew that they were going to hear a song they really liked, and that really was the beginning of her coming back on to the live scene. It gave her some confidence. She was well-loved. She wasn't on stage for very long. It was just dipping your toe in and realising that the water was actually extremely warm. She got rid of her stage fright, she started her own live career, and we all know what happened. By the time she was killed, she was really enjoying playing. It was such a pity. She loved The Pogues. They loved her as well. She used to enjoy the dancing with MacGowan at the end of 'Fairytale Of New York'. They would always do this little dance, and he'd hit on her a little bit."

Again, the band were supported by After Tonite, a young band from Coventry who had as their mentor and producer the former Specials guitarist Lynval Golding. Every night after their own set, trumpet player Eli Thompson and saxophonist Brian Clarke would join The Pogues on stage for the likes of 'Fiesta' and 'Metropolis'. Golding himself would come on for the encores, singing and playing guitar on a joyful, brassy cover of The Specials' Top Ten hit, 'A Message To You, Rudy'.

"It was great, that tour," says Andrew. "It was a real buzz having the extra people."

The band would expand even more when they arrived in London for an unprecedented six sold-out nights at the Town & Country Club [March 14 to 19] and an add-on at Brixton Academy [20]. Pogues fever was running high.

Joe Strummer had another type of fever that week. He wasn't feeling well at all, but nothing was going to keep him in his sick bed when The Pogues were playing just a few miles away. To miss this would have been "stupid", he said.

Backstage at the Town & Country on St Patrick's Night, Strummer talked to a video crew who were filming the event, showering every member of the band with compliments. Darryl and James were the anchors, "holding the whole thing down". James was also a wonderful showman whose hard work showed in the amount of sweat he produced. Jem, he declared, was "the Bill Wyman" of the band – "Without him, they're all going to float away in the air." Shane was "the poet" and "one of the finest writers of the century". Strummer praised Spider's quick wit and exceptional humour and said of Andrew: "He's not clobbering any more. He's got great feeling." Philip's rhythm guitar playing was "really the tops", and Terry was "the master musician of the band".

It was a mad and marvellous gig, both musically and visually. The brave souls at the front strained against the barriers, arms in the air, as the whole crowd surged and bounced up and down with abandon. By now, The Pogues had so many great songs in their armoury that it was hard to cram them all in, but they played a dazzling selection that ran from 'Dirty Old Town', featuring Andrew on harmonica and James on mandolin, to the raucous chorusing of 'Turkish Song Of The Damned', with Spider and Kirsty whirling round, arms linked, in a spontaneous burst of high spirits.

MacGowan played rhythm banjo and bodhrán when his right hand wasn't curled round the microphone in the classic pose, cigarette smoke rising from his fingers, and various group members attempted the tricky art of harmonising with him - Terry in 'The Broad Majestic Shannon', Philip in his own 'Thousands Are Sailing' and Kirsty in 'Fairytale' and 'Lullaby Of London'.

'Thousands Are Sailing' took on a pacey immediacy and Strummer led the band through 'London Calling' with his usual urgent authority. 'Fairytale Of New York' had already established traditions that are still observed today, the fake snowflakes falling on the stage and the audience's bellowed response to Shane's "I could have been someone": "So could anyone!"

St Patrick's Day was visibly acknowledged by the bunches of shamrock on Fearnley's accordion, Chevron's black hat and MacGowan's stripey T-shirt. The Pogues' matching suits were a thing of the past by now. Some members, including Spider, still favoured formal wear. Philip especially cut a dash in a black two-piece with a long, billowing jacket, seen to dramatic effect with all his spinning and dancing. Others – Darryl, for instance, and a baseball-capped Andrew and Jem in a regular, striped shirt - were more casually presented.

The celebrations really got under way with 'Fiesta', which triggered an explosion of streamers, party string, party poppers and more snow, most of it ending up on the heads of the musicians, and the fun-time atmosphere held up through 'The Irish Rover'.

The encores began with Andrew Ranken creeping towards the front of the stage, bent double, for a delightfully macabre rendition of 'Worms', before a cast of thousands took to the boards for 'A Message To You, Rudy'.

There were people everywhere – The Pogues, Kirsty, Strummer, Thompson and Clarke, Joey Cashman playing sax and Paul Taylor playing jazz trombone, and singers suddenly appearing from nowhere around microphones. It was beautiful chaos, continuing into 'The Wild Rover', which lured Andrew back out from behind his massive drumkit. Fearnley, meanwhile, strode around offering swigs from what looked like a bottle of champagne.

Another eminent musician joining The Pogues on stage on the tour was Steve Earle, although he was on a plane headed back towards America when the St Patrick's performance was taking Kentish Town by storm. Earle's guest spot involved the band playing 'Johnny Come Lately', a song they recorded together at this time for his *Copperhead Road* album. His journey was as pleasant as the king-size hangover he took back with him to the United States.

"But it was worth it," he wrote, years later, in his liner notes for the reissued *If I Should Fall From Grace With God*. "For four minutes on four consecutive nights in the spring of 1987, I had been a Pogue." Clearly, he meant 1988.

"It was good," nods Andrew. "He was all right at that stage, but he was getting a bit naughty. He ended up with a major drugs problem. Of course, he's completely straight now."

The tour had been a healing experience for Kirsty MacColl, who would continue to turn out for Pogues gigs and TV appearances in the UK and Europe. It also had a unifying effect upon the band members, who could plainly see that they were now among the country's top live acts.

"I think things between us were pretty much all right," says Jem. "The tour went well and everyone enjoyed themselves."

Terry Woods adds: "The Pogues is like some type of juggernaut. It takes off and rolls over everything. There's huge power in the band. For a band that isn't a conventional rock band and doesn't use conventional rock instruments, we tend to be able to power up with the heaviest. And I don't know if we've ever managed to achieve that power on a record."

The Pogues' next single release had caused some argument within the group. MacGowan insisted that 'The Broad Majestic Shannon' was the ideal follow-up to 'Fairytale Of New York', but the eventual choice was 'If I Should Fall From Grace With God'. It was backed with 'Sally MacLennane (Live)' and, on the 12-inch, a live version of 'A Pair Of Brown Eyes'.

Philip Chevron says: "We've always put out singles in the wrong order. They put out 'If I Should Fall. . .', which we knew wasn't a hit. There were two obvious follow-ups, both brave choices but which would have been better choices: 'The Broad Majestic Shannon' and 'Thousands Are Sailing'."

Andrew voices the opposing view: "I'm pretty sure I would've gone for 'Fall From Grace' because 'The Broad Majestic Shannon', although it's a lovely song, is another ballad. It's not anything like the same subject matter, but I think I almost certainly would've felt it was too similar in form and that it would be better, instead of a medium-paced romantic ballad, to do some sort of out-and-out fast rocker."

'If I Should Fall From Grace With God' failed to replicate the success of its predecessor, stalling at Number 58 at the beginning of March while the UK tour was in full swing. It was only a minor blip in the scheme of things.

Frank Murray sums up The Pogues' situation at that time: "Everything was good. There was a great record [album] out. We'd done our first Wembley show, then we did six nights at the Town & Country and a seventh night at Brixton Academy. We were flying, you know."

Darryl Hunt: "'Fairytale' became a major hit and everything went into another world. In a way it went into a world where it was harder for everybody. Once you get more people involved in an organisation... it's almost like a universal law: the more you expand, the more bodies become part of your orbit. You get more disparate. Communication became more difficult. It affected the unity of the group a little bit. It's knowing how to deal with it.

"It's the same in business when companies expand and expand. Accountants tell them they have to expand. It's almost like, nothing lasts forever. Expansion leads to decay as much as anything else. It's very difficult. You have eight people, and to handle it all the same at the same time... We could feel it was getting harder to keep all the strings attached.

"I think we did not too badly. We actually survived and we didn't go bankrupt or do anything silly. We managed to run the group and pay the bills. We have to give ourselves a bit of a pat on the back. By that time, our albums were being released all over the world."

As Terry Woods puts it: "We were flavour of the month and the treadmill became increasingly fast."

The Pogues had no chance now of solving their long-standing problems with touring. The kind of success they may once have dreamed of came at a high price. *If I Should Fall From Grace With God* had created a whole new audience. More people in more places wanted to see them, and they would be on the road almost solidly between albums, which was draining, physically and creatively. There was no longer any time to go into a studio just to try out ideas, to write as well as to rehearse. From press to promoters, everybody wanted a piece of the action.

"It's just old-fashioned rock'n'roll pressure, where more people want more of you and there just aren't enough slices to go round, but that's something every band experiences," says Philip Chevron. "I suppose the difficult thing was that as the pressure piled on and built up as we got more popular, there were more and more demands, and you spend half your time explaining yourself to people.

"What everybody really wants when they meet The Pogues is, 'How was it really?' and you can't answer that without opening your soul to them, and it's a hard question to face day after day. You're constantly leaving yourself emotionally exposed, and then all the other issues filtered in... I'd say it started to get bad soon after *Fall From Grace*. There were moments of respite."

The new-found fame and glory brought with it with the extra pressure of expectation. The band had to be good on stage, they had to be professional, since fans were paying more to see them play in bigger venues. There was another challenge stored away at the back of their collective consciousness, and that was the knowledge that *If I Should Fall From Grace With God* was going to be a hard act to follow.

All of this took a heavy toll on MacGowan, a reluctant frontman in the first place, who became the focus for the sudden rush of attention. Shane had long predicted his own fame, or infamy, from the early days of his conversations with Dee O'Mahony and the regulars in The Cambridge. He hadn't minded being pictured on the covers of music papers and magazines. He hadn't objected too strongly to anything that was written about him, since he considered that any press was good press. At the same time, he hadn't intended to be singled out as a star in The Pogues. He'd wanted Spider to share the singing, and he'd been a great believer in the original six-person frontline.

MacGowan had formed the band to reinvigorate Irish music, to make it live for audiences of every kind who might never otherwise have appreciated it, and he had succeeded. His vision of The Pogues as the ultimate good night out, the providers of rousing up-tempos that people could sing and laugh and dance to and thoughtful ballads that they could sing and sway and shed a tear to, had been enthusiastically taken up around the world, and now it was all turning into a business.

The democracy that had been central to The Pogues' organisation (although their democratic decisions were now usually subject to Frank Murray's approval) was also beginning to infuriate MacGowan, who was needled when band votes went against him, exasperated that his views could be so easily dismissed by the majority. Perhaps he was starting to feel sidelined, insulted. Gradually, he withdrew from his bandmates. He drank. He spent whatever spare time he had with Victoria in Thailand, where drugs of every description were freely available. He continued dropping acid.

The rest of The Pogues were by turns bemused, concerned, frustrated and angry – although an unexpected by-product of their predicament was that several members would emerge as confident songwriters, not through desire, design or ego but simply because they had to keep coming up with the goods when MacGowan would not.

Shane MacGowan was getting tired of being in The Pogues, although he didn't say so, and it would be some time before anybody realised it.

They hopped off to Europe only days after the British tour ended, and they went down as sensationally as they had done on home ground. Then in June, they flew once again to Canada and the States, where one of their opening gigs was at LA's open-air John Anson Ford Theatre. Here, James Fearnley met up again with his actress pen-friend, Danielle von Zerneck.

"We got together there," says James. "And then we went to her flat and we danced to Thelonius Monk in her living room. Then she flew off to New York next morning because she had to go to work. In that October, we went on holiday to St Martin's in the Caribbean for about 10 days, and that was the beginning of it, really."

James and Danielle would be married a year later.

For Terry Woods, the LA gig brought back memories of Ireland. He explains: "Years ago in the old Irish ballrooms, the men would be on one side and the women on the other. It was like that when we did this gig in LA. The Pogues were becoming flavour of the month, especially with America and Irish America. Backstage in the hospitality area, The Pogues were on one side and all Hollywood was on the other side, and they were looking at us and we were looking at them. Jack Nicholson was at that gig.

"They were terrified of The Pogues, the Americans. They thought we were like a bunch of mafiosos that came out of Italy. They didn't know what to make of it all. Where U2 could crack middle America, I don't think we could ever have done that."

There was no such A-list glamour in the next part of the itinerary, a back-to-basics club tour that took the band, for the first time, across the southern states of Texas, Louisiana, Alabama and Georgia. Driven around in a bus which rather cheekily displayed the sign "Nobody You Know" above its front windows, The Pogues had to pull out all the stops to win over virgin audiences in the clubs and bars of cities such as Dallas, Austin, New Orleans, Birmingham and Atlanta.

Sean O'Hagan, covering the great adventure for *NME*, reported that in Tommy's Club, Dallas, the band played "a careful, understated set that would surprise those weaned on the excesses of London or Glasgow". In the Liberty Lunch in Austin, they persevered through almost insufferable heat,

Big Charlie keeping his charges refreshed with supplies of iced whiskey and orange juice. Here, "They receive the sort of welcome most bands would be glad to get going off", carrying on to provoke "total uproar" with 'Bottle Of Smoke' and setting off a near riot when they opted to call it a night after three encores. In Tipitina's – Professor Longhair's club in New Orleans – the show was "more animated than Dallas but a lot less wired than Austin". O'Hagan added: "This is another 'listening crowd' who applaud the band's dexterity as well as raising the roof for the more crazed outings."

There were several interesting additions to the set including two new Shane MacGowan songs, 'NW3' and 'Boat Train', Steve Earle's 'Johnny Come Lately' and, as a final encore, a cover of the Stones' 'Honky Tonk Women'.

O'Hagan noted: "These days, The Pogues approach the kind of on stage togetherness reminiscent of the Stones' lazily effective blues or vintage booze-stained Faces shows. There's a cohesion and interplay that few live bands seem capable of."

Despite the group's developing internal problems, things had not yet become so terrible that an outsider would notice anything amiss. Philip remembers: "We figured out a way of not going insane. We were eternal optimists. There was always the chance that Shane would be brilliant, and he frequently was. He could look completely out of his head and sing like an angel. But it was very much an up-and-down graph. The troughs were coming more often than the peaks. We became adept at compensating for it within ourselves as a band and making it still work for us musically. Part of that was just responding to Shane if he went out of time, even. There were times he'd fall back – 'Am I going to go with him or am I going to go with James, and where's Andrew going to go?' You have a split second to make the decision. It's one of the things that makes you proud of your craft, or not. There were a lot of compensatory moments, even at its lowest ebbs."

The band members were writing on the road, including MacGowan, who came up with 'USA' and 'Cotton Fields'. Like *If I Should Fall From Grace With God*, The Pogues' next album, *Peace And Love*, would reflect the places they had been visiting rather than dwelling on the streets of London and the green hills and fields of Ireland – although neither of those core inspirations would be forgotten or neglected.

Chevron continues: "There were times when the music was exceptionally good. I took notice of those moments because they were so precious – 'That's why I'm here. Actually this is great. Me and Andrew and Darryl have hit a groove here that's straight out of heaven. We're only conduits for it.' That came simultaneously with 'yer man' slurring a vocal in front of it. We learnt how to separate the awfulness and the beauty of what was going on.

"I remember the moment I got the idea for 'Blue Heaven' [a *Peace And Love* song]. It was in New Orleans. There's something about the city. I suppose there's some great sort of force there that really isn't a part of America at all, although it's geographically located within the United States. I thought that was very interesting and wanted to write a song that reflected that and how I myself was feeling – part of something but completely disconnected.

"I got this riff for it, a Professor Longhair/Dr John sort of thing. I did it at a soundcheck one day in Birmingham, Alabama - an outdoor gig at the Schloss Foundry. It was a converted iron foundry, all rusty and everything. The moon was behind us. It was so romantic, but in this strange, weird place with a contradictory, complex history of racism and the Ku Klux Klan. It happened in this soundcheck at that moment, wonderful stuff, in a glade of trees. We were so locked in a groove you couldn't have sliced it with a cheesewire. Me, Darryl and Andrew got into a lot of that rhythm section stuff around that time – a unit within a unit. But it's fair to say it's the only time that 'Blue Heaven' completely made sense. It just refused to replicate itself in the studio, and I think I'd agree with the fans that it's one of the worst songs The Pogues have ever recorded."

New Orleans became a favourite tour destination for many of the band, including Andrew Ranken. He says: "We played there more than once. It didn't do us any good, but it was a fantastic place. I loved going there, and I'm very upset by what's happened to it."

The city was devastated by 2005's Hurricane Katrina – a disaster which also exposed the divide between the rich white inhabitants and the poorer black population. In everything from the TV coverage of looting to the rescue efforts and the rebuilding programme, the blacks were seen to be treated as lesser citizens.

Andrew: "I remember playing at Tipitina's, Professor Longhair's club – who's a great hero of mine. I always used to walk around places just to get the feel of them, and we were staying in this nice hotel in the French Quarter. On the day of the gig I asked them the way to Tipitina's. They said, 'Just call a cab.' I said, 'I want to walk.' They said, 'You can't walk through that area.' 'Why not?' 'Cos that's a black area.'

"A lot of American cities are like that. Once you get out of the town centre, you're into ghettoes and shanty towns. And I did walk it and, of course, it was completely fine. It was virtually all black but it wasn't particularly run-down or rough, and there were lots of people sitting out on their porches looking at me – 'Jesus, look at this idiot walking.' But, I mean, I saw that so many times in the States. Places are really so divided, not necessarily just in the south. Washington is really awful. Detroit. It's pretty much all over, I think. LA, of course, is pretty horrendous in that respect."

It was also in New Orleans – a little later in the band's career – that Andrew would make a stand for a separate hotel room. By this time he was sharing a hotel room with Philip.

"I'm quite amazed how long we put up with certain things," Ranken comments. "The band had been going for several years by now. I was suffering from this very unpleasant complaint, cluster headache, on this particular tour. Philip was as sympathetic as he could be."

"There were times when I would be bringing him towels full of ice cubes, just to douse the agony," remembers Chevron.

Andrew: "One of the things about this is that you actually just need to be on your own, however nice or well-meaning other people might be. You need privacy to bang your head against the wall in. I said to Joey, I think, 'I just have to have my own room.' So I got a single room, which was great. And then I thought, 'Well, I'm not going back to sharing a fucking room after this,' and I didn't. And then, of course, the others said, 'Well, if *he's* having a single room. . .' I was thinking, 'We should've done this years ago. We're sharing so much of our lives anyway, we could at least have a room to ourselves at night.'

"Of course, there was never any question about Joey and Frank having single rooms. They always had them. It came down to money. The reason we were sharing rooms was obviously because it was cheaper. At the end of the day, I just wasn't prepared to go on working like that. I didn't mind settling for less money if it meant having a better quality of existence. I think we'd all had the wool pulled over our eyes to some extent. We probably really did believe that, financially, it was impossible."

It was a busy summer. In addition to the usual round of European festivals, The Pogues released 'Fiesta' as a single, recruiting comedian Ade Edmondson to direct the video. The shoot took place in Barcelona and the ensuing promo captured all of the whoosh and fizz of the song itself, which charted at Number 24 in July. Its B-sides were 'Sketches Of Spain' and, on the 12-inch, 'South Australia', a traditional sea shanty sung by Terry Woods.

"I thought the video was great," remarks Andrew. "It looks really good. It was a hoot to make it, and Ade was fine. He was a very proficient director and he was a nice geezer."

Nice, but not hilarious. "These people never are," says Andrew. "I mean, he wasn't unfunny, but if you met him, you wouldn't think, 'Oh my God, this guy's a brilliant comedian.'"

James Fearnley had a less enjoyable time, for various reasons. One was that Edmondson managed to burst the bubble of innocent fun that surrounded James's pin-up image.

"It was kind of flattering really," says James. "I don't think I'd ever considered myself to be particularly good-looking, but then people kept saying I was 'the Cary Grant of the group'. I enjoyed wearing the suits and I kind of enjoyed being Cary Grant for a bit, but then Ade Edmondson said, 'You're the sex symbol,' and I had to sit on the chimney top of this building and I had to 'smoulder' into the camera. I felt so uncomfortable, not right at all. I'm glad it never made it into the video."

There were other problems too. "Shane was losing it," recalls Fearnley. "He was wandering round Barcelona with a Samurai sword and he didn't know where he was. He was going seriously off the rails, I think, at that time. In the 'Fiesta' video, I remember me and him dancing on a table top. It was really funny. I'd been drinking all afternoon. I've got an accordion on my chest and we're holding one another and dancing, and all of a sudden the table's over and I'm flat on my back with the accordion on top of me and Shane on top of the accordion. I'm so lucky I didn't break something. Shane was being a bit of a twat to me. There's a piece on the rooftops, and I remember Shane grabbing hold of my hair and pulling me about for some reason. I don't suppose he would know why, but I didn't enjoy that particular day."

It was at some point during that summer that MacGowan went careering off the rails once too often. Frank Murray says it was his "first intervention", and it happened shortly after Dave Jordan's wedding day. That's when Murray saw trouble brewing.

"We were down in County Cork," says Frank. "The wedding reception was in Youghal. I wanted Shane and [The Clancy Brothers'] Liam Clancy to meet. Liam lived in Ring in Waterford. I made some calls and this friend of mine brought Liam down. I was bringing him to Shane and saying, 'This is Liam.' Shane put up this limp hand, and he wouldn't even look at the man who was supposed to be one of his heroes. I'm starting to feel embarrassed about the whole thing. I had to draw Liam away and say, 'He's not himself.' I probably should have said, 'He is being himself.'"

Subsequently, the entourage travelled up to Dublin. "I heard reports of Shane in this club," relates Murray. "His face was painted again and he was knocking over drinks and stuff. I was told he'd taken a handful of Ecstasy."

Murray hot-footed it to the club: "He was going round and his eyes were popping out on stalks and he looked close to death, so I got a shock, and I was taking him out of the club and the two of us were having an argument in the street there in Dublin. I went off to speak with Terry O'Neill, who was our publicist at the time, and we called a doctor for Shane. We started making enquiries about somewhere Shane might go. He was going back to an apartment his cousin [Carmel] had, and he tried to jump out of the car that night when it was going down the road on the way to his cousin's.

"We heard about this, and then he'd locked himself in a room over at the apartment, so we got this doctor to come over and see him. We spoke to his sister Siobhan and she was very worried about him, and his cousin was worried. Eventually we went over with the doctor to him, and we needed two doctors to sign him in. We got some other doctor out of bed. He came over and we got Shane signed into St John Of God's in Dublin. When he was going away, he was like a ghost. I didn't think he was going to come out alive.

"Then I went round and saw him the next day. He wanted to sign himself out. I think he stayed in for an extra day and then I had to fly back to London. And then I was hearing all kinds of things about his behaviour and getting all kinds of flak from his family. They came to London and they were talking to me. While they were there, they got a phone call saying Shane had tried to jump out of a window somewhere. Then they withdrew all their objections to me. I think they felt it was my duty to babysit him and make sure he couldn't drink. I was always trying to get Shane to stop and be healthy. My friend Philip Lynott had died from all these excesses. But I could only do that to some extent.

"So then we got Shane over to London and we put him in a place off the King's Road. He started signing himself out of there within a day or two again. His so-called friends were always bringing him in packets of speed. You couldn't keep an eye on all these people. They'd be the first to criticise myself and the band, all standing on the sidelines. We'd done everything we possibly could. Shane was three times in rehab while I was managing the band. When he went into these places, even afterwards, people were always bringing him in speed, coke, whatever he wanted. It made all the attempts in there laughable."

Victoria Clarke was not with Shane when the dramas erupted in Dublin. She'd flown back to England in a huff after catching him in bed with a groupie in the city's Blooms Hotel.

In *A Drink With Shane MacGowan*, the singer claims that the trouble started because he drank too much poteen, an illegal and extremely strong Irish spirit made from potatoes. He then collapsed and woke up tied to a stretcher. Against his will, he was admitted to St John Of God's hospital where he "raged and screamed and yelled and banged my fists against the wall for a day or two". Then, changing his tactics, he adopted a charming and apologetic demeanour with which he negotiated his release.

Heading back to London under the supervision of his cousin Carmel, MacGowan got no further than Dublin International Airport. With their flight delayed by six hours, he settled down to pass the time drinking Long Island Iced Teas. This had several interesting repercussions. First, he fell asleep at the bar. Then he deliberately attacked a male passenger for no reason at all. Finally, he tripped and barged straight into a female traveller, accidentally knocking her bag across the floor.

The airport police, he claims, had already been watching him, but were prepared to overlook his behaviour on the grounds that he was *Shane MacGowan*. The woman was not so impressed. She insisted on pressing charges, although she withdrew them the next day. In the meantime, MacGowan was informed that he could either go to Mountjoy Prison or St John Of God's.

Returning to the hospital, he found that a charm offensive wouldn't work this time. Instead, "they certified me insane and kept me in". It was only by agreeing to attend Narcotics Anonymous sessions that he gained his freedom, and he found group therapy "a load of old crap". He added: "I think piss artists and junkies are whingeing toads who should help themselves. I've always helped myself."

MacGowan and Victoria had some talking to do when they were finally reunited. Clarke revealed in the *Daily Mail*: "I told him that it was over if he couldn't be monogamous. He wasn't keen at first but he agreed and asked me to come on the road with the band."

Victoria had long been uncertain of Shane's faithfulness while he was away on tour. He rarely phoned when he was supposed to. If she called his hotel, he would be out. She admitted: "I spent the whole time sulking or in a rage of jealousy."

And so in 1989, Victoria gave up her job as a sales rep and went on to tour the world with her boyfriend: "I flew to Australia, Japan and America with The Pogues. We travelled around in stretch limos and stayed in five-star hotels."

At this stage of the band's career, stretch limos were not the usual means of transport, although they did turn up from time to time. Some members, including Jem Finer, refused to ride in them.

It was a lifestyle to which Victoria adapted with ease: she confessed that she enjoyed MacGowan's generosity, which endowed her with designer clothes and celebrity parties. However, Clarke did not take kindly to being largely ignored or dismissed as "the little woman" of the great star.

She said: "If you're content to be part of the wallpaper, then you're fine. Unfortunately, I discovered that I had more of an ego than I'd bargained for. I wanted attention, too."

In October 1988, The Pogues went to Japan, and it was there, in a country with no historic links to Celtic music, that they realised the simple, human power of what they played, the ability to communicate without words. Due to the language barrier, the idiomatic nature of the lyrics, the references to Irish names and customs, the preponderance of mind-boggling words such as 'Cuchulainn' and Shane's often impenetrable way with a vocal, few of the fans would have had any idea what on earth they were going on about. Yet, there they were, girls and boys, rocking out like there was no tomorrow while the group served up a delicious concoction of age-old favourites and newer material including 'USA', 'Boat Train', 'Johnny Come Lately', 'Honky Tonk Women', a Pharoah Saunders tune called 'Japan' and a preview of the forthcoming single, 'Yeah Yeah Yeah Yeah Yeah'.

"I have long believed that the connection people feel to The Pogues' music happens beyond the actual language we use," said Chevron recently, adding: "A whole new generation of Japanese fans now sings along, word-perfect, when we play there."

MacGowan, for all of his recent misadventures, was clearly thinking on his feet. He didn't miss the heckling from one fan in Tokyo who seemed to be yelling, "Shane, you're ugly!", immediately hitting back with, "It doesn't matter – I'm rich!"

Japan loved The Pogues. It still does.

Frank Murray, in the meantime, had been looking ahead to the next album, the band's fourth. With Stiff Records dead and buried, ZTT had done a perfectly acceptable job with The Pogues' record releases and had managed to recover some of its earlier losses with the income from *If I Should Fall From Grace With God*. Now, however, it was time for the band to move on again.

"We'd been to court with Frankie Goes To Hollywood," said ZTT's Jill Sinclair. "I went and had a meeting with [Warners'] Rob Dickens, who was Chairman of the BPI at the time, about appealing the Holly Johnson case."

Dickens had assumed that Sinclair was coming to him for a chat about The Pogues.

"Everybody knew it had been quite a hard time for me with Stiff," continued Jill. "Rob said, 'I thought you might want to sell me The Pogues.' I was a small company and I certainly still am. The Pogues were characters, and they would have been better off in a larger organisation. That then helped me too. It helped me get the bank off my back and pay back a little bit more Stiff money. I sold my [Pogues] contract on to Warners. I basically stepped out of the way and let Warners take over the record side of the contract, but we kept their publishing. So then we were still involved and, in fact, we still publish Shane and I've signed bands with Terry Woods. I'm a big, big fan of The Pogues. I think they're fantastic."

Frank Murray sums it up: "She sold the contract. We got The Pogues away from ZTT and fully with Warners. That was for *Peace And Love*."

At the same time, another business problem was being solved, and that was the question of publishing and royalty percentages for those members of the band not named as principal songwriters. Andrew Ranken had dug his heels in, declaring that he was ready to walk if the perceived imbalance was not corrected.

"There were things that to me were not very fair and that I kept banging away about and eventually got improved," explains Andrew. "I felt that the people who were named as the writers of the songs were earning an amount of money that was quite disproportionate to what the rest of us were getting. In a lot of cases, although not all cases, the songs were largely a joint effort. To my mind, U2 did the right thing by always splitting everything equally. It seemed the best way to avoid having these arguments.

"Yeah, people wrote the tunes and wrote the words but there was more to it than that. This is an old argument that lots of bands have. If you say that a group has this chemistry and it couldn't be the same if different people were in the group, then you're saying that everybody contributes something to the way that group sounds. If you're saying that, which everybody was saying about The Pogues, you can't then say, 'Oh, but some people are going to get paid ten times as much as the other ones.'

"I did think that everyone getting exactly the same was a bit of an extreme position because I recognise that not everything is completely co-written by everybody. But being a bolshy bastard, I said everybody should get the same, knowing full well that nobody would agree to that, and that we'd negotiate from the two extremes and meet somewhere in the middle, which is what ended up happening. I don't think it took that long because I was quite upset about the whole thing, to the point where I threatened to leave the band if it didn't change. We did come to an agreement and we've never had problems with it since."

Murray reveals that the agreement entitled the rest of the band to 30 per cent of the publishing income earned by the credited songwriter/s, adding: "To me it's always right that the other members of the band should get some money. I'd been through this before with Thin Lizzy. Everybody gets out there and they're all enjoying themselves and then suddenly they see one guy picking up all of this money and they're not getting any. The Pogues had input into the arrangements and the songs and they went on the road and played them. I think Shane accepted the deal all right, but if you'd tried to make if 50/50 I think he would've caused trouble, if not at the time certainly later on down the road."

The band ended 1988 with a round of German dates and a Christmas tour of Britain and Ireland, Kirsty MacColl turning out to thrill the already euphoric crowds with her inimitable recreation of MacGowan's shrewish wife amid the snow showers of 'Fairytale Of New York'. Again, in a confirmation of her recently recovered self-confidence, she remained on stage to join in the singing and general hilarity of the show. The tour came to an end at Dublin's Point Depot on December 22.

In the space of three days, The Pogues had proved their continuing pulling power in London by headlining both Wembley Arena and Brixton Academy (December 17 and 19), although they were coming to accept that, with the one obvious exception, they were not a singles band - which said more about the radio programmers and the record-buyers than it did about the group.

Their latest offering, a stand-alone single called 'Yeah Yeah Yeah Yeah Yeah', was produced by Steve Lillywhite and it was a real departure, a stripped-down, raw and choppy slice of R&B with a call-and-response chorus that would've been no embarrassment to the classic British rhythm and blues groups of the Sixties. Andrew Ranken remarks: "You wouldn't say it was pioneering if it was the Spencer Davis Group, but it might be pioneering for The Pogues."

"The single was very different to a lot of Pogues stuff, but that's fine by me," says Jem. "It was a good track, a good laugh."

Darryl told *Melody Maker's* Jonh Wilde: "'Yeah Yeah' is probably the sexiest record we've ever made, really pumping it out."

"It's raw lust and emotion," said Spider, in a separate interview with Wilde.

Ade Edmondson again directed the video, a recreation of Sixties pop-TV shows with The Pogues – featuring Spider on harmonica and Jem on sax – performing to a studio audience. Opening in black and white, the video tips a fond hat to *Ready Steady Go!* and *Top Of The Pops*, Mary Quant make-up, micro-mini-skirts, mod suits and op-art graphics. Suddenly everything turns psychedelic, bursting into colour at the point that a flying saucer shoots out of Jem's exploding head – an idea of MacGowan's.

"I was very happy for my head to explode," confirms Finer. "Ade was a fun guy, clever, not an idiot. Those two videos, 'Fiesta' and 'Yeah Yeah Yeah Yeah', were very colourful and had a lot of humour in them. They were really good."

The single, backed with 'The Limerick Rake' and, on the 12-inch, a studio version of their regular encore 'Honky Tonk Women', peaked at

Number 43 in December. This was no reflection on The Pogues' general standing: they were right at the top of their game.

"I think we felt that we could really start calling the shots in a way that we hadn't been able to before with anybody, in terms of where we played and when we played and what we recorded," remarks Andrew. "But I think I personally was being very naïve thinking that, because one album that goes into the Top Three for not very long actually isn't enough. And it was obvious that the way being suggested that we should go was the way that was increasingly anathema to Shane... which is the whole stadium-rock thing."

CHAPTER 24

Peace And Love: The Irony

Joey Cashman doesn't beat about the bush when he talks about the *Peace And Love* period in the documentary *If I Should Fall From Grace: The Shane MacGowan Story*. The Pogues, he says, were jealous of Shane.

"There was an underlying sort of resentment against Shane in the band because all the media would want to speak to Shane," Cashman declares. "They liked to think about themselves as a band where everybody had an equal input and equal importance. So sometimes I felt that people were objecting to his opinions not based upon his actual opinions but simply because they just got fed up with it being Shane, Shane, Shane, Shane. . ."

"It was never my band," remarks MacGowan. "We were a democratic band and then in the end, like, I wasn't involved in the democracy any more. The system was to blame, you know. We thought we could beat the system and we couldn't."

In *A Drink With Shane MacGowan* he insists: "I never liked the idea of working in a democracy. . . No, I need to be in charge of it all, you know. I can't work otherwise. When I write stuff, I can't have any musical democracy involved in it."

He explains: "I wanted democracy but I think if I had done a bit more leading, things would have been better. A democracy can still be led. . . Harold Wilson knew how to lead a democracy. People do want to be told what to do, to a certain extent."

Today, he says: "All the time you're getting on each other's tits and when you've got this bloody democratic rubbish – it seems to me, Frank had to be a dictator of some kind. I took all this democracy with a pinch of salt. As long as I didn't have to go out there and be the frontman doing a set that was far too long far too many times a month far too many times a year for far too many years, as long as they were prepared to give me a little bit of

329

trust on some basic points, that was fine by me, but even if they weren't, I thought, 'Fuck it, I'll just have a good time,' and after a while I started saying, 'I'm not having a good time any more,' and they were saying, 'Well, nobody is.'"

It's fair to say that things were not altogether peaceful and loving when The Pogues went back into RAK with Steve Lillywhite in the spring of 1989 to record their new album.

Cashman's accusations of jealousy are met with varying responses from the band members.

"That's bollocks," James retorts, hotly. "Shane was getting the attention a lot of the time because of his indisputable prowess at writing songs. It goes without saying that the songs are Shane MacGowan, basically, and his poetry, and he was the main songwriter and the source of everything. And also he was one of the most interesting people that you could see interviewed, ever. There's no fucking around. He is what he is. When he gives forth it's just *pure*. And funny."

Andrew Ranken feels there may have been a grain of truth in Joey's outburst although, "It misses the point."

"It makes it sound like we were all terribly jealous," continues Andrew, "but it wasn't that at all, really. I think it was quite understandable that Shane would get a lot of attention, but the thing that pissed people off was that it happened more and more that people would come to interview us and talk to us and the only thing they'd ask about was, 'How's Shane?' And you just wanted to say, 'Well, go and ask Shane yourself.' And it was like nothing mattered apart from Shane. It did feel as though we were being treated as Shane MacGowan's backing band, and he was the only one that made any decisions, and he was the only creative input, and that was the thing that pissed people off."

Frank Murray says: "To some extent, yes, the others may have been resentful of the attention Shane got. I'd say they probably felt like all of the glory was going on to Shane as the songwriter, but I must stress this – their arrangements, and what they brought to the table, was incredible. I've seen Shane arrive in a rehearsal room with some lyrics and an idea, and I've seen what they've turned it into. James, Jem, Terry. . . and Andrew's drumming is always bang on. I think they probably felt that their contribution was ignored. And I think they were right to feel like that."

Of Shane's complaints about the democracy, Andrew laughs: "It wasn't really a true democracy. We would often take a vote on things, and that's good. I think we were, on the whole, reasonably fair to each other. I think Shane missed quite a lot of important, decision-making meetings and we ended up acting on his behalf at times when maybe the outcome wasn't what he wanted, but he hadn't been there to put his point of view. I also think there were probably times when things that he thought were good ideas we didn't agree with, and he was simply out-voted. If that's what he means by the democracy not working for him, that's hard luck, I'm afraid. He had a few really hare-brained ideas that he would've liked to try out, and we did experiment with a few things he was keen on doing which I don't think the rest of the band were that mad about. We had a shot at them to see if they'd work and basically ended up thinking, 'No, that's not the way to go,' which he may have been disappointed about.

"I don't think Frank ever wanted it to work as a democracy anyway, because Frank wanted to be the boss, and I think his attitude was divide and rule. The main area where it was obvious was the touring schedules."

Jem Finer contends: "I think the democratic process was going to the extremes of democracy, where things break down because everything is too democratic and, at the same time, there's no common connections any more. I don't think Shane was marginalised by any concensus. If there's any marginalisation, it was a result of his state of mind. Otherwise, he was in the same ultra-democratic boat as everyone else."

Philip Chevron: "Shane's whole idea of the band as a democratic one in the first place was that he understood, 'We've got a bunch of people who are in their own right hugely talented. It would be a shame not to show their talent.' In one sense, *Peace And Love* was fulfilling his own view of the band – perhaps at the wrong time and for the wrong reason. We had to cover up for his inadequacies."

Referring to the number of non-MacGowan tracks on the album, Chevron continues: "This didn't happen because we thought it was a really good assertion of how powerful this band is – 'Alongside Shane, here's all these other great talents.' It came out as compensating rather than complementing.

"Shane himself mistook the messages here. Certainly we weren't as intimate with him as we used to be. He was a hard person to be familiar with. He was on a different fucking planet and also off on these personal philosophical and artistic journeys, turning his hotel room and himself into a work of art. There was something going on we weren't party to. We couldn't be a gang saying, 'How can we make this into Pogues stuff? How can we make this fun?' People were feeling increasingly isolated for their own personal reasons anyway.

"Any one of us could have said the same thing: 'Where has this democracy got to?' Because of his tendency to think the world revolved round him, Shane didn't realise that. It was all because we proved democracy doesn't work. If he'd been in the position to be autocratic and say, 'This is the way we're going to do this,' and it had legs, we would've gone there, I think."

"It wasn't really that democratic," insists Frank Murray. "Sometimes democracy reigned and sometimes it didn't. I made decisions and I wouldn't consult the band unless I had a doubt in my head about something. Then I would talk it over with them. But generally speaking, they just wanted to do their gig and go home. In the beginning, I made lots of suggestions, but after *If I Should Fall From Grace*, I did that less and less. I felt they wanted more control over their stuff. You can see the change. There's quite a large change in *Peace And Love*, and there's different writers involved. It's spread more over the band. But Shane wasn't exactly coming up to rehearsals with great ideas and saying, 'I've got these songs.' Somebody had to fill in the gaps."

MacGowan has always spoken with great affection about the early days of The Pogues, days when they were young lads together in a transit, all for one and one for all, drinking and raising hell and being "intensely loyal" to each other.

But as time went on, he says, he felt division and paranoia, a problem which he traces back to the development of two separate touring groups within the band – the "mad" group led by himself and Spider and the "sensible" group consisting of Pogues who didn't want to be wasted all day and night.

Andrew Ranken sees this as a simplistic view of things: "Superficially, it's obvious where you'd put certain people in the two groups, but if you look at it in more detail, it doesn't really work that well. For instance, it would be very easy to say that someone like Spider was a serious hell-raiser and had a very cavalier attitude to everything but, in fact, Spider has been one of the mainstays of the group since the word go, and he's always been very committed to the group and to the audience. Apart from the odd moment, he's always taken his responsibilities very seriously about putting on a good show and giving people value for money and being an entertainer. Whereas, personally, I do care, but there's times when I couldn't give a fuck, really. There are different areas where people are more sane or less sane in terms of what they actually do within the group."

MacGowan has also stated that the band went "downhill all the way" after *If I Should Fall From Grace With God*. In *A Drink With Shane MacGowan*, he rages: "We became a rock band, we became what we hated most, what we were rebelling against, what we most tried to avoid becoming."

Tied in here was Shane's disinclination to be professional. This became an important issue with The Pogues' growing success, their promotion into bigger venues and Frank Murray's belief that they could break America – a place that MacGowan had grown to hate, with the exception of a few stimulating centres such as New York.

Again in *A Drink With...*, MacGowan insists that, "I wasn't interested in being professional. I was interested in being real."

"What do people actually mean when they say that?" wonders Andrew. "Presumably what they mean by 'professional' is being squeaky clean and turning up on time and getting out of bed. Shane is a musician – that's his profession. He's a professional musician. What was becoming a problem was that we were playing to bigger and bigger audiences. We did and we didn't go the stadium-rock route. We didn't go the whole hog. We'd got to a point where that was a direction that was open to us, but it would have required a lot more self-discipline, and it does, I think, take a lot of the spontaneity out of things.

"If you're going out in front of however many thousands of people, a lot of it just comes down to economics. The amount of money involved in staging those kind of shows and the amount of money people are paying to go and see them, you can't afford to fuck up, and if you do, you end up getting sued right, left and centre, and it all becomes a horrible sort of evil mess, and you end up being under this enormous pressure just to deliver a show that may not be terribly inspired, but it's reliable. And I think probably to Shane more than anybody, that was the kind of thing that was completely divorced from what he wanted to do.

"There was a fairly steady sort of grumble that gradually became louder and louder. I felt quite mixed about it because there was a big carrot there and we could have gone on to do bigger things. We were in quite a strong position and that made me think, 'Well, maybe we can do bigger things, but we can also do them on our own terms.' And I don't know that I'd thought it through terribly well or realised the implications of it because, in retrospect, I don't think that was necessarily true, largely for the economic reasons and also for personal individual reasons as well. Nobody had ever been into the idea of long-term touring."

The touring problem was still casting shadows over the band. "We eventually realised that one of the reasons it suited Frank having us out on the road the whole time was that he was making a packet out of it," continues Andrew. "To put in extra shows was always lucrative for him, but it wasn't always so for us. It just became silly sometimes. He'd be swanning around in limousines and hotel suites and we were still sharing rooms and taking the bus. I think we suffered from the 'naïve band' syndrome."

Darryl Hunt agrees: "I felt the group was being used in the wrong way. That's how people earn money out of you, when you're touring. They don't have to get out of bed. When you're in the studio writing or rehearsing, you're not earning anybody any money until the album is out. For eight people to be banging away and touring round the world and for everybody to keep it together, it doesn't happen.

"I would talk a lot with Jem and Philip mainly. They felt a little like that, that it was a treadmill we couldn't get off. There were bills to be paid. Probably one of our faults was we'd brood on it rather than just confront people about it. We should've been more communicative with the management. Whether that would have helped Shane or not..."

Quite apart from the long absences from home, there was another aspect of touring that Andrew, and other members of the band, came to loathe and despise. "There was a forced attempt to live out the 'rock'n'roll myth'," reveals Andrew. "Generally, we were always well-behaved. I don't think we tried to throw our weight around and be rude to people just as a matter of course. Frank seemed to have this attitude – 'Well, you're supposed to do that. That's the way bands behave when they're on the road.' And I always thought, 'I don't really want to be like that,' and for a long time, I had this idea that it would be nice if bands could change all that around somehow. It would've meant bands getting a lot more politicised, because I began to see the music industry as just a microcosm of the worst aspects of capitalism, and I thought if enough musicians stood up and said, 'We don't want to do things this way,' we could actually do something about it.

"But it seems that there's not enough people interested in trying to change anything. It still goes on, all the exploitation and the endless touring and the making of albums. But one thing that I started to find more and more disillusioning was how self-important the actual music industry is, and how they regard musicians as just the workforce. They're sitting there in their comfortable offices ordering you to go out and make money for them, and most of the time they haven't got a fucking clue whether it's good music or not.

"The more I saw that side of it, the less I wanted to work in that way. However, that coincided with being on a treadmill that was virtually impossible to get off. There were contracts to fulfil and managers whose pockets needed lining and there did come a point – I can't tell you exactly when it came – where we, maybe not consciously, made a decision to start extricating ourselves somehow. I'm not even saying it was a collective decision. I think people went about it in different ways. Part of what happened to Shane was his way of extricating himself."

All this discontent was churning away in the background when The Pogues returned to RAK Studios.

With the exception of their annual St Patrick's Day gigs, held this time, victoriously, at the Brixton Academy on March 17 and 18, they'd had a couple of months off to prepare for the sessions, which MacGowan certainly appreciated. He says, "That lay-off was quite good. We could relax a little bit. Not very much, but a little bit more. We'd been on the road solidly for several years and we were starting to cool it down a bit. That's where *Peace And Love* came from."

Perhaps MacGowan relaxed a little too much. When the group reconvened to start recording, it was clear that their singer was on "a different fucking planet", as Philip so delicately puts it. Not only was he drinking heavily and taking enormous quantities of acid, he had also fallen deeply in love with the Acid House scene, and was determined to bring its influence into The Pogues' new album. 'Yeah Yeah Yeah Yeah Yeah' was an attempt to introduce a new type of danceability into the music, although it didn't turn out quite the way Shane had envisaged. Now, he intended to take things further. He arrived at the studios with only half a dozen songs. It was up to Jem Finer, Philip Chevron and Terry Woods to supply the rest of the material for the album.

Frank Murray: "When it all became very serious was when Shane started mixing everything together. I don't know whether he was doing acid or Ecstasy and drinking on top of it and whatever else he wanted to do. Things started to go a bit weird during the recording of *Peace And Love*. That's when the first cracks started in everything, both with Shane and with the band themselves. He'd be trying to talk to someone and it's like he wasn't there. He'd turn up for sessions and he wouldn't sing. We'd get nothing done.

"At one time during the recording, I had to get him out of Paddington Green nick because he was going across a pedestrian crossing and I don't know whether he kicked a police car or something, so he got nicked. During the recording of that album, I had to get him out twice. I guess that's when it really started to get out of control, and I think around that time was when he started to think really about leaving the band."

Murray describes his reactions to Shane's condition: "First of all, there's sadness. That's what hits you first. Then you feel sort of impotent; there's nothing you can do about it. I could get promises out of him but they'd never really last. He was also at the time going backwards and forwards to Thailand and he was getting every kind of drug you could possibly get over the counter there, and he was coming home with them.

"The Pogues had become very, very big. Shane was getting money and I think he wanted to stop and do whatever he wanted to do. There's a certain discipline attached to being in a band. At a certain place at a certain time, you have to go on tour or you have to get together on an airplane. You've gotta be sober. You can't be legless when you're going on to the stage, and I had various conversations with him about this."

Andrew adds: "Shane really was a worry. A lot of the time he seemed hell-bent on destroying himself, although there were others [Philip, Terry and Spider] that ended up in a bad way as well. It's quite remarkable that they've recovered so well. We all had our moments. In a way I've been lucky, myself. It's quite an irony really, but this awful cluster headache thing that I suffer from has probably done quite a lot to help me live longer, cos it means giving up drinking for long periods of time. And there have been other, outside influences which have always been very steadying for me and for others as well – relationships and children, things like that. There were times when I found it very difficult to communicate with Shane. That was usually, to put it mildly, because he was out to lunch for a lot of the time. I think he was taking acid every day in large quantities. He never did anything by halves.

"He was withdrawing from the songwriting and the performance a bit at this time. He was becoming erratic onstage: he was fucking up more. It got worse and worse. It's understandable if you forget the odd line or whatever, but when you're forgetting whole verses or you start singing completely different songs to what the band are playing, it becomes more serious. Spider and Darryl and myself were having to cover up for him and fill in the bits he was missing out. We were also doing more songs without him, which was to some extent was a product of the fact that there were several people in the band capable of writing songs and it was always supposed to be some sort of democracy, so it was fair enough that people had the chance to give their songs an airing if they were felt to be up to scratch."

MacGowan's unpredictability, infuriating enough in his own circles, could become outrageous in his dealings with the outside world.

James Fearnley gives one example: "During the recording of *Peace And Love*, we were contacted by the family of a kid who'd been in a car crash and was lying in a coma in hospital somewhere. We were asked to record something for him – he was such a fan of The Pogues – that might assist in his recovery, something that might lift a corner of his injury and bring him back to daylight. So we put something on a cassette for the kid, you know, like, 'This is The Pogues and we hope you get better.' 'This is Jem.' 'This is Philip.' Shane wanted to contribute too, but his contribution, it was clear, was going to be a matter of shouting into the microphone, 'WAKE UP! WAKE UP!' We respectfully and painstakingly discouraged him from doing such a thing, pointing out that the tape would be as much for the ears of the kid's parents as for the kid himself. It was a difficult hour or two."

The Pogues approached the recording sessions with a mixture of confusion and practical resolve.

Philip explains: "We were aware that the record company would be really pleased if we were to come back with *Fall From Grace II*. But you can never allow yourself to be intimidated by expectations. We were like a sponge – wherever we went in the world, we absorbed music and influences and culture and, in as much as it was a diary of the previous two years, and because so many of the songs were written on the road, this album was always going to be different.

"We'd proved on *Fall From Grace* that people's expectations of us were rubbish. Nobody expected 'Thousands Are Sailing' or 'Lullaby Of London' or 'Fairytale'. If we were to pay attention to what people hoped we were going to do, we'd never have moved anywhere. It's the sort of thing that Elvis misunderstood about us. We just had to make the best album we could. On the other hand, there were a number of factors conspiring against it. It was very evident that Shane was going completely in the wrong direction, taking way too many drugs and drinking too much. It was a way of coping with things. He was a shy man who never wanted to find himself in the position he was in. It took him many, many years to be comfortable with being 'that Shane MacGowan'."

At the same time, the prevalence of cocaine in the studio meant that some of the songs suffered a surfeit of window-dressing. Various members of the band were going through crises in their personal lives, and nobody was quite sure what to do about MacGowan's Acid House obsession.

"The way that Shane was was making things quite difficult for all of us," says Andrew. "Things were pretty nebulous as to what we were trying to do, what direction we were trying to go in. I think a lot of that was cos we couldn't come up with any clear plan of action because Shane was really quite unreliable and unpredictable, and it was becoming increasingly obvious that he wasn't happy with working the way we had been.

"I think we were floundering at that stage. At the same time as we were losing our focus, we were actually in quite a strong position, so it was quite ironic really that when we probably could have been sort of pushing ahead and establishing ourselves more forcefully, we weren't able to do that because of internal difficulties."

Jem Finer: "We were at a point where we could've become really massive as a band, and it's possible Frank thought we had to come up with a record that would make us big in America. It was recorded in a way we hadn't recorded before. We'd recorded the backing tracks pretty much live in the studio and then fixed things and added things. With this one, each instrument was recorded separately, which gives a much cleaner sound, a more slick, produced sound. That was done very consciously by Steve with the idea of making a record that would be more likely to crack the mass market of America, as I understand it. It was a horrible way to record. It's very laborious and boring, but I think it sounds good."

James Fearnley dislikes specific treatments on some of the album tracks, contending that, "The production values threaten to nail the record firmly in the Eighties. I'm thinking of the weird vocal treatments and the phased accordion in 'Cotton Fields', the horrid echoes of Philip and Terry's voices in 'Young Ned Of The Hill' and elsewhere. And the whistle doesn't cut through all that much on the record."

Finer was unable to enter into his usual writing collaborations with MacGowan: "I'd taken these songs along, in the way I always had, and expected him to change things a bit, but he felt they were finished. And I think he thought his songs were finished as well. There was a lot of problems around the making of the album. There had been a time when Shane had a very rigorous approach to writing songs, endlessly re-editing and re-writing, but round this period, one rather had the feeling that the publicity had gone to his head, that anything he wrote was a 'work of genius', so some of the stuff that he brought along was very hard to make sense of, and it took more work for the band to create arrangements.

"And that was complicated by Shane's vision for what sort of record he wanted to make. It seemed to be quite a different vision than everyone else's. He wanted to make an Acid House record. And Shane did literally try and make an Acid House track in the studio - a 20-minute drum-machine track with him ranting 'Contact yourself!' over it."

According to Steve Lillywhite, that particular gem "fell by the wayside" somewhere along the line.

Fearnley points out: "Shane wasn't the only person who was getting into that sort of music. I remember talking to Philip about the cut-and-paste type of music-making, which was a really exciting subject, and Jem was getting into sampling and indeed so did I on one occasion. Jem had been talking to The Edge as well about how he got his sounds. And Darryl was going to raves."

Darryl enjoyed the rave scene so much that he started turning his hand to DJing around this time, getting behind the decks at London's famous Turnmills club and in various venues across Europe, notably Germany and Portugal. So it wasn't as if MacGowan's bandmates were stubbornly refusing to appreciate his latest influence. In fact, they experimented with several of his ideas before concluding that Acid House music played on folk instruments didn't really work, at least for The Pogues. But some of MacGowan's notions paid off creatively.

"A song like 'White City' is a quintessential Shane song," says Jem. "It's got a great melody and a simplicity, in the best sense of the word. And I can remember that we were just playing it like a Pogues song and Shane started going on about making it into an Acid House song. Of course, it still sounds like a Pogues song. I think Shane made Andrew do this very fast hi-hat pattern on it, which somehow filtered out of this Acid House obsession, and also something happened to the bassline, which became more fluid. Rhythmically, it made the song much more interesting. So it wasn't all bad. It was just that it was a new kind of struggle to contend with."

MacGowan later commented: "If you listen to *Peace And Love*, you'll find that all my tracks are in the house beat."

The struggle was further complicated by communication problems: "If you put yourself in a radically different state of mind from everyone else, then it's kinda hard to be on the same wavelength," reasons Jem, "but that's not everyone else's fault. People always tried very hard to understand Shane's ideas and to make some sense out of them."

"He was definitely distancing himself," adds Andrew. "He never really made it clear, I don't think, what the problems really were, and there seemed to be this constant sort of dichotomy going on as to whether Shane thought we should be more diverse or we should be more back to the Irish roots. He changed his mind about everything every five minutes. It was never really clear what he thought the musical direction of the band ought to be, or whether it should be all of them combined in some way, which I suppose is what we were trying to do with *Peace And Love* – some ghastly amalgam of everything and the kitchen sink."

The Pogues' traditional Irishness would not take centre stage this time around. "We were all feeling very restricted by it," admits Ranken. "The attitude of sticking shamrock on everything we did seemed to extend to the sort of music we were expected to play. All of us had a much wider range of musical interests and we felt that it was a good enough group to be able to encompass all or some of those interests, and why the hell shouldn't we? It was our band. And I think there was probably some sort of feeling that we weren't a bona fide Irish band anyway – we were a London band with Irish influences. Those influences had been very prominent, but they weren't by any means the whole picture.

"We felt we were just giving a bit more space to the other influences and not chucking out the Irish side of things by any means, but maybe moving it to one side a bit, giving it less of a central position. It didn't really work for a lot of people.

"We went for this all-out approach, chucking in everything, which in retrospect I think is a dangerous road to take. At the time it all seemed quite exciting and when you're in a good recording studio with a good producer, you do have a huge amount of scope to try different things. Unfortunately, we weren't very good at putting the brakes on, and I think it did start to get out of hand. We were all suffering from a lack of direction, really. I think what we needed from Shane was a much clearer overview. He was possibly the one person who could have said, 'Look, this is bollocks, we're really going up our own arses here and we need to strip it all down and get much more focused on what we're trying to do,' but unfortunately he was away with the fairies a lot of the time. We weren't really sure what we were doing, although I'm not sure that we were actually admitting that to ourselves at that point. I think we were desperately hoping it was all going to work out okay."

MacGowan refused to sing, or couldn't sing, certain songs, and when he did, his vocals were not as strong as they'd once been. Steve Lillywhite was faced with a very different band to the one who had recorded *If I Should Fall From Grace With God*.

"We couldn't quite reconnect with the magic," sighs Lillywhite. "The diversity that worked so well on *Fall From Grace* didn't work so well on *Peace And Love*. MacGowan hadn't written so many songs, and there was song-writing from other members of the band. The songs that were a bit outside their realm didn't work so well. 'Fiesta' had worked well, but maybe 'Blue Heaven' didn't work so well within a Pogues album. A great song for something or somebody else, maybe.

"I think MacGowan's voice had become weaker. I made a mistake with *Peace And Love* in mixing his voice quietly, which made a weak vocal worse. If I'd turned it up, I could've made a weak vocal better. I should apologise to him for that. I feel it could've been a much better album if the vocals, even if they were weak, had been louder in the mix. Quite often he would slur his voice a lot, so I would actually move the voice forwards in the track. Now you can do it really easily. In those days, it was quite a big job. I did that on a couple of tracks to try and get his voice more in the right place."

Lillywhite, like the rest of The Pogues, was a little baffled by Shane's Acid House ambitions. He remembers: "Shane had been getting into club culture, and I wasn't quite *au fait* with what he was doing. He was the one member of the band I didn't sit down and discuss things with. I didn't have a one-on-one personal relationship with him. We never quite connected. Maybe we were doing different drugs. We were all taking lots of cocaine. MacGowan was taking acid and ecstasy. But it really was the music that was the main reason. It just didn't slot together as well. We're talking magic – things that make it brilliant rather than just great."

Jem Finer is one of those who believes that cocaine was a hindrance rather than a help. He says: "I would say that too many people in the band were taking too much cocaine. It definitely had an effect on that record. I've always hated cocaine, and I think it's responsible for a lot of rubbish that happened round the band. People often turn into complete arseholes – not always, but creative ideas fuelled by cocaine are often just shit. That probably is a problem. There was a lot of over-indulgence, musically. Things became over-complicated and lost, and I think it became very hard for Steve to actually mix the record, cos he ended up with so much stuff and everyone wanting their stuff to be heard. The collective ego of the band got fragmented into individual egos. I found it really, really tedious and frustrating and disheartening. I'm sure I talked to Andrew and Darryl and James quite a lot about it, cos I always did, and I would have talked to Shane but I found him rather hard to talk to at that point.

"'USA' [a percussive drama] is a case in point of sheer over-indulgence. I've got some tapes somewhere of mixes of that that are just incredible where it's quite sparse. It had this amazing, brooding menace to it, and that sort of got lost. People kept overdubbing stuff more and more and it just lost a lot of its power."

The overdubs include a helicopter and the sound of an exploding bomb, and some band members still feel very positively about the track.

"People were coming and going a lot at that stage," carries on Jem. "I'd go off home after a while cos I didn't fancy staying around half the night listening to people doing overdubs. This whole record was made in a very fragmented way because people were doing their tracks one at a time. It could almost have been a band of people who never actually saw each other. Every day or two, you'd get a new cassette with the latest rough mixes. There could've been 20 versions of one track, and you could hear how it went from something very bare to a point where there was an absolutely perfect balance of instrumentation and then going over the top to sink under its own weight."

James Fearnley admits: "There was a bit of cocaine going around. Steve would disappear from time to time and there was a little room at RAK that he would invite people into. It was like a signal for those who were interested. When I was a squatter in Westbourne Grove, cocaine was really fantastic. It made me feel like I was the most important person in the world. I used it, though rarely and at times of inattention, during my Pogues career. I did take it at some points I'm sure in the earlier days. But I became uninterested and somewhat scornful of it on account of what I saw it doing to people, which made me want to avoid those who were using it. Thereafter I came to abominate it on those grounds and on the grounds of what the manufacture of it, and distribution, did to Colombian culture."

James was once again delighted to take up his role as the overdub king, working with Lillywhite on the arrangements and instrumentation, and hoping that the work he produced was "clean and assistive", not self-serving or aligned to any coke-addled extravagance. The band were joined in the studio at various times by string arranger Peadar O'Riada, strings and brass arranger Fiachra Trench, a brass section comprising the usual suspects - Eli Thompson, Brian Clarke, Paul Taylor and Joey Cashman - plus the group's King's Cross friend Rick Trevan on tenor sax, percussionist Gasper Lawal, and Kirsty MacColl on backing vocals.

The Pogues themselves had expanded their weaponry. Jem had spent a year building a hurdy-gurdy at home, an intricate and challenging task, and now he wanted to experiment with it. The hurdy-gurdy creates a droning sound which gives space and atmosphere, and it appears to a greater or lesser degree on almost every track on *Peace And Love*. In fact, Finer still has that instrument at home, although he quickly had to have a new one made for live work because the original was "unreliable and cranky".

"It did add a lot to songs like 'Misty Morning, Albert Bridge'," says James. "I think that kind of drone was quite important musically for a while. It's a great instrument." Inspired, James bought a hammered dulcimer, which he played on a couple of tracks on *Peace And Love*, commenting: "I love the rolling rhythm type thing you can get out of it."

Finer says: "We did a lot of playing round with new instruments, more than on previous records. 'Down All The Days' is a good track. It's got this lovely floating feel, and then I put the hurdy-gurdy on it to make the drone space, and James played the hammered dulcimer. That track's an example of where it really all worked."

The melodically attractive 'Down All The Days' is a song about handicapped Irish writer Christy Brown, who is immortalised in the movie *My Left Foot*, and its effects include the clicking of typewriter keys tapped by the group's old friend Kathy MacMillan.

Then there was Andrew's drumkit, which had grown yet again. Undoubtedly this facilitated the album's opening drum flourish, leading into 'Gridlock', and the theatrical displays of 'USA', but even Ranken became embarrassed by its size: "I think everything was getting a bit overblown, and the instruments went on a diet after that."

Fearnley adds: "I can be bossy and resistant and I resisted going to a full drumkit for as long as I could. Possibly Shane's quarrel with the group, where he accused us of being a stadium band, set in when we got a full drumkit. I don't know."

Some of the memorably experimental tracks involve Jem Finer. 'Gridlock', a sprightly jazz instrumental and a co-write with Andrew, was a natural successor to 'Metropolis', but there was no attempt this time to work in an Irish compromise. The brooding atmospheres of 'Tombstone', harking back to the vastness and the wildness of Australia's natural landscapes, were captured using not only the hurdy-gurdy but an aboriginal instrument called a bull roarer.

Says Jem: "It's basically a piece of string, several feet long. We used that in the studio in a big room, roared it round and worked out ways to make it sound really big, and it had this weird rhythm to it which we built the track around. And then this guy Gasper Lawal came along and played a lot of percussion on it.

"The intention had always been for Shane to sing it, but he wasn't interested. I like very much the way Terry sang it, although it would have been better if Shane had sung everything. I guess he was in a bloody tricky situation. There were more and more people writing stuff that just didn't mean anything to him. That's the case with 'Tombstone', I guess, whereas 'Misty Morning, Albert Bridge' was a song he really identified with, and he gave a great, heartfelt performance."

Contrastingly, 'Night Train To Lorca', with its Spanish-style cittern and brass arrangement, creates a soundtrack to the journey Jem and his family undertook every year as they drove to the town of Aguilas in Spain for their annual holiday. In the writing, their car turned into a train.

A more familiar Pogueishness arises in Terry Woods' contributions, with 'Young Ned Of The Hill', accelerating from slow, funereal beginnings, voicing a traditional Irish protest: *"A curse upon you Oliver Cromwell/You who raped our motherland."* James says: "We all agreed it would be great to have this hole punched in it and to explode out of the hole. It was really exciting to figure that out. And it's got an unhinged, ska-type backbeat."

'Gartloney Rats', a song about the band Woods was playing in, for pints, before he was called up to The Pogues, is tremendous fun, whirling round the dancefloor with its skirts flying as the words tumble out almost too quickly to distinguish.

MacGowan's 'Boat Train' is equally amusing, a rattling account of a disgraceful journey by train and ferry from Dun Laoghaire to London, complete with spoons and Spider's best punky backing vocals. 'London You're A Lady' lacks the character and distinction of MacGowan's most accomplished compositions. James, however, is a fan of the music if not the words: "It's almost profligate. There isn't the kind of poetry in it that I'd become used to from Shane. But it's fantastically sung and the arrangement is weird and original. The strings are just dynamite. The tune is, I think, a Carolan tune, baroque in style, just fabulous."

'Cotton Fields', an innocuous countrybilly track, features Andrew

Ranken's voice alongside MacGowan's. "I think Shane was a bit wrecked," says Andrew. "So we kind of doubled up his voice with mine just to give it a bit more weight. That was symptomatic of what was going on with Shane at the time. There's a lot more people than Shane singing on that album. Philip did a couple of vocals with him too. He was bowing out quite a lot."

Chevron adds: "'Down All The Days' was the song Shane took the least care of. It ended up not even having a full lyric. Under pressure from Steve, I had to write the second verse for it. I don't think Shane realised these weren't even his words that he was singing."

Jem Finer remembers this differently, suggesting that, "Both Phil and I contributed to a second verse which Shane then rejected, coming up with something of his own."

Meanwhile, Philip, with Kirsty on backing vocals, brings a touch of pop melody to the party with 'Lorelei', the song of a siren on the River Rhine luring sailors to a watery grave, played by instruments including the hurdy-gurdy and the hammered dulcimer, electric guitars and Ranken's harmonica. 'Blue Heaven', however, came as a great disappointment to Philip and co-writer Darryl Hunt, who had experienced its true power outdoors in the shadow of the iron foundry in Alabama.

Philip says: "It actually should have worked with just bass, guitar and drums. Instead of that, we went the other way. There's fucking everything on there, like the brass section. At one stage, Lillywhite makes the track speed up. None of that should have needed to be done. We should just have waited until we got the right groove on it. It was a brilliant central idea badly executed by the band and the producer."

Fearnley adds: "I have to say I wasn't a great fan of that song, although I did have a rather nice piano solo on it that I recorded with Steve – who then wiped it by mistake."

The album's most enduring tracks are songs The Pogues still play today: Finer's ballad, 'Misty Morning, Albert Bridge', a beautiful and dignified expression of longing, of missing someone, accompanied by trumpet, Fearnley's trilling mandolins and a string section that hints at Puccini; and Shane's galloping 'White City', laced with concertina and accordion – a traditional tune with new words lamenting the loss of the old west London greyhound track in particular and the pillars of working-class life in general: *"And the car parks going up/And they're pulling down the pubs/It's just another rainy day."*

Despite the tremendous problems and uncertainties surrounding the recording of *Peace And Love*, despite the fact that it lacked the cohesion of its predecessor, despite the booze and the acid and the cocaine, the self-indulgences and the inconsistencies, it would emerge as a braver, more expansive, more interesting album than it has received credit for, at the time or since.

Still, the irony of the title, compounded by a front-cover photo of a boxer (with an extra finger on his right hand), said everything about the state of play in The Pogues' camp at the time, although they told enquiring journalists that peace and love, indeed, was something to aspire to.

"At some basic level, our sense of humour never quite deserted us," asserts Philip. "It was the opposite of what was going on. There was so much turmoil.

"At one stage, Steve wanted to call the album 'World Music'. Everywhere we went, 'world music' was the buzzword. Steve was trying to think of what would make the record company happy – 'Let's make this The Pogues' world music album.' It was the hook that would get the album off the hook. Then he could say, 'It's meant to be overdubbed and over-produced and over-arranged cos the band are playing on all their world influences.' But the whole point of The Pogues was to tell people where we were at. If we couldn't be honest about ourselves, we were nothing. We all stood behind *Peace And Love* because it was an honest album, even in its flaws. If there was disharmony, we said so. It was called *Peace And Love* because it was ironic, because that's what was going on: disharmony.

"I think we must've nearly killed Steve Lillywhite, cos he refused to do the next album. He refused to work with us ever again. He said, 'We've done what we can together. Let's leave it at that.'"

James Fearnley's mind had not been entirely on the recordings. He was thinking of Danielle in LA.

He confesses: "To go to the studio, I'd walk up Lamb's Conduit Street every day, and then as you go past Coram's Fields [a children's park], and the road leads round to the west, I said to myself, 'That's the direction I want to be going.' That came into my head every single morning – 'I want to finish this and I want to go west.' I wanted to go off and be with her in California. It's the beginning of my centre of gravity moving elsewhere.

"I was very, very much in love with Danielle, which I still am. Then, it was searing. I had to figure out how to work in London and be in love in LA. I suppose it was a matter of, 'The tour's going to start on this particular day – turn up.' There's something romantic as well about the wrench of being severed from your loved one and flying off and having a difficult few weeks of pining and playing and being with your ghastly family – something of putting your knapsack on your back and walking up the gangplank and sailing off to sea, and there's Molly left behind on the quayside. . ."

Later in 1989, James and Danielle would rent their first flat in LA, and The Pogues' accordionist would become an international commuter.

Philip Chevron was also pining for his partner, although this was simply one of several major anxieties in his life. "I was turning inward," he reveals.

Philip and Darryl had gone to support their team, Nottingham Forest, against Liverpool in the FA Cup semi-final being played at Hillsborough Stadium, Sheffield, on April 15. And they had watched helplessly as 96 people died in a massive crush in the crowd.

"We both had nightmares afterwards," says Philip, "seeing things coming through the walls and that vision of people being crushed against fences knowing that those people are dying and there's nothing you can do. You're on the opposition stand surrounded by policemen with Alsatians, and you literally, physically can't be there. A lot of that stuff played into the imagery of 'Blue Heaven'.

"I was aware for the first time that my drinking was becoming a serious problem, and also I was using it to cover up my unhappiness. My father fell seriously ill and looked like he was going to die. In fact, he lived another eight years. The whole Hillsborough thing had happened and my emotional life was in chaos. I had a boyfriend, Achim, who I couldn't spend enough time with. He was living in Hamburg. I remember us being in Copenhagen and we had to fly down to Italy to do a week's TV shows in Rome and I said, 'I can't do this unless I stop off in Hamburg.' So I'd fly to Hamburg, get a message to him, he'd come out to the airport, we'd have a coffee and I'd be on the next plane out again."

Achim inspired Chevron's 'Lorelei'. Says Philip: "We'd played the Lorelei Festival [in July 1988] and he was telling me the legend as he knew it, about the temptress luring all these sailors on to the rocks. There was something about the way he told it that personalised it for me. I used the imagery in that to explain how it felt to be away from somebody as often as I was away from him."

Explaining the background to the relationship, he explains: "I'd had a long experience of being in love with somebody who didn't reciprocate it. For the first time in many, many years I was with somebody I cared about who was also gay. The whole life I was living conspired against that, and I didn't know to what extent I was important to him. All this was generally making me very unhappy. My sense of self-possession was slipping away. I suppose everybody to a greater or lesser extent felt that during that period. It's all there on the vinyl.

"We had to spend more time out on the road. Bills were coming in, and we ran a very expensive ship. We had our road crew on full wages all the time we weren't on the road. Everything was very costly, and there were eight of us, not four. We did actually have to keep working to keep the thing afloat. All of that fed into the general madness and the sense of being a hamster on a wheel.

"At one level, you're just crying out – 'Will somebody hear that I'm in fucking pain here?' And I think we all had to figure out ways to internalise it. The one person who was most seriously at risk from all this and who was taking it most personally was Shane. It was his way of coping with it. We, in order to protect him from it, were internalising it.

"You're aware that you yourself are developing a problem that seriously needs to be addressed and it's not going to be addressed because it's always going to be hiding behind the apparently greater problem of Shane, which is very convenient for an addict. That's where you're going to hide. And you will hide there until you can't hide any longer. There's no avoiding that people aren't noticing the extent of your problem. It's just that they've got their own shit to deal with. That had a very negative effect on me. I felt sort of let down that somehow my cries for help weren't being heeded. I realise this was an exceptionally irresponsible and stupid attitude to take, but it's a measure of the extent of the problem I had.

"Things often get expressed by people getting drunk and moaning to each other in hotel rooms, so all of that was very corrosive. None of this is to deny that there were some great moments of joy and happiness and laughs, but they became fewer. The gaps between the fun, joyous, happy moments became ever wider."

Chevron also became aware, in 1989, that *The Sun* newspaper was on his trail, planning to run an exposé on his homosexuality. Consequently, he added two new tracks to The Radiators' re-released *Ghostown*, one of which, 'Under Clery's Clock', was an openly gay song.

"I did it just to deprive them of their nasty little Page Five feature. All they got in the end was a miserable article about gays taking over the music business – 'They're everywhere! They're even in The Pogues!'"

Andrew Ranken had been having a tough time of it too. Such were his troubles that The Pogues were often the last thing on his mind. "Myself and my partner Deborah had been trying to have a child for a while," he reveals. "It must have been just after *If I Should Fall From Grace With God* was finished, in 1987, that she had her first ectopic pregnancy and we lost the baby, which was absolutely awful. There was a nice Italian restaurant round the corner from the studio, and I remember going round there to celebrate when we first found out she was pregnant. In the early stages, we thought everything was regular and normal. And then subsequently she had a second ectopic pregnancy and we lost that baby as well. The second one happened when we were in Japan. If you've had one ectopic pregnancy, there's more of a chance that you could have another one. And if you've had a second one, there's very little chance that, apart from IVF, you're ever going to have a natural pregnancy because they cut bits out of your tubes.

"From the first ectopic pregnancy onwards for the next few years, my mind was really on other things, and what was happening with The Pogues became less and less relevant. It paled into insignificance. I was opting out of a lot of interviews by this stage. For a long time I wasn't in the mood to talk about the band at all, especially to people just endlessly asking, 'What's Shane up to?' But the group were fantastic. I really value all the things they did for me. They helped me through some incredibly difficult times."

CHAPTER 25

The Bob Dylan Disaster

They were still putting on a hell of a show. And the weekly music papers – usually so fickle and contrary - still loved them. The St Patrick's concerts at Brixton had garnered rave reviews, with *Melody Maker*'s Paul Lester coming to a remarkable conclusion: "St Patrick is caught with his hand up a woman constable's skirt. Yeah, one of *those* nights. The Pogues will take you *higher*, to be sure."

The audience was "gorilla-shit crazy, completely and utterly bonkers", wrote Lester, who also reported favourably on MacGowan's beard – a "handsome thicket of facial hair" - and on the new songs that the band were trying out live, including 'USA' and 'Lorelei'.

The Pogues were supported by Sons Of The Desert who played "rollicking good-time ballroom mini-blitzes" and were briefly co-managed by Frank Murray and Joey Cashman. "I left them in the office one day with Joey," remembers Frank. "When I came back, he'd kicked them out. He'd done the right thing."

April, May and June 1989 brought selected European gigs and festival appearances. On June 10, they supported UB40 at Birmingham's St Andrews football ground, and in a chilling echo of the Hillsborough disaster only two months earlier, a crush at the front of the stage three songs into The Pogues' performance resulted in 100 fans being injured. For Philip Chevron and Darryl Hunt, this must have brought back all the shocking memories they were still trying not to dream about.

The band immediately left the stage while teams from St John Ambulance dragged bodies out of the moshpit. It was later stated that The Pogues' prompt action and a quickly co-ordinated response from the emergency services had together prevented a major tragedy. The group resumed their set after order had been restored and the casualties taken away from the pitch.

One eye-witness in the audience told an *NME* reporter: "I saw about 25 people pulled out of the crowd during The Pogues' first song, mostly young girls who were there to see UB40 and didn't know what to expect at a stadium gig. Pogues fans were jumping up and down behind them and the kids were being crushed at the front. It was pandemonium for the first couple of songs. A lot of them were carried away on stretchers."

A spokesman for The Pogues commented: "People were being squashed at the front, so the band decided it would be best if they left the stage to let things calm down."

"If a bunch of people got killed at one of our gigs I wouldn't ever play again," said Shane MacGowan, five days later. "I'm not interested in causing a single piece of human suffering just for the sake of a fucking pop concert."

MacGowan was talking to *NME* writer Edwin Pouncey in Lausanne, Switzerland, where the band would later that evening play a headlining show at the Hot Point Festival. He spent part of the interview talking excitedly about Acid House music and his experiences of it in clubs, and also about his favourite holiday destinations of Thailand and Greece, where the cost of living was "fuck all".

Pouncey had heard an advance copy of the new album and he was impressed by the group's expanding musical horizons, stating, "*Peace and Love* is The Pogues' latest LP, a record which sees them moving out of the atmosphere of the public bar and on to the stage of a large stadium. Here the band can stretch out and show that it's not just tradition they can tangle with." He added: "Pogues purists (if such animals exist) may be slightly awestruck to discover that the experiment which brought to life a creature like 'Yeah Yeah Yeah Yeah Yeah' is still alive and well and refusing to go back into its box."

Considering the group's huge live popularity, Shane remarked: "We used to play in bars and have the audience, together with most of the band, lying on the stage. . . now we're playing big stadiums. We used to be able to hear what we were playing. . . now we can't. But they're not listening anyway. . . They don't have to listen because we blast it out, unless it's a bad night. Obviously a bad night didn't mean shit when we were playing in bars. A bad night now, though, is like, 'Oh dear! Wet my knickers in front of 10,000 people.'"

Asked if he still enjoyed performing, he said: "Not much. There's the odd time when you get a rush, like when you play London, Glasgow or Belfast."

The Pogues were by now including almost all of *Peace And Love* in their live set, alongside crowd-pleasers such as 'Bottle Of Smoke', 'The Irish Rover', 'Streets Of Sorrow/Birmingham Six' and 'Honky Tonk Women'. Pouncey picked as his highlights "the all-out, almost TV cop show soundtrack sound of 'Gridlock'" and Finer's hurdy-gurdy solo in 'Misty Morning, Albert Bridge', which had just been released as the first single from the album. Backed by 'Cotton Fields' and 'Young Ned Of The Hill', with a dub version of the latter track appearing on the 12-inch, the single reached a top position of Number 41.

Problematic to the bitter end, *Peace And Love* did not arrive without a struggle or two. Frank Murray wasn't thrilled with the finished product, and Warners didn't know how they were going to promote it. Both Murray and Rob Dickens wanted to ditch Philip Chevron's songs, 'Blue Heaven' and 'Lorelei', feeling they strayed too far from the identifiable sound of The Pogues.

Murray: "I wasn't entirely happy with the material. Everybody was scrambling to get a track on the album. There were some very good tracks on it, but the chemistry within the band was becoming fragmented and the splits were starting to show. It was sketchy. It didn't have the vision of some of the other albums. There were a couple of songs that shouldn't have been on it. I tried to get them removed. Rob Dickens called me, saying the same thing. I remember calling Philip and saying I didn't think they were Pogues songs."

Chevron retorted: "They're Pogues songs, because somebody in The Pogues wrote them."

Philip continues: "When the album was delivered to the record company, Rob Dickens said, 'Oh my fucking Jesus, how am I going to market this?' He felt that both of my songs had to go. Obviously, he told Frank this and Frank said, 'You're going to have to be the one to tell Chevron.' At the time, I was staying at the Gresham Hotel [in Dublin] for a couple of weeks. Rob Dickens phoned me up at three in the morning, we spoke from then until seven o'clock, and he never did talk me round. He offered me my own solo deal. I said, 'I'm just not fucking interested. I'm in The Pogues, these are Pogues tracks and they're staying on the album."

Murray says: "Personally, I think he should have taken the solo album deal, but I didn't want to start getting into fighting any more. I was tired. There was also the responsibility of taking away two songs that Philip was going to earn off. You have that to think of. It was Phil's decision. I just told Rob Dickens the songs were staying on."

The predictable problem with the artwork then reared its head, according to James: "What appears on the inner sleeve is what we wanted to have on the front and we went to great lengths to put it together with Philip Hardaker [who was responsible for the montage]. We had a photo session with candles and flowers and all of us in suits, and we had the whole thing set up. But then Shane didn't show up and it was all wasted."

The photo session had in the first place been an idea of Marcia Farquhar's.

Released at the end of July, the album reached a respectable Number Five, although for the first time in their career, The Pogues were faced with mixed reviews. Many critics were impressed by their adventurousness, but others were lukewarm.

"That's okay," says Murray. "I always thought the band were big enough and talented enough to overcome that."

Jem: "I was disappointed. I had the feeling that people were looking for *Fall From Grace Part II*. I did realise that maybe the cohesion from *Fall From Grace* was lacking, but I also felt *Peace And Love* was strong enough to deserve a better listening, and it would've been nice if people had taken it on its own merit rather than trying to put it next to what had gone before. Of course they never do that. You go into that territory where the band just has to plough its own furrow and 'fuck the critics' sort of thing, which we've always done anyway.

"The fragmentation that occurred was due to the fact that the democratisation had gone to extremes. Everyone was writing songs by then, or a lot more people were, and there was an attempt at least to represent their writing on the record. And I think that might actually have made it a weaker record. *If I Should Fall From Grace* was a record made with a great deal of focus and common direction, and I think that got lost in *Peace And Love*. But the other way to look at it is that it's actually a really interesting album and it's the band being a lot more experimental in ways of creating sound. I prefer to think of the record in this spirit."

"I think it was a worthy follow-up," says Darryl. "I couldn't understand why it was panned so much when there was such quality stuff, very good tunes on there, like 'White City' and 'Misty Morning, Albert Bridge'. We were bound to be criticised because it's impossible to match *If I Should Fall From Grace With God*. But it does affect you a bit. You want people to like what you do. Everybody likes a good review. It didn't do us that much harm, though. People were still very positive about us."

Philip Chevron adds: "We all knew we had to stand behind the album. There was no point in being despondent about it. I think it disappointed people when it came out, but it's common to hear people say that when they went back to it, they discovered a much better album than what they'd remembered."

Paul Verner, The Pogues' lighting engineer, was supposed to be on the wagon. He was reputed to have been putting away two bottles of brandy a day at one stage, and after a series of alcohol-related health scares was sternly warned that if he didn't stop drinking, he'd die.

James Fearnley remembers one ominous episode in Scotland: "We were at Glasgow Barrowlands and Paul had an alcohol attack of some kind. He was the colour of pus and he had no fucking idea who we were, no clue what was going on. He was gone. That was one of the most distressing things."

Paul, described by Shane MacGowan as "the nicest, kindest guy you could ever meet", made efforts to dry out, but he struggled with sobriety and he managed to hide his lapses, even from the band.

James says: "I shared a room with Paul for the longest time and he kept his secret so well. He was drinking the whole time, and I didn't know. I just thought the room smelt a bit funny. It must have been fumes or something."

Verner suffered his most serious collapse to date when The Pogues went to Canada and America to play a series of dates with Violent Femmes in July 1989. "We'd gone down to Irvine or somewhere south of LA to do a gig and he wasn't very well on that occasion," remembers James. "He was pale as anything. Jem went to see him in his room in the Hyatt House Hotel and he was in an awful mess – his guts had just exploded."

He was rushed to LA's famous Cedars Sinai Hospital. "There was the usual Euro outrage at United States medical insurance and the appalling likelihood of the County Hospital downtown if someone didn't come forward with a credit card," says Fearnley, adding, "This was the one big harbinger of the likelihood that Paul was going to die."

Verner, thereafter, made concerted efforts to stay on the straight and narrow and he succeeded, for the time being.

Shane MacGowan has stated on more than one occasion that The Pogues should have knocked it on the head after *Peace And Love*, claiming that he tried to leave the band and had been persuaded not to.

In *If I Should Fall From Grace: The Shane MacGowan Story*, he says: "The touring was getting to me... the constant arguments and stuff. We were starting to sound tired and jaded, and sounding like we should call it a day. We should've called it a day at that stage. But making *Hell's Ditch* was a ridiculous mistake...

"They said, you know, 'We don't really want you to go. We need you,' you know, all this, 'Give us a couple more years.' And then, like, because... I was easily persuaded to carry on... 'Things will get better.' Well, things got worse."

MacGowan says now: "I don't really know what was going wrong. The road crew, the management, the production manager, the tour manager –

they were all part of this big happy family but it just became an ordeal, particularly for the frontman, which I didn't want to be anyway. Most of it was really good fun. I can't remember when it started becoming an ordeal. It happened gradually. It was getting a bit fragmented, the group. Maybe they did want to go in different directions. It was an Irish band... To be quite honest, I can't remember what the problem was. I think all five Pogues albums are fine. Yes, actually, I do like *Peace And Love* otherwise I wouldn't have let them put it out. I've always said *Peace And Love* would be recognised as the great album that it is one day."

This is not quite what he said in *A Drink With*... where he described it as "one really dodgy album" and elaborated: "I started to really lose heart, I didn't think there was a way out."

Shane stated that he had been "in control" of the first two albums and had only just managed to keep control of the third after fighting for it, adding that things deteriorated after *Peace And Love* and "all the squabbles about publishing money... because I made more money than them, because I wrote the majority of the songs. And I was always out-of-it."

A little further into his tirade, he decided that "half of *Peace and Love* is all right – the half I wrote!" And he concluded that the fans tolerated the broad range of the material only because more familiar Pogues fare such as 'White City' came as part of the deal, declaring: "When a band has reached sort of legendary proportions, the audience will put up with just about anything."

It should be pointed out that *A Drink With Shane MacGowan*, compiled after Shane had left the band, was published with a last-minute disclaimer on the final page. Titled "Uncoditional [sic] Apology", it reads: "I was speaking from the heart when I spewed this stuff. I was a stranger in my own soul. To those who can accept it particularly The Pogues family including Frank, I offer uncoditional love. To those who can't I'll see you at the gates of hell – Shane MacGowan."

For their part, The Pogues have no recollection of MacGowan saying that he wanted to quit the band, or of persuading him to stay. They recall only that he was becoming increasingly remote.

"I certainly don't remember pleading or cajoling with him to stay, nor do I remember him saying he wanted to leave," says Andrew. "I can quite imagine him saying, 'Oh God, I don't want to do all these gigs,' and somebody else saying, 'Sorry, you've got to or you're going to get sued.'"

Jem concurs: "I don't remember him saying, 'Look, I'm leaving.' It didn't occur to me. If anything, I was probably more concerned whether we could actually finish a record or whether the band would carry on existing, but I don't think I thought of it in terms as simple as Shane saying, 'I'm leaving.'

I find it hard to remember my feelings from day to day. It was bloody stressful. Probably the whole thing was a bloody crisis."

"People must've realised that we were quite a volatile combination and might just explode at any moment and that would be that," agrees Andrew. "I did feel that would happen at one point, probably right from the start, because we always had quite a punk ethos and we owed quite a lot to bands like the Sex Pistols, and the fact that they split up as soon as they did... I always saw that as a possibility with The Pogues, that we arrived with a bang and we'd just as suddenly go out with a bang.

"But as for splitting after *Peace And Love* – well, it probably would have mattered to me, because apart from it being an income, I was still getting quite a lot of enjoyment out of the band, even though things were messy. And I didn't really have anything better to do, and it was still providing me with some sort of focus and structure, which I was very glad to have at that stage. Even though I was becoming more detached from the day-to-day running of things, the actual work involved I quite relished.

"I do think it would have been a good idea to call a halt and review the situation and try to work out how or whether we wanted to carry on, but I think there was an awful lot of contractual stuff that I doubt we could've wriggled out of easily at that point. And there must have been a feeling that we'd actually done very well – 'We'd be a bit mad to throw it all away.' If we had split up at that point, I think it's much more unlikely that we would ever have got back together again. The sense of failure would have been much greater. We didn't feel things had really run their course and however much I felt things were going wrong, I still thought it was worth persevering with and that, with or without Shane, it was still a good band and still popular."

Talking of MacGowan's dissatisfaction, James comments: "This had been in development for quite a long time, where his way of telling us that he couldn't do this any more came out in a language of painting himself blue in New Zealand and finding happiness in ranting to a drum machine and taking acid and ecstasy and whatever else he was taking. It's hard to know if he would have done that anyway or whether he was putting himself apart in order to say, 'I want to leave.' It's a very unclear sort of language."

For Spider Stacy, MacGowan's withdrawal from the rest of the group was an especially bitter pill to swallow. Spider had lost his partner, the other half of the old double act, the one person with whom he could enjoy a high-powered battle of wits.

Still flying the flag for alcoholic excess, Stacy found his one-time drinking buddy and fellow mischief-maker just as difficult to reach as everybody else did, and he didn't like it.

"Not only was Shane physically removing himself, but he was disappearing into this chemical sort of oblivion," says Spider. "I did react very badly to the way that he was, but I myself was not exactly *compus mentis* at the time. I would just get really, really angry. I'd be very short with him. It could be that some of it was me taking out on Shane what I should have been directing at myself. My reaction may have been in some ways an exaggerated one, although the way he was acting was making things very, very difficult."

However, Stacy was beside himself with anger, genuine anger, when MacGowan let the band down, big-time, on their next American tour.

On August 26, 1989, they played a headline gig at the Reading Festival, which had just been taken over and dragged out of the dark ages by the Mean Fiddler Organisation. Their performance had been well-received, with *NME*'s David Quantick swept away by "the increased wonderfulness of The Pogues".

In September, they flew out to America for the most prestigious dates of their career, supporting Bob Dylan at six concerts in southern California before heading off to other states for their own headlining tour. It seems that Dylan had personally asked for the band, having heard about them from his son Jesse, a confirmed fan. And the word was that he was really looking forward to seeing them play.

Unfortunately for everybody, Shane MacGowan didn't get on the plane. Frantic transatlantic phone calls ensued, with Shane complaining that airline staff kept banning him from boarding because he was drunk.

"They wouldn't let me on an airplane," says MacGowan. "They said I wasn't fit to fly. Three days in a row me and Charlie MacLennan tried to get on a plane. He used to live with me and my other half, Victoria. And he was our production manager, road manager – he ran the show on the road, which isn't to say that Frank didn't come on tour, but there were a lot of other people involved."

Some of The Pogues accepted Shane's explanation. Others didn't. Now they were in California, about to play in front of Bob Dylan, and their singer was still in London. Once again, Spider had to deputise, but this was a far cry from belting out a few songs in the 100 Club or a bar-room somewhere in Sweden.

"My take on it for a long time was that he hadn't tried as hard as he might have done to get there," says Spider. "I was really fucking angry then because I had to sing and I really, really didn't appreciate it. Out of all the things he did when he was fucking around, it was the one I was pissed off about because I wasn't ready for that. I did have to get up in front of all those people, opening for Bob Dylan, and make a prat of myself. For a start, I only knew half the words. Obviously, we tailored the set accordingly, to make it as easy as possible. It was nerve-wracking. I didn't know how to sing properly. My throat got really tight and I think my voice got all sort of... [helium-squeaks] The only song I remember thinking, 'That one went all right,' was 'White City', cos it was in the right key.

"We didn't know at that time that Shane wasn't going to show for any of the Dylan gigs, although it was at the back of our minds. I was just thinking, 'Thanks a fucking bunch, Shane. Thanks a million.'"

Journalists from all over the world had arrived to report on the shows and The Pogues were bombarded with questions about their missing vocalist at a time when they still didn't know what had really happened or when and if MacGowan was going to turn up. And so they closed ranks, avoided questions wherever possible and gave evasive answers when put on the spot.

The result was a rash of rumours: Shane had quit the band; Shane had stopped touring; Shane was seriously ill; Shane was in hospital. Shane was none of these things. Where he actually was, at least for some of the time, was in a bar.

Another first-night disaster befell the group when their instruments failed to arrive. Andrew remembers: "We'd arrived on Labor Day [celebrated on the first Monday in September]. When we got to the airport, we got our personal baggage but the guys dealing with the freight weren't working, so we couldn't get our instruments out of the airport. We panicked. Luckily we had a few contacts who went rushing round trying to borrow banjos and accordions and things off people. I think we probably used Bob Dylan's drummer's kit. We begged, borrowed and stole things, and we got by just about, although it was a complete shambles."

The reviewers were generally understanding and kind. *NME*'s Jane Garcia wrote: "Although Spider has many strong points – tin whistle-playing and a friendly manner, for example – singing is not one of them. But he's game, and the audience, who have turned out in unusually high numbers for an opening act, seem appreciative of the band's efforts."

The Pogues had hastily re-arranged their set to include a number of instrumentals. Terry Woods and Philip Chevron sang their own compositions from *Peace And Love*, leaving Spider to deal with 'White City', 'USA' and 'Yeah Yeah Yeah Yeah Yeah', while Fearnley gave displays of showmanship at the centre of the stage.

Dylan met his support band only once, venturing out from behind his wall of security on the first night to shake their hands as they came offstage and exchange a few words. He'd watched the set but passed no comment about it. After that, they didn't see him again, except on stage. They did, however, see Bruce Springsteen, who visited their dressing room at the Greek Theatre, an outdoor venue set among trees in Los Angeles.

It was later officially announced that Shane had been "unable to travel due to nervous exhaustion".

"I was so fucking disappointed," recalls Frank Murray. "I don't buy Shane's excuses. I don't buy it. I don't know whether he bottled it. Maybe he thought it would be too much pressure. If it had been two or three years earlier, he would've been there in a flash, but I think he'd been worn down by all the drink and the drugs.

"His family were in town and he'd been up all the night before his first flight, drinking with them in a hotel. He left the hotel room well drunk and we were told he turned up at the airport legless with a bottle of gin in his hand, swigging from it. He wasn't allowed on the plane. That was fine. It was an early-morning flight and I knew there was one in the evening at six o'clock. I said to Charlie, 'Get him a hotel room and get him back for the six o'clock flight.'

"Shane and Charlie had become very close. They were drug buddies and they were living together as well. Charlie would try and cover up a lot for Shane. So there was a story concocted that Shane went in to take a leak and Charlie was wondering after about twenty minutes what's keeping him and went into the loos after him and Shane had gone. They say Shane then went back to the airport. He never went back. He was staying in Montagu Square in an apartment there. This woman [Kathy MacMillan] was his landlady, and Shane had been doing his usual, 'I'm ill, I'm sick, I'm too tired.' Women particularly used to fall for this a lot. They'd be on the phone – 'Don't you know Shane is ill?' I'd get the strangest calls from the strangest women who'd probably known Shane for two days. Anyway, he kind of had a shoulder to cry on there."

Victoria Clarke later stated that she'd spent four days with MacGowan in a hotel at Heathrow Airport, adding: "Unfortunately because of the large quantities of cough mixture and gin that Shane was consuming, British Airways kept refusing to allow him on any of their planes. When he finally got on a plane it took four people to escort him and he screamed the whole way to Dallas."

"At that point," says Jem, "Shane probably was saying he was leaving the band. I can remember talking to him on the phone from America and not really getting anywhere with him and thinking, 'Maybe that's it. Maybe he is leaving the band.' I'd imagine I was saying, 'Come on, come and do this and see how you feel and we'll talk about it and if you feel like leaving at the end of it, then fair enough.'

"I don't know who persuaded him to come in the end. He didn't come until after the Dylan part of it was over. I didn't particularly sympathise with his version of events. If you really want to get on the plane, you try to make sure you put yourself in a state where they're going to let you on. I think that's a bit lame. I just don't think his heart was in it, for whatever reasons, but the whole thing was fucking annoying."

Andrew Ranken gives Shane's story the benefit of the doubt. He says: "I've always been a huge Bob Dylan fan and I thought it was a major coup to get on that tour. I've never understood what Shane's problem was except that I think he'd been on one of his holidays in Thailand. I think he was certainly doing opium when he went there, but God knows what else as well. He did that a couple of times, went off to Thailand and thoroughly indulged himself and came back in a state where he wasn't fit for anything. He was stopped from boarding a plane. That's fact. Two or three times he wasn't allowed to get on the plane cos he was too out of it. I thought, 'What a twat.'

"I think he may have realised that he wasn't in a fit state to perform properly. Maybe he was doing us all a big favour by not turning up. Dear old Shane – thank God he didn't come! It could've been a disaster! Who knows?"

Spider also sees a certain humour in the situation: "I do remember backstage at one of the Dylan gigs, all the Californian [Hell's] Angels were there. I was just thinking, 'It's a good thing that Shane isn't actually here.' I could just see an unpleasant situation developing if he took exception to them."

Stacy agrees with Jem that the most probable explanation for Shane's missing the flights – either by accident or design – was that he "wasn't that bothered about going".

Darryl suggests, thoughtfully, that the airport staff in London "could've handled it better – they didn't have to give him so much trouble". And he says of Shane's no-show, "There might have been a psychosomatic thing going on. Maybe he wanted to stay on the sunny side of the street. Maybe there was a Bob Dylan thing going on – he was very keen to see us and I think he recognised in Shane a fellow story-teller, a poet. Shane could've been quite freaky about even working with him. Shane's quite shy sometimes. Bob Dylan was pretty disappointed."

Philip Chevron agrees: "Shane's always been a bit angsty, reserved or stand-offish, with people who would be his peers. There are very few people in his class who he actually knows, partly because he's shy and partly because he hates the implied competition. Bob Dylan – if you want to get on an airplane, you can get on an airplane. Shane didn't want to be judged alongside Bob Dylan. He loved Tom Waits but he had no interest in hanging out with Tom as the rest of the band did. What he has is so precious and personal to him that he hates to feel it's under challenge or under question. Even if there's a possibility of that, he backs off."

MacGowan shoots back, perfectly: "After doing a single with The Dubliners and having Terry Woods join the group, you know what I mean – I'm not going to get fazed by Bob Dylan."

He casually adds: "Dylan is all right. He's a nice guy. He's always been courteous to me. Jesse Dylan was a good mate, with Los Lobos and stuff in California. That was a fun part of California, but that was basically Mexico. I mean, Jesse, he used to hang around the studio. He liked his old man's stuff, but he liked The Pogues' music. He was younger than us – but not much younger."

James Fearnley drew a direct comparison between MacGowan and Dylan when he recently watched the acclaimed Dylan documentary, *No Direction Home*. He adds: "In the same way as Dylan, Shane – whether or not he would agree with me – is just like a vessel through which traditional music is coming. He's part of a tradition that pre-dates him by hundreds and hundreds of years, and all he's doing is stepping into it and wading up to his neck in it. To some degree he might feel a bit loath to take credit for music that's been going on for hundreds of years."

MacGowan's unwillingness to admit his own exceptional talent is legendary. Ask which of his songs he's most proud of and he'll answer, "I'm not fussed. I prefer singing other people's songs anyway." Talk about his body of work and he'll say, "If you check the credits then you'll find that the Pogues albums I was on, I probably wrote about half the tunes, as much as anybody writes a tune. Other people in the group wrote tunes, and you arrange the rest."

In an interview with *The Guardian*'s Dave Simpson in 2004, he summed up his life's work in six short words: "I just wrote a few songs."

"He's never been a great one for taking compliments," affirms Spider. "His poetry is everything, I think. It's the soul of the band. It articulates the soul of the band with the music. It's that kind of whole gutter-poetry thing, but it's also there in the music as well. That's what really gets the magic, it's the way the songs are played. The words are fantastic. They're always really, really good. He knows what he's doing. He always knows what he's doing."

Chevron: "In the minibus in Germany, on my first tour when I was standing in for Jem, I had a long chat with Shane about his work. I said, 'You realise you're really one of the greats.' He said, 'Really?' I said, 'You're up there.' At this point I think he realised it might be true, because it was coming from me. Anyone else might have had an agenda. All I wanted to do was be in the band.

"To me, the songs are all about how you are in the world with other people, and I don't think anybody's expressed it as well as Shane MacGowan has in many, many years. He's very protective of his legacy, and our legacy. He's hugely proud of it. He knows better than anybody how good it is. Once he gave himself permission to say, 'Okay, this is great,' he's his own best critic. Anyone who's any threat to that legacy or how valuable that is, is a potential source of enmity, and basically they're a cunt."

They didn't put the bunting out for Shane when he finally arrived in Dallas for the first date of the band's own tour. He didn't say a lot about his absence, and it seems that his bandmates didn't really want to get into that discussion.

"Relations were rather strained, understandably," says Andrew. "I also think he was still having a massive comedown from his Thailand experience. I don't think he was on very good form at all, and I don't think we were very sympathetic."

"He wasn't in a great state," confirms Darryl. "He had a situation where it didn't look as if he'd been treated fairly. I didn't see the point of asking him about it. The rest of the tour went okay, but it was a bit worrying, a bit tense. He didn't particularly like America. The bullshit factor in America is so huge it gets people down. For a country that does produce so much amazing stuff, it's still culturally bereft."

Philip remembers that despite everything that had happened, he wholly enjoyed the musical experiences of a tour that took The Pogues around the southern and eastern states of America.

"We were on our game as a live band," he says. "There were times when Shane was really bad and unreliable. It made us all the more distressed but all the more committed to each other as musicians. It was one of the most exciting tours we did musically, the '89 US tour, from the point of view of a band completely in the zone and intuitive with each other. Stuff started happening that made us realise we could hold our heads up in places like Austin and New Orleans. We made damn sure that we put our whole heart and soul into the 90 minutes we spent on stage."

Jem Finer has no such happy reminiscences. He says: "I don't think the atmosphere was that pleasant for a while, and I don't think Shane was in particularly good shape or mood. We schlepped across America and gradually things evened out. I don't have any good memories of that period. It was all just very difficult and unpredictable. There's lots of times I wondered whether I should still be doing it, but there's something about giving up in the face of adversity that I find quite hard. I'd rather give something up when it's going well. But when things are going well, you never think about giving them up, so that never happens. Something was up. The future of the band was precarious."

CHAPTER 26

Gudbuy T'Shane

There was some good cheer for The Pogues when on October 7, 1989, two days before his birthday, James Fearnley married Danielle von Zerneck. It was, says James, "a big LA wedding" held in a marquee in the English setting of Buckland, Worcestershire.

He adds: "People still talk about it to this day. It was a fantastic wedding."

The morning began with a champagne breakfast at a café in nearby Evesham, organised by best man Jem Finer.

"I'd talked to Danielle about asking Kathy Burke to be the best man," confides James. "But then we both agreed that Jem should do it."

The guest list was international, with friends and family flying in from LA and arriving from London in a specially chartered bus. There is in fact more than one small town in England called Buckland and, if legend is to be believed, Shane and Victoria managed to visit all of them before finally pitching up at the correct place with "a crap wedding gift".

It may have been crap, but Fearnley still keeps that set of laminated stills from the video of 'Yeah Yeah Yeah Yeah Yeah', made into place mats. "Was it a joke, playing on the wedding vows?" James wonders. "It did happen to be the only Pogues video I didn't appear in. . ."

By the time of the best man's speech, the drinks were in full flow. "I rather think Jem made a good speech," says James, vaguely. "I don't remember anything about it except that there were bets on how long it was going to be, and Darryl won."

Close attention was paid to the hospitality. "We got Hofmeister lager in for Kathy Burke, because I knew she liked that and nothing else," says James. "Apparently in the afternoon, she went up to the bar and said, 'I don't suppose you've got Hofmeister lager,' and the barman brought up a case of it. Everybody was pretty well looked after, I'd say."

The Pogues played a European tour in November and a Christmas jolly-up back home to wind up what had been a stressful year.

Philip Chevron, surveying the new decade, realised that things could only get worse if he didn't somehow get a grip. He became the first member of The Pogues, other than Shane, to seek help for his alcoholism.

"People had found various ways of retreating from the madness," he recalls. "In Shane's case, he'd discovered Thailand as a source of spiritual rejuvenation. People have various ways of recharging themselves. At the beginning of 1990, I had my first serious attempt at rehab. I went into St Luke's Woodside Hospital in Muswell Hill. I'd reached the point where I just didn't want to go down any further."

Philip was reeling from the cumulative effects of the previous year's events: "There was the whole chaos of the *Peace And Love* experience, and my boyfriend, Achim, was ill from HIV, which was induced by his heroin addiction rather than sexually transmitted.

"I hadn't realised the extent of his heroin addiction. It's weird how addicts become mutually self-denying. I was in denial of his illness and he was in denial of mine. He was very seriously ill and, in fact, he died a couple of years later, which was another grand trauma.

"I was becoming so divorced from everybody and everything, and so unhappy. I was becoming more and more closed up and isolating myself from the band on the road. I still needed to do gigs and I still needed to drink the alcohol, but I was happier not having to deal with everybody else's pain – Andrew's bellicosity if he got too drunk, or Shane's drug-addled mind. I took to my room and drank myself stupid from the mini-bar. I drank as much as I needed to stay on an even keel. You reach a point where it's pointless to be drunk. You just reach a level that you want to maintain."

Philip had been living in a flat at Regent's Park during the *Peace And Love* era, and had then tried living back in Ireland, in Dublin, which didn't work out. Returning, he entered St Luke's. "It didn't last long," he admits. "It didn't really work the first time. You just haven't surrendered yet. At some part of it, you always think, 'I'll give up when I have to surrender, but not until then.' But it sowed the seeds of knowing what I needed to do."

Chevron took a flat nearby, in Muswell Hill, and stayed sober for a few months. "I didn't like it," he confesses. "I was going through a state of being 'dry drunk'. You haven't done anything to address all the issues that made you drink, so when you stop drinking, you're left with the problem.

"AA works so well. They give you the tools to deal with the person underneath and to recognise that person as being valuable. That takes some doing. It's a tough call. It requires a fair amount of dedication and commitment. Nobody gets sober without that commitment and dedication. You have to remind yourself of what you liked about yourself, if you ever did. I wasn't at the stage where I was ready to face that."

Philip still had mountainous problems to face in his relationship with Achim. He recalls: "He was frantically trying to get hold of me at one stage, and I didn't realise he was in a hospital. I didn't have a home phone for three years. If the office needed to get hold of me, they'd have to send somebody up to my flat at Muswell Hill. At one stage, Achim's hospice somehow managed to get hold of me to say he would very much like to see me before he died.

"He arrived in a wheelchair to one of the gigs in Germany, with his nurse. I spent his entire visit in a fog of denial that this was happening to him and to me. I got very, very drunk for the first time in a long time. I was oblivious to his pain in the midst of mine. All the other shit. . . it was just one thing too much, and I wasn't there for him because I couldn't be there for him. I still very much regret that I couldn't have been there for him when he was dying. And anyway, the whole Pogues situation had become such a rollercoaster that there wasn't any time to be there for him.

"I couldn't take him with me. If he needed nursing, that was out of the question. He just wanted to spend one more happy evening with me. I suppose I didn't really take it on board that he was dying, to my eternal regret. I was surrounded by people who appeared to be dying.

"I've forgiven myself for it, but it's still an ache that it all ended so badly. I didn't find out he'd died until a month later. I had to visit the grave without his family knowing I'd visited it. It was just awful. Awful."

Chevron had fallen well and truly off the wagon by the summer when the band were recording *Hell's Ditch* – their fifth album, and their final one with Shane. "I was taking drinks on the quiet," Chevron confides. "I don't know if the band did or didn't know, but they didn't say."

It seems that the band, and producer Joe Strummer, were fully aware of Philip's setback. Meanwhile, the Pogue who actually did manage to stop drinking, at some point that year, was Terry Woods, who went cold turkey. "When I was on tour," says Terry, "the drinking got a bit silly, and it got even sillier. There were a number of things, family problems and all the rest of it. It became very apparent that I was out of control. At the end of the day, the choice was that I drank – or that I stopped drinking and had a family. And I wanted my family.

"It was getting in the way of me doing things that I wanted to do. Drink fools you into thinking you're very busy and doing lots of things when in actual fact you're doing nothing except drinking. I didn't attend AA or anything like that. That wouldn't be my kind of scene, standing up talking about things.

"One of my problems was going into places where I was known and people buying you a drink and not having the moral fibre to say, 'I don't want a drink.' It was easier to take it. Once the gate's open, the gate's open. So I stayed away from my usual haunts for a while. Gradually I went back and I was drinking mineral water and nobody pushed the issue."

One might imagine that the real test for Woods would be in his next close dealings with The Pogues. He comments: "Everybody else in the band was still the way they were. But I'd made up my mind that it was over for me, so it wasn't that difficult."

The Pogues had released 'White City' as a single in August 1989, just a month after *Peace And Love*, and it had bombed. Backed with 'Every Man Is A King' and with 'Maggie May (Live)' and 'Star Of The County Down' additional on the various extended formats, it failed to trouble the Top 75. No further cuts from the album would be released: The Pogues' next single, in May 1990, would be another collaboration with The Dubliners, featuring 'Jack's Heroes' and 'Whiskey In The Jar', which reached Number 63.

It was decided that the band should proceed with their next album as soon as possible, although before that happened, there was still a little more touring mileage to be got out of *Peace And Love*. In February 1990, they made their second trip to Australia and New Zealand, hoping that this time Shane would keep his clothes on and his paints in their box. Fortunately, he did. On this particular trip, it was James Fearnley who lost his mind for a while.

"When we went to Byron Bay," relates James, "someone went off farming for [magic] mushrooms and came back with some, and I had the most awful time with them. As soon as I took some of them, I wished I hadn't. It was horrible. So I went up to Charlie and I said, 'You've got to get me out of here. I can't handle it.' He kept on slurring, 'Wait a minute.' The minute turned into 20, and then 40 minutes. We were at somebody's pool at a house somewhere near to the hotel. Then Charlie said, 'I've got to take Shane and Victoria back to the hotel, and I'll take you as well.'

"In this car there was Shane and Victoria in the back and me and Charlie sitting in the front, and I was aware of the darkness out of the side of the car and the dashboard all lit up. Shane was Han Solo, Charlie was the Wookiee, I was Luke Skywalker and Victoria was Princess Leia. We zoomed along this mainly flat road with bumps in it every now and again. It was like going into warp speed with all the characters from *Star Wars*."

March found the band back in America. They celebrated St Patrick's Day in New York, where they had a fervent following, with a gig on March 16.

On the big day itself, they appeared on *Saturday Night Live*, the classic late-night comedy and music TV show, hosted by Rob Lowe.

There were more European appearances throughout the spring and summer, but the big project was *Hell's Ditch*. The question was - who would produce it and where would they record it?

Philip: "People weren't falling over each other to produce The Pogues. They must have checked out Steve Lillywhite's work with *Peace And Love* and realised he must have had his work cut out. Stories of Shane's reality were filtering out. The Bob Dylan no-show had happened. It's just, 'Don't touch that band, they're bad news.'"

But there was one person who could be depended on: Joe Strummer.

"At this stage, I think Joe would've been dreading calls from Frank Murray," says Philip. "But Joe was a trouper. Without fail, he took the call, and *Hell's Ditch* was the cavalry riding to the rescue."

Murray reveals: "I thought Joe Strummer would be some kind of unifying force. They all respected Joe, and he wasn't going to over-produce the album. Shane was in a weird state at the time. He was falling out with the band, and you can hear that on some of the songs. There's that line in 'The Sunnyside Of The Street' – *'I will not be reconstructed.'* There was a few things there."

Again in the interests of band unity and with a view to keeping the members focused on the task at hand, Murray booked The Pogues into Rockfield residential studios in Monmouth, Wales. "People would probably get away from everything in London," hoped Frank. "And Shane would be away from a lot of smack dealers and stuff like that."

Heroin had crept quietly into The Pogues' world and now, says Murray, "It had become more overt."

It would finally become public almost ten years later with Sinead O'Connor, a close friend of Victoria Clarke, reporting MacGowan's possession of heroin to the police in Kentish Town, reportedly for his own good, while Shane retaliated with accusations of publicity-seeking.

It was a beautiful summer, the World Cup was on, and all of the band bar MacGowan delighted in the rural lifestyle at Rockfield. Darryl and Andrew could often be found strolling alongside the River Wye when they weren't recording or breaking out of sessions to catch an important match on TV. James Fearnley watched foxes creeping around the hay bales in the early mornings, and was thrilled to see a hawk at close range. Whatever the problems of the recent past, the group members had carried on writing and had plenty of new material, much of which had already been worked out with Shane and then rehearsed and demoed.

MacGowan absented himself from the studio for long periods, taking off with Victoria at a whim, and when he was present, he behaved awkwardly, unreasonably. His alienation from the band was almost complete. Still, he contributed handsomely in terms of songs – the 'Thailand trilogy' is a worthy achievement by any standards, particularly 'Summer In Siam' – and he stayed for long enough to put down vocals for nine songs out of 13 (the others supplied by Spider and Terry).

The Pogues' long-standing friendship with Strummer and his extraordinary patience were key to the success of the sessions. Few producers coming cold into the scenario could have handled Shane MacGowan, and fewer still would have stuck around to try. It was felt, too, that Strummer was the right man to help the band get back to basics: they'd decided to return to a more immediate approach to recording.

"Joe had his work cut out," says Murray. "You'd have to wait until Shane was in the mood to sing. Maybe at 2am or something he'd say, 'Okay, I'll sing now.' Joe never complained. He wasn't a judgemental person. He was the kind of guy, if Shane wasn't there, he'd get something else done, and the band had enough songs to record that they'd written themselves."

Spider adds: "Joe really had to work the songs out of him. Shane really wasn't in a very good state when we did that. His singing was done virtually line by line."

"Joe was incredibly enthusiastic, incredibly intense, determined to get it right," remembers Darryl. "He really wanted to do a good job. But he had a hard time. He remembered us from two or three years ago, and he thought, 'I'm not getting the group that did *Fall From Grace*.' He probably would've liked the group that Steve Lillywhite had. It was harder to pull the strings together. It was getting quite hard work."

So fastidious was Strummer that he kept a notebook, with drawings, detailing everything they did in the studio.

Philip Chevron saw the Rockfield experience as a recreation of the old hippy *cliché*, the band getting their heads together in the country, and despite the problems in his personal life, he enjoyed it immensely. He says: "It was very much a good idea and it fitted into Joe's way of working with us. Joe liked communal living. The one person who got out of the loop was Shane. He just decided, 'This is far too fucking rural for me. If I want to get my head together, I'll do it on a beach in Thailand.' Which, to some extent, he did. 'And then I'll come and do the vocals when they need me.'

"Joe had to set up a little vocal booth for him outside on the patio, to record his vocals in the open air. Luckily the weather was okay for that. I don't know why he didn't want to go into the studio, having not wanted to be involved in a rural environment. When he does get down there, he's the one who decides to stay out in the open. It might have been him being contrary. He was determined to get the vocals down as quickly as possible and fuck off back to London or Thailand.

"There were no hard feelings cos he actually delivered more than he delivered on *Peace And Love*. We always preferred to have Shane around. If we can get him to articulate whatever it is he's trying to fucking say, it's always worth hearing. However, we had kind of got used to him not being around and it wasn't a great hardship to do the album without him."

Strummer later told Ann Scanlon, for *NME*, that his role was dictated by the fact that The Pogues had worked out the material before entering the studio. "So it wasn't a question of producing it," he said. "It was a question of producing an atmosphere inside which the musicians could operate. And that was the first time that all eight Pogues had been recorded together – I mean, can you imagine putting a band like this in one room and then having Shane MacGowan out on the verandah? I put him outside because I understood that he didn't like being inside in a booth with headphones on."

There are places where *Hell's Ditch* shines and shimmers and glistens; often it conveys a cheeriness and conviviality quite remarkable in a band who were wondering what kind of future they had, and how long their singer could carry on. 'The Sunnyside Of The Street' sounds as bright and uplifting as its title. 'Rain Street' is fleet-footed, irresistibly sassy. '5 Green Queens & Jean' runs with a country-flavoured tunefulness. Less Irishness and more snap, crackle and pop music: that's the general story of the album, with Spanish, Greek and Middle-Eastern aspects woven in. At the other end of the spectrum, the warm, late-night romance of 'Summer In Siam' evokes the rich contentment of MacGowan's days in Thailand, the "perfect peace" that he later explained could be achieved by anyone because it's "about a state of mind, not a place". It features the talents of Dubliner John Sheahan's daughter, Siobhan, playing the harp.

"*Hell's Ditch* had a sunnier outlook," agrees Chevron. "It's a happier album, and one that was turning the corner for us. It's not the same band that made *Peace And Love*. There's that optimism about it. It's well named. The Pogues' motor had got stuck in this ditch. You have to get the fucking van out of the ditch at some point. The album reflected that. We were stepping on the reverse pedal.

"Every record we made reflects very accurately where the band was at, creatively, emotionally, physically, in terms of capability. By the time we got to *Peace And Love*, you feel like the band are falling apart. The album sounds torn. How much darker can this thing get? We somehow came out of this awful fucking storm to the other side. *Hell's Ditch* feels more pastoral."

Astonishingly, MacGowan would later accuse his bandmates of wilfully abandoning the group's essential Irishness, despite also admitting that he "wasn't in the mood" to write any such songs himself for *Hell's Ditch*. This was the same Shane who had recorded a 20-minute Acid House track, 'Contact Yourself', for consideration in *Peace And Love*.

"They were trying to force Irish music out altogether, which is insane," he complained in *If I Should Fall From Grace: The Shane MacGowan Story*. "I was saying, 'Well, what do you mean? That's what we do is Irish music.' Like The Specials did ska and The Rolling Stones did R&B. What we do is Irish music, raw Irish music, emotional dance music with guts, and [it] by-passes the intellect and hits you in the gut and hits you in the heart and hits you in the soul."

"I think that's bonkers," replies Jem. "For example, there's three songs that Shane really wanted to do – 'Summer In Siam', 'Sayonara' and 'House Of The Gods', three Thailand songs. That's completely down to him. He's writing those songs. At the same time, there were songs like 'The Last Of McGee' that I wrote which is a completely archetypal Pogues Irishy song, and that didn't get on the album. One of the songs Shane objected to not getting on was 'Pinned Down', a weird dub track which he wrote after watching some programme about the liquid cosh being used on some people in mental institutions.

"So (a) he's upset because it's not Irish enough but (b) he's upset because a track of his, a weird psychotic dub recording, didn't get on. I don't think anyone was trying to stop the band being Irishy. I don't think anybody was trying to stop Shane doing anything. This Irishy thing had been spinning off in all directions, a lot of which were to do with him."

Jem and Shane, despite the latter's subsequent complaints about the album content, had returned to a more collaborative way of working. 'The Sunnyside Of The Street' matched MacGowan lyrics to Finer's title and music, while Jem wrote the instrumental half of '5 Green Queens And Jean' and 'Hell's Ditch' combined tunes that each had. Finer says of the night-marish visions of the title track: "I remember saying to Shane that I thought the lyrics were really brilliant, but that they needed toning down to make it not so much XXX to the max but just XX certificate. And so he wrote them into the form they are now."

Jem's own song, 'The Wake Of The Medusa', returns to the subject of the Gericault painting that the band had adapted for the front cover of *Rum Sodomy & The Lash* and the instrumental 'Maidrin Rua' started out as a tra-ditional jam in the studio, led by Terry Woods, which Strummer recorded and liked.

★

Few would have expected Rockfield to be haunted, especially not by someone who's still alive.

"There were some strange sounds going around in the studio that [engineer] Paul Cobbold rather mysteriously put down to the fact that Robert Plant of Led Zeppelin had recorded there," reveals James. "Every now and again you'd pick up a high-pitched distant wailing noise that Paul said was the ghost of Plant, notwithstanding the earthing problems that I think they had at the studio."

Cobbold is clearly a man of imagination, capturing thunder-and-rain sounds for *Hell's Ditch* by holding a microphone out of his bedroom window one night during a storm.

In some of the other varied effects, the sound of Joe Strummer's Morris Minor engine is incorporated into 'Rain Street' at Andrew's suggestion, and the sizzle in 'Summer In Siam' involves an uncoiled length of snare wire.

Fearnley, as usual, was fascinated by the studio processes, proposing the bell at the start of 'Rain Street' and playing mandolin on a track called 'Aisling', which didn't make the final cut.

"This upset Shane quite a bit on one of his returns from London," says James. "I remember him not liking the idea of the mandolin at all, but then it might be true to say that my relationship with Shane had been steadily getting worse over the years if, first of all, he could be bothered to think that he had a relationship with me by the time of *Hell's Ditch*." James adds that, "I tended to want to keep out of his way, unless circumstances absolutely demanded it. I still loved his songs, with exceptions, but he was far gone, I think, for most of us, certainly me."

The Pogues' memories of Rockfield are as much to do with the social aspects of the visit as with the music they recorded. James describes the illicit thrill of sneaking meat from the fridge as he started to give up his vegetarianism, and of overhearing disturbing rows when some of the band's partners came to visit. Philip talks about Joe Strummer and how The Pogues turned him on to "the beautiful game".

"There was great camaraderie and it extended all the way through," says Philip. "I loved Joe so much, and to spend that time with him was great. He drove me back to London in his battered old Morris Minor. He usually had a mountain of tapes. He said, 'Have you got any tapes you want to play? I'm sick of these.' I had *Pet Sounds*. I stuck it on and we played it all the way back. I think he genuinely didn't know the album."

Unlikely as it may seem, some members of The Pogues eventually ended up in a terrible argument with Strummer over the tracklisting for *Hell's Ditch*. Having settled on a selection that suited everybody, they were then informed by Joe that Terry Woods' track 'Six To Go', an unusual, percussive chant which had been previously deemed unsuitable, was now to appear on the album replacing Jem Finer's 'Curse Of Love' and MacGowan's 'Pinned Down'.

Jem: "I would imagine Frank got on to Joe saying, 'You fucking take that off and put Terry's track on.' So Joe phones me up and says, 'This is the way it's going to be.' I said, 'That's nonsense. You're going back on what you said. I think it's a really bad idea. It disrupts the flow of the record, it dilutes the record, it's not what everyone wants.' Joe ended up coming round to my house with Spider, who he'd got on his side, at about six in the evening. He didn't leave until 3am, during which time I tried to throw him out a few times, cos I was sick to my back teeth with the two of them.

"Marcia had gone round to see Shane and Victoria and leave us to it. Joe had come round to persuade me that this new tracklisting was the way it should be. We spent the whole night arguing about it and trying out different combinations of songs and trying to find compromises, interspersed with calls to Shane, which was quite funny cos Marcia was there. Shane and I were unified in what we wanted. About 3am, it ended up Joe or whoever got their way. It wasn't going to change. I've always found that pretty annoying. He later apologised to me about it. We didn't fall out as friends, though in that instance I was pretty pissed off with him! I don't think it was purely his idea. There was some politics going on."

James Fearnley, back in LA after the sessions, pitched in by telephone. He says: "I remember talking with Joe on the phone and losing my temper about it. It seemed to me that 'Six To Go' had been planted in the running order by Frank. My trouble with it was that it was a song so way outside the aesthetic, somehow. Without wanting to sound pretentious, there was always an aesthetic to try to be true to, shifting and ephemeral as sometimes things like that are. I mean, there we all were ranged about in the courtyard of Rockfield with our percussion instruments: someone with an agogo [a type of drum] and claves and maybe a vibroslap – it was all very Theme Park and the only thing missing was the bong to contemplate on."

MacGowan was additionally upset at the omission of 'Aisling', a song which was later popularly covered by Christy Moore, and the instrumental 'Squid Out Of Water'. He later said that he was depressed at his decreasing control over the contents of the band's albums, a situation which became "unbearable" with *Hell's Ditch*.

He contended: "I was writing good songs and they were getting left off and writing mediocre tripe and it was getting put on."

In *A Drink With. . .* he added: "All I wanted off Frank was to be able to run the group the way I wanted it, musically. . . artistically. Which Jem had always left up to me as well."

"Rubbish!" reports Finer. "I'd never left anything up to anyone completely!"

Naturally, problems arose over the cover art. Marcia Farquhar had made a popular suggestion that the Hell's Ditch of the title could be represented as a jump at a racecourse. However, it had already been agreed that Joe Strummer's artist friend and collaborator Josh Cheuse should do the artwork. He produced an illustrated map, rather like an old pirate's treasure map.

Says James: "Josh had been around for such a while that he seemed part of the fabric, in spite of the fact that Marcia had always been a colour with which we were all dyed, if I'm not being too fanciful. Hers was a great idea, but we were too cowardly, I think, to dump Josh."

Frank Murray felt that the sleeve looked very "indie", and reveals that Warners found it difficult to market.

He adds: "There were a lot of good songs on the album but, again, it was like The Pogues were almost running away from their past stuff. I thought there was still a lot of challenges left in Irish music."

"*Hell's Ditch* is a flawed masterpiece," announces Spider. "If Shane had been in a little bit better health, it would've been a much, much stronger record."

And MacGowan considers: "Joe did a great production, but I don't think he had much to do with the final mix. It wasn't me either. It could've been a better album, yeah, but they all could have been better albums. We weren't after perfection."

The Pogues began a major British tour at the end of September 1990 to coincide with the release of *Hell's Ditch*.

'Summer In Siam' had been released as a single a couple of weeks earlier. Backed with 'Bastard Landlord' and with 'Hell's Ditch (Instrumental)' and 'The Irish Rover' additional across the formats, it was unlucky not to climb higher than Number 64 in the chart: it remains one of The Pogues' most admired songs.

The single was attended by a video which the band would be happy to disown, shot by punk film-maker Don Letts, now an award-winning director. He was a highly respected figure. "That didn't mean he was any good," snaps Jem. "I could be quite horrible about Don Letts. I thought it was a sort of stereotype that was being portrayed as someone's vision of Thailand."

The video was set in a sleazy sex club, with the band playing on stage as an alternative entertainment to the naked women on swings and so on.

"That was quite insulting to the integrity of the band, to the people of Thailand and the viewers of videos on television," continues Finer, who realised Letts's intentions the minute he walked into the film studio and saw the set. "It was a *fait accompli*. The whole thing was a depressing experience. I remember not looking forward to seeing the video and then seeing it and my worst fears being confirmed. It's a shame, cos it was a really brilliant record."

Darryl Hunt agrees: "I think Andrew felt that it was a lot of gratuitous shit as well. There wasn't much subtlety to it. It looked like a Bacardi ad or something. Perhaps Don Letts was going through a dodgy part of his career. When everything's going really well, you always meet the people who are hot, like an alignment in the stars. Positive energy attracts positive energy. It was getting harder. We felt by then that things were sliding a bit."

The tour dates opened with two shows in Cambridge and three in Glasgow Barrowlands, where *NME*'s Barbara Ellen caught up with the band, both to review and interview them. Whatever was going on behind the scenes, The Pogues were still packing a jubilant punch in the concert halls with an unflagging 24-song set including half-a-dozen from *Hell's Ditch*.

Ellen reported pandemonium and teary emotion in the audience and excitable scenes on stage with Philip Chevron "running around like he's got a helicopter trapped in his trousers". She added: "At one point I swear I saw his bow-tie rotating." As an added attraction, the great blues–rock singer Frankie Miller joined the band for 'Honky Tonk Women', all wrapped up in an overcoat and scarf.

The Pogues, Ellen declared, were "the drinking woman's crumpet", and she paid one of the most memorable compliments to Shane in the band's entire history: "MacGowan might resemble a testicle with teeth but *listen* to the man, *look* at the way he smiles when Frankie Miller waltzes on... He's like an intelligent footballer – unique, *beautiful*."

However, Ellen hadn't travelled to Scotland simply to gaze upon a beautiful testicle. She'd come to ask the band about the rumours that surrounded them, and about the tone of recent press coverage which had speculated, none too diplomatically, that MacGowan was not long for this world.

"I'm tired of reading about my imminent death, know what I mean?" retorted MacGowan, who had, in truth, been warned at some point during 1990 that his life was in danger, and on doctor's orders, had taken time out and stopped drinking for several weeks.

Ellen pressed on, asking MacGowan if he had ever considered leaving the band. "Ha! I'll leave any fucking time they want!" joshed the singer, deflecting the real question. She further enquired about his reputation for missing or ruining gigs and the "disunity" that this had created. Spider jumped in: "Things did get a bit shaky but it would completely unfair to blame Shane entirely. There's an element of truth in it. He kind of wandered off for a bit...but it's far from the whole story. Things have been said recently about The Pogues growing apart – not just by Shane, by various people – but it has to be borne in mind that it's all heat-of-the-moment stuff. This tour is the acid test. It's early days yet but it's great so far."

Darryl Hunt enjoyed the tour but acknowledges the underlying tension: "It was a bit like, 'Are we going to get through another year?' We were getting a bit worried then. Lots of things...the state of Shane, how long he could carry on. I was very aware of Shane's frustrations, but a lot of the time we didn't know what those frustrations were. They'd manifest themselves in him getting harder to work with.

"I think we felt we could've spent a lot more time at home writing and recording and developing other aspects of the group. Instead we were going to Norway to play a small club in Oslo. There was a bit too much agenting going on. People were making money out of the group. I just felt we were missing a lot of opportunities to develop – writing for films, getting into other things."

Andrew Ranken says of the tour: "Shane was more and more off in his own world. It all became increasingly strained. I think we all developed strategies for coping with it as best we could. We had to be prepared for the worst, really, and if things went okay, well, that was a bonus, but we couldn't expect that to be the norm.

"As well as the musical side, there was the whole business of getting from A to B. It always increases the tension if you're hanging around for somebody and you don't know whether they're going to show up or whatever. Myself and probably everybody retreated into their shells to some extent."

Ranken believes that some of MacGowan's dissatisfaction came from the expectations placed upon him as a frontman: "Shane is quite a contradictory person. He quite likes being in the limelight some of the time, but other times it's the last thing he wants. And I think being a frontman is a very difficult job. Unfortunately for Shane, with his appearance and the way he comes across, it's obvious people are going to focus on him, and people in the business exploited that to some degree. I mean, he tried doing all sorts of things like playing other instruments on stage, but he was always first and foremost the lead singer in the band. There wasn't really any way round that. Although other people did sing some of the time, he was obviously the main man and I think it's fair to say that's the way the fans perceived it and wanted it as well."

Contrary as ever, when asked if he became fed up with always being the focus of attention, MacGowan stares and says simply, "No."

The tour carried on around the British Isles, taking in a headline at

Wembley Arena before continuing to Europe and finally returning for a trio of gigs at Brixton Academy on December 7, Dublin Olympia (9) and Camden Electric Ballroom (10).

By now, they were including the 1935 Cole Porter standard 'Miss Otis Regrets' that they had recorded with Kirsty MacColl for the AIDS benefit compilation album *Red Hot + Blue* and which they had also released as a fund-raising single. Kirsty was on hand to sing her part live on both that and 'Fairytale Of New York'.

Hell's Ditch, meanwhile, charted at Number 12.

"I always knew Shane was going to leave the band," says Frank Murray. "Always knew. Just his behaviour for a start. I want to say this in the kindest possible way – he didn't have the balls to tell the band he didn't want to stay, because he felt responsible: 'If I leave, these guys are fucked.' Not in a big-headed way. By the same token, Shane didn't do very well after he left the band either. They both needed each other. Shane needed The Pogues and The Pogues needed Shane."

MacGowan seems to confirm Frank's theory in *A Drink With Shane MacGowan*, stating that "it was more out of a sense of responsibility that I kept on doing it". Since the band had started together, he felt duty-bound to see things through, one way or the other, with his colleagues, even though he was desperately tired of touring. The result was that he often felt angry going on stage night after night – in which case it would be a great show. If, on the other hand, he felt self-pitying or miserable, then he would "drink myself stupid" and consequently screw up his performance. Even more extreme, he claims that there came a point, at gigs, that "the music had gotten so far away from what I wanted to do that all I was interested in was fucking them up".

It's been widely suggested that MacGowan was actually asking to be sacked without having to say so; without having to be the one to upset the applecart. Yet in *A Drink With...* he insists that he saw a possible way forward.

"I thought everything would be all right if we could get rid of Frank..."

Murray had quite correctly predicted Shane's eventual departure from the group, but what he had not foreseen was his own. In the early spring of 1991, The Pogues attended a meeting at their manager's office in West Hampstead Mews at which they informed him that they no longer required his services.

They'd been aware of a clause in their management contract which stated that if they were without a record company, or without any recording obligations to a record company, for a specified number of months, they could cease their relationship with Murray's company, Hill 16. That situation was about to arise, because they had fulfilled all of their obligations to Warners with the delivery of *Hell's Ditch*, and the allotted time had nearly elapsed without any new developments relating to their record deal.

For Murray, it was just another regular meeting at which he intended to tell the band what he was organising for them in the months ahead.

He remembers: "They came along and there was Shane and Spider, Darryl, Jem and Andrew and Philip. James and Terry weren't there. [They were at home in LA and Ireland respectively.] Here's what I had lined up for them. I had The Chieftains' shows at Brixton Academy. And I [they] also was going to do a single, 'The Battle Of New Orleans', with Lonnie Donegan. And a WOMAD gig in Yokohama. And I was discussing the first Lollapalooza tour in America for the summer. I was in the middle of negotiating a new record contract, Warner Brothers against EMI. That was just a brief outline. I pointed all this out. Then Jem kind of looked at me and said, 'We don't want you to be the manager any more.'

"My management contract was going to run out in May, so I thought we would've renegotiated it. Of course I was shocked. I was stunned for a few seconds. I think I said, 'Why?' 'We just want to do it ourselves.' Spider went to say something like, 'Hey, guys, I think we should think about this,' and about three of them looked at him as much as to say, 'Spider, shut up.' And that was it."

"Frank said, 'I didn't see it coming,'" recalls Philip. "He burst into tears. There was a big, awkward silence in the room. Nobody wanted to see him as upset as he was."

Spider confirms: "I felt sorry for Frank because he was part of the family, I guess. I really liked him as a person, and I suppose I felt it was something that was so abrupt and final and quite horrible. But it had to be done. Everybody else was just so pissed off with him, and I certainly wasn't going to go against them.

"If I remember it rightly, we arrived at the office and after the initial pleasantries Frank said something about a new contract, and Jem said, 'Well, we don't want to sign it.' Afterwards, when the rest of the band were leaving, I said, 'I'm going to hang around,' and I stayed at the office with Frank and Joey."

Joey Cashman says: "When they fired Frank, I was in another room and he came in and he said, 'You won't believe what they've just done.' I had a good idea, cos I'd fucking warned him, although the band hadn't told me about it exactly, cos I was his partner. Frank said, 'I think they're going to ask you to step in and as far as I'm concerned, you'd be mad not to,' which was pretty magnanimous."

Cashman did indeed take over the reins of management, although he too would be fired a couple of years down the line.

Shane MacGowan says today: "I didn't feel good about sacking Frank. Unfortunately, it was a democracy."

Jem takes issue with this pronouncement, stating that the decision had been unanimous. He adds: "It's never nice to tell someone something they don't want to hear and something that was going to cause all kinds of ructions. We'd all spent a lot of time together. It wasn't just like saying, 'Cheerio' to someone. It was bound up in all kinds of history and legal shit as well, and financial implications.

"I was elected to be the person that told Frank. He wanted to talk about what we were going to do for the next year, but before we did that, we had to tell him we didn't want to make plans for the next year with him. He was very shocked. He asked everyone individually if that's what they wanted to do, and everyone said yes, but it wasn't easy for people to say that."

Philip: "We sacked Frank because he had stopped listening to us when we told him about what we wanted to do. We didn't want to tour the way we had been touring. He comes from this rock'n'roll thing, all lads together out on the road. We were people with kids and wives and girlfriends and other lives. We didn't want to be the bride of rock'n'roll, but he was still pursuing it. He kept saying, 'Just give me one more year, let me take you to Madison Square Garden, then you can relax.' At every stage it was the same – "*Then* you can relax, *then* we can talk about it.' The carrot started being dangled further and further away.

"And then there was the great emotional blackmail – 'If you stop touring you'll stop selling records. You just need to do one more tour, one more tour...' and we realised when we split up that our records didn't stop selling. That's when I got really angry. We were on this constant rollercoaster and the only way of stopping it was to throw Frank off.

"We didn't always go into battle with him over issues that nevertheless were quite important to us, so there were all these underlying resentments about things we didn't challenge because it was too much effort. You've gone Frank's way without him realising you resented it. It was corrosive to the point where you think, 'I'm not in control of this, somebody else is, and I've allowed them to be in control because I didn't want to be shouted out.'

"Then there were things that Frank bullied through, album titles, artwork or whatever, and there was the old 'divide and rule' thing which created a culture of suspicion. Frank did have his bullying tendencies, which was one of the things that led to his departure from the band. There were times when I felt very intimidated by him. It reached a point where I couldn't stand to be in the same room as Frank alone. He would get edgy and start whistling.

"It wasn't an easy job managing The Pogues, and there were elements of it that were way beyond the call of duty with Shane, which Frank strove manfully to deal with. He'd say The Pogues wouldn't be what they are without Frank Murray and to some extent he's entitled to say that. But ultimately, we weren't prepared to put ourselves sufficiently in his hands. If it just came down to one problem that was it. The fact that he could never quite accept it – that was why he had to go in the end.

"I'm on very good terms with Frank these days, but that's mainly because I don't work with him. Having said all that, it was delightful to meet him at Christmas [2004] and give him a hug and say, 'Nice to see you,' and mean it."

Some of The Pogues have complained that while Murray was a hands-on, rock'n'roll manager, there was nobody left to mind the shop while he was off on tour with the band. They felt that the business side of things could have been organised more efficiently, and they had also come to regret the percentages they had agreed with Frank.

"We're partly to blame for whatever money Frank got that made us feel uncomfortable as time went on," says James. "Terry was very conflicted cos Terry and Frank had been firm friends for a long, long time. I remember Anthony Addis, our accountant, saying something like, 'You can't live beyond your means.' And Terry said, 'I don't have any means to live beyond.'

"I remember being at a hotel in Annecy [France] and something had been going on between Frank and Terry. I remember Terry walking over to the window and he just ran his fingers down the woodwork and he said, 'Oh, Frank, why have you forsaken me?' It was like a trough in a relationship that had been quite a solid one."

Murray comments: "The thing is, Terry never called me afterwards. Nobody called me or spoke to me. Everything that went on about that hurt me enormously. Enormously. I'd been associated with everything that they'd done. I did a lot for that band, simply because they weren't interested. When I was working years ago with Thin Lizzy, Phil [Lynott] would always be on the phone – 'What about this? What about that?' The Pogues weren't like that."

Terry Woods' years-long friendship with the man who had given him a job in The Pogues had been compromised for some while by the band's growing antipathy towards Murray. "Frank was a bit like the rest of us," comments Woods. "He got into the enjoyment of it all. It would have been better if he'd had a business partner so they could have made some decisions that would have been beneficial both to him and the band.

"I was caught in a very strange position. I was in the band but I was always Frank's friend. I found it very hard to deal with. The Pogues worked very, very hard but we weren't receiving the type of recompense we should have been. I was struggling financially, and I had a young family. We may have got accolades musically, and we may have been feted in fucking China or whatever, but putting bread on the table was the reality. It caused an awful lot of stress in my life. I got a telephone call from Marian once when I was in Paris saying, 'The bank won't give me any more money. You're going to have to get me some money and come home.' In the middle of a tour I had to get some money off Joey Cashman and fly home and give it to Marian.

"The sad thing was, it was Frank's vision that had developed the band to where it went. If he'd only had the vision to involve himself with a businessman who could come in and partner him. I wasn't the only one feeling like this."

Woods was uncomfortably aware of the mood in the band and could see the writing on the wall for Murray. "I'd tried to warn Frank on various occasions that he needed to look at his role in the whole situation, but by the time he tried to act upon it, it was too late. I felt very torn. Frank had a go at me after the meeting for not being there, but I didn't even hear about it until a couple of days afterwards. By that time Frank had reached fever pitch in his anger. What was I going to say to him if I did ring him? 'I told you so'? I couldn't have changed anything. The only thing I could have done would be to say, 'If Frank is going, I'm leaving.' I was in an impossible position. But I would still regard myself as being very close to Frank."

It wasn't a clean break with Murray, according to Jem. "Things became quite difficult for a while," he explains. "He actually refused to believe he wasn't the manager and he kept carrying on as if he was for a bit. I don't think he thought what we were doing was legal. We had to ask our lawyer to sort it out, basically. It went on for a few weeks."

Rather than enter into protracted legal proceedings, The Pogues' lawyer worked out a severance deal with Murray.

Later that year, in the autumn, the band released a compilation album, *The Best Of The Pogues*.

Murray: "For some reason, they took my name off everything. They wouldn't say thank you to Frank Murray, even though I was involved in every one of the things. It was done on purpose. They thanked everybody. They probably thanked the dogs on the street. That was really, really mean-spirited and it really hurt me as well. I didn't see why it should have to come to that. My daughter had just been paralysed in a diving accident. I was trying to deal with that thing at the same time. It shattered me for a long, long time."

"Took his name off what?" wonders Jem. "I don't know what he means by that. Also, we did a benefit for his daughter at the Electric Ballroom. We were incredibly sympathetic."

The Pogues played a disastrous gig at the Fleadh Festival – an annual gathering of Irish and Irish-influenced musicians - at London's Finsbury Park on June 2, 1991.

Zane and Dave Jennings, reviewing it for *Melody Maker*, noted of Shane: "He doesn't *actually* fall over. But he does sound severely slurred, lurches around with a drink in each hand and mis-times things to a comical degree... he's in a world of his own and his voice is a barely audible whine. Here only in spirit, you might say." Zane and Jennings left the festival with "a sense of genuine, heartfelt disgust".

By contrast, six weeks later, appearing with The Chieftains at Brixton Academy, MacGowan was on marvellous form. Sadly, this had become a rare thing.

Says Andrew Ranken: "It had been getting progressively worse with Shane. We just couldn't rely on him at all. He was often so out of it that if he got round to singing the songs at all, he was usually singing the wrong song, and the wrong words to the wrong song as well. There were at least a couple of occasions where he just about made it through the first couple of songs and then left the stage and disappeared.

"We'd had to evolve a means of coping with it, and so for quite a while Spider had been covering for him on vocals, and myself and Darryl were doing bits as well. A lot of the time, the audience didn't realise that Shane wasn't actually singing. As long as they could see him up there, they presumed that that was where the voice was coming from.

"It had got really difficult getting him on to planes and stuff like that. Shane had had problems with Frank for quite a while, so I think we did hope that once Frank had gone, that would ease the pressure a lot for Shane, but unfortunately it didn't seem to make much difference. He was in pretty bad shape, really, and unhappy. He didn't want to be doing it. He needed the break and he wasn't getting it. I imagine he felt nobody was listening to him or taking him seriously. The only way he could get out was to go so far off the rails he couldn't get back on them."

MacGowan's derailment finally happened in Japan in September.

"'Sacked' is a very brutal word," says Jem. "If one's honest, then he was sacked. It got to a point where we all felt we couldn't stand the situation of trying to go on tour with Shane or work with him at all. We had about nine months or a year's touring booked ahead, and it just seemed like it was going to be impossible. He was taking all sorts of stuff, and it wasn't making him happy. It was making him incapable of functioning as a human being in any way. He was beyond anyone's help.

"We had two weeks in Japan, and we only did four concerts. Two of them Shane didn't make. One of his missed gigs came from falling out of the van [some say it was a taxi] and landing on his head."

The band members realised they had two options. One was to split the group, which no one wanted to do and, besides, there would have been endless complications over their contractual commitments. The other was to dismiss MacGowan, not only for the band's benefit but for the good of his own health. They held a meeting in a hotel room, and Darryl Hunt was elected to suggest to Shane that he might prefer not to be in The Pogues any more.

"For once, I didn't have to do it," says Jem. "I said it was something I just couldn't do. A large part of me just wanted to stop the whole thing. I was very torn. We'd been through a lot together, and it was a horrible conclusion."

Spider was extremely distraught, having been a close friend of Shane from the outset. He remembers: "It was really, really tough on everybody. It was far, far worse than Frank. Getting Darryl to tell Shane was an act of collective cowardice, and I'm fully including myself in this. I think it was felt that Darryl would be the most diplomatic."

MacGowan reacted with dignity.

Darryl: "It was an awful thing to have to say to somebody you respect so much. I've always had a very high regard for Shane, and it was a great disappointment to us all. He said, 'What took you so long?' Which I suppose was him saying he wasn't angry about it. I genuinely think he didn't want to let us down, which is why he hung in there longer than he should've done, even though he was making it worse for himself."

"I remember him saying, 'You've been very patient,'" adds Jem. "I thought that was a measured response from someone who had some comprehension of something, a passive acceptance, maybe even relief. Maybe he was admitting he'd been pushing things and finally we'd twigged."

Asked if MacGowan could have been deliberately putting himself in a position where the band had to fire him, Finer responds: "If that's the case then he did his job very well. It might have been easier for everyone then if he'd just said, 'I'm leaving,' and left. I imagine he felt a responsibility that he couldn't do that, and if that's true, then I'm very sorry that he was made to feel that way. I'm not holding any grudges against him. I'm just sorry that it all turned out that way, for whatever reasons."

According to Spider, there was some suggestion at the time that MacGowan might be able to continue as a creative, non-touring member of

The Pogues. He says: "It was originally put that it would be a Brian Wilson situation where he would write and we would tour. At the same time, I think everyone knew it would never work out like that. It would be inevitable that we'd go our separate ways."

The weekly music papers revealed the news on September 21, 1991. The lead story in *Melody Maker* announced: "Pogues frontman Shane MacGowan has left the band – and he's being replaced for the rest of their world tour by Joe Strummer."

CHAPTER 27

'I Am Going, I Am Going...'

"I was relieved," says MacGowan, looking back at his dismissal. "They let me off the hook. I'd been trying to leave the group for three years. There was too much touring for everybody. It wasn't fun any more. Going to places was fun, being in Japan was fun, but America was unbearable. I mean, the US of A - what is there to like about it? I see them committing fucking genocide and being a royal pain in the arse. I like hanging around New York for a few days and going out to play gigs. I like Mexico and all that, hanging out.

"But I wasn't prepared to do endless touring and because of all sorts of bloody reasons, mainly to do with the business, we were getting stiffed right, left and centre once they smelt blood. I kept doing it for a bit longer, a bit longer, a bit longer. It didn't feel like I was leaving the group that I'd joined several years before."

The band were equally relieved. They were finally free of the dread that came with the two possible outcomes of every working day: that Shane wouldn't turn up, and that Shane would turn up. At the same time, they faced a future without one of the most gifted and revered songwriters in the country, a singer whose inimitable vocals, unique charisma and dental originality had become synonymous with the name of The Pogues.

Terry Woods has come to believe that the group, given the right information, could have dealt with the situation before it got out of hand. He says: "What none of us realised was that we were doing well enough to take time out. We could've made sure there was money in the bank and given Shane a bit of time to recover. We didn't know we could afford to do that. It would have done every one of us the world of good. So poor Shane – it was like travelling the world with a cardboard cut-out. The best thing for us all would have been to stop for a month or two, gather our breath and then decide what to do next."

Philip Chevron agrees: "If people had realised we were disintegrating and taken it seriously, we would've just taken some time off. Shane wouldn't have had to leave. The rest of us were always trying to find some way of accommodating everybody else, trying not to add to their misery. Shane didn't have that inbuilt mechanism that stopped him infringing on other people's lives, so he became very obviously the person who was disintegrating – 'They're going to push me to the edge, I'm going to go to the edge.'

"As far as he was concerned, he was being driven there anyway and he might as well do it on his own terms. He took all the drugs, he drank all the drink. He did it in the fashion of all these suicidal poets he worshipped that were always looking into the abyss. He was never, ever going to avoid looking into the abyss, because he was one of them. He was Shane MacGowan: 'Only on my terms.'"

Philip had been carrying around a mental snapshot of something that had happened in France in 1986 and was, he'd been sure, a portent of disaster. He reveals: "In France, Shane was regarded as some sort of cultural icon. The media were besotted with this drinking poet from Ireland. They thought they had the new James Joyce on their hands. On this occasion, Shane had collapsed after a gig and he was carried on to the bus by two of the roadies and followed by 20 members of the French fucking press with cameras and notebooks. At that moment, this overwhelming feeling, really bad, really negative, came over me: 'This isn't the way it's meant to be and it can't end well. This is not what I want happening to my friend.' Somehow it was all in this one image. It became an over-riding thing at the back of my mind, always, that Shane was never going to be able to cope with it. He was always going to have to be somebody's performing fucking seal."

James Fearnley alone had wanted to keep MacGowan in the band, and only then because of an ingrained protestant work ethic. He admits: "It seemed to be a bit wussy at the time that we should sack him. We'd dragged him round the world with us so far. Why couldn't we drag him round a bit more? That's the way I felt about it all. It was so selfish on my part to want to keep him on. To be truthfully cruel to myself, I was channelling my dad – 'You don't give up, you just do it and I don't care what condition you're in, you've got a responsibility,' and all that kind of crap. When you let somebody go, it seems so final. It's scary. You're on your own, you don't really have a songwriter and you've got no singer."

The Pogues considered their new dilemma. Who could possibly step into the shoes of Shane MacGowan?

Joe Strummer, as usual, was delighted to come to the rescue, accepting the position of lead singer and guitarist temporarily. The Pogues would now be able to go ahead with the American tour which was scheduled to start towards the end of September, followed by dates in Europe, the UK and Ireland and, in 1992, Australia.

Strummer was an inspired choice. As Andrew remarks, "It went a long way to satisfying people who were disappointed that Shane wasn't there because we could say, 'Well, all right, we haven't got Shane but look who we *have* got.' And it worked really well. Joe was a fan. We had a lot of good times with him. It was very enjoyable."

Their first outing was nevertheless tinged with sadness. Flying out for the opening US tour dates at New York's Beacon Theatre on September 26 and 27, the band were without their long-time lighting man, Paul Verner, who had just died.

Jem: "Paul drank a lot and he got very ill, so he gave up drinking, which was a struggle. And then one Christmas he went and had a couple of drinks and he started drinking again. I think there came a point where he couldn't really cope with what he was doing, and I think Frank and us decided it was better if he stopped doing the lights until he got better. He got cirrhosis of the liver and went yellow, the colour of mustard, and died in hospital."

The entourage included a new member, Andrew Ranken's six-month-old son Daniel. After suffering the heartbreak of two ectopic pregnancies, Andrew's partner Deborah Korner tragically died two weeks after giving birth to Daniel, in April 1991. A shocked Andrew suddenly became a single parent.

Andrew and Deborah had not expected to conceive in the first place: the ectopic pregnancies had made this highly unlikely.

"We did, miraculously, manage to have a child against all the odds," explains Andrew. "It was a complete fluke. They hadn't quite sewn up one of the tubes properly so this sort of commando sperm managed to find its way through and it all happened naturally. However, two weeks later, she died. She had an aneurism. Probably the stress and the strain exacerbated it. She must have always been susceptible to it but we never knew. So that was really out of the blue."

The Pogues, for all their troubles, seemed like a good place to be. "I was very keen to work as much as possible because it was a good distraction," says Andrew. "It was actually really helpful and very therapeutic. I was on my own looking after Daniel, but I had a lot of help. I employed a couple of people as nannies and he came on the road with me. I did miss the odd gig here and there that I just couldn't do for one reason or another but, generally speaking, I carried on doing the tours and Daniel came too. I thought it was rather lovely having this baby on board."

Andrew appointed his first nanny in time for The Pogues' American tour with Strummer. He says: "I had this woman called Frances who we knew from way back because she used to do catering for bands, and she'd done catering for us on some tours, and she was also the mother of Joe Strummer's [first] wife Gabby."

The tour moved from New York to Boston, Toronto, Chicago, Vancouver and San Francisco, where *Melody Maker* caught up with the band. At this stage, they were publicly insisting that there was every chance of MacGowan returning to the line-up. He was still a member of the group, he was simply having a rest and when he had recovered his health, he would be welcome to come back. Strummer said he was "keeping the seat hot" for Shane.

Meanwhile, MacGowan was back in London with a partially paralysed hand caused, reportedly, by a trapped nerve, telling everyone who would listen that he'd been sacked by The Pogues and was "glad to be out of it". He considered Strummer a "great choice" as his replacement, and had chatted to Spider and Jem on the phone about how the tour was going.

How it was going was very well. The Pogues' regular followers were joined by a contingent of Clash fans and they came together with frantic enthusiasm for a set that incorporated three of Strummer's most popular live songs, The Clash's 'London Calling' and 'Complete Control', and 'I Fought The Law', the 1966 US hit by The Bobby Fuller Four originally recorded by The Crickets which The Clash covered. The band also included 'Straight To Hell' and 'Brand New Cadillac', which both The Pogues and, more famously, The Clash, had played frequently in concert.

Darryl remembers: "We did a really good, wigged-out version of 'Straight To Hell' with Joe. He'd go into raps for about ten minutes. He'd dub it up."

"We actually did something new with it and brought it to a new place," adds Philip.

Darryl continues: "Joe absolutely loved the band, and he really enjoyed doing it, although it was quite hard in a way to go on and sing Shane's songs."

There were some – 'A Pair Of Brown Eyes', 'A Rainy Night In Soho' and, of course, 'Fairytale Of New York' – that were too obviously associated with MacGowan for Strummer even to think of attempting, but The Pogues' repertoire was comprehensively represented by favourites such as 'Dirty Old Town', 'Turkish Song Of The Damned', 'Fiesta', 'Thousands Are Sailing', 'Body Of An American', 'Metropolis', 'Yeah Yeah Yeah Yeah Yeah' and 'Johnny Come Lately'. Alongside these reassuring old friends, the newer additions from *Hell's Ditch* – 'Sayonara', 'The Sunnyside Of The Street' and 'Rain Street' – sounded perfectly compatible; worthy of their place in the set. It was a show that really did seem to please everyone. By the time the group had played two nights at LA's Wiltern Theater, the audiences had become so out of control that The Pogues were banned from ever coming back.

All of the band were delighted to have Joe Strummer as their frontman, especially Spider Stacy.

"I was really, literally in the same band as Joe Strummer!" he marvels. "It was the only reason I ever wanted to be in a band in the first place, so I could be in a band with Joe Strummer – and here I was in a band with Joe Strummer. A small part of me was a little bit disappointed that I wasn't going to be the singer, but a bigger part of me was absolutely delighted, sad little thing that I am, that I was going to be in a band with Joe. It was great. It was really, really good. It had been difficult before that, really hard-going, and suddenly it wasn't. He was very easy-going. He was incredibly enthusiastic. It was just really good for the morale. Joe gave us the legs to continue."

Andrew believes that Strummer brought a new quality to The Pogues: "There were times when I thought it sounded absolutely brilliant, because he was such a tough, straight-ahead guitar player. It gave it quite a punk feel, a real edge, and it was very powerful."

Jem adds: "He was a really great person to have around. He was very sociable and always trying to make a party happen. He was a very good conversationalist. He was a very different character to Shane. He took on the role of being the frontman in a way Shane never did. Shane never had to try – he just does what he does. The world revolves around him, in a sense. Joe's from the school of frontman who takes the responsibility on himself. It was kind of interesting to have that different experience of working with a lead singer. And it was such a bloody relief after the difficulties of working with Shane, where we didn't know what was going to happen next, to get up on stage with someone who was taking that responsibility on to the maximum extent."

The Pogues, energised, carried on with a European tour and arrived in the UK and Ireland in December for a string of dates that included London's Brixton Academy on December 11 and an added show at the Town & Country Club the next night.

Home audiences proved to be as welcoming as the Europeans and Americans, although Joey Cashman identified a partisan element and acted quickly to disarm it. He says: "Joe came into a very different situation after Shane. At the Brixton show, I went out on the stage to make sure everything was okay. I looked out in the crowd and across the balcony was a banner that said, 'Have You No Shane?' I thought, 'That's smart. That's funny. It's very heavy for Joe.' I went up to the guys. I said, 'That's a brilliant poster, but you know fine that Shane isn't playing. You know Joe's singing and you know you're only going to upset him, so I'm asking you, I'm not telling you – would you mind taking it down for Joe's sake?' and they took it down."

Somewhere along the line, The Pogues' eccentric director friend Alex Cox had caught a show, and he came to a surprising conclusion. "There was this moment that I realised The Pogues wanted to be The Clash," he declares. "You saw that nobody in the band really wants to be in a London-Irish tin-whistle band. Every one of these guys wants to be in The Clash – the spirit of rock'n'roll, the spirit of revolution. We *all* wanted to be in The Clash - they really were the only band that mattered – but not Shane, because Shane was himself and he wanted to do his thing. So that was interesting."

Obviously, this raises howls of protest: "Absolute shit!" "Ridiculous!" "Moronic!" "Meaningless!" "Insulting!" Only Spider is prepared to indulge Cox's vision for a passing moment, remarking: "I do understand why he thought that. Maybe everybody in The Pogues secretly wanted to be in a band with Joe Strummer!"

He adds, more seriously: "We did 'London Calling', 'I Fought The Law', 'Straight To Hell'. . . I think Joe slotted in absolutely naturally. So even when he was singing The Pogues' songs, you'd say, 'That's The Pogues with Joe Strummer singing.' Anyway, there was a whole lot more of us than there was of them [The Clash]."

For Christmas, the band members received a Harrods hamper from Warners. It had been a while since their last one. During 1991, their record releases had enjoyed varying degrees of success. A reissued 'Poguetry In Motion', featuring a Steve Lillywhite remix of 'A Rainy Night In Soho', had scraped a Number 67 placing in September. The compilation, *The Best Of The Pogues*, issued in the same month, returned the band to the albums chart at Number 11, and 'Fairytale Of New York' was re-released for Christmas with 'Fiesta' as its B-side and 'A Pair Of Brown Eyes', 'The Sickbed Of Cuchulainn' and 'Maggie May' added across the formats. It registered at Number 36.

Says Philip: "We got the Harrods hamper the first time we did a good job for them. We got that in 1987 and 1988. In 1989 we got the magnum of champagne. It starts to taper off. I remember one year we got this trinket from Tiffany's. I said, 'That's it, we're fucked.' They don't realise you're aware of the pecking order. They, unwittingly, are giving you signals. There's always some fucker telling you you're no longer the bee's knees. That's showbusiness."

Somewhere towards the end of the year, Frank Murray bumped into Shane MacGowan. They had both turned out to see Dr John at the Jazz Café in Camden.

Says Murray: "We were having a drink and Shane said to me, 'I thought when you went, Frank, we'd stop touring, but they're playing more fucking gigs than ever.'"

The Pogues were back out on the road in March 1992 for a tour of Japan that had recently been added to the schedule. The band had dared to hope that Strummer would stay on permanently: they'd discussed it with him and he'd seemed keen. But even though they continued to enjoy a good relationship with Joe, and even though he was still excited by the chance to explore new musical directions with the group's varied instrumentation, he was finding it difficult to settle into his role. And there was an element in The Pogues' following who were finding it difficult to accept Strummer in MacGowan's place.

"He was a very different frontman to Shane," explains Philip. "That was appropriate to the way the band had developed. It was a very interesting time, but it was experimental. We wondered whether it might work in the long term. But the one person who kept appearing onstage was the ghost of Shane, and it was never going to stop getting in the way, however brilliant it was with Joe. It was like Banquo's ghost, and that dispirited Joe and us, cos we realised we weren't going to be able to move on with him, unfortunately."

"There was talk of him joining, but I think he felt a bit awkward, usurping," suggests Darryl. "He felt it would be a bit cheeky. He had this sense of unease about him. It's funny, cos he always said to us, 'You've gotta think of Shane like Brian Wilson... he's out there... he's taking a sabbatical.'

"Joe had no problems getting on with everybody although he was quite solitary sometimes. He liked his own little space. Often we'd start off together in the same dressing room and then he'd construct his own space or get his little dressing room where he could be by himself. As the tour progressed, he seemed to withdraw more into his own space. I think it got him through it. I think he just needed to get away from everything. He probably felt the pressure and responsibility. He had to be Shane, in a way. Just as it would have been hard for Shane to be Joe, I think Joe felt that it was great to be doing it but a bit uncomfortable as well."

Jem: "We were going to go to Australia after Japan, and at that point, Joe decided he wanted to stop working with The Pogues and go back to whatever he wanted to do as himself. He said, 'Okay, I'll do Japan,' so we scrapped Australia and that was the end of that phase. I was kind of sad, cos there'd been a plan to start writing and make a record. It would have been interesting, but I respected his wishes."

"How unbelievable it would have been had it run its full course!" sighs James. "I suppose we expected us all to make a record, and he would sign a contract and he would get out of his responsibilities with CBS. Joe sounded kind of positive about it – 'Yeah, yeah, that's a really great idea, man.' It was all too good to be true. I think he was playing for time to see how he felt, leaving his options open, not burning bridges. We genuinely liked each other. I think he had to have a think away from the tour buses."

Darryl feels that there was an element of unfinished business about the Strummer era. "I was sad that we couldn't have continued a bit and done a record together," he admits. "It would have been a legacy to leave behind of that period."

Terry Woods says: "Joe was great. He was a real centre forward and I loved that about him. But The Pogues with Joe was a different animal, and we'd have had to become a further different animal for it all to work. We all would have had to change somewhere. In retrospect, for him, it was probably the right decision, but it was disappointing because it was back to the drawing board."

The Pogues had been putting their house in order. After splitting with Frank Murray, they had retained the services of their accountant Anthony Addis. And it was Addis, with a lawyer, who negotiated The Pogues' next recording contract with Warners. They had also taken on Joey Cashman as their manager, although they were not expecting him to assume all of Murray's previous responsibilities.

"We said, 'What we want is somebody who does the day-to-day work,'" states Philip. "We didn't want any grand ideas. Essentially, it was an administrative job, and all the main decisions we took ourselves because we weren't going to make the same mistake twice. Increasingly, we made decisions with Anthony Addis. I suppose Joey enjoyed the idea of being manager. He did what he was supposed to do and he did it quite well."

"It was fine," says Jem. "We basically said to Joey how we wanted to work, what we wanted to do and when, and he organised things. Joey knew the ropes."

"I came in to change strings," says Joey, "and at one time I was stage manager, production manager, T-shirt designer, stage designer and piss artist. I was really eager to work. Once I start something, I get really speedy and I want to do it."

"After a while he realised he was being severely underpaid for it," continues Philip, "but it wasn't something we could remedy because we'd made it clear it was going to be on a wage basis and, secondly, we didn't know how it was going to work out. Eventually, I suppose, he got a bit disaffected. We'd laid out the terms of how we were going to do this and he either accepted them or not, but they weren't going to suddenly change. Joey at various points got raises and so forth."

The band had also formed a company, Pogue Mahone Ltd, and they had started tightening their spending. There was to be no further abuse of expenses.

Philip: "There was a time where Charlie MacLennan considered it fine just to pick up parking tickets. If he needed to stop somewhere, he'd inevitably get a ticket. He'd put it down to expenses, because he wasn't going to spend an hour travelling round London looking for a parking space. Which is okay until you find Camden Council is taking The Pogues to court for unpaid fines totalling £5,000. These are expenses we didn't even know about until after the fact. Restaurants had a tab. Everything was expense account. Everything was being paid for by The Pogues."

The group were also anxious to budget properly for tours, and to turn down work that was unlikely to produce any financial return.

The Pogues were unhappy about the idea of bringing in an outsider, and so they decided that Spider would become their full-time vocalist. He'd stood in for Shane on many previous occasions, most memorably during the Bob Dylan dates, he was popular with the audiences, he knew the material inside out, and his earthy, English, punky singing style would hopefully bring a new and different quality to the band.

Says Spider: "I was really nervous about it but also I was drinking a lot, so a drunk arrogance swaggered into town."

He would be the first person to admit that he wasn't really in the best condition to take up the frontman's role in The Pogues. "Generally I was too messed up at that time," he confesses. "Everything was kind of like slipping through my fingers. The times when I wasn't actually drinking too much, I was fine, but you really can't be drinking like that and singing at the same time. It was difficult to maintain focus."

"Spider was getting himself into a bad state at the time and we did realise that," confirms Andrew. "We tried to impress on him that he needed to take it seriously and do it properly and try to sort himself out, but it was beyond that."

The Pogues had already been through this all before with MacGowan. "Well, nothing compares to that, really," muses Ranken. "But it was pretty depressing just watching another person falling apart. Having said that, Spider actually managed to keep things together remarkably well most of the time, but the cracks were beginning to show and they were getting wider all the time. Spider made a huge effort. I just don't think he was fully up to the job. He carried on, but his singing was getting worse and he was just destroying himself, pretty much."

James Fearnley remembers thinking that Spider was "losing it a bit" at the time of the *Hell's Ditch* recordings at Rockfield. And then, says James, "We replaced one singer [MacGowan] with another one who couldn't sing as well and didn't write as many songs as the last one did and was as much of a fuck-up as the original one had become. It was out of the frying pan and into the blazing furnace. I hoped that Spider was up to the job."

"Much as I love Spider," says Terry Woods, "he didn't have the vocals to hold The Pogues together. He was always struggling. I couldn't have held The Pogues together either."

They were still determined to keep the band intact. For one thing, their record company advance had already been swallowed up by debts incurred previously, and they obviously had no wish to be asked to pay it back. For another, they felt that as musicians, they still had untapped potential. Finally, no one at that point wanted to face the uncertainty of life without the group.

"You have a kind of momentum, and you have your wage coming in, and I'm not saying that's the most important thing," continues James. "You work in a band for 11, 12 years and you think, 'That can't be it. We're all mates, we all love one another and we're so connected on a level that we don't experience with most other people. Why should we stop? Let's see what this is like. It can't be as bad as it looks.' But as much as I love Spider, at that time it was very difficult working with him."

The band went into rehearsals to work on new material, with a view to recording for a new album later in the year. Spider, Jem, Terry, Andrew and Darryl were all writing – although Philip Chevron, that most accomplished songsmith, was not. He hadn't contributed to *Hell's Ditch* either.

"I had great plans but none of them came to fruition," reveals Philip, whose alcoholism had now started to affect his health and who had started to suffer from black-outs. "I was suffering from writer's block mixed up with self-esteem issues – fear of my own work, fear of my own talent, complete mental shit. It's not possible to write songs from a position of torment, even if they're about torment. That's what's wrong with 'First Day Of Forever'."

This was a Chevron song which would later appear as a B-side, and it was the last composition of his which The Pogues would release.

"It has many good qualities," considers Philip. "But it failed dismally in communicating what it was about. I just wasn't well enough to be able to do that. The whole period of being in The Pogues coincided with a huge period in my life of low self-esteem and inability to do what I was good at, a lot of which was camouflaged in many ways by the fact I was the guitarist in a successful band. At a certain point in *Hell's Ditch*, I realised I was loving what I was doing. I loved the whole getting away from it. I loved so much being the guitarist. I was afraid to do anything that might upset that. Why fuck with something if it's working for you?"

The Pogues spent the summer of 1992, as usual, touring festivals around Europe. Such was the affection in which they were held that few critics were prepared to damn their performances. Generally, they applauded the group's persistence and courage. But the ghost of MacGowan continued to haunt the stage and the reviews.

At the Fleadh in Finsbury Park in June – a headlining show - it wasn't only the ghost of MacGowan who turned up, but Shane himself. Speculation swept the festival that he might join his old mates onstage for a song or two, but it was not to be.

Andrew Mueller, reporting for *Melody Maker*, commented: "MacGowan, the man who made it all possible, stands by and watches balefully as the band play his songs." Of The Pogues, he wrote: "And they're still precious, in their own unkempt fashion, a law unto themselves, one of rock'n'roll's happier accidents. But only a fool would argue that there isn't something missing."

Earlier in the day, one member of the audience, watching The Saw Doctors, was heard to remark: "These wankers think they're writing songs that people will sing in pubs 200 years from now, but they're not. MacGowan already has, but I don't think he realises it."

The band had not been happy with the selection on their best-of compilation, released the year before. It was always going to be an impossible task to pick out a single album's worth of songs from such an exceptional repertoire, but various members felt that it didn't really represent the cream of the crop. There was no sign of 'The Sickbed Of Cuchulainn' or 'The Old Main Drag', 'Turkish Song Of The Damned' or 'Summer In Siam'.

The Rest Of The Best, a second volume released in June 1992, gathered up many of the glaring omissions, and although it didn't enjoy the big chart showing of its predecessor, it drew a satisfying line under the MacGowan phase of the band's career. The album included 'Honky Tonk Women', a song that the lads had cranked out in a soundcheck once, with Spider singing, and thereafter played at gigs as an encore.

It was issued as a single just a few weeks before *The Rest Of The Best*, not only to draw attention to the album but to introduce the idea of Spider as the band's new vocalist. Backed with Jem's 'Curse Of Love' and accompanied by 'Infinity' and 'The Parting Glass' on the 12-inch and CD formats, it charted at Number 56.

These releases gave The Pogues a bit of breathing space, some time to plan their next move without fear of being forgotten. For the rest of the year, they were hidden away working on new material, although they did emerge in December for British dates, including a night at the Brixton Academy, and a handful of German shows just before Christmas.

There was no chance that the band would even consider trying to recreate the sound and style of their years with MacGowan. They had to move on from that and come back with a fresh personality that reflected their developing musical interests.

With this in mind, Jem Finer took the ambitious step of asking Brian Eno to produce the next album. He said no. "I thought maybe he didn't realise we were interested in seeing how we could expand into some new, unknown dimension," says Jem. "So I wrote him a letter. He was very nice. He wrote one back and said, 'Sorry, I don't mean to sound rude, but it's not something I think I could really help you with.' But what did come out of that was that a collaborator of his called Michael Brook became interested."

John Leckie – famed producer of Radiohead and The Stone Roses among others – had also expressed a willingness to be involved, but The Pogues could not afford his expertise. And so in the early part of 1993, they and Michael Brook teamed up for the album that would become *Waiting For Herb*. The recordings took place back in the basement at Elephant Studios. After the luxury of such facilities as Abbey Road and RAK, this completed rather a depressing full circle for The Pogues.

"Oh, the ignominy of returning to Elephant where everything was filthy beige and familiar and very much, sometimes, the other side of the bell curve of our career," says Fearnley, who was nevertheless thrilled that the band had decided to record 'Drunken Boat', his one and only songwriting contribution to The Pogues.

"Without the support of Jem and Darryl particularly, I wouldn't have gone on to think of myself as someone who could possibly write a song or two, which I have done since, though I'm hardly prolific. Once the stone of Shane had rolled away, I was so glad I could write a song for the group. Shane's obviously up there with the best songwriters in the world ever, and if you're playing accordion for the guy, what are you going to write a song about? I had such fun writing 'Drunken Boat'. There are lots of words, and the whole song's about The Pogues and our life together, with a homage of sorts to Deborah Korner in the verse about turning the table upside down and sailing round the bed, which was a story Andrew told me about him and her when they were stoned – and that homage being a homage to all the people that died or could have done or looked likely to. Spider loved the song. His encouragement meant a lot to me and he should have done it proud, but he was in a place at that time that wouldn't permit him to do so.

"I could have fucking killed him the day he was first due to sing

'Drunken Boat'. I was so looking forward to it. When he arrived, he was so drunk and incapable of doing it that I lost my temper. I went into the room where he was and shouted and shouted at him."

Spider admits: "I know I had to do the vocals for the album twice. The first time they must've been all over the place. I was really, really irresponsible, doing all the sort of stuff that you shouldn't do. The second time, Michael Brook was renting a house in the Harrow Road and I went and did them there. It took two or three days. I couldn't piss about. I couldn't just go to the pub for hours and then turn up. I hadn't been singing for very long at all by the time we did *Waiting For Herb*, and I don't think the vocals are actually very good on it, but it was what I was capable of at the time."

Stacy did, however, write a song for the album: 'Tuesday Morning' would be a Top 20 hit when it was released as a single. "That's a fucking brilliant song," laughs Spider. "Probably the best song The Pogues ever did apart from 'Repeal Of The Licensing Laws'! Better than all that old Irish shite. . ."

'Tuesday Morning', a straightforward pop tune, began life as a tiny scrap of music with a title. "The title just stuck in my head," says Spider, "and I think I wrote the whole song in about 15 or 20 minutes in Molly Malone's in Stoke Newington."

Waiting For Herb is an extremely diverse album touching on everything from mainstream pop to country blues, Middle-Eastern innovation to hard-edged new wave and sensitive balladry. Terry Woods's folksy jig, 'Haunted', a ghost story, comes closest to the old sound of The Pogues, which is only otherwise recalled by the presence of the usual instruments, minus Stacy's whistle, and not by the songs.

Finer's hurdy-gurdy and Fearnley's hammered dulcimer return to the fold, along with mandolin, sax, bouzouki, piano, clarinet, strings, Hammond organ and ukelele. Additionally, the band brought in two percussion players, one of whom, David Coulter, would later join the line-up. Presumably as the result of lessons learned from *Peace And Love*, the album manages to sound clean and uncluttered despite the multitude of instruments.

James Fearnley played his usual role in the overdubbing, labouring over his efforts in both London and LA, in a rented studio. "I could be the overdub king without anybody bossing me about," he says.

The chief songwriter for the album was Jem Finer, who contributed several of his own compositions and three co-writes. Of his own songs, 'Small Hours' makes for a gentle and ultra-sensitive evocation of night-time loneliness, featuring Debsey Wykes, Darryl's friend and James's ex-girl-friend, on backing vocals, and 'Once Upon A Time', a sad, romantic ballad originally written with Rod Stewart in mind. At the other extreme, 'Pachinko' runs at a gallop and incorporates a maddening chorus that sounds like a nursery rhyme. This is the story of Jem's repeated attempts to master the Japanese game of the same name in some of that country's many dedicated Pachinko parlours.

He remembers: "I took James and Andrew and Paul Scully and Darryl, and I was trying to play it and nothing was happening again. This old man came and put his hand on my hand and moved my hand to all the right places so, in the end, I hit the jackpot. And he mysteriously disappeared. He was like a kind of ghost figure. It was all very dreamlike. Then we went and spent all the money I'd won on saki and beer. It ended in James having a nasty accident in the car park of the hotel. The hotel was on a hill and he decided to ride down the hill in a baggage trolley. . ."

Two of Finer's collaborations were with Andrew Ranken, who had worked with him on 'Gridlock'. "I never used to feel that I could write stuff that fitted with The Pogues," explains Andrew. "I tried to write some Irish songs, but they didn't work and it was only when the music got more eclectic that I felt able to do things that did work. Plus it takes me about 100 years to write a bloody song."

'My Baby's Gone', sung by Andrew, is a powerfully moving reaction to the loss of Deborah. "Unlike most things I write," he says, "that just came out in a complete rush. It came out in about five minutes."

The story for the percussive, Eastern-flavoured 'Girl From The Wadi Hammamat' came from a passage in a book by novelist and travel writer Bruce Chatwin. Says Jem: "There's this bit about a goat herder in the Sudan singing a song about a girl from the Wadi Hammamat. I said to Andrew, 'I wonder what this song is? We should write it.'"

Ranken supplied the lyrics, which include the line, *"She is as sweet as a green parakeet"* – a reference to the new woman in his life. He reveals: "By this time I'd met Jane [Perrott]. She actually replaced Frances as Daniel's carer. Frances's mother got ill and she had to go and look after her. I'd met Jane a couple of times before, because she's a sister of Paul Scully's wife." Andrew had also fallen asleep on a table backstage at the Self Aid gig with Jane's brother.

"The first time I really got to know Jane, she came on holiday with me to look after Daniel," recalls Andrew. "I went with Paul Scully down to west Cork, and we were staying on this farm and we had this room where in the evenings we used to get some bottles of wine and sit around drinking, and it became known as the 'green parrot lounge', cos there was a little wooden green parrot in there. So there was a very flimsy connection there to the 'green parakeet'."

Andrew and Jane became a couple some time later, and in the winter of 1993, she moved from Ireland to London to join him. They now have a daughter Nell, eleven at the time of writing.

Waiting For Herb was also noteworthy for the emergence as a songwriter of Darryl Hunt, whose contributions 'Modern World' and 'Big City' bring a punkish energy to proceedings. Darryl was also beginning to take an active role in the studio.

Producer Michael Brook was not the sort of person to befriend the groups he worked with, but all of the band remember him as a punctual, friendly, humorous and likeable character. Jem considers he did "a good job". Andrew and James are among those who disagree.

"I think the production was a bit too clean for us," decides Ranken. "I felt it was a mistake for us to go back to Elephant. We thought we might recapture some of the early magic, but it wasn't a very happy process, generally. I felt like it was clocking in and clocking off. When we worked there before, we created our own sort of atmosphere, but with *Waiting For Herb* I didn't feel that really happened."

Fearnley: "I thought Michael Brook was great but his work was awful. He took the tapes off to Peter Gabriel's studio complex, biosphere, Avalon, crop circle, whatever it was, and fucked around so much with the sounds and everything that I've had no desire to listen to it since. And I'm hard put to remember many of the songs on it. Oh, yes, there was 'Pachinko' with its silly lyrics and the challenging banjo part which Jem and I played together. And then 'Girl From The Wadi Hammamat' which contains the theme from *Lawrence Of Arabia* but backwards, or backwardish. Leastways, we used to do it live that way. What else? I got to play clarinet, after starting lessons with a guy on Southampton Row, a guy called Harry Conn who had rooms with interior windowed partitions with lace and a piano and piles of music books and everything covered in dust. I enjoyed playing clarinet on the road in Germany, in the echoey toilets, Yiddish tunes mostly, or something from Tchaikovsky."

The Pogues had been searching for a strong, new identity, but *Waiting For Herb* did not create one. While it certainly contains some worthwhile Pogues tracks, it throws a spotlight on the disparate forces at work within the band rather than establishing any purposeful direction, or finding another niche.

Andrew: "We were definitely floundering a bit. We didn't come up with a cohesive whole."

"There's a lot to speak highly of in *Waiting For Herb* as well," ventures Philip. "But there's always going to be a problem – Spider was singing most of the stuff. His voice doesn't have the range of colours that Shane's does. As he's gotten older, he's learnt how to alter the timbre a bit and use it to its advantage. Spider learnt how to sing from Johnny Rotten records and he ended up with his own voice, but only by default."

A Pogues album wouldn't be a Pogues album without an issue of some sort surrounding the cover art. For James Fearnley, this was all bound up with the title.

"Oh, how I had problems with that title," he declares. "It came from a pornographic magazine or something, but it took on accretions of meaning with which I wasn't comfortable – which presupposes comfort with the pornographic source, which shouldn't be inferred. Unless there was something I wasn't getting, herb was marijuana, in which I had not had much interest since finding my toothbrush in the fridge in the Seventies and otherwise becoming speechlessly paranoid if I happened to allow myself to get stoned in some expression of bonhomie that looked like a good idea at the time.

"In order to bring the album title round to something I was comfortable with, I suggested the cover should be Samuel Beckett's tree at the beginning of Act Two of *Waiting For Godot*, where one leaf can be seen to have grown over the interval. That got nowhere and the next thing I know is that the matter has been given over to the record company album sleeve designer. The next thing I experience is bafflement tinged with a certain amount of awe at the resources at album sleeve designers' fingertips." The artwork shows a man with his feet up, reading a newspaper.

"Anyway, to my mind a pretty crap album all round, though at the time it didn't feel like that," contniues James. "A lot of it seemed to be characterised, for me, by a sort of troglodytic husbandry in the bowels of some cave by underlings who are undertaking what they think might be the work expected of them by the departed Great One – a sort of hobbit thing without Gandalf, all very worthy but not quite there."

'Tuesday Morning' was released as a single in August 1993 backed with Chevron's 'First Day Of Forever'. The extra tracks across the formats were 'Turkish Song Of The Damned (Live)', 'London Calling (Live)' and 'I Fought The Law (Live)', the latter two with Joe Strummer.

It reached Number 18 which gave The Pogues an instant morale boost: for a moment, after all they'd been through, their post-MacGowan career was on the up. "We thought we were going to do okay," says Darryl. "We were going to places like Germany and doing good business, and selling places out."

"That was really good," says Jem who, along with other members, had helped translate the tune in Spider's head into living, breathing music. "Although I'd never give any great credence to what happens in the hit parade."

"It was what they call a radio-friendly song," says Andrew. "A lot of DJs seemed to pick up on it. At the same time, I'm not sure how representative it was of The Pogues. I'm not sure what was, really."

Waiting For Herb was another commercial success, entering the chart at Number 20 in September 1993, although critics internationally were unconvinced. For every *San Jose Mercury News*, which decided that the album "bristles with traditionalism and modern punk fervor", there was another grouchy reviewer somewhere else, like the *St Louis Post-Dispatch*, comparing The Pogues to "a competent, Irish-flavored band covering Clash or Tom Waits material". The *Irish Voice* pronounced that listening to the album was "similar to buying a seat to a Broadway show only to find that the star has gone sick and has been replaced by an understudy".

"I think there's some good songs on the album, but ultimately, we were on a hiding to nothing," says Jem. "We didn't have Shane with us any more and I seem to remember some of the reviews saying, 'There are some good songs here that are worthy of The Pogues but without Shane singing what's the point?' If we'd been a new band and we'd made that record, it would probably have been quite well received. It was an impossible situation. We were always going to be compared with what he'd been and what we'd been."

The Pogues, nevertheless, fulfilled their promotional responsibilities, with Spider shouldering much of the work. He gave endless phone interviews to journalists around the world, and in October 1993 made an appearance on the leading American TV chat programme, *The David Letterman Show*, with the band's guitar tech Paul McGuinness[*].

"The rest of the band were on holiday," says Spider. "We had a new record label in America [Chameleon] and we had to do all this press. We had one vaguely realistic chance of getting anything approaching a hit single in America – 'Tuesday Morning' - and it was scuppered. I was like the new drunken lead singer and I go off to the States with our roadie to do the most watched chat show in the world. It was quite funny. The record label and the people from the TV show wouldn't let us out of the building once we'd arrived. You're hanging around for ages. We just wanted to go to a bar across the street on the corner. They weren't having that. They sent runners down to get pints of Murphy's. Then we did 'Tuesday Morning' with the house band."

The Pogues took to the road for most of September, October, November and December and half way into the next year to promote *Waiting For Herb* across Europe and America.

"We had a bit of euphoria at first," remembers Darryl. "We'd got a single back on *Top Of The Pops*, and we gained a lot of new fans, particularly on the continent, who only knew the new stuff. There was a degree

---

[*] Not to be confused with U2's manager.

of success, but our home market was getting harder. It's very difficult to get up to the same level we were at before to maintain momentum. Once you're on the downward hill, it's very hard to get up again. There was quite a bit of criticism when the album came out. We didn't feel it was going very well any more. Things started to tail off. I felt disappointed. We had a great group."

There were more upheavals in store for The Pogues when, first, James Fearnley and then Terry Woods announced that they were going to leave.

James had become a father for the first time with the birth of his daughter Martha on February 4, 1993. He and Danielle had looked around a few flats in north London with a view to buying there, and at one point made an offer which eventually fell through. However, the arrival of Martha led to their decision that they should settle permanently in LA.

Says James: "I was a father and I had to be nowhere else but at home with my family. At the same time, we decided that the thing to do was to have grandparents who were close by. My mum had died in 1991, not long before or after Deborah died. That was a big year in everybody's lives in The Pogues, that was. (My dad died after that, in 2004.) If we lived in LA, we'd have grandparents."

Fearnley was now unwilling to keep travelling backwards and forwards across the Atlantic, and so it was unfeasible for him to remain in The Pogues. He talked things over with Danielle and then with Jem, over breakfast one morning in a café in Lamb's Conduit Street, WC1 – a short walk from the place where the story of The Pogues had started all those years ago.

"Jem and I are dead close like that," says James. "I told him what I was thinking of. He seemed to be disappointed. I felt shit because I'm very loyal to Jem. He's been very loyal to me. The last person I'd want to bugger up is him."

Fearnley decided to break the news officially to The Pogues at one of the summer's European gigs, in Switzerland. He can't remember the name of the town, but he can remember everything about his journey there, and his apprehension about telling the band.

He says: "I'd made my way from Los Angeles and was getting to the rather mountainous resort place we were going to be playing. On the train from the airport out to the resort, which ran alongside one of those Swiss lakes, who should be on board but Simon McCorkindale, whom I'd actually met before with his wife Susan George, at dinner somewhere in Kensington. Susan George is a very touchy-feely sort of person. I didn't go over to say anything to McCorkindale on the train because I was far too nervous about meeting up with The Pogues with my news.

"I rang up all the band members when I got there to summon them all to a room. Darryl, I remember, was very angry, which took me by surprise, and once the announcement had been made, I thought that I'd be marked in some way – 'not to be fraternised with' or something – but everyone was exceedingly charming about it and Darryl seemed to have overcome his anger."

James offered six months' notice so as to give the band time to work in a new accordionist. He continues: "Over the next six months, I became more and more alarmed that the rest of them didn't seem to be doing much about replacing me. David Coulter was playing with us at the time, didgeridoo mostly, and percussion stuff. He seemed to be the guy to replace me, though eventually it was James McNally, who I'd never had much of a relationship with despite [his band] Storm opening for us for a long time. I found him on the cheesy side, actually, as a human being and, come to think of it, on the musical side too after hearing 'Fairytale Of New York', the instrumental version he did with everyone but me playing on it, or so it seemed at the time, when Paul Scully played me it once."

"I think if everything had been going smoothly and successfully, then maybe James would have carried on," says Andrew. "But there was still a lot of pressure to tour and do lots of gigs. That was getting harder and harder for James and I think a lot of the fun had gone out of it, a lot of the magic, and I think it was quite soul-destroying. I was absolutely sorry to see James go. To my mind, he was irreplaceable, really. James McNally was a very talented musician, but he's not James Fearnley. I don't know anyone who can play the accordion like James Fearnley. He's quite unique."

James's last appearance with The Pogues came at the end of a run of UK gigs at a familiar venue – the old Town & Country Club in Kentish Town, now known as The Forum – at Christmas 1993.

He remembers: "Shane and Joe [Strummer] were both at the gig and I think I'm right in saying they both performed. I don't remember what Shane did, what he sang. At the end, in 'Fiesta', I remember sinking to the ground and they all sort of gathered round me in a huddle. I won't forget that.

"As a gift, my parents-in-law put Danielle and myself up in The Savoy for the last shows in Kentish Town. It was a brilliant and swank leave-taking sort of thing with the Thames outside our window, and then getting the plane the day after the last show to start a new life somewhere else."

Martha was joined by a new sister Irene on September 14, 1996.

Terry Woods had other grounds for wanting to leave – musical and financial reasons - although he stayed on into the new year of 1994.

Woods, who had been brought into The Pogues because of his fine pedi-

401

gree in Irish and Appalachian music, now found little outlet for his talents. He wasn't in love with the latest experiments. He says, "Musically, we were going through the motions. I felt the band became a bit disparate. One minute we were playing jazz and the next minute we were playing rock and I felt the Irish music at that point was getting a bit of lip service. I felt we'd gone into areas of music that wasn't where the audience of the band expected us to be. As a result, some of the audience were nonplussed by what the band wanted to deliver for them.

"We weren't going anywhere. It was as if we'd done the business when Shane was there and it wasn't going to happen again. I was incredibly sad when it all fell apart that night with MacGowan. He was one of the main reasons I joined the band. It was his visions of Irish music that intrigued me and I realised that The Pogues without Shane was going to be a different beast. There was no focus.

"The final thing was, we did a tour in Germany [autumn 1993] whereby we were guaranteed X amount of money. All the costs were being borne by the German promoters, but at the end of the day, there was no money. Everybody was doing their best, but the band's finances had spiralled out of control.

"Also, I'd reached the stage where when we were going places I couldn't be bothered leaving the hotel apart from doing the gigs. That seemed to me, 'Hold on, this is wrong.' If you were on holidays you'd be dying to go out and look around.

"James had admitted he was leaving anyway. The band had become tired and The Pogues to me were a big band and I regarded them as being very strong and powerful, and I certainly didn't want to be around when it became a whimper, which I felt was going to happen.

"I was winding down in my mind. We were going to be doing this American tour in the spring of 1994 and I thought, 'Oh, I can't do that again, go away for that period of time and not earn any money.' I informed everybody that it was over for me. They'd kind of known. I'd said I didn't think I was going to be hanging around for too much longer. I'd said it the summer previous when James had said he was quitting. He acted on it more quickly than I did. There was a bit of a to-do when I did leave, with the financial ramifications. I got legal representations over here [Ireland] and dealt with the band's representation, and it was finally sorted out."

"I didn't feel good about Terry leaving at all," comments Andrew. "He was another kind of irreplaceable member of the band. He was becoming quite withdrawn and not really communicating what was going on, but I think it was quite obvious that he wasn't really happy. I think the lack of clear direction in the music really bothered him. There was less and less of the Irish stuff. I know Terry was in dire straits financially. He had two kids and a big house in Ireland."

"I don't know what happened with Terry," says Jem. "We kind of stopped talking. I don't think it was done in the most amicable way on either side. He just sort of stopped. It was done more by absence."

Philip: "Terry had been proclaiming for the longest time, in business meeting after business meeting, that if the band's business matters could not be put on a more understandable footing – ie you're offered work, a fee is mentioned, you do the work, you get paid – he would have no option but to leave as neither his bank manager nor his wife could operate under the status quo, in which payment was erratic and unpredictable. We all felt victims of this to a greater or lesser extent, but Terry's circumstances seemed to be more critical...

"Ultimately, as the situation never improved, Terry had no option but to announce his departure. Eventually, he said, 'I'm sorry lads. I'll do this last album with you [*Waiting For Herb*] but after that I'm off. Terry once told me that it was costing him money to be on the road with The Pogues, a situation his wife could never fathom. I can't convey how this is possible but, trust me, it is. I believe Terry began to feel marginalised in other ways too. He had to fight to get 'Haunting' taken seriously and recorded for *Waiting For Herb*.

"Crucially, the absence of Shane and the imminent departure of James radically altered the chemistry of the band. Where before, the balance had been self-correcting when ego or self-indulgence loomed, that seemed to evaporate.

"There were, without question, too many Indians all trying to be chiefs. The appearance of David Coulter and James McNally was never going to affect this much, as the remaining Pogues adopted a 'what we have, we hold' approach. David and James brought their own fresh grievances about pay and status which were, largely, ignored. With Terry's departure, it was no longer a band I felt I had much, if anything, in common with."

Unsurprisingly, then, Philip Chevron would be the next to go.

CHAPTER 28

In The Death Of Afternoon

Philip was desperately ill. He dragged himself around Europe and the UK for the last four months of 1993 as The Pogues went on the campaign trail for *Waiting For Herb*. And then came 1994 and another American tour that included dates in Boston, New York, Philadelphia, Montreal, Toronto, Detroit, Chicago, Vancouver, Seattle, San Francisco and LA, concluding on March 31 with a show at Hollywood's famous Viper Room, which had opened the year before.

The band had employed on a session basis percussionist David Coulter, who played fiddle, mandolin and tambourine, and Storm's James McNally, replacing James Fearnley on accordion.

At every gig, they managed to win over audiences who were neverthe-less still grumbling about the absence of MacGowan, and their reviews were by turns encouraging, disparaging and fair-to-middling. The *Boston Globe* enthused: "There was bark and ferocity last night during the septet's 85-minute rip-snorter of a set," while *Newsday* shook a weary head: "Watching The Pogues stagger through this disheartening display, one could envision a dilapidated version of the young boxer on the cover of 1989's *Peace And Love* stubbornly taking a beating rather than falling down and acknowledg-ing the end of a once-glorious career." Taking a seat on the fence, *The Gazette* in Montreal said of the band's performance: "It didn't erase the visions of what Could Have Been, but it worked as a life-affirming reminder of the necessity of moving on…"

Most of the critics paused to mention the old news of Shane MacGowan's physical decline but in lauding Philip Chevron's rendition of 'Thousands Are Sailing', failed to notice that he too was in a wretched con-dition.

"As my alcoholism got worse, physically I got worse as well," says

Chevron. "It became harder to eat. I had to constantly rest - effectively just do the gig and go back to sleep. I was becoming increasingly frazzled by the whole pace of the thing."

Despite the group's intention to cut down on touring after leaving Frank Murray, they'd firstly had to honour their contracted bookings. Now, they found they had to tour to try and stay in the game.

"If anything, it sped up as we sold less records," says Philip. "It came to a head for me when we arrived back in London from LA. Myself and Paul Scully and a few of us were staying at a hotel in Heathrow cos we had to go to Belgium the next day to do a gig. The hotel was being decorated, it was noisy, the rooms weren't booked properly, and we had to wait for hours while they found spare rooms. Something just clicked in my head and I said, 'I'm not doing it any more.'

"James had left. He'd been getting charged for commuting – 'You've got to pay your own fare to rehearsals.' He'd feel, 'Don't punish me for living in LA.' A number of things built up for him that made it less and less like fun and more and more like hard work. Terry left soon after that, partly cos James had gone but mainly because he couldn't get any sense out of the band. To me, it just didn't feel like The Pogues.

"Spider's alcoholism got worse in that period, as did mine. The hardcore fans didn't accept Spider as a singer any more than they'd accepted Joe. Spider struggled with it. It was a pretty heavy-duty responsibility, and he wasn't able to shoulder it. All the stuff that was already falling apart fell apart more when they had this extra pressure on them. There was a very gradual fading away. I liked James McNally and David Coulter as people, but they weren't Pogues."

Chevron played the gig in Belgium and then took six months' sick leave. He remembers: "Often you feel something and you discover other people are feeling it as well. They all had decided to take six months off. It didn't matter what was in the diary, it was getting dumped."

Philip went home to Nottingham where he had been living since leaving Muswell Hill in 1992. He still lives there, in the suburb of West Bridgford, south of the river. "I moved to Nottingham because that's where my team were," he says. "I became a Forest fan quite late in life. Darryl was a Forest fan and never shut up talking about them. I was quite scathing about football. As a kid, I just hated it. Darryl said, 'Let me take you to a game and see if you feel differently about it.' So he did, and I did.

"It wasn't like if somebody had taken me to Arsenal or Spurs or something. I just really liked the way they played. I completely understood the whole Brian Clough football philosophy. It coincided with what I thought was a beautiful way to play football. It really would only have been Forest;

not necessarily the same Forest who are now scrambling to stay at the bottom of the third division. They were on the way to winning a couple of league cups and things. They were figuring quite highly in the first division. I'm still in touch with some of the players including Stuart Pearce, who went on to manage Manchester City.

"I was going up to Nottingham for home games, which weren't home games for me, and league cup games and things. And I just grew more fond of the place the more I saw it. I also liked the price range of the houses. I was able to buy a whole house for what I would have spent on a one-bedroom apartment in London. I live beside the river, near Trent Bridge cricket ground, and round the corner from the City ground where Forest play. I'm five minutes away from the theatres and the railway station and the shops."

Chevron had tried to buy a home in Dublin in 1990 and as a result of the red tape that he encountered, will never live in Ireland again: "I had come to the notion that, after 13 years in London and flushed with success, the time might be right to re-establish my Irish roots. In order to qualify for either the mortgage or the insurance on the mortgage, it was required that I take an HIV test, as an apparently high-risk category. It was not specified if this was because I was a Pogue or because I was openly gay and, rather than ask, I just got on with the damn thing. The test came back HIV negative, as I had supposed it would, but I was turned down for my mortgage anyway. When I asked why, I was given the Kafka-esque explanation that I was turned down because I had been required to do an HIV test! This news was transmitted to me by an office junior, by phone, to my hotel room in Tokyo.

"I understand the law about these things may since have changed in Ireland, but if so, it came too late for me. My battles against injustice and homophobia in Ireland had all been uphill. If the new, liberal, forward-thinking Celtic Tiger was still requiring me to fight on even the most mundane of levels at the age of 33, it would have to have its Brave New Ireland without me. There and then, in my Tokyo hotel room, I vowed I would never again be a permanent resident of Ireland. I have now lived in Britain for 29 years."

Shane MacGowan, on the other hand, has grown closer to his home country over time, has become more conspicuously sentimental about it, and regularly retreats to the old family farmhouse in Tipperary.

Philip, for his part, does not trust the "brave new dawn". He sees in Ireland a new capitalism, a cynicism and disillusionment - "probably because Irish society has been let down by the church and the state so much" – and a lack of compassion for immigrants.

He concludes: "What's always been important in Ireland is spirituality, in the fields, in the stones, in the music, in the stories - not what people brought to bear in terms of money. There's something timeless that goes beyond, probably into other dimensions we're not aware of. There's an essence there that goes beyond some 24-year-old fuckpig who's got a degree in economics and thinks he knows the way forward for Ireland. They're making a grotesque error in redefining themselves as a capitalist nation. To me, Ireland's great so long as I'm a visitor there and I know the door's open when I want to leave."

Spider was still hitting the bottle with a vengeance, although he'd made one effort to sober up in the summer of 1993, after a particularly bad experience in Portugal while The Pogues were touring *Waiting For Herb*.

James Fearnley starts up the tale: "It was probably before the gig. We were up on the top floor of this hotel with white tablecloths, glittering silverware and glasses and folded napkins, like a formal dinner in this fancy penthouse restaurant with a bow window looking over some Mediterranean town. Up comes Terry, running up the stairs - 'Help, help, come and help me!'"

Something had happened to Spider. In one version of the story, he was in his hotel room banging his head against the wall. In another version, he was throwing up uncontrollably at the bottom of the stairs. In every version, he ended up in hospital.

Spider: "I think I broke my collarbone on a marble bar in the hotel, just falling into it. And everyone in the band said, 'You should really do something about this.'"

And so he jumped on the wagon, not entirely whole-heartedly. "I kind of knew I had to do something," he remembers. "But at the same time, I didn't really want to. I was okay for about six or seven weeks. At first it probably wasn't too bad. But, of course, I didn't really want to stop drinking, so I started again."

The rest of The Pogues were hardly thrilled, but they didn't come down too heavily on Spider. "I think a certain amount of general fatigue had set in," says Stacy. "They'd already been through all this with Shane. It's just the curse of people who don't know when enough is enough. I'm sure no one was happy about the situation, but what can you do? They don't want to spend their whole time being a nursemaid to somebody who should be able to work things out for themselves. I'm certain that my drinking didn't do anything to further the band's cause."

Fearnley remembers Spider coming out to LA on a couple of occasions to visit a girlfriend who lived there. "He was once walking down Western Avenue in Los Angeles and he gets mugged and has all his money taken off him," says James. "He was pretty out-there. I remember making myself instrumental in extricating him and his girlfriend at the time from a bad situation. He'd become involved in some imbroglio which required Danielle and I getting them both to what was the Holiday Inn in Hollywood to extricate them from the imbroglio. The loan of money was involved. That was one visit."

On another visit, in the summer of 1993 – after *Waiting For Herb* had been recorded but just before the touring began - James, Danielle and baby Martha became involved in some extraordinary shenanigans, with Spider jumping in and out of vehicles when they attempted to deliver him to the airport. There was, says James, "a person" involved.

Spider, experiencing only the haziest reality outside of his failed attempt to get sober, felt like a "spectator" as James and Terry left The Pogues and Philip went off, sick. "More and more bits were coming off the original thing, the band as everybody understood it," he reflects. "I was looking at it in slow motion, probably. It still was The Pogues, because there was enough of the spirit left, but not enough original members. Everything had changed. The vague memory I have of that period is of watching it all happen but not really feeling that I was involved. I'd chosen to isolate myself to a certain extent."

The Pogues spent the second half of 1994 rehearsing and making demos, with Philip Chevron's guitar tech, Jamie Clarke, standing in for him. They were preparing for what would be their final studio album, *Pogue Mahone*.

In September, Philip travelled down from Nottingham to see how things were going. With his six-month rest period coming to an end, he was theoretically gearing up to return to the band. But his recovery hadn't gone to plan.

"He was not in a great way," says Darryl. "He had problems to deal with."

Chevron's problems were probably much worse than anyone realised. "I literally wasn't eating at all," he says. "My stomach had closed up. I wasn't able to keep food down when I did eat, and I was in constant pain. I needed to get out of the vicious circle of just being dependent on alcohol.

"The band were recording demos in Camden and I went to hear how the album was shaping up and to be perfectly honest, I didn't like it. It sounded to me like pub rock. The music had lost any character it had in terms of being distinctly Irish or distinctly punky. It felt competent, well-played and boring.

"We went down to the pub for a drink, and we had this meeting. Jamie Clarke had substituted for me on a temporary basis. He'd fitted in quite well, as I knew he would. He'd made his presence felt, he'd become invaluable to the arrangements, and he'd helped Spider write something. No one knew to what extent I was prepared to re-commit to the band. They hadn't seen me in months. The meeting broke up all smiles, all cheery – 'Hope you can make it to rehearsal next week.'

"I booked myself into a hotel in London, bought two bottles of Bacardi and said, 'I need to think this through.' I gave myself two days. I was a wreck. I thought, 'Will I ever get well if I'm in this band?' I was beginning to see there was more to it than going off the road, resting for a while and per-suading myself not to have a drink. I needed more time than the six months I had allowed myself to 'get better'. Six weeks, six months, six years – it was all irrelevant if I did not actually address the problem with some sort of commitment. Being in the band seemed to simply confuse the issue.

"Apart from the fact I was disintegrating, I had to remind myself I didn't really like these demos very much, and I hadn't forgotten how awful that last tour had been for me, how ghastly and hopeless the whole thing was, and how much I missed James and Terry."

Philip spent his couple of evenings in London seeing shows, something he hadn't done for several years, and it occurred to him that he might have a future in the theatre.

"I went back to Nottingham," he recalls. "I slept on it another night and phoned Jem. I said, 'I'm sorry, I just can't do this.' I told him calmly. It was a decision made in regret. Nothing became more important to me that year than rescuing myself from the brink of disaster."

Chevron's royalties from album sales and from 'Thousands Are Sailing' as a song in its own right had been building up. He realised that he had a financial cushion and could afford to take more time off to attend to the "life and death nature of my health concerns".

He reveals: "I went into hospital in January 1995 for the second life-saving attempt to mend my diseased liver. Five weeks later, I went direct from hos-pital to the Nottingham Clinic, a Priory-type place, for six weeks of rehab."

Philip adds: "As soon as I possibly could after that, I wrote a long and detailed letter to The Pogues, care of Jem, explaining something of the dark journey I'd been on for the past two or three years, and how I now felt I finally had a future worth looking towards."

That future, for the time being, did not include The Pogues, although he kept in touch with his former bandmates. "I was giving my recovery a chance," he explains. "I needed to devote a year to making that my priority above everything else."

Philip was making plans to write a musical, and he was taking tentative steps towards that goal. He says: "One of the first things I did when I got sober in 1995 was to gingerly get back into songwriting as the thing that I do. It's an even more terrifying thing when you come to it sober where you've kidded yourself for years that you need to take lots of drink and cocaine or whatever to concentrate. But, of course, I'd written songs all through my teens with none of that shit going on, and I'd forgotten that."

Not that Chevron was ever a major coke-head: his drug was alcohol. "I didn't take cocaine on a regular basis, but drugs were there from time to time," he admits. "I can't say I was ever a coke addict. Jem would say there was a lot more coke taken than there probably actually was."

The outcome of Philip's return to writing was revelatory: "Much to my amazement, I can still write songs, and even better songs."

"Philip was too ill physically to go out gigging," says Andrew Ranken. "But I think he was most probably feeling the same as a lot of us – that the thing had become quite directionless, and it didn't seem like it was really going anywhere any more, and we weren't really enjoying it."

Andrew was losing interest in The Pogues. His main priority was Daniel: "I was trying to bring up my son, and a lot of the things that were going on in the band just went completely over my head. I wasn't paying attention a lot of the time."

Jem Finer was also experiencing mixed emotions. He explains: "James and Terry and Philip left and the other three people started playing with us and I think we did some touring. We all got on very well together and we had quite a laugh and we had good audiences. It wasn't like they disappeared at all. There was a feeling, on the one hand, that it was actually fine because we were enjoying ourselves and people were enjoying watching the band.

"But also, my heart was not quite in it. In a way, it didn't feel like The Pogues. It just felt like running something down. It sort of happened gradually. It felt a bit like fighting against the tide to keep something afloat when really it was probably better to let it sink. The more you carry on, the more commitments you've got. Really, there comes a point where you have to say, 'Commitments be damned.' But there was a feeling of wanting to see something through and trying to make something work. Then it was time to make another record, cos that's what you have to do."

"I think we were sticking two fingers up to a few people," comments Andrew. "*Waiting For Herb* had been slated a few times and some people had said we were washed up and finished and the band was no good any more and blah blah blah. We thought we'd make a really good album and just say, 'Actually, no, we can still do it.' And, in fact, it started off really well."

Jem: "We went back to the old routine of rehearsing and going through lots of stuff and we started doing these demos in June or July 1994 – the World Cup was on – in a little studio in Chalk Farm."

Philip Chevron had not been impressed by the demos, although he liked much of the new material when he heard the finished album. For Andrew Ranken, this worked the other way round.

He says: "The demos were the best thing we'd done for ages, I thought. It all seemed to gel. It was really happening, and everyone was really pleased. And it was one of those ridiculous things where we just should've kept the demos. We'd got the album. And then we just went and made it worse. Sometimes you shouldn't listen to people when they say, 'Oh, but those are just demos.' Sometimes you have to stick your neck out and say, 'They're as good as you're going to get,' instead of wasting weeks and thousands of pounds in posh studios tinkering. The demos were much better than the finished bloody album."

The Pogues had hoped to acquire the services of producer Mike Thorne, who had worked with Soft Cell and Wire. Thorne was interested but unable to take on the job at the time. And so they were introduced to Steve Brown, who had produced pop acts ABC and Wham!, goth rock bands The Cult and Balaam And The Angel, and Welsh agit-prop heroes Manic Street Preachers. In his days as an engineer, Brown had also been behind a host of punk records, rock albums by the likes of Thin Lizzy and Status Quo, and Wizzard's epic studio singles 'See My Baby Jive' and 'I Wish It Could Be Christmas Every Day'.

The Pogues went back to RAK studios, where Andrew became disenchanted with Brown's production work and Darryl, reportedly, agreed with him. "It was awful," declares Andrew. "This twat who produced it, Steve Brown, had this bee in his bonnet about making a better album than Steve Lillywhite had done, and I really didn't enjoy it at all. He kept making me do things to click tracks, and I just don't get on with click tracks. I persevered, but my heart wasn't in it. We were trying to get back to basics in a way, trying to do something fresh and immediate and spontaneous and that's what we did when we recorded the demos. We ended up in the studio just getting very jaded and not playing as well, and it was a shame, really."

Jem Finer judges Brown less harshly: "I don't think it was the best partnership in the world, but it wasn't the worst," he reflects. "It all seemed to take a very long time.

"By then, Spider was starting to have severe problems and it was rather hard to get vocals out of him. He was in a right old state. Very bad. It didn't help the process of recording. On *Waiting For Herb*, he'd tried to take it seriously."

"I did miss my regular comrades," adds Darryl. "It was really disappointing to have lost James and Terry, and to see that Philip was finding it difficult to work with us. We just had to get on. We had a job to do and bills to pay. The three different members who joined were very good and I enjoyed working with them, but I can't deny I'd like to have gone back to the *Fall From Grace* line-up.

"It's very difficult when you're in a group. You don't see it in perspective. You always think, 'This is bigger than the sum of its parts.' In hindsight, I think maybe a break might have been better."

To an outsider, *Pogue Mahone* doesn't sound like a bad album at all. There's a lively musicianship at play throughout the songs, and a much more focused ambition. To a great extent, the songs recall The Pogues' twin strengths of old, their headlong Celtic flings and their melodic ballads. Close your eyes and you can almost hear Shane MacGowan rasping along with the punky charge of 'Living In A World Without Her', the cavorting 'Bright Lights' or the high-spirited 'Tosspint'.

Two rather more unusual songs stand out from the others, 'Oretown' for its insistent drone and Andrew's 'Four O'Clock In The Morning', a deeply personal account of crisis and death, musically as blue and heavy as its subject demands. In quite the opposite mood is a song co-written by Andrew and his old friend Stephen Skull. Dating even further back than their days together in The Stickers, 'Where That Love's Been Gone' with its jovial banjo is an infectious and tuneful proposition.

Darryl Hunt, for his part, was clearly in love, contributing the haunting big ballad 'Love You Till The End' and co-writing with James McNally another romantic declaration, 'Living In A World Without Her'. Darryl was in a relationship with his future wife, Claudia Poeschl, whom he'd met in Munich and bumped into in London, accidentally, at the beginning of the Nineties. They would marry in 1997.

The new hired hands brought a diversity of instrumentation to the album. McNally contributed uilleann pipes, piano and whistles as well as accordion and David Coulter played mandolin and ukelele in addition to his array of percussion instruments. The band additionally brought in cellist Caroline Lavelle, who'd previously worked with Siouxsie Sioux, Graham Parker and Peter Gabriel, fiddlers Jon Sevink and Anne Wood, and once again Debsey Wykes to sing some beautiful backing vocals.

There are two covers on the album. One is a Jem Finer rewrite of Bob Dylan's 'When The Ship Comes In'. "I arranged it and I wrote the whole tune that goes with it," says Jem. "I did see if I could get a share of the publishing on it, but I was told no by Dylan's people!"

The other is a happy-go-lucky, banjo-a-go-go version of Ronnie Lane's 'How Come' which was suggested to the band by Rob Dickens at Warners, after they had finished the main recordings. He also suggested they should record it with a different producer "who knew how to make hit records".

After the success of 'Tuesday Morning', Warners had obviously become concerned when its follow-up single from *Waiting For Herb*, 'Once Upon A Time', made much less of an impact. Backed with 'Train Kept Rolling On' and with 'Tuesday Morning' and 'Paris St Germain' additional to the 12-inch and CD formats, the single had reached its top position of Number 66 in January 1994.

Producer Stephen Hague, a veteran of New Order, Pet Shop Boys and Blur, was chosen to craft The Pogues' next hit single. "It felt like we were being bribed," recalls Jem. "We were being told by the record company, 'If you don't do this you're not going to get any support from us.' So we did it with Stephen Hague, who was a nice guy, actually."

"I'd actually always been a really big fan of Ronnie Lane, but I didn't think it was a very good idea in terms of a Pogues single," adds Andrew. "I felt it was a bit sort of clutching at straws, and I didn't think we needed to be doing cover versions."

Darryl: "We were in a position, unlike with Shane, where we weren't strong enough to say, 'Take something of ours for the single.'"

Once again, Jem Finer contributed considerably to the album. The Irish-tinged ballad, 'Anniversary', is a song he'd written on a snowy day in Boston on March 12, his wedding anniversary, while he composed 'Bright Lights' in response to 'Big City', Hunt's song from *Waiting For Herb*, as an allusion to the old blues song, 'Bright Lights, Big City'. Extending the joke, Finer adds: "Andrew was going to write one called 'Gone To My Baby's Head.'"

'Tosspint' grew out of an obsession with Rabelais and a fascination with the paintings of Hieronymus Bosch and Pieter Bruegel. What sort of music were their characters playing?

"I decided it would be very loud and raucous," says Jem, "and so I wrote a song about a day in the life of a Rabelaisian character called Tosspint and tried to make it sound a bit medieval, as it were. I don't think it's altogether successful."

Clearly, the song that means the most to Finer is 'Point Mirabeau', a translation of a poem by Apollinaire which he set to music. He explains: "My father had once translated it, and I found the translation in a little tin box of his precious things – photos, old letters and stuff – that he left to me when he died. I remembered he'd once said to me, after I'd written 'Misty Morning, Albert Bridge', that it would be great if we could turn this translation into a song.

"So in this box of memories was an old typed-out version of his translation but also a letter he'd written to me, cos obviously he knew that at some point he was going to die. Some years previously, he'd had one of his heart attacks and thought his time was up. He wrote letters to everyone and when he didn't die, he put them away. The letter said, 'I'd love you to turn this into a song.' I had to re-translate it, based on what he'd done, because it didn't really work lyrically, and I wrote the music. I think very much he would have liked it."

The album artwork presented the usual problems. "The record company came up with a dreadful idea," says Darryl, who resolved to come up with an alternative. "I had the idea for using lettering and Claudia designed it all. We did it together. We had a weekend to rush it out quick."

There was consternation at Warners when their high hopes for 'How Come' were disappointed. Released in September 1995 backed with 'Eyes Of An Angel' and live versions of 'Tuesday Morning' and 'Big City', it failed to enter the Top 75. *Pogue Mahone*, in the shops a month later, didn't chart either.

Philip Chevron comments: "I actually think the first half of the album is among the best things they ever did. The first side is a strong piece of work. The whole first sequence of five or six songs is really good. It didn't deserve to be dismissed as it was."

"In some ways I prefer *Pogue Mahone* to *Waiting For Herb*," says Spider. "I quite like it. But there wasn't another album left in the band after *Pogue Mahone*. We realised that it needed to have the proper people in it for it to work."

The Pogues went out on the road with Jamie Clarke replacing Philip on guitars. They toured throughout the autumn and into the next year, which helped neither their album sales nor their personal satisfaction with the band. By this time they had parted company with Joey Cashman and were under new management. "I think Joey left at RAK studios while we were recording," says Jem. "He had developed very bad personal problems... and that wasn't very helpful."

"He had become a bit unreliable," adds Spider.

Cashman then took up a new position as Shane MacGowan's personal manager and buddy while The Pogues appointed his replacement, Tim Collins, from a professional management company based in Brighton. Collins had previously worked with Siouxsie Sioux.

"I just turned round one day and there he was," says Spider. "I never liked Tim's attitude. He probably didn't like me. You know some people just rub you up the wrong way? Maybe I'm being completely unfair to him. In fact, Louise and I went to Reading Festival some years later and Blur were playing. He was working with Blur, and he wouldn't let us up on the side of the stage to watch them. I just didn't like him."

Jem Finer disagrees. "He was very helpful," he says. "He was a 'proper manager' and he tried to do things very professionally."

Unfortunately for Collins, he was taking over a band that was reaching the end of the road, literally and figuratively.

Philip Chevron turned out to see his old friends at Nottingham Rock City. He remembers: "The place was half-full. It should have been chock-a-block, with demand for a second show. I got up and played with them on a couple of numbers. They were just falling apart and they seemed unhappy, although they were saying all the right things to big it up.

"What I didn't quite realise at the time was how much all of them hated that period. They really, really hated it. I think Spider found it a complete and utter misery. The whole thing was looking like a bad space to be in. I sensed almost instantly that Jem was not going to be doing this for much longer. If he feels something, everybody else becomes aware he feels it. People knew how to read him very well. That's part of Jem's strength and his charisma.

"Also, in the middle of this, I suppose I was like a beacon of hope. I arrived entirely sober, having done rehab, been in AA and been on the dry for quite a few months at that point. They could see the change. There's life beyond The Pogues, in other words. I was talking about this musical I was going to write and I was well on the way to doing it. You could go and have a life. You don't have to settle for playing to a half-full house at Nottingham Rock City.

"I was painfully aware that The Pogues were on the slide. In *Spinal Tap* terms, they were going on before the puppet show. They were playing at smaller places."

Andrew agrees: "It was quite soul-destroying. I think we ended up in a position where we realised we could go on doing the same circuit forever with any old line-up as long as there was a few of the original members in. But it wasn't a very exciting circuit, and the gigs were slowly shrinking. It just became like hack work. We were enjoying it less and less.

"I just felt like the bollocks had gone out of it. It just wasn't the same. There was increasing friction. It was getting very difficult with Spider. He was getting too ill to carry on, and the new guys were becoming increasingly difficult to work with as well. They all had their own projects going on at the same time and they were double-jobbing a lot of the time and getting quite unreliable and forever demanding more money. It all just became meaningless. We were going through the motions. There wasn't any kind of cohesion within the group. It just wasn't working, really."

At the beginning of 1996, Warners announced that they were dropping The Pogues, and plans for their next single, a Stephen Hague remix of 'Love You Till The End', were immediately withdrawn. This was a devastating blow to Darryl Hunt, its author.

"In many ways, at the very end, it had almost become Darryl's band," says Philip. "He'd become one of the main songwriters and engines of the band, and he had the enthusiasm to drive things forward."

This had indeed been a remarkable journey for the man who had started out as a driver, a roadie and a target for Shane and Spider's relentless piss-taking. "The single was all ready to come out," says Darryl, "and they decided they weren't going to release it. Of course I was very disappointed. It could have been like 'Tuesday Morning', something different that worked."

Jem Finer was furious: "The thing that was very annoying was that having done everything according to Rob Dickens's plan, the record company didn't then support the album terribly well. It came out at the same time as a Simply Red record or something like that, which got all their attention, and our record was left to sink. I felt we'd compromised ourselves to go along with their judgement, and they didn't even bother to uphold their side of the bargain by pushing the record.

"When Warners said they weren't going to take up their options for any more records and they weren't interested in us any more, I decided I was certainly not interested any more in trying. Everything was run down to an extent that I just wanted to quit. We had a meeting round Andrew's house and I said, 'I'm gonna stop.' As usual we had a lot of touring lined up into the summer. I said, 'I'll do the concerts until the end of July and then I'm stopping.'"

Philip: "Joe Strummer once said, 'Jem is like the glue that keeps the whole thing together.' Once Jem left, that was the end of it."

The other band members decided then that it wasn't worth struggling on.

Touring through the first half of 1996, The Pogues played in Europe and America and Europe again, with Jem, Darryl and Andrew often having to cover for Spider on vocals, in the way they once had for MacGowan. And then it was July.

Spider: "I remember we were doing a festival in France and I collapsed. It was the second or third time I'd collapsed with some sort of alcoholic seizure. I went to hospital. The band were going off to play some gigs in Prague, I think, and I was in London recovering from the French thing. They couldn't take me abroad, so they arranged one last gig at the Boston Arms pub in Tufnell Park so that I could actually be there. Which is really going out with a whimper rather than a bang."

It was the whimper that Terry Woods had feared.

"It was very poignant imagining them all in that place, come sort of full circle, and learning since how miserable the occasion seemed to be," says James Fearnley.

"Shane came up at the last gig as well," reveals Spider. "He said, 'Thank God that's all fucking over.'"

Despite the trials and tribulations of their last few years together, the end of The Pogues was a crushing experience for almost everyone involved.

Darryl: "It seemed like all the planets were lined up saying, 'That's it, boy. It's time to knock it on the head.' I got quite depressed. It was a very bad time for me. I'd been working with the group for 14 years. It gets into your blood. I found it very difficult. At the same time, my mum had died that year. My father had died a few years before. Claudia and I were living in Munich and we were planning to get married and move back to London. I didn't realise at the time how badly I'd taken it, the loss of my group and the loss of my parents. I didn't know I was in quite such a bad way as I was."

Andrew Ranken was more relieved than anything else when the end came. He says, "Daniel was growing up and I wanted to be at home more with him. It was just getting to the stage where I was looking for nurseries and things and just needing to be at home more and more. When we did call it a day, for me it was quite good timing."

"I was very depressed," admits Finer. "I felt that I'd put a lot into writing stuff. For the last album in particular, I tried to write in a style that I thought was what people wanted from the band. In a sense, I was compromising myself. I wasn't necessarily writing what I wanted to write. I remember the reviews for *Waiting For Herb*. Some of them seemed to be saying, 'This isn't The Pogues.' Then there was this one review for *Pogue Mahone* and it said, 'It sounds like a parody of The Pogues.' I thought, 'This is totally pointless.' Creatively, it had become a dead end. On the one hand, people were never going to accept it for what it was, but on the other, it had run its course. I started thinking, 'What the hell are we trying to do?' It left me in a state where I didn't want to be playing songs or writing songs.

"By then, I'd started work on 'Longplayer' and I just wanted to concentrate on that and to really just submerge myself in a whole different way of looking at sound and music. And I've been doing it ever since."

'Longplayer' is a 1,000-year long piece of music which began on January 1, 2000. In its present incarnation as a computer programme, it can be heard at listening posts in London and Nottingham, Alexandria in Egypt and Brisbane, Australia, and also globally via a live internet stream.

Jem then made an album, *gtr*, which experimented with using the techniques of computer-generated music in live performance with instruments, and he followed on with two more. *Visionary Landscapes* was made as a collaboration with Andrew Kotting. A meeting of electronic and folk music, it was originally performed as a live soundtrack to projections of out-takes from *Gallivant*, one of Kotting's films, as part of the seminal Visionary Landscapes festival at Cecil Sharp House. *Bum Steer*, by [one-man-band] DM Bob and Country Jem, is a more traditional entertainment. Finer was also in the London Electric Guitar Orchestra for several years, playing improvised music.

A blend of science and art lies at the heart of a series of projects, including the making of films in zero gravity aboard a Russian "vomit comet", with Ansuman Biswas.

Between October 2003 and 2005, Jem was artist in residency in the Astrophysics department at Oxford University. Among the diverse outcomes of his time there – films, installations and sculptural observatories – was a band formed with members of the department, Big Eyed Beans From Venus.

In September 2006, Jem was due to finish work on a new composition, taking the form of a sonic sculpture titled 'Score For A Hole In The Ground'. Partly funded by prize money from the PRS Foundation, Finer having won the 2005 New Music Award for his proposal, this is to be found deep in a forest in Kent.

On the lighter side of things, Jem has formed an (occasional!) performing band with his daughters Ella and Kitty, called The Good The Bad And The Ugly. He continues to work across a wide spectrum of disciplines, from "fucked-up country music and rock'n'roll through experimental sound work to conceptual art".

Spider Stacy finally faced his demons in 1997 and gave up alcohol for good – too late for The Pogues, but not too late for himself. He formed a band with Andrew and Darryl, at whose suggestion it was named Wise Men. Several months later, first Ranken and then Hunt dropped out without having progressed much beyond the rehearsal stage. Spider recruited new members, removed the overtly Poguish flavours of the music, steered it into a more electric direction and renamed the band The Vendettas. In 2001, he played a handful of gigs in America using a Pogues covers outfit, Boys From The County Hell, as his backing group. This adventure went under the name of Spider Stacy's Pogue Mahone.

One of Spider's proudest achievements was to play at Kirsty MacColl's last-ever gig at the Shepherd's Bush Empire in October 2000, contributing tin whistle to 'Fairytale Of New York' (Shane's part in the duet being covered by Sonny George) and singing along on the choruses of 'There's A Guy Works Down The Chip Shop, Swears He's Elvis'. Another huge thrill was to perform onstage with Patti Smith and her guitarist and bassist, Lenny Kaye and Tony Shanahan. This happened at a folk night forming part of London's Meltdown festival, curated by Smith in June 2005. Spider sang 'Joe

Hill', backed by Kaye and Shanahan, and then accompanied Smith and her band on tin whistle for an old English folk song that Stacy had heard for the first time during the soundcheck.

In other activities, Spider has performed and recorded with Filthy Thieving Bastards, an offshoot of Bay Area punk band The Swinging Utters, playing whistle and singing. He also contributed to a 96-day sound score composed by Susan Stenger for an art installation at the Musée Art Contemporain gallery in Lyon in 2006. Soundtrack For An Exhibition included a feature film and paintings which were "in confrontation . . . with the soundtrack and each other" so that the music functioned "not as a sin-gular experience but as a score evolving over time".

At the time of writing, Spider was planning his wedding in Las Vegas to Louise Nevill, his partner since 1997.

Darryl Hunt moved back to London from Munich when The Pogues split and married Claudia in 1997. After his stint with Spider, Andrew and Wise Men, Hunt pursued his Bish project, releasing an album, *Bish*, in 2001 and performing live shows which included Shanne Bradley on bass. He worked on other solo material and joined a band of multi-instrumentalists called The Marseilles Figs whose music he describes as "sort of quirky, sort of acoustic and electric moods". He still DJs and has completed production work for various musicians in Munich.

He and Claudia separated after seven years of marriage, and he now shut-tles between London and Munich where his former wife lives with their daughter Sophie, seven at the time of writing. "It's still quite tough," he says. "I still miss Claudia. It's lonely not having a partner by your side. And I'm missing Sophie a lot. I think we should be a little bit nearer than 1,000 miles apart. It's tough to deal with every day. Times for me are in turmoil at the moment, but they're better than they were. It won't last forever. It'll be better when I'm more of a dad, make me feel a bit stronger."

Andrew Ranken, after The Pogues, started playing with an outfit called Nigel Burch & The Fleapit Orchestra, and was involved with them for several years. He then picked up with some of his old friends from The Operation to form The Mysterious Wheels, for whom he sings at occasional gigs. He still plays drums with The hKippers, a long-running band per-forming "stupid world music", and he has appeared on two of their albums, *Gutted* and *Filleted*, plus another yet to be released. For anyone lucky enough to be invited, he holds jam sessions in his front room on Sunday afternoons with The Mysterious Wheels' Paul Seacroft (ex of The Selecter) and another friend who lives in the same street in north-east London.

Philip Chevron continued his recovery and is still sober. He released two compilation albums of Radiators material – *Cockles And Mussels*, a best-of, in 1995, and *Alive-Alive-O*, a collection of live and rare studio songs, in 1996. He reformed The Radiators in 2004 in Dublin under the name of The Radiators Plan 9. They played gigs and TV shows before recording a new album, provisionally titled *Trouble Pilgrim*, which was awaiting a release date at the time of writing. Former Pogues bassist Cait O'Riordan, then living in Dublin, joined the band for its resurrection, but she departed in 2005 due to personality clashes and band politics.

Says Philip: "She has screwed up opportunity after opportunity for years, and it's all of her own making." The band have now reverted to their original name of The Radiators From Space.

Philip is nearing completion of *Jack Rooney*, the musical he began in 1996 with Nick Robbins, his studio collaborator, and writing partner Declan Lynch. He has already recorded 18 tracks with guest vocalists Spider Stacy, Andrew Ranken, Kirsty MacColl, Sarah Jane Morris, Ronnie Drew, Lila Macmahon and Niall MacMahon. Kirsty's contribution, 'Manhattan Moon', was the last recording she made before her untimely death only days later. It has already slipped out to the public on a career retrospective, *From Croydon To Cuba*, released by EMI/Virgin in 2005.

Work on the musical had to go on hold in 2001 when the first Pogues reunion happened and Lynch started concentrating on his novels. The most recent, *The Rooms*, tells a perhaps familiar story. It is, says Philip, "about an ex-drunk who writes a musical called *Jack Rooney*"! Chevron intends to complete the project – set in an Irish-American milieu - in 2007, by which time he and his team will have taken the opportunity to address questions posed by 9/11.

Philip has also started some other theatre pieces, although his next major project is likely to be his first solo album. He has already forged alliances with country, blues and Tex-Mex musicians in Texas with a view to creating "quite a rootsy album – an Irish album made in Texas".

James Fearnley turned out to see The Pogues play LA in 1994 at the Wadsworth Theatre, only a few months after he'd left the band. He found it disappointing: "It didn't seem right with the likes of McNally and Coulter and Clarke, great musicians as they are. I remember the charge I wanted to get, but it didn't happen for me, not with just four of my cohorts remaining in the band."

James was enjoying an informal musical life in LA, playing a series of regular hootnannies at friends' homes with actors Kieran and Dermot Mulroney. Brad Pitt was among the guests and Melissa Etheridge was the "musical heart" of these gatherings, knowing "tons of songs and the words to all of them". James and the Mulroneys were finally invited to join Zander Schloss's outfit The Low & Sweet Orchestra, which included accordion, banjo, mandolin, cello, dobro, viola and violin. They signed a deal with Interscope, spent a "shitload" on videos, recorded with Neil Young's producer David Briggs before he died, released an album, *Goodbye To All That*, in 1996 and finally split when the prospect of a three-month tour arose. James, Kieran and Dermot were not prepared to take on a tour of that length.

Next, James formed a band called The Cranky George Trio, featuring a fiddle and cello player, and they still perform around the greater LA area. The Trio, perversely, has four members, with James playing a snare drum with a foot pedal. He says: "The material is quite different from The Pogues, although we're good at the 'rumbly stuff' as well, and there's a kind of sea-faring element to it and imagery from fairgrounds *et cetera*." Cranky George are liable to cover James's Pogues song, 'Drunken Boat'. The bass player is Brad Wood, who has produced Smashing Pumpkins, Liz Phair and Ben Lee among other artists.

Fearnley has also continued with his writing, working seriously on songs for the first time and starting a novel. He attends a writers' group, has been at writers' retreats in Virginia and Georgia and had a reading of his material in Beverly Hills.

Terry Woods stopped playing music altogether after the Pogues years and formed a management company, working with an "absolutely stunning" rock'n'roll three-piece band from the north west of Ireland called The Marbles, whom he signed to ZTT.

Terry was later, somewhat reluctantly, persuaded back into playing by Shane MacGowan, who phoned with the idea of forming a group including Liam Clancy and Ronnie Drew. Gathering at Clancy's home in Ring, Waterford, the four had a great time playing together, and although the collaboration was destined to fizzle out, it reawakened Terry's love for making music. He says, "I took the instruments out and I enjoyed it so much I didn't want to put them back. I found it to be therapeutic."

This, in turn, led to the second coming of The Woods Band which was another enjoyable but ultimately unrealistic undertaking. "It was going to be incredibly disparate," admits Woods. "I felt we needed something to put a handle on it. I parked it. It has remained parked. I've taken the wheels off. There's no engine, and the petrol tank has gone. Literally, as I parked it, The Pogues thing started up again."

Terry, who is now living with Marian near Cavan, County Meath, has become involved with a number of bands and a young Irish musician whom he's producing.

Cait O'Riordan split from Elvis Costello in November 2002. He married actress Diana Krall the next year. Cait then joined the reformed Radiators with Philip Chevron but left under a cloud in 2005. She has become an expert mountaineer, scaling peaks around the world, and was last thought to be planning a move from her home in Dublin to the UK.

Frank Murray moved to the States where he has returned to his love of the theatre.

Jamie Clarke went on to form a speed-folk band called Jamie Clarke's Perfect. Based in Germany, they have released a string of albums, the live ones including a number of Pogues covers. James McNally has recorded a series of "world fusion" albums with Afro Celt Sound System, released a solo album, *Everybreath*, and also worked with Ronan Keating, playing whistle and accordion, and programming. David Coulter has recorded in his own right and in collaboration with a host of other musicians and artists. He hooked up with the Museum Of Modern Art in Oxford as a musician and sound artist, and he also became a lecturer in music and performance at Stratford-Upon-Avon College.

And then there was Shane MacGowan.

After leaving The Pogues in Japan in 1991, Shane became involved in a number of collaborations. He recorded a duet with Nick Cave – a cover of Louis Armstrong's 'What A Wonderful World' – which was released by Mute in December 1992. It reached Number 72. There were link-ups with Breton folk singer and harpist Alan Stivell and a French band, Soldat Louis. He also formed a short-lived group called The London Contemporary Five, and early in 1994 accepted an invitation from Van Morrison to perform 'Gloria' with him at The Brits, the event thus bringing together Ireland's two grumpiest singers. In August that year, MacGowan appeared as a guest vocalist on 'God Help Me', a track on The Jesus And Mary Chain's Top 20 album, *Stoned And Dethroned*.

By now, MacGowan was about to launch his solo career with a backing band called The Popes, having spent a year hidden away in Dublin (at Bono's house and then at a private address with Victoria) and London, writing, rehearsing and recording. The Popes included rhythm guitarist Mo O'Hagan and bassist Berni France from The London Contemporary Five. France was an old friend of Shane's dating back to his college days in Hammersmith. Presumably this is the same Berni with whom he formed his first band, the long-haired Hot Dogs With Everything, as a teenager. Also in The Popes were guitarist Paul McGuinness, banjo man Tom McManamon, former Exploited and Boothill Foot-Tappers drummer Danny Heatley and whistle player Colm O'Maonlai.

MacGowan told an interviewer: "The Popes are just doing what The Pogues were doing until it went wrong."

The first single, 'The Church Of The Holy Spook', was welcomed by serious music critics, although it created something of a controversy with its cover photograph of a bearded, bare-chested MacGowan in a crucifixion pose. At the time, Shane said of his religious philosophy: "I believe in one great spiritual entity which the Catholic church calls God and which I call the Tao. It's the same thing... the mandala of Christ, the crucifix, is a strong protective thing and guide. I feel a lot better with a Gaelic cross around my neck." The single reached Number 74 when it was released by ZTT in September 1994.

Its follow-up, 'That Woman's Got Me Drinking', caused even more of a stir when it became known that heart-throb actor Johnny Depp – at the height of his love affair with Kate Moss – had contributed some guitar parts. Depp appeared with The Popes on *Top Of The Pops*, carried out joint interviews with Shane, and directed and appeared in the video, playing a drunk to MacGowan's straight barman. MacGowan and Depp had met in Dublin in a late-night bar some years previously and become firm friends. MacGowan would later appear as an inebriated minstrel in Depp's 2004 movie, *The Libertine*. The single hit its peak position of Number 34 in October.

The album, *The Snake* – produced by MacGowan and former Pogues soundman Dave Jordan - was released the same month. Widely received as a fine return to form for MacGowan, it mixed traditional Irish up-tempos and ballads with R&B, rock, rock'n'roll and a hint of jazz, and made Number 37. It included MacGowan's love song 'Aisling', which had been discarded by The Pogues. Guest musicians included Jem Finer and Spider Stacy, along with former Thin Lizzy guitarist Brian Robertson and Dubliners John Sheahan and Barney McKenna.

Shane was still in demand as a collaborator. In 1994, he sang 'Spancil Hill' on Irish TV with Christy Moore. He went on to record duets with Sinead O'Connor (a new version of 'Haunted') and Maire Brennan of Clannad ('You're The One'). Both songs wound up on film soundtracks, the former in 1996's *Two If By Sea* and the latter in 1995's *Circle Of Friends*. They were subsequently added to a repackaged version of *The Snake*. 'Haunted' became MacGowan's most popular single for some while when it was released by ZTT in April 1995, scoring a Number 30 placing. He did even better a year later with a chaotic version of 'My Way', fuelled by the spirit of Sid Vicious. It registered at Number 29, helped along no doubt by its use on a TV ad for Nike trainers, although MacGowan himself disliked it. In 1996, he sang with Kylie Minogue, PJ Harvey and others on 'Death Is Not The End', a track from Nick Cave's *Murder Ballads* album and, in 1997, he was one of the featured artists on the BBC's 'Perfect Day' film. He also recorded a couple of tracks with Ronnie Drew.

MacGowan had been having his health problems. At the end of the Eighties, he'd been suffering from stomach ulcers. By 1993, he'd been ill with alcoholic hepatitis and was having regular hospital appointments to check up on his liver, but was still admitting to taking cocaine and speed-balls, a mixture of heroin and amphetamines, and he was spending his days and many of his nights in Filthy McNasty's pub in Islington, run by his friend Gerry O'Boyle. In 1996, he was said to be run down and, later, on the wagon. If that was true, it didn't last long. By the time *Loaded* journalist Ben Marshall met him in 1997, he was drinking Martini by the pint and half-pint. He was also recovering from a broken hip.

MacGowan told Marshall: "I have suffered, because life is suffering, but it's also fucking pleasure. You can't separate the two. If you didn't have pain, then you wouldn't realise when you're having pleasure. It's partly knowing that it's not going to last that makes happiness so wonderful. It will be struck down in the end, so you've just got to grab it while you can. That's the thing everyone misses; I'm just having a good time.

"I'm just following the Irish tradition of songwriting, the Irish way of life, the human way of life. Cram as much pleasure as you can into life, and rail against the pain that you have to suffer as a result. Or scream and rant with the pain, and then wait for it to be taken away with beautiful pleasure."

He also admitted: "I have been strung out on heroin. Ages ago now... I'm not sure I was an addict, but I do know that heroin's not a problem, providing you can get hold of it. Spirits are a problem when you can't get hold of them and an even bigger problem when you can. I tell you, if I was on a death-trip, I'd still be drinking spirits... I've tried everything. Speed, smack, coke, crack. Every drink you could possibly imagine. I tried it because I was curious and inquisitive."

Two years later, Sinead O'Connor reported MacGowan to the police in Kentish Town after apparently witnessing him taking heroin at his flat in London. The *Sunday Independent* later quoted her as saying, "I reported him to the police for his own good. I never wanted him put into prison, because drugs are freely available there, but ordered into a rehabilitation programme."

MacGowan was furious, at first accusing O'Connor of chasing publicity, but he later stated that her action served as a "wake-up call", with the result that he discontinued his relationship with smack. "I'm very grateful to her now," he told one journalist.

There had been deaths in his close circle. In March 1995, Dave Jordan – who had left The Pogues to work with MacGowan – was found dead from a heroin overdose in a Paris hotel while on the road with The Popes. Both Jordan and his wife Elizabeth had expressed their worries at his taking the job in the first place.

Terry Woods remarks: "I had a long conversation with him before he went back in. I'd asked him did he think it was a wise thing to do. It was a good way of him earning the money that he bought his house with, but it wasn't worth dying for."

James Fearnley: "I do remember getting wind from Elizabeth about DJ's fears about finding himself working with Shane. It's awful, really, to remember that Frank presented DJ to The Pogues in whatever year that was and to be told that DJ had been back in his hometown to clean up from heroin and that his job for us was his first since his rehab."

In July 1995, an Irish friend called Brian Ging died in Shane's flat in Blackstock Road, north London, from a mixture of alcohol and opiates. The next year, in October, Big Charlie MacLennan, who had also defected to The Popes after allegedly being sacked by the Pogues, died from a heart attack. Paul Scully is now the last man standing of The Pogues' "big four" road-crew characters.

"It was recklessness to the point of suicide," comments Joey Cashman. "Charlie got a huge amount of heroin and cocaine and he put out these massive lines and that's really what killed him. Now if you'd gone up to him and said, 'Charlie, that is ridiculous,' he'd just turn round and say, 'Why don't you mind your own fucking business? I know what I'm fucking doing and I don't give a fuck if I die anyway.' He'd been taking drugs all his life. He knew his limits. He didn't do it to die, but it's a form of suicide.

"Charlie was a complete professional. He knew every venue in the world. We used to go into airports and we'd hear, 'Hiya Charlie.'"

James Fearnley last saw Charlie in LA: "He parted the crowd ahead of me, leading me backstage at the House Of Blues to play accordion on a couple of songs with The Popes – where Shane introduced me as 'one of the bosses that sacked me'."

In May 1999, Robbie O'Neill – the eldest son of The Pogues' Irish publicist Terry O'Neill – died from a heroin overdose at MacGowan's flat in Savernake Road, north-west London. The post mortem revealed that he was not a habitual user.

Responding to the series of tragedies, Shane commented: "I don't want any of this shit [heroin] in my house. My place is my place."

The year 2000 brought the death of Kirsty MacColl on December 18 in Cozumel, Mexico. Kirsty was killed, aged 41, by a power boat speeding through restricted waters where she was swimming with her sons. Kirsty's mother Jean now leads the Justice For Kirsty campaign which is dedicated to finding and bringing the culprit to accountability. So far, it has proved impossible to subpoena the boat's rich and influential owner.

425

Jean has stated that, "Whenever I hear Kirsty's singing it gives me pleasure and joy."

On December 22, 2002, Joe Strummer died suddenly at 50 from heart failure at his Somerset home after returning from a walk with his dog.

Spider: "Kirsty's death was just horrible, so shocking that it almost hasn't sunk in still. It was such a horrific thing to happen. Joe's death was really sad, but Kirsty's was a violent death whereas the manner of Joe's passing was very peaceful. He was at home, in his chair. Kirsty's was of a different order entirely. When it happens to a friend of yours..." The Pogues, without Shane, had recorded two tracks with Kirsty – 'The One And Only' and 'All The Tears I Cried'.

MacGowan And The Popes went through some line-up changes. Paul Conlon and next John Myers replaced O'Maonlai on the whistle. Then Kerina joined on accordion and whistle, and Bob Dowling replaced Berni France. MacGowan began work on new material, co-producing with Brian Robertson. A single, 'Christmas Party EP '96', was released in November 1996, but failed to chart.

The next year, MacGowan recorded a track called 'An Irish Airman Forsees His Death' for a tribute album to the Irish poet WB Yeats, who had written a popular poem of the same name.

1997 also saw the release of the new Popes album, *The Crock Of Gold*, which reached Number 59 early in November. It came with a cover painting by MacGowan, who has given the original artwork to Joey Cashman. In some quarters, the album was welcomed with great excitement, with *Loaded* declaring that it was MacGowan's best work since *If I Should Fall From Grace With God*, although in others it was considered a poor follow-up to *The Snake*. One reviewer said it was "at times easier on the ear but hardly threatened to set the pulse racing". It was a less varied offering than its predecessor and MacGowan preferred it to *The Snake*. He said later that he had a "nervous breakdown" over its disappointing performance.

The Crock Of Gold was Shane MacGowan's last album.

Epilogue

It was Anthony Addis – the band's former accountant - who put the wheels in motion for a Pogues reunion in 2001. It wasn't a new idea; it had been suggested several times before. But this time, as Darryl would undoubtedly say, the planets seemed to be in the correct alignment.

The proposal was to reform the eight-man line-up that had recorded *If I Should Fall From Grace With God* – Jem Finer, Spider Stacy, James Fearnley, Andrew Ranken, Philip Chevron, Terry Woods, Darryl Hunt and, of course, Shane MacGowan – for a run of Christmas concerts. There would be no new recordings and nothing to sell except for a set filled with classic Pogues favourites.

Some members of the band were immediately interested and others approached it with a degree of caution, but the unknown quantity was MacGowan. Would he agree to take part? And if so, would he prove to be any more reliable than he had been during his last days with the band?

Joey Cashman, Shane's personal assistant - in fact, his manager in everything but name - had a lot to do with securing his co-operation. Jem Finer played a major part on behalf of the other Pogues.

Finer wasn't immediately taken with the suggestion of a reunion. He recalls: "It was the last thing I wanted to do. It had been proposed before a few times and it had conveniently gone away, but it wasn't going to go away this time. I thought, 'I don't want to do it if Shane doesn't want to or if he's going to be completely crap and horrible to work with.' I didn't want to go back to what we'd had before.

"I phoned him up and talked to him and he said he'd like to do it in theory. I said, 'What if I come over and visit you in Tipperary and we talk about it?' and he said, 'Yeah, come over.' So I went over, I think in September that year, and visited him and we talked about it. I just thought

427

it was worth a try. I thought maybe something could be healed. It seemed very sad the way everything had ended up."

That was how Terry Woods felt. He explains: "The Pogues were too big a band to go out with a whimper. I was quite delighted about the reunion. It appeared if nothing else that we could put a proper full-stop after The Pogues."

With everyone in agreement, Anthony Addis consulted with Simon Moran, a personal friend and the boss of leading promoters SJM, and a list of UK dates was drawn up.

"I was really quite gobsmacked by the whole thing," says Spider. "For a long time, I'd accepted that it was over, that The Pogues' story was finished. Then Jem phoned me up. I was very, very surprised. I'd have thought that Jem would simply have not wanted to do it, although I think he did find it all a bit painful, the way that it came to an end.

"When Louise and I saw the dates, we thought, 'Two Brixtons! That's a bit ambitious, isn't it?' Next thing we know, they're all selling out, so it was very exciting, that run-up to the first show."

As for the participation of his old sparring partner, MacGowan, Spider says: "People have this idea that there was a lot of acrimony, especially around Shane leaving. It was a really, really painful thing to have to do and probably we didn't do the right thing, or we didn't do it in the right way, but there was never any bad blood about it. Jem and I played on *The Snake*, and I've played with The Popes many times. But I was surprised that Shane agreed to be involved in the reunion. I thought he'd put himself beyond the pale a bit with Victoria's book."

Published earlier in 2001, *A Drink With Shane MacGowan* is jointly credited to Victoria Mary Clarke and Shane, and it takes the form of a series of conversations between the co-authors, recorded over an unspecified period of time and then faithfully transcribed, warts and all. There are sections where MacGowan hits out generally at The Pogues and also attacks individual members of the band and its organisation, viciously enough that, in a clear-headed moment, he made the sudden decision to post-script the book with an apology.

In subsequent interviews, he was keen to point out that, "It was not written by me", and in a typical explanation, he would insist: "It's just a garbled bunch of tapes of me out of my brains talking to my missus. You should take it as a funny book."

Terry Woods agrees that it's "very funny" although, according to Philip Chevron, other band members found it upsetting. Frank Murray certainly did. He fumes: "It's a lot of rubbish, lies and fantasy talk."

Shanne Bradley remarks: "Funnily enough, my daughter bought it for me this Christmas [2005]. I have avoided reading it cos it makes me angry. There are lots of myths in it."

Darryl simply remarked that he intended to write a sequel: *A Cup Of Tea With Darryl Hunt.*

Spider reasons: "You have to remember the circumstances in which the conversations were recorded. Shane was lashing out. It's how he was, maybe, at the particular time she happened to record what he was saying that particular evening. It might not have been how he was feeling that particular day or the following morning. Or he might have held those opinions. The other thing is, Shane is Shane. Every now and again he may say stuff that could be construed to be quite hurtful, but you have to let it be hurtful in order for it to be hurtful. You have to bear in mind who's saying it. Everybody in the band is capable of giving as good as they get."

Philip Chevron develops the argument: "Shane's always made nasty comments about The Pogues. I instinctively understood it's part of the territory, part of the vaudeville. There's a certain degree of entertainment value in it and one thing that I never allowed myself to forget with Shane is that he's an entertainer. He knows how to play the game. He absolutely knows what he's doing, why he's doing it and what effect it's likely to have."

As a strange sort of bonus, says Philip, "It played into the drama when we had the first reunion. The audiences, the media – they thought hell would freeze over before we'd get back together again."

Shane and Victoria had been having their problems as a couple. Victoria later told the *Daily Mail* that after suffering two nervous breakdowns, she had moved into a separate flat in north London.

By 1994, living with Shane in Dublin, she had started to feel trapped: "Although there were plenty of stars to hang out with, lots of parties and so on, we were both unhappy there. By then, I'd realised that my life and my career – I'd started writing celebrity interviews for newspapers and magazines – were totally tied up with Shane's.

"I'd set out to save him from himself and it hadn't worked. I also saw that looking after him was a way of not having to think about my life or where I should be going."

Clarke came to believe and accept that MacGowan's excessive habits were part of the creative process and, realising that he was not going to change his lifestyle, decided that if she couldn't beat him, she might as well join him. She then, for a while, "went off the rails" on drink, tranquillisers and, occasionally, cocaine.

"I think I was having a nervous breakdown," she stated. "I thought about suicide and I'd walk in front of cars, not caring if I lived or died."

The groupie problem had also reared its head again. MacGowan had managed to be monogamous for a while after Victoria's last ultimatum, but had given in to temptation once more and the ensuing ructions exploded at Waterford's Tramore Festival (where Shane, finally, got to support Bob Dylan).

"Shane and I had a huge fight in his dressing room, in front of Bob Dylan and his roadies," said Victoria. "I was bashing Shane around the head with my handbag and Bob was laughing his head off. Then I got very drunk and we broke up – unofficially – for a few months. We ended up back in London and lived together for a while, but I had another nervous break-down and had to move out. I couldn't function and live with him."

Clarke reported that by 1996, MacGowan had calmed down a great deal and was responsibly taking charge of The Popes. She was optimistic enough about their future to think of marriage, although she specified that they would have to live in a house sufficiently large to accommodate their incompatible habits and preferences. In that same year, she appeared in a Channel 4 documentary called *Rock Wives*.

In a *Daily Telegraph* feature about the show, Victoria talked about her "ultra-white, scrupulously tidy, no-smoking" house – the opposite to Shane's which was "indescribable". She also looked back on some of MacGowan's more unpredictable moments – the time he stubbed a ciga-rette out on a dog in Trafalgar Square, and the acid-informed occasion in Kathy MacMillan's flat when he literally ate chunks out of a Beach Boys album.

Clarke asserted that she had stopped sacrificing her own career for MacGowan's, assessed the high levels of attention demanded by certain people in the public eye, and added: "You need to be aware that you have a life of your own and you are not responsible for the life of your rock star. Once you have these two things figured out, you can live happily ever after."

Unfortunately for Shane and Victoria, the ever-after turned out not to be so happy, with Clarke since calling time on the relationship. Allegedly, she was on the road with MacGowan when he took a female fan to another hotel room. However, Victoria remains a close friend and confidante to Shane, and she still accompanies him on tours.

The crunch time for The Pogues' reunion arrived with the rehearsals. It was then that they would know for sure whether things were going to work or not.

Spider: "The weird thing was that once we started playing together, everything seemed so natural and normal, like not very much time at all had gone by. It was exactly like the old days. There had never been anything between us that couldn't be fixed. There was nothing that needed to be patched up. Any bad blood that may have existed had been forgotten."

"It was very much like finding the common feeling amongst us all that had been lost over the years, which was very wonderful," adds Jem. "It was like finding something one thought was dead when actually it had only been asleep."

The schedule included two dates in Manchester, at the Academy and the Apollo on December 15 and 16, Glasgow SECC (17), Birmingham Academy (18), Dublin Point Depot (20) and three nights, the third added due to ticket demand, at Brixton Academy (21, 22 and 23). It was a far cry from the Boston Arms.

Philip Chevron's friend, singer Lila MacMahon, sang the female part in 'Fairytale Of New York', and The Dubliners joined the band on stage in Ireland. James Fearnley says: "Barney had to be guided across, and he sat on a stool. It says something about the relationship we've had with The Dubliners that we took time to actually greet one another on stage in front of 9,000 people – 'Just wait a minute, we have to do this.' And then to play a song with them... it was just a great thing to be able to do."

"I'd really run out of steam by 2001, so I was glad to go on the road," says Darryl Hunt. "I was very happy – I thought it was a bloody good group - although it took us a while to get used to things. It was a bit hairy. But it was great to go out on stage and see how much people cared about the group and Shane as a singer and songwriter. And we got paid well. If you do something that's fun and you're getting paid for it, what more can you ask for?"

All of the band have stressed the efficiency of Anthony Addis – now their manager – in ensuring their prompt and proper payment.

The audiences were rewarded with a reinvigorated Pogues, playing with all the wild energy of their youth but the powerful dynamics of their long experience. Revisiting some of the greatest and most ageless moments of their career, from 'Streams Of Whiskey' to 'Sally MacLennane', 'A Rainy Night In Soho' to 'Sayonara', they were in capable hands with Shane MacGowan, who was taking this reunion thing seriously.

"Some of the versions Shane's been doing are better than the album versions," says Darryl. "His voice has got a really good quality to it. It's deeper and stronger. In versions of 'A Rainy Night In Soho' and 'The Broad Majestic Shannon', there's a passion that I hadn't heard in years."

The band enjoyed the tour so much that they agreed to a couple of major gigs in 2002, appearing at the Fleadh Festival in London's Finsbury Park on June 8 and also laying on a treat for Dublin audiences at the city's RDS.

Everything went quiet in 2003, apart from the release in June of the doc-umentary, *If I Should Fall From Grace: The Shane MacGowan Story*. Subsequently issued as a DVD with a cover photograph that illustrates exactly how MacGowan stares in horror when someone dares to say, 'I'm sorry, I didn't hear that,' it was premièred internationally at selected venues in major cities. James Fearnley was invited to represent The Pogues at a Q&A session after the screening at the Egyptian Theatre in Hollywood.

He remembers:"A guy in there was so outraged by Shane. He might have been coming from a Californian point of view where people are looking after themselves with healthy diets and not smoking and taking lots of exer-cise and stuff. And honestly, he was so outraged that somebody like Shane should actually exist in this day and age, and that nobody had ever done an intervention or something.

"This guy threw me so much that I didn't know what to say, because I'd been put on the spot. I kind of felt a little bit guilty that I was in part way responsible for Shane being like that. In some people's view, I might have enabled him in 'self-destruction' or whatever. It was probably my upbring-ing that made me feel guilty.

"But on account of that guy, I've had a think about it and now I think I appreciate more what Shane's up to than probably I ever did. In a com-pletely happenstance way, Shane is having a look at the cosmos closer up than certainly I can. It's really good for humanity to have somebody out there fucking it up. The absurdity of life is going to bring out somebody that just exists on the brink of something all the time. Shane couldn't function if he weren't on that brink. He could stop drinking and whatever else he medicates himself with, but he would still be on the brink. Seriously, I think there's no way of avoiding that. He's staring into the void, and I don't want to do that.

"He's embracing things that lots of us daren't and he's telling us what he can see in his songs. I think he's donated himself to the vagaries of the cosmos and that's what makes him what he is. We need people like Shane around, because they've got a point of view that's pretty unique and valu-able. He's full blast on the prow of the ship and he's taking everything. And it's life. I don't mean death or anything. He's out there saying, 'Bring it on.'"

2004 brought another tour and an extra member to the stage. Cait O'Riordan had bumped into Shane MacGowan at Christmas 2003 in the foyer of the Shelbourne Hotel in Dublin, just after closing time. They hadn't met for 17 years.

"Remember me?" she asked. "I used to be in your band."

A year later, Cait joined The Pogues for a December tour, following the re-release by WEA of all seven Pogues albums, remastered and extended with extra tracks relevant to the period of the original recordings.

Cait sang Kirsty MacColl's part in 'Fairytale Of New York', performed her own old showstopper, 'I'm A Man You Don't Meet Every Day', and contributed backing vocals.

She said afterwards: "To be given this second chance was amazing. I felt very grateful for that."

However, Cait carried her gratitude and enthusiasm for the reunited Pogues a little too far. Amid rumours that she tried to stage a one-woman coup to secure for herself a bigger role in the band, she succeeded only in screwing up the position she did have, and she was consequently banned from any further tours.

The group members are unwilling to discuss what happened in any detail. Spider says: "Some of us were really excited at the prospect of Cait joining us in 2004 and some of us were a bit wary. I have to say that the way it's panned out, the ones who were wary were probably right to be wary. It all got a bit ugly. On stage, she was great, and it could have been really, really good, but unfortunately, it wasn't to work out."

Andrew, who had not been on speaking terms with O'Riordan when she left The Pogues originally, says: "I tended to give her a wide berth when she came back. She played very well, but things very quickly became problematic."

It was in 2005 that things really took off for The Pogues. By now, the word "reunion" was sounding a little inappropriate. They had become an occasional and, once again, enormously popular band, playing live dates and manageable tours at their own pleasure without having to worry about record company commitments or expectations.

Says Andrew Ranken: "We've got to the sort of position I had hoped we could get into way back then, where we're doing a few big shows but much more at our own convenience."

After a one-off show at Guildford's Guilfest, The Pogues undertook a short Japanese visit in July, with a Spanish festival appearance in September. The Christmas tour of major venues in Ireland and the UK, which included three heaving, delirious gigs at the Brixton Academy, found the group on more vibrant form than they'd been in for a very long time, with MacGowan charismatically mooching around the front of the stage alongside James Fearnley, still jumping and crashing to his knees despite the huge bulk of accordion on his chest, and a swirling Philip Chevron. In Dublin at the Point Depot, Terry's wife Marian had the unusual experience of seeing both of her husbands on stage, with Terry having invited Keith Donald to play saxophone on 'Fiesta'. And Shane enjoyed the experience of going to

Rehab – a club night at the Voodoo Lounge where he DJed with old mucker BP Fallon.

By now The Pogues had arrived at an irresistible setlist which showcased the broad talents of the band members and usually included 'Streams Of Whiskey', 'If I Should Fall From Grace With God', 'The Broad Majestic Shannon', 'Turkish Song Of The Damned', 'Young Ned Of The Hill', 'Rain Street', 'White City', 'Tuesday Morning', 'The Old Main Drag', 'Sayonara', 'Repeal Of The Licensing Laws', 'The Sunnyside Of The Street', 'Body Of An American', 'Lullaby Of London', 'A Pair Of Brown Eyes', 'Thousands Are Sailing', 'Dirty Old Town', 'Bottle Of Smoke', 'The Sickbed Of Cuchulainn', 'Sally MacLennane', 'A Rainy Night In Soho', 'The Irish Rover', 'Star Of The County Down', 'Fairytale Of New York' and 'Fiesta'.

Despite the familiarity of the songs, various Pogues had moments they looked forward to, or found unforgettable.

Philip: "'The Old Main Drag' is a defining Pogues song. It's obviously about a teenager with nowhere to live. Obviously he's a rent boy for a while. He sees characters around who could be him when he's their age. They also came to London with dreams that didn't get fulfilled. To see Shane MacGowan singing that song in Brixton Academy is a deeply moving experience. He himself is living proof of the song, living the exist-ence that he speculated, although of course he's Shane MacGowan and he's in The Pogues and he's not somebody sitting outside the tube station drink-ing VP sherry. But he could be, and he knows that. And I could be. Shane's best songs are always on the edge of that very thin line that separates fortune and misfortune, and that's universal."

James Fearnley cites different emotional highlights. He says: "One of the thrilling things with being on stage with The Pogues – I like to go far right when we're doing 'Streams Of Whiskey' and stand dead close to the front and watch everybody in a line. They all step up to the microphone and sing, 'I am going, I am going,' and when they've finished, everybody takes a step back, all in one. Oh God, it gives me the heebeejeebees, that does. It reminds me of walking to the Pindar Of Wakefield for our first-ever gig, a line of guys all out to do business. It's cool. It's way cool.

"And it's such a thrill to have Andrew do that 'clackety-clackety' at the beginning of 'Sally MacLennane' and keep it going for as long as he can keep it up. And I love the instrumental solo in 'Sally', a little respite in the hell-for-leather flurry of it all, even if it just lasts eight beats."

The Pogues had recruited a number of female singers for 'Fairytale' as the tour moved from city to city, among them Cerys Mathews, Aisling Bowyer, Jem's daughter Ella Finer and Katie Melua, who performed the song with the band on the Christmas edition of *The Jonathan Ross Show*.

The single had been re-released, with the proceeds benefiting homeless charities and, also, the Justice For Kirsty campaign, for which The Pogues collected at Brixton.

Spider issued a statement reading: "The single isn't about making money. It's about justice for Kirsty. Jean [Kirsty's mother] has spent the last five years trying to get at the truth and she is making good headway. But the guy in question is one of the richest men in Mexico and is able to buy the best lawyers. When I first heard of the campaign, I didn't see the point. It's all an uphill task and Jean is an old lady. But I was wrong. She is getting close to finding justice for Kirsty."

The single, voted the best seasonal song ever by VH1 viewers, reached Number Three in the Christmas singles chart.

"I was so excited," says Steve Lillywhite. "That song is like a great wine. It seems to improve with age."

As further evidence of the escalating interest in The Pogues, the BBC broadcast a making-of special about 'Fairytale Of New York' in December, while the band were on tour.

Ella Finer made most of the 'Fairytale' appearances during the December dates. Jem explains how this came to be: "The suggestion was made by Darryl, I think. Ella's a really good singer. I was asked what did I feel about it. It wasn't something I would've encouraged because I wouldn't want to put one of my kids into that situation where they're open to all the possible negativity that can come from the press or public, or even people carping within the band. I felt very nervous about it. I talked to Marcia and I think she felt the same. All the other people in the band wanted her to do it – if there was anyone that didn't, then we would have felt she shouldn't do it. But we felt that Ella was a grown-up and if that's what people wanted her to do, it was for her to make the decision. She said yes, and she was really brilliant."

The tour was filmed for a documentary of the band being made by James's wife Danielle, in collaboration with director Nora Meyer, who had previously made a film about Oona King and George Galloway, and boom man Tom Sheahan. James, meanwhile, drew on his writer's instincts to document everything that happened to The Pogues in 2005/2006 in infinitesimal detail in what he calls the Bloguemahone, still showing on the band's official website. Some of this was published first in *The Independent*, having been specially commissioned.

Not all of The Pogues were delighted when, on February 2, 2006, they were presented with a lifetime achievement honour at the Meteor Ireland Music Awards in Dublin, a ceremony at which they also performed 'The Irish Rover'. Hosted by Patrick Kielty, the show was broadcast three days later on RTE television.

Philip Chevron comments: "I thought it was just licking the ass of the Irish music business, but I was out-voted over it. I really thought it was about selling mobile phones, and not about them saying, 'Well done, lads.'"

The next month, some twenty years after they first went to the States to quaff and raise hell with their Limelight VIP cards and to start building a grass-roots following in New York and the surrounding areas, The Pogues returned for a string of dates arranged round St Patrick's Day, all of which sold out. As on the initial visit all those years ago, they didn't travel too far afield, playing shows in Washington, Atlantic City, Boston and New York, and the crowds attending their gigs included everyone from Steve Lillywhite to Frank Murray to Kate Moss.

Shane MacGowan had viewed The Pogues, in the days after he left, as something of a ruthless organisation - "And the next scapegoat's head would be cut off, and then people are even leaving before their heads get cut off." Today, he believes the band can co-exist indefinitely due to the more flexible working arrangement, stating: "I think we'll stay together. Nobody's interested in doing all-year-long tours."

Jem Finer adds: "It's nice. It's like doing it outside the business. The business is very much the thing that helped to destroy The Pogues in the first place. We can cut out the middle man. There's no pressure. It's not like we're on this wheel where we constantly make another record and rehearse and tour, and each turn of the wheel meaning you had to do it again and again. It's a much nicer way to exist, just getting together and playing a few concerts.

"There's an advantage in that what we were doing had a certain timeless quality anyway. It's not so much a nostalgia thing, it's something that still makes sense. One of the gratifying things is that there's a whole new audience. We always did have a very wide-ranging audience in terms of age, but what's happening now is very satisfying."

Terry Woods: "Anthony has actually made it financially viable for The Pogues to do what we do nowadays. He's very fastidious about it, which I very much appreciate."

"It's been really encouraging," comments Andrew. "At best, Shane is a bit unpredictable, and on odd nights he's been a bit ropey, but on the whole, he's been pretty solid and at the last gigs we did, he was the best I've heard him for donkey's years. The band's got really good again, it's enjoyable and it's fun. I'd be mad not to do it."

Philip Chevron describes the atmosphere today with The Pogues – who are set for another UK and Irish Christmas tour at the end of 2006, preceded by gigs in Japan and California. "We're going through a process at the moment where we're finally beginning to take on board the fact that we're older and can't necessarily do things the way we used to, and that we have to be more sensitive to each other's physical needs," he declares. "In our day-to-day business negotiations we decide how many gigs we're going to do on a tour, where we can take a day off, whether we need to do four days in a row somewhere. All of this is The Pogues being businessmen. I need to just rest a bit between gigs. Andrew has this recurring cluster headache that can take him at any moment. Terry has a problem with his back. Just stuff that happens with old men. The reality of it is that we don't see that much of each other. Shane has his posse up in The Boogaloo, and we all have home lives. On tour, we have our social life. I still believe to this day, now that we're old and boring and sober, that we still do all the right things for the right reasons, and it's still as playful as ever it was. It's just that we're different. People tend to exchange news about how their daughters are doing in school or college, or how their parents' health is, the things that middle-aged men actually talk about. Dressing-room conversations now revolve around prostate glands and the need for stronger spectacles. It's a real loving relationship where everybody has been around each other long enough to talk about anything, and we do."

Philip carries on, jokingly: "Never were more smart men assembled in one group to create a whole so idiotic and stupid – so many politics and fragile egos and sensitivities to remember. Everyone now has their own emailing style, which we've had to get used to. That's more fuel for tension. One or two people always have the knack of writing an email and pressing the 'send' button before they should. It's just another new aspect of The Pogues we never expected we'd have to deal with back in 1984. Whatever the next technology is, we'll have to figure out how we write to each other in that as well."

The Pogues have arrived at ways of avoiding discomfort on the road. "One of the reasons I love touring with them so much these days is that I do it entirely on my terms and those terms manage to suit the band," continues Chevron. "What you want and how you want things to be... things we were too timid to stick up for first time around.

"Also, it's taken many years to realise that it's okay to *miss* stuff, to go your own way, to create your own way of doing things. It's part and parcel of being in a band where you're surrounded by seven equally stimulating human beings that you're afraid to miss anything."

Some of the band's earliest supporters and associates have been to see the reunited band, with varying reactions.

Dee O'Mahony, who turned out for one of the 2004 gigs, says: "I found it really painful to see Shane, compared to how sparky he used to be. I know the flashes are there. I don't need to say I'd ever write Shane off. I still thought he was amazing, but it's a different experience. Every time I might find myself mentally thinking, 'He's lost it,' he'll come out with some kind of comment or you'll hear him snarl a lyric and he'll just let you know that the tiger is still there somewhere."

Shanne Bradley has a word of good cheer about MacGowan. She says: "Shane isn't sad, so nobody else ought to be. I saw him in Eire playing a couple of gigs. He was in great form and we enjoyed the craic!"

Dave Robinson comments: "The band with Shane back is something really interesting. It's a natural progression. The Pogues are seen as a seminal font of Celtic psycho music, which is all based around the idea of them. A real musical movement has come out of it, which is doing very good business in the States – Flogging Molly *et cetera* [others being The Tossers and Dropkick Murphys]. If Shane can get it together, and when he has a little respect for the music he's performed, it's got to work better."

Frank Murray responds with his old managerial eye for cash and a suggestion that the band should return to the treadmill they are only too happy to have escaped: "They're making themselves a lot of money, and I'm glad they're doing it, but there's one thing I feel is missing. There's no creative process going on with them as a band. They're not striving to make a record or anything like that. But as long as Shane stays fit and healthy, it should work out."

The worst problems Shane has been presenting The Pogues with lately are run-of-the-mill things – turning up early when he isn't expected, or changing a setlist around at the 11th hour.

Says Chevron: "We know to keep the setlist as far away from Shane as humanly possible. Never bring a setlist to within a mile of him. New people in the crew, it's the first thing they get told. Every time we move a song, it shifts the whole balance of the show – and half an hour before the show, it's not something you can really do. Fortunately Shane doesn't do many soundchecks. We rehearse without him and do soundchecks without him and we hope he won't turn up too early, cos he'll just get in the way. He can wreak utter chaos. He tends to know when he's needed although, occasionally, just in case anybody gets too comfortable with that, he'll turn up before anybody else.

"This is the part he does understand: that absolutely no situation exists where he can be out-of-it at a gig and not deliver. People are employing you, and you know you're not going to get asked back if you fuck up. His duty is to get out there for two hours and deliver. We've come to learn that he doesn't let us down any more. At the very least, he delivers a show and sometimes he does even more than that. We're always on good form, but when he's on good form as well, the whole thing just catches fire. We're inevitably better than we were the first time around."

Shane has now become inseparable from his cousin Sean who carries out the role once occupied by Big Charlie MacLennan and Joey Cashman. On a voluntary basis, he organises MacGowan's day, looks after him and keeps him company at night, on and off the road.

And as for the other members of the band – well, they're still alive, although at one time there were grave worries for Spider, Philip and Terry.

James Fearnley: "It's really great to look around at them. Spider and Philip could easily be dead now from alcoholism. They were handing themselves the black spot, so to speak. Terry was having a hard time too, but I don't think I feared for his life as much as I did for Spider and Philip."

Chevron: "The Pogues proved that you can be completely out to lunch and still be a pop star, and you can be a Pogue and still live to tell the tale years later. We've survived. We're not dead and our lives have changed for the better in many ways."

And above all: "We've learnt over the years that we're all indispensable, that the only way it really works is when the eight of us are all together."

Pogues Discography

SINGLES

Dark Streets Of London/And The Band Played Waltzing Matilda
Initial Limited Edition 7"
Pogue Mahone Records PM1 (May 1984)
Stiff BUY207 (June 1984)

Boys From The County Hell/Repeal Of The Licensing Laws
Stiff BUY212 (7") (October 1984)

A Pair Of Brown Eyes/Whiskey You're The Devil/Muirshin Durkin
Stiff BUY220 (7" & 12") (March 1985)

Sally MacLennane/The Wild Rover/The Leaving Of Liverpool
Stiff BUY224 (7", 12" & cassette) (June 1985)

Dirty Old Town/A Pistol For Paddy Garcia/The Parting Glass
Stiff BUY229 (7" & 12") (August 1985)

POGUETRY IN MOTION
London Girl/A Rainy Night In Soho/The Body Of An
American/Planxty Noel Hill
Stiff BUY243 (7", 12" & cassette) (February 1986)

Haunted/Junk Theme/Hot Dogs With Everything
MCA1084 (7" & 12") (August 1986)

The Irish Rover/ The Rare Ould Mountain Dew/The Dubliners Fancy
(without Pogues)
Stiff BUY258 (7″ & 12″) (March 1987)
with The Dubliners

Fairytale Of New York/Battle March Medley/Shanne Bradley
Pogue Mahone NY7 (7″, 12″ & CD) (November 1987)
with Kirsty MacColl

If I Should Fall From Grace With God/ Sally MacLennane (live)/
A Pair Of Brown Eyes (live)
Pogue Mahone FG1 (7″, 12″ & CD) (February 1988)

Fiesta/ Sketches Of Spain/ South Australia/ Sally MacLennane (live)/
A Pair of Brown Eyes (live)
Pogue Mahone FG2 (7″, 12″ & CD) (July 1988)

Yeah Yeah Yeah Yeah Yeah/ The Limerick Rake/Honky Tonk
Women/Yeah Yeah Yeah Yeah Yeah (Long Version)
WEA YZ355T (7″, 12″ & CD) (1988)

Misty Morning, Albert Bridge/ Cotton Fields/ Young Ned Of The
Hill/Young Ned Of The Hill (Dub Version)/Train of Love
WEA YZ407 (7″, 12″ & CD) (1989)

White City/ Everyman Is A King/Star Of The County Down/
Maggie May (live)
WEA YZ409 (7″, 12″ & CD) (1989)

Summer In Siam/The Bastard Landlord/Hell's Ditch (instrumental)/
The Irish Rover (7″ Version, with The Dubliners)
WEA YZ519 (7″, 12″ & CD) (1990)

Jack's Heroes/Whiskey In The Jar/Whiskey In The Jar (Extended Version)
WEA YZ500 (7″, 12″ & CD) (1990)
with The Dubliners

Miss Otis Regrets/Just One Of Those Things
Chrysalis CHS 73629 (7″, 12″ & CD) (1990)
(B-side is Aztec Camera performing Do I Love You)

POGUETRY IN MOTION
A Rainy Night In Soho (Remix)/London Girl/The Body Of An
American/ Planxty Noel Hill
WEA YZ603 (7", 12" & CD) (1991)

A Rainy Night In Soho (remix)/Squid Out Of Water/Infinity
WEA YZ603 (7", 12" & CD) (1991)

Fairytale Of New York/ Fiesta/A Pair Of Brown Eyes (live)/The Sick Bed
Of Cuchulainn (live)/ Maggie May (live)
WEA YZ628 (7", 12" & CD) (November, 1991)

Honky Tonk Women/Curse Of Love/Infinity/The Parting Glass
WEA YZ673 (7", 12" & CD) (1992)

Tuesday Morning/First Day Of Forever/Turkish Song Of The Damned
(live)
WEA YZ758-1 (7", 12" & CD) (1993)
Disk 1 of 2
Tuesday Morning/London Calling (live)/I Fought The Law (live)
WEA YZ758-2 (7", 12" & CD) (1993)
Disk 2 of 2

Once Upon A Time/ Train Kept Rolling On/Paris St Germain/Tuesday
Morning
WEA YZ771 (7", 12" & CD) (1993)

How Come/Eyes Of An Angel/Tuesday Morning(live)/Big City (live)
WEA WEA011 (7", 12" & CD) (1995)

ALBUMS

RED ROSES FOR ME
Transmetropolitan/The Battle Of Brisbane/ The Auld Triangle/Waxie's
Dargle/Boys From The County Hell/Sea Shanty/Dark Streets Of
London/Streams Of Whiskey/Poor Paddy/Dingle Regatta/ Greenland
Whale Fisheries/Down In The Ground Where The Dead Men Go/Kitty
Stiff SEEZ55 (October 1984)
WEA Records 244 494-2
Enigma 4XT-73225
The Enigma Cassette & CD (4XT-73225 & D2-73225) also contains:

Whiskey You're The Devil, Muirshin Durkin, and Repeal Of The
Licensing Laws

RUM, SODOMY & THE LASH
The Sick Bed Of Cuchulainn/The Old Main Drag/Wild Cats Of
Kilkenny/A Pair Of Brown Eyes/I'm A Man You Don't Meet Every
Day/Sally MacLennane/Dirty Old Town/Jesse James/Navigator/Billy's
Bones/The Gentleman Soldier/And The Band Played Waltzing Matilda
Stiff SEEZ58 (August 1985)
WEA 244 495-2
The CD and Cassette versions also include A Pistol For Paddy Garcia

IF I SHOULD FALL FROM GRACE WITH GOD
If I Should Fall From Grace With God/Turkish Song Of The
Damned/Bottle Of Smoke/Fairytale Of New
York/Metropolis/Thousands Are Sailing/Fiesta/Medley (The Recruiting
Sergeant, The Rocky Road To Dublin, The Galway Races)/Streets Of
Sorrow/Birmingham Six/Lullaby Of London/Sit Down By The Fire/The
Broad Majestic Shannon/Worms
Stiff Records CDNYR-1 (January 1988)
WEA (Pogue Mahone NYR1)
Island 90872-2 (Different Cover)
The CD version of this LP also includes South Australia and The Battle
March Medley

PEACE AND LOVE
Gridlock/White City/Young Ned Of The Hill/Misty Morning, Albert
Bridge/Cotton Fields/Blue Heaven/Down All The Days/USA/Lorelei/
Gartloney Rats/Boat Train/Tombstone/Night Train To Lorca/London
You're A Lady
WEA (Pogue Mahone NYR-2) (1989)
Island 422-842-838-2
Formats: LP, Cassette, CD

HELL'S DITCH
The Sunnyside Of The Street/Sayonara/The Ghost Of A Smile/Hell's
Ditch/Lorca's Novena/Summer In Siam/Rain Street/Rainbow Man/The
Wake Of The Medusa/House Of The Gods/5 Green Queens And
Jean/Maidrin Rua/Six To Go
WEA (Pogue Mahone 9031-72554/2) (1990)
Island 422-846-999-2

THE BEST OF THE POGUES
Fairytale Of New York (with Kirsty MacColl)/Sally MacLennane
(live)/Dirty Old Town/The Irish Rover (with The Dubliners)/A Pair Of
Brown Eyes (live)/Streams Of Whiskey/A Rainy Night In
Soho/Fiesta/Rain Street/Misty Morning, Albert Bridge/White
City/Thousands Are Sailing/The Broad Majestic Shannon/The Body Of
An American
WEA 9031-75405-2 (1991)

ESSENTIAL POGUES
The Sunnyside Of The Street/If I Should Fall From Grace With
God/Lorelei/Thousands Are Sailing/White City/Fairytale Of New
York/Fiesta/Rain Street/Turkish Song Of The Damned/Summer In
Siam/Misty Morning, Albert Bridge/Blue Heaven/Honky Tonk Women
/Yeah Yeah Yeah Yeah Yeah
Island 314-510610-2 (US) (1991)

WAITING FOR HERB
Tuesday Morning/Smell Of Petroleum/Haunting/Once Upon A Time/
Sitting On Top Of The World/Drunken Boat/Big City/Girl From The
Wadi Hammamat/Modern World/Pachinko/My Baby's Gone/Small Hours
WEA 4509-93463-2 (1993)
Chameleon/Elektra 61598-2

POGUE MAHONE
How Come/Living In A World Without Her/When The Ship Comes
In/Anniversary/Amadie/Love You 'Till The End/Bright
Lights/Oretown/Pont Mirabeau/Tosspint/Four O'Clock In The
Morning/Where That Love's Been Gone/The Sun And The Moon
WEA 0630-11210-2 (1995)
Mesa-Blue Moon 92684 (1996)

THE POGUES, THE REST OF THE BEST
If I Should Fall From Grace With God/The Sick Bed Of
Cuchulainn/The Old Main Drag/Boys From The County Hell/Young
Ned Of The Hill/Dark Streets Of London/The Auld Triangle/Repeal Of
The Licensing Laws/Yeah Yeah Yeah Yeah Yeah/London Girl/Honky Tonk
Women/Summer In Siam/Turkish Song Of The Damned/Lullaby Of
London/The Sunnyside Of The Street/Hell's Ditch
WEA 9031-77341-2 (1992)

THE VERY BEST OF THE POGUES

Dirty Old Town/The Irish Rover (with The Dubliners)/Sally
MacLennane/Fiesta/A Pair Of Brown Eyes/Fairytale Of New York/The
Body Of An American/Streams Of Whiskey/The Sick Bed Of
Cuchulainn/If I Should Fall From Grace With God/Misty Morning,
Albert Bridge/Rain Street/White City/A Rainy Night In Soho/London
Girl/Boys From The County Hell/The Sunnyside Of The Street/Summer
In Siam/Hell's Ditch/The Old Main Drag/And The Band Played
Waltzing Matilda
WEA (April 11, 2001)

VIDEOS/DVDs

THE POGUES: LIVE AT THE TOWN AND COUNTRY

The Broad Majestic Shannon/If I Should Fall From Grace With God/A
Rainy Night In Soho/Thousands Are Sailing/Fairytale Of New
York/Lullaby Of London/Dirty Old Town/London Calling/Turkish Song
Of The Damned/Fiesta/The Irish Rover/Worms/A Message To You
Rudy/The Wild Rover
Virgin SVG1013 (1988), app. 59min.

COMPLETELY POGUED: The Story Of The Pogues In Their Own
Words And Music (Documentary)
Contains interviews and concert pictures with The Pogues.
Start, Audio & Video SVG1013 (1988), app. 55 min.

POGUEVISION (Videos)
Streams Of Whiskey/Miss Otis Regrets & Just One Of Those Things
(with Kirsty MacColl)/Jack's Heroes (with The Dubliners)/Summer In
Siam/White City/A Pair Of Brown Eyes/Dirty Old Town/Fairytale Of
New York (with Kirsty MacColl)/Fiesta/If I Should Fall From Grace With
God/Yeah Yeah Yeah Yeah Yeah/Misty Morning, Albert Bridge/A Rainy
Night In Soho
WEA 9031 75483-3 (1991), app. 47min

STRAIGHT TO HELL (Movie)
An Alex Cox/Dick Rude penned film directed by Alex Cox. A send-up
of spaghetti westerns featuring The Pogues, Elvis Costello, Joe Strummer,
Courtney Love, Dennis Hopper, Grace Jones, Zander Schloss, and many
others.

Island Pictures (1987)
Key Video 3859 (1987), VHS
Island (2001), DVD, app. 86 min

IF I SHOULD FALL FROM GRACE: THE SHANE MAC-GOWAN STORY (Documentary)
Contains interviews with Shane MacGowan, his family, friends and band-mates, with archive and new footage filmed in London and Ireland, and live and video clips. Originally produced for Ireland's national television, then had a cinema release in 2001.
Weinerworld (2003), DVD, app. 110 min

Acknowledgements

First and foremost, I would like to say a huge thank you to The Pogues – Philip Chevron, James Fearnley, Jem Finer, Darryl Hunt, Shane MacGowan, Andrew Ranken, Spider Stacy and Terry Woods – for the many hours of interviews that form the basis of this book. I'd like specially to mention James and Jem who gave assistance and advice beyond the call of duty.

A number of people have been kind enough to share their time and memories: I'm very grateful to Shanne Bradley, Stan Brennan, Buttz, Joey Cashman, Alex Cox, Phil Gaston, Steve Lillywhite, Patricia Mitchell, Frank Murray, Dee O'Mahony, Dave Robinson and Jill Sinclair.

I have appreciated the patience and help of Marcia Farquhar, Louise Nevill, JP and Marian Skeffington Wood.

Bouquets to Maria Jefferis and Kerry Lake for their friendship and invaluable research – and high fives to Colin Harper, Mick Houghton and Kris Tait for their generosity.

Chris Charlesworth – respect! I have welcomed the opportunity, encouragement and understanding.

I'm delighted to raise a toast to my lovely friend Sharon Ortega, to Stephanie Jones for the diversional reading and to Spike for the sometimes chaotic company.

I would like to take this opportunity to remember Nancy Clerk, Stu Devillier (Stu P Didiot as was), Desperate Dave Burns, Rene Berg, Speedie and Elric.

Finally, I must express my endless devotion and gratitude to Nigel and Eve O'Brien who have, as always, given their whole-hearted help, support and love throughout this project.